BEHAVIOR MODIFICATION IN CHILD TREATMENT

an experimental and clinical approach

BEHAVIOR MODIFICATION IN CHILD TREATMENT

Robert M. Browning and Donald O. Stover

Routledge
Taylor & Francis Group
LONDON AND NEW YORK

First published 1971 by Transaction Publishers

Published 2017 by Routledge
2 Park Square, Milton Park, Abingdon, Oxon OX14 4RN
711 Third Avenue, New York, NY 10017, USA

First issued in hardback 2017

Routledge is an imprint of the Taylor & Francis Group, an informa business

Library of Congress Catalog Number: 2008039945

Library of Congress Cataloging-in-Publication Data

Browning, Robert Mitchell, 1938-
Behavior modification in child treatment : an experimental and clinical approach / Robert M. Browning and Donald O. Stover.
p. ; cm.
Originally published: Chicago : Aldine, 1971.
Includes bibliographical references and index.
ISBN 978-0-202-36293-9 (alk. paper)
1. Behavior therapy for children. I. Stover, Donald O. II. Title.
[DNLM: 1. Autistic Disorder--therapy. 2. Behavior Therapy. 3. Child. 4. Infant. 5. Neurotic Disorders--therapy. WS 350 B885b 2008a]

RJ505.B4B76 2008
618.92'89142--dc22

2008039945

ISBN 13: 978-1-138-51931-2 (hbk)
ISBN 13: 978-0-202-36293-9 (pbk)

Preface

This volume is devoted to the quest for practical knowledge concerning child and family behavioral disturbances. A wide abyss has long existed between the pure behavioral research of the university setting and the treatment demands made on the practicing clinician. Meaningful applied research may assist in bridging that gap. A satisfactory applied research program must stand in systematic relationship, on the one hand, to the accumulated findings of university-oriented pure research, and, on the other hand, to the needs and demands of the real-life problems of patients and practicing clinicians. Applied researchers must (1) use knowledge of basic psychological processes to develop practical treatment procedures, and (2) define clinical problems in such a manner as to stimulate investigation of related problems by pure researchers. Although the benefits of such a scientific approach have long been apparent in medical research and engineering, they have seldom been realized in psychological research.

One major drawback to the development of significant applied psychological research has been the inadequacy of psychological technology to deal scientifically with the myriad complexities of human behavior in other than the contrived, controlled, and sterile atmosphere of the experimental laboratory. Most of this book is devoted to the presentation of a scientific attitude and some beginning technical methods for arriving at a meaningful system of applied research into the complexities of child and family behavioral disturbance.

However, practical considerations have long been a far more serious obstacle to the development of applied research. Throughout the country there has been an almost complete lack of encouragement and support for those clinical facilities which could most productively conduct research programs. As a nation we spend enormous sums of money on, and give tremendous prestige to the applied scientists who produce, better medicines, more potent fertilizers, longer-lasting paints, and faster rockets. Historically, we have seen the value of training the engineers who take basic knowledge from the scholars and apply it to the solution of mechanical problems. By comparison, we spend virtually nothing to encourage the engineering of solutions to the problems of human behavior and relationship.

The authors have been privileged to work in one of the few settings in this country that encourage and demonstrably support applied research into human problems. The Children's Treatment Center was established by the Wisconsin State Legislature to provide a total program for emotionally disturbed children and their families. Significantly, the founders of the program made responsibility for research a specific charge of the enabling legislation. Under the very able leadership of Martin Fliegel, M.D., the Center has developed the kind of administrative structure, staff, and intellectual climate conducive to productive research efforts. Although patients are admitted primarily to meet current research needs and interests, the research program has been developed without sacrificing the clinical goal of providing the very best possible treatment for each patient.

This book reports one aspect of the Center's developing program. It is the first and we hope a preliminary report of an expanding program. The authors sincerely hope the Wisconsin leaders who have so patiently supported our program will, in this volume, see some beginning return on their very large investment.

The research presented in this volume was accomplished only with the magnificent assistance of those who worked directly with the project. Their contributions of time, creativity, and personal devotion were more extensive and diverse than we can describe. We hope they will accept the following simple listing of their names as a token of our deep appreciation.

Duane Alwin; Genevieve Baker, M.S.W.; Kay Benisch; Brian Boegel; Judy Borree, M.S.W.; Glenn Bradfield; Patty Burmeister; Ellen Cunningham, M.A.; Mary Eickelberg, R.N.; Mary Ann Fahl; Mary Finnigan, R.N.; Steve Finnigan; Steve Folstad; Arthur E. Gatenby, M.D.; John Giebink, Ph.D.; Richard Hanish; Marek Hann, M.D.; Judy Harris; Don Harvey; Nancy Heath, M.A.; Judy Herberger, M.S.W.; Tom Hughes; Bobbi Johnson; Griff Johnson; Claire Kemp, M.S.W.; Molly Kirley, R.N.; Reggie Korolev; Nancy Krinsky, M.A.; Carrie Kuiper; George Langley; JoAnn Langley, R.N.; Robert Leff, Ph.D.; Lyle Lenzendorf; Mike Levin; Janet Loeb, Ph.D.; Eugene Messina; Jean Miller; James Mills; Donna Morrissey, M.S.; Charles Norman; Edward Orman, M.D.; Gail Osborne; Susan Pemberton, R.N.; Charles Perso; Liz Pierson; Vernon Post; Mike Price; Susan Raddatz, R.N.; Rose Mary Rapp, M.A.; Dan Reimer; Vincent Ritacca; Marsha Rubinowitz, M.A.; Betty Rulff, M.A.; Gerri Ryan; Isabel Schleicher, R.N.; Olive Schneider, R.N.; John Schutz; Carol Spanjar; Marion Thorson, R.N.; Connie Traut; Ruby Turner, R.N.; Sandy Wendling; Naomi Nelson, B.S.; Jeff Wheeler; Al Wilhite; Art Williams; Roselyn Wiltgen, R.N.

All of us are indebted to the entire staff of the Children's Treatment Center who consistently supported our work.

Contents

CHAPTER ONE

The Experimental-Clinical Method

The scientific method must be the basis for treatment of psychologically disturbed persons. The clinician should identify and measure behavioral problems in the same manner that the physical scientist approaches any natural phenomena. As an applied scientist, the clinician should combine basic psychological knowledge with current observations of his patient to form testable treatment hypotheses. Factual understanding of the patient's behavior derived from experimental tests of these hypotheses should then be the basis for the design and execution of a total treatment program. Finally, the clinician should be capable of objectively evaluating his treatment procedures and, consequently, his understanding of the patient. This technological ideal is the experimental-clinical method.

Experimental methods are seldom employed in current clinical practice. Most clinicians have difficulty accepting science as even one of the boundaries of practice, and would vehemently reject the proposition that scientific methodology should stand as a central pillar of treatment. Instead, they state that the complexities of human feeling and action cannot be measured and that the treatment of unique individual behavior is the proper province of art.

Traditionally, there has been a marked difference between the scientific and the clinical approaches to the problem of psychological disturbance. Arising from philosophical questions about the nature of man, and motivated by a search for knowledge, the scientific orientation has become formalized in the pure research of academic psychology. In contrast, the clinical approach has its roots in the humanistic tradition and is motivated by the desire to alleviate human suffering by treating disturbances of individual functioning.

As clinical psychologists, the authors have been acutely aware of the continuing antithesis of scientific and clinical approaches to human behavior. Our training included a heavy emphasis upon academic psychology, experimental method, statistical design, and the other accoutrements of pure behavioral research. However, we were also deeply immersed in clinical problems and traditional treatment methods. In our training, as in our current view of the field, we could seldom find useful relationships between the experimental approach of the university and the practice of the clinic. As clinicians, we have been deeply concerned about the complexities of individual human behavior and we have shared with our clinical colleagues the conviction that the uniqueness of an individual personality can never be comprehended within the rigid rules of the currently revered behavioral science methodologies. As scientists, however, we have valued a degree of preciseness, experimental control, and predictiveness that the vagaries and ambiguities of the usual clinical methods are unable to provide. The great masses of scientific data contained in archival journals relate only peripherally to the human problems that arise daily in a clinic. There is a plethora of studies on basic learning processes, unconscious motivation, perception, and the physiological correlates of behavior, but the gap between these experimental studies and the patients in our offices is great. Integrity prohibits their direct application with anything less than intense skepticism. We regret the absence of a meaningful technological literature and are unwilling to accept in its place the lore of traditional clinical practice which, be it analytic, phenomenological, or behavioral, is replete with subjective evaluation, dogmatic belief, and mystical thinking. Thus, we have found ourselves in conflict between the apparently antithetical values of behavioral science and clinical practice.

Despite the apparent contrasts, the motives of clinical and experimental approaches may be complementary. Emphasis upon the disparities has hindered development of meaningful research on clinically critical aspects of behavior, and treatment methods have scarcely improved since the historically prominent psychiatrists first attacked the problems. A technical integration of craft and art, such as exists in engineering or medicine, could enhance the goals of both scientist and practitioner. Accomplishment of an integrated technology would mean the rejection of contrived manipulations, complex experimental designs, esoteric statistics, and overly sophisticated measurements. Equivalent cynicism must be directed at treatment methods that rely upon intuition and hunches while failing to accommodate objective results. From clinicians though, we accept the positive value of working to assist suffering persons find more satisfactory behavioral adjustments; from scientists we accept the value of efforts precisely to predict and control the behavior of clinic patients. The scientific and clinical traditions have much to offer humanity; but their current separateness can lead neither to efficient treatment of disturbed individuals nor to complete understanding of human behavior.

We hope that an eventual integration of scientific method and therapeutic craft will permit knowledgeable treatment. This book reports our initial attempts to work within the experimental-clinical method. It is our first approximation to the ideal of making clinical practice an applied science.

Science Versus Practice

Before proceeding with a detailed description of experimental-clinical methods, we shall more specifically examine the differences between science and practice. The clinician and the experimenter differ in their use of basic theory, the independent variables each espouses, their definitions of dependent variables, their attitudes toward prediction and control of behavior, their conception of the variabilities of behavior, and their goals concerning the generality of knowledge about human behavior.

Clinicians have preferred comprehensive theories of total personality; experimentalists have insisted upon precisely formulated conceptions. The broadly encompassing and thoroughly literary clinical theories generally fail to meet basic scientific criteria. Their concepts are difficult to define in terms of the operations that could be used to measure them. The interrelationships of concepts in clinical theories are usually difficult to specify. Even when operational criteria are applied to measure the strength of a cathexis, the quality of identity formation, or the extent of libido drive, the resulting definition fails to capture the essence of the concept as a clinician would employ it in his daily practice. By far the most unacceptable aspect of many clinical theories is that they in no way specify the conditions under which they would by proven inaccurate. This, of course, is a basic criterion of any scientifically acceptable theory. At the other extreme, many of the most scientific theories are but miniature theories relating to highly restricted fields such as immediate memory or psychophysical judgment. Although relevant as building blocks for a pure science of behavior, these limited theories offer little promise to the practicing clinician. The clinician holds no antipathy for precisely constructed theory, nor the experimentalist for comprehensive theory. However, the present state of the science indicates that the achievement of both goals in a common theoretical framework will not occur soon.

The argument between global and molecular theories is irrelevant to clinical practice. If molecular theories are available and seemingly valid for dealing with even limited aspects of a given patient's behavior, they should be applied and used to give treatment direction. Where precise notions are not available, the clinician can do no harm by falling back upon more global notions of personality so long as he recognizes their limitations, directs his work toward the development of more scientifically acceptable approaches, and, most important, refuses to adopt status quo attitudes about sloppy theorizing.

In accepting scientifically weak theories, the clinician permits himself to follow a poorly blazed trail often meandering far afield from the proper goal of objective practical treatment procedures. Since clinical theories rely upon concepts that are not easily related to touchable, visible realities, the clinician often accepts diffuse definitions of dependent variables. The patient comes to him with a referral complaint—specifically, a behavior or set of behaviors disturbing to himself or others. Rather than defining observable behaviors, typical clinical theories emphasize feeling states, cognitions, complexes, and other hypothetical constructs.

The clinician seldom contracts with the patient to change the patient's behavior. He does not promise to eliminate rages or produce a higher rate of smiling. In fact, the advice has often been that it would be dangerous to make a direct attack upon "symptoms" of underlying disorders. The underlying disorders are considered the cause, and the "symptomatic" behavior, the effect; but seldom is the mechanism by which cause and effect are supposed to be related clearly specified.

As clinicians, we maintain that a change in the referral behavior is the appropriate goal of treatment. As scientists, we assert that referral complaints are appropriate dependent variables. To meet scientific criteria, some observable and specifiable behavior must serve as the dependent variable under study, and definable treatment manipulations must be designed to produce change in that variable. Clinicians often begin with this point of view, but shortly find themselves concerned wtih more abstract concepts that are only vaguely related to the original behavior problem. Early therapy notes may discuss the referral behaviors in detail, but subsequent accounts will be filled with discussion of changes in other areas. Seldom is the relationship between the original dependent variable and the apparent new variables of interest made explicit.

The clinician is also guilty of an inability adequately to define his independent variables or treatment manipulations. Once again the problem is related to the clinician's acceptance of imprecise theory. The favored forms of treatment, such as milieu therapy, family therapy, and psychotherapy often defy operational definition. Thus, no two practitioners may be expected to perform similar treatment procedures. How could one hope to replicate another's interpretations? How can one describe precisely what is meant by encouraging dependency, providing structure, permitting catharsis, or supporting the ego? Favored treatments are so global in their description that it would be difficult to duplicate them. Further, in general practice treatment methods are so confounded that assessment of their interactive effects would be virtually impossible. A controlled attempt is seldom made to evaluate the effects of a particular kind of interpretation or reward procedure on a patient's behavior. The impreciseness of description of independent variables in common clinical practice has led to comments like "Psychotherapy is an undefined technique applied to unspecified problems with unpredictable outcomes. For this technique we recommend rigorous training" (Raimy, 1950, p. 93). If treatment is to be a technology, it will be necessary to specify more clearly what the therapist does.

One can be equally critical of the scientist. His productivity to date has given us little that would successfully objectify the clinical task. He busies himself with watching college sophomores pursue rotors with metal sticks which electrically and quite operationally measure performance. His dependent variables are usually irrelevant to the complex human issues faced in the clinic. The clinician seldom cares how well his patient can memorize a list of nonsense syllables, discriminate the weights of tin cans, or salivate at the sight of the word "meat." The contrived manipulations of most psychological experiments seem to have limited clinical value. Do messages mixed with static coming through earphones to a college sophomore in a communications laboratory have any significant relationship to the communication breakdown that leads to the dissolution of a family? Does being told that your score on an experimental task is subnormal compare with the experience of having a frustrated teacher shout "stupid" at you? Is a hypnotically induced sense of guilt similar to the feeling that arises in a child when his father commits suicide? Although similarities may exist, the distance between such contrived laboratory situations and the impact of the human events that comprise clinical cases is far too great to permit meaningful application. The findings of the laboratory often seem useless to the clinician precisely because they are the result of laboratory manipulations. He demands that research be performed in the context of real situations with real people under real stresses.

The artificiality of some laboratory research is not sufficient reason to explain the clinician's usual indifference to behavioral science. After all, many competent studies have been conducted under highly naturalistic conditions. Even naturalistic studies fail to provide the clinician with the kind of information he needs in his daily practice. For example, the extensive literature on early deprivation (e.g. Yarrow, 1961) clearly indicates an association between maternal deprivation and later deviances in intellectual and social functioning. However, the literature does not tell the clinician how a given individual will be or has been affected by deprivation, nor how to formulate specific treatment programs to alter the behavior of a particular patient. The clinician must ask, not "what are the general effects of deprivation?" but rather, "what are the specific effects of deprivation for this child?" Because the clinician sees his patient as a unique individual with highly idiosyncratic problems, studies providing general conclusions about the average effect of some independent variable seem to offer little promise of meaningful clinical application.

This brings us to an essential difference between clinical and experimental approaches to human behavior. The clinician and the experimentalist seek and require totally different kinds of predictions. Experimental psychology has long been enamored with predictions based upon groups of subjects. To write a paper acceptable to the prominent journals that maintain the standards of the science, a researcher must provide a study consisting (at its simplest level) of a randomly selected pool of subjects divided into two groups, each of which receives specifiably different treatment manipulations. If the null hypothesis (that the population means for the two groups are the same) is rejected, the researcher generally concludes that the treatment manipulations have important significance with respect to the dependent variable. The procedure, of course, overlooks the fact that *"there is really no good reason to expect the null hypothesis to be true in any population"* (Bakan, 1966, p. 426). As a review of much of the published literature will quickly reveal, experimenters often find statistically significant differences, but the extent of correlation between their dependent and independent variables is so small that the finding may have virtually no psychological significance. Anyone who has conducted a typical group study is aware that examination of individual data often results in the conclusion that the treatment manipulation had little or no effect upon many of the subjects. The statistics, even if they could be shown to be logically related to the usual conclusions from such studies, would still leave us with the finding that the treatment effect works for most but not all subjects.

The clinician cannot be satisfied with a finding that works for most individuals. He must choose a treatment technique that will have a maximum effect upon the behavior he wished to change in a particular person. Further, his interest and concern are centered upon the oddities of each patient's behavior. For example, most of the children described in this volume had normal hearing, so their hearing capacity was of no special interest to us. One of them, however, was nearly deaf, and this was of enormous interest in our clinical investigations of his behavior. By the very nature of their work, clinicians are confronted with behaviors so unusual that they defy any grouping. The experimentalist often criticizes clinical studies because they do not meet the criteria of random sampling. Indeed, random sampling of subjects is virtually impossible when one is studying deviant behavior. Clinically relevant behaviors are unique entities which can seldom be lumped together across groups of individuals. Every child seen in the clinic has a unique learning history which accounts for his abnormal behavior. For this reason the clinician needs information which will permit accurate clinical prediction about the relevant behaviors of each individual child.

Statistical and clinical prediction cannot be compared fairly because their end goals differ. Actuarial prediction is intended to make statements such as, "most persons of this type will respond in X manner to Y treatment." Clinical prediction has as its goal statements such as, "this person will respond in X manner to most circumstances of Y type." The actuarial prediction has applied value for the program administrator or planner. For example, a welfare director may base his planning upon a prediction that 50% of the juveniles in a particular ghetto area will become delinquent unless assisted by prevention programs. Such predictions are of little use, however, to the clinician who works in a prevention program in that ghetto area. His responsibility is to single individuals and he must be able to predict relationships between specific environmental interventions and delinquent behaviors for single individuals on his case load.

The inability of research to provide clinically applicable data has often been simply attributed to the relative youth of behavioral science. As research continues, this argument runs, sufficient knowledge will be gained to permit individual clinical prediction. Ultimately we shall know enough about the myriad variables which affect human behavior that we shall be able accurately to measure these with respect to a single person, and predict what specific treatment will alter his behavior. The history of the physical sciences would certainly lend support to this view; a century ago few would have believed it possible to understand and control circumstances so as to permit placing a satellite in exact orbit about the earth. However, even if extensive basic research will improve prediction of individual behavior, that improvement is many decades away from today's clinician. Our viewpoint is that, even given vast amounts of basic knowledge, the clinician will still be grossly limited in understanding the highly idiosyncratic problems of individual patients. The inevitable uniqueness of a person's developmental history means that major aspects of his behavior will be lawful only onto himself. Gordon Allport, whose writings have enormously influenced our own position, put it succinctly :"The true goal of clinical psychology is not to predict the aggregate, but to foretell 'what any one man will do.' In researching this ideal, actuarial prediction may sometimes help, universal and group norms are useful, but they do not go the whole distance" (Allport, 1961, p. 21).

The experimentalist would have his findings apply to a broad class of persons while the clinician wants his findings to apply to a sphere as limited as all of a particular kind of behavior in a single individual. Because the respective universes to which they must generalize their findings differ, clinicians and experimentalists should and do sample differently. The experimentalist samples from a population of persons; the clinician, from a population of behaviors in a single person. The experimental psychologist aims his research at understanding the variability of behavior between groups of persons who differ because of some treatment manipulation or because they were selected according to some organismic factor. His basic measure is the mean score for a group of individuals, and differences between individuals within a given group are classed as error variance. The clinician is interested in understanding the conditions of the experimentalist's error variance. The clinician's subject is the one who produces the statistically rare score. Consequently, the clinician's basic measure (if only he would use measures) would be an individual's average response over many repeated occasions; and his error variance would be differences in that individual's behavior under a given level of a specified independent variable. His interest would be to understand the conditions necessary for that individual's behavior to differ from its average. His findings would be generalized to permit the control of future behaviors of his subject.

Clinicians and behavioral scientists do not, as is sometimes supposed, differ in their wish to improve their knowledge or understanding of human behavior, nor in their wish to control or predict behavior. Rather, it appears that they differ in terms of the kind of knowledge they select as a goal. The experimentalist has typically concerned himself with obtaining findings that have wide applicability or broad generality. The clinician criticizes these findings because, from his viewpoint, they have often been formulations about trivia. The generalities of the scientist have not typically been useful to the clinician in dealing with the extremely idiosyncratic aspects of behavior that he sees in the clinic. The clinician finds himself needing, not to know general laws of behavior, but rather to know a law which will permit him to predict and control the behavior of the individual patient who sits before him at the moment. Where the behavioral scientist has typically taken all human beings, or all sixth-graders in a given school district, or all schizophrenics, as his population of inquiry, the clinician has typically sought to take all of the behavior of the individual patient as his universe of inquiry. What knowledge he has the clinician wishes to generalize to this patient, not to all persons. This is his responsibility as a practitioner.

The lack of communication between experimentalists and clinicians does not exist because either is any the less concerned about human welfare than the other or any the less concerned about factual knowledge than the other. The major point of stress has come because the behavioral scientist has traditionally considered the only proper universe of scientific inquiry to be the large population of persons. He has felt that the only useful scientific fact is the one that is broadly generalizable to many persons. On the other hand, it has been unfortunate that clinicians have failed to see the applicability of scientific methodology to the study and treatment of their patients. The difference need not be one of sciences versus art, or of humanitarianism versus cold logic. Behavioral scientists may properly take as their responsibility the determination of laws of behavior applicable to all persons or definable groups of persons. However, just as legitimately, the clinician may take as his proper responsibility the discovery of laws relating to the behavior of a single individual, and the prediction and control of that individual's behavior. As the science grows, the approaches of clinicians and experimenters must merge. The experimenter's general laws are useless if they do not ultimately apply to the single individual who is seen in the clinic. The clinician's work is equally useless if it cannot ultimately stand the scrutiny of scientific evaluation.

We are concerned with the development of an experimental-clinical method that is based upon scientific fact and aimed at efficient treatment of individual behavioral disturbances. We hope to rely upon scientific tradition for precise theoretical concepts, testable hypotheses, definable treatment procedures, and objective evaluation of results. From the clinical tradition, we hope to adopt the intensive study of individual behavior as well as humanistic concern for the relief of suffering.

Idiographic Experiments

The union of science and practice can be achieved by applying experimental methods to the study of single cases. Our plea is not for the highly literary case reports often found in clinical writings, nor for overly stylized experiments. The experimental-clinical psychologist should answer clinically relevant questions with experiments that achieve a practical level of methodological sophistication. We ask that experimental methods be used in each clinic case to answer the questions: "What is the behavior to be altered?" "What are the factors that control that behavior?" "What is the best technique to alter the behavior?" "How successful was the technique that was used?" These are tactical questions often asked by the clinician, thoroughly amenable to the application of scientific methodology, but all too often unstudied.

Although frequently discussed in psychology, the idiographic experiment has received only limited application and respectability as either a clinical or a scientific procedure. (Allport (1960, 1961, 1962), a strong proponent of idiographic methods, emphasized the uniqueness of the human organism. He felt that only limited aspects of an individual personality are held in common by other men, or even by other men of a given culture. The vast reaches of humanly significant traits he felt were unique to the single individual. Thus, to understand any single man, one would need knowledge of that man's own unique personality. In so speaking, Allport sounded like a clinician, but he clearly disavowed the notion that commonness is the province of science, while uniqueness is the province of art (Allport, 1961). On the contrary, he concluded that the science of personality needed to develop a procedure that could adequately deal with unique traits if it was ever to make knowledgeable predictions about or for individuals.

Classificatory methods and actuarial approaches to the study of human behavior were viewed skeptically by Lewin (1935). Counting the frequency of events or the common characteristics of different persons or groups of persons appeared to him to be an initial aspect of the science of behavior. The unique event was indeed seen as important in all of science, and the unique individual or behavior of importance in psychology. It would not be satisfactory for the science of behavior to dismiss the problem of uniqueness as one that could not be meaningfully studied.

The single-subject experiment certainly has received its greatest use and development from the operant conditioners using the procedures of the experimental analysis of behavior. Much of that methodology has been put in clear conceptual form by Sidman (1960), who has outlined the logical procedures, experimental designs, and research methodology for the conduct of single-subject studies. The limitation of the usual group studies and the fallacious conclusions that can result from the common practice of averaging data from many subjects are emphasized in Sidman's work. The designs and procedures he discusses establish the methodological goal of achieving maximum control over dependent variables. Although the experimental analysis of behavior has achieved scientific respectability, its applications have been primarily limited to problems in basic research.

A historical review by Dukes (1965) emphasizes the importance of the $N = 1$ study in the broad perspective of psychological science. During the past 25 years, over 200 single-case studies have appeared in the major psychological journals, and have covered virtually every area of psychology. Historically, single-case studies have provided "many instances of pivotal research" (Dukes, 1965, p. 74) and are seen as important for a variety of situations beyond the usual clinical case study.

Despite the attention idiographic methods have received, only a handful of investigators have attempted to exploit fully the single-case experiment in clinical practice. Outstanding among these is Shapiro, who with his colleagues has presented a variety of methodological and case examples of an experimental-clinical psychology (Shapiro, 1961a & b; Inglis, 1966). In recent years idiographic studies have also increasingly appeared in the growing literature on behavior modification (Bandura, 1961 & 1969; Leff,

1968; Gelfand & Hartmann, 1968). The behavior therapists seem to be establishing a new legitimacy for idiographic research methods and introducing to clinical practice an increased reliance upon scientific objectivity.

Unfortunately both critics (Breger & McGaugh, 1965) and apologists (Rachman & Eysenck, 1966) for behavioral treatment seem to feel that clinical work should be evaluated according to the procedures of the academic psychologist. Breger and McGaugh criticize the lack of controlled studies, while Rachman and Eysenck appear to argue that such studies will be forthcoming. By controlled studies is meant the same kind of large group studies that have for the most part produced inconclusive results concerning the effectiveness of therapy. In the midst of proper challenges to and defenses of learning-theory treatments, both behavior modifiers and their critics may overlook the significant methodological innovations these new techniques have brought to the clinic. In individual cases, behavior modifiers are attempting to specify independent variables, to manipulate these systematically, and to measure reliably the effect. Missionary fervor for or against a particular form of therapy has often been seen in the past, but the introduction of scientific procedure with the individual clinical case is by far the most exciting contribution of the behavior modifier.

Although we emphasize the importance of scientific method, we also feel that the clinician, in designing idiographic studies, must maintain a healthy perspective about the usual requirements of the academic psychologist. Despite the undisputed value of experimental control, he must ask himself whether the degree of preciseness employed in a study is truly appropriate to the problem being investigated. For example, the general rules of scientific psychology require evidence that measures employed have a known degree of reliability or that the chosen experimental designs control for suspected confounding variables. Yet, if the experimental-clinical psychologist abides strictly by such rules, he is unlikely to produce meaningful research. By the time the perfect design and ideal measurement of a dependent variable have been developed, the individual case for which these tools have been designed will have received some form of treatment (even in the absence of scientific methodology) and will have passed beyond the clinic walls. Consequently, in developing idiographic studies, the experimental clinician must strive for a degree of preciseness that is compatible with the urgency and practicalities of the treatment situation. Methodological sophistication should not be so idealized that a study can never be accomplished with the current patient; nor should it be so completely renounced that the clinician relies entirely on his own subjective judgment.

For the experimentalist, the idiographic experiment may be as important as the more commonly accepted group study. Science can just as legitimately advance itself with the study of individual cases as with attempting to demonstrate general principles with large groups of persons. If, as many would contend, pure curiosity is a proper motive of science, then the scientist can as reasonably be interested in the universe of a single individual's behavior as in that of many individuals. In fact, the detailed study of a single individual can provide the evidence to disconfirm widely held generalizations about behavior (Dukes, 1965). The collection of a number of similarly conducted idiographic studies may provide a sound basis for the formulation and test of a general law of behavior. Ultimately, the idiographic experiment places constraints upon the scientist that may unfortunately go overlooked in group studies. To demonstrate an effect in an idiographic study, the experimenter must be able to eliminate sources of error that would simply be "averaged out" in a group study.

Before concluding this discussion of the idiographic experiment, we should make explicit our assumptions about the commonness or uniqueness of human behavior. With Allport, we assume that each individual is a unique entity. As clinicians, we find ourselves particularly interested in unusual and deviant behaviors of our patients. Nevertheless, we assume the existence of general behavioral laws which may be abstracted from the observation of the unique behavioral traits of many persons. We would, however, make the distinction between the content of an individual's behavior and the process by which that behavior occurs. The content of a person's behavior would be expected to be predictable only on an idiographic basis, whereas behavioral processes would be common for all or at least for large classes of persons. For example, from learning theory we might predict that the consistent performance of a given behavior will depend upon its schedule of reinforcement. This prediction is based upon a general behavioral law concerning the process of behavior. Such a law would be broadly applicable. However, the functional conditions for reinforcement may be quite variable for different individuals. One child may be adequately reinforced by a pat on the back, whereas for another the same pat may serve as a punishment. The values of different reinforcers (or the specific contents of behavior) would be expected to be dependent upon the given individual's particular developmental history. Even given broadly applicable psychological principles such as "the law of effect," the scientist still needs to conduct idiographic experiments to determine the specific application of these principles. These specific applications will be lawful only for the individual subject. Evidently, neither a totally nomothetic, nor a totally idiographic, science could adequately encompass the clinician's task.

Given that the experimental-clinical method has all the values we have expounded, one may ask why idiographic experiments have so seldom been used in clinical practice. Certainly there is nothing in the concept of the experimental-clinical method that differs radically from the technologies of engineering or medicine. The method of idiographic experimentation has probably not been neglected because practitioners have a basic distrust of scientific procedures. Rather, idiographic experimentation goes unused because the method itself has been inadequately developed. In our own work, we have found that almost every case presents new methodological problems. Measurement, design, and evaluation problems occur with each new behavior that is studied. Often it appears that the resolution of these problems in a particular case would take longer than treatment needs could possibly warrant. In fact, at this point the experimental-clinical method may well be inefficient precisely because so much time is needed to develop the tools that can be used for the relevant idiographic experiments. Therefore, a major goal of our work has been to begin the development of measurement and design procedures for the efficient conduct of idiographic studies. Such knowledge is not readily available in the research literature nor provided in standard training programs. Experimental-clinical methods will not become an established fact until a variety of investigators take their development as a major task.

THE RESIDENTIAL TREATMENT CENTER

A residential treatment center is ideally suited to the development of experimental-clinical methods. Patients undergo an intensive, long-term living experience within the treatment facility. In our own facility, the Wisconsin Children's Treatment Center, almost all of the child's behavior occurs under the direct and continuous observation of trained staff. The clinician need not be satisfied with limited observations in school, the child's response in a therapy room, or parental reports of the child's behavior. Instead, every aspect of the child's day—the way he gets up in the morning, how he dresses, the way he eats, his disputes with peers, his episodes of creative play, his struggles with reading, and other daily situations—is available for observation and controlled study.

As has been emphasized by some pioneers of residential treatment (e.g., Bettelheim, 1950; Redl & Wineman, 1951), such centers permit a greater degree of environmental control than is typically available in an outpatient setting. The staff can provide consistent and continuous management of the child's total environment. Staff behavior can be highly controlled, the physical environment can be altered, the child's experiences with other children can be precisely structured. In short, the environment can be constructed to conform to treatment plans and research.

Although our studies have been made easier by the intensive residential setting in which we work, experimental-clinical methods are also relevant to other complex but less controllable environments. The work of Allen *et al.* (1964) and Harris *et al.* (1964) in a nursery-school setting, of Becker *et al.* (1967) and Thomas *et al.* (1968) in elementary schools, and of Patterson *et al.* (1968) in children's homes are representative examples of experimental-clinical work in less controllable settings than our own.

Subjects. Children present particular advantages as subjects in experimental-clinical work. There are fewer ethical problems involved in accepting total responsibility for the control of a child's environment, for few would question the responsibility of adults to establish broad value and behavioral goals for children. From a purely experimental view, children are desirable subjects in that their learning history is brief and they may be expected to respond relatively promptly to the imposition of treatment techniques. Since the total life of the child is available to the scrutiny of adults and since he is so dependent upon adults, the design of a total treatment program for children can be carried out more easily than would be possible for adult subjects. Thus, the research can be done in a more controlled fashion and the experimenters can have prompt feedback of the results of their work.

Our subjects are all children who required separation from their homes for treatment purposes. Two groups were studied. One was composed of young (three to seven years) severely disturbed (psychotic, autistic) boys and girls. The other group was composed of nine- to twelve-year-old boys who, although less disturbed, had been extruded from home, school, and community because of a variety of severe behavior problems. A more detailed description of the children and their families is contained in Chapter 2.

Theoretical Orientation and Experimental Variables. Once we had chosen the residential treatment setting and the disturbed children for our forays with the experimental-clinical method, our next task was to select a theoretical orientation and to specify the experimental variables to be studied. We would need to work within the framework of a scientifically acceptable theory whose concepts would assist in the operational definition of independent and dependent variables.

Learning theory as developed in the psychological laboratory appeared to meet a variety of scientific and practical requirements. In the clinical area, learning theory has recently proven highly productive—particularly in providing directions for idiographic studies. While presenting general hypotheses such as "the law of effect," learning theory is also flexible enough to account for specific individual differences in the operation of basic principles. Thus, the theory is quite suitable for applying basic behavioral principles to the problems of unique human subjects. Learning theory appeared capable of providing adequate definitions for independent variables to permit the precise specification of the treatment milieu. The learning theorist's emphasis upon observable dependent variables also seemed to promise direction in the task of applying experimental-clinical methods to the treatment of children.

For purposes of experimentation, we wanted to select independent variables consisting of specifically defined treatment techniques. For example, we were not interested in studying the effects of such broadly defined techniques as a benign environment or family therapy. Such techniques seemed too gross and all-encompassing in their definition, and consequently would not permit precise cause-and-effect findings. Our choice was to examine the treatment environment in much more detail. Thus, we wanted to know the effect of particular kinds of childrens' activities upon changes in behavior. We wanted to study the effects of specific actions taken by staff members toward children. For example, what is the effect when a staff member shouts angrily at a child for a particular response as opposed to praising him for some other incompatible behavior? In short, we studied treatment techniques which would answer the common questions of parents and child-care workers, "What should I do when the child does . . . ?" or "How do I get him to do . . . ?" We assume that certain general attitudes on the part of treatment personnel and attributes of the treatment environment were interactive with the treatment programs, upon which we shall speculate in subsequent chapters.

Similarly, the dependent variables needed to be clearly specified. We were not interested in studying changes in grossly defined feeling states, or traditional diagnostic classifications. As our dependent variables, we wished to study the specific behaviors that comprised the referral complaints of parents and community. Thus, we wanted to study the effects of our treatment conditions upon behaviors such as tantrums, fighting, disorganized speech, isolate behavior, encopresis, arguing, swearing, crying, etc. These, we hoped, would be objectively observable dependent variables.

The object of our experimental-clinical studies has not been to answer questions such as "What is the effect of residential treatment upon childhood psychoses?" or "What is the effect of benign adult attitudes upon thought disorder?" Rather, our experimental questions have taken the form: "What is the effect of token reinforcement upon the development of speech behavior?"

Our committment to learning theory and behavior modification techniques is secondary to our concern for the application of experimental-clinical methods. The method of applying scientific procedures to the treatment of each case should be equally possible within other sound theoretical frameworks. The variables selected for manipulation and study might differ, but the general procedures of hypothesis formation, measurement, and use of experimental design would remain similar. The setting in which we work, our particular subject population, and our own training biases have led us to select the learning-theory approach. However, at a time when relatively little is entirely valid, we hope that clinicians will increasingly apply scientific methods to separate fact from myth in their everyday work.

The Experimental-Clinical Studies

The remainder of this book reports on the behavior modification programs that have been conducted with disturbed children at the Wisconsin Children's Treatment Center. The basic intent of these studies has been the development and demonstration of experimental-clinical procedures.

The research has been the result of the efforts of all of our staff. Consequently, we have provided in Chapter 2 a general description of our treatment groups. Presentation of the data would be meaningless without prior discussion of the selection, training, organization, and total functioning of the staff groups. The staff have consistently given of themselves to provide the children with excellent care. Bettelheim (1950) was no doubt correct in stating that "Love Is Not Enough," but were love enough, the children in our units would have shown the quickest behavior changes ever recorded. Beyond providing loving, sensitive care to the children, our staff have (as will become clear from the studies) contributed to every aspect of research design and data-gathering. The organization, devotion, and morale of the staff were essential to the total experimental-clinical enterprise.

During the course of these studies, by far the greatest number of problems have been in the areas of experimental design and measurement. In many situations, good experimental-clinical studies have not been completed because a major amount of our time has necessarily been devoted to these more basic problems. We hope that our experience in some of these difficult situations will provide at least minimal aid in solving similar problems as they are encountered by other investigators. Consequently, Chapters 3 and 4 have been written to discuss issues of design and measurement in experimental-clinical procedures.

In the course of this project we have considered and experimented with a broad range of treatment techniques. Chapter 5 summarizes our thoughts and representative data on a variety of behavior modification techniques. A recurrent concern in all of our work has arisen because of some of the peculiar effects of social reinforcement with our children. Several studies of social reinforcement are therefore combined in Chapter 6.

A number of detailed case studies are included in Chapter 7, giving a day-by-day account of experimental-clinical procedures in action with individual children. These cases are intended to illustrate the values of constant monitoring of treatment effects, as well as the values of providing total milieu planning for the treatment of disturbed children.

We hope that the contents of this book will be a first approximation to the experimental-clinical model. Firmly committed experimentalists may find some of our solutions to design and measurement problems unsatisfactory. Firmly committed behaviorists may find some of our discussion too introspective. Traditional clinicians may desire more consideration of cognition and feeling states. Our own awareness of these differences is heightened by the fact that we feel that an adequate experimental-clinical psychology can test all of these different orientations.

Many new treatment methods have met with enormous initial success and exuberance, only to be followed by periods of increasing ennui as professionals find them relatively unsuccessful and impractical. The stage of excitement over the initial success of behavior modification is rapidly drawing to a close as more and more persons ask cogent questions about its overall applicability. For example, Gardner (1968) asks for evidence that behavior modification programs can be carried out at the ward level by regular staff, that such programs produce long-term gains, that multiple behaviors can be treated, and that there exist efficient behavioral measures for evaluation. We believe our studies provide data relevant to all of these questions. But more important, we hope that experimental-clinical procedures will provide a guideline for answering the many relevant questions that should be raised whenever any treatment method is used to alter disturbed behavior. We offer the following report of our studies as initial evidence that treatment of disturbed individuals can indeed eventually achieve the status of an applied science.

CHAPTER TWO

The Residential Setting and Treatment Groups

Total Programming

Our treatment approach assumes that significant aspects of the child's behavior either are or can be brought under the control of his immediate environment. The day-long living situation of the residential treatment center provides an endless series of opportunities to stimulate and reinforce desirable behavior patterns. To accomplish this goal, however, the clinician must determine each of the events which occur in that day-long environment. "Therapy" does not occur just during a specified hour when the child is in a playroom with the "therapist." Education does not occur solely when the child is sitting in a classroom with a "teacher." Behavior is being shaped just as much when the child is brushing his teeth or watching the cook prepare a meal. Presumably, whoever is spending time with the child can have a direct effect on his behavior and learning. It is likely that the effect any one person or setting has on the child's behavior is a direct function of the length of time the child spends with that person or in that setting. Thus, the real *therapists* in a treatment center are those persons (i.e., the child-care staff) who spend the most time with that child. Hence, the behavior of the child-care staff must occur according to treatment plans in order to have the desired results in the child's behavior.

The Residential Setting and Treatment Groups

CHILDREN'S TREATMENT CENTER— PURPOSE AND HISTORICAL DEVELOPMENT

The Children's Treatment Center was formed by an active public group interested in the development of treatment, training, and research programs for severely disturbed children. This founding group recognized that the needs of disturbed children could not be met adequately in large state hospital programs. They also realized that costs of intensive treatment were high, while the effectiveness of such programs was relatively low. Clearly, applied research was needed to seek out improved treatment methods. Further, there was a desperate need to provide clinical training for mental-health workers. Finally, this group recognized that an emotionally disturbed child may often be the product of a distressed family. Treatment of all family members would have to be available if the children were to readjust to the mainstream of home and community living.

According to legislative mandate, the Center opened in 1963 as a tax-supported facility charged with the treatment of disturbed children and their families, the conduct of applied research, and the training of personnel in all of the mental-health disciplines. As a small (capacity for 30 in-patients) facility, it was hoped the Center would provide research, training, and demonstration programs that could serve as the basis for future development of state services to disturbed children.

THE RESIDENTIAL CENTER AS A CONTINGENT ENVIRONMENT

The kinds of institutional environments into which children may be thrust have been variously described along a continuum from benign to punitive. In the purely benign environment the child is well fed and clothed, granted his desires in everything, and rarely if ever frustrated. At the other extreme is the punitive environment of the old-time reform school or understaffed orphanage. Although these two extremes contrast greatly, they are equally useless in their ability to promote behavioral growth. Indeed, they are identical in that rewards and punishments are not clearly contingent upon the child's behavior.

We have employed the term "contingent environment" to describe our therapeutic milieu. The optimal contingent environment is one in which a child's behavior results in clearly defined consequences. These consequences, be they rewards or punishments, are training conditions designed to lead to the child's acquisition of socially acceptable behaviors. To make maximal use of residential treatment, the child's entire day should be brought under the control of such contingencies. There must be a minimum of "floating" time wherein neither the child nor the staff are engaged in therapeutically planned activities. "Free time" should exist for the children only when they have progressed to sufficiently complex levels of behavior that they require decreased staff supervision to manage effectively.

In the contingent environment there are a minimum of locked doors, fences are unnecessary, and uniforms are replaced by street clothes. The children's behavior should be controlled by the reinforcers typical of his community, not by keys, fences, or authoritarian dress. If there is sufficient total programming for each child, and staff available as he needs them, he will neither be disposed to run away nor need constant monitoring lest he run. Youngsters will have nothing to run away from or to, if the program is adequately rewarding. Children often run away from the boredom and punishment of residential programs. In the contingent environment of the residential setting, all staff at the facility are involved in the programs. Staff, ranging from superintendent to kitchen personnel to psychologists to engineering crew, should identify themselves as part of the treatment environment for the child and understand that they are working there, not only for their living, but for the treatment of the youngster.

Total programming is based on a few simplified principles of learning theory. For example, independent of those physiological variables which may render the disturbed child likely to acquire the strange responses which led to his having been diagnosed as such, the child did in fact learn these responses. It is predictable that the responses or habits, desirable or undesirable, will have generalized to a multitude of stimuli in his environment and can be evoked by those stimuli. One can predict that the abnormal responses themselves serve as stimuli capable of eliciting chains of abnormal habits. Although the early training conditions remain speculative, a child acquires secondary reinforcers which are unique to his own learning history. The child may also have acquired many behaviors which are self-reinforcing, such as rocking or twirling. Social reinforcers, therefore, can interact with the child's own reinforcers in maintaining certain responses.

Some children may have very few reinforcers, or socially unusual ones. Nevertheless, when the child is admitted, his referral behaviors, directly or through some indirect chain of responses, operate or are maintained by some reinforcement contingencies which are available on some unknown schedule. This myriad of generalized responses, unidentified and with interactive reinforcers and schedules, remains unpredictable to the clinician. There has yet to be performed an experimental analysis of behavior that predictably observed and recorded the multitude of responses and their naturally available reinforcement schedules. However, accepting some simple facts of behavior, one may presume that, as he extinguishes or punishes certain undesirable responses, he will have some effect in decelerating related responses. Also, if the treatment program allows the child to rehearse previously acquired undesirable responses, that effect will generalize to related responses (Buell *et al.*, 1968). Thus, one has to control all the behaviors of the child in order to reinforce differentially the available and preferred responses as well as those to be acquired, and to extinguish or suppress the "abnormal" behaviors which necessitated the child's referral. This attempt to achieve continual and pervasive behavioral control is total programming.

To attain such a treatment model is in some respects comparable to scientifically rearing a normal child, a feat accomplished quite expertly but in total scientific ignorance by most people. However, with the emotionally disturbed child, the clinician has to extinguish numerous habits while simultaneously teaching new responses. Parents must extinguish and punish also, but the emotionally disturbed child is defined in part by the many responses which parents, schools, and professionals have been unable to suppress (or to teach). So the optimal rehabilitation program would control all behaviors. By control, we do not mean behavioral restriction as found in a prison. Rather we mean identification and prevention of the occurrence of those stimulating and reinforcing conditions maintaining the deviant behaviors, and the systematic presentation of conditions designed and measured for their success in helping the acquisition of desirable social responses.

The patient's parents are required to participate on an increasing schedule in the total programming model for two reasons. First, they must ultimately assume the social responsibility of training their child. Second, many of the child's deviant responses are evoked and maintained, however innocently and inadvertently, to some degree by the parents. Thus, they must be interacting in a training program with their child so that their unsuccessful parental behaviors can be eliminated and replaced with the techniques staff have identified as more effective with their child.

Since it requires so long to identify the child's deviant responses and to test various treatment procedures, the parents generally do not come in more than once a week for the first few weeks. The parent-training schedule is expanded progressively until they have again assumed total responsibility for their child while simultaneously adopting those programs we have constructed for training their youngster.

During the course of the child's treatment program, the staff all rotate continually in conducting the multiple-treatment programs such as those described in the section on case studies. This staff rotation is to assure optimal generalization of treatment effects. Each child's program begins with a very delimited environment, such as working with only one staff member in the child's room. The child's environment expands gradually as his behavior improves. Total programming, then, is simply defined as shaping, involving multiple and concurrent behaviors. The mechanics and the logistics of administering a program with multiple and simultaneous responses are exceptionally difficult. As in any shaping program, one must be prepared to "back up" when one has advanced a child too rapidly. At such a time, one drops back to an earlier level of the program and proceeds at a pace which is more likely to assure success.

The various treatment programs should be monitored constantly to see whether one should proceed to train more complex responses. The data in the experimental designs discussed in this book do not incorporate the habit interactions which comprise a child's total behavior, and which ideally should be understood and used to advantage in a treatment program. The studies presented unfortunately imply that each habit was autonomous and independent of all other responses—an interpretive error but not intended by the data.

DEVELOPMENT OF INDIVIDUAL TREATMENT GOALS

Clinical judgment plays a crucial role in the selection of treatment procedures and behavioral goals for a child. There is not a book of tabled social behaviors considered to be appropriate at given ages for children of cultural subgroups. At the beginning of the program, treatment goals are generally derived from the referral behaviors of the child. Seldom do the referral behaviors which are discussed in the diagnostic evaluation include all of the disturbing components of a behavior that are treated. Globally descriptive behaviors are usually referred to as requiring treatment. It is only after the child has been admitted and observed for several weeks that the staff are able conjointly to decide upon the specific behaviors which should be decelerated or acquired. The clinician supervising the treatment group generally makes the final decisions on the treatment behaviors. Other clinicians may well have chosen different responses and treatment procedures. Not only is there considerable behavioral variance among children, but also among clinicians establishing treatment programs. This variability is further reason for using same-subject methodology performed in a scientific manner to control for this difference among investigators.

The behaviors chosen for study among the children described in Chapter 7 did satisfy several criteria which may be helpful to other investigators establishing such programs. First, the behaviors under treatment had to be observable, discrete responses which all staff could agree upon. Unfortunately, reliability studies were not performed for the numerous responses which were investigated, for reasons of expense and our inability to provide meaningful interpretation. The behaviors chosen for treatment had to be measurable by being counted with a hand tally counter, a check mark, or simply a notation of the presence or absence of a given class of behavior. The behaviors chosen for treatment had to be such that their deceleration or acquisition would make the child more amenable to receiving positive social reinforcement and acquiring normal responses in his own environment.

The kinds of treatment goals described above assume clinical responsibility performed under the discipline of the scientific method. This responsibility for the patient's welfare in a scientific framework is contrasted to the numerous university research projects in which scientific rigor may be stringently present, but total clinical responsibility is often absent. Our treatment programs were not scientific in every aspect. For example, placement of a youngster in a public school was usually not conducted under a data-oriented program, nor were the purchase of new shoes, haircuts, etc. Hundreds of decisions that comprise clinical responsibility in the treatment of these youngsters were made in addition to those made in our experimental treatment of a few behaviors.

DEVELOPMENT OF TREATMENT PROGRAMS

Group Goals. The difficulties of administering highly individualized programs can frequently be simplified by placing the children in relatively homogeneous treatment groups. If the children are of approximately the same age, and at similar levels in verbal and physical skills, portions of programs can be conducted at a group level. Among our older children, we maintained a nine- to 12-year age range and restricted admission to boys. Programs for activities like dressing, bathing, group games, and meal-time behavior could often be directed on a group basis. In Chapter 3 we seek a method for establishing and assessing performance with respect to certain group behavior goals. When we found several children to be deficient with respect to a subset of these goals (e.g., table manners), we often found it was possible to use the same treatment technique simultaneously with all of the children. In establishing group goals, the clinician must, however, be careful that he is not overlooking the particular needs of an individual child. If a child fails to respond to a group type of treatment procedure, the clinician should immediately assess this idiosyncracy of the child's behavior and, if necessary, design a more individually oriented treatment approach.

DISCHARGE CRITERIA AND PROCEDURES

The decision to discharge a child from the treatment program was contingent on more than the data accumulated for acquisition or extinction of specific behaviors. A variety of information was involved in the decision to discharge a child, with academic success one of the foremost prerequisites. It was the return of the child to functioning at his grade level, or at a level consistent with his intellectual abilities, which comprised school success. The child's discharge required that there should be the minimum of staff supervision necessary for the child's maintenance of optimal social behaviors in residence, in the public school setting, at home visits, and in play with his peers in the community. When the child is discharged, there must be a willingness not only of the staff to allow the child to leave, but also of the family to accept the child back into the home. Not only must the child's behavior be satisfactory to his parents and peers in the community; his parents also should be in control of that behavior—capable of maintaining the preferred behaviors and identifying reoccurrence of nonpreferred behaviors. There should be such a gradual fading of the child out of the residential program that there is little surprise on the day he packs his belongings and returns home. Local agency responsibility should be established to assure that lines of communication will be maintained between the family and the treatment setting after the child has been discharged. This is necessary not only for the accumulation of follow-up data, but also to provide channels of communication between the family and the residential center in the event that the child's adjustment to the community begins to deteriorate. The parents should be sufficiently educated that they will seek the assistance of the treatment facility if problems do arise, even years after discharge. There are other realities which enter into the decision to discharge the child, such as the necessity of freeing a bed for an emergency case.

It requires considerable courage on the part of a clinician to return a child to the residential center when his behavior deteriorates at home. Returning the child to the treatment program because of a retrieval of the original referral behaviors, or the acquisition of new behaviors, indicates that the clinician has accepted the treatment responsibility for the child.

STAFF CREDENTIALS

The staff credentials discussed here include the child-care workers and nursing personnel who were primarily responsible for the treatment programs which are described in this text. The treatment groups were supervised by psychologists in conjunction with social workers. Occupational therapists, teachers, and members of other disciplines were also involved. The child-care worker is primary to the success of the treatment model as described herein. Preferably, the child-care worker should be of above average intelligence and should be employed on a full-time basis. We hope that child-care workers will eventually establish a professional position, training for a degree comparable to a bachelor's degree with a major in child-care work, and that there will be appropriate and competitive salaries available for those who achieve that professional position. The child-care workers who accumulated the data contained in the case studies were capable of such an education and some were then involved in acquiring a bachelor's degree. The training of the child-care workers involved either a full-time six-week program conducted at the Center, or a grant-supported program designed to train child-care workers for institutions throughout the state. The training program consisted of courses taught by social workers, psychologists, psychiatrists, occupational therapists, educators, and nursing personnel on job skills necessary to the child-care worker, and advanced courses on behavior modification and the research conducted at the Center. Child-care workers included in the research groups also had on-the-job supervision. The individuals who were in the programs at their inception had taken a number of training sessions on learning theory and research methodology that would be used in the programs. Periodically, we would review the status of the research at meetings in addition to the usual hours at the Treatment Center. Child-care workers in the research groups were kept up-to-date on relevant literature by the senior investigators.

Staff Problems. The treatment techniques for the case studies presented in Chapter 7 were carried out by supervised child-care workers and nursing staff. Since these persons were primarily responsible for the treatment programs, it is appropriate to discuss some of the staffing problems which can interfere with the optimal functioning of an experimental-clinical program. The following discussion will focus on the necessity for having well-trained nursing and child-care staffs and on the kinds of problems of which one should be aware and should minimize.

Although it may be denied by some professionals, we contend that the nursing and ward staffs in most inpatient residential settings have always assumed primary responsibility for patient management, and therefore most treatment effects. This argument is easily substantiated if one simply contrasts the number of hours per day the patient is receiving direct treatment from a psychologist or psychiatrist to the hours he spends in the ward setting where the environment is controlled completely by nursing and aide staff. Furthermore, we maintain that in most residential settings the amount of therapeutic endeavor by the professional staff is inversely related to the severity of emotional disturbance in the patient. For example, as in many state hospitals, at the beginning of a patient's first admission to the residential program his chances are maximum for receiving a limited exposure to either individual or, more likely, group psychotherapy. If the patient demonstrates quick remission, which is most likely to occur during his first admission, he will remain in that professional treatment setting for the duration of his residential care. However, if the patient does not remiss quickly, it becomes increasingly likely that he will be discharged from individual or group therapy so that patients who are more likely to profit from therapy will be allowed their turns. The result of this very economical decision is that, as a patient becomes worse or remains very disturbed, he will be placed in the back-ward settings, where his direct professional therapy decreases and his contact with nonprofessional care increases progressively. This is the strange dilemma of many state-supported residential facilities where there is an inverse relationship between optimally trained therapeutic intervention and the severity of the patient's disturbance. Perhaps this dilemma served to perpetrate the myth that the traditional treatment procedures were of value, when in fact they were reserved for persons most likely to remiss whether or not they received that treatment. The kind of ward management performed by minimally trained and supervised aid and nursing-level staff has been the subject of popular novels (e.g., Kesey, 1962).

It is of historical interest to note that early investigators of behavior therapy, particularly those innovating new programs, were often allowed to use only the most regressed backward cases in the hospital setting (e.g., Aylion and Michael, 1959). The behavior therapists have accepted that challenge and have repeatedly demonstrated treatment effects where traditional therapies were ineffectual. Furthermore, these early studies employed ward staff who had to be trained to perform the treatment programs.

Since the treatment methodology presented here relies substantially upon child-care workers and nursing staff, we shall present some of the problems which may hinder optimal functioning of such treatment programs. It has been our experience that one outstanding indicator of a poorly functioning group (i.e., psychologists, social workers, nursing, child-care worker staff composing a team), or a treatment team with problems, is a decrease, if not an absence, of humor among the staff. When staff members are incapable of joking, if there is little laughter, or if certain members are essentially squelching humor, there are not sufficient adult kinds of social reinforcers available to maintain optimal performance and cooperation among staff. If the staff members, specifically the child-care workers and nurses, are not interacting positively, one may suspect that they will not work well with the children. Furthermore, it seems justifiable to state that a staff member who is unable to joke about his own behavior, or about his shortcomings in conducting certain programs, will be lacking in the objectivity necessary for performing an experimental-clinical treatment program. The team leader should demonstrate that correction of staff behavior, unless it is extremely serious, should be done with a certain amount of jest so that the staff member does not feel too suppressed, since this would risk generalizing to desirable aspects of his work. We do not mean to imply that the investigators are so humorous that they are unconcerned whether a treatment program succeeds or fails. The heartbreak of an ineffectual treatment program is difficult to accept no matter how objective one tries to be about the data. However, a treatment team is not going to function well unless there is considerable positive social reinforcement available among all members, and the extent of this is well represented by the amount of humor shared by the group members. Furthermore, staff members who are incapable of laughing spontaneously and frequently are certainly not very likely to be positive reinforcing agents for young children. Affectively flat staff members are unlikely to be reinforcing to other staff members, and one may expect that such persons will take criticism seriously and negatively, regardless of how the group leader presents the criticism. A staff member's inability to demonstrate that he is capable of socially acceptable humor may be one criteria to make him ineligible for membership in a treatment team.

Staff members should be encouraged to speak freely about the behavior of any given child as well as about any staff problem. If a staff member simply detests the behavior of a certain child, he should have the privilege of voicing that reaction, not only for the sake of speaking freely, but in order that something will be done about the behavior of the child. If this level of communication among staff members is lost or never originally established, the investigator will be existing in a communication vacuum. One of the communication dilemmas of many state hospitals is that a rigid chain of command is established, and the professional staff are told by the nurse what she understands they wish to hear. Such a rigid communication structure fosters false impressions about the behavior of the children as well as the effectiveness of treatment programs. All treatment staff should have the same freedom of speech; they should have the same recognition from the professional staff. This means, then, that the child-care worker and nurse both have the privilege of questioning a management order by the professional staff. We feel it is a privilege of *trained* ward staff to question any program, since they are the staff who are performing those programs. However, we suggest that ward staff should make their discussion on the efficacy of a treatment program dependent upon data, not simply on value judgments of what they consider to be the most efficacious program. Furthermore, we feel it is not of value to foster free license to chronic complaining among staff. With the experimental-clinical model, the questions and criticisms formed by the staff members should be subjected to the same evaluation as any treatment program devised by the psychologist. It is justifiable for a child-care worker to question the psychologist about the theoretical rationale for a given program if it is not understood by him, but it is not his prerogative to sabotage a program by failing to comply with a management order because he did not speak up when he had a question. A breakdown in communication among the treatment team occurs when professional staff members leave management orders like prescriptions, and the nursing staff then assign the work to the child-care staff. Two problems are likely to emerge in such instances. First, the psychologist will not be acquainted with many of the finer nuances of behavior that are crucial to establishing the most beneficial treatment program for the child. Second, in such circumstances, the nursing staff are assigned the responsibility for overseeing the treatment program, and it is the ward staff that will be in charge. Furthermore, the ward staff may be expected to be increasingly reluctant to do the extra work which is involved in behavior therapy programs when that work is in no way shared by the professional group leader.

A failure to train new staff to the standards of previously hired staff accounts for many of the staffing problems we have observed. Child-care worker staff at the Treatment Center are typically college students hired for a limited term of full-time employment, plus bright high school graduates. These persons seem motivated and able to perform the treatment programs more effectively than the underachieving high school graduates who are often the only other ones who would aspire to or compete for the poor salaries available for ward staff in some state hospitals. Employing college students has given impetus to our programs, but the problem of staff turnover is serious and constant. Every spring we may expect a certain percentage of staff to leave, to the detriment of the program. Since it requires approximately six to nine months of intensive work and feedback for a staff member to be optimally effective with children, it is crucial that an ongoing training program be maintained. We have observed that at the beginning of a new research project the required staff are equally trained. However, as the program progresses and as staff leave and new members join the group, there may be a decline in the effectiveness of treatment programs simply because the new staff were not so trained as the original staff.

Child-care workers and nurses who have previously worked with traditional treatment programs often voice the complaint that experimental-clinical programs are "unnatural." The complaints are usually directed at management orders involving very specific and rigid ways of responding to the child, an unnatural response mode for most persons. It is helpful for such staff members to monitor the data of the treatment programs at frequent intervals so they may have the feedback of the effectiveness of their work. It may be helpful to explain to the staff members that the treatment programs are indeed "unnatural" ways of dealing with children for them, and to assure them that after a few months they will become habitual. Failure to acquaint the child-care workers and nursing staff with the data which they accumulate is an easy mistake for the senior staff member to commit and one which should be prevented. It is usually reinforcing for staff to examine the data illustrating how effective they have been with a particular program, or to give them evidence to substantiate why they will need to alter an ongoing program. This is particularly true for slow-effect treatment programs, such as teaching a three-year-old autistic child to stop crying by having a time-out contingent upon that response. The treatment effect may require a long period of time (e.g., several months), and to offset the staff's discouragement in conducting that program, frequent examinations of the data will show if there is a preferred trend to the treatment condition. The data themselves may comprise a mutual reinforcer for all the research personnel and they should be used as such.

Failure to specify exactly the training programs staff members shall administer throughout the day often leads to a stagnating program. The treatment programs should advance in levels of complexity until eventually they approximate the behavioral expectancies of the normal environment to which the child shall return. If a child does not progress, his behavior becomes increasingly obnoxious to the staff, making it less likely that staff will be able to function effectively as positive reinforcers for the child's desired behaviors. Thus, staff boredom with a program may be a function of the psychologist's failure to design goal-directed treatment activities. Designing programs which demand increasingly complex responses of children is difficult. Psychologists are not trained in "what children do" during the day for successive periods of time. Occupational therapists are often familiar with child behavior expectancies and have been allied with our research projects in designing activities in which the children were trained.

We have observed that child-care worker and nursing staff may fail to reinforce continually newly acquired and more complex behaviors in the children. This problem of the staff's failure to reinforce at a sustained high rate often occurs with children who have progressed from very low to highly complex social behaviors as a function of a successful program. The staff members seem to fade their reinforcement ratio naturally, since the child is "doing as expected" and there is the absence of negative behaviors which previously demanded the staff's attention and served as a reminder to demand positive responses. The child who has progressed optimally receives less attention as the staff focus on the more disturbed youngsters in the treatment group, with the unfortunate result that the child retrieves some of the old behaviors to operate for staff attention. Since a major goal of a treatment program is to train behaviors which will be maintained in the home environment, the treatment reinforcement schedules should eventually be comparable to those available to the child in his school and home. However, we are often confronted with the problem of the staff's thinning out their reinforcement schedules much sooner than would be desirable, i.e., before the behavior has generalized sufficiently. It is necessary to monitor the staff periodically to assure that they are maintaining the reinforcement rates planned for a child. One way to control this problem is to show the staff by demonstration, or by referral to prior studies, what occurs when attention is given to the negative behaviors of a child, and what the effects are of decreasing a high reinforcement ratio for a newly acquired response.

The following problems were derived from discussions with staff members associated with one research group. The discussions dealt with what conditions contributed most to problems among staff and in performing the treatment programs both in our research facility and in a traditionally oriented state hospital.

Fatigue was a major problem the staff felt interfered with their performance, particularly on the weekends when the staff ratio was lowest. The staff working with the group of young psychotic children often had four children for one staff member for entire shifts on weekends, with no assistance from other research staff such as occupational therapists, school workers, or psychologists. The staff members complained that they would become so tired that they could not maintain a decent semblance of the treatment program for all the children, much less obtain accurate behavioral counts. They also complained that, when fatigued, they found it very difficult to reinforce the diversity of habits currently being trained. They also stated that the children would become particularly hyperactive when the staff ratio was low and the children would retrieve more of their old attention-getting behaviors. The result would then be that the staff member would become less positively reinforcing, more punitive, and his control of the childrens' behavior would crumble. This effect was repeatedly seen in the data for weekends when many of the undesirable behaviors would accelerate for the youngsters.

The staff related that the absence of desirable interstaff communication would be most likely to interfere with the establishment of experimental-clinical programs in state hospitals. Most of the staff members had had experience in such facilities. For example, the staff members questioned whether the child-care worker staff would be able to relate information pertinent to child behavior at the same level of influence as nursing staff. They felt that the interprofessional rivalries existent in many large hospital settings would prevent the child-care workers from having equal authority in reporting on the children's behavior. Staff members explicitly stated that it had been their experience in many facilities that there was a hierarchy among the different professional groups that did not engender interactive communication among staff. This breakdown in communication was reportedly most apparent at the time of shift changes, when the new staff, would be briefed on the children's behavior for the previous shift, and also during staff meetings.

The staff also agreed that the difficulty in acquiring accurate data throughout a shift was a third problem. Problems like the failure to take the counters along with them when beginning a new activity, or trying to recall the frequency of a behavior while a child was taken from one activity to another, produced unreliable data collection. The staff were cognizant of the necessity of agreement among staff as to the kinds of behaviors being counted, as well as the necessity of logging every occurrence of the response. They concluded that it would be better to have a few accurate counts rather than many unreliable counts.

A fourth problem related by staff was that of rivalry between groups—not a problem unique to the Children's Treatment Center. They were referring to other groups employing different theoretical orientations in their treatment approaches. Rivalries would develop particularly when children from one group were having difficulties with children from the other. At such times, perhaps, it would be best to separate the groups until the children were in better control, or to combine staff so that they may together control all the children. This leads into the next problem, which was that of limited space. Limited space is perhaps characteristic of most residential settings for emotionally disturbed children. The lack of space during the winter is disabling to a program, particularly when the program involves working with children on a one-to-one basis. There is no solution for this problem except pressing for building funds.

A sixth problem which the staff suspect would interfere with the development of similar programs in other state-supported facilities was that of using food as reinforcers, and also punishment programs employing electric shock. State laws, or directives from state mental health services intended for the necessary humanitarian treatment of patients, may make it impossible to use primary reinforcers, regardless of the available research supporting such a decision. The humanitarian appeal behind such laws, designed to prevent the medieval practices of punishment that plagued state facilities for decades (the remnants of which are still with us), is obvious. However, one is confronted with the humanitarian decision of refusing to employ a successful treatment program for children in which food may be used contingently. This problem must be dealt with at the state level as well as within each agency. At least with the experimental-clinical model, one would be able to substantiate whether a desirable effect did result from a program using food as a reinforcer or for certain punishment contingencies; this would be the most satisfactory justification to the humanitarian.

Another problem cited by the staff was the lack of facilities and equipment, such as certain playground items, that would engender responses they were attempting to teach. This problem arises from the available budgets for many mental health facilities—budgets which are almost universally inferior. Inclusion of a well-trained occupational therapist who had had experience with children minimized our problem of lack of funds for equipment. The education of an occupational therapist trains him to use a variety of commonly found items in most ingenious ways to elicit desirable responses that are then available for reinforcement.

A final problem which the staff described at the traditional state hospital was lack of dedication or loyalty among staff. More broadly stated, their accusation is directed at the many large programs with an orientation which maintains neither mutual reinforcers among staff nor job-related reinforcers other than salary. The staff illustrated this problem by referring to facilities where it is impossible for staff members to interchange working hours because of bureaucratic entanglements. In discussing this problem, the staff members frequently referred to the personnel often hired in state facilities, e.g., the "man off the street" who was hired to work as a custodial attendant but never trained as such. A treatment team simply does not function with that quality of personnel. In the behavior modification programs described in the journals and presented in this book, the qualifications and training generally required of institutional aids would not be satisfactory. It is foreseeable that in the near future two years of college education will be required, as well as an intensive in-service training program. Some states (e.g., Illinois) have already created professional child-care career positions, thereby recognizing that persons most directly responsible for treating the patient in the residential setting should be trained for the job.

We have not conducted a formal study to isolate what behaviors or relationships effect the most desired staff cooperation necessary for an experimental-clinical treatment program. We have emphasized the "team" approach as the necessary model for conducting such treatment programs. The "team" is not a hierarchal status group in which there is an unyielding chain of command comparable to what one would find in an army or in many large agencies. Perhaps the model we are trying to present for the treatment program is the kind of "team" one finds in a good home. We are advocating that all members on the treatment team are the temporary "parents" of the child in residential care. In addition, all of the team members, or "parents," should be trained so that they are able to communicate on the same level. Furthermore, they should all have the same privileges of communication, and they should all be equally aware of how effective the treatment programs are for "their" child in treatment.

We recommend strongly that the investigator, regardless of his professional training, should have his office in the immediate setting where the children are in treatment. In the large hospital using the experimental-clinical model, the clinician's office should be on the ward with the children. If there is a cottage system such as at the Children's Treatment Center, the clinician's office should be in the cottage. When one accepts someone else's child for residential care, he is assuming the responsibility of the parents. The treatment program should be designed to approximate the normal environment in which the parents reside at home with the children. It is reasonable, then, that the investigator be in as close physical proximity to the child as possible, just as a parent would be. There are other reasons for the clinician to have his office in the ward setting. First, the clinician is able to monitor the staff and to provide them with the feedback necessary to correct their errors and reinforce their competence. Second, it is important that the investigator work with the child or children just as are the child-care worker and nursing staff. Location on the ward is not a treatment panacea. When the investigator's office is where the children are residing, he is able to monitor the treatment program better, and he will be conducting some of the treatment programs himself along with the other staff members. The authoritarian model of the professional staff member leaving management orders to the discretion of senior ward personnel, typically a nurse, is a model likely to guarantee that that professional staff member will be ignorant of what is occurring on the ward. We also suggest that the clinical investigator should be responsible for working on the ward when there is a deficit in available staff. The clinical staff should assist in cleaning up fecal smearing as well as providing the model for shaping speech in a psychotic mute child. The clinical investigator should be active in every aspect of the treatment program, and he should never expect anything of his staff members that he is unable to perform himself—from janitorial duties to data analysis.

CHILDREN IN RESEARCH GROUPS

The children whose case studies are presented in Chapter 7 were members of one of two research groups. One research group was composed of boys, aged nine through twelve years chronologically, who were referred with a variety of diagnoses ranging from borderline psychoses, neuroses, and psychopathy. Some of the boys had natural parents, some had foster parents, and some were eligible for adoption. The second research group was composed of male and female children referred as autistic or schizophrenic. Their chronological ages ranged from three to seven years at date of admission. These children had to have real or adoptive parents at date of admission. The data derived from these two research groups are not restricted to the particular cases presented. We should like to emphasize that the data are relevant to the experimental-clinical method. This is not a text on how to treat neurotic or psychotic children; it just happens that these were the dominant diagnostic classifications of the children in the research groups. The same methodology, i.e., experimental methodology with observable dependent variables, would be generalizable to an adult alcoholic or psychotic. It is, of course, hoped that the treatment techniques and hypotheses which have evolved from the case studies will assist measurably with programs for similar groups of children. However, the message of this text is methodology, not technique.

The children in the research group for psychosis were referred with the diagnosis of childhood autism or schizophrenia. Some of the children demonstrated obvious neurological signs, although at date of admission none was sufficiently compliant to permit administration of a neurological examination, much less a psychological test battery. The children's differential diagnosis distinguishing autism from schizophrenia and isolating retardation or brain-damage variables was not pursued. It was recognized that there were no reliable discriminatory diagnostic variables as evinced by the lack of agreement on diagnosis among referring agencies. It was an admission requirement that children have no speech, be devoid of compliant behaviors, demonstrate aggressive behaviors; the presence of self-destructive responses was optional. Each child's admission to the group had to be the family's last resort, implying that all other attempted treatment programs had been unsuccessful. One reason for this was that we wanted assurance that the parents had finished "shopping" for quick cures and had accepted the behavioral status and prognosis of their child. This assurance was maintained in most but not all cases. These children demonstrated disturbed sleep patterns, toilet training was not required, eating problems were dominant, and a variety of bizarre responses and stereotyped behaviors were characteristic of each child. It was impossible to predict each child's potential intellectual functioning. It was repeatedly explained to the parents that we were unable to make such predictions, that our goals would constantly be reformulated, and that we would strive for acquisition of normal behavioral patterns. We explained that the treatment techniques traditionally employed were ineffectual, that their child was in a research program where we could make no guarantees, but that we would at all times keep them informed of their child's progress. Regardless of our attempts to be objective, the parents invariably became increasingly optimistic, which made it difficult for both investigators and families to maintain their objectivity about the children.

The children did not show physical abnormalities which would be suggestive or indicative of primary mental retardation. Functional retardation was obvious, since the youngsters did not even demonstrate sufficient behavior for us to assess intelligence. Medication was discontinued for all youngsters prior to admission, so there were no drug-induced or drug-suppressed behaviors. The children were administered no psychiatric drugs during residency because we wanted each child to be optimally amenable to the treatment programs. This decision does not imply that psychiatric drugs were of no value for these children; it simply means that we were neither conducting a formal drug study nor intending to investigate the interactive effects of medication on the treatment programs.

It was intended that the parents reside within a 50-mile radius of the Treatment Center, because of the requirement of increasing visits. This qualification was not enforced, and some parents lived farther than 100 miles from the Center. This distance did interfere significantly with the parent-training program as well as with reintroducing the child into his environment. Such problems as this convinced us of the necessity of the regional treatment center model, which is in contrast to the traditional state hospital system.

FAMILY TREATMENT

It is the success of a family therapy treatment program which will assure that a child's treatment effects will remain permanent. It has been our contention, reflected in other literature in the field, that optimal child treatment cannot be conducted independently of the family constellation. The following discussion will present the treatment model used with the parents of the children described in this text. The family therapy program as described is in the pilot stage of development and there has been little data accumulation. However, we do consider the family therapy program to be as important as the child's individual treatment program.

Contract between Family and Treatment Center. When a child is referred to the Treatment Center, a verbal contract is established with the parents during the course of the diagnostic evaluation, which typically requires three consecutive half-day visits at the Treatment Center. The parents agree to remain involved with their child during the course of his treatment in the residential program. It is repeatedly implied that we shall not allow the parents to reject the child, that, if they fail to keep their scheduled appointments and to work as intensively as we expect them to, we shall go out into the community and bring them to the Center. The entire family is involved in the evaluation, which is performed by the professional staff who would be working with the family and child if he is accepted for residential treatment. The social worker usually serves as the spokesman for the family. All members of the family are requested to explain why they have sought the services of the Treatment Center, which makes it clear from the very beginning that the youngest to the eldest of the family is part of the referred child's problem and may be an integral member of the treatment team. The parents are made aware that behavioral changes will be expected of the referred child, as well as with all members of the family as they interact and maintain the child's deviant behaviors. Psychological evaluations, educational testing, psychiatric interviews, and social histories are accumulated during this diagnostic evaluation. The family is observed as a unit during meal times at the Center, eating with the other children in a dining hall. If there is an agency involved in the referral, a person from that agency must be present during the evaluation and interpretation. This is required because, if a foster family or adoptive plan will eventually be integrated with the treatment program, it will be assured that more than one agency will have a continuing obligation to the child. The diagnostic team also arranges for a home visit during which several members of the professional staffs will visit the child's home for most of a day to obtain observations and hypotheses regarding the child's behavioral difficulties and how the family members are involved with them. Video tape equipment may be taken on home visits to record those instances on which hypotheses about the child's behavior may be based.

During the course of the evaluation, it is clarified that the parents are not relinquishing custody of their youngster to us and that we consider them at all times to be responsible for their child's behavior. It is the role of a treatment program to determine which treatment techniques will be most effective in teaching the child appropriate behaviors, to train the parents to use the treatment programs, and to monitor their success. It is our contention that the parents must be able to maintain the habits that the child is taught while in the residential program. We recognize that one cannot control the post-residential environment to which the child will be discharged. Furthermore, we are aware that once a habit is acquired, it may forever be retrievable to the child. This means that a youngster may quickly reinstate the previously acquired abnormal habit patterns which necessitated his original referral. It is the parents' responsibility to be able to retrain the preferred behavioral patterns learned in the treatment program if some of the old habit patterns appear. It is assumed that if a child has acquired a combination of abnormal behaviors in the home environment, then acquires more appropriate responses in the residential treatment center, and is then discharged back to the original environment, those earlier referral behaviors are likely to be reinstated. Therefore, the model of the program is to teach the parents the appropriate parental skills so that they may maintain the acquired behaviors of the child when he is discharged to the home. The parents cannot perform such a duty by visiting a youngster in an unstructured manner once a week. Some parents have spent up to 20 hours per week working individually with their child. This family treatment program suggests that a regional model would be most appropriate for residential treatment.

Parental involvement by continued responsibility for the child during a treatment program is not a new concept in the field. The literature is replete with family therapy techniques in which family involvement is emphasized. This is particularly apparent in the multiple-impact therapy approach (MacGregor *et al.,* 1964).

The contract with the family requires a complete explanation of the treatment techniques relative to their particular child's problems. It is made clear to the parents that there are no guarantees of treatment effects for their child. Staff try to be realistic in explaining the child's status to the parents. All data are available to the parents during their scheduled visits, and they are free to enter the nursing station at their own discretion to review the data. If the parents are not showing an appropriate degree of interest in their child's advancement, then staff impose upon them to review the data for themselves. It is made clear to the parents that miracle cures are not available in the field of child treatment. It is emphasized that they have to become as proficient as our staff in maintaining the treatment programs for their youngster before they may expect to see a substantial generalization of the treatment effects toward them.

It has been our commitment to the parents that the Treatment Center will always be available to the family and their child if further problems develop within the family. This family contract is necessary to interrupt the "clinic shuffle" in which parents and child seem to shuffle from one clinic to another for successive diagnostic evaluations with no long-term treatment responsibility being assumed by any one agency.

Part of our contract requires that there shall be an open-door policy with the parents. If it is ever necessary for keys to be used for locking doors, such as a quiet room, the parents will be given those keys during their visits with the child and be instructed in the appropriate use of them. Parents are not restricted to certain times for their visits. The parents are not given the message that they report to a reception area and wait until a professional has time to see them at the latter's convenience. Appointments, of course, are made for a family therapy interview. However, the parents are made aware that they may visit at any time, and the usual courtesy of giving some forewarning of at least an hour is appreciated but is certainly not mandatory. We want to maintain the attitude that the child is the parents' responsibility, that the child is never removed from that responsibility, and that the parents always retain the privilege to visit and work with their child in addition to any scheduled hours under staff supervision. Parents maintain their responsibility in other forms such as allowances, clothes, paying for trips, birthday parties, etc.

This contract with the family involves all the professional staff. The child-care workers and nurses who assume primary treatment responsibility with the children are instructed to have coffee breaks, even meals, with the parents. These staff members must feel sufficiently comfortable eventually to go into the parents' home with the youngster during the gradual return of the child to his home environment.

Didactic Program. Didactic training is an integral component of the treatment program with parents. The parents are provided information, such as Patterson's manual (Patterson & Gullion, 1968) and similar materials on using behavior modification techniques in the home. Other investigators report encouraging results of using parents as the therapists for their children (Hawkins *et al.,* 1966; Patterson, WPA Paper, 1959; Wahler *et al.,* 1965; Wetzel *et al.,* 1966; Zeilberger *et al.,* 1968). The didactic program with the parents is to train them how to administer the treatment techniques we find to be most effective with their youngster. This program requires the parents to visit on an increasing schedule, which is usually more convenient for mothers than fathers. Evening visits are necessary for many parents, as well as weekend visits when the parents live a considerable distance away. It is preferable that parents live within a half-hour's driving distance from the Treatment Center. This distance means that, should a crisis situation arise which could be a profitable learning situation, the parents can be called to work with their child. Reviewing video tape recordings of parents working with their youngster has been of instructional value. The parents observe other staff working with their child and are then requested to model the staff's implementation of the treatment techniques. The data from the various treatment programs are explained to the parents, as well as their theoretical rationale and how they are to be used most effectively.

A child-care worker or nurse is assigned to each family and is responsible for providing the parents with the feedback of how well they are working with their youngster. Not only are these staff members responsible for tracking the parents during their weekly sessions with their youngster, they also serve as representative of the child during the family therapy sessions in which that child-care worker will be involved. The child-care worker or nurse assigned to each family is the child's representative not only in didactic training, but also in planning for eventual discharge. It is this staff member who is most likely to have the information available during the family therapy sessions to clarify the parents' difficulties in learning the techniques insofar as this inability interacts with marital problems or other difficulties unique to either parent.

The child-care worker or nurse may also use the cumulative recordings obtained during training sessions with the parents to inform them of their success in training their youngster. These data may be provided simply in the form of counts or by cumulative recordings explained to the parents. This information is obtained by a remote counting and recording device for which the cottage has been wired. There are several locations in the cottages where a staff member may plug in a small hand-held box containing several buttons which, if pressed, operate a cumulative recorder as well as electromagnetic counters located in the office. Thus, responses and reinforcement rates, etc., may be recorded during the parents' training sessions with the child by the observing staff member. Data of this sort are included in the family therapy data of the case studies in Chapter 7.

The staff members also provide the family members with information regarding their success in working with their youngster during the home visits. It is the child-care worker assigned to the family who will initially accompany the social worker and psychologist and who will be the last person fading from the home visits. It is this staff member who will visit the home on an increasing schedule which will gradually be diminished as the parents acquire the necessary skills, and who will provide decreasing supervision to the parents during the home visits.

Traditional Family Therapy. All families involved in the two research groups were involved in traditional family therapy. Traditional family therapy is superficially described as professional staff members discussing with parents what kinds of problems exist in the home relevant to the entire family, and particularly as these problems interact with their acquiring the parental skills we are attempting to teach them. These weekly sessions are directed by the social worker, and may include a child-care worker or nurse and quite often the psychologist assigned to the group. The social worker assumes primary responsibility for these sessions, which are often held in the evenings that they are convenient for both parents to attend. Thus, there is a multiple therapist relationship with the parents. The primary function of all treatment programs with the parents is to teach them the skills necessary for their child's eventual discharge to the home and the community. However, individual as well as marital problems are often accompanied by emotionally disturbed children and must be dealt with if one is to expect maintenance of the treatment programs with the child upon his eventual discharge. Traditional family therapy is not a requirement for the acceptance of a child to the Treatment Center. However, the professional staff are insistent upon such a level of involvement and make every endeavor to have the parents in a family therapy program.

Termination of Family Therapy. The didactic training with the parents cannot be separated from the traditional family therapy program. Data have not been accumulated thus far to suggest such a separation, nor do we know how to separate the multitude of interactions which must exist between the two procedures. We have concluded that didactic as well as family therapy can be terminated when several response criteria are judged by the staff to have been met. For example, when the parents were clearly aware of the expectations they provided their child, and could predict his response, they had profited optimally from the program. The training seems to be successful when the parents have response expectancies which are consistent with the child's skills and are advanced at a rate of progression which assures more success than failure. The parents should be able to control their child without a child-care worker or nurse assigned to them for constant supervision in the home setting or at any place in the community. In other words, the parents are no longer dependent upon our staff for maintenance of their child's newly acquired behaviors. We expect that with a successful conclusion of didactic training the parents are able to enjoy their child, i.e., the child has acquired positive reinforcing value to the parents, to a degree greater than that which was apparent when the child was admitted.

Upon conclusion of the family treatment program the parents' guilt regarding the child's behavior should be subdued or, at best, understood. It is preferable that they have an acceptance of the child's social and academic achievement and his anticipated potential. It is necessary that the parents advance beyond the guilt aroused by their inability to control their child and their chagrin over staff members' being more successful. This guilt seems to dissipate when they have acquired the skills taught to them so that they are no longer dependent upon the staff. We try to reduce their guilt by informing them that they did not intentionally train their child to be emotionally disturbed.

One should be confident at the conclusion of the family training that the parents are able to identify any ensuing problems which may arise in the child after his discharge. It is important that the parents are able not only to identify the behavior, but also to control it and reinstate the preferred behaviors, and to seek our consultation when these goals cannot be achieved.

Guidelines for Future Development of Family Therapy. We suspect that for optimal generalization of treatment effects as much time will be required in the parent-training and family therapy program as is used in the child's treatment program. Just as the child has to acquire new behaviors, the parents have to acquire new habits of child-rearing which are often contrary to those which may have been rehearsed for several years and which sustained the child's referral behaviors. Their erroneous child-rearing practices may be as durable as the child's responses which were so acquired. It may be found that the parents' reinforcers which inadvertently maintain their child's behavior may be as unusual as the child's. Just as some children's social reinforcers may require counter-conditioning, it may be found that the parents will require a comparable training program. It can be predicted that staff will have to spend greater intervals of time in the home with the parents and child to produce more effective generalization of treatment effects and parental skills as originally trained in the residential setting. It can also be anticipated that the cost of such residential programs will increase enormously with this greater family involvement.

If foster care or adoptive plans for a child become necessary, this decision should be made early in the child's treatment program. It may be optimal that the foster parent be selected from a pool of trained foster parents associated with the residential center. These parents should be trained and involved in both the family therapy and the didactic training program just as the natural parent of the child would have been if he were available. Not only should there be an adequate monetary reimbursement to the foster parents for this degree of involvement, but also an appropriate degree of social reinforcement that is seldom extended to foster parents.

CHAPTER THREE

Measurement

The experimental-clinical method requires the use of experimental designs in routine clinical practice. The critical elements of an experimental procedure are the measurement of dependent variables and the systematic presentation of independent variables. Pure behavioral research provides the guidelines for measurement and design in experimental-clinical studies but, unfortunately, fails to answer many of the specific questions which arise in making practical application.

Idiographic studies, as described in Chapter 1, present difficult measurement and design problems. The measurement procedures and experimental designs that have proven highly satisfactory for nomothetic or laboratory studies often appear irrelevant for idiographic research. The naturalistic setting of experimental-clinical studies rarely permits the precisely mechanized measurement that is possible in the laboratory. Favorite laboratory forms of experimental control rely upon pools of subjects randomly assigned to different treatment conditions. Idiographic experiments, however, require the use of subjects as their own controls. Thus, idiographic and naturalistic aspects of experimental-clinical studies require many innovations in measurement and design.

The present chapter discusses some of our attempts to resolve measurement problems. Chapter 4 will focus upon the attributes of various experimental designs for idiographic studies. This distinction between measurement and design is arbitrary, since in actual practice the choices of measurement procedure and experimental design are interdependent.

Common Forms of Clinical Recording

The commonly accepted forms of clinical observation and recording are unsatisfactory in an experimental-clinical study. Most clinical measurement seems to consist of subjective and frequently biased observation. Our dissatisfaction with these commonly accepted clinical procedures and our initial solutions to the problems will be illustrated by a discussion of the kinds of measurement and recording that we found ourselves using prior to the introduction of experimental-clinical techniques.

PSYCHOLOGICAL TESTING

The traditional psychological evaluation was the major formalized measurement procedure. This consisted of the usual two-hour sample of the child's behavior in response to such instruments as an individual intelligence test, the Rorschach cards, and the Thematic Apperception Test. From these restricted behavior samples, we were attempting to predict the day-long activity of the child as it might occur under totally different conditions. Although the intelligence quotient may predict school performance, it seldom provides specific information about the materials and approaches the teacher should use with the child. The Rorschach may provide information about the child's thought patterns and emotional distortions, but it seldom suggests how these responses might be elicited or altered in the child's natural environment. The Thematic Apperception Test may disclose the child's attitudes toward various figures as they are represented in the stimulus cards, but again, it does not specifically disclose how he will respond to similar figures in real life. The traditional psychodiagnostic evaluation demonstrates the child's response to a relatively specific situation at an isolated point in time. Specific information or hypotheses about the child's past learning experiences and his future performance in other situations are not provided. The evaluation itself is based on a structured interview and the child's response to it may or may not be related to the behavior he demonstrates in school, with siblings, or with his parents.

Despite this dim view, traditional psychological assessment does have a deserved place within the experimental-clinical psychologist's toolbox. Psychological tests often are an efficient means of beginning the evaluation of a child. Intelligence estimates, as well as the diagnostic information of projective tests, provide initial directions for the measurement task. However, they are never sufficient for designing a complete treatment program for a child. Often psychological evaluations may be of assistance in the formation of hypotheses to give new directions to treatment programs. A specialized intellectual assessment (such as a detailed analysis of profiles of the Wechsler Intelligence Scale for Children or the Illinois Test of Psycholinguistic Abilities) may be useful in suggesting reasons why a particular teaching program produces poor results and could thus suggest new approaches. If a child fails to respond to staff in an expected or understandable manner, projective or interview data may suggest hypotheses about how to change his behavior. In such instances, the test should be used to establish hypotheses that can be validated. Thus, the psychological evaluation is best used in preparation for, or supplementation to, treatment studies

Our major criticism of the psychological evaluation is that the data are too distant from critical referral problems. If the child's ongoing behavior in school or home is the focus of concern, then some means to measure this behavior adequately is necessary. The clinician need not be concerned about the child's response to him, his questions, or his test instruments. The important data are the child's behaviors toward teachers, his peer group, or his family. Consequently, these latter *in vivo* data need to be the focus of measurement in treatment programs.

NARRATIVE CHARTS

In a residential treatment center, *in vivo* data are readily available but difficult to record. In our setting, the children were spending their entire day with trained staff members. The psychotherapists, child-care workers, nurses, and teachers are skilled observers of child behavior, and their experiences with the children yielded many promising observations. Descriptions were available of the child's reactions to the important people in his life, his productivity in school, his motor skills, his relationships with other children, his many individual behavior strengths and weaknesses.

The various staff members conscientiously recorded their observations of the child in daily narrative charts. These were lengthy descriptions of whatever seemed significant to the worker who had spent time with the child. The charts focused upon clinically important behaviors and invariably proved to be interesting narratives. Unfortunately, they were relatively useless in evaluating treatment techniques or changes in the child's behavior.

By their very nature, narrative charts result in irretrievable data accumulated in an unsystematic fashion. For example, one might be concerned about the amount of isolative behavior a child is currently showing. A common question would be, "Is he isolating himself as much as he was three months ago?" A search of the previous charts might reveal no comments about isolativeness. Did this mean that the child had not been isolative three months ago, or had he been isolating so much that the behavior was unrecorded because all staff were aware of the obvious severity of the problem? Or perhaps comments about isolativeness were omitted because some other behavior was of more concern. Narrative charts are of little use because the same questions are not asked and answered in the charts on successive occasions. One staff member may write pages about isolative behavior; another may write about fighting. Are the different emphases because the behavior differs, or because different staff are sensitized to different aspects of the child? For scientific adequacy, dependent variables must be measured in the same manner on different occasions. The procedure of narrative charting is insufficiently formalized and standardized to meet criteria for obtaining reliable data.

Measures, whether qualitative or quantitative, must be reducible to numerical representation. No matter how insightful the narrative chart is, it is virtually impossible to translate the observations into a numberical format. For example, two staff members may each record "Bob was doing a lot of fighting today." We do not, however, know that the word "fighting" refers to the same behavior, qualitatively, for each staff member. Nor do we know that "a lot" of fighting means a similar quantity to each staff member. One staff member may be describing three fistfights, while the other may be referring to several loud verbal arguments. Unless we can reduce the observations to numbers that hold the same quantitative and qualitative value for each observer, the data will be useless for making objective comparison of the child's behavior at different times.

RATING SCALES

A variety of behavioral rating scales (e.g., Ross *et al.,* 1965; Quay, 1964; Borgatta & Fanshel, 1965; Spivack & Swift, 1966) have been developed for use with children. Such scales, primarily designed for program evaluation research, generally consist of a large number of items to be rated by a teacher, parent, or other person well acquainted with the child's behavior. Ratings are usually intended to be repeated periodically, e.g., every one to six months. A number of these scales have been factor-analyzed (e.g., Quay *et al.,* 1966; Ross *et al.,* 1965; Borgatta & Fanshel, 1965) and satisfactorily meet criteria of reliability and validity when applied to relatively large groups of children and observers. Some scales also seem to be useful with small groups of subjects and to yield sufficient inter-observer reliability (e.g., Stover & Giebink, 1967) to permit their use by different observers at different times as would be required in a treatment situation.

Rating scales of this type, however, have limitations for application within the experimental-clinical method. Since children are rated on a large number of behaviors or traits, changes in the most important behaviors of a particular child may be masked in the data summary. The idiographic orientation, as currently used, assumes that only a few individual behaviors will be of critical importance in describing either the disturbance or response to treatment of each particular child. Because it spans an entire range of behaviors, the rating scale tends to obscure variability in the few behaviors that are clinically important for the individual child. Allport (1962) illustrated this point with data obtained by Conrad (1932). In Conrad's study, teachers were asked to rate children on 231 common traits. They agreed poorly when all 231 traits were considered, but when permitted to rate the child on only those traits that they considered to be of "central or dominating importance in the child's personality," they obtained very high agreement with each other. Allport summarizes: "This result shows that low reliability may be due to the essential irrelevance of many of the dimensions we forceably apply to an individual" (Allport, 1962, Page 418).

The well-developed behavior rating scale is capable of reliable and valid measurement of gross behavioral changes and, as such, does have a place in the evaluation of treatment programs. We used the PASS (Ross *et al.*, 1965) in this manner with the older group of boys. Tables 3.1 and 3.2 give examples of this type of data for two of the children in our studies.

Table 3.1. Examples of PASS Scores on One Child at Ten-Week Intervals

Week	*1**	*3*	*15*	*25*	*35*	*45*	*55*	*68***
I. Aggressive	41	29	31	30	32	35	37	2
II. Withdrawn	14	18	8	9	14	17	16	6
III. Pro-Social	8	19	16	16	15	14	23	31
IV. Pass-Aggressive	20	18	17	17	20	19	22	5

*Completed by the child's teacher prior to his admission to CTC.
**Filled out by public school teacher after treatment.

According to Table 3.1, this boy was rated high on the Aggressive and Passive-Aggressive dimensions prior to his admission to the Children's Treatment Center, and very low on these dimensions by his public school teacher after his discharge from the Center. Also, he was rated high on the Pro-Social dimension by his new public school teacher. During his stay at the Treatment Center, his successive ratings on the four dimensions were fairly stable.

Tabie 3.2 gives the scores for a second boy who showed a decrease on the Aggressive, Withdrawn, and Passive-Aggressive dimensions, and an increase on the Pro-Social dimension as compared to rating on the PASS prior to his admission to the Treatment Center.

This kind of data may be useful, but it fails as a thoroughly experimental-clinical measurement procedure. For example, we cannot from such data relate change or lack of change to particular treatment procedures. We would submit that the reason most research on the effects of therapy is ignored by therapists is because only such gross evaluations have been used, and the details of the progress of treatment (i.e., the effects of specific therapeutic maneuvers), cannot be discerned from the data.

Table 3.2. Example of PASS Scores on One Child at Ten-Week Intervals

Week	*1**	*3*	*15*	*25***	*35*
I. Aggressive	50	34	40		39
II. Withdrawn	15	10	8		4
III. Pro-Social	5	26	22		33
IV. Pass-Aggressive	24	20	21		11

*Completed by teacher patient had two years prior to admission to Center.
**Form not completed by teacher.

Requirements of Measurement in the Experimental-Clinical Method

Each of the common forms of recording observations in the clinical setting has particular drawbacks. The psychological test, although often a sophisticated measurement tool, seems largely artificial and distant from the real-life data that are required. The narrative recording of trained therapists and child-care workers provides *in vivo* observation, but fails to meet scientific requirements for reliable numerical data. Rating scales generally meet these latter criteria, but are unsatisfactory because of their nomothetic nature.

Experimental-clinical methods require measurement devices which will meet the usual criteria for reliability and validity. The method of observation must be formalized and systematic; it must repeatedly ask the same questions about behavior and answer them in the same manner on different occasions. The variability of a measure must be primarily attributable to changes in the behavior and not to the observer or his method of observing.

Beyond these basic requirements, the experimental-clinical method demands that the measure be directly related to the *in vivo* behavior of the clinic patient. Consequently, the measurement device must have a high degree of face validity as an indicator of the real-life behavior of the individual being studied. We hope that the clinician's careful use of experimental design will further support the construct validity of the measure by demonstrating that particular treatment procedures will produce predictable variations in the measured dependent variable. Perhaps most importantly, the measure must provide meaningful idiographic data. What is measured must be a salient behavior for the individual being studied. The behavior must be important as a direct target of clinical manipulation and control. This latter criterion presents some of the most difficult problems for the experimental-clinical method. The clinician cannot simply go to a grab-bag of dependent variables, but rather must use clinical judgment in selecting for observation those behaviors which are indeed relevant to the treatment of the patient. Although similar or even identical behaviors may be relevant for many subjects, the clinician must use caution in making a *carte blanche* application of the same measurement procedures to each case. One may not presume response commonality across subjects. Each case requires individual analysis and decision about what behaviors are to be selected for detailed observation, for the results of studies will be as relevant as the behaviors observed and treated. The clinician's value system figures importantly in the selection of patient behaviors to be treated.

Finally, certain practical requirements must be met in the development of experimental-clinical measures. Since the aim is efficient scientific treatment of disturbed persons, the measurement devices must be both economical and practical. The various methods described below differ in cost both in training the observers and in planning, conducting, and summarizing the observations. Some methods require an investment in mechanical apparatus; some must be performed only by a highly trained observer who has no other responsibilities. Some procedures require no equipment other than a pencil and paper and can be performed by a minimally trained child-care worker during the course of his other duties. For some methods, the analysis and summary of data are complicated; for others, very simple. The ultimate efficiency of any observation method is a function of both the cost of obtaining the observations and the usefulness of data obtained.

To obtain a description of any single behavior, a variety of basic behavioral measures would be necessary. Examples of measures which would provide an optimal response description have been provided by Pascal and Jenkins (1961) as listed below:

frequency	amount
latency	variety
rate	surrounding conditions
intensity	direction
duration	correctness

Such a complete description of behavior would, at the current stage of research, be logistically and financially impossible to procure in the clinical setting. Consequently, the most critical behaviors must be selected for measurement in the simplest and most succinct form. Frequency of response occurrence is typically the preferred measure; short narrative charts may be logged concurrently to monitor for qualitative changes in the behavior. Duration of the response is often the second preferred response measure in our studies.

The following is a discussion of the major techniques we have used to measure behavior.

SCREENING INSTRUMENTS

An initial problem in the treatment of a child is the selection of what behaviors shall be trained and what responses deleted from his response repertoire. In every case there invariably are two or three critical behaviors which have resulted in the child's referral for residential treatment. These referral behaviors are generally the complaints by parents and/or teachers about the child's disruptive or inappropriate behaviors, which may include bizarre gestures, tantrums, fighting, and isolativeness. Many clinicians would agree, however, that the task is not only to eliminate these primary referral behaviors but also to teach appropriate behaviors to replace the inappropriate responses as they are extinguished. According to our experience, the absent positive behaviors are of greater clinical importance than the more dramatically obvious negative behaviors. For example, the child who engages in profuse perseverative speech will also be observed as deficient in appropriate conversation. As much of our subsequent data will demonstrate, the most effective way to eliminate many inappropriate behaviors is to shape the culturally expected behaviors for the situations which previously evoked the child's negative behavior. To achieve this, the clinician needs some criteria by which to select those behaviors that are deficient. Absences of behavior do not always stand out so clearly as could be desired. For example, for use with the group of older boys, we developed a screening instrument to select behaviors which were missing or occurring inconsistently in the child's repertoire. To develop this instrument, we defined those behavioral goals which we would maintain for most of the patients. These goals were established from a review of developmental literature. Thus, we established behavioral goals for meal times, school, getting up, going to bed, free time, and structured activity times. General descriptions of these goals composed a brief behavior rating scale. The staff would complete this scale on each child every three weeks. The scale served as a screening device to select behaviors that had to be modified for each child. Since this particular instrument was developed with reference to a specific sample of children, it is not applicable to all treatment populations. Such measurement instruments are useful in the initial development of a treatment program and for the general review of a child's progress. This is not a sophisticated research instrument, and the data from it are seldom summarized with the intent of demonstrating treatment effectiveness. The results of the instrument, however, are useful in defining more specifically those behaviors which need to be studied with a given child. This instrument is often the first step in defining behaviors which will be measured subsequently either by behavioral charting or time-sampling procedures.

The children should be routinely screened for the levels of both appropriate and inappropriate behaviors which might otherwise be overlooked. It has become increasingly apparent that many inappropriate behaviors may be missed because the staff adapt to the high rate of occurrence. On the other hand, staff attention may be dominated by prominent negative behaviors to the exclusion of positive behaviors. We have often had the experience of becoming satisfied with a child's behavior only to discover, when we began placement in the home and classroom, that there were still levels of inappropriate behaviors sufficiently high to guarantee a poor adjustment outside of the Treatment Center. Consequently, we used the two screening devices described below to monitor ourselves to assure that we were attending to and establishing programs to deal with behaviors that would need modification prior to the child's eventual discharge from the treatment program.

One useful method of screening for negative behaviors was to have several staff members review long lists of inappropriate behaviors with special reference to each child in the group. For this purpose, we found the Deviant Behavior Inventory (Novick, Rosenfield, and Block, 1966) to be particularly helpful. This is a list of 237 deviant behaviors often encountered in preadolescent boys. Although the list is extensive, it by no means covers the variety of problem behaviors which we observed at the Center. The staff member reviewing the list generally found himself reminded of several behaviors in each child which should warrant our attention. Such a review is made approximately every three weeks for each child. The negative behaviors which had been checked by the staff can be classified in reference to those which are currently the subject of treatment programs, those which should be placed on the treatment schedule for the near future, and those which can be safely ignored at the present time. The instrument was valuable in the evaluation of the child's progress but, more important, it stimulated development of specific measurement and modification procedures related to particular behaviors which might otherwise go unattended.

Research Notes. Research notes maintained by the child-care staff are a second method of screening for behaviors which should be treated. Research notes are a less formalized method of data collection than would be represented in behavioral charting or in behavioral sampling techniques. In research notations, the instance of a behavior is recorded with respect to time and place, and the observer also makes relevant narrative notes which may lead to subsequent development of methods for obtaining accurate measures of the behavior as well as hypotheses concerning events which may control the target behavior. The kind of research notes to be maintained varies with each individual case. We were concerned with maintaining a day-by-day behavioral notebook much as a chemist or biologist would keep in following his experiments on a given topic. Research notes differ from narrative charting as previously discussed in that the observations to be described are limited according to one or more specific criteria. For example, we might ask our staff for specific notes concerning the child's response to situations demanding spontaneous play. We might request notes describing situations in which a particular kind of tense, anxious behavior is evoked in the child. In some cases we have been concerned because staff may complain that a child is constantly behaving in ways which they find grossly irritating but they may be unable clearly to define the behaviors to which they are reacting. In such a case, we might ask the various staff members to record each instance in which the child evoked their reactions of discomfort or annoyance. Their task would be to describe in considerable detail both the situation and the child's behavior. By collecting a series of such notes from all of the staff over a one- or two-week period, we can often identify the primary behaviors that are causing difficulty and require modification.

Several examples of different research notes we have used will more clearly define the technique. One important place for research notes is in the conduct of a behavioral shaping program. A standard form of behavioral charting or behavior sampling is virtually useless as a measurement of effectiveness of shaping procedures. This is true because the definition of the behavior to be counted would have to vary with each subsequent step in the shaping program. In shaping speech the behavior of interest at the beginning of the program might be any kind of vocalization, whereas at a later point in the program, the recorded behavior would be the clear vocalization of a complex verbal request. At some point in the program, imitation of complete sentences would be the reinforced behavior, and still later the spontaneous production of complete sentences would be the criterion response. Thus, one satisfactory way to record a shaping program is to maintain research notes which indicate the date and time of the treatment session, the criterion response being worked with at the time, the number of trials performed in that session, and the type of reinforcement contingencies being used. Further, the worker would need to note observations relating to establishing response criteria for future sessions, changes in reinforcement schedules, methods of presentation of material, etc. At the beginning of such a program, it would be impossible to specify clearly what data will be gathered in each step of the program and how the data might best be summarized. Programs in which qualitatively different behaviors are being successively taught differ from programs which are designed to vary the frequency of some response. In the second case, it should be possible to specify in the design of the study the exact nature of measurement and manipulation at each point in the study.

In another example, the staff were impressed that an eleven-year-old boy demonstrated excessively immature behavior for his age. They reviewed expected behavioral descriptions derived from developmental surveys (Gesell & Ilg, 1946) and were convinced that the child did not engage in many of the physical activities expected of boys his age, nor did he have the expected levels of self-maintained interest in a wide variety of projects and activities. The staff did not have available a detailed picture of the kind of mature and immature activities in which the boy engaged. Further, we had no evidence of the amounts of time he spent in various activities. This information could be the basis for a shaping program to create a more normal behavioral repertoire. The staff were asked to record in their research notes information on each activity the child entered spontaneously, the kind of activity, with whom he played, and the duration of the activity. The notations were the foundation for the treatment program established for this youngster.

Another kind of research note which is often helpful is a modification of the "critical incident technique" (Flannagan, 1954; Pascal & Jenkins, 1961). In the critical incident technique staff are instructed to record each incident of a particular kind of behavior or a particular kind of situation to which the child is exposed. Certain kinds of data are collected around each incident. The staff were requested to describe the incidents according to three categories. Their task was to describe the situation which they believed stimulated the target behavior, describe the behavior in detail, and finally to describe any events which may have reinforced the behavior. Thus, the recording consists of three columns in which are noted stimulus situations, child's behavioral response, and the consequences of the child's behavior, respectively. This kind of research note, if conscientiously maintained by the staff, may be of assistance in generating hypotheses concerning the child's behavior. For example, one can readily predict those situations in which a particular behavior is likely to occur and can specify more clearly the form of the behavior for subsequent definition in behavioral charting and behavioral sampling. The method is of value in formulating hypotheses concerning reinforcement contingencies that maintain the behavior. The hypotheses arising from critical incident recording can then be submitted to test in controlled experimental designs. Although research notes are of the greatest usefulness in the screening and hypothesis formation stages of treatment programs, we have found them to provide us with data for evaluating a treatment program. This is particularly true when the important aspect of the treatment program has been to produce a variation in the quality of a particular habit, rather than in the quantity or amount of the behavior.

BEHAVIORAL CHARTING

The behavioral chart has been our most frequently applied measurement procedure. The previous method of narrative charting was changed to a systematic numerical format. Staff members maintained day-long counts or tallies of the occurrence of particular target behaviors for each child. Generally the staff members carry small tally counters, such as a stock clerk's counter. We have found the wrist counter often used by golfers to be highly unsatisfactory. The following are some examples of behaviors counted in this fashion: tantrums, hitting, smiling, changing the topic of conversation, whining, complaining, implusive actions, and provoking peers. Once clear operational definitions have been established, a well-trained staff member can maintain from five to ten counts of such behaviors while fulfilling his clinical responsibilities of playing with and training the children. Up to four or five behavioral counts may be maintained on each child at any given time. Some of the behaviors thus counted may be under baseline observation, while others are being exposed to particular treatment conditions. Only behaviors of relatively high frequency need to be tallied on counters. Low-frequency behaviors, such as those which occur less than five times per day, can usually be reliably remembered and the tally written down every few hours.

In the research groups, behavioral counts are totaled and entered in the children's charts twice daily. These data-gathering periods correspond with the usual staff working shifts of 7:00 A.M. to 3:00 P.M. and 3:00 P.M. to 11:00 P.M. These two behavioral counts per day seem to provide adequate units of measurement for most of the behaviors observed. The subsequent summarizing of the data is generally handled in one of two ways. First, the data may be transformed to a frequency graph from which changes in the day-by-day rate of the behavior can readily be seen. As an alternate method, the mean rate of the behavior may be computed each week and these means then become the major unit for review or analysis.

In actual practice, the behaviors to be recorded in behavioral charts are selected by the leader of the treatment group. He relies upon the case history and the observations of the staff to determine which behaviors are most critical for observation and modification. Through joint discussion during weekly rounds, the members of the treatment group decide upon an operational definition of the behavior and clarify for themselves just when a particular behavior is or is not to be tallied. Observing and discussing particular examples of the behavior usually helps all members of the group come to a working agreement about behavioral definitions. At times we have also used video tape recordings of the child to assist us in defining the target behaviors. Naturally, some behaviors are much simpler to define than are others. Different staff members can more easily agree upon definitions of "swearing" or "hitting" than upon definitions for behaviors such as "provoking other children" or "seeking affection." The clearer the definition of the behavior, of course, the better are the chances of maintaining more reliable observations.

Accurate and consistent scores on behavioral charts would be relatively easy to obtain were it not for the child-care worker's many other responsibilities. Generally, the worker does not have the children under his direct observation at every moment. He must attend to more than one child at a time, and when one child in the group is having extreme difficulties the staff member may be so occupied with him that he misses counts on the other children. In actual practice, the person working with a particular child changes frequently, and often these changes of direct responsibility occur when there is no time for the first staff member to hand the counters on to the second staff member. In such cases, one of the workers may have to make a mental note of the counts until he reaches the person who has the counter and then record his tally. To maintain adequate behavioral counts, the staff must be thoroughly familiar with what is being counted on each child, and must constantly remind themselves of the counts despite the many other demands for their attention. An additional problem is that many behaviors tend to change in quality from one situation to another, and in particular as a treatment procedure begins to take effect. No matter how careful the original definition of a behavior, the staff members are constantly faced with living examples that are difficult to judge. At such times, they must make quick subjective decisions. All of these factors would be expected to contribute to the unreliability of the behavioral chart.

Since behavioral charting is conducted under a broad range of circumstances with a wide variety of behaviors, there is no thoroughly satisfactory way to judge its reliability. Several types of studies, however, have been conducted to obtain sample reliability figures. Basically, we have been most concerned about the differences in the scores that are attributable to different observers.

Behavioral Charting: Reliability Study 1.[1] In the first study, the scores of child-care staff were correlated with those of a research assistant whose training and familiarity with the counts were comparable to those of the child-care workers. The special observer was assigned to follow a particular child-care worker and maintain counts on the childrens' behavior in the same manner as the worker. The child-care worker performed his usual duties, and the observer did not work with the children. The observer made his observations in a series of randomly determined time blocks of 15 minutes' duration. At the conclusion of each such 15-minute block, the child-care worker and the observer recorded their tallies on the data sheets. Some of the behaviors thus observed were occurring with very low frequency while others were high-rate behaviors. For the low-rate behaviors, a 15-minute unit of observation was unsatisfactory, since it resulted in many blocks with zero entries which produced a markedly skewed distribution of scores. In such cases, a larger number of 15-minute blocks were obtained and these were combined into larger units such as 30-minute or 45-minute blocks for purposes of analysis. An arbitrary criterion of approximately six pairs of observations was required before reliability coefficients were computed for any particular behavior.

Rank order correlation coefficients were computed to assess the agreement between the child-care workers and the trained observers for each behavior which had been charted in this manner. These correlations, along with the definition of the behavior being tallied, the number of observation blocks, and the median score obtained by child-care workers and observer are summarized in Table 3.3.

The first reliability study demonstrated reasonable levels of consistency in the data obtained from behavioral charts. Despite the many diverse factors which would be expected to produce capricious variations in the behavior counts, the correlations in Table 3.3 indicate relatively good agreement between child-care workers and a specially assigned observer.

Encouraged by these initial results, we proceeded to conduct a second and somewhat more sophisticated study of the consistency of behavioral charts. The first study had several major shortcomings. Foremost was that the observer and the child-care worker could be aware of each other's counts and consequently could have biased their data in an effort to obtain favorable reliability. For example, if the behavior being observed were also undergoing some specific treatment, the observer would know each time the child-care worker counted the behavior because he would see a reinforcement or punishment being administered to the child. The observer

1. The authors wish to acknowledge Donna Morrissey and Duane Alwin, research assistants, who were primarily responsible for the design and conduct of these reliability studies.

Table 3.3. Behavioral Charting Reliability

Study 1: Correlations between observer and child-care worker staff

Child	*Behavior Count Observed*	*Number of Samples*	*Sample Time (min.)*	*Median Count Obtained*		*RHO between Observer and Staff*
				Observer	*Staff*	
Art	Swearing	11	45	5	5	.94
	Staff praise for not swearing	10	15	2	2	.91
Bob	Compliance	14	15	4.5	3.5	.83
	Noncompliance	14	15	0.5	0	.70
Bill	Compliance	6	15	4	1	.66
	Noncompliance	6	15	2	0.5	.88
Ric	Clinging to staff	12	30	1	1.5	.97
	Use of pronoun "I"	36	15	2	2	.88
Roy	Compliance	18	15	3.5	3	.83
	Noncompliance	18	15	2	2	.57
Ted	Compliance	57	15	2	2	.81
	Noncompliance	19	45	2	0	.59
	Praise from staff	57	15	13	13	.64

was also writing down the child-care worker's tally every 15 minutes, and hence was well aware of discrepancies between that and his own count. Since the observer was following the child-care worker, the data provide no information on the extent to which the observations were valid. That is, there is no information on how much behavior goes uncounted because the child-care worker is called away from the child or because he is working with several children at once. To meet these objections, the following study was conducted.

Behavioral Charting: Reliability Study 2. Two research analysts who had had extensive training and experience in making observations of this type as well as the regular child-care workers were used in the second study. Initially, the research analysts familiarized themselves with the behaviors to be charted by reviewing the current behavior counts with the staff in each of the research groups and spending time in informal observation of the children with the child-care workers who were maintaining the counts. When the two research analysts felt they clearly understood and could agree with each other and with child-care workers about the definitions of the behaviors, they began the actual data collection.

Sampling was again conducted in 15-minute blocks. Twelve samples were used for each behavior studied, but as in the previous study for samples of low-rate behaviors, they were based on blocks longer than 15 minutes. The two research analysts were assigned to observe two behaviors simultaneously in one child. In this study, their task was to follow that child regardless of whether the child-care worker was with the child or not. They did not, however, interact with the child or carry out any child-care tasks while observing. At the end of each 15-minute block, the observers tallied their counts and the child-care worker tallied his count on the data sheets. None of the three persons was aware of the tallies made by the others. As a further guarantee that observations were made independently, only behaviors that were on baseline measurement (i.e., no response of the child-care workers was contingent upon the behavior) were used in this study.

The results were summarized in the following fashion. Rank order correlations were computed first between the two trained observers. These correlations are interpreted as a measure of reliability under optimal conditions, i.e., assignment to observe just two behaviors in a single child without concurrent responsibility for managing any of the children. Next, the average of the two research analysts' scores for each observation block was computed. These averaged scores were then correlated with the counts obtained by the child-care worker. This latter correlation was interpreted as a measure of the extent to which a child-care worker operating under the usual demands of his job achieved agreement with the optimal measure obtained by the research analysts. The resulting correlations for the observations of thirteen behaviors are summarized in Table 3.4.

The first column of Table 3.4 shows that the research analysts learned to agree quite satisfactorily on the definitions of the thirteen behaviors. Although their correlations ranged from .67 to .98, eight were greater than .80. The Kendall's W (Siegel, 1956) was performed to assess reliability among the research analysts and the child-care worker. Again, the scores varied considerably, from .73 to .97. The third column in Table 3.4 shows the correlations between the averaged scores of the research analysts and the care-worker that ranged from a low of .49 to a high of .97. The last two columns contain correlations between each research analyst and the child-care worker they were monitoring at the time for all thirteen behaviors.

The data suggest that there is considerable variability in the reliability of behavioral charting as it has been employed in our studies. However, it is interesting to note that many of the correlations were very respectable, supporting our procedure of having the child-care worker staff perform be-

Table 3.4. Reliability Study 2

Correlations among research analysts and child-care workers on behavioral charting

Child	*Behavior Observed*	*Time of Sample (min.)*	*Spearman R between Res. Analysts*	*Kendall W between Res. Analysts and Child-Care Worker*	*R. between Mean Res. Analysts Scores and CCW Scores*	*R. between Res. Analyst 1 and Child-Care Worker*	*R. between Res. Analyst 2 and Child-Care Worker*
Sharon	Compliance to verbal request	15	.96	.94	.91	.91	.86
	Noncompliance to verbal request	15	.71	.80	.74	.62	.80
	Gross aggression	30	.95	.89	.79	.81	.77
	Low-level aggression	30	.77	.73	.49	.44	.60
Heidi	Compliance to verbal request	15	.97	.97	.95	.96	.94
	Noncompliance to verbal request	15	.98	.94	.88	.87	.88
Roy	"Brush-offs"	15	.65	.75	.73	.82	.48
	Impulsiveness	15	.67	.86	.97	.90	.83
	Speech (complete sentences)	15	.97	.93	.85	.85	.84
James	Positive transitions	30	.86	.82	.61	.63	.65
	Negative transitions	30	.83	.84	.76	.72	.73
	Swearing	30	.93	.90	.83	.83	.79
John	Compliance to verbal request	15	.78	.80	.66	.54	.79

havioral charting concurrently with their other duties. Unfortunately, we could not ascertain what conditions were responsible for the decreased reliability for some of the behaviors. It seems reasonable that eventually we shall develop a procedure periodically to sample for reliability of behavioral charting, so that, when poor reliability is discovered, steps can be taken to rectify that problem.

In reviewing these data, one should realize that during a reliability study the staff are likely to produce biased data. The experienced child-care worker or nurse is quite aware of the problem of reliability, and is most likely to be more consistent and accurate when he is aware of being observed.

Behavioral Charting: Reliability Study 3. The purpose of this study was to evaluate certain aspects of the behavioral charting procedure used in the experimental-clinical approach. A superficial inspection of the behavioral charting would suggest that it is simply recording the frequency and occasionally the duration of responses. However, the complexity of counting behavior arises from the situational context in which it must be performed. Staff members must maintain several behavioral counts on each of several children during most of the entire work shift, in addition to conducting the treatment programs and child-care activities that compose their daily routines.

This study was designed to evaluate the agreement among staff members counting the same behavior in an artificial setting, i.e., from a video tape recording. It was also intended to demonstrate the effect of training staff to identify the behavior upon their agreement in counting that behavior at a later time.

In cases where an acceptable degree of inter-rater reliability is difficult to achieve, the problem may lie with the kind of behavior being measured or the definition given the behavior, rather than with the observers accumulating the behavioral counts. In addition, if the frequency graphs which appear throughout this book mean anything at all, one must be able to assume that the behaviors were studied consistently. That is, when it is stated that "staff counted temper tantrums during baseline and treatment conditions," can it be assumed that all staff counted those responses uniformly? Can it be assumed that all staff were operating with the same definition of the behavior, thus agreeing on its occurrence or nonoccurrence, and thus being able meaningfully to differentiate it from other behaviors?

Central to the behavioral charting measurement procedure is the presumption that behavior may be viewed as a series of discrete events occurring through time. Also, any behavior which would be subject to measurement must present certain observable characteristics which distinguish it from other behaviors. Therefore, as standard procedure in devising treatment programs for a child, the staff attempt to define the behaviors of interest as clearly as possible. From this, one assumes that the staff members perform the measurement procedures uniformly and that the counts reflect valid, unitary dimensions.

A second aspect of the study is whether the agreement among staff members can be improved if they conjointly decide upon one definition of the behavior and as a group rehearse counting the agreed-upon response as observed in video tape sequences. In order to accomplish the goals of this study, it was necessary to postpone an intended treatment program for problematic behavior of one child. One youngster was beginning to provoke a specific peer with increasing frequency. This provoking behavior was retained on baseline during the course of this study. In performing this study, two requests were made of the staff members: (1) to ignore the provoking behavior and respond to it only when it became unbearable for the provoked peers; and (2) not to discuss any aspects of the behavior in question among staff members, except when asked by the investigator. As far as could be ascertained through close association with the staff and children during the time period occupied by the study, these two objectives were fulfilled.

Two ten-minute video tape recordings of a situation in which the provoking response was almost always encountered were prepared in a natural setting. One staff member and the two children, the provocateur and the peer most often provoked, appeared in the tapes. The recordings were made in the same room at approximately the same time on two different days. The frequency of the behavior was such that each tape could be broken into ten one-minute, consecutive time samples. The tapes were comparable in most respects, except for the relative frequency of the response both within each one-minute sample and during the entire ten-minute viewing. It would have been desirable to obtain comparable samples, but such behavioral constancy is seldom available in naturalistic studies. These video tapes were used for the reliability study, which was conducted as described below.

An experimental and a control group composed of five staff members each were formed. The staff were nursing, child-care worker, research analysts, and a social worker, all of whom were attached to research groups using behavioral charting.

Two ten-minute video tapes were made of the above-mentioned child provoking the other child. The child would directly hit, or almost hit, the other child, which would invariably engender a counter-aggressive response. The study was devided into three steps. In step one, both the experimental and the control groups viewed the video tapes. They were simply requested to count the frequency on which the child provoked during each of the ten-minute video samples. Staff in both groups were requested to use their own definition of "provoking." Staff in the experimental group received a Kendall's W of .787, and the control group a W of .814. These coefficients of reliability suggest that the staff were in fair agreement on their observations used in behavioral charting of the provoking response. They had all had experience in charting similar provoking behaviors with other youngsters.

In step two, the experimental group conjointly reviewed the video tape used in step one. For approximately fifty minutes they discussed the definition of provoking and viewed samples on the tape until they felt certain that they all agreed upon the common definition of the response they had decided upon. Immediately after the training sessions were completed, the staff were again requested to view the entire ten-minute segment of the video tape. For the successive ten one-minute samples, the staff now received a Kendall's W of .905. It was also noted that staff who contributed most to the Kendall W in step one maintained their position of being the most reliable observers, i.e., their correlation with the first and second viewings remained constant. The staff who did most poorly in their agreement with the other staff during the first viewing improved the most after the second viewing following the training session.

In step three, the second video tape was shown to both experimental and control groups. Again, the tape was separated into ten one-minute samples. The experimental group was told to record the frequency of provoking responses as they had agreed upon that definition in step two. The control group was simply requested to count the provoking responses without the benefit of reaching a group consensus on the definition of the response. The experimental groups' Kendall's W was .963, and the control group received a W of .902.

The data suggest that staff with experience in behavioral charting do acquire good agreement in their common definitions of behavior. The data also suggest that discussion, in conjunction with video tapes, does facilitate their agreement in observing behavior. There were confounding variables in the study. For example, the tapes were not comparable in frequency of provoking responses, the control group did improve substantially between steps one and two, and all the staff had considerable experience in behavioral charting. It would be expected that the training effect, i.e., discussing and conjointly reaching a definition of the observed behavior, would be more obvious with less experienced staff. In support of this hypothesis, it was found in the experimental group that the staff who improved most from the training sessions had been attached to the research group for the shortest time.

The data of these reliability studies do not account for errors of measurement that often appear to result from subtle changes in the quality of the child's behavior. For example, in one case, behavioral charting of "demands" and "polite requests" were being maintained for a very bossy, demanding boy. After obtaining a satisfactory baseline on these two behaviors, treatment was instituted. Treatment consisted of profusely reinforcing the "polite requests" and ignoring the youngster's "demands." Several weeks later, the staff concurred that the treatment had been highly successful; they felt that demands had been reduced significantly. The behavioral charts, however, thoroughly indicated that the rate of demanding was unchanged. The staff, who are usually willing to defer to the summaries of their own behavioral charts, on this occasion argued vociferously that the counts did not adequately represent the boy's behavior. There appeared to be various degrees of "demanding." Previously, all of the boy's demands had been of an extremely obnoxious and insistent quality. This extreme form of making demands now appeared to be fading out, but in its place the boy was engaging in demands of a much milder form. However, both forms of demands were readily included under the definition of this behavior. Thus, the behavioral count remained constant, although the general quality of the behavior was judged to have improved. With hindsight it is apparent that the data could have been more accurate had we tallied extreme and mild demands separately. Unfortunately, these qualitative changes in the behavior are difficult to anticipate. In the present case, further maintenance of the count ultimately resulted in a decrease of both forms of demands and a concomitant increase in "polite requests."

Another problem in behavioral charting is that the circumstances under which behavior is observed tend to change during the progress of treatment. For example, the older group of boys were exposed to a total shaping program in which the general staff expectations and environmental structure were constantly being altered to approximate normal environmental expectancies. Early in the program, each child was handled with maximum structure on a 1:1 relationship with staff; later, he was given greater freedom and responsibility. Naturally, the closeness of observation varied directly with the amount of staff structure each child received. Thus, behavior counts may tend to decrease simply because the child was less closely supervised than previously.

At times, this problem may be circumvented by expressing the behavior count as a function of the number of opportunities observed which could elicit the response. The counting of compliant behavior provides a good example of such a case. Compliance is defined as obedience to specific requests made by staff members. A simple count of the number of compliant responses occurring each day will not provide an adequate measure because the number and kinds of requests change with the progress of treatment. During his first weeks at the Center, a child may be specifically told when to get up, what clothes to wear, to brush his teeth, to clean his room, and to go to breakfast. Once he begins to anticipate and comply with these many simple requests, the staff find themselves making fewer but more complex requests of him. Now, the staff member may simply awaken him in the morning. The dressing, tooth-brushing, room cleaning, and walking to breakfast may all occur without further direction from the staff. As a result, the rate of compliance may remain the same or more likely decelerate while the child is actually becoming more obedient and amenable to adult direction. Consequently, both the number of requests made of the child and the number of compliant responses made by the child are counted. Compliance is then expressed as the percentage of all requests which are met with compliance.

In other situations, this problem may be solved by maintaining a count of two incompatible behaviors, one of which is to be accelerated while the other is to be decelerated. The previous example of demands and polite requests is a case in point. Here, the treatment would be designed simultaneously to reduce the amount of demanding the child does and to increase the number of polite requests he makes of staff. A score based upon the ratio of the counts of the two behaviors may be used to evaluate treatment effects. Thus, it is assumed that, although the absolute number of demands counted may vary because of factors such as the amount of time staff spend with the child, the ratio of the undesirable behavior to the incompatible positive behavior will adequately reflect treatment progress.

The method of observation may have a directional effect on the behavior being monitored in behavioral charting. It is infrequent that one performs a study to determine just what effect, constant or varying, behavioral charting has on each behavior studied. It is suspected that the more the patient is unaware of the manner in which the count is recorded, the less likely will the method of observation inadvertently reinforce the response. Figure 3.1 contains a same-subject study in which we investigated the effect of method of observation upon accumulating a baseline of inappropriate vocal responses (i.e., "barking" response, Chapter 7, case study 5). Five twenty-minute, randomly obtained samples were acquired for: (1) recording response frequency with a remote counter, the control unit of which was plugged into the wall and observable by the child; (2) recording the responses with a tape recorder which was observable by the child; and (3) recording with a hidden counter which was unobservable. As Figure 3.1 indicates, the child "barked" most frequently during the "presumed baselines" obtained when he could see the staff push the counter button, secondly to a tape recorder operated by staff, and least frequently when he was unaware that his behavior was being observed. The data indicated to us that the child's awareness that staff were attending to the response would accelerate the behavior. The study also provided the hypothesis that for this child, his "barking" response was an operant response for a variety of social reinforcers.

Behavioral charting is difficult and costly to maintain over a prolonged time span. Since there is a limit to the number of counts that staff can reliably obtain, all of the important behaviors for an entire group of children cannot be charted at all times. Consequently, judgment is required to determine which are the most important behaviors for charting at any given

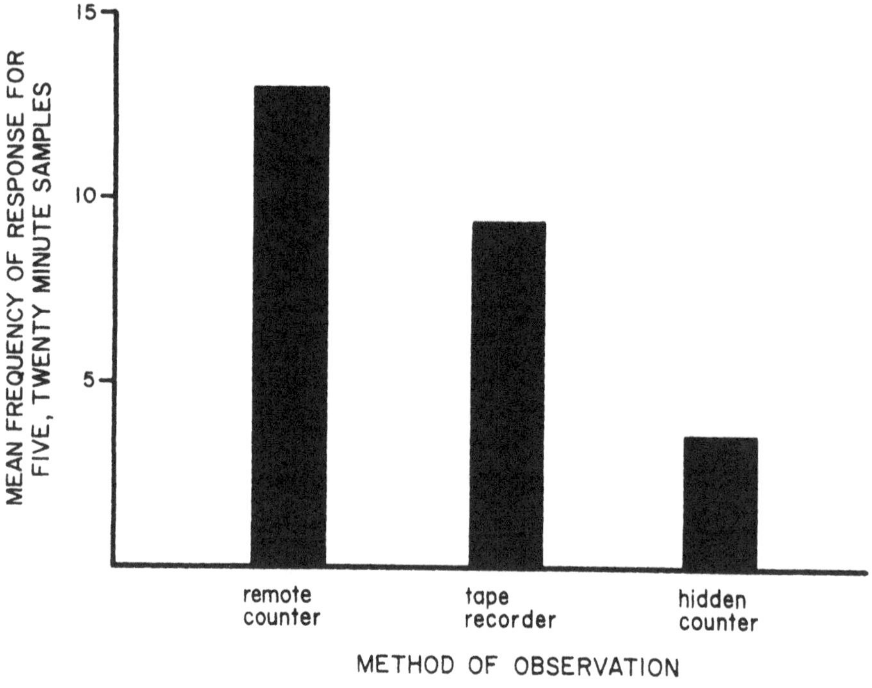

Figure 3.1. Mean Frequency of Inappropriate Vocal Responses as a Function of Three Observational Methods

time. Usually, this problem may be resolved by using a count during a baseline period and during the initial phases of treatment. Once it has been determined that a particular treatment procedure is effective, the behavioral charting may be temporarily dropped while the treatment procedure continues to be performed. Later, the counts can be reinstated to insure that the expected treatment effects have indeed occurred. By discontinuing and reinstating the behavior counts in this manner, we can obtain adequate data on a greater number of behaviors.

One modification of behavioral charting is useful for obtaining continuous measures of a large number of behaviors. With the group of older boys, the staff not only maintained behavior counts but also completed a series of true-false items at the end of each 8-hour shift. The true-false items are simple behavioral statements such as "demonstrated appropriate mealtime behavior," "made his bed and cleaned his room," "in bed on time," etc. The items review the child's response to various aspects of the program day. Although more subjective than behavioral counts, these items are useful as a means for evaluating the child's overall performance. The data from true-false items are usually summarized on a weekly basis and, where appropriate, we may add together groups of items to produce a single performance score for the child's week. Such data highlight the child's general progress and call attention to behavioral areas that may require new or specialized treatment.

The true-false chart may be used to maintain follow-up data on a behavior that has previously been carefully counted. For example, behavioral charting indicated that swearing had been virtually reduced to a zero level for one child. Thus, it was no longer necessary to maintain a daily count on this behavior and the charting was changed to a simple true-false item. If we should in the future find that this item was being marked "true" with a high frequency, this would be an indication that the previous treatment had lost its effect and more careful study of the behavior should again be instituted. Although such a chart is largely insensitive to small changes in behavior, it will serve as a simple method for obtaining a continuous check on the state of any behavior.

Behavioral charting is probably the most widely applicable and economical measurement system to use. Measurement can be performed by regular child-care workers in the process of their ordinary duties with the child. A variety of behaviors can be monitored, and the measurements, as subsequent chapters will illustrate, usually adequately reflect the effectiveness of a variety of treatment procedures. Behavioral charts are, however, by scientific standards, unsophisticated and crude measurement systems. They often reflect only gross changes in behavior and frequently miss important qualitative features of the behavior. Perhaps the biggest drawback is their inability to provide data which will demonstrate moment-by-moment variations in a behavior. For example, a day-long count of swearing does not indicate under what circumstances the swearing will occur with greater or lesser probability. The child might accumulate the same count of 200 swearing responses per day whether these occurred aimlessly throughout the day or in a single five-minute angry outburst. Thus, behavioral charts are generally insensitive to variations brought about by fluctuations in the stimulus condition.

Despite its limitations, the behavioral chart appears to be basic to any experimental-clinical procedure. The other measurement systems described below are intended to expand upon and compliment behavioral charts, but at least to date, it does not seem that any of these can successfully supplant the behavioral chart in all circumstances. Of the various measurement systems we have worked with, the behavioral chart comes the closest to meeting our requirements of achieving a compromise between scientific and clinical criteria for measurement.

CUMULATIVE RECORDING

One of the most analytic measurement procedures used in experimental laboratories has been the cumulative recording of free operant behavior, as illustrated, for example, in Ferster and Skinner's (1957) studies of reinforcement schedules. Cumulative recordings permit accurate observation and discrimination of subtle changes in behavior rates. Unfortunately, this type of recording has seldom been applied to the observation of ongoing, natural human behavior. For example, we have little information concerning the day-long variations in the rate of inappropriate behaviors of disturbed children. What are the hour-by-hour or minute-by-minute variations in the occurrence of the clinically relevant behaviors of a disturbed child during the course of his typical day? What environmental events might be found responsible for these variations? To begin to answer such questions, we have developed a system for obtaining cumulative recordings within the normal living situation of the children.

Cumulative recorders were mounted in a central location and the cottages were wired to permit the remote operation of the cumulative recorders from any part of the living units. In practice, an observer who has been assigned to record a particular behavior carries a small remote-control box by which all observations are recorded. The remote unit can be plugged in at a convenient location in the cottages. Buttons on this unit control all four functions (paper drive, reinforcement pen, event pen, and response pen or stepper) of the cumulative recorder. After locating the child to be observed, the observer plugs the remote counter into a convenient outlet and starts the paper drive on the recorder. When the target behavior occurs, the observer momentarily depresses the button that operates the stepper pen. If a predetermined type of reinforcement occurs contingent upon the behavior, the observer also depresses the button that activates the reinforcement marker of the recorder. In practice, the observer also maintains a series of narrative notes concerning the observation situation. These are coordinated with the cumulative record by using the event pen of the recorder.

We have used cumulative recordings for basically two types of studies. First, they have proven invaluable in understanding ongoing day-long variations in behavior. Few behaviors occur at a consistent rate throughout the day, and, in fact, most are erratically influenced by understandable, but often difficult to discriminate, changes in the child's environment. The cumulative recording and its associated narrative chart have been useful in formulating hypotheses about environmental factors that influence these critical behaviors. An example of this is contained in case number 5, Chapter 7. Hypotheses arising from the cumulative records may subsequently be tested in more highly controlled studies. Second, cumulative recordings have been useful in situations where a treatment technique is tested in a miniature experiment. Because of its sensitivity to small variations in the rate of the behavior, the effects of different treatment conditions can be promptly assessed. An example of this latter type of study is presented in case number 1, Chapter 7.

The cumulative recording is an expensive measurement tool both because of the cost of the apparatus and because a special staff member must be assigned to make the necessary observations. However, it is a sophisticated measurement procedure and has been found to be particularly applicable in the study of relatively high-rate behaviors. In a number of cases to be detailed later in the book, cumulative recordings have been invaluable in the initial development of treatment hypotheses.

RANDOM TIME SAMPLES

The time-sampling technique appears to be the most successful procedure when a study requires precise measures obtained over a relatively short time span. A block of observations is collected under each condition of the experiment, and the summary scores for each block of observations are used to evaluate the differences between treatments. Each block consists of a predetermined number of brief observation periods. During each of these observation periods, the observer tallies the number of occurrences of the target behavior in the same manner as would be done in behavioral charting. Generally, a block consists of 10 to 20 observations collected at randomly determined times over a two to- three-day interval. The observations themselves may be of three to 45 minutes in duration, depending upon the demands of the particular study.

With a moderate amount of prior planning and careful adherence to the predetermined procedure, time samples can be relatively easily collected and will provide satisfactory measures. Carefully collected behavioral samples may be expected to be sensitive to small differences in behavior. Consequently, they are especially useful in the conduct of miniature studies designed to evaluate several hypotheses about what might be the best treatment procedure to use over a prolonged period of time. Since only small portions of the child's behavior are sampled, problems of sampling bias can well influence the data. Consequently, inferential statistics may be indicated to determine if the results may be safely generalized to larger samples of the child's behavior. Such inferential statistics are, of course, irrelevant when behavioral charting is used where all occurrences of the target behavior are recorded over a relatively long time period.

In some circumstances, the random time-sampling technique is indicated because it employs an especially assigned observer rather than a child-care worker who must carry out other duties at the same time. Often accuracy of observation depends upon a highly trained observer who will not be distracted by other duties. In some circumstances, a child-care worker may be unable sensitively and spontaneously to perform a prescribed treatment procedure if he must also bear the burden of maintaining the evaluative data. Finally, there are many studies where it is essential to take major precautions against having the worker unwittingly bias the data because of his confidence in or distaste for a particular treatment technique. The familiar "blind" techniques of drug studies are, of course, a case in point. An example in our studies might be a situation where we want to obtain a measure of the amount of praise a child receives from staff. Only the rare staff member could fail to bias a count of the number of times he praises the child if he were maintaining the count himself. If a third person observes such a behavior without the staff member's at the moment being aware of the count, a more accurate measure may result.

Under ideal conditions, the behavior-sampling technique would provide the best controlled method of obtaining experimental-clinical data. Unfortunately, it is rarely possible to conduct a study with rigid adherence to the ideal requirements of behavior-sampling. The chief problem is to achieve truly random time samples. The usual clinical setting places many practical obstacles in the way of meeting this criterion. Scheduling of the observer's time is frequently a major obstacle, particularly if they are part-time employees, and therefore the time of observation would have to be biased in conformity with the observer's work schedule. If a regular child-care worker is used to make such observations, it is usually necessary to bias the observation time in conformity with the rest of his schedule. Variations in the child's schedule, such as occur frequently in a flexible treatment program, may also bias the observations. For example, a change in a parent's visiting time or unforeseen changes in the school schedule could interrupt a previously determined schedule of observations and thus have a biasing effect upon the data. Therefore, most of the data that we have obtained with the time-sampling technique do not rigidly meet the requirements of random selection of time samples. Wherever time samples have been biased in some fashion that could reasonably be assumed to have an effect upon the data, we have made note of it in our discussion of the study.

In using random time-sampling, there is sometimes difficulty in determining the duration of each observation. The best rule of thumb seems to be to make a single observation sufficiently long that relatively few of the observations will result in zero entries. Thus, for a very high-rate behavior, short observations of one to three minutes will often prove satisfactory. When a much lower-rate behavior is being studied, however, the length of the individual observation must be extended in order to avoid having a high number of samples in which the behavior does not occur, since this would produce a skewed distribution that would enormously complicate the problems of statistical analysis.

One of the major drawbacks in the behavioral-sampling technique from a clinical standpoint is that the results do not often lend themselves to providing immediate feedback to the staff. Unlike behavioral charting, it is not possible from random samples to determine the day-to-day status of a given behavior. Consequently, staff may tend to rely upon their own subjective judgment of the status of that behavior and not have the objective feedback that so often provides important reinforcement for them in their efforts to carry out difficult management procedures. A set of behavior samples may take three to four days to collect and then an hour or more to summarize and to analyze statistically. The consequent delay in feedback of data is seen as a major drawback to the use of behavior-sampling techniques in the day-to-day evaluation of a treatment program. A related problem, of course, is that where programs are evaluated by behavior-sampling techniques, a more highly trained staff with time set aside for statistical analysis is required. Consequently, this technique would be less applicable in minimally staffed facilities or in outpatient treatment where most of the measurement must be carried out by the child's family.

BEHAVIORAL CODING SYSTEM

A somewhat different method of behavior sampling is incorporated in the Behavioral Coding System, an instrument that has been under development at the Treatment Center. With this procedure, a very large number of extremely brief observations are made of a child's behavior. These brief observations are selected according to a predetermined random schedule as with the previously described time-sampling methods. At the time of the observation, the observer codes the child's behavior according to a scheme of between one and 20 behavioral categories. The coded observation is based upon the child's behavior during a one-second interval. Thus, at the predetermined time, the observer notes what the child is doing and then codes that behavior according to the categories being used. A simple presence or absence indication is made for each behavior on the checklist.

Approximately 200 such one-second observations are usually made over a predetermined time interval and randomly covering particular kinds of environmental situations for the child. In this manner, a large number of observations can be collected with relatively little observer time, since each observation itself requires only one second. Although the observer codes only the behavior occurring at the target second, he is allowed to code that behavior according to inferences he may make from the total enviromental situation and from other behaviors occurring both before and after the target second. For example, if the observer looked only during the target second, it would often be difficult to judge exactly in what category the child's behavior belongs. However, if the observer has been on the scene for a few minutes preceding the moment of the observation, he will have a better understanding of the total environmental context of the behavior that occurs at the target second.

This method of observation is appropriate to a wide variety of measurement situations. In actual practice, however, we have been developing a set of 20 behavioral categories that may be used in its entirety when observing according to the Behavioral Coding System. In practice, the observer codes the child's behavior into only one of the 20 categories for any observation. However, it is also possible to include additional behavioral codes as may seem appropriate with any given child. Thus, for example, we might include "bizarre behavior" as an additional category with a psychotic child. Also, one of the major aggressive responses used by a child may be biting, which could be included as an additional category. In that case, both "aggressive" and "biting" would be scored simultaneously.

The method of sampling discrete moments in the child's behavioral day has special advantages for certain measurement problems. For example, with both behavioral charting and random time-sampling, the observer must judge when a particular kind of behavior has begun and when it has terminated. With almost any behavior, this is a difficult judgment and one that is prone to much subjectivity. Even a behavior as simple as "swearing" presents difficulties for observers, for they may not be able to judge how many instances of swearing have occurred in a given outburst. Or, with "helping behavior," it may often be difficult to judge whether three small helpful behaviors have occurred or one single helpful behavior. The coding system avoids this problem of the observer's having to judge the onset and termination of a particular behavior. The behavior either is or is not occurring at the moment of observation.

There is a rationale for selecting a one-second time interval for the Behavioral Coding System. Originally, the intent was to use a short period of time primarily to permit a large number of observations with a minimum of observer time and to avoid the above-mentioned problem of judging the beginning and ending of a particular behavior. Ten-second samples of behavior were used in our original studies. However, the resulting inter-judge reliability figures were discouraging. To obtain better understanding of our reliability problems, we applied the behavioral coding system to video taped recordings of children's behavior. At this point it was discovered that the major source of disagreement seemed to occur when two observers would emphasize earlier or later portions of the behavior in a particular ten-second period. The source of this disagreement thus was not the definition of the behavior being observed, but rather the fact that observers tended to emphasize different sections of even so short an observation as ten seconds. The reliability was thus improved by shortening the observation itself to a split second.

Another major goal in our work with the Behavioral Coding System has been related to the definition of behaviors to be observed. In behavior modification, workers have tended to emphasize easily defined behavior often to the exclusion of more complex behaviors that may be of more meaningful clinical concern. For example, few behavior modifiers can be satisfied with broad categories such as "aggressive behavior," because they find it difficult to achieve inter-observer reliability. Instead, then, they tend to define more precisely the behavior to a category such as "hitting." We felt that it might be possible, by using a method such as the behavioral coding system, to establish a relatively finite list of broad classes of behavior that could nevertheless be reliably observed. Thus, a single class of behavior such as "aggressive" might include hitting, swearing, throwing objects, kicking, biting, spitting, etc. From the common-sense point of view, such a total class of aggressive behavior would be of more clinical interest than would be any one of the sub-behaviors included in that class. One would certainly want to modify the whole class of aggressive behaviors rather than one or two of the specific behaviors within it. Particularly in our older group of children, the single behaviors in such a class did not occur with great consistency, but by lumping them together as "aggressive," one would see the total class of behavior occurring quite consistently. A child might show hitting today and biting tomorrow, and to achieve meaningful measurement, one would have to count all of these precise behaviors or class them together. Consequently, the present set of 20 classes of behavior has been used.

The Behavioral Coding System demonstrates certain possibilities as an evaluative instrument as well as an instrument for use in particular treatment studies. Table 3.5, for example, gives the results of observations from 16 of the categories in the Behavioral Coding System for one child in his own home in relation to his mother and two weeks later at the Treatment Center in relationship to the Center staff. The results seem to show the effect of a change in the gross environmental situation to which the child was exposed. It is of particular interest to note that in the home situation the child was scored 48% of the time as engaged in rebellious behavior, while at the Center the same score dropped to 7%.

Table 3.5. An Example of Data Collected on a Child prior to Admission to CTC and Shortly after Admission, Using the Behavioral Coding System

	Mother		*CTC Staff*	
	Frequency	*% of Total*	*Frequency*	*% of Total*
A. Assertive	3	1.5	—	—
B. Directive	24	12.	3	2.
C. Intrusive	14	7.	—	—
D. Pleading and clinging	—	—	—	—
E. Dependent	6	3.	2	1.
F. Compliant	7	4.	114	9.
G. Rebellious	94	48.	10	7.
H. Helpful	2	1.	1	0.7
I. Aggressive-sadistic	—	—	1	0.7
J. Withdrawal	13	7.	—	—
K. Kindly, friendly	9	4.	37	25.
L. Giving direct reinforcement	—	—	5	3.
M. Giving recognition	11	6.	14	9.
N. Attention to observer	—	—	3	2.
O. No observation possible	—	—	3	2.
P. Attention to task	14	7.	56	38.

One of the things data from the Behavioral Coding System highlight is the great percentage of time that even the most disturbed children spend engaged in essentially appropriate behavior. In the clinical situation, one is often overwhelmed by the inappropriate behavior and tends to overlook the high percentage of time that the child may actually engage in desirable behavior. Thus, data from an instrument such as the behavioral coding system may be especially useful in highlighting those positive behaviors that can be strengthened in shaping programs to combat many of the child's negative behaviors. Often such behaviors are already occurring at a fairly high rate and hence can be relatively easily strengthened as behaviors that are incompatible with the less desirable acts in the child's repertoire.

The Behavioral Coding System shares with all time-sampling systems a major deficiency. It tends to provide only biased data of low-rate but nevertheless important behaviors. For example, the coding system includes the category "assaultive behavior." With our older children, assaultive behavior can be a major problem even though it may occur but once every two weeks. If it is that infrequent, the chances of its being noted during the Behavior Coding System observations would be very slight indeed and the data would show no difference between a clinically troublesome level of assaultive behavior and zero assaultive behavior. Thus, time-sampling procedures such as the Behavioral Coding System should not be used to evaluate clinically important behavior that is occurring at a very low rate.

The Behavioral Coding System as presented here is an example of a different type of time-sampling procedure. Although this instrument is not fully developed as yet, it seems to present some interesting possibilities for future work.

DURATION AND TIME-ON-TASK MEASURES

Frequency of response is not always the most sensitive indicator of a treatment effect. Duration of response, often in addition to frequency counts, provides a more meaningful dependent variable. For example, frequency counts of temper tantrums may be very misleading. We have frequently observed that at the beginning of treatment (e.g., two-minute time-out contingent upon each temper tantrum), there may be six tantrums per day, but each lasting 45 minutes to an hour. As this behavior begins to extinguish, there will initially be an increasing frequency of tantrums with a concomitant decrease in the duration of the tantrum. In such instances, it would be preferable to monitor the effectiveness of the time-out procedure with a stop watch as well as a hand tally counter.

Many of the positive behaviors we are attempting to develop in the children would be difficult, if not misleading, to measure simply by frequency of response. Cooperative interaction with peers, a social response preferred to be accelerated, may be more meaningfully measured by the amount of time the child is engaged in such behavior than by the rate of occurrence of such instances. To illustrate, we wished to assess if in the classroom the amount of appropriate work behavior in contrast to class disruptive and non-work behavior, such as day-dreaming and talking, differed. In this instance, a definition of "on-task" behavior was agreed upon and careful observations were made of the amount of time the child spent "on-task." The teacher had a control panel containing switches and clocks for each child. When the child was working appropriately, the teacher would turn on a clock which also turned on a light which was mounted on the child's desk. The elapsed time on-task was recorded in ratio form to the total time spent in class.

Time on-task has also been used effectively in measuring appropriate isolative and parallel play, which has to be taught to many of the children. The preferred duration of response measure would be to have a concurrent frequency of response count. A duration measure is more expensive and difficult to obtain than a single frequency count. This problem may be delimited by coordinating the accumulation of the duration measure with a sampling procedure.

Summary

The measurement techniques presented here are intended only as initial developments. The orientation of measurement procedures in the experimental-clinical method should satisfy several requirements, including: (*a*) to measure the behavior intended to be treated, so that it is as independent as possible from the observer; (*b*) to minimize the presumption of response commonality among children, i.e., emphasize the idiosyncratic approach; and (*c*) to measure the simple behaviors which are readily discriminatable from other responses. Our orientation has been to avoid measurement techniques which are not directly sensitive to the treatment procedure, and particularly those which are designed for group descriptions.

Our work to date has focused upon the child's responses, and has been oblivious of antecedent stimulating and contingent reinforcing conditions. The next logical step would be to develop measurement techniques which would assess the variety of stimulating and reinforcing conditions maintaining a response under treatment. The next level of complication is to employ the assumptions of learning theory in interactional form, as contrasted to the simultaneous treatment of habits as if they were nonrelated.

It should be recognized that the value of a treatment technique is never greater than the validity of one's measure of the dependent variable. A goal for the experimental-clinicians will also be to devise ways to assess the reliability of his measures routinely and without biasing the data at the time the reliability study is performed.

CHAPTER FOUR

Same-Subject Experimental Designs

The experimental-clinical model, as discussed in this book, gains its value by methodology and not necessarily by the treatment techniques which may be evolved from the employment of the method. Our primary purpose is to promote a scientific-clinical method; it is not the purpose of the text to substantiate certain behavior-therapy techniques which may have resulted from our studies. Recognizing that the experimental-clinical method allows for development of new treatment techniques, we do not consider the techniques derived from the studies as panaceas. The important point is that we never consider a treatment technique currently in use as a finished procedure, but rather presume that existing techniques can be improved. The experimental-clinical methodology makes such improvements possible.

As previously mentioned, learning theory was used in developing the treatment techniques studied because of the objectivity provided by that theory; its postulates permit predictable hypotheses about treatment outcomes, and it is conducive to studying relatively clean dependent variables when investigating single habits or habit groups. The entire historical development of learning theory is consistent with the experimental-clinical method, since the investigator is required to use a degree of experimental design, or control, to ascertain if the independent variable was responsible for the predicted variations of the behaviors under treatment.

Same-subject designs provide a variety of advantages for individual treatment programs. One rationale for using these designs is to avoid the between-subject variance found in group studies. A second justification for same-subject designs is our assumption that, although the same laws of learning apply to all individuals, idiosyncratic learning histories preclude the assumption of commonality of responses to same stimuli or response rates to different reinforcement schedules. Another reason for the employment of experimental design is that one can continuously monitor the treatment program with a subject—typically not the case in group studies. The use of experimental designs and monitoring of data enables an investigator to determine what conditions are responsible for sustaining the behaviors. These rationales for using the experimental-clinical method will be, in theory, acceptable to many clinicians, but, in practice, seldom used because of the expense in time and money. Furthermore, many of the current clinical treatment models or theories are not amenable to measurement as demanded by the experimental-clinical method.

The major value of using experimental design is that the clinician more readily maintains a scientific attitude toward his patient. More specifically, the scientific attitude is that one may have as much pride in discovering the source of his error as in finding the source of his success in any treatment technique. The scientist values learning, even if that means learning he has been ignorant up to the latest studies. Such an attitude is seldom incorporated in the traditional clinical approach, in which a combination of personality theories govern the treatment techniques, and acknowledgement of failure holds no value, but more often triggers justifications to explain why the patient did not improve. The clinician employing the experimental-clinical model is not compelled to rationalize his failures; he is responsible for the behavior being treated.

Most of the data contained in this book are in the form of graphs and descriptive statistics, seldom in the form of inferential statistics. A detailed explanation of single-subject designs and the role of statistics in such methodology is provided by Sidman (1960). In using same-subject designs, one seldom resorts to inferential statistics, since by selecting a single subject he has circumvented the between-subject variability characteristic of group studies. Occasionally we have used sampling procedures and inferential statistics to demonstrate treatment effects with a single subject. We propose that it is reasonable for one to define a population in terms of responses contained within one subject and to make predictions from a base rate as contrasted with a treatment procedure. Rather than dismissing error variance, it is the aim of the well-documented same-subject design to deal directly with a source of variability that may confound a treatment variable. This variability is discovered by monitoring the data continuously while using the subject as his own control during the institution of several treatment techniques. Furthermore, in the methodology contained in this book, we are concerned with the individual, we are not really concerned about group trends. In many respects, the same-subject design is more exacting on the investigator, since in a large group study a statistically significant effect may be demonstrated when in fact the procedure involved would be clinically senseless because the effects were not sufficiently generalizable to enable prediction of how any particular subject would respond.

Statistics were not considered applicable in many of the studies, since the treatment goals were designed to show an "either-or" effect. For example, the typical treatment goals are to show the presence or absence of a given behavior or behaviors, after which the investigator may also be interested in the rate of acquisition or extinction of the behavior elicited by the treatment procedure. Thus, the investigator is interested in a graph illustrating whether he has been able to elicit or eliminate a given behavior. If the desired result failed to occur, a different treatment technique may be tested. In review, many of the studies were primarily concerned with acquisition and extinction, and secondarily with the rates of those behavioral changes.

At the current stage of our research, the treatment goals selected for the patients would be considered naïve in comparison with selecting goals based upon developmental norms acquired from the literature. Frankly, the investigators used considerable bias in selecting what the preferred behaviors would be in any given treatment program; seldom was a program devised in which the behavior to be acquired was based upon available accumulated evidence contained elsewhere in the literature to indicate the criteria for an age-appropriate response. Developmental goals were used in training speech. It is currently beyond the scope of this book to discuss what would be preferred behavioral goals; our text is limited toward methodology which may make it possible to approach the treatment goals. The experimental-clinical method demands that the investigator make a hypothesis about the behavior he is treating, to make a prediction of what the behavior change or approximation to that change shall be, and to determine under one or more conditions the best procedure for achieving the predicted behavior change.

There are guidelines for selecting the experimental designs discussed in this chapter, and one has the option of shifting from one experimental design to another. There are precautions of which an investigator should be aware in selecting experimental designs. For example, one guideline is that the investigator should not select a design which is likely to guarantee the patient's rehearsing retrieval of an undesirable habit because of excessive replications of treatment programs. These precautions will be emphasized in the discussion of the particular designs presented in this chapter.

There is one point of departure in the same-subject designs contained here as contrasted to those discussed by Sidman (1960). In Sidman's text, the studies cited referred primarily to experiments with animals whose entire lives had been under rigorous experimental control. Thus all relevant independent variables are controlled and consequently stable baseline rates of behavior occur. When dealing with the massive unknown learning history of a human subject, one can seldom obtain a stable baseline. Only a few of the major contingencies controlling a human subject's behavior are ever identified. At best, in our studies we obtain what may be described as uncontrolled baselines. An uncontrolled baseline is the measure obtained by observing a behavior that is not currently exposed to a formal treatment program. Preferably, the uncontrolled baseline would be a naturalistic observation. Unfortunately a well-trained staff may confound a naturalistic baseline because they habitually and inadvertently conduct favored treatment programs.

In an uncontrolled baseline condition one allows the child to operate for the preferred reinforcement contingency or contingencies, maintaining the behavior under observation. Perhaps as a function of differences in staff experience, one can expect variable baseline rates depending upon the schedule of reinforcement the different staff members make available to the child. Such problems in obtaining a baseline are the reason that one may not generalize excessively from a same-subject study to similar subjects in other facilities. Staff using the same treatment procedures may have subtle differences in reinforcement contingencies and ratios available for the child during acquisition of the baseline conditions. Furthermore, the maintaining reinforcement contingencies may differ between subjects, and the baseline data would never disclose such idiosyncracies in responses to social reinforcers. This point deserves some elaboration. In the experimental-clinical method, the data do not warrant generalization to ostensibly similar cases. It is reasonable to test the efficacy of the same treatment techniques with presumably similar subjects, but still one would be required to use an experimental design to assess the effectiveness of the treatment technique for each patient.

When using the experimental-clinical method, one would not be justified in accumulating a number of similar cases for eventual generalization from such data as if they were indeed group data. A reason that one is unable to generalize from accumulated case studies is that the subjects were not obtained randomly, they were not assigned to treatment conditions randomly, and they were not likely to have received similar baseline and treatment conditions, because of the vast differences between treatment facilities or the differences within the same facility over time. The accumulation of case studies may engender useful hypotheses, but if the hypotheses are going to be tested in group form, that substantiation comes from conducting the group study; it does not rest with generalizing from accumulated case studies. It is our contention that if one feels he has a treatment technique worthy of generalization as demonstrated from successive same-subject studies on that technique, the valid step would be to obtain a group of subjects and, consistent with the requirements for conducting a group study, assess the effectiveness of that treatment condition.

Same-subject design data are often criticized for their failure to generalize to group behavior. Perhaps the predictive restrictions of the same-subject study are no worse than being unable to predict individual behaviors from group data. It is apparent in parametric statistics that the prediction obtained from group data can be applicable only with an estimated degree of error established from those samples to comparable samples. These kinds of data certainly put the clinician at a loss in many instances, since he is dealing with the individual rather than large groups.

Conducting idiographic studies stimulates development of new and various kinds of treatment techniques for similar habit patterns. It may be considered of value that the increased variability among treatment techniques promotes growth in the field, and that it is not productive for the understanding of human behavior to rehearse the same treatment procedures over and again. A basic contention of any investigator working with various cases across time is that whatever techniques are currently employed may be improved upon, and that such improvement will be developed by testing various treatment techniques in a well-monitored manner. The designs in the remainder of this chapter are recommended for long-term programs in which the behaviors treated are monitored either by sampled time intervals or during the entire day.

In these designs the symbol *A* will represent a baseline condition which may be assumed to have been obtained under uncontrolled conditions unless stipulated otherwise. "Uncontrolled conditions" means that the behavior was not under any prescribed staff-controlled reinforcement contingency, but that the subject was allowed to operate for whatever reinforcement contingencies he desired, and the staff were instructed to respond however they wished to the child's behavior. It is recognized that if staff are trained in conducting numerous reinforcement programs then an uncontrolled baseline is impossible to obtain, since the staff will reinforce, punish, and ignore behaviors selectively. It is also recognized, but unfortunately not prevented, that successive samples of baseline behaviors will never be valid comparisons of return-to-baseline procedures. Valid replications may not be acquired once a treatment technique has been conducted because it is doubtful if the patient will have a social environment comparable to the environment present during the original baseline condition, particularly if there were any positive effects with the treatment procedure.

The symbols *B, C, D,* etc., will represent different treatment programs. Thus, the common experimental design, *ABAB*, represents one successive replication of both the baseline and a treatment condition. There is little doubt that a baseline condition is a variation of a treatment program, since one presumes that those reinforcement conditions available to the subject during the baseline maintained his behavior under observation. One may identify the baseline conditions typically employed with human subjects as an observational condition as contrasted to a treatment condition. Perhaps an accurate distinction between the baseline and the treatment condition is that the baseline condition represents an observational period during which the investigator has no control over the reinforcement contingencies but assumes that the subject is operating for reinforcers which maintain the behavior for which the child had been referred to the treatment facility. This definition of the baseline is contrasted to the return-to-baseline conditions which are available to the investigator working with animals under a laboratory setting where the baseline condition is greatly controlled and, in fact, is a treatment program with as much control as is available in any *B*, *C*, or *D* conditions. In addition, sampling for the baseline is not so simple as is implied in the above discussion. The method by which observations are recorded during the baseline may have a significant effect upon the rate of the behavior. The reader is referred to the previous discussions on methods of observations upon rates of behavior to indicate how crucial it is to isolate which variables are responsible for maintaining the behavior during a baseline condition.

B *Design*

The *B* design is simply the administration of a treatment technique for which no baseline was obtained. Traditionally, this would be comparable to the investigator's relying upon observations obtained during therapy to demonstrate behavioral change during the course of therapy. The investigator simply monitors certain behaviors during the course of the treatment program on the assumption that any changes in the rate of the dependent variable are a function of the independent variable or treatment program. The *B* design is gaining in popularity simply because it is easy to administer, it is comparable to the traditional method of assessing the effectiveness of psychotherapy, it is inexpensive, and it easily provides a compromise to the clinician who is gradually making a transition to behavior-therapy procedures.

Figure 4.1 illustrates a study employing a *B* design. The graph contains mean frequencies for five-day intervals for a five-year-old schizophrenic child who was being taught to approach, sit next to, or sit on the laps of staff for an interval of time. The criterion interval of time that was minimally acceptable for reinforcement was rather short, typically being less

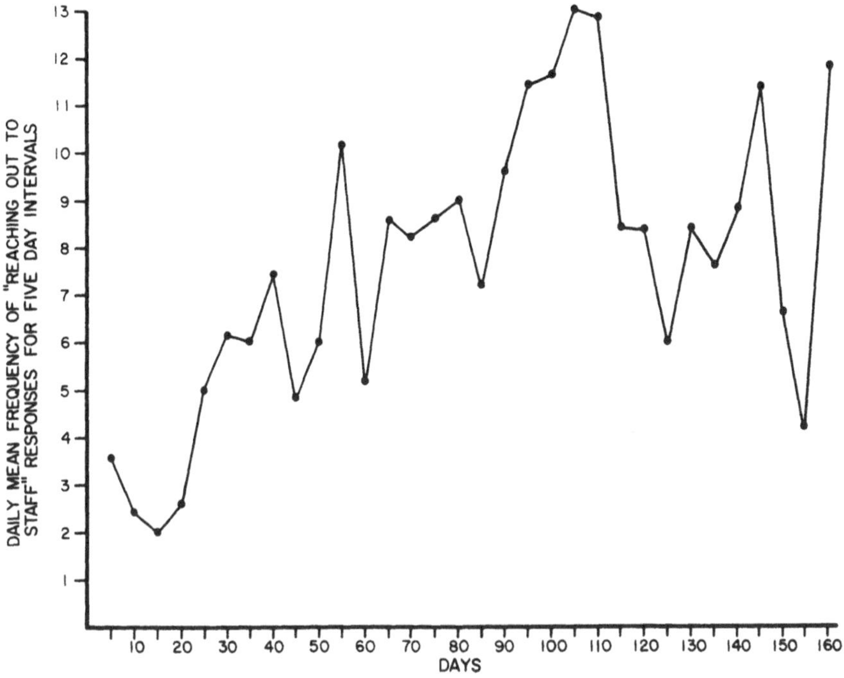

Figure 4.1. B *Design: Effect of Positive Reinforcement on "Reaching out to Staff" Responses in a C.A. 5, Schizophrenic Child*

than two minutes, and the response duration was seldom longer than three minutes. The treatment technique which comprised the *B* condition, or independent variable, was simply giving the child an M & M candy each time he approached a staff member as described above. When the response was occurring at a level of eight to ten times per day, the staff "naturally" faded out the candy reinforcement condition on the presumption that it was not so necessary, since it could now be replaced by more preferred social reinforcers. Figure 4.1 shows a slight acceleration of the approach response with the child. The *B* design illustrated here is certainly the crudest of the experimental designs; in fact, one cannot reasonably call it an "experiment," since there is a complete absence of control or comparison between two independent variables both monitored by the same dependent variable. Although no experimental control is demonstrable with the *B* design, at least it is an attempt to monitor data, the results of which may direct the investigator to test other procedures until a desired effect is obtained.

Figure 4.2 illustrates another *B* design. The dependent variable was the

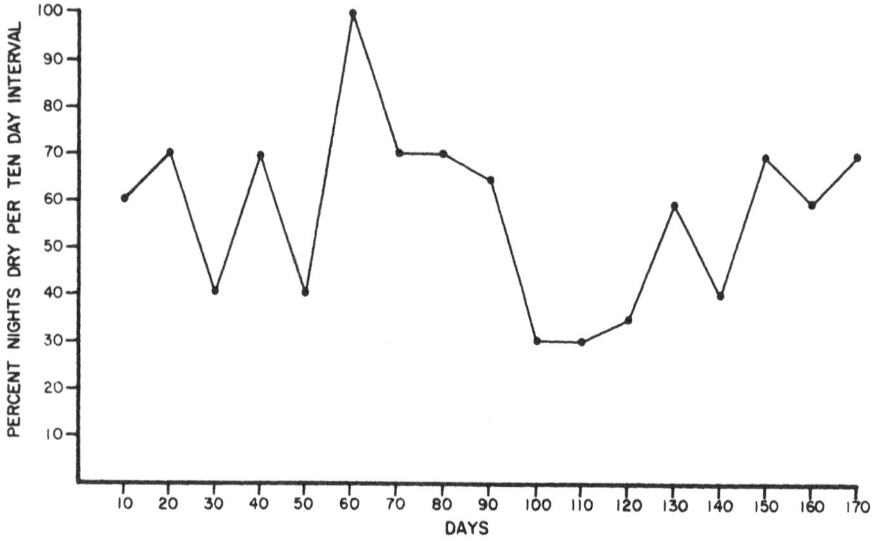

Figure 4.2. B *Design: Effect on Enuresis of Awakening a Child Two Hours after a Sleep*

percent of nights dry for each 10-day interval for an enuretic child. The measure was obtained by simply requesting staff to record whether the bed was wet or dry for successive nights. A baseline measure had not been taken for the study, so that even with a spectacular deceleration or acceleration of the rate of dry nights, the investigator could not with reasonable assurance assign the treatment effects to the presumed independent variable. For example, in reference to Figure 4.2, if prior to treatment the child had a baseline average of 30 percent of nights dry for each 10-day interval, then the treatment program which was employed would have appeared significant.

The treatment technique, or independent variable, was simply to awaken the child at 10:00 P.M. each night, which was on the average two hours after the child had fallen asleep. The treatment program of awakening the child is often a recommended procedure prior to resorting to the "bell and pad" conditioning technique for enuresis. The investigator wished to ascertain if the treatment procedure would have the desirable effect of training continence during sleep, and he hoped that bladder tension would eventually awaken the child. Actually, this was a rather preposterous predicted effect, considering that awakening the child was not contingent upon any degree of known bladder tension. Figure 4.2 illustrates that there were no acceleration or deceleration effects associated with the treatment procedure. Such apparent nonsignificant data could easily lead one to conclude that the treatment procedure was ineffectual. However, since there was no comparison with a pretreatment measure of percent of nights dry per 10-day interval, one is unable to determine if the procedure of awakening the child had a preferred treatment effect. The failure to compare the dependent variable against successive or simultaneous administration of two independent variables is the primary disadvantage of the *B* design. Although the treatment technique may demonstrate a definite acceleration or deceleration effect on the behavior being measured, one cannot conclude with confidence that the independent variable was the necessary and sufficient condition for the rate change. In reference again to the enuresis graph in Figure 4.2, if the treatment effect did not produce an incipient acceleration or deceleration effect, but rather had an immediate invariant and constant effect, it may have been a spectacular change from the rate of enuresis prior to that date. Unfortunately, such a stabilizing effect of the treatment program on enuresis would not be demonstrable with the *B* design. The *B* design is not recommended as a preferred experimental-clinical procedure, since it does not impart information about possible variables responsible for behavioral change because experimental control is absent.

Reliance upon differential rate changes for successive time intervals during a *B* design study, such as comparing 10-day intervals during the treatment procedure interval to demonstrate a trend in rate change of the measured behavior, is not considered an adequate experimental approach. The expected error incurred by comparing successive time intervals during the same treatment interval is that the dependent variable is being observed only during the administration of one independent variable, and the investigator is left with verbal argument to substantiate that any rate change was a function of that independent variable alone. It remains unknown if the rate change might have occurred without the presence of that independent variable, or perhaps after its absence. The treatment effects in such a study may be accounted for by any number of spurious variables which were not controlled by the investigator; the information imparted by such studies may thereby be misleading and the extent of its error would never be known.

The inferential error incurred from a *B* design is comparable to the one so prevalent in the clinical field. Many a clinician is content to hypothesize from either previous or similar cases, and most often from theoretical orientations, that he knows which variables were responsible for the behavioral changes without having resorted to any experimental manipulations. There is a trend in the field to rely upon the simplified *B* design, since, if a desirable treatment effect does occur, that becomes sufficient evidence to substantiate the hypothesis. Moreover, the obvious fact remains that as same-subject *B* designs using the same treatment procedure accumulate, they will be misinterpreted and popularized as group data. Thus, the clinicians will be deciding that the variables which were responsible for an acceleration of a particular response were derived from studies for which no experimental control existed. The error then committed is comparable to that in the field of clinical psychology today. That is, the clinician presumes which variables are in control, and regardless of whether that clinician is analytical in orientation or presuming to be a behavior modifier, any social reinforcer so inferred as an independent variable in a *B* design is endowed with as much scientific credence as the weakest of mentalistic terms. The investigator should be aware of the limitations of the *B* design, since it imparts little information; it does not promote formulation of new hypotheses and it leads to inferences not warranted by the data. We regret that we have resorted to this design so frequently in our case study data; the above precautions should be recalled when reviewing that data.

BC *Design*

The *BC* design is a comparison of differential acceleration or deceleration rates of behavior between two successively administered treatment techniques. The optimal methodological development of the *BC* design would require replication of the two treatment conditions, and preferably a counterbalancing of the order of treatments. Unfortunately, both replicated and counterbalanced designs are often economically unrealistic same-subject designs; furthermore, with successive replications, one runs the risk of training the child to retrieve an undesirable habit as well as to make the habit more resistant to extinction by virtue of the replications which place the behavior on an increasingly thinner schedule of reinforcement. This methodological error has not been confirmed by the investigator; it is presumed as an error, and considering the ethical issues involved the eventuality of such error should be avoided. The implied danger is not restricted to replicating a *BC* design, but applies to any replication design in which an undesirable behavior is inadvertently strengthened because of the experimental design.

Figure 4.3 illustrates the differential effects of one-minute and two-minute time-out procedures on gross-testing responses in a five-year-old schizophrenic child. The definition of gross testing was a combination of hostile responses which included hitting and kicking staff and children. The time-out condition, or independent variable, required staff to walk or carry the child to the quiet room, shut the door, and, without showing his face in the observation window, leave the child there for the one- or two-minute time-

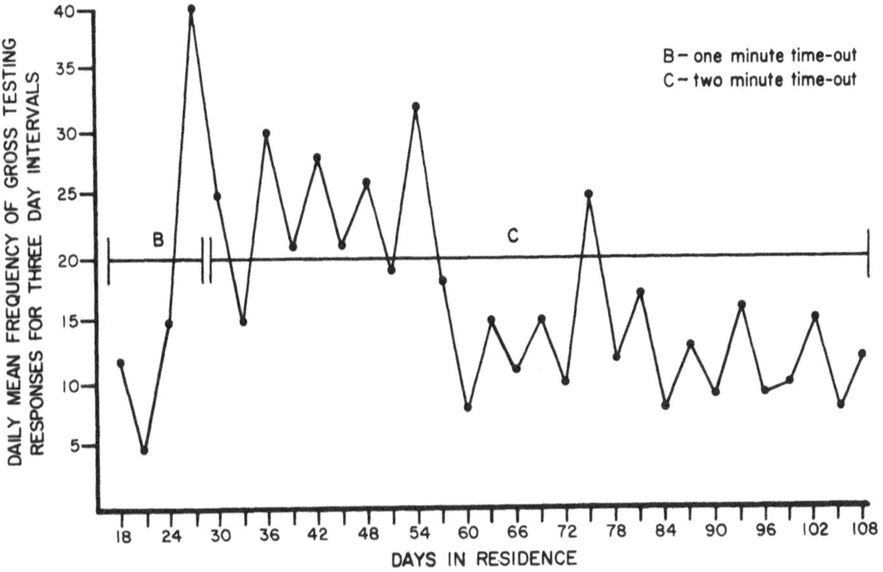

Figure 4.3. BC *Design: Effects of One- and Two-Minute Time-Outs on Daily Mean Frequency of Gross Testing in a Schizophrenic Child*

out as indicated by the treatment procedure in effect at the time. The quiet room was a single bedroom devoid of furniture and decor. The windows were not screened, nor did the room have the appearance of a security cell that is so characteristic of many institutions. In the case of this particular child, the time-out condition was often conducted in places where a quiet room was not available. At those times, the staff would take the child, sit him down, forcibly if necessary, and sit behind him so that he was unable to see the staff directly. The staff member would hold the child firmly in that position by the upper arms, which were held to the child's side for the required time-out interval. The latter procedure was a contaminating variable for assessing the singular effectiveness of using the quiet room for the time-out procedure, but one may presume the same ratio of trials employing the time-out condition of staff holding child was constant throughout the treatment conditions tested. Figure 4.3 shows that the one-minute time-out procedure employed for the 24-day interval was related with an acceleration of the gross-testing response. Unfortunately, the design does not compare the acceleration effect with a baseline. However, the acceleration effect within the one-minute time-out condition was obvious, and when the two-minute time-out procedure was initiated resultant gradual deceleration effect of the *C* condition was in marked contrast to the treatment effect noted in the B condition.

One criticism of the *BC* design in this particular study was that the one- and two-minute time-out treatment intervals were not used the same number of days. However, if one compares the first 24 days of both time-out treatment conditions, it becomes apparent that a deceleration effect was occurring with the longer time-out contingency. However, it still remains uncertain if the treatment effect might not have occurred if a one-minute time-out procedure had been maintained rather than our having changed to the two-minute condition. An initial acceleration effect of a given treatment procedure is not unusual, and this may have been what occurred during the one-minute treatment condition. Such an acceleration would be predictable on the basis of learning theory, since, during the extinction schedule of a given response, quite often the subject will operate more frantically for the preferred reinforcer, which is now unavailable, before the response begins to decelerate. More substantial credence would have been lent to the study of preferred time-out intervals for the child's gross-testing responses if at least one replication had been conducted.

AB *Design*

The *AB* design is a comparison between a treatment technique and a behavioral baseline. In conducting such a treatment procedure the investigator should be cognizant of the problems associated with securing a baseline condition and comparing it with the *B* treatment procedure. These problems involve knowledge of the conditions under which the baseline was obtained, and whether a stable rate of behavior was obtained during the baseline condition. Figure 4.4 illustrates the results of a series of behavior-modification procedures designed to assist in the eventual counter-conditioning of enuresis in a psychoneurotic child. The baseline was almost perfect for eight and one-half years, i.e., the child had always been enuretic. The succession of treatment procedures designed for the child are described in greater detail in the article entitled, "Operantly strengthening UCR as a prerequisite to counter-conditioning enuresis" (Browning, 1967b). The treatment problem, in summary, was that the child would not awaken when the bell rang as triggered by the "bell-and-pad" conditioning apparatus used with enuresis. Two previous attempts to counter-condition the enuresis had failed in the two years before the study commenced. A program was designed to awaken the child at any hour during the night, using a low-level intensity bell which would not awaken other children but yet would eventually awaken the patient. Once the child had been condi-

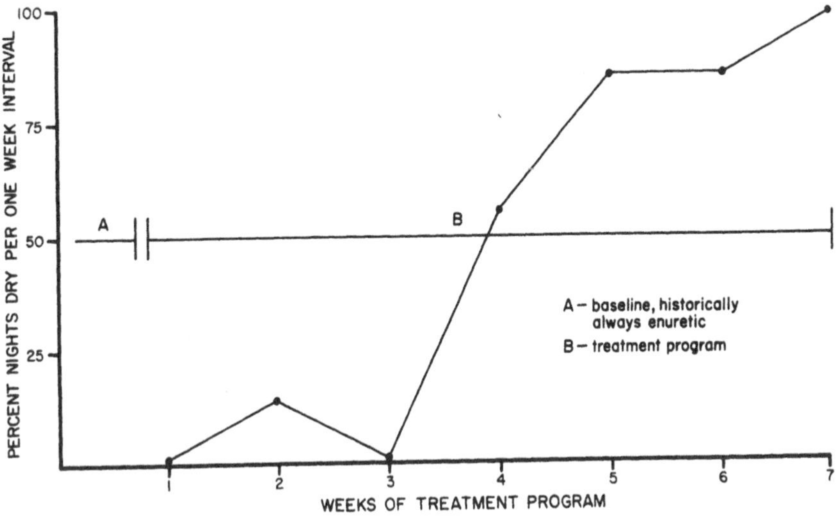

Figure 4.4. AB *Design: Effects on Enuresis of Operantly Strengthening UCR (Awakening to a Bell) and Counter-Conditioning Program*

tioned to awakening to the bell, from in the waking stage to in deep sleep, the bell-and-pad technique was initiated. Figure 4.4 shows the effect of the bell-and-pad conditioning procedure once the child had been trained to awaken to the bell. The baseline, or *A* condition, was zero percent days dry, and after a seven-week interval of the treatment program, the child was dry all nights of the week. The acceleration effect of the conditioning program was quite obvious, since the baseline was essentially perfect. An *ABAB* design, or replication of the study, was not considered necessary to demonstrate experimental control. The experimental control was documented, since previous attempts to counter-condition the enuretic response had failed because a prerequisite response of training the child to awaken to a low-level intensity bell had not been trained. The reader will note that the dependent variable monitored a series of two conditions: conditioning the child to awaken to a bell and then conditioning bladder control with the bell-and-pad conditioning apparatus.

Figure 4.5 illustrates a second example of a study using an *AB* design. The subject was an eight-year-old child with a history of brain injury and a concomitant diagnosis of childhood schizophrenia. The child seldom smiled, so it seemed warranted to teach the response by reinforcing increasingly better smile responses. The *A* interval, or baseline, is contained in

Figure 4.5 and is contrasted to the *B* treatment interval, shown as positive reinforcement on the graph. The positive reinforcement was a combination of social reinforcement (positive evaluative statements) from staff that served as discriminative stimuli and receiving candy, all contingent upon all smile responses during the entire day. The candy reinforcement was gradually faded during this study as the smile response became increasingly prevalent, although social reinforcement remained steady for a longer interval. Unfortunately, the data do not show the qualitative change in the smile response. A qualitative change is more difficult to measure,

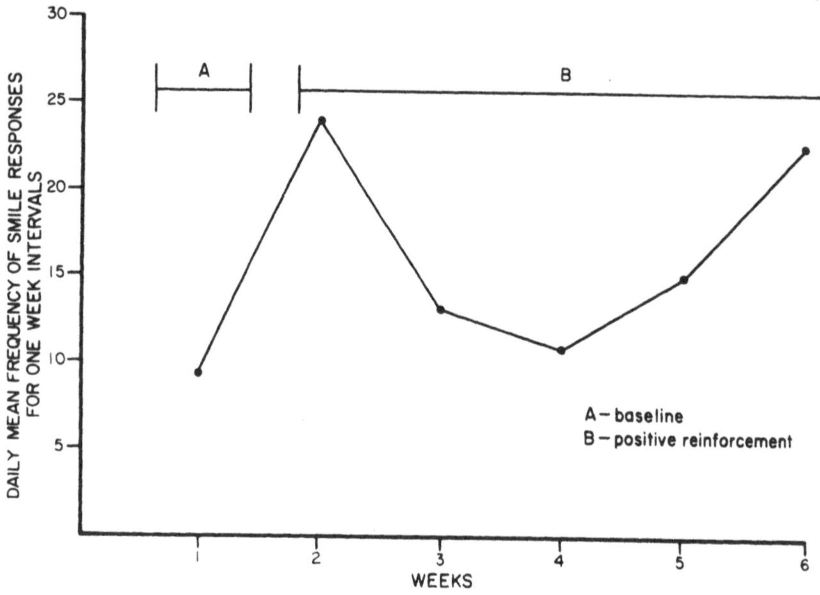

Figure 4.5. AB *Design: Effect of Positive Reinforcement on Smile Response in a C.A. 7, Schizophrenic, Brain-Injured Child*

since one is required constantly to change the dependent variable, i.e., to count frequency of increasingly more categories of a similar response. Such a measurement problem is characteristic for all studies of shaping a new response. The treatment phase of Figure 4.5 shows an initial acceleration, then deceleration, and finally acceleration to the point where the program was stopped because selective reinforcement of the smile response was no longer necessary. Apparently the smile response was now being maintained by the child's social environment. The smile response, once acquired, confronts the investigator with the problem found in studies on mutism after speech has been acquired and generalized. The problem is that the investigator loses control of the reinforcement contingencies maintaining the response, which would negate an *ABAB* replication type of design. In this study, the *ABAB* design would have been desirable, but the simplified *AB* design relating the treatment condition with a previous baseline was judged acceptable. One of the reasons an *ABAB* replication could not have been employed with this child's newly acquired smiling response was the impossibility of obtaining the degree of control necessary to demonstrate a replication. It would be extremely difficult to request staff not to reinforce the child's smiling response, since we suspect they were also being reinforced by the child's smile.

The *AB* design described above allows for better control of the independent variable than the simple *B* design because there is comparison between two treatment conditions monitored by the same dependent variable. The *AB* design is likely to be incorporated by investigators using the experimental-clinical method who do not have the staff time and control necessary for the designs which will be presented later. The baseline condition may be obtained quite conveniently on an established ward setting, or, in some instances, in an outpatient setting using parental assistance in collecting the data. The *AB* design may be described as having some semblance of experimental control.

ABC *Design*

The *ABC* design comprises comparisons among two treatment techniques and a baseline. The *ABC* design is inferentially weak, since order effects remain uncontrolled when one is comparing the treatment conditions against an original baseline, and when there may be some accumulation effects from earlier to later treatment conditions. This problem of order effects remains uncontrolled in the majority of designs in which several treatment conditions are studied successively. The *ABC* design is of value in the experimental-clinical setting when one finds that the *B* condition in an *AB* design fails to produce the desired treatment effect, but the data stimulate formulation of a new treatment hypothesis which is incorporated in a modified *B* treatment procedure which may now be labeled *C*.

The *C* condition is then installed to determine if it has a greater desired effect on the responses found in the *B* condition. Perhaps such a procedure can be described as a clinical investigator's trial-and-error method in which his errors are being compared against previous trials, but reflect more reasonable experimental control than the procedures previously mentioned. The fact that a trial-and-error approach is suggested is not derogatory; the well-monitored trial-and-error approach has probably evoked more significant scientific productivity than any other approach.

Figure 4.6 shows an *ABC* designed study in which successive treatment procedures were tested for differential effectiveness in reducing frequencies of temper tantrums in a five-year-old schizophrenic child. To reiterate, the rationale for using an *ABC* design is that, when the *B* condition does not effect the desired control as is preferred or hypothesized, a new technique is devised and tested.

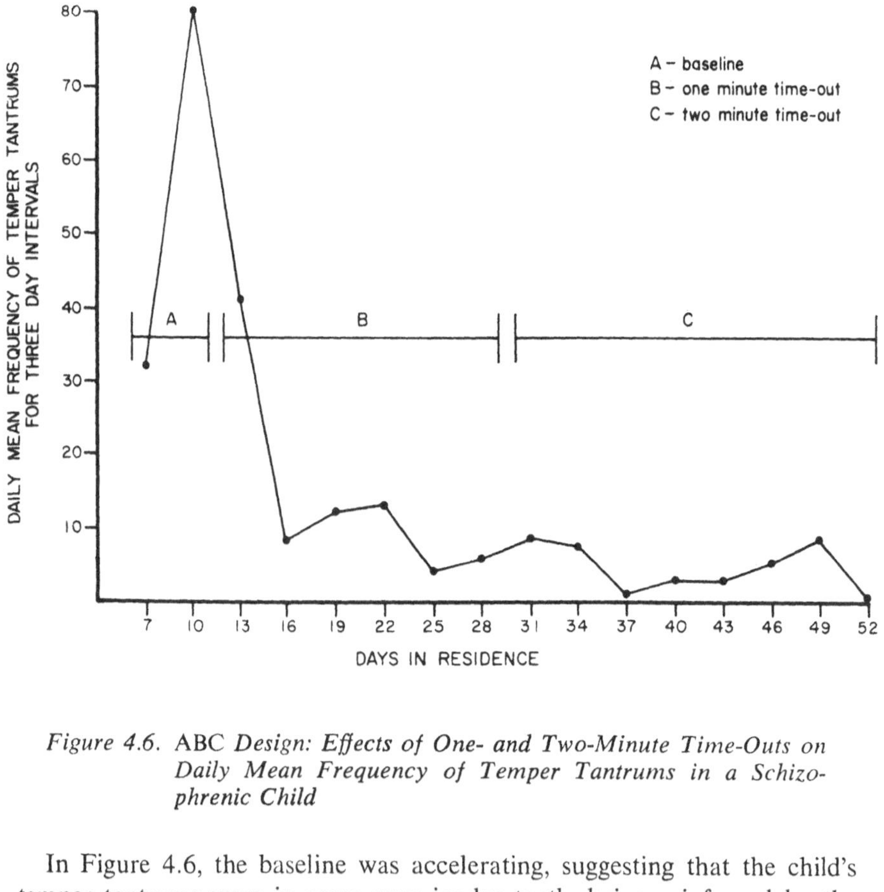

Figure 4.6. ABC *Design: Effects of One- and Two-Minute Time-Outs on Daily Mean Frequency of Temper Tantrums in a Schizophrenic Child*

In Figure 4.6, the baseline was accelerating, suggesting that the child's temper tantrums were in some way inadvertently being reinforced by the staff, most likely by their means of observation. The one-minute time-out procedure effected a rapid deceleration of the frequency of temper tantrums. Although it is not depicted in Figure 4.6, there was also a marked diminution in the duration of temper tantrums with successive trials of time-out procedure employed. It has been our experience that it is preferable to obtain duration as well as frequency of temper tantrums, since duration is often the first measure to be sensitive to a treatment effect. The one-minute time-out procedure appeared to have reduced the frequency of temper tantrums to a range of eight to ten per day, but the treatment effect was not considered optimal, since there were temper tantrums which occurred at the times most undesirable for staff to conduct a total program involving several children. At this point the two-minute time-out treatment technique, or *C* condition, was initiated. The two-minute time-outs showed a continued deceleration of the tantrum response, and although not illustrated entirely on the graph, the outcome of the treatment condition was to reduce the behavior to an occasional temper tantrum, and that final rate was not considered unusual for a five-year-old who may be expected to test his social environment.

ABA *Design*

The *ABA* design provides more demonstrable control of a single treatment condition under investigation than the previously mentioned designs. With the *ABA* design, one is able to demonstrate that the treatment variable, or combination of variables, was responsible for the alteration of the behavior under investigation. If the *B* condition varies the rate of the behavior differentially from that found in the initial baseline, and if during the replication of that baseline the original behavioral rate is reinstated, one generally concludes that the *B* condition was primarily responsible for the rate change.

A complete replication of the study would provide the improved design defined as the *ABAB* design, in which treatment and baseline conditions are both replicated to demonstrate control. Actually, one of the few instances in which an *ABA* design would be recommended is if one were to test whether a treatment condition was effective by returning to baseline, and if that were demonstrable, and for the sake of reducing staff time involved in observing and recording the subject's behavior, to schedule the treatment program thereafter without further monitoring of the data.

If the staff note a marked reversion of the undesirable behavior following application of an *ABA* designed study, then observing and recording of the behavior would be reinstated. It is often desirable that staff occasionally resample the behavioral rate after the *B* condition has been put into effect, or at least be alerted to inform the investigator if the undesirable behavior is reoccuring, which would then indicate further study of the treatment program. Figure 4.7 shows an example of an *ABA* design study in which a treatment condition was tested for its effectiveness in reducing

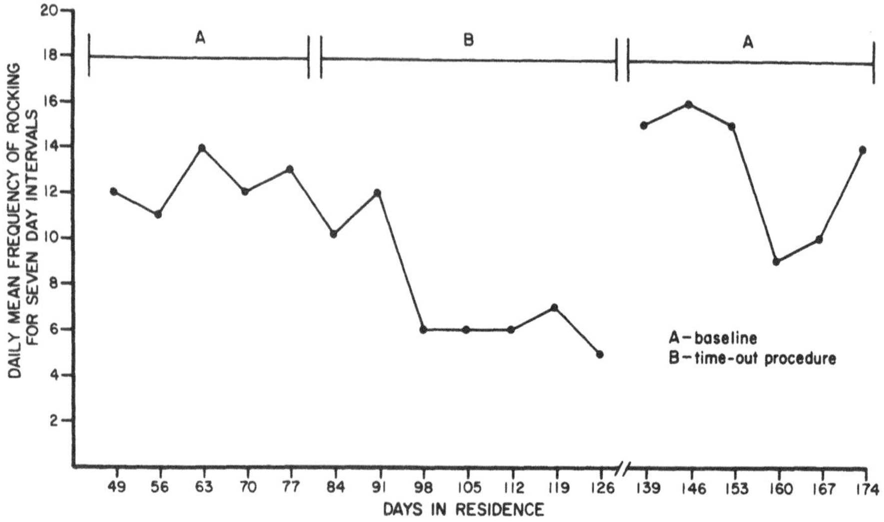

Figure 4.7. ABA *Design: Effect of a Time-Out Procedure on Rocking Response in a C.A. 7, Schizophrenic, Brain-Injured Child*

a rocking response in a seven-year-old schizophrenic, brain-injured child. The data are plotted by weekly averages. The response of rocking was defined as his swaying back and forth while sitting, standing, or lying on the bed. The duration of the response was not recorded, and again, although it is more difficult to obtain both time and rate measures simultaneously, the duration of the response is the dependent variable most likely to show an initial treatment effect. The treatment condition was simply to request the child to leave the room where the rocking response was occurring, and to return when he was "finished" rocking. If the child returned and commenced rocking again, he was *benignly* requested to leave the room and come back when he had finished rocking. Each time the child returned, staff greeted him with profuse expected positive social reinforcement and commented on his not rocking at that particular moment. Thus, the rocking response was not reinforced positively or negatively in a verbal manner. The treatment technique was essentially a time-out procedure, coupled with a rehearsal to success technique, the duration of which was determined by the subject himself. Perhaps the procedure could be described as a self-controlled procedure for decelerating the rocking response. The return-to-baseline interval demonstrated that the behavior did approximate the level at which it was previously occurring, in fact, it appeared to be slightly elevated. Unfortunately the child was discharged from the program prior to our having installed the *B* treatment condition for a sufficient interval to determine its long-term effectiveness. It was later discovered that when the child was returned home, the parents did not conduct the above, or any, program for controlling rocking behavior. In a short time there were reports that the rocking response was again occurring at a high rate. The reported acceleration of rocking at home suggested that some reinforcement contingencies, in addition to possible reinforcement characteristics of the rocking response itself, were again available for the behavior. The retrieval of rocking at home also raised the disturbing hypothesis that replication only placed the response on a thinner schedule, and possibly trained the child for quicker acquisition of the response the investigator wished to extinguish.

ABAB *Design*

Perhaps the *ABAB* design has gained the widest acceptance as a valid experimental design for same-subject studies, although there are problems associated with its use. One of its major disadvantages is that one never really returns to the *A* condition and successive replications may be expected to contaminate later treatment programs. There is also the importance of the skill of the investigator using the *ABAB* design to its most sensitive advantage. For example, the investigator is cautioned against continuing the initial *B* condition for too long an interval of time if there is a definite treatment effect, since this may guarantee such generalization of treatment effects that returning to baseline will be less likely to occur. This is a design problem which was mentioned earlier in regard to mutism, i.e., the more successful the treatment program, the more difficult it becomes to demonstrate a return-to-baseline effect.

Another disadvantage of the *ABAB* design is that successive replications may have the deleterious effect of training the child to retrieve the undesired habits more quickly. And as previously stated, because of the thinned reinforcement schedule resulting from replications, this is likely to render the habit more durable. If the *B* treatment condition intervals are short enough to show treatment effects, but not of sufficient duration to establish strong generalization effects, one is essentially training the child how to retrieve the old habit more rapidly, and perhaps extinguishing the more weakly acquired, but desirable, treatment effects. In a molar perspective, one creates this same problem simply by removing the child from his home environment (baseline), training new behaviors in the residential setting (treatment *B*), and then returning him home (baseline) where recidivism occurs. The treatment program should be designed to assure that "return-to-baseline" effects do not occur, because if they do it is obvious that the child has not acquired and generalized the desired behavioral change. Whether or not replications are involved in one's design, ethical considerations are involved in the selection of any treatment procedure as well as in the experimental design employed in the experimental-clinical method. There is the very real danger that excessive replications may be simply training the child for recidivism, thus making a mockery of long-term follow-up studies on the effectiveness of experimental-clinical programs. Many behavior modifiers choose designs with the contention, which is reflected in the arguments proposed by Lovaas (1967), that if one has the conviction of his treatment techniques the return-to-baseline condition is not likely to be deleterious. However, conviction is data, the accumulation of which could be detrimental to the child. The argument for replication designs seems warranted if the treatment condition is definitely put into effect for sufficient intervals of time to guarantee complete generalization of the desired response. The ethical error which may be committed would be to conduct an *ABAB* design with some undesirable behavior and then to cease the study simply because the investigator has obtained the desired data, after which he returns the child to an uncontrolled environment where the behavior is likely to be retrieved. In such an instance, all the investigator did was assist in strengthening the initial habit which he had been studying, for which he received a publication and possibly a professorship. Such disregard for the total treatment of a patient would certainly constitute unethical practice for the experimental-clinical investigator who has assumed clinical responsibility for the treatment of his patient. Another clinical limitation of the replicated design is especially important with older children and adults. Most often, the subject must be kept "blind" as to the nature of the study being conducted. He may well feel that the change of treatment procedures during an *ABAB* design is capriciousness on the part of staff. In such an instance the repeated replications can only serve to reinforce his feelings of distrust and suspiciousness.

Figure 4.8 shows a typical *ABAB* design study conducted at the Treatment Center. The child was a ten-year-old, borderline schizophrenic youngster. He had particular difficulty in complying with staff requests to cease an activity in which he was currently engaged and to begin another task appropriately. When such requests were made for transitions from one activity to another by staff, the child would typically become disruptive and demonstrate bizarre motor and verbal behaviors. These behaviors which manifested the child's refusal to participate in a new activity were described, counted, and charted as "negative transitions." A "positive transition" was defined as a compliant response to a staff request when the child did move to a new activity without demonstrable negative behaviors and immediately participated in the second activity. Figure 4.8 shows in the ver-

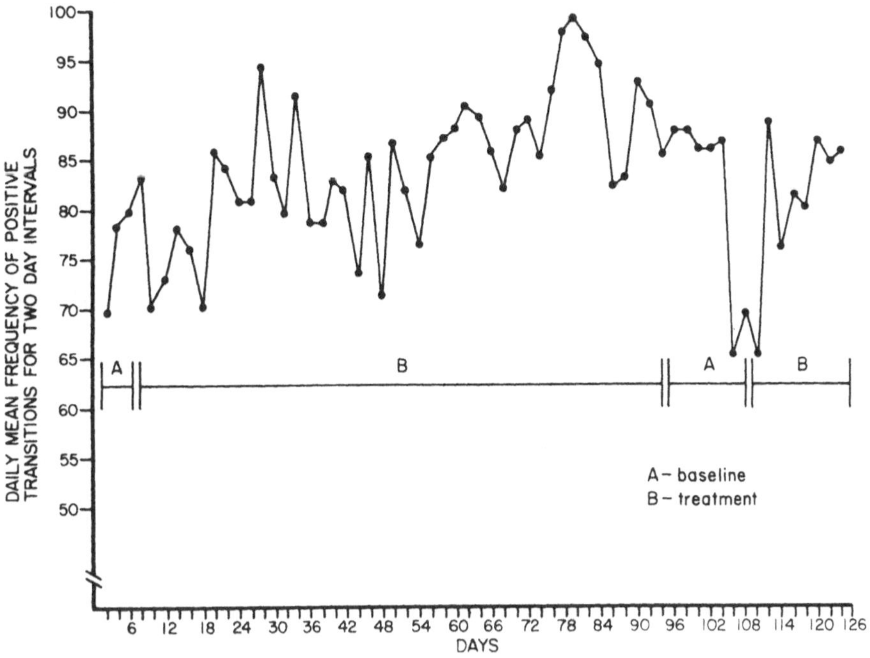

Figure 4.8. ABAB *Design: Effect of Positive Practice on Daily Mean Frequency of Positive Transitions to New Activities*

tical column the percent of all transitions occurring during each successive day when the child responded smoothly and positively. The baseline condition shows that 70% of his transitions were positive, and also illustrated that this was an unstable baseline as evidenced by some acceleration of positive transitions during the baseline period. Perhaps it would have been advisable to conduct the baseline interval longer to ascertain if the rate of positive transitions would have stabilized. However, since each child is on several programs conducted simultaneously, one often finds a general, although gradual, facilitation of desired behaviors. Furthermore, the staff are over-trained on reinforcing compliant behaviors, and although they may try to ignore compliant responses during a baseline interval, they often forget the management order and inadvertently reinforce the response. We suspect that these uncontrolled conditions were responsible for the unstable baseline.

The treatment condition conducted during the *B* phase of the study was described as "positive practice," which was defined as requiring the child to rehearse a transition until it was completed successfully. The staff would remove the child from the room and require him to reenter and rehearse the transitional period, repetitively if necessary, until the child had completed a positive transition. He was socially reinforced when the desired response finally occurred. When the child engaged in a new activity without negative behaviors, profuse positive social reinforcement followed and the new activity commenced. During the baseline condition, a count was recorded, unknown to the subject, of the frequency of positive and negative transitions. The *B* condition showed a gradual acceleration of positive transitions, even to the extent of one day in which 100% of all transitions were positive. The return-to-baseline condition showed a marked drop in the percent of positive transitions. Replication of the treatment condition in comparison to both baseline conditions demonstrated that the treatment procedure did accelerate positive transitions. Following the experimental investigation, the treatment technique of positive practice, reinforcing all positive transitions, and rehearsing negative transitions to success, was adopted as an integral part of his total program.

Figure 4.9 illustrates an *ABAB* design study used to test the effectiveness of a five-minute time-out technique for negative behaviors in a psychoneurotic, ten-year-old child. Negative behaviors were defined as the child's defiantly screaming "No," and refusing to comply with a verbal request from a staff member. Such behavior, often described as noncompliance, is characteristic of the habit patterns which initiate a child's referral for residential care. The child's noncompliance was described as "negative behavior" because he was so vehement in his screaming of "No," accompanied by an assortment of escape responses which included sitting immobile, running, swinging, and swearing. The treatment condition, *B*, was a five-minute time-out in the quiet room. In conducting the treatment program with this particular child, the staff did not verbalize what the child had been doing wrong, but simply carried or walked him to the quiet room, deposited him, and shut the door for the five-minute interval. The child had a long history of hearing adult verbal explanation associated with his negative behaviors, and we suspected that further verbal cues to label the behavior would only result in a prolonged treatment interval. The negative behavior was high and variable, and in fact 216 incidents were logged for one day during the first baseline condition. The treatment program decisively decelerated the response, as may be seen in Figure 4.9.

The return-to-baseline interval showed a slight and gradual acceleration; this baseline replication served as an example of how the treatment condition had been maintained sufficiently so that generalization effects were so strong in the training program that one could not readily demonstrate an unquestionable return-to-baseline effect. This slight acceleration in the

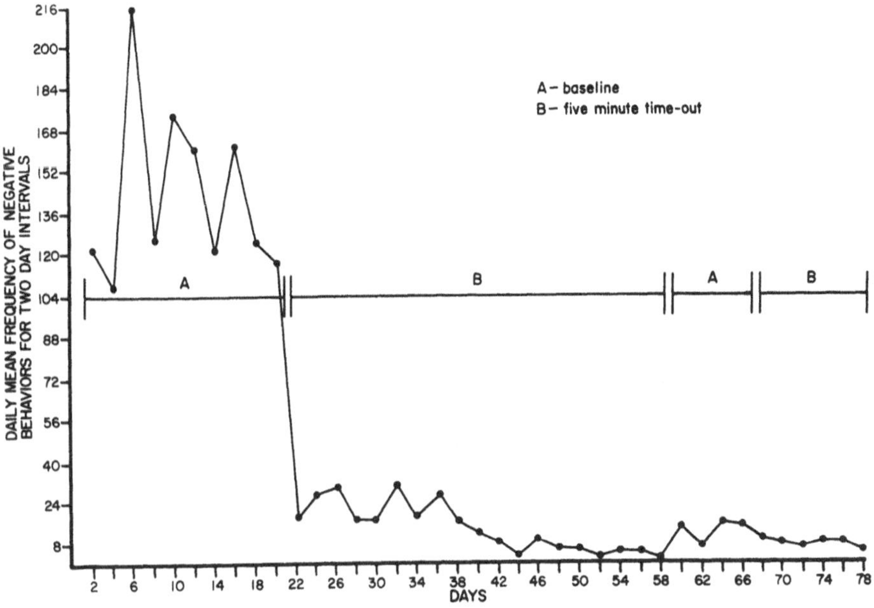

Figure 4.9. ABAB *Design: Effect of a Five-Minute Time-Out on Negative Behaviors in a C.A. 10, Neurotic Child*

baseline replication demonstrated that the negative behaviors were beginning to return, much to the dismay of the staff involved in the study. An investigator does have an obligation to the staff who are performing experimental-clinical techniques, since they are the ones who contend with the aversive behaviors under treatment. This is a serious problem in a program employing the treatment model described herein, since one has to train not only the child, but also the staff. Staff are required to tolerate many extremely undesirable behaviors with children in residential care and any reduction in those behaviors is likely to be reinforcing to staff. The return-to-treatment interval *B* in Figure 4.9 shows that the negative behaviors were again decelerating, much to the enjoyment of all the staff. The treatment conditions were maintained throughout the child's stay at the Treatment Center and eventually declined to the point where the child seldom made a visit to the quiet room.

In acquiring a baseline, we usually record the data under uncontrolled conditions. That is, the experimenter is seldom aware of what reinforcement contingencies are maintaining the behavior being monitored, much less the schedule of the reinforcers. Therefore, the dependent variable which is being tracked in the baseline interval is being monitored only one way, by its presence or absence, and not in relation to conditions suspected to be associated with its presence or absence, as are *B*, *C*, and *D* treatment conditions. An obvious fault with the baseline measure obtained under uncontrolled conditions is that during a *B* treatment condition one may inadvertently be reinstating the same reinforcement contingencies or some approximation of those conditions which were available during the baseline period, but only on a different schedule. If that occurs, one may simply be studying schedules of reinforcement and be completely unaware of it. Furthermore, one may be unable to replicate very closely the baseline conditions, since one is never aware of what the schedule of reinforcement was for the behavior. These problems exist for all designs in which baseline intervals are recorded. This discussion is not intended to degrade baseline counts, since it is the baseline interval which informs one of the gravity of the problem and promotes formulation of a treatment hypothesis. Perhaps in many instances it would be most advantageous to drop the baseline and replace it with experimental analyses of behavior to ascertain the maintaining reinforcement contingencies.

ABACD *Design*

One may find after replication of the baseline that the treatment condition had a weak or negligible effect, which may convince one to alter the design and test successive treatment conditions until a desired effect is found. In some instances, such a procedure may simply be a method of describing a program of successive treatment techniques devised to approximate the normal environment. A successive treatment design lends itself to monitoring a total residential program composed of a series of treatment techniques for each child. This design is a combination of an *ABA* design, as well as *BCD* type of design. It is a play upon words to use all the symbols of *ABC*, etc., since all that one is doing, in as controlled a manner as possible, is comparing successive treatment techniques against a replicated baseline. Quite often the design is simply a means of repairing an *ABA* study which has failed. The optimal design would conduct successive experimental studies interrupted by return-to-baseline intervals. However, if one is returning to baseline between successive treatment condition studies, one has the problem training the child to extinguish the treatment effects performed by the staff. Furthermore, the problem of order effects remains open, regardless of the care taken to establish baseline replications.

Figure 4.10 illustrates a study where one-, two-, and five-minute time-out contingencies were studied successively for their relative decelerating effects on noncompliant responses in a seven-year-old schizophrenic child.

The noncompliant responses were defined as adamant refusals to comply with verbal requests made of the child by a staff member. The child would be asked to perform a simple task, and his characteristic responses would vary from sitting, folding his arms, or walking away and simply paying no attention to the staff member's request. The frequency of the noncompliant responses is quite easy to record since a verbal response was the discriminative stimulus for the measured response; the child's response to the staff's request was simply counted on the hand tally counter as a compliant or noncompliant response. The base-line condition shows the daily fre-

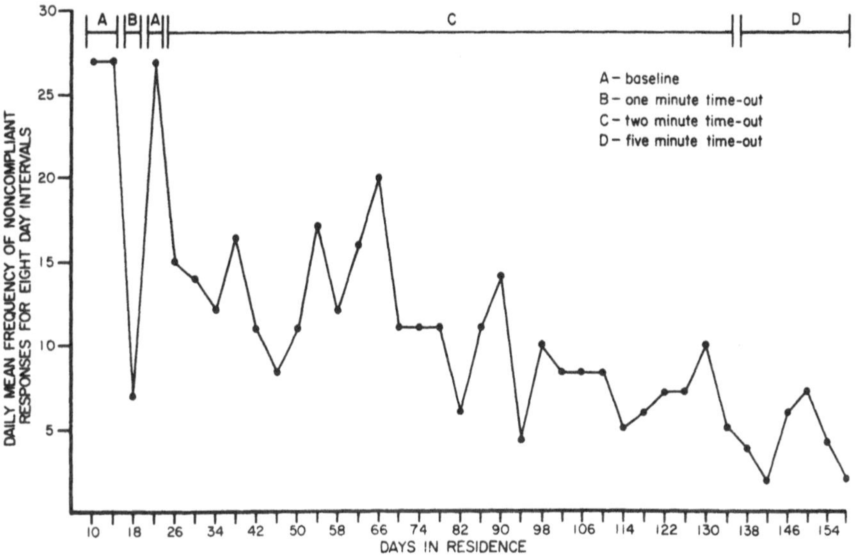

Figure 4.10. ABACD *Design: Effects of One-, Two-, and Five-Minute Time-Outs on Noncompliant Responses in a C.A. 7, Schizophrenic, Brain-Injured Child*

quency of the noncompliant responses—roughly 28 per day and relatively stable. The *B* condition of the one-minute time-out for noncompliant response effected immediate and marked deceleration of the response, and the child did return to baseline quite quickly. Previous experience did assist us in conducting the initial *ABA* phase of the study, since once the deceleration was noted, then a return-to-baseline program was initiated and expected control was demonstrable as the child quickly retrieved his old habits of noncompliance. The next treatment condition studied was a two-minute time-out, to determine if it would effect any greater diminution of the behavior than had occurred with the one-minute time-out. The initial effect was a quick deceleration, although not so great as that which was noted in the initial *B* treatment condition of the one-minute time-out procedure. The two-minute condition was maintained for a considerable interval of time, as indicated on the base of the graph. Eventually, a five-minute time-out procedure, *C*, was begun because the behavior appeared to have leveled off at a fairly stable rate of noncompliance and we wished to extinguish the behavior further. The five-minute time-out was an effective step in decelerating the response and that program was then installed as a permanent management order, for the duration of the child's residence, for his noncompliance to verbal requests.

In a clinical setting where one is faced with the economic facts of providing behavioral change, one may find it advantageous to use successive treatment programs and retain that program which is providing optimal rate change. For example, one may try treatment technique *B* for a given interval, and upon being dissatisfied with the results, switch to treatment *C*, eventually proceeding to *D* or *E*, etc., until a desirable effect is produced. This method is rather poor in design, but has value as pilot work for another subject with similar behavior as the one under treatment at the time. Thus, if one is working on a program to teach a child speech, successive methods may have to be attempted before one is found to be most effective. If staff time is available, one can firm up such a method with a design having a return-to-baseline interval separating each successive treatment condition attempted, although we caution that problems exist in such a procedure. If an investigator is able to be objective about his treatment techniques, and has pride in identifying the source of error in a given procedure, it is advisable to stop the unsuccessful program and return the child to baseline while devising a more effective program. Perhaps the most difficult part of this procedure is informing the parents that what one has been doing thus far has not been successful.

ABACA *Design: Successive Treatments Design*

A successive treatments design requires the return-to-baseline condition to be replicated successively for the comparison of two or more treatment techniques. The design not only compares one technique with the other, but also demonstrates control of the independent variables by baseline replications. As discussed in the previous simultaneous treatments design, there are problems involved in using any return-to-baseline procedure to an extreme, such as staff's becoming less capable of ignoring high-rate aggressive behaviors during baseline periods. Figure 4.11 illustrates a study in which two different treatment conditions were tested for their comparative effects on decelerating a swearing response in a ten-year-old, borderline schizophrenic child. Each column of the histograph is composed of 20 three-minute samples obtained over three days. The baseline condition shows that a 30-second time-out technique reduced the frequency of swearing by half, and the return-to-baseline condition demonstrated control effected by the time-out technique. Samples were all obtained during meal-

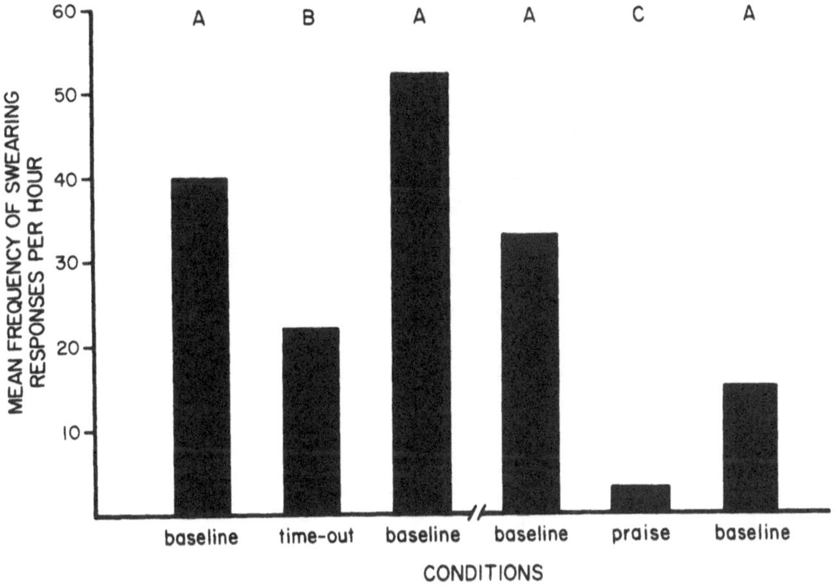

Figure 4.11. ABAACA *Design: Effects of Two Treatment Conditions on Mean Frequency of Swearing Responses*

time. During the time-out condition, the child was required to sit back in his chair away from the table and was unable to participate in the table conversation or to continue eating with the rest of the group for the duration of the time-out. The *C* treatment condition of the *ACA* procedure was conducted several weeks after the previous *ABA* program. The *C* condition consisted of staff's using a small pocket timer which was set for increasing time intervals of not swearing. For example, following a one-minute interval during which the subject had not sworn, and the timer bell had rung, the child was then reinforced with social praise for that interval of time of no swearing. This was a self-control shaping technique, used to train the subject to use verbal expressions other than swearing. Perhaps some investigators would make the misinterpretation of calling the treatment methodology as reinforcing "no" behavior, which is a rather naïve statement considering that instead of swearing, the child was being reinforced for using another kind of verbal response. The data show that the praise condition for the alternative verbal response was more effective in decelerating the behavior than the initial time-out condition. The child's return-to-baseline data show that the return was not so spectacular as the one that occurred following the time-out condition, which may suggest that generalization effects were better for the praise condition. A program using praise for increasing intervals of time of not swearing was then initiated with the subject in his total program.

The successive treatments design lends itself to short experimental studies testing differential treatment programs to determine which ones are most effective for the desired response change. The treatment intervals in an *ABA*, *ACA* type of design should not be of long duration because of the dangers previously mentioned on successive replications of a baseline.

B
|
A—C—B or C or D Design: Simultaneous Treatment Design[1,2]
|
D

The purpose of the study was to test the efficacy of a same-subject design applicable to a residential behavior modification program employing cottage staff as behavior therapists. The *ABAB* same-subject design was often inadequate for assessing treatment programs, for the following reasons:

1) It was often difficult to establish a stable behavioral baseline. This problem was typically a function of the procedure by which staff counted the incidence of the behavior to establish a baseline. To illustrate, Figure 4.12 shows the baseline of verbal responses described as "bizarre speech" charted for daily occurrence for a seven-year-old schizophrenic child. The graph demonstrated a treatment effect, although a program had not been instituted. Investigation revealed that when the subject spoke bizarrely, staff would leave him to notate the tally and content of his speech. Staff

1. The authors wish to thank the following staff members, whose encouragement and participation made this research possible: Edward Orman, M.D., Violette Solem, R.N., Richard Ostwald, R.N., Jo Ann Christianson, R.N., Mabel Stamn, R.N., Thomas Hiebel, and James Roth.

2. Reprinted with permission from *Behaviour Research and Therapy*, 1967, 5, 237–243. A same-subject design for simultaneous comparison of three reinforcement contingencies, by Robert M. Browning. Copyright 1968 by Pergamon Press, Ltd.

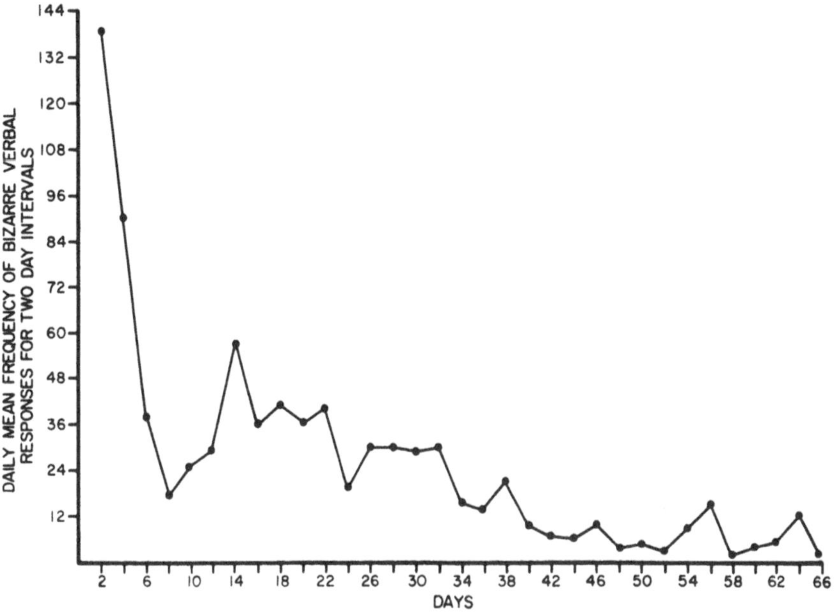

Figure 4.12. Example of Unstable Behavioral Baseline of Bizarre Speech in a Schizophrenic Child

were thereby inadvertently extinguishing his bizarre speech by ignoring it, which in turn negated continued use of the *ABAB* design because of the failure to establish a stable baseline (Sidman, 1960).

2) A second disadvantage with the *ABAB* design occurred during the return-to-baseline *A* period. It was frequently observed that a treatment procedure *B* would effect a desired behavior change, but this effect would be irreversible during the return-to-baseline period. The *ABAB* design restricts one to concluding from such data that the treatment condition was either ineffective or confounded with other conditions (Sidman, 1960). Confounding has been the rule rather than the exception in such instances. To illustrate, Figure 4.13 shows the last 42 days of a 122-day treatment period and 20 days of the return-to-baseline interval. The treatment condition was designed to reinforce audible speech in a mute child by making all staff attention and requests contingent upon audible speech. The initial baseline was stable; the child never replied audibly when spoken to, he merely followed instructions and communicated his needs through sign language. The child's mutism declined progressively and continued to do so following cessation of the study. It would have been erroneous to inter-

pret the data as indicating an ineffective treatment condition. It was learned that the treatment condition had been confounded by the child's being reinforced for audible speech during the return-to-baseline period by peers, siblings, teachers, and parents. Perhaps the irreversible treatment effect could have been avoided if the treatment condition had not been maintained for such a long time period. It has been observed that the *ABAB* design is most suitable for testing treatment conditions which have an immediate but short-term effect.

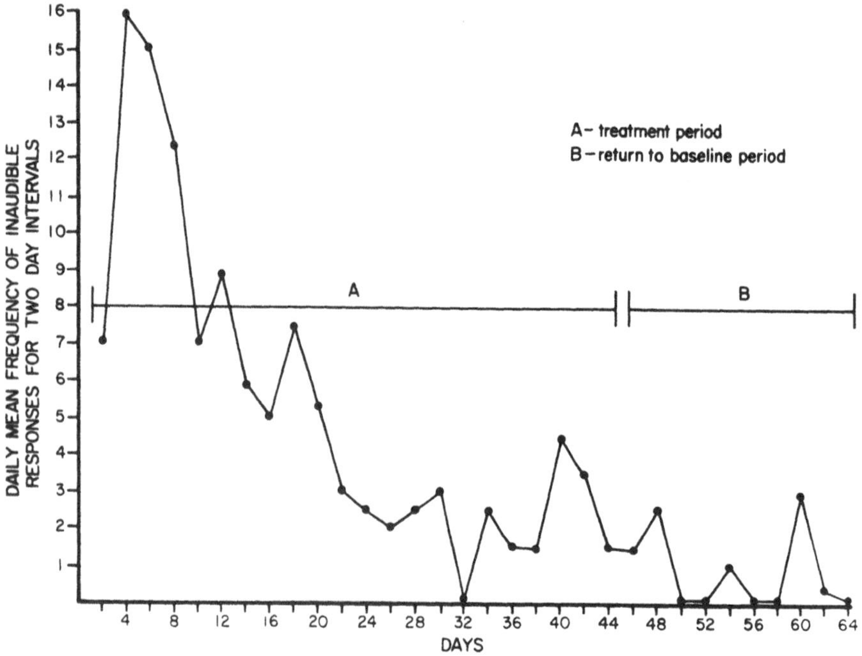

Figure 4.13. Example of Failure to Return to Behavioral Baseline Following Treatment of Mutism

3) Another problem arose when we tried to replicate conditions of the original baseline during the return-to-baseline period. In studying the effectiveness of social reinforcers employed by staff who were with the child on a daily basis, we found it difficult to replicate staff's baseline conditions of dispensing various reinforcers to him. If staff obtained his behavioral baseline in an uncontrolled method by counting his behavior and responding to him however they pleased, they would have had considerable difficulty recalling the social reinforcers used, much less their schedules. If one

had all staff respond to the child's abnormal behavior in a consistent manner and were fortunate enough to produce a stable baseline, staff were often reluctant to reinstate the baseline conditions following a successful treatment program. For example, if treatment *B* successfully extinguished the child's assaultive behavior (which was aversive to staff), staff were unlikely to be enthusiastic about reinstating it. Thus, the *ABAB* design requires not only that the child receive an extinction period, but also that staff be extinguished in employing the treatment condition whose effects may have been quite reinforcing for them. Presumably this problem could be circumvented by having the child in different cottages during the *A* and *B* periods, although this would generate other problems in the total treatment program.

4) Economy was another requirement the *ABAB* design often failed to meet. For example, it was frequently necessary to determine which of several reinforcement programs would be most effective in controlling a particular behavior. To test each condition successively by an *ABAB* design would require considerable time, and even then treatment sequence effects would remain an uncontrolled variable.

The design described here avoids some of these characteristic difficulties of the *ABAB* design. The design is symbolized below:

$$\begin{array}{rcl} & B & \\ & | & \\ A - & C & - B \text{ or } C \text{ or } D \\ & | & \\ & D & \end{array}$$

Symbol *A* represents a behavioral baseline, preferably obtained under uncontrolled conditions as previously described. *B, C,* and *D* in the vertical arrangement represent three treatment conditions, which in this study were three social reinforcement contingencies for one behavior. The three conditions were administered simultaneously and successively by three groups in counterbalanced order.

Thus, three reinforcement contingencies were available to the subject at all times and, in the course of three equal time intervals (e.g., three weeks), from all persons or groups. The final period, symbolized as *B,* or *C,* or *D,* indicates that the treatment condition effecting the most desired behavior change was programmed for continued use with the child. The following is an example of a same-subject study using the design.

METHOD

Subject. The child was a nine years and eleven months old male admitted for residential treatment with the diagnosis of psychoneurotic reaction, anxiety reaction. He was under no medication during the course of the study. One of his dominant abnormal behaviors was "grandiose bragging." Grandiose bragging was defined as the subject's relating an expansive and untrue tale, most often in reference to himself. His bragging was so blatant that there was little difficulty with inter-staff agreement. Nine days after his admission, his grandoise bragging was placed on an uncontrolled behavior charting program for four successive weeks. Staff would count and chart the daily occurrence of his bragging during those hours he spent with cottage staff. The charting program was devised so that staff periodically cross-checked each other for inter-observer agreement.

Three social reinforcement contingencies were observed to be administered on variable schedules by staff and peers during the baseline interval. Occasionally the subject received interest and attention for his bragging, sometimes he was verbally admonished for such blatant lies, and infrequently he was totally ignored. It appeared warranted to test for the differential effectiveness of these three hypothesized reinforcement contingencies in extinguishing his grandiose bragging. The three reinforcement conditions will be symbolized hereafter as: $B =$ positive interest and praise (e.g., "That's interesting, tell me some more."); $C =$ verbal admonishment (e.g., "That doesn't make sense, you're lying."); $D =$ purposely ignoring his bragging.

The experimental design described above was designed to identify the differential effectiveness of the three reinforcement contingencies. The final phase of the study enacted a 100 percent schedule of the reinforcement condition which effected the greatest diminution of the subject's bragging.

Procedure. After staff had obtained the four-week baseline, they were requested to obtain an additional week's baseline under a controlled condition. The controlled baseline was to ignore the child's bragging but to chart its frequency. The controlled baseline period was not a formal period of the design; it was of experimental interest as an illustration of how the method of observation may alter a baseline.

During weeks six, seven, and eight the three reinforcement conditions were conducted simultaneously and successively by three groups of two staff each. The order in which staff groups administered the reinforcers for each successive week was counterbalanced for sequential order of treatment conditions in accordance with the requirements for a 3×3 Latin square design. Group 1 administered the B condition in week one, C in week two, and D in week three. The order of treatments by weeks for group 2 was C, D, B; the order for group 3 was D, B, C. Each staff was requested to count each bragging incident directed to him by the child and to time the duration of the incident with a stopwatch. It was decided to time the bragging incidents since it was suspected that treatment effects would be reflected in diminished duration of the response before frequency declined.

In review, the child had three reinforcement contingencies available for his bragging. It was hypothesized that his bragging was an instrumental response for attention and that he would seek out and brag to the most reinforcing staff and shift to different staff on successive weeks as they switched to the subject's preferred reinforcement contingency.

RESULTS

Figure 4.14 illustrates the mean frequency per week of the child's bragging throughout the study and for each of the three reinforcement contingencies during weeks six, seven, and eight. It was apparent that the controlled baseline period (week five) produced a decrement in the child's bragging, showing the necessity of obtaining a baseline under conditions which do not prevent stable rates. Table 4.1 presents both mean frequency and duration of bragging for each week of the experimental period. Benjamin's (1965) Latin square for using the subject as his own control was performed

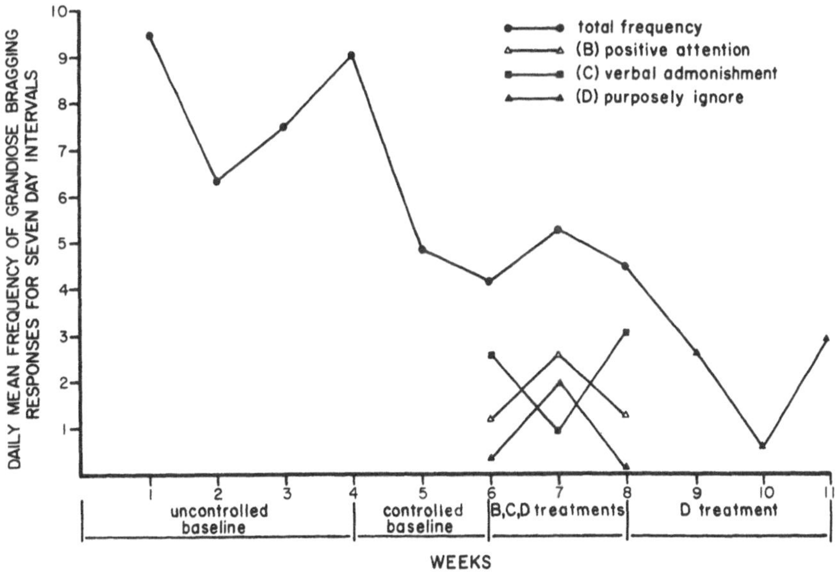

Figure 4.14. Total Mean Frequency of Grandiose Bragging Responses Throughout Study and for Each Reinforcement Contingency during Experimental Period

Table 4.1. Mean Frequency (F) and Time in Sec of Grandiose Bragging for Each Reinforcement Contingency for Each Week of Experimental Period

	Weeks of Experimental Period							
	Week 1		*Week 2*		*Week 3*		*All Weeks Combined*	
Reinforcement Contingeny	$\overline{M}$(F)	$\overline{M}$(sec)	$\overline{M}$(F)	$\overline{M}$(sec)	$\overline{M}$(F)	$\overline{M}$(sec)	$\overline{M}$(F)	$\overline{M}$(sec)
B Positive Attention	1.14	57.57	2.57	330.00	1.29	160.71	16.7	181.43
C Verbal Admonishment	2.57	295.71	0.86	42.29	3.00	372.86	2.19	239.29
D Purposely Ignore	0.29	17.14	1.86	99.29	0.14	8.57	0.76	41.65
B, C, & D Combined	4.14	366.43	5.29	478.57	4.43	542.14	4.62	462.38

to test for differential effectiveness of the three reinforcement contingencies on both frequency and duration in seconds of bragging. There were no differences among treatment conditions when the data were analyzed by the number of times the child bragged under each condition ($df = 2$ and 6, $P < 0.05$). Table 4.2 shows that a significant treatment effect was found when data were compared on time in seconds spent in bragging by the subject ($df = 2$ and 6, $P < 0.05$). Duncan's new multiple-range test (Edwards, 1960) was used to test for mean differences of time spent on bragging under the three reinforcement contingencies. The child responded significantly less under the *D* condition of staff's purposely ignoring his behavior than under either the *B* ($P < 0.01$) or the *C* treatment ($P < 0.01$). Verbal interest and praise (*B*) effected significantly fewer responses than the condition of verbal admonishment ($P < 0.05$). Since ignoring the child's bragging was the most effective procedure for extinguishing the response, staff were requested to continue with that treatment.

The significant square uniqueness term of the Latin square reflects, in part, the differential effectiveness of the cottage staff's employing the social reinforcers. Although it was not an objective of this study, the design and statistical analysis would enable an investigator to identify which staff would serve as the most effective behavior therapists to administer the selected treatment technique with the patient.

DISCUSSION

The design presented herein appears to have applicability to a residential setting where cottage staff serve as behavior therapists. The design does

Table 4.2. Latin Square Analysis for Differential Time on Bragging in Seconds among Three Reinforcement Contingencies

Source	df	*MS*	*F*
Group	2	809505.56	1.34
Error	3	604666.56	—
Weeks	2	64851.39	—
Treatments	2	758693.06	5.19*
Square Uniqueness	2	1995847.23	7.67*
Error Residual	6	146152.77	—

* $P < 0.05$

have value in the clinical research setting where one requires a short-term, ideographic study to test which of several reinforcement conditions will produce the desired behavioral change. One cannot always predict by clinical judgment the effects of a particular reinforcer for a child; in the case just described, an ostensibly negative social reinforcer (verbal admonishment) significantly increased the frequency of the subject's grandiose bragging. The advantages of the design are (1) staff are not required to replicate a baseline period as demanded in the *ABAB* design; (2) several reinforcement contingencies may be compared simultaneously by counterbalancing for sequence effects; (3) an appropriate statistical test is available for such a same-subject design (Benjamin, 1965); (4) the design satisfies the basic requirement of a same-subject study of demonstrating that the behavior varies in relation to treatment conditions.

Summary and Conclusions

We have reviewed a number of experimental-clinical designs for idiographic studies. These range from the simple *B* design through replicated designs such as the *ABAB* to one example of a simultaneous comparison design. Although some designs obviously provide more convincing data than others, no single type of design is suitable for every idiographic study. Further, no design would seem capable of providing a "perfect" study that demonstrates experimental control beyond all doubt. However, it is equally clear that some form of design and measurement is preferable to total reliance on subjective judgment in evaluating treatment results.

Successive treatment designs have a particular drawback in that their conduct requires a considerable period of time. A one-week interval for anything other than the initial baseline is generally far too short to permit us reliably to assess treatment effects. Ideally, since stable baselines are virtually impossible to obtain, the *A* phase of the study would be two or three weeks long. Unfortunately, it is seldom clinically or ethically feasible to delay this long in beginning treatment. In a similar manner, successive treatment conditions use up valuable time. One cannot fairly assume that other things are not happening to or changing for the child while successive treatments are being tried.

For these reasons, designs which utilize simultaneous comparisons of several hypothesized treatment techniques are clearly preferred to designs using successive treatment conditions. The simultaneous design clearly requires greater skill on the part of the investigator and considerably more planning and organization for the child-care staff. To date we have only rarely employed simultaneous comparison designs. However, an area of experimental-clinical practice which needs development is the improvement of techniques for conducting simultaneous comparison studies. One possible method, not discussed above, would be to obtain measures on three or four behaviors while applying treatment to only one of these. Thus the other behaviors might serve as the control condition for the treated behavior. Variations of this type of design would include making predictions about the generalization of the treatment effect among a series of behaviors which were not directly treated. We hope that other investigators will pursue the creative development of such new techniques.

CHAPTER FIVE

Treatment Techniques

Reinforcement Contingencies

Reinforcement is a dominant procedural term referred to in the treatment methods described in this text. The reason for applying certain components of learning theory, such as reinforcement, and particularly for adapting the model of logical positivism as exemplified by Skinner (1938, 1953), is that they are so adaptable to the experimental-clinical approach. The experimental-clinical treatment model parallels Skinner's experimental approach in which theory is de-emphasized and experimental method determines what facts of behavior are accepted as predictable. The experimental-clinical model promotes an empirical approach to the patient, with an underlying presumption that whatever behavioral facts are learned today may be elaborated upon in the future. Such an approach seems logical at the current stage of psychological research, since it restricts one from adopting a rigid theoretical position by promoting a constantly changing and searching approach to treatment problems. The experimental-clinical method is not limited to learning theory; it is suitable for testing the efficacy of other theories used to establish treatment techniques. It is recognized that other theories and treatment approaches, particularly psychoanalysis, will have difficulty in allowing the imposition of observable dependent variables and precise application of specific treatment techniques.

To reiterate, only a few simplified learning terms were used in designing the treatment techniques used in the research described in this text. Disagreement persists in the literature on the definitions of the learning terms which were employed. The following definitions are provided for the most prevalent learning procedures used. These procedural terms will be defined as operationally as possible.

Positive reinforcement is a procedure in which the presentation of a stimulus condition is contingent upon the sequential occurrence of a stimulus and a response and increases the frequency of that stimulus' evoking the response. A primary positive reinforcement contingency is one which has an accelerating rate change effect on the behavior without prior training. A secondary positive reinforcer is a procedure in which the positive reinforcement contingency acquires its accelerating behavioral rate change effect by previously being paired with a primary reinforcement contingency and thereby acquires a discriminative stimulus value for that primary reinforcement and a semblance of its reinforcing effect.

The actual procedure by which secondary reinforcements are acquired is largely presumed in this text. Perhaps the numerous social reinforcers, defined in this text as secondary reinforcers, are acquired by being paired with numerous and previously acquired secondary reinforcers and not primary reinforcers. It is our hypothesis that many social reinforcers exist independently of primary reinforcers and do not require retraining with primary reinforcers to maintain their effectiveness. We suspect that the primary reinforcers have more universal effects at young ages, i.e., at less than two years of age, and that the social reinforcers are more idiosyncratic in their effect because their acquisition was a function of each person's own unique learning history. The hypothesis that social reinforcers are unique to each person's learning history means that one cannot presume commonality of social reinforcers in the clinical setting, and this is more the case with an emotionally disturbed than with a normal child. This hypothesis provides additional support for the idiographic studies promoted by the experimental-clinical method.

This definition of positive reinforcement requires the measurement of a change in the rate of a behavior. The procedure, as well as the measurement, are both considered necessary for the identification of a positive reinforcement stimulus. This, of course, means that positive reinforcement, as well as the other reinforcement and punishment terms defined below, are established a posteriori. Such a procedural definition is compatible with the experimental-clinical model in which the evidence of a term remains empirical, i.e., one decides whether a stimulus presented to a child was indeed a reinforcement by a change in the frequency of the child's response rate. The preferred operational definition of reinforcement as stated above would require that the response rate be monitored not only by the frequency of the response but also by its relation to a particular stimulus or stimuli. Most of the data contained in the studies herein monitor only the response rate and do not relate this to a concurrent count of the stimuli eliciting the response.

Negative reinforcement is a procedure in which the absence or termination of a stimulus, contingent upon the sequential occurrence of an eliciting stimulus and its response, increases the frequency of that stimulus to evoke the response. A primary negative reinforcement is one which effects a response acceleration without prior training. Secondary negative reinforcements, such as a negative social reinforcer, are those that are acquired by being associated with primary negative reinforcers and serve as discriminative stimuli for those primary reinforcers. A negative reinforcer is defined in part by an accelerating behavioral rate change. It has been our experience that a negative reinforcement contingency is really defined by what behavior the observer wishes to count. This may be misleading, as the following example illustrates. Presume that faradic stimulation derived from a grid on the floor is used with an autistic child to condition the child's approach responses to an adult. The shock is turned on, and if the child approaches the adult, the shock is terminated. Termination of the shock is an avoidance paradigm, since the child can prevent the occurrence of the shock or terminate it by the approach response to the adult. One would probably define the faradic stimulation as a negative reinforcement procedure, since the approach rate to the adult is accelerated. However, if the dependent variable were to count autistic mannerisms, or perhaps rate of avoiding the adult, while the child was walking about on the electric grid, it would be observed that these mannerisms and avoidance responses would decelerate. With these latter dependent variables, the shock would be defined as a punishment contingency, since its presence effected a deceleration of the autistic mannerisms or avoidance responses of the child. This example illustrates how the definition of these terms are a function of both the procedure and the dependent variable. The relationship between procedure and measurement in defining reinforcement as a treatment condition is crucial to designing treatment programs. Our having measured the wrong behavior probably accounts for many of our ineffectual studies. To illustrate, during the first year of the research program for psychotic children, 26 studies were conducted, three of which resulted in significant data and one in suggestive data, and the remaining studies were total failures. Measurement of the wrong behavior was responsible for most of the failures.

Punishment is defined as a procedure in which the presentation of a stimulus following the sequential occurrence of stimulus and a response decreases the frequency of that stimulus to evoke the response. A primary punishment condition would be a stimulus which would decelerate behavior without prior training. A secondary punishment contingency would be a stimulus which would acquire a decelerating effect by previously being paired with a primary punishment condition and thereby acquiring discriminitive value for the primary punishment stimulus. We are defining punishment by a procedure as well as by a measure of decelerating behavioral rate change. It is required that a stimulus decelerate behavior to be identified as a punishment; if it failed to do so, it would not be defined as a punishment stimulus. Of course, the question always remains, "How much of a deceleration is necessary for the contingency to be acceptable for the definition of a punishment stimulus?" One may wish to delegate that decision to statistical probability, for other investigators' replicated rate changes may be sufficient evidence.

When reinforcers, particularly social reinforcers as defined above, are used, there are a few procedures which assist in their effectiveness. The procedures which will be discussed represent only a few of the variables which affect the rate of response acquisition and are only a few of the variables identified in the experimental literature. For example, we try to present a reinforcement contingency as quickly after the response occurs as the staff can. The emphasis on decreasing the latency between response and reinforcement has been followed in the use of food for reinforcing speech, attention, etc., with psychotic children as well as with the use of social reinforcement with adolescent and neurotic youngsters. The rationale for reinforcing as quickly as possible is to avoid inadvertently reinforcing the wrong response by delay of the reinforcement. Close observations of children show that there is usually a very rapid sequence of behaviors occurring much of the time, and a delay of even a few seconds is sufficient for one or more responses to follow the one which the investigator wished to reinforce. The unfortunate result is that the investigator accidentally trains the wrong response. It is usually our management order not to attempt to reinforce a response if the staff member is unable to reinforce that response as quickly and as optimally as possible, particularly if the child is nonverbal. When verbal children are involved, the reinforcement contingency may be explained and identified, although it is hypothesized that even this delay is not ideal.

The staff members are urged to make their social reinforcements loud and clear. One reason for this request is to assure that the child does respond attentively to the reinforcement contingency. A second hypothesized reason, which is an interpretation of contiguity learning theory, is to assume that the reinforcement contingency "separates out" the response to be rewarded from those associated responses which are not to be accelerated. Such a hypothesized effect of "separating out" a response may sound quite speculative, but when one is working with a child emitting a high rate of numerous kinds of behaviors, many of which are chained so that there is a progression from appropriate to inappropriate responses, the clinician is interested in separating the earlier preferred responses from the later emerging incorrect ones. Actually the staff are requested, although they seem to do so naturally, progressively to fade the intensity of their social reinforcement as the child's behavior approximates that which is acceptable for discharge. This order is designed to insure that their social praise is more compatible with what would be available to the child in the normal environment. With the young psychotic children, particularly during the early months of training, it is necessary literally to shout one's positive evaluative statements at the child in order to elicit an attentive response. The necessity of intensifying the reinforcer testifies to the weakness of the emotionally disturbed child's social reinforcers and in fact may be indicative of the necessity of strengthening those reinforcers by pairing with primary reinforcers.

The staff are alerted to the gradual acquisition of behavioral chains which may be established without their awareness. For example, one autistic child was observed repeatedly on video tapes so that we could ascertain what conditions were responsible for her progressive acquisition of mild provocative responses toward one of the other children. It was observed that the staff members would mildly reprimand the child for these low-level aggressive responses, but their social punishment was not sufficiently strong to decelerate the behavior. It was noted that every seventh to tenth provocative response the staff member would strongly reprimand the child and then direct her into a more productive activity away from the other child and immediately strongly and profusely positively reinforce the child's initial compliant behavior. These replicated observations corroborated that the child was demonstrating mildly provocative behaviors to elicit staff's eventual positive reinforcement; the staff's mild reprimands were only discriminative stimuli heralding an impending positive social interaction which was predictable every seven or tenth provocation. The staff had inadvertently established a behavioral chain in which the child would command staff's attention by mildly provoking other youngsters so that eventually she would attain a 1:1 positively reinforcing relationship with the staff for a short interval of time while they redirected her into a more constructive activity. Frankly, it is almost impossible to observe the acquisition of these behavioral chains by oneself; it requires the replicated observation of another staff after the response chain has become predictable. We have found video tapes to be helpful in conducting such behavioral analyses.

Treatment programs using both primary and secondary reinforcement contingencies are begun on a 100% schedule, i.e., every response occurrence is reinforced, to promote a quick and high rate of response acquisition. As the desired behavior becomes available to the child and predictable on the 100% schedule, then the schedule is gradually faded. It has been our hypothesis that the staff naturally fade their schedule as the child's behavior becomes more predictable. At times the staff may decrease their reinforcement ratio too rapidly and the response deteriorates. When such extinction effects are caused by thinning a schedule too soon, the staff "back-up" to a high ratio of reinforcement once again to re-establish the behavior at the preferred high rate.

All staff members are informed of the requirement of approximating the normal environmental reinforcement schedule with each child. In theory, this sounds reasonable; in practice, it is currently impossible to achieve. The reason for this is that we are never really sure of what reinforcement schedule will be available for certain behaviors for the child in the normal environment to which he will be returned, much less the nature of those reinforcers. One way to circumvent this problem is to train the parents so that they are at least predictably capable of reinforcing the child's behaviors on some schedule. It has been our experience that the emotionally disturbed child requires more social reinforcement than is usually available in the normal environment to which he is discharged. This means that the child's behaviors maintained by the inpatient reinforcement schedules, may be placed on extinction when he is discharged. We suspect that such drastic alterations in reinforcement schedules account for much of the recidivism seen in children after residential care. It is also our recommendation to avoid treatment programs which rely predominantly on primary reinforcement and/or token reward systems, since these are so unlike the reinforcement contingencies which will be available to the subject upon his return to the normal environment. Although primary and token reinforcement techniques may be effective in quickly making behaviors available to a child, they should be faded quite early in a program. With older youngsters, it may be preferable to avoid a token economy and rely on weaker social rewards, particularly as the discharge date approaches.

Drive is defined in our treatment programs as a procedure involving a deprivation schedule of some reinforcement contingency. Hunger drive, which may be defined as time without food, is a procedure which is likely to enhance the effectiveness of food for reinforcing given behaviors. It is our recommendation that programs involving alterations in a child's hunger drive be conducted under close supervision. A management order for increasing drive, such as a delayed mealtime to increase hunger, should be coordinated with the response increments which are to be reinforced in the shaping session by using food as a reinforcer. The success of a treatment program is determined by the extent to which one is successfully able to reinforce the preferred behaviors. If the response increments are too difficult for the child to acquire, or if other prerequisite behaviors are not already available to render the child amenable to learning the response increments, a drive state will be of absolutely no value and there will be no training effects. In fact, if one is unsuccessful in training the child when drive has been increased, one is only constructing a very pervasive punishment program which may be expected to generalize to much of the child's behavior. It is a real concern that some investigators, under the guise of varying a child's drive state to enhance his learning, may be inadvertently punishing the child by failing to coordinate the drive condition with response approximations which the child is capable of attaining.

With many psychotic children, there are at first few social responses occurring during the day that are appropriate and would predictably elicit social reinforcement from their normal environment. The residential treatment program is an artificial environment, but one from which one hopes the normal environment may be approximated. The early stages of a child's program should have heavy reinforcement, so as to accelerate a variety of pro-social behaviors and to diminish the possibility of establishing a paradigm for depression, as defined by the absence of reinforcement for the child. Many of the social behaviors initially reinforced may appear insignificant, but they may be essential as prerequisite responses for acquisition of more complex social behaviors. In the absence of this profuse social reinforcement, not only are behaviors being extinguished, but the reinforcers themselves may be extinguished as effective. This profuse reinforcement is important particularly with psychotic children for whom these reinforcers may already be very weak in their effect and may become progressively ineffectual as reinforcers by thinning of the schedule. The staff are informed that, if they are having difficulty in reinforcing the child, they should "back-up" to simpler response levels for which they can reinforce successfully. If one has been reinforcing a child for cooperative play and it is observed on a particular day that these responses are not being elicited, rather than leaving the child on an extinction program, one should "back-up" and reinforce the child for parallel play. In such a case, if the child had not been reinforced for an approximation of cooperative play, one could expect an acceleration of random behavior to occur in the child's attempts to elicit some reinforcement from the staff member. The staff member should prevent this behavior decay by making the social reinforcement contingent upon very specific and currently available responses of the child that have been highly reinforced in the past and then to progress to more complex levels of behavior. If the staff member simply ceased reinforcing because the child was unable to demonstrate the preferred behavior, one could expect the emotionally disturbed child to demonstrate what we would describe as a frantic operation for the available reinforcers, most likely using some abnormal behaviors which are still dominant in his response repertoire.

Specific Applications of Reinforcers

There are currently no rules for determining when primary or secondary reinforcers should be applied in the treatment program of a child. Clinical judgment decides when a child's reinforcement program should be composed of primary as contrasted to secondary reinforcers. One source of information that may assist staff in deciding whether the program should be dominated by either primary or secondary reinforcers is simply to find which contingencies are effective for the child. With many preverbal psychotic youngsters, the secondary or social reinforcers are often ineffectual, perhaps even of questionable polarity, and would not be of value at the beginning of a child's program. For such youngsters, the primary reinforcement contingencies may be necessary to counter-condition the social reinforcers, or perhaps to increase their effectiveness, or to teach the prerequisite behavior of speech that is so necessary to enhance the social reinforcers. Secondary reinforcement programs should also be analyzed in terms of what particular reinforcers will be effective. To illustrate, we had conducted a speech program for a schizophrenic child that unfortunately did not accelerate speech, but in which tokens (marbles) could be exchanged for preferred foods. The program was a failure simply because the child was unable to discriminate which reward should be eaten, i.e., the reinforcement contingency was too complex for the child. Another program with the same child involved dispensing tokens contingent upon imitative speech responses. The error was that the child was unable to count conceptually, so he was totally unaware why one token could not be redeemed for the same items as five tokens.

One problem we have encountered with the use of tokens with psychotic children is that the delay of reward is too long. Even with the older neurotic children of average and above intelligence, the token systems were only used sporatically to engender certain preferred responses. The token systems would then be discontinued and the behavior maintained on social reward contingencies, which are more compatible with the reinforcers available in the normal environment. We feel it would be a disservice to a child to discharge him with behaviors maintained by a token economy. The child would be returning to nothing more than a complete extinction schedule where it would be predictable that the original referral behaviors would be very likely to emerge in the child's attempts to elicit some reinforcement from his environment.

A major part of establishing a reinforcement program is teaching the staff how to employ the reinforcers. This requires monitoring the staff and providing them the feedback when they reinforce either correctly or incorrectly in their use of social praise as well as during mealtimes when primary reinforcement programs may be used with the psychotic children. This kind of feedback may be derived from on-the-ward participation with the staff or through video recordings. It has been our experience that staff usually complain that it feels unnatural to socially reinforce behavior on a 100% schedule. For the beginning staff, a 100% schedule usually does consist almost exclusively of saying "good boy." However, when there is sufficient staff interchange that different staff are working together through shifts, they acquire each other's reinforcement patterns and social reinforcement variability may be facilitated among the staff members. If the staff member is becoming stereotyped in his method of reinforcement, this should be corrected. It may be erroneous to presume that a staff member will necessarily use those social reinforcement contingencies which are most effective for him. We suspect that some staff members are able to identify those kinds of social reinforcers with which they are most successful with certain children, whereas other staff members may be using quite dissimilar reinforcers with the same child. We have not investigated this area, but it is one crucial to the future development of treatment techniques using social reinforcers.

Type of Reinforcers

A. SPECIFIC VERBAL STATEMENTS

We have classed the social reinforcing statements used by staff in two categories, specific and general verbal statements. The definition of these techniques is rather self-explanatory. A specific verbal social reinforcement would be certain statements which would be used by all staff at all times for a particular child. These statements may be delimited to something like "good," or "I like the way you did that," or some other such statement. Use of these circumscribed statements provides more control as defined by being able to identify exactly what social reinforcement contingencies were available from the staff. Although more control may be gained by the specific verbal reinforcement statements, such a procedure is less comparable to the normal environment. In the normal environment, one may expect a variety of social reinforcers to be elicited by the child on various schedules. Since it is the normal environment to which one is attempting to return the child, it seems that it would be unrealistic to use specific statements throughout the program.

B. GENERAL VERBAL STATEMENTS

We suspect it is preferable for staff to use general verbal statements. Thus the staff member uses that social reinforcement contingency of his choice, and this choice may constantly fluctuate and change. The presumption, of course, is that the staff member is able to discriminate which reinforcements are most effective for certain responses in a youngster. This presumption is fallacious and presumes a degree of clinical judgement which we are unlikely to be able to attain. However, general verbal reinforcement statements are more compatible with the premise that one cannot assume commonality of social reinforcers across subjects as well as across clinicians. For example, one staff member may be able to reinforce a child with a smile and pat on the shoulder, whereas if another staff member used the same social reinforcement contingency the child would aggress.

Typically, general verbal reinforcement statements are less controlled than specific ones because the staff are allowed to use those statements which they use most habitually. It is erroneously assumed that the staff are capable of discriminating their own optimal reinforcers. Perhaps one procedure to make them so would be to employ experimental designs to identify which reinforcers each staff member uses most effectively with a child (Browning, 1967). This could be done by the staff member's working with a youngster in a controlled setting on a specific task which would assure a high response rate. The staff member would then test differential effects of several reinforcers to ascertain which would vary the response rate in the most preferred and predictable manner. If all staff members use different reinforcers at different rates, even if it is established that the staff are using those with which they are most effective, there is still less control over the behavior. That is, with such variance among available reinforcers, one would be unable to identify what were the necessary and sufficient reinforcement conditions that varied the response rate for the child. It appears that identification of optimal reinforcers is completely open to research.

Especially with our older group of youngsters, who are psychologically much more nearly intact and who usually have complete verbal repertoires, we have found several problems in the use of general reinforcing statements. In addition to the confused nature of social reinforcers, as noted in the studies of Chapter 6, we have often observed that a youngster may at one time be pleased and proud to receive a reinforcing statement from the staff, whereas at another time he will totally reject the reward. We have often observed children in the early stages of treatment being stimulated by social reinforcers to engage in negative behavior. Haim Ginott (1969) proposes one very plausible rationale for this effect. In his parents' manual, he comments that a praise statement which is too general, such as, "You are such a good boy," may be rejected because the child recognizes it as fallacious. Ginott's recommendation is that praise statements should be worded in such a way that the youngster knows that he is being praised for a specific act that has pleased the adult, not for his entire being which he may or may not feel is praiseworthy. If this point is as important as Ginott stresses with the normal youngster, it certainly is far more important with severely disturbed youngsters. Their histories have included many experiences in which they and others have seen them as inadequate persons. The related explanation is that most of these disturbed youngsters have experienced many negative consequences in situations in which they have become psychologically close to other persons. Thus, particularly with our older group of youngsters, we have commonly observed high levels of anxiety aroused by efforts of staff or parents to achieve emotional closeness with them. The child may be refusing social reinforcers because these are perceived as an adult's moving close to the youngster and arousing anxiety. This anxiety may be terminated by the youngster by his refusing the compliment or resorting to inappropriate behavior that once again separates him from the adult.

We have used two approaches to combat this problem. The first consists of positive practice that will be discussed in detail later. In this approach, when a staff member observes that a child has refused a compliment, he calls the youngster's attention to the fact. He may say, "Jimmy, what did I say to you?" If the youngster denies having heard the praise, the staff member may repeat it. He may then ask, "Do you think I meant what I said?" Or, "Do you think you deserve such a complement?" The staff member continues to discuss the incident until he succeeds, even if for only a moment, in obtaining a genuine response of acceptance of the praise by the youngster. This procedure is then repeated everytime the youngster appears to reject or ignore a social reinforcer from the staff. The discussion with the youngster of the praise situation aften reveals interesting feelings he has about being praised and what he believes adult praise to mean. For example, many children will say that the staff praise him automatically and without true feeling. Since this conclusion may often be valid, helping the child to express his feeling may force the staff to evaluate whether the treatment techniques are merely the mechanical carrying out of a set of management orders, or a part of our total value system about this child and how to help him. At other times a youngster may, for example, reveal that he holds unreasonably high expectations for himself and consequently cannot accept praise for behavior that isn't up to his own standard. Danny, for example, was academically two years retarded and reacted quite negatively whenever his teacher praised him for good work on a spelling test. He could not accept praise for a good grade in fourth-grade spelling words when he felt he should be at the sixth-grade level.

With some youngsters, we have used an opposite approach. Recognizing that the implied closeness of praise is threatening and to be avoided at all costs, we have permitted the child to maintain his social distance from us, while gradually introducing praise to his program. For example, Micky, in his first weeks at the Center, would almost invariably respond with totally negative behavior every time he was praised. Consequently, we shifted to a program of token reinforcement. Instead of praising him, the staff would give him a token for each behavior we were attempting to accelerate. The tokens could be used to purchase a variety of rewards, ranging from candy and material goods to off-grounds trips with staff and time alone to talk to a staff member at bedtime. Initially, the staff would only occasionally accompany the presentation of a token with a direct praise statement. Gradually, they gave more and more praise until praise accompanied every token and then continued gradually to shift until praise occurred for every positive behavior but tokens for only some of these behaviors. His choice of back-up reinforcers to purchase with the tokens also showed an interesting progression—from the purchase of immediately available material goods toward an increasing tendency to purchase activities and periods of relationship with staff.

C. TOKENS

Frequently tokens, which may be exchanged for more basic rewards, serve as a convenient means for reinforcing desired behavior. We have not implemented a total token economy in any of our groups. In only a few cases have we placed multiple behaviors of any one child under token reinforcement. More often we have used tokens to initiate new behaviors after which the tokens are phased out as other more readily available social reinforcers take effect.

Our experience has conformed with that of many investigators in finding that tokens are most effective if the youngster can select from a variety of back-up reinforcers to purchase with his tokens. Often a "cafeteria" of items for which the tokens may be exchanged is the most efficient means of accomplishing this. At times we have prepared a catalog of the rewards the youngster may purchase with his tokens. An obvious but often overlooked rule is to seek the child's own opinion as to what items he would like to purchase with tokens and attempt to include these in the catalog. If forethought is used in the development of the token catalog, rewards that will promote other desirable behaviors can be included. For example, our token lists usually vary from immediately available trinkets and candy to the inclusion of special trips and items of higher value. Since we generally wish to promote increased relationship between staff or parent and the child, we try to make enjoyable social interactions part of the rewards the child may buy with his tokens. For instance, the reward items may include a cake mix which the child could bake with the help of his mother, or the possibility of going out to dinner with a staff member of the child's choice. Sometimes when we have had more than one youngster on a token program at the same time, we have been able to promote cooperative behavior by offering bargain prices for highly valued activities, e.g., operating the electric train, if two youngsters will pool their tokens in order to share the activity. The problem of maintaining a balanced token economy is often complex. Inflation can occur in this miniature economy as well as anywhere else. A youngster may find himself with many more tokens than there are things to purchase, or the requirements for earning tokens can be so stringent that he quickly becomes discouraged about his ability to earn any of the back-up reinforcers. The constant changing of prices in order to keep a balance in the economy is usually detrimental to our task of helping the child to learn to trust adults.

Many older youngsters may see token programs as the crassest sort of attempt to control and manipulate their behavior for the convenience or gratification of the adult. If the youngster's preception is correct, as is sometimes unfortunately true, a drastic reorientation of staff values and feelings about that child must be undertaken. On other occasions, staff's motivation may clearly be an unselfish attempt to help the child develop confidence in his own ability to function competently, but because of the way the child has been controlled in the past, he will be unable to accept the program in a spirit of mutual trust. Many of our children are initially enthusiastic about a token program but rapidly seem to become satiated with this form of reinforcement, and consequently their new behavior performance rapidly decays. The most parsimonious explanation of such an effect is that the back-up reinforcers are insufficient or that the shaping program has not been adequately spaced, as is sometimes the case. However, it should not be overlooked that frequently the youngster simply cannot trust that the program could benefit anyone except the staff. As discussed in Chapter 6, social reinforcers and general attitudes toward other persons may be distorted, confused, and peculiarly polarized. Thus, the chief reinforcer for some children is to frustrate the goals and aspirations of the adults who work with him. With such a youngster, almost any mechanically designed and performed behavior modification program will be doomed to failure because he will get his greatest "kicks" from seeing the staff's plans frustrated. Hastily conceived token programs are by far the easiest prey for this sort of youngster.

It is important that the design of any token program include a plan for eventually eliminating the tokens. Various procedures may include permitting the subject eventually to purchase his own release from the token system by earning a sufficient number of tokens; pairing the tokens with social reinforcement and then thinning out the schedule of token reinforcement; or simply dropping the token altogether once the behavior has reached a sustained level. The last of these alternatives is least satisfactory, since it makes no particular assumption about what other reinforcer will subsequently control the behavior. By far the best is some system which will permit the behavior to come under the control of self-reinforcement and/or commonly available social reinforcement. For example, if a youngster learns via a shaping program that has been reinforced with tokens that he can tie his shoes, button his shirt, and buckle his belt independently, his pride in this accomplishment, the convenience of being able to dress himself, and the pleasure of adults with his growth will probably outweigh the tokens in reinforcement value.

Before concluding these brief considerations of token systems, we would like to describe one case in which the employment of tokens was somewhat unusual and was designed to meet many of the problems discussed above. In this book, we frequently emphasize the importance of a twofold approach designed to eliminate inappropriate behaviors while simultaneously reinforcing appropriate responses. In this case, a token system was combined with a mild punishment condition and applied to the total milieu treatment for an eleven-year-old boy. Our goals were to achieve adequate levels of behavioral response within the residential center and to have the youngster ultimately maintain the new behavior under conditions approximating those he would encounter once discharged from the Center. The youngster had been admitted to the Children's Treatment Center two years prior to the beginning of our first experimental-clinical treatment group. At his admission, he was showing an overwhelming amount of aggressive and destructive behavior. More bizarre behaviors, such as smearing feces, twitching, smelling and licking foreign objects, were also present. His interests were noted to be peculiar and his orientation feminine. He initially demonstrated much whining, screaming behavior and was particularly inept at forming any close relationships with staff or peers. During two years of intensive psychotherapy and exposure to a benign milieu, many of the more bizarre behaviors disappeared and he formed a few limited but tenuous relationships. His anxiety, depression, and basic attitudes about himself had undergone little meaningful transformation.

When we began to redefine our milieu program for Don, we found he was able to stimulate only a minimum of positive regard from staff. Day after day the staff notes described him as "provocative, sarcastic, and hyperactive." He seemed to be becoming increasingly sophisticated and cruel in his verbal provocation of peers. He resisted or defeated any efforts of staff members to form relationships with him and his silly hyperactive behavior was seen as a constant annoyance. Although he was capable of many cooperative friendly behaviors, these often received little attention from the staff because of the pervasive effect of his more prevalent negative behavior.

An initial effort was made to control his silly, hyperactive, and provocative behaviors with a punishment while providing constant social reinforcement for more desirable behavior. When he became silly or provocative, he was given one warning to stop the misbehavior. If the same or a related disturbance occurred within the next ten minutes, the staff member took him without discussion to the quiet room and locked him in for a five-minute time-out. All staff were alerted to provide praise or any other social attention for constructive participation in activities, initiation of pleasant conversation, or cooperative behavior with other boys. Several factors made the strengthening of appropriate behavior less effective than hoped for. First, although staff had a clear notion of what behaviors they did not wish to see, we were unable to be explicit about behaviors we did wish. Second, Don himself understandably had only a diffuse notion about what the adults would see as positive behavior. His own ability to perceive, accept, and value social reinforcement seemed extremely limited. He literally did not seem to hear praise when it was given.

Because of the ineffectiveness of social reinforcement, a token reinforcement system was developed to strengthen appropriate behaviors. He received tokens whenever a positive behavior occurred, and the tokens could later be exchanged for back-up reinforcers. The major innovation with the tokens was an attempt to provide Don with a precise description of the behavior being reinforced. This was accomplished by having the staff member write on a small card a brief description of the behavior for which the card (token) was given. We hoped that, by specifying the positive behaviors in this manner, we would become more alert to the many reinforceable behaviors that we knew were occurring. Examples of the messages written on the tokens are as follows:

Pleasant conversation when you woke up.
Polite—you nicely talk about plans for a pet.
You pleasantly accepted responsibility.
Set a good example in church.
Helped a friend.
Good table manners.
Asked me for help when you needed it.
Handled your anger well.
Did more than your share in clean-up without complaining.
Discussed your plans for your home visit with staff.
Offered part of your dessert to the others at the table.
For encouraging the group to discuss activity plans for tonight.
For being honest during a game of pool.
Fun to be with.
You accepted praise nicely.
Played well in tag even when you were losing.
Included Mike in a "secret" instead of making him feel like an outsider.
I liked the way you tried to get Mike back into the soccer game after he quit.
You sought me out pleasantly for a talk.
Pleasant teasing with staff.

While he wrote the card, the staff member was able to keep Don close to him and talk with him about what was being written. At the end of the day when Don turned in the cards for credit, one of the staff members would spend about ten minutes discussing the contents of the cards that had been earned.

This program was initially explained to Don as a means to help him learn specifically how staff wanted him to act and a means to encourage him to behave in ways that would bring him more happiness. He chose his own back-up reinforcers and, to our pleasure, included at the top of the list the privilege of staying up a half-hour later in the evening so that he could play a game or converse with staff.

The second major innovation in this particular token program was a method for eventually eliminating the tokens. This was accomplished by gradually encouraging Don to write the good behaviors on the cards and dispense them to himself. Ultimately, he wrote all of the tokens for himself and then reviewed them with the staff in the evening. He was allowed gradually to become more careless about this, and instead of writing the card immediately following his behavior, he would wait until a moment of free time to write an entire stack of cards. Finally, he came to us saying that he felt that he no longer needed the tokens, we concurred, and the system was discontinued.

Table 5.1 summarizes the design of the study and the results in terms of the mean number per week of uncontrolled silly and hyperactive responses. In this case, the baseline is estimated but it should be noted that the universal opinion of the staff was that this baseline estimate was far too conservative. The time-out condition produced a drastic reduction in the hyperactive behaviors during the next 12 weeks (*B* phase of the study). Further

Table 5.1. "Uncontrolled Silliness" Responses for Each Phase of the Treatment Program

Phase	*Week*	*Program*	*Weekly Mean Number of "Uncontrolled Silliness" Responses*
A		Baseline (estimated	140.
B	1–12	5′ time-out	4.8
C	13–26	5′ time-out tokens written by staff	1.5
D	27–30	5′ time-out writes own tokens	1.0
E	31–42	5′ time-out no tokens	.6

reductions occurred during phases *C* and *D* when both cards and time-out were in effect. This effect was maintained with time-out during phase *E*. During the course of the token reinforcement, Don earned an average of 17 cards per day. The number of cards per day was quite variable but stayed at approximately the same rate from about the 5th day through to the conclusion of the token program. Charts of qualitative change in his behavior were most encouraging. Initially, staff found they needed to stretch themselves to write any kind card. Thus, behaviors they were able to observe were things such as "nicely asked for help," "helping a friend for a few moments," "pleasant conversation." The behaviors reinforced later in the program were much more complex and included such things as "nice job handling teasing from staff with appropriate replies and knowing when to stop," "staying out of arguments that Mike and Doug were in," "helping Mike learn a new game," "talking about your worries and concerns over your home situation." Don was discharged from the Center shortly after the *E* phase of this study, and no major behavioral problems have been reported since.

D. SPECIAL DISCRIMINATIVE CUES FOR REINFORCEMENT

Frowns, smiles, and other approach responses may all become discriminative cues indicating that a more basic reinforcement may be forthcoming. Such learned cues are of course essential in bridging the gap which naturally occurs in the normal environment between the occurrence of a response and the actual presentation of a primary reinforcer. Many of our children are neither able to discern such subtle social reinforcement cues nor have an accurate understanding of how their behavior operated to control those cues from other individuals. They are especially unskilled in (1) identifying when they have pleased another person, and (2) recognizing how their behavior thus operates to alter conditions so that reinforcement may occur. For example, in the school setting, the desirable behaviors are those which are pleasing to the teacher, result in new learning, and produce good grades. As a total class, these might be described as on-task behaviors and thereby distinguished from nonattending and disruptive behaviors. We find that many of our youngsters do not clearly discriminate the on-task behaviors. Consequently, a teacher offering social reinforcement and punishment periodically for off-task behavior may be quite inefficient in teaching the child to discriminate the difference between on-task and off-task behavior. To resolve this problem, we decided to provide a cue which would always be present when the youngster was on-task and absent when he was off-task. Thus, he could learn that, when the cue was present, conditions were right for subsequent reinforcement to occur. Further, we hoped that this cue would become paired with the actual responses he was making so that the responses themselves could become cues or secondary reinforcers.

The cue which we ultimately employed for a number of in-school studies was a small electric lamp mounted on each youngster's desk. When the youngster was on-task the lamp would be lit, and when he was off-task the lamp would be off. In the first case of this sort, we connected the lamp in a series with an electric clock. Thus, when the child was on-task, the teacher would activate a switch that turned the clock and the lamp on. When the child daydreamed or engaged in disruptive behavior, the teacher would turn the switch off, thus turning out the lamp and stopping the clock. It was explained to the child that he would earn tokens based on the amount of time he accumulated on the clock and that when the teacher felt he was working appropriately she would turn the light on. In this way, he would know when he was earning tokens. The time on the clock was added up at the end of each teaching session and tokens that could be exchanged for other items were paid to the child. The more time he accumulated on the clock, the more tokens he would earn. In the first study of this sort, the youngster spent part of his day working under conditions with the clock and light and the remainder of the day without these cues. An independent observer took samples of the child's behavior according to the Behavioral Coding System discussed in Chapter 3. He would observe the youngster every 20 seconds and score the behavior in which the youngster was engaged at that instant. Six hundred such instantaneous observations were made during the on-clock condition and 608 observations during the off-clock condition. Table 5.2 summarizes the results of these observations for six different behavior categories. The first category, competitive behavior, is defined as a behavior in which the subject is attempting to make himself look better than others by being boastful, challenging, comparing his work

Table 5.2. Percent of Total Frequency of Behavior Occurring during Each Experimental Condition

	On-Clock (N = 600 obs.)	*Off-Clock (N = 608 obs.)*
Competitive	.7%	2.6%
Friendly-cooperative	7. %	6.9%
Withdrawal	1.5%	3.2%
Attending to assigned task	73. %	31. %
Receiving positive reinforcement from teacher	20.5%	11.6%
Receiving social punishment from teacher	.6%	6. %

with others, interrupting, and intruding upon others. The friendly, cooperative category includes all efforts to initiate friendship with other children, cooperate with them, make polite comments, and give approval to others. The withdrawal category was scored for any moves away from the teacher or other children in the class, for example, by daydreaming, isolating himself, or not responding to others. Attending to assigned task was scored when the youngster was engaged in work as assigned by the teacher. This definition depends upon his eyes' being focussed upon the expected work or upon the teacher if she were giving instructions, manipulating the pencil appropriately, or reciting as required. The category receiving positive reinforcement from the teacher includes the teacher's making any socially reinforcing statements to the youngster or giving any form of positive attention to him. Social punishment from the teacher included her prodding him to get to work as well as making disapproving comments about his behavior. As can be seen from the data, attention to task was almost double in the on-clock condition over off-clock. Friendly cooperative behaviors, which one would not expect to be particularly altered by the teacher's control of the clock, remained about the same under both conditions. Interestingly, competitive behavior, a major problem for this youngster, came under better control during the on-clock condition. The teacher herself was particularly interested in the data on her behavior of reinforcing the youngster. Nothing in the study had given her any direct instructions about the socially reinforcing statements which she would make to the youngster; she was allowed to praise or disapprove of his behavior as she ordinarily would with any of the children in her class. He earned almost twice as much praise from the teacher during the on-clock condition than during the off-clock, but more interesting was the enormous increase of negative statements from the teacher when the clock was not operating. The teacher herself commented that she appreciated the light and the clock because it made it unnecessary for her to make negative statements to the youngster. She elaborated that her own displeasure with him could readily be handled through turning the clock off and thus it helped her to control what she occasionally felt were biting negative remarks to the youngster.

The technique of having a cue which can be constantly present when appropriate behavior is occurring seems to merit further investigation. To date, we have only been able to carry this out successfully in the school setting where a device such as a light can be readily present and easily observable by the child.

E. FOOD

It has been hypothesized and demonstrated that social reinforcers may be acquired secondarily by being paired with primary reinforcers. The primary reinforcement contingencies suspected to be most responsible for this remarkable conditioning effect under naturalistic circumstances are reduction of hunger and cessation of pain or discomfort, i.e., usually the termination of a deprivation schedule. For example, an infant after several hours of food deprivation receives food from its mother who in turn acquires secondary reinforcing value by being associated with the food. The verbal statements, changes of the mother's facial expressions, and other stimuli concurrent with food presentation eventually acquire value as social reinforcers and are all presumed to be learned by some distant or close associations with the reduction of hunger or other primary reinforcers. Social punishment stimuli become effective as behavioral suppressors by being paired with some painful stimulus, which could be an auditory stimulus such as a loud yell, or more direct such as a spanking.

John B. Wolfe demonstrated in 1936 that poker chips could acquire secondary reinforcement value for chimpanzees. The subsequent literature is replete with the methodology used experimentally to demonstrate the acquisition of secondary reinforcers. It was Lovaas (1967) who finally put this laboratory-demonstrable knowledge to practical use by employing food as well as termination of electric shock to condition positive social reinforcers with autistic children. Lovaas also employed shock with these children to suppress aggressive and self-destructive responses. Food has been used as a reinforcer for training new responses and for conditioning social reinforcers with autistic children, as presented in Chapter 7 below. The following discussion centers on the technology of using food as a primary reinforcer as an integral part of a treatment program.

It was often found in dealing with the autistic children described in Chapter 7 that foods available at mealtimes were not effective primary reinforcers. In fact, the children were usually existing on very restricted diets, i.e., eating only a few preferred foods which did not provide sufficient daily nutrient requirements. Because of this behavioral deficiency, it became apparent that our first treatment program would be to condition a variety of foods as reinforcers before they would be used to condition new behaviors, or to strengthen previously acquired descriminitive stimuli such as social reinforcers, or to build in totally new behaviors, such as speech, attention, and compliance. We have conditioned a variety of foods to serve as more effective reinforcers in three different ways, all of which are illustrated in the case studies #1, #2, and #3. One method is to seat the child alone at mealtimes with a plate of food available at the meal but devoid of the highly preferred foods on which the child was subsisting at date of admission. No social proddings are given to encourage eating; in fact, the youngster is left completely alone. This method simply allows food to reinforce itself by permitting sufficient hunger drive to build up and being sure that one does not contaminate the program by constantly encouraging the child to eat. This paradigm is comparable to what would be devised for a case of anorexia nervosa in which the refusal-to-eat behavior was being maintained by social punishment stimuli, or perhaps by positive social reinforcement expressed as a function of someone's genuine sorrow over the patient's debilitated condition. Usually the social reinforcers responsible for non-eating have not been identified, and in such instances it would be preferable to delete all social reinforcers, and with the naturally occurring condition of hunger drive, allow the patient to operate for food at his own rate.

A second method to accelerate eating a variety of foods and to increase their effectiveness as reinforcers is a modification of the above procedure but designed for the youngster who starts to have tantrums and throws food when left at the table alone. This kind of behavior, which is disruptive to other staff and children in the dining area, often occurs because the youngster is seeking some social attention for that behavior. To handle this problem we constructed a chair with which one can administer an instant time-out for aggressive behaviors occurring during mealtimes. The chair, which is described in case #3, has a tray built in front of the child as well as sliding doors which, when shut, block the child's view of the staff member or other persons seated before him. The staff member sits before the child with the sliding doors open and does not say anything; he merely offers each successive bite of food to the child. For each time that the child knocks the food away or in some other form aggresses, the sliding doors are shut for a time-out which usually lasts no more than one or two minutes. After completion of the time-out, the doors are reopened and the food which was last offered is again presented. If the child is spitting or knocking away nonpreferred foods, that particular food is presented until an appropriate response occurs, after which we recommend a preferred food be offered.

The third means of conditioning various foods as more effective reinforcers is described in case #2. In that case the child existed on toast and cookies. A program was developed in which the preferred food was used to reinforce the nonpreferred food. His receiving decreasing pieces of cookies and toast was contingent upon his eating increasing bites of the nonpreferred foods. The reinforcement schedule was progressively thinned from 1:1 to a 1:4 fixed ratio schedule. Thus, on day one, meal one, the child received an entire piece of toast for eating a minute bite of potatoes, and for successive meals the amount of the toast was diminished and the amount of reinforced foods increased. Again, if on a given trial the child was refusing to eat a particular kind of food, only that food would be offered, until it was eaten appropriately or the alloted time for the meal had terminated. At the next meal, the new foods would be presented in a random manner; we would not use the foods from the previous meal in the next.

There are numerous procedural points pertinent to an effective reinforcement program using food. Cooperation with the kitchen staff is one crucial point. In many institution settings, the kitchen is completely divorced from the clinical program. We have found it advantageous for the kitchen staff to be involved on the treatment team, since they simply have the reinforcers we are discussing. The kitchen staff in a reinforcement program have to alter their schedules for cooking and cleaning to fulfill the requirements of the treatment program, and this can be an inconvenience.

We seldom use candy as a reinforcer simply because it satiates drive quickly, i.e., you cannot use many candies before the child is full, and this has the unfortunate effect of ruining the next meal as an effective reinforcer. Moreover, autistic children already have enough difficulty with stable eating patterns without our accentuating their problems by relying upon foods likely to have high preference value. We have used cookies during early parent-training sessions to guarantee success, but this procedure is faded rapidly. We have used dried fruits quite frequently in the early months of a child's program, for two reasons. The dried fruits may be included beneficially in the child's diet, and second, they assist in relieving the constipation which is so characteristic of the children who had restricted diets when first admitted. The dried fruits were then gradually faded as normal elimination habits were acquired.

During those meals when food was not used exclusively to reinforce secondary reinforcers, speech, etc., because of insufficient staff coverage, the food was used contingently for appropriate table manners. At these times, the staff members would not allow a child to eat unless he held the fork correctly or other appropriate table manners occurred that the staff member was training the child at the time. Since all the autistic children reported here had confounded social reinforcers at date of admission, we have made it standard practice always to precede presentation of food as a reinforcer by some positive social reinforcement statement to facilitate conditioning of the latter. For example, if we are teaching speech, the speech model is presented, the child imitates with an acceptable approximation to the model, the child is verbally praised, and then, almost simultaneously with the verbal statement, is given a bite of food. With this procedure, the speech response as well as social reinforcements are being conditioned. In our program, social praise is used to reinforce speech as it is elicited during the remainder of the day, i.e., exclusive of mealtime conditioning programs.

Strengthening Social Reinforcers

Our experience has been that both the young psychotic children and the older primarily neurotic children in our research groups respond in unusual ways to social reinforcement. One of the basic tasks in dealing with the emotionally disturbed child is to strengthen the effectiveness of various social reinforcers which will be available to him in the environment outside of the Treatment Center. Unfortunately, the basic literature provides very little information concerning the acquisition of social reinforcers. These problems are discussed in more detail in Chapter 6, but at the present juncture, we would like to present several methods which, although they have received little controlled study, seem to be of value in strengthening social reinforcers.

As already mention, whenever food is used for particular training programs, social reinforcement is given immediately preceding the presentation of the food. A similar procedure is generally followed whenever our older children are placed on token programs and whenever reinforcers like stroking or cuddling the youngster are used. In addition, we have made use of a "reinforcer cabinet" as a means of providing incentive to the older youngsters and also, we hope, as a means of strengthening social reinforcement. The reinforcer cabinet contains a variety of toys and foodstuffs from which the children may select freely whenever taken to the cabinet by a staff member. In addition, we also make available a wide range of more expensive and highly valued toys and games in the reinforcer cabinet. These are not given to the youngster outright, but when he has a trip to the cabinet, he has the choice of taking one of these games or toys for a period of play. Staff are instructed to back-up their social reinforcement periodically by giving a youngster a trip to the cabinet. Thus, for example, a staff member might say to the youngster, "I really am pleased with the way you worked in school this morning. In fact, I think that merits a trip to the cabinet." In a given day, a youngster may receive a large number of social reinforcers, but only a few of these would be immediately backed-up with a trip to the cabinet. Later in his experience at the Center, trips to the cabinet are thinned out considerably until this kind of special reward is on the same basis as it might be in an average home.

The success of social reinforcers is dependent upon the development of a comfortable and close relationship between the adult presenting the social reinforcement and the child. Consequently, during the initial days of the youngster's experience at the Center, we make every effort to establish a close relationship between him and one or two staff members so that these persons acquire a high reinforcement valence for him. At this stage of treatment, we seldom make basic reinforcers contingent upon specific positive behaviors of the child, but rather attempt to make them contingent upon the youngster's presence with a particular staff member. Thus, the staff who are initially working with the youngster in a 1:1 relationship will attempt to use a wide variety of activities that are highly gratifying for the child. Cooking and eating activities are, of course, generally very popular with the youngsters as are activities such as listening to stories or playing quiet table games. The staff member uses all of these kinds of activities, as well as his wide repertoire of skills in relating to children, to promote himself as a person of value to the child. It is hoped that when this staff member praises him, the social reinforcement carries some genuine meaning. Later, of course, the praise of that staff member and others who by then have formed a relationship with the youngster is used to shape particular behaviors.

Shaping Techniques

It is probable that many responses are learned independently of other responses, i.e., their acquisition is not dependent upon nor influenced by generalization gradients established by previously acquired responses. However, most social behaviors are thought to be learned in incremental steps with a myriad of generalization effects differentially accelerating and decelerating the learning of different responses. Shaping, or a successive approximation of a response, is a procedure by which one systematically trains a complex response by successively acquiring and extinguishing prerequisite responses which are increasingly comparable to the goal response. This is no more complex than recognizing that children must sit, crawl, stand, and then walk before they are able to run. In most instances, shaping is a method of acquiring and extinguishing a succession of responses where the previous response is required to learn the next response, and all incremental steps are trained to the same cue. Many responses do not require all the prerequisite steps which may have been acquired and extinquished in a step-like order. It is likely that with children many of these hierarchal response steps are confounded with maturation in which prerequisite physiological developments must occur before the acquisition of a particular response is possible. It is difficult for one to separate maturational variables from learning variables, particularly with psychotic children. The only evidence we have accumulated relevant to such a problem are the speech data in case study #1, where we were able to identify a discrimination deficit as primarily responsible for the failure to shape speech responses.

Training complex behavior through incremental steps is the foundation of curriculum construction in a public school setting. Shaping is what the mother does who requires her child to use a spoon with increasing dexterity in successive meals. These training skills are employed naturalistically by people; perhaps they acquired the skills by imitation. The fact that parents have always been training extremely complex behavior in their children, without having the vaguest idea of what were the necessary techniques responsible for training their children, illustrates the goal of psychology, namely, to learn what we have been doing all along.

In the research program described in this book, the child-care worker and nursing staff were trained in the use of shaping. They are encouraged, in fact, expected, constantly to devise techniques to shape the many responses disturbed children need to be taught. Occupational therapists with pediatric specialities are particularly adept in establishing hierarchies of responses which approximate desired goal behaviors in children. This has been our experience, particularly in constructing fine and gross motor training programs for the children. The following cases illustrate some innovative uses of simple reinforcers for shaping playground behavior with a few psychotic children. In one instance, a youngster was unable to pedal a tricycle. He would sit on the tricycle, rock gently a few times, grunt often, and then sit immobile until removed from it. A staff member took several small chocolate candies and used these as rewards for the following steps: (1) gently, then strongly, flexing one thigh muscle, then both alternately; (2) pushing against the tricycle pedal by alternately flexing each thigh muscle; (3) pushing the pedal one-half inch, then one inch, then for increasing increments. The child was rewarded for these steps until he pedaled completely unassisted. It required five days with approximately 45 minutes' training per day to teach the child how to pedal the tricycle.

Another youngster was terrified of swings. The child had daily sessions of sitting beside and on the lap of the staff member at decreasing distances from the swing. During these sessions, she would be rewarded with small preferred candies. Within one week she was eating the candies beside the swing, then on the lap of staff while swinging, then on the swing by herself, and within two weeks she was being pushed gleefully on the swing. The candy reinforcers were gradually deleted, since the swing itself had now acquired reward value.

The above child was unable to play on the slide; she refused to climb independently, much less assisted, and she would refuse to slide down. An ingenious staff member took her to the slide one afternoon directly after the child's nap when she was quite hungry. The staff placed small candies on each step of the slide and the child devoured them oblivious to the height she had climbed to procure each one. When at the top she started to panic, but upon sighting the enormous pile of candy at the bottom of the slide, she promptly slid down—and her fear of the slide decelerated correspondingly. Several more trials on successive days were required to extinguish her fear response completely, but after that she continued to enjoy the slide without requiring external reinforcements. Numerous examples comparable to these occur continually in the research program.

Shaping is a procedure which has not gained much acknowledgement in the literature. There have been numerous studies demonstrating that one can train single responses in various groups of subjects, but it is a minority of investigators who have been systematically studying the multiplicity of variables which interact in shaping a response. This research is crucial, since the acquisition and extinction of successive habits compose a much more complex operation than acquisition of a single response. This area seems to be overlooked by individuals who reference single response training studies with retarded subjects and maintain that with sufficient trials they could learn almost any response, and completely fail to recognize how few responses are acquired in the isolative manner characteristic of many of the experimental studies from which their hypothesis was derived.

The procedure of shaping is teaching the subject a response(s) which is a prerequisite to acquiring another response(s), which is a prerequisite for acquisition of another, et cetera. The earlier acquired responses may never again be utilized after they have succeeded in preparing the child for a new response. In some instances, these preparatory responses may remain in the response repretoire or assist in training a multitude of skills which branch off from that prerequisite response. In conducting a shaping program, one can be assisted by certain procedural points.

For example, many persons have became quite skilled in shaping behavior, like graduate students working in psychology laboratories training animals to press levers—hardly comparable to the skill demonstrated by many kindergarten teachers who are able to train group behavior in a matter of weeks with 25 children. It is always more difficult to shape/train behaviors in human beings than in lower animals, simply because of the more kinds of responses which may be emitted by humans. In shaping, one must try to stimulate, or wait for the occurrence of, a desired response which is reinforced as soon as it occurs. The child is likely to be demonstrating numerous responses simultaneously, increasing the risk of inadvertently reinforcing the wrong response during the shaping program. Thus, it is crucial that the reinforcer be contingent upon the correct responses, and if there is some undesirable concurrent response occurring, then it is preferable not to reinforce but to wait, hoping that there is sufficient response variability so that the desired response is reinforced the most and the other concurrent error responses are being inadvertently reinforced on a thinner schedule and do not acquire the dominance of the desired response.

Shaping is difficult to perform with emotionally disturbed children. As one is trying to reinforce a desired response, some undesired/abnormal response may occur which should be punished. For example, if one is continuously punishing aggressive behaviors while trying positively to reinforce speech as well as maintaining eye contact, a response contamination may occur. If the response to be punished is occurring and is so decelerated, the risk of generalization effects increases, so that not only are temper tantrums decelerated, but also speech rate. For instance, during training quite often trial-and-error responses are elicited, and there may not be much variability among these responses. These trial-and-error responses should not be punished, but they may be ignored. If they are punished, the effect may be to decelerate the rough response approximation so necessary for shaping.

To illustrate, a parent was trying to teach his child how to complete lotto puzzles. The puzzles were simple pictures cut in half, several of which were placed in a pile; and the child was instructed to match the pairs. It was observed that the child was using many trial-and-error responses in matching the lotto pairs. The father was reinforcing 94% of all correct responses, but in the frustration of observing his child make so many error responses, he began inadvertently and mildly punishing the error responses by saying, "No," "That's not correct, keep trying." The effect of this mild punishment was inadvertently to pair an ostensible social punishment stimulus with trial-and-error responses, and in a few minutes decelerated all trial-and-error responses. Thus, a very well-intentioned parent, who reinforced correct responses quite effectively, had accidentally decelerated the problem-solving behavior which this particular child was capable of performing, namely trial-and-error responses. The few correct responses made and reinforced became dominant, trial-and-error or random problem-solving behaviors were extinguishing, all of which was a paradigm for teaching a responseless child with stereotyped behaviors. The developing stereotyped behaviors were that the child was rehearsing the few correct responses she happened to have made over and over.

This father's mistake has been committed by us innumerable times. As response approximation which is usually slow and variable, occurs, the staff would often think that the child was "holding out," being obstinate or perverse, and could have easily performed the response if he so wished. It required many experiences before we realized that our clinical judgments had disguised the data. Patience is a virtue of the greatest necessity in shaping and it took us many trials to learn that we were not going to teach the child most effectively by being angry at him for not being able to learn quickly.

In initiating a shaping program, one should establish the successive response steps before proceeding. Shaping has been considered an "art" by many, and is thus relegated the same validity as traditional psychotherapeutic endeavors. It is recognized that one must constantly revise the response steps with the data acquired during the shaping program. Reasons for establishing the response steps before shaping are: (1) to promote hypothesis formation, a necessary procedure for idiographic studies; (2) to make the data public and replicable; and (3) to guarantee that staff will be reinforcing the same responses, thus facilitating communication among staff.

Behavioral goals should be established prior to commencing a shaping program, because it requires the staff to decide what behavior is comparable to that which will be expected in the normal environment. Unfortunately, this is seldom possible with the young psychotic child. Quite often a behavioral goal will be consistent with the expectancies for a normal child of average intelligence, but when psychotic behaviors have been decelerated, one may find that the child is to some degree retarded. Thus, one must often reestablish the behavioral goals, which should always be explained to the child's parents.

We frequently found it necessary to "back-up" in a training program. "Backing-up" is defined as reinforcing a previously trained response which was a prerequisite response to the current response being trained but which the child has been unable to acquire. One should not be reluctant to "back-up," although this does impart a sense of failure to a clinician. However, in support of the investigator's pride, it testifies that he is cognizant of the child's progress, which is certainly a worthwhile goal of which to be proud. When backing-up, sometimes it is necessary only to reaccelerate a previously acquired response before continuing on with the program. In some instances, it is necessary to back-up and proceed again, but at smaller response increments.

One danger in a shaping program is overtraining at a particular response level. This is an easy error to commit simply because it is reinforcing for staff to maintain a particular level of compliance such as a child's sitting still and coming when called. The danger of maintaining such behavioral plateaus is that it increases the likelihood of regressing to that level if later more complex levels of behavior are extinguished. This hypothesis is based on the Dollard and Miller (1950, p. 171) interpretation of regression. Also, if the response is overtrained, it becomes more difficult to extinguish when progressing to the next response. There are no formulations which can tell one how to avoid these problems.

A shaping program should progress in steps which are most likely to assure continual and incremental success. If the response hierarchies are too dissimilar, facilitory generalization effects will not occur for successive responses. The results of maintaining too difficult response goals are that:

(1) the child will experience more failure; and (2) the treatment program will take too long, which is expensive and makes it difficult for the total program to function optimally. It is essential that the response increments be in small enough steps so that the child will receive considerable positive reinforcement. The reduction of reinforcement is tantamount to a paradigm for depression, i.e., extinction of reinforcers. If the steps are too difficult and only assure error responses, the likelihood is high that this will engender some conflict behavior and increase the probability that the child will retrieve referral behaviors to operate for previously preferred and available reinforcers—a regression paradigm. Thus, acceleration of negativistic or depressive behaviors during a shaping program may indicate that the investigator has not been shaping the desired responses at small enough response gradations.

Ignoring error responses seems to be the most effective procedure for separating out correct and incorrect responses. Punishment may generalize to desired responses if it is carelessly applied to error responses. If the child is producing only error responses, the absence of reinforcement itself may decelerate those trial-and-error responses and make it more difficult to teach the response. In the event of such response depression, one has several alternatives: (1) accept a rather rough approximation to the response; (2) back-up to an earlier-acquired response level and begin over again; and (3) variably reinforce error responses with the hope that acceptable response approximations will eventually be emitted.

The case studies described in Chapter 7 contain numerous examples of shaping. These cases are first approximations to synchronized application of conditioning procedures. It is stressed in the case studies that in establishing a total program, we should coordinate the various shaping programs so that they interact to facilitate each other. Just as we teach a mute child to initiate a blowing response as the first step in a speech program, there are beginning or prerequisite responses which must be trained before other shaping programs may begin. For example, a child must learn to sit still and pay attention before a speech program may commence. The treatment program directors in conjunction with the treatment personnel must determine the hierarchy of responses.

Let us make a closing point in this brief discussion of shaping; all treatment staff should be aware of each response increment currently being trained with the several simultaneously trained responses for each child. This may be achieved by having staff rotate among the children throughout the day, rather than having one staff work individually with just one child. Furthermore, such staff rotation should facilitate generalization effects. It is most advantageous if the parents can participate in all treatment programs to assure that generalization is greatest toward them.

Prodding

Prodding is more than a command for a child to "come here." We feel that prodding should be a discriminative stimulus for work, or perhaps a compliant response which if not made will result in punishment, or if commenced will result in positive reinforcement. The verbal social prod, then, indicates a rather complex response sequence. The response may be an avoidance of punishment, and it may at the same time be an operant response for positive reinforcement. A management order using prodding cues for a child should not be one which is totally punishing. If the program is one in which the child is continually requested to perform some response in avoidance of punishment, the effect is likely to be deleterious to the child's total treatment program. Avoidance behavior maintained under such a paradigm is likely to produce stereotyped responses and a pervasive deceleration of desired and appropriate response variance to the social prod. We feel that it is most effective for the social prod to serve as a discriminative stimulus for positive reinforcement. Such a paradigm is likely to engender more approach responses and more response variability, and thereby make it more likely that the child acquire increasingly complex responses. There is a problem which we suspect results from the use of social prods. As the social prod acquires a discriminative stimulus value, it is concurrently acquiring some reinforcing effects. It is then possible for the discriminative stimulus effect to develop into the form of a response chain, as, e.g., in the case of the child who does not perform and thereby elicits social prods to which he will respond for the impending positive social reinforcement. Thus, the child has the staff member on a schedule of prodding that eventuates social reinforcement for both. This problem could be diminished by reinforcing all compliant behavior on a shaping program and resorting to social prods as little as possible. One danger of prodding, then, is that the prod will serve as an independent reinforcer maintaining noncompliant behavior.

It has been observed of some psychotic children that social prodding in the form of strong requests to participate in an activity with other children or with a staff member often stimulates avoidance responses. It has also been our observation that such avoidance responses had also been elicited and maintained by numerous social proddings by the parents prior to the child's admission. The child had been trained to noncomply to social prods because the parents would soon cease their requests and allow the child to return to his preferred, albeit asocial, but reinforcing activity. Thus, inadvertently, the child had been trained to tolerate increasing frequencies of prodding by the parents to attain his preferred reinforcers of being left alone. Again, this merely illustrates that the effectiveness of social prodding is idiosyncratic to the learning history of the child.

Role-Playing and Direct Instruction

Various forms of role-playing and direct verbal instruction should, of course, be used to promote behavioral change. Primarily such techniques serve to increase the child's awareness of available reinforcement contingencies and to raise the position of desired behaviors in his total behavioral hierarchy. Obviously, direct instruction must be used creatively if it is to be effective. Most disturbed children have received far more than their share of useless lecturing, moralizing, and general harping about their behavior. Direct instruction must relate to needs the child himself experiences and must be enjoyable in its own right if it is to be useful.

Our staff have used a variety of methods for direct instruction, varying from the simple, one-time hint, "If you get in bed quickly we will have time for a story," to far more elaborate instructional programs. For example, on one occasion a child indicated he was fearful of going on a pending home visit because he would need to travel on the bus alone. The staff member improvised a game, "riding the bus," in which all the elements of buying a ticket, speaking to the driver, taking a seat, identifying his stop, and claiming his baggage, could be rehearsed in a pleasant, relaxed manner with the help of staff and other children.

Presumably a didactic procedure promotes verbal mediation of overt behavior with respect to particular stimulus conditions. In one study conducted at CTC (Giebink, Stover, & Fahl, 1968), verbal responses to frustrating situations were used to mediate disturbed boys' overt behavior in the same situations. Frustrating situations that typically occur at the Center were presented symbolically in a simple table game. The youngsters had to locate appropriate "response cards" to pair with each frustrating situation in order to make a "move" in the table game. The game rewarded the child for being able verbally to describe an appropriate behavioral response for each of the frustrating situations. Measures in this study included a verbal test and behavioral observation during the actual frustrating situation. The children demonstrated both improved verbal and improved behavioral responses to the frustrations after instruction via the table game. The performance increase, however, was not so marked as the improvement in verbal responses. This suggested that direct instruction might increase the probability of the overt response, but direct reinforcement of the overt behavior would also be needed to strengthen and maintain the new overt response.

Modeling and Imitation

Bandura's and Walters' text (1963) contains a very enlightened discussion of the value of imitation in acquiring social behaviors in children. We have used some of their findings in our programs, but systematic experimentation has not been completed as yet.

That the role of imitation is necessary in the acquisition of appropriate social behaviors becomes very obvious in the residential center. It also becomes apparent that the residential setting is an unfortunate environment for a child because it provides many socially inappropriate models among his peers. The few children within a residential center who are close to discharge have available to them a host of inappropriate social models. We attempt to counteract this problem by entering the child in public school as soon as our special classes have brought academic and social behavior to a reasonable level. Thus the children are admitted to the community public school while still in residence at CTC, thus providing them with appropriate behavioral models. Also, early public school placement allows us to monitor the child for academic problems, generalization of treatment effects, and development of new problems. Our preference for exposing the child to a normal environment often dictates against placement in a special class for the disturbed where the frequent high levels of inappropriate behavior might be modelled.

The role of imitation in the acquisition of social behaviors becomes particularly apparent with psychotic children as soon as they begin to acquire speech and a few complex social behaviors. During the acquisition of these imitative responses, these children are controlled less by the clinicians and more by their peer group. In the residential center when the dominant peer models are acting-out neurotic youngsters, the "flowering" psychotic children are exposed to these inappropriate models and begin to acquire neurotic behavior patterns. We have observed instances in which nonaggressive schizophrenic children acquire aggressive response patterns after they have begun to acquire speech and the more complex fine and gross motor skills necessary for interaction with peers.

We have observed that imitation figures strongly in the acquisition of certain abnormal behavior patterns. For example, there was a child referred for a variety of problems, one of which included mutism. The mutism was selective because it was established from many people that the youngster was able to speak, in fact did speak fluently, when at home. During the initial diagnostic interview with the entire family, a staff member asked one of the parents to describe what they considered to be the child's major problem. The mother replied in a barely audible whisper—so low that all staff had to lean forward and listen quite attentively to hear her say —"The child's major problem is that she does not speak." The child had simply imitated the verbal behavior of her mother to get considerable attention from her mother. Just as the mother was able to control others with diminished speech intensity, so was the child able to employ the same response and thereby avoid attending school (where she had been a failure) and remain home with her mother, who was highly reinforcing.

There are a few treatment techniques which we use in a standard manner and which are relevant to modeling and the acquisition of social behaviors. For example, staff standardly reinforce behavior acquired by the child in the public school that is appropriate, particularly if the staff think the behavior was acquired by modeling. This is simply using the technique of reinforcing the child for imitating a preferred response. For example, whenever the young psychotic children model the staff, they are socially rewarded, regardless of whether the response was age-appropriate or not. After modeling becomes dominant, then we reinforce more specifically. We also attempt to expose the child as much as possible to the normal peer environment, which includes summer camp, public school, excursions into town, and various other activities. These occasions, we hope, allow the child to imitate more appropriate peer models than are available within the treatment setting. We attempt to avoid some models, particularly the analytic one of having children strike an inflated toy clown on the presumption that it will discharge their hostilities. It has been established (Bandura & Walters, 1963) that children who merely watch other children aggress either against other children or even inanimate objects will in turn acquire more aggressive behaviors. It is our contention that aggressive behaviors are not responses which need to be taught to most emotionally disturbed child.

In the early stages of training the young psychotic child, we often use modeling in its most primitive form. The child will be requested to observe the staff member, and if he is unable to imitate the staff member's behavior, such as in gross motor training, the staff member will physically move the child through the motions of imitating the staff member's response while constantly reinforcing the slightest approximations on the child's behalf to comply with the modeling. Shaping is used in conjunction with modeling in our treatment programs in a standard manner. If a child who walks on tiptoes is unable to imitate a staff member's walking from heel to toe, the staff member will physically move the child's foot through the appropriate imitative movements. For successive trials the assistance rendered in modeling the staff's gait is diminished until the child is able to imitate the staff member unassisted.

The staff will reinforce a peer model if he provides an appropriate model to one of the other children, and particularly if the child imitates the model. There are two reasons for this social reinforcement. First, we would suspect that the child imitating the peer's appropriate response would receive some vicarious reinforcement (Bandura & Walters, 1963) from observing the model's being reinforced; and second, we would wish to reinforce the model for the correct behavior in anticipation that the behavior would occur at a later time to the advantage of the model as well as to the observing child. Then, third, we would reinforce the child for imitating the model simply to increase the probability of that response's occurring again in imitation.

Training Supportive Behaviors

Inappropriate behaviors often develop under stimulus conditions where the child is incapable of producing the expected desirable behavior. Staats and Butterfield (1965) give the example of a child who demonstrated negative behavior in school while being unable to read at the grade level to which he was assigned. After a successful reading program, the youngster no longer needed to use disruptive behavior to achieve social reinforcement in the classroom. Frequently, a child will be argumentative or quarrelsome in a group game and unable to produce sportsman-like behavior. He may avoid many kinds of activity and isolate himself simply because he does not have the requisite skills for the activity. Endless therapizing directed at the child's self-consciousness or isolativeness may be useless if he does not have the particular skills needed to gain at least some recognition in a particular social activity. For this reason, a treatment program should direct itself to improving the child's skill level in all areas in which he must function, no matter how "unpsychological" some of the areas may seem. This is generally recognized for problems such as teaching bladder control, or polite conversation, or reading skills. In many other areas, however, the point is often missed.

Most of the children admitted to the Treatment Center are found to be extremely deficient in many motor skills. Consequently, early in each child's program a simple evaluation is made of his physical skills, particularly those necessary for his successful participation in age-appropriate play activities. Subsequently, he is provided an individually designed skill-building program to overcome his most marked deficiencies. The following are examples of some of the skill areas which would be assessed and developed for a ten-year-old boy.[1]

Arm and Torso Control

Skill: Two-handed throwing.

Behavioral goal: To throw a basketball accurately using all passes 25 consecutive times at 15 feet.

1. The authors wish to acknowledge Mr. John Shutz, who took primary responsibility for developing these skill-building programs.

Method of development: Rolling, underhand throwing, overhand throwing, bouncing. Increase speed and distance at each step of program.

Skill: Underhand throwing.
Behavioral goal: Throw a softball underhand accurately 25 consecutive times at 20 feet.
Method of development: Rolling, tossing with roll, throw. Increase speed and distance at each step. Achieve progress by using small playground ball, bean bag, fleeceball, softball, football, etc.

Leg Control

Skill: Straight, coordinated running.
Behavioral goal: Run 50 yards in eight seconds.
Method of development: Walk, jog, run.

Skill: Kicking a moving object.
Behavioral goal: Kick a slowly rolled large playground ball 40 feet and within a 90-degree arc five consecutive times.
Method of development: Kicking without object, kicking stationary object, kicking moving object.

This same step-by-step training of skills for activity areas may be facilitated by using physical education manuals, e.g., Boyer (1965) and the President's Council on Youth Fitness (1961). In our program we generally make certain a child has the skills for a simple activity before exposing him to the stress of more difficult activities. Thus a child would be given many experiences making puddings or simple candy before being exposed to the activity of baking a cake. This point may seem redundantly obvious, but we have had the repeated experience of seeing a new staff member or a parent wonder why a ten-year-old boy who has not learned to play dodgeball always gets into fights when thrust into a game of touch football.

Positive Practice

Positive practice is a procedure whereby the clinician requests the child to repeat a particular response until it is emitted correctly, or at an acceptable criterion level necessary for reinforcement in a shaping program. Positive practice is conducted throughout the day concurrently with other treatment programs. To illustrate, if a child is asked to brush his teeth and the child says something which the staff member cannot understand, the child may be requested to rehearse that verbal response until it is comprehensible to the staff member. The rationale for positive practice throughout the day for improved responses is that if an error response does occur, it may be expected to generalize and therefore be more resistant to extinction. We have observed in our speech-shaping programs that, if the training occurs only at mealtimes, during the rest of the day the child may be rehearsing error responses or, more likely, remaining mute. For this reason, the staff members constantly try to elicit speech and require the child to rehearse until an acceptable response is made. This, of course, involves considerable prodding during the day, but also makes an enormous amount of positive social reinforcement available for successively approximating particular responses during the positive practice sessions. In the residential setting one has the capability of reinforcing a variety of responses in an ever-increasing or expanding environment, while using all employees in the setting in conducting a positive practice program (Browning, 1967).

One must be careful in establishing positive practice programs to be sure that the rehearsals to success do not acquire a noxious valence. We attempt to avoid such a "negative practice" effect by having an abundance of positive reinforcement available for each approximation to criterion level of the response during the rehearsals. If the positive practice sessions for certain responses during the day are becoming punishing, then the program should be backed-up to easier response levels where the child may succeed and again achieve positive reinforcement. A subsidiary goal of a positive practice program is that the child will eventually rehearse the response himself without being requested. It is hoped that eventually the corrected response acquires a reinforcing value for the child as a function of the positive practice programs with the staff. This is comparable to the notion that performing the correct, or a preferred, response becomes reinforcing for a child, which would certainly be a worthwhile behavioral goal.

Positive practice, then, is not simply prodding a child where an avoidance response would be elicited. Positive practice is requesting the child to rehearse a response which the staff member knows the child can produce and which will not evoke an avoidance response. One rationale for positive practice is that it provides the child with more opportunities to rehearse a desired behavior throughout the day and to attain profuse social reinforcement. This differs considerably from a kind of shaping program in which one simply waits for the child to make a preferred response which the clinician may then reinforce. Often the staff do reserve positive practice for spontaneous occurrences of behavior that are currently being trained in more structured training programs throughout the day. When these spontaneous behaviors, which have been trained but which are not occurring at criterion level, occur, positive practice is employed. An example would be speech, when the child uses a speech response which is not comparable to that which he is able to perform as evidenced during the specific training sessions during mealtimes. With the occurrence of such responses, the staff member would require the child to repeat the response over and over, assisting as necessary, until the child is successful. Considerable positive reinforcement is provided for the child's attempts to model the staff member correctly. Positive practice should not be confused with negative practice in which fatigue effects are being paired with elicitation of the response.

Extinction

We define extinction as a procedure in which the response-maintaining reinforcers are no longer available for the occurrence of the response. It is crucial that the reinforcer never be contingent upon the response during extinction; it must be a 100% continuous nonreinforcement program. If a response is reinforced at all, this is merely thinning the reinforcement schedule, which would make the response more resistant to extinction. The intermittent reinforcement actually runs the risk of strengthening the response as measured by resistance to extinction, i.e., resistance to a continuous nonreinforcement program. It is hypothesized by the investigators that, as one approximates the normal environment in training a child, one comes close to extinction schedules for reinforcers maintaining the social behaviors of the child. It is crucial that a method be devised by means of which one can efficiently and inexpensively assess the kinds of reinforcers and the ratio available for certain social behaviors in children before they are discharged. It may be that the schedules are so thin in the normal environment that the emotionally disturbed child's newly acquired behaviors will extinguish before they are rewarded. It is not that all social settings have certain responses in children on extinction schedules, it is simply that the child's behavior may be extinguished before the reinforcement maintaining the behavior is forthcoming. The necessity of maintaining 100% continuous nonreinforcement on an extinction schedule should be reemphasized to staff constantly. One cannot impress it enough upon the staff that it takes only a few instances of inadvertently and accidentally reinforcing an abnormal behavior to maintain its resistance to extinction when the child is returned to the normal environment. Perhaps we are unable to be socially programmed to the extent necessary for complete extinction of socially abnormal behaviors. For example, in all of the responses which we have monitored for long intervals of time for all-day counts, e.g., longer than two years, it has been observed that the response may be absent for weeks or months and then intermittently occur only to disappear again. One may question if it is ever possible to have an extinction schedule for social behaviors in consideration of the hypothesized myriad of generalization effects among the child's response repertoire. Thus, wherever possible, an extinction schedule should be accompanied by a program to strengthen an appropriate behavior which will be incompatible with the extinguished response.

Punishment

Punishment is often described as an aversive stimulus, although this does not necessarily have to be so. Punishment has been defined for our treatment techniques as a procedure in which the contingent presence of a stimulus decelerates a particular response. Some investigators may wish to define the removal of a particular reinforcement as a punishment paradigm. We would define the procedure of removing a reinforcer with a corresponding response deceleration as an extinction schedule. The use of punishment is a social fact; it is used quite liberally in the rearing of many children. The employment of punishment in a treatment program for someone else's child involves considerable ethical responsibility, as described in the concluding chapter of this book. In the studies contained herein, the most severe punishment stimulus used was that of faradic stimulation, which effectively saved the child's life. The most typical punishment condition was social admonishment.

Punishment or the suppression of behavior is tantamount to death. By punishment, one is essentially destroying behavior which does involve ethical responsibility on the part of the clinician. It is our strong recommendation that one should be concurrently teaching appropriate behavior whenever a punishment condition is being employed in the treatment program for a child. The assumption of responsibility by the clinician in teaching a child social behaviors is comparable to the life and death of the patient, since behavior is as much life as is a heartbeat. Punishment has been a primary procedure of making children responseless in some custodial hospital programs so that they are not a nuisance to the staff members. These punishment programs range from days in the quiet room to the contingent administration of depressants to children who are causing a disturbance. We admonish those programs, particularly those under the guise of behavior therapy, which state that they are "controlling" the child's behavior. We feel that such programs are more comparable to jails which have assumed the role of making the individual socially unresponsive. Punishment is a dangerous treatment technique, since it does not promote growth in a child, i.e., acquisition of new behaviors. Punishment often provides an aggressive model for the children to imitate. Punishment invariably fosters escape or avoidance behavior in children. Punishment serves as a generalized behavioral suppressor, and quite often the clinician is unaware of what preferred behaviors are being suppressed by the punishment contingency. Punishment entails ethical responsibilities for the clinician that are not always assumed by most residential centers. Punishment implies to the child patient that it is a preferred child-rearing practice. One may suspect that the child reared under punishing conditions may use the same conditions in rearing his own children—which may interact with the hypothesis that emotionally disturbed children grow up to rear emotionally disturbed children. We feel that the child exposed to punishment conditions either personally or as an observer is more likely to use those techniques in raising his own children. For that reason, since punishment is dangerous, one should use care in its administration in a child's treatment program. When one is treating children in a residential center, he is assuming parental responsibility for that child in the parent's absence; and this includes teaching him appropriate child-rearing practices comparable to or better than those he would acquire in his own home.

Time-Out Procedures

A. STRAIGHT TIME-OUT

A time-out condition is an extinction procedure for decelerating an undesirable response. In administering a time-out condition, one is removing the child from some environmental condition(s) which is reinforcing the undesirable response. The teacher who requires the youngster to leave the room and stand in a corner for "clowning" in the classroom has administered a time-out condition. The time-out condition, was to remove the child from the peer reinforcers which were maintaining the disruptive behavior of the child in the classroom.

As may be seen in some of the studies contained in the chapters on design and on case studies, we have used time-out conditions quite frequently to decelerate aggressive and tantrum behaviors. The conditions under which we would employ a time-out involved children for whom social punishment stimuli either were ineffective or would inadvertently accelerate the response which we wished to decelerate. The time-out condition varied in the manner in which we would remove the child from the presumed-to-be reinforcing conditions. Typically, we would not have experimentally identified exactly what social reinforcement contingencies were maintaining the behavior which we wish to extinguish. We would usually raise some hypothesis as to why the child was operating with the inappropriate behavior, but the time-out condition would be administered without the necessity of determining what the reinforcers were. The time-out condition was administered in several ways: the first means would be by placing the child in a bedroom which was devoid of furniture and decor; a second procedure would be by placing the child in his bedroom for the required time-out interval; a small, quiet booth was constructed which was used in the classroom setting as well as in the youngster's room. As the child acquired greater behavioral control and it was less necessary to rely upon a closed room, the staff would use a corner or a chair in a remote part of the room, or a seat by a tree while outside, for the required time-out. As the case study data show, the time-out intervals varied from one minute to five minutes in duration, except for one case study in which the child was kept in the quiet room until the tantrum behaviors ceased, which at most was for 45 minutes to an hour during the initial weeks of the treatment program. The means of employing a time-out were arranged on a gradient. The gradient progressed from very strict control and complete absence of possible social reinforcers, such as the quiet room, to more of a self-control measure and complex time-out conditions such as sitting beside a tree for a moment while playing outside. These time-out conditions progressed as the child's behavior was extinguishing so that they progressively approximated that time-out condition which would be like that expected to be administered in the child's natural environment. The environmental time-out contingency to be approximated would be simply ignoring the response when it occurred, with that extinction procedure being an effective one. Such a time-out condition as ignoring the response was approximated from using the quiet room, progressing to the bedroom, to the child's sitting on a chair in the corner, to his being removed to the periphery of an activity, to eventually our ignoring his response.

We have observed that if one progressed too rapidly from the close control of the quiet room setting to a greater self-control condition such as the child's sitting on the periphery of a group activity, it could result in the child's failing to have a time-out. For example, if one removed a child from an activity and sat him down on the ground away from the group and the child continued to aggress or make inappropriate responses, the time-out procedure would not be effective, since he could elicit some kind of social reinforcers to maintain that behavior from staff or peers. Once again, the progression of the techniques used to administer the time-out procedure involved a shaping program, or successive approximation. We have preferred to use the time-out condition quickly with little or no verbalization except during the latter stages of the time-out techniques when verbal mediation would be indicated. Staff were typically required not to admonish the child when a time-out procedure was administered. Although children may perceive a time-out condition as punishment, this is not essential. Time-out is an extinction program in which one is trying to remove the child from reinforcing conditions maintaining some inappropriate response. The time-out conditions as discussed here are not in any way comparable to the seclusion orders in effect in many institutional programs. Seclusion orders are ones in which the child is removed from the group for abnormal behaviors, usually aggressive responses, and placed in a "padded cell" for extended intervals of time, even days. Such barbaric orders are not time-outs from reinforcers eliciting the behavior. Seclusion orders, and even long time-out orders such as 15 minutes, remove the child from the program to which he was admitted to learn new behaviors. While the child is in a quiet room he is unable to learn new responses. Extended time-outs and seclusion do not assist a total program; they simply diminish the time during which one is able to teach new and desired responses. A danger with a time-out condition, as well as with social punishment contingencies, is that untrained staff may use these contingencies vindictively toward the children. Extended time-out contingencies are not recommended for several other reasons. One is that while in the quiet room, the child may be behaving appropriately at some point but will be receiving no reinforcement for that behavior. The quiet room setting, at least for any extended interval of time, is more likely to elicit asocial behavior, which would only augment the isolative social responses of a schizophrenic child. We suspect that the seclusion practices of many hospitals only assist in training withdrawal behavior in a child. Duration in a quiet room setting is fertile ground for rehearsing stereotyped behaviors with the psychotic individual.

B. "STOP-THE-WORLD"

"Stop-the-world" is the term our staff use for a technique chiefly designed to achieve compliant behavior from a child after a specific request has been made. Basically the method is designed to deprive the child of any reinforcement for any behavior until compliance with the original request has been achieved. The technique might be applied whenever the child is stalling, complaining, or simply avoiding a specific task. At this point the staff member attempts to bring all events in the child's environment to a complete halt. For example, the child has been asked to make his bed, but keeps inviting other children to join him in playing with his cars. The staff member directs the children elsewhere, stating, "Bob can play with you when he finishes making his bed." The child is not served a meal, permitted to go out to play or to keep an appointment to see his parents until the original task has been completed. The first few times this technique is used with an extremely noncompliant child, the staff can expect to wait a long time for compliance. A wait of several hours, or even of a full day, was not unusual with our nine- to twelve-year-old boys. However, after the staff succeeds in holding out on the first few occasions, delays become infrequent and of short duration.

Using Situational Control to Strengthen Desired Behavior

Various interpersonal behaviors of a child are elicited by relatively specific interpersonal situations. A given child is assumed to behave according to a hierarchy of available responses to any given stimulus situation. For example, in a situation involving an adult's making a request of the child, the child may—to differing degrees of probability—respond with compliant, cheerful, cooperative, sulking, pleading, or attacking behaviors. These different responses have correspondingly differing degrees of desirability in our culture. The task of treatment is to increase the probability of desirable responses and decrease the probability of undesirable responses.

Among disturbed children, the undesirable responses occur at a high rate and interfere with the production of desirable responses. Frequently, too, the high rate of occurrence of undesired responses produces a reaction from others in the environment and the youngster is either deliberately punished or receives various kinds of uncontrolled negative feedback.

One method of increasing the relative frequency of desired responses is so to control the stimulus situation as to permit primarily stimuli that lead to the appropriate response. Thus, if a rejecting or attacking response is more likely when the interpersonal situation includes not only the requesting adult but also several peers, it would be beneficial to control the situation so that the child's peers are not present and the adult's request has a higher probability of evoking a cooperative response. At a later point, after the desired response has been well established, the more complicated situation in which peers are present can be introduced gradually and thus with greater success. This approach is consonant with accepted techniques for training such responses as motor or academic skills. For example, in teaching reading, one initially introduces a small number of words. The child's vocal response to these visual stimuli is over-learned before new words are presented. Gradually, the reading stimuli are made more and more complex. It would be unlikely that the child could learn to read were he faced initially with the task of making responses to thousands of different stimuli. In such a situation, a majority of his responses would be incorrect and go unreinforced or punished. Inappropriate reading responses would continue at a high rate. Further, in the relative deprivation of positive reinforcement, other more reinforcing behaviors, such as withdrawal from the teaching situation or aggression, would be likely to occur. This same logic can be applied to the analysis of interpersonal situations where the child does not consistently produce appropriate social responses.

Using a graded system of management orders, i.e., a level system, we control the child's exposure to various interpersonal situations. The situations in which it is highly probable that the child will produce desired behavior are maximized. Second, the child's exposure to any stimuli that would lead to undesired behavior is minimized. Gradually, as the desired behaviors are strengthened, the child is exposed to situations in which they might previously have occurred. Thus, he is initially exposed to simple, easily managed situations and later, gradually presented with more complex and difficult social situations. The procedure is analogous to shaping.

Basically, it is assumed that the 1:1 child-adult relationship is the simplest, for here most behaviors can be adult-directed, limited, and reinforced. There is a maximum opportunity to prevent the occurrence of inappropriate responses and capitalize upon the occurrences of appropriate responses. The most complex interpersonal situation is assumed to be the one in which a variety of adults and peers are present, and the child's behavior must be determined by a complex interaction of the behaviors of all of the other persons, with reinforcement often being quite delayed. Thus, at admission to the Center the child is placed on the lowest level of the program—he is on a 1:1 relationship with the staff member at all times. He is seldom exposed to any interaction with other children and spends most of his time within the limited confines of the cottage. When satisfactory behavior consistently occurs at this level, he can be advanced to the next level, where he is permitted slightly more freedom and a beginning interaction with other youngsters. From there, a gradual progression occurs through a number of levels, each one permitting the child more freedom and exposure to a more complex situation, and requiring from him greater responsibility and higher behavioral performance.

The exact management orders contained in a levels system should be developed with reference to the treatment setting, the ultimate behavioral expectations established for the children, and the particular children being treated. With our group of 9- to 12-year-old boys, we developed a system of twelve levels. With several outpatient children, we have helped the parents develop simplified levels systems aimed at more limited behavioral problems. Although the actual management orders for a levels system are extensive and detailed, it may assist the reader if we provide a few examples from the system we used with numerous inpatients.

At admission a youngster was usually placed on level two. The management at this level provided for close supervision on a 1:1 relationship with a staff member. The child's physical boundaries were primarily restricted to the upstairs area of the cottage living unit. He ate his meals alone with this staff member. He was permitted to be outdoors for a maximum of four 15-minute periods each day, and was allowed no activity or play time with other children. High gratification activities (such as candy-making, water play, or use of mechanical toys) were used extensively. Staff maintained high levels of social and, if appropriate, primary reinforcement. Special attention was given to the reinforcement of the relationship with staff and of compliant behavior.

Three or four days at this initial level were usually sufficient to produce consistent levels of positive behavior. The child would then be moved to level three, where more time outside was permitted, some interaction with small groups of peers was encouraged, and family visits to the cottage were allowed. At level four, the child was being gradually introduced to our intramural school by means of visiting the classroom or going along with staff to meet the other boys at dismissal time. At level four the staff still maintained close supervision, but no longer carried an exclusive 1:1 assignment with the child. On level five, the child was permitted to play outside for half-hour periods with no direct supervision. He was introduced to large group activities and began a regular classroom schedule. His first home visits could occur at this level. Level five management orders prohibited the use of the quiet room for time-outs or assaultive behavior. Both child and staff were required to handle such situations as they would in a home or school where a seclusion room would not be available.

Subsequent management levels gradually increased the complexity of activities to which the child was exposed and emphasized increasing opportunities for self-reliant behavior. For example, on level nine, the child was entered in our local public school; on level ten he was receiving extended home visits. At level eleven he was being introduced to a variety of community activities, such as a Scout troup, a Saturday afternoon at the movies, or solo trips to the public library. By now he was spending as much time in his own home with his parents as he was at the Center under staff supervision. Level twelve consisted of his final discharge from living at the Center and shifting to weekly outpatient visits. These outpatient visits would consist both of family therapy sessions and, where appropriate to the child's needs, participation in milieu activities.

The management orders contained in the levels system provided a constant set of guidelines for staff to use in training each child. Although applied flexibly and altered in accordance with each child's needs, these management orders provided an overall behavioral curriculum for each child, whose movement from level to level was decided by the entire staff after a review of behavioral data and the staff's subjective impressions of the child's performance. For each level the child was given a typewritten card which outlined the rules of that level and made note of behaviors the child must especially work on to achieve his next level. Most of the children carried these cards with them or pinned them to the wall in their rooms. Generally, achievement of a new level was accompanied by feelings of pride for both child and staff. We attempted to interpret to the child that his achievement of the next level was concrete evidence of his growth and increasing mastery of his problems.

After the initial few weeks at the Center, each boy's inappropriate behaviors would usually stabilize at a relatively low rate. We attempted to hold negative behaviors down while increasing the stress placed upon the child by moving him to a less structured level of management. Typically, movement to a higher level was accompanied by a temporary increase in negative behaviors and then stabilization at the new level. If a child's behavior became worse and remained that way, he was moved down one or more levels in the system and thereby given more structure. Although children often perceived upward and downward movements in the levels system as specific rewards and punishments, our intention was primarily to modify the overall level of structure given the child in order to promote the highest possible rates of positive behavior and permit staff to give high levels of positive reinforcement.

Our particular set of management orders included one punishment level, known as level one. Repeated serious misbehavior, such as violent assaultive attacks, could result in movement to level one. On level one all personal possessions were removed from the child's room and he was required to stay in his room in pajamas. Meals were served in his room on a tray, and he was permitted virtually no social interaction with staff or peers. He might be kept on level one for one or two days. Level one was used only for repeated serious incidents in an attempt to highlight the importance of the behavior. The child was required to conform to level one limits before he could once again move up through the entire series of levels.

Systematic Desensitization in the Milieu

The classical methods of reciprocal inhibition are frequently difficult to employ with the severely disturbed anxious child. He is often so anxious, negativistic, or hostile that direct training in relaxation is impossible. Consequently, the treatment program must make use of common events in the milieu to reduce stimulus specific anxieties. An obvious example would be to help a child with a fear of swimming by promoting water play in the bathroom, walks to the beach, skipping stones, wading in shallow streams, etc., gradually working up to the point of the child's full immersion in the water and beginning swimming lessons. To accomplish this type of progressive desensitization staff must be extremely skillful in (1) observing the child's varying degrees of anxiety in response to specific events in the milieu, and (2) creatively manipulating the everyday environment to pair relaxation stimuli with gradually increasing anxiety stimuli. Often this pairing must occur on the spot as opportunities present themselves. For example, one water-phobic youngster had resisted all carefully planned efforts to desensitize him to water. No matter what the staff did he would refuse to go any further than the water's edge. Finally on an overnight camping trip one of the staff noticed that he showed a particular fondness for the air mattress and put this observation together with the fact that the only place the child really appeared relaxed was in bed. The staff member took advantage of the moment, cancelled a previously planned hike, and subtly encouraged the boys to discover that the air mattresses could be dragged to the beach and floated. Within ten minutes the previously water-phobic youngster had forgotten his fears of water and his negativism at staff for trying to persuade him to swim. He shortly was seen splashing and floating on his air mattress with the other boys.

On other occasions a child can be quickly helped through fears if a detailed desensitization program is worked out. One boy was extremely fearful of being hurt in any physical activity. A series of hierarchies was constructed to help him deal with this fear. One of these programs worked specifically on his fear of being hurt by a thrown ball. Another dealt with his fear of joining in an activity of rolling down a small hill in a large cardboard barrel. Those two hierarchies are detailed below as examples. The staff worked with the boy on each hierarchy for about 15 minutes a day, using the boy's verbalized anxiety and physical appearance as cues of when to expose him to stronger or weaker fear stimuli. He was not exposed to the next most-feared situation on the hierarchy until he appeared comfortable at the current level.

Ball-throwing and catching progression

1. Kick large playground ball around cottage
2. Hand soft red ball back and forth to staff
3. Toss soft red ball
   a) staff throws softly and directly into his hands
   b) start at 3 feet and gradually increase to about 10 feet
4. Staff stands about 4 feet away, and throws ball less accurately
   a) to one side
   b) in front of him
   c) toward his face
5. Increase distance and repeat number 4.
6. Repeat above steps but bounce ball at him.
7. Stand about 6 feet apart. Throw to his hands, but gradually throw harder
8. Repeat, gradually combining all previous steps, and varying the distance between staff and him
9. Repeat previous steps with soccer ball
10. Repeat previous steps with basketball
11. Repeat previous steps with softball
12. Repeat previous steps with hard baseball
13. Repeat previous steps with football

Barrell Roll Progression

1. Playing near blue tube (a cloth crawl-through tube about 6 feet long)
2. Touching blue tube

3. Crawling in tube
4. Playing near barrels
5. Touching and kicking barrel
6. Crawling in and out of barrel
7. Rocking slightly in barrel
8. Rolling from smaller to longer distances on level ground with staff controlling the barrel
9. Rolling down slight inclines
10. Rolling down the hill in the barrel

The items in these hierarchies were selected after discussion and play observation with the boy, and the order in the hierarchy was established on the basis of the boy's reaction to trial runs at the activities. This boy subsequently used his learning in these two hierarchies to design his own desensitization programs for his fears about going to religious instruction classes and entering public school.

Desensitization programs require considerable skill, sensitivity, and flexibility on the part of staff. The staff can make rigorous observations to identify fear and relaxation stimuli, but they must be extremely creative to be able correctly to put the two in juxtaposition as milieu events may permit. One staff member described at a staff meeting how he succeeded in helping a child with a fear of group participation and an inability to share his possessions with other boys.

"Well, I had tried this summer several times to get Bill involved in some kind of group behavior and singing was the one thing, on camping trips, we had tried, I had tried, we had tried to make very simple songs, tried to get him just to clap his hands, to do anything like that, so he could get involved in some sort of group process from singing to playing games, that kind of interaction. He just shied away from it completely. Last night I was in his room and he wanted to play the guitar. So, we started playing the guitar a little bit and I showed him the few chords that I knew, and while I was playing the chords, I was singing a note, along with each chord--woo, woo, woo, woo, up and down, as the chords went. And all of a sudden, just totally spontaneously, Bill joined in, doing the same thing. So, I played them, and played them—those four chords back and forth again and again, and then Bill did them, and so I helped him to learn those four chords. Then he kept singing as he played and I kept singing as he played. And pretty soon we're singing very loudly, and Ken sort of stopped at the door, and I said, 'Can you sing along, Ken?' And he said, 'Sure,' And he just walked in, and sat down and *he* sang along and Bill continued to sing, and louder than ever. And, so we're going, and Ken picked up the guitar and I was surprised to see that he could play *Tom Dooley* and a couple of other things, and he started playing and then we started singing words rather than just going up and down the scale with the chords, and Bill sang the words right along with us. Then Joey walked in and just started singing along. And Bill just continued, as loud as ever, and then, after it was all over, he said, 'Could I show the boys the chords that you showed me?' I said, 'Yes,' and he showed the chords and continued singing as he went along, while he was showing them the chords. I just couldn't believe it. He was letting them use *his* guitar. It was really the most spontaneous thing I've ever seen Bill do in that kind of an activity. It was really great! It was just really a pleasant experience for me. Things started going so well I just kinda got wrapped up in it. It was just so different, it was, it was like suddenly a whole new self-image had developed, you know, in Bill—he was assertive and just really responsive to everything that went on in there. Like I was telling Chuck, maybe the guitar is his thing. He's found his thing."

CHAPTER SIX

Unexpected Values of Social Reinforcers

A cursory review of studies in which social reinforcers are varied as independent variables may lead one to the erroneous conclusion that there is commonality of effects for social reinforcers. The term "generalized reinforcer" (Ferster & Skinner, 1957) has not been defined to imply that the reinforcer has generalized to a cultural group, but that the reinforcement contingency has an effect on particular responses under certain discriminative stimulus situations for certain individuals. Examples often provided of generalized reinforcers include social attention, affection, tokens, money, and school grades. These examples are classes of contingencies that may be applicable as generalized reinforcers for a person's response repertoire, and they may indeed be effective for a large group of individuals.

When one is confronted with the realities of clinical treatment, one realizes that social reinforcers must be defined as unique to each person's learning history. Positive and negative conditioned reinforcers, aversive stimuli, generalized reinforcers of various kinds, in principle may describe how groups of individuals learn, but when one is identifying the unique response repertoire of a patient the particular stimuli acquiring these reinforcement characteristics will be idiosyncratic to each individual. Social reinforcement contingencies are presumed to be acquired by being paired with primary reinforcement contingencies. The primary reinforcers with which the social stimuli are paired to acquire reinforcement effects may be a single primary reinforcer, or numerous primary reinforcements, and thereby become defined as a generalized reinforcer (Ferster and Skinner,

1957). Assuming that social reinforcers are acquired in this manner, one may not presume commonality of social reinforcers across individuals. We do assume some degree of commonality of social reinforcers in the society in which a child is raised. Unfortunately, there are no available data to indicate which social reinforcers are predominantly common to a group of people. The notion of "expected social reinforcers" is used frequently in this text, but each child's abnormal behavior must be studied in terms of the uniqueness of his own social reinforcers. The uniqueness of those reinforcers may have more meaning if contrasted to the more dominant social reinforcers available to the child in his natural environment.

It is essential, for the accurate use of the term "social reinforcers," that one identify the specific contingencies available to each child and their relative effectiveness. One cannot presume commonality of learning history across subjects in the acquisition of their respective social reinforcement contingencies. One does presume that there is some commonality within a culture of those social reinforcers that are effective for a child.

It is demonstrable in the learning-theory model that secondary reinforcers may be acquired by being paired with primary reinforcement contingencies. This has been well documented since the pioneering work of John B. Wolfe (1936) on secondary reinforcement. Unfortunately, it has not been clearly demonstrated that social reinforcers are acquired historically by being paired with primary reinforcement contingencies. This learning procedure is speculated, and the paradigm has been demonstrated in the laboratory (e.g., Lovaas *et al.,* 1966). It is suspected that stimulus conditions of comfort and pain serve as a primary reinforcer in child-rearing. The painful or primary aversive stimulus condition may vary from a spanking, or perhaps the case may more universally be that of loud shouting at the child of the conditioned aversive stimulus, with the strong auditory stimulation being the primary aversive stimulus. Lack of affection or withdrawal of affection is also presumed to be responsible for conditioning social reinforcers. The question remains of how conditioned social reinforcers acquire their autonomy, so that they do not have to be "backed-up" with primary reinforcers periodically (Wike, 1966). We suspect that most social reinforcers become generalized reinforcers, and not because of being paired with numerous primary reinforcers. It is our hypothesis that social reinforcers serve to condition other social reinforcers. The discriminative stimulus conditions maintaining the operant behavior continue to do so because of the variety of social reinforcers available for the behavior. Thus, there is never mass practice on a particular social reinforcer so that it extinguishes, but it continues to be trained on a thin schedule as a generalized reinforcer. The breakdown of such a reinforcement condition would ultimately lead to that behavior which we describe as depression, or the extinction of available social reinforcers.

We suspect that social reinforcers become autonomous, in fact, they may be more aptly described as primary reinforcers, since they may become the most dominant reinforcers. It is obvious that individuals will die for anticipated social reinforcers which they will never receive, such as dying for a patriotic cause. Humans will starve themselves for social reinforcers. This is presumed to be the case in anorexia nervosa, since it has been demonstrated that social reinforcement maintains non-eating behavior. The treatment demonstration of anorexia nervosa does not substantially indicate that it is entirely determined on a behavioral level. It may be that there are physiological determinants for non-eating behavior that can be maintained and reversed behaviorally. In any event, it is demonstrable that one may starve himself to death in order to receive social reinforcement of various kinds. We had a very clear example of this problem with an autistic child, eight years of age, who was referred to the Treatment Center when she was seven. One of her dominant problems was that she preferred to eat only cookies of various kinds, a sustained diet which had resulted in an extremely poor physical condition at date of admission. The first step in her program, as with many of the autistic children, would be to teach her to eat a variety of foods at age-sufficient quantities. The program was initiated in which decreasing amounts of preferred foods (cookies), and later the foods which became reinforcing, were used to reinforce her eating of non-preferred foods. This program was effective, within a six-month interval, in teaching the child to eat a variety of foods. When she had been at home, she maintained her diet by having temper tantrums on a negative reinforcement schedule for her parents. If she were not given the preferred food, she would have a temper tantrum which would cease—and serve as a negative reinforcement—when her parents gave her the preferred kind of cookies. It became apparent at the conclusion of the food-shaping program that she still had staff on a negative reinforcement schedule. Staff members had to eat beside her at all meals and allow her to touch them in a certain autistic manner lightly on the arm, or else she would throw her food about, have a temper tantrum, and knock items off the table. Thus, she still had the problem of eating to reinforce adults for sitting beside her on a 1:1 basis at all times and agreeing to be touched on the arm lightly throughout the meal. She was operating for social reinforcement, i.e., to have staff seated beside her, by eating food. It was our conclusion that social reinforcement was more basic than food was for this youngster.

A program was established in which staff attention in the form of sitting beside her with body contact were diminished on successive meals. This program followed one in which she had been allowed to enter the dining room and to go to the table and eat if she preferred. In that earlier program she had refused to eat except for small amounts of breakfast for a one-week interval. Her refusal to eat was almost too much for the staff to bear. During the course of one meal, the investigator removed her from the room on the premise that all the social reinforcers available in that room, although not given to her directly, historically signaled that she would receive some kind of reinforcement. It was observed that when she was removed from the room during mealtime she would persist to work her way around to the door so that she could see clearly and listen to everything that was transpiring in the dining room. It was hypothesized that she was working for those social reinforcers which were historically available for non-eating behavior. The program was then begun in which the investigator or staff would take her and seat her at the table and hold her by the collar of her shirt in the chair. She was a slight child, so this was rather easy to do. During the meal, initially she would swing her arms about and try to knock all the food off the table and refuse to eat. The staff member would wait until she settled, after which he would then offer a small tidbit of a preferred food (such as bread, or other foods available in the meal). As she began to operate for that food, they faded the amount of holding her physically and being seated beside her for successive meals. Thus, the staff were using social reinforcement in the form of holding, touching, and being seated beside her as the reinforcement condition to train her to eat without having staff on a negative reinforcement paradigm.

In this case social reinforcement was used to condition eating appropriately. We now had to make social reinforcement decreasingly contingent upon eating unassisted. Again, as in any shaping program, we had difficulty in measuring the effectiveness of the program simply because the response being trained would change on successive days. The case studies in Chapter 7 contain instances in which food was not reinforcing to a child, and had to be conditioned to acquire reinforcing effects for the eventual acquisition of appropriate social reinforcers.

It is our hypothesis that the unique value of social reinforcers for each child is crucial to the explanation of that child's emotional disturbance, as well as to the treatment for that problem. There has been emphasis placed on unspecified social attention as the maintaining reinforcement contingency for a disruptive behavior that would lead to the diagnosis of the emotional disturbance. Historically, there has been considerable emphasis placed on the responses which lead one to define and individualize emotional disturbance, and there has been some emphasis on stimulus conditions, but both stimulus and response have been considered as unaffiliated with certain reinforcement contingencies as variables in emotional disturbance. It is our conclusion that it would be erroneous to separate stimulus, response, and reinforcement in the understanding of any habit patterns leading to the identification and treatment of emotional disturbance.

Deviation from presumed group norms for stimulus, response, and reinforcers seems plausible in the definition of emotionally disturbed behavior. As previously stated, it is unfortunate that there are no standards currently available on appropriate social behaviors for certain cultural groups. One has to use what is simply identified as clinical judgment in concluding that certain responses, stimulating and reinforcing contingencies, are abnormal and lead to the diagnosis of emotional disturbance. We are identifying emotional disturbance as a socially deviant pattern of behavior, rather than as an internally driven problem. This is not to presume that all behaviors described in the case studies were acquired exclusively by social learning. There is considerable research indicated for identifying those conditions which are organically determined but behaviorally maintained that may help us in understanding autistic children.

It is hypothesized that the social reinforcement contingencies maintaining emotionally disturbed behavior are at variance from what may be expected in the normal population. Obviously, the emotionally disturbed child did not receive the usual forms of social reward for these disturbed behaviors. In fact, these children are prone to receive social punishment and, in many instances, it may be such conditions which maintain their abnormal behaviors. If this is a correct assumption, it becomes obvious that exploring the uniqueness of each child's reinforcers that maintain his deviant behaviors is necessary before explaining and treating his inappropriate behaviors. The study described below was the first really to support our contention that reinforcement contingencies maintaining abnormal behavior must be studied individually.

The intent of the study was to determine if negative practice would be a recommended technique for symptom control of Gilles de La Tourette's disease (Gilles de La Tourette, 1885). Kellman's (1965) excellent review of the literature on this syndrome provides a summary of the dominant symptomatology as well as the relative effectiveness of numerous treatment procedures. The symptomatology of this disease includes coprolalia, echolalia, and numerous tics and mannerisms which follow sequential patterns unique to each individual. The etiology of this syndrome is considered to be functional (Dunlap, 1960; Eisenberg *et al.*, 1959), although the possibility of neurological involvement remains in question (Wechsler, 1952). It appears that chemotherapy has been the most effective treatment procedure, with phenothiazines and piperazines being the most consistently effective medications for the symptom control of the tics and mannerisms characteristic of this disease (Kellman, 1965).

Since negative practice has been so successful in eliminating single and multiple tics of a functional etiology (Eysenck, 1960), it seems reasonable to suspect that the tics and mannerisms of Gilles de La Tourette's Disease may also be amenable to such treatment. The reader is referred to Eysenck's text for detailed studies on the procedure of negative practice. Yates (1958) discusses the learning theory relevant to the effects of negative practice. In simplified terms, negative practice involves having the subject deliberately rehearse as accurately and rapidly as possible the tic desired to be eliminated for a given period of time.

The following is a preliminary study on the effectiveness of the method of negative practice. It was designed so that accurate data could be obtained from a single subject who was available for a limited time. The rationale of the study was that if one tic could be effectively controlled with the technique of negative practice, then we would be warranted in conducting later research designed to employ systematically this technique to control all of the tics present in patients demonstrating Gilles de La Tourette's Disease. The study was divided into two experiments. The first was a test of the effectiveness of negative practice; the second experiment was an investigation of the reinforcement conditions responsible for the acquisition and extinction of the tics in the patient.

Experiment I

METHOD

Subject. The subject for this case study was a 14-year-10-month-old male schizophrenic who also demonstrated the symptomatology characteristic of Gilles de La Tourette's Disease. This adolescent had demonstrated schizophrenic behavior since he was eight years old, and the tics and mannerisms were sufficiently present when he was ten so that a formal diagnosis of Gilles de La Tourette's was made then. The patient was definitely psychotic throughout this study. He had been in residential treatment at the Children's Treatment Center for two consecutive years, and there was no significant reduction of his schizophrenic behavior during the course of this study. The predominant symptoms which warranted the diagnosis of Gilles de La Tourette's Disease in the patient were as follows: coprolalia, verbal outbursts, fingernail-snapping, extending and jerking forearm, rotating shoulders, raising foot and touching heel, foot-tapping, dragging foot while walking and running, eye-blinking, raising of eyebrows, spitting, coughing, and guttural "CH" sounds while speaking, repeated touching of objects, ritualistic mannerisms when performing routine activities, wiggling of ears, head-jerking, facial distortions, twisting of chin, hitting abdomen with right hand, bending forwards and backwards at the waist, pushing off with one foot when beginning to walk, and repeated smelling of objects. It was obvious that this patient would be a difficult subject for the study, since he was almost incapacitated by these tics and he was also psychotic. This subject's attention span was delimited, his motivation to perform in any activity was extremely low, and his cooperation with the study was variable. He had two complete neurological and EEG evaluations, both of which failed to reveal evidence of neurological dysfunction. The subject received medication (Mellaril, thioridazine, 25 mg., three times daily) before, during, and after this study.

Procedure. The design of this experiment involved four steps. The first was to choose one of the most dominant tics present in the subject. His eyebrow-raising tic was chosen, since it was observed to be one of the most consistently present. The second step of this experiment was to obtain an operant level of the incidence of the eyebrow-raising tic. This operant level was established by taking three-minute time samples twice daily during which a frequency count was taken. One time sample was taken just prior to breakfast and one in the evening after supper. Precaution was taken to insure that the subject was unaware that he was being observed. Frequent checks were made on agreement between observers, and it was found that the frequency counts always agreed within one to three counts. These differences occurred when the subject was not facing one of the observers. This step of the experiment lasted for eight days.

The third step involved four weeks of treatment during which the subject received 17 negative practice sessions on the eyebrow-raising tic in the investigator's office. Each treatment session lasted 23 minutes: four 5-minute negative practice periods with three 1-minute rest breaks between the practice periods. The subject did not practice alone in the cottage, as would be recommended procedure with this technique. In this study, the subject frequently had to be reoriented to the task, and he was encouraged and praised by the investigator when he cooperated optimally. During each treatment session, he was not engaged in conversation with the investigator. The cottage staff and the subject's therapist were requested not to change their reaction to his tics. The subject received medication and psychotherapy long before, during, and after this study. Since these treatment conditions had previously been ineffective in reducing the tics, and were held constant throughout this study, treatment effects were not considered to be a function of either chemotherapy or psychotherapy.

The fourth step of the experiment was four consecutive weeks of post-treatment observation, derived by continuing the twice-daily time samples throughout this phase just as they had been during the pre-treatment and treatment phases of this experiment.

The design of this experiment enabled the investigator to compare the incidence of the eyebrow tic under three conditions. The pre-treatment phase yielded the operant level, or base-rate occurrence of the tic; the treatment phase demonstrated the immediate effect of negative practice on the eyebrow tic; and the post-treatment phase offered data pertinent to the continuing effects of the treatment procedure.

RESULTS

Table 6.1 shows the mean number and the standard deviations of eyebrow tic frequencies as observed in the cottage time samples during the pre-treatment, treatment, and post-treatment steps of this experiment.

Table 6.1. Mean Eyebrow Tic Frequencies Derived from Daily Time Samples before, during, and after Negative Practice

	Treatment Condition		
	Baseline	*Negative Practice*	*Return to Baseline*
Number days per treatment condition	8	27	21
Number time samples taken	12	39	36
Mean tic frequencies	53.33	14.15	14.69
Standard deviation	35.17	10.17	16
Range	122	39	61

Figure 6.1 graphically illustrates the effect of negative practice on the incidence of this tic as observed in these daily 3-minute time samples. It is interesting to note that not only did the tics diminish drastically in this short-term treatment, but that there was also a corresponding decline in variability. Although there was an increase in variability during the post-treatment phase, the mean frequency of the tic was comparable to that which occurred during negative practice.

DISCUSSION

The results of the first experiment of this study led to two tentative conclusions. The first was that negative practice was an effective procedure for the control of tics in Gilles de La Tourette's Syndrome. The second was that the tics of the patient's syndrome could be modified as separate habits.

What may be an appropriate explanation for the effectiveness of negative practice in this particular case? The usual explanation for the effects of negative practice is derived from Hull's Theory (Yates, 1958). In simple terms, the $_{s}I_{r}$, or the habit of not responding with a tic, acquired greater strength than the habit of responding with a tic. It is theorized that during massed practice, reactive inhibition (I_r) maximizes to the point where the subject is unable to rehearse the habit, and this resultant behavior, or habit, of not responding $({}_{s}I_{r})$ is reinforced by the drive-reducing effects of the rest period. However, there were two cues derived from the study which led the investigator to suspect that the acquisition of these tics, as well as the effectiveness of negative practice, could be explained better in terms of social reinforcers.

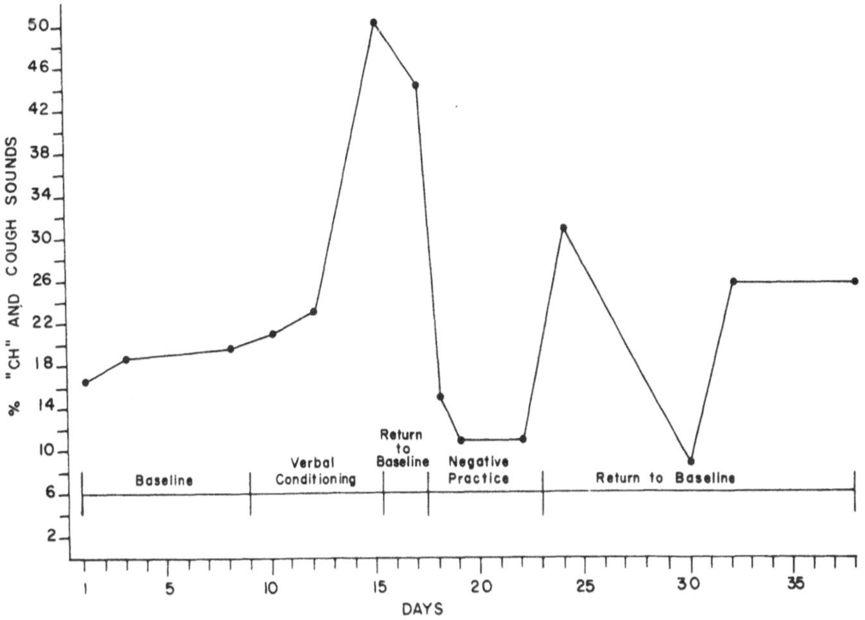

Figure 6.1. Mean Eyebrow Tics for Successive Days before, during, and after Negative Practice Sessions

The first cue stemmed from the investigator's reactions to the subject's variable cooperation during the negative practice sessions. The investigator noted that on the data sheets he had recorded that he was verbally reinforcing the subject by saying, "very good," "good job," "you're doing very well now," when the subject was cooperating best during the negative practice sessions. These responses by the examiner would be expected to act as positive social reinforcers. When the data were considered, however, it appeared that during negative practice the tic responses were being evoked in the presence of the investigator's verbal praise, which would be expected to act as a positive social reinforcer, and yet the tics declined in frequency. This cue suggested that the investigator's verbalization served as a social punishment for this subject's behavior.

The second cue relevant to the development and continuation of the tic behavior in this subject was that his parents were extremely irritated by his tics. A study of the subject's social history indicated that he has never been able to display overt aggression behaviors toward his parents, since such reactions would result in punishment regardless of how warranted the aggressive responses may have been. However, his parents regarded his tics as beyond his control, and although they were obviously irritated by them, they would not punish him overtly for their occurrence since he was not held responsible for them. The subject also stated he could not control his tics. Thus, in retrospect, it impressed the investigator that the parents' response of manifesting irritation in the form of facial expressions and verbal comments, which would be expected to serve as social punishment in most cases, in this instance served as positive reinforcers for the subject. The investigator suspected that the tics of this subject could be described as alternate aggressive responses which were reinforced by responses of others that reflected their irritation and annoyance with his behavior. This interpretation was supported by observations in the cottage. One observation which suggested that the subject's tics and mannerisms were alternative aggressive responses was that these behaviors would diminish drastically whenever he became overtly aggressive. It was also noted in the cottage that when attention was directed toward his tics they would increase in frequency. Quite often the attention which was focussed toward these tics was one of slight annoyance by the staff members. Although staff members made an effort to ignore these behaviors they would occasionally express their distaste for them, implying that these tics were on a variable ratio schedule. This, of course, assumes that the staff members' negative responses were serving as positive reinforcers for this subject.

Thus, it impressed the investigator that the reinforcers for the tics in this subject were actually what would be expected to be social punishment stimuli, and that many expected positive social reinforcers would have the effect of social punishment stimuli for him. If this reversed polarity of presumed common social reinforcers was correct for this subject, one would hypothesize that the frequency of a given response in him would be diminished by being paired with a positive reinforcer and that the same response would be increased in frequency if paired with what would be expected to be a social punishment stimulus. The second experiment of this study was designed to test these hypotheses.

Experiment II

METHOD

Procedure. The method by which these hypotheses were to be tested was to take one characteristic tic-like response of this subject and determine if it would increase in frequency when paired with a typical aversive social stimulus, and also decrease in frequency when paired with a typical positive reinforcer during negative practice sessions. The response chosen was a guttural "CH" sound which was invariably accompanied with a cough. This tic-like response was prevalent in the subject's response repertoire and was considered to be a symptom of Gilles de La Tourette's syndrome.

We also decided to take two other verbal responses and pair them with what ostensibly would be considered positive social reinforcers while the "CH" sound was paired with a social punishment stimulus. These two verbal responses were the words "owl" and "box," which the subject talked about incessantly in the cottage and which were considered to be part of his psychotic ideation.

The design of this study involved five steps: (1) to obtain a baseline level of the "CH," "owl," and "box" responses; (2) to conduct verbal conditioning sessions in which the "CH" response was socially punished and "owls" and "boxes" were positively reinforced; (3) to cease reinforcing these responses to ascertain if extinction would occur; (4) to subject the "CH" response to negative practice in conjunction with positive reinforcement; and (5) to determine, during a post-treatment period, whether the "CH" response would return to the baseline level.

This entire study took 38 days. The first step involved days 1 through 8, during which three 3-minute speech samples were recorded in the cottage by a research assistant to obtain the operant level of the "CH" verbal tic and verbalizations dealing with owls and boxes. These speech samples were recorded on days 1, 3, and 8. During these speech samples, the subject was requested to talk on any subject he wished.

The second step of the experiment was a verbal conditioning regimen on days 9, 10, 11, 12, and 15. During this verbal conditioning regimen, 3-minute speech samples were obtained in the cottage on days 10, 12, and 15. The verbal conditioning regimen involved bringing the subject to the investigator's office and requesting that the subject talk for 35 to 45 minutes on any topic he wished. The investigator did not direct the conversation and responsed only to direct questions. During verbal conditioning, whenever the subject made the "CH" and cough sound, the investigator would always turn toward him and frown in a disparaging manner. Thus, the "CH" verbal tic-like response was paired 100% of the time with what would be considered a social punishment condition. Whenever the subject said the word "owl," the investigator chuckled in a good-humored manner; whenever the subject mentioned the word "box," the investigator said, "uh, huh," and turned toward him in an attempt to convey interest in the topic. The words "owl" and "box" were thus paired with a response by the investigator that would be expected to serve as a positive social reinforcement with most children.

The third step involved days 16 and 17, when the previously positively reinforced and punished verbal responses were no longer reinforced by the investigator, in order to determine if extinction would occur. Speech samples were taken in the cottage on both of these days. All verbal conditioning and extinction sessions were tape-recorded and analyzed for percent of verbalizations which were "CH" sounds and total frequency of the words "owl" and "box."

The fourth step of the study involved days 18, 19, 22, and 23, when the "CH" sound was subjected to negative practice according to the same procedure used with the eyebrow-raising tic in the first experiment. The subject was requested to rehearse this "CH" sound as rapidly and accurately as possible. While he was cooperating in rehearsing the tic the investigator would verbally reinforce him by saying, "You're doing a good job," "Very nice," "That's right," "Good," and "Keep it up, you're doing a good job now." During each of the four negative practice sessions, there were four 5-minute periods of practice with three 1-minute interperiod rest breaks.

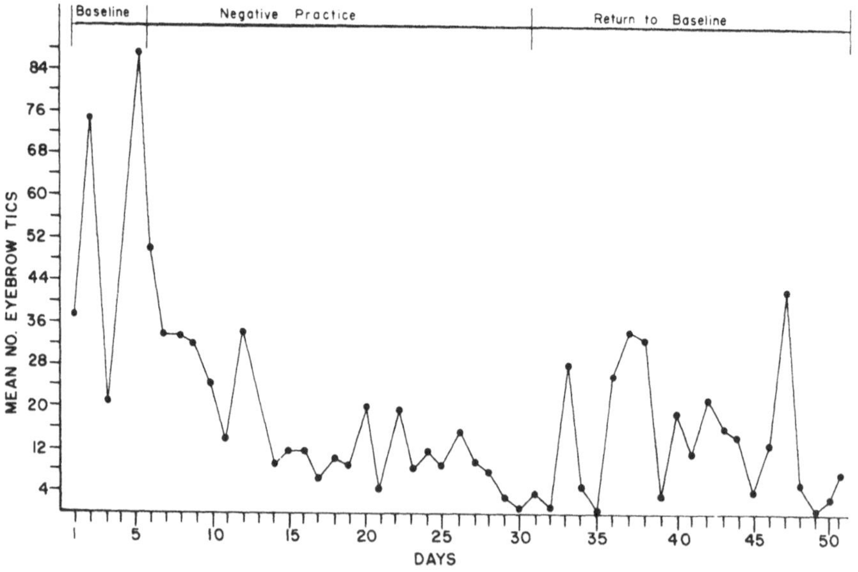

Figure 6.2. Per Cent of Total Verbalizations Which Were "CH" and Cough Sounds for Each Speech Sample Taken in Cottage during Successive Treatment Conditions

Speech samples were recorded in the cottage by the research assistant immediately after each negative practice session.

The fifth and last step of the study was the post-treatment period, which lasted for days 24 through 38. On days 31, 33, and 38, speech samples were taken in the cottage in order to determine whether the response rate increased or decreased.

RESULTS

Figure 6.2 graphically illustrates the percent of "CH" and cough sounds derived from the fifteen tape-recorded speech samples taken in the cottage during this study. Table 6.2 also shows these same percentages in relation to the treatment conditions of pre-treatment, verbal conditioning, extinction, negative practice, and post-treatment. During verbal conditioning, the "CH" sounds had been paired with the examiner's facial scowl and the frequency of that response doubled. There was only a slight decline of this response during the extinction phase. During the negative practice sessions

Table 6.2. Per Cent Total Verbalizations Which Were "CH" and Cough Sounds and References to "Owls" and "Boxes" during Speech Samples in Each Treatment Condition in Experiment II

Treatment Condition	*Day Speech Sample Taken*	*% "CH" and Cough Sounds*	*References to "Owls"*	*References to "Boxes"*
Baseline	1	17	—	2
	3	19	2	—
	8	20	—	—
Verbal Conditioning	10	21	—	—
	12	23	—	—
	15	50	—	—
Return to Baseline	16	47	—	—
	17	44	—	—
	18	15	—	—
Negative Practice	19	11	—	—
	22	11	—	—
	23	31	—	—
Return to Baseline	30	9	—	—
	32	26	—	—
	38	26	—	—

the response diminished drastically, as was also found in the experiment with the eyebrow-raising tic. When negative practice ceased, the response rate again increased, was initially variable, and then approximated the pretreatment level. This effect suggests that the negative practice accompanied by verbal reinforcement was an effective procedure in controlling the verbal tic response.

Table 6.2 indicates that the subject seldom referred to either "owls" or "boxes" during the speech samples taken in the cottage. These data seemed rather incongruous in consideration of the cottage staff's report that these topics dominated his conversation. The investigator reexamined the speech samples derived by the research assistant and found that on the first sample she had said, "Everyone's always telling me how you talk about 'owls' and 'boxes,' but you've never talked to me about them. Why don't you tell me about them?" This request by the research assistant was spoken in a manner which conveyed interest, but, as would be expected for this subject, such a response apparently served as a social punishment and he ceased speaking of "owls" and "boxes" in her presence. However, according to staff reports he continued to speak on these topics in the cottage, and as evidenced in Table 6.3, he repeatedly referred to "owls" and "boxes" in the first verbal conditioning session with the investigator. These verbal responses were almost completely extinguished in the investigator's presence during the verbal conditioning sessions when they were paired with what the investigator considered to be positive social reinforcers.

Table 6.3. Per Cent Total Verbalizations Which Were "CH" and Cough Sounds and References to "Owls" and "Boxes" during Verbal Conditioning and Extinction Sessions in Experiment II

	Treatment Condition						
	Verbal conditioning sessions					*Baseline sessions*	
% "CH" and cough sounds	11	20	15.8	7.4	22.2	21.4	23.9
References to "owls"	29	—	—	—	1	2	—
References to "boxes"	16	—	—	—	2	—	1

Table 6.3 shows the percent frequency of the "CH" sounds and the usage of the words "owls" and "boxes" present during the five verbal conditioning and two extinction sessions of this study. On day 4 of the verbal conditioning period there was a drastic reduction of the "CH" and cough sounds, suggesting that the investigator's facial scowl was at that time serving as

a social punishment. However, the interesting point was that on that day the subject was overtly angry toward the investigator, and expressed this by calling him "stupid," and making numerous other derogatory remarks including a threat to rearrange the furniture in the office in a rather violent fashion. This behavioral change was in agreement with the cottage staff's observation that when the subject does respond with overt aggression there is an immediate reduction of his tics. This clinical observation was interpreted to support the hypothesis that these tic behaviors are alternative aggressive responses.

General Discussion

This study revealed some rather interesting information on the treatment of Gilles de La Tourette's Syndrome as well about as the role of social reinforcers in the acquisition of these abnormal behaviors in this subject. The first experiment indicated that negative practice can be an effective procedure for the reduction of the numerous tics and mannerisms which characterize this syndrome. The results also suggest that Gilles de La Tourette's Syndrome can be treated as a series of simple learned habits, which implies that, although the etiology of this syndrome may be organic, it can be functionally maintained. The data supporting these two conclusions are tentative, since this is a case study which merits systematic replication with similar cases, and since the tic was not subjected to complete extinction.

The second experiment was suggested by a few incidental cues which led the investigator to test the hypothesis that the effects of negative practice for this subject could be best interpreted in terms of social reinforcers. The second experiment was also designed to investigate the reinforcement conditions under which the tics and mannerisms of this syndrome were acquired by the subject. As we mentioned, the investigator noted that he had been inadvertently pairing what would be considered positive verbal reinforcement with the tic which the subject was rehearsing during negative practice. This suggested that the experimenter had either violated strict negative practice procedure, or that verbal reinforcement had absolutely no effect on this subject's behavior, or that these verbal reinforcers had acquired a punishing valence for this subject and were indeed responsible for the treatment effect. These possible explanations had to be investigated, since they were so contradictory. A review of the subject's social history and current behavior in the cottage strongly suggested that these tics were acquired as alternative aggressive responses and were reinforced by attention from his parents and cottage staff. The quality of this attention would be expected to act as a social punishment for the average child, since it included annoyed glances and derogatory comments about the grotesqueness of his behavior. However, if these tics are viewed as an alternative aggressive response, they were highly effective in irritating other persons, which apparently has acquired a strong reinforcing value for this subject's behavior. The social reinforcers which would be expected to serve as positive reinforcers, such as various forms of verbal praise, had acquired a punishment value for this schizophrenic boy. The second section of our study was a test of the effectiveness of what ostensibly appeared as positive reinforcers and social punishment stimuli in the control of abnormal behavior.

When the subject's "CH" and cough verbal tic was paired on a 100% schedule with the investigator's disparaging frown, the relative frequency of that tic doubled in his free conversation with the investigator. At the same time the incidence of speaking of owls and boxes, that characterized his conversation in the cottage and in the school, dropped out in the investigator's presence after being paired with what would be described as positive social reinforcement. When the "CH" and cough verbal tics were subjected to negative practice and also paired with positive verbal reinforcement, the frequency dropped below the baseline level. This negative practice of the verbal tics served as a replication of the first section of this study and, in conjunction with the verbal conditioning data, demonstrated that this behavior could be varied by reinforcement conditions.

This information sheds considerable light on the abnormal behavior of this adolescent. For example, since social punishment stimuli are paired with deviant behavior in our society, and since punishment stimuli had acquired a positive valence for this boy, it is no surprise that his abnormal behavior has been sustained. Also, some of the usual positive social reinforcers have acquired a punishment valence for this youngster, which probably explains why psychotherapy and the employment of positive social reinforcement that characterized his residential treatment had failed to alter his behavior.

This child was described as having reversed polarity of expected social reinforcers. This interpretation was probably oversimplified. Subsequent studies revealed that the expected direction (i.e., acceleration vs. deceleration) of emotionally disturbed children's reinforcers may vary with different persons, concurrent stimulus conditions, etc., but are all unique to each child.

This single-subject, single-response study was a combination of several pilot studies in which we were attempting to identify what was maintaining the abnormal behavior of the child. In this experimental study, it was apparent that the child's abnormal behaviors of the tics were maintained by the converse of the expected social reinforcers to maintain or accelerate behavior. This complete deviation from the expected social reinforcers for maintaining behavior we have identified as "reversed polarity" of social reinforcers. This is clearly demonstrable in the case of Heidi in Chapter 7. It has been our experience that the social reinforcers maintaining abnormal behavior patterns are usually at variance from those expected to be positive or aversive social stimulus conditions as available in the child's normal environment. Thus, if the child's abnormal behavior is being maintained by punishment conditions, and by its deviation it elicits such a stimulus contingency from the social environment, it is obvious how the home, school, and playground may all serve to maintain the child's deviant behavior. In such instances, it becomes apparent that it would be desirable to program the child's total environment to counter-condition such reinforcers and behaviors.

Parents of disturbed children frequently report that praise and reproof have little effect upon their children's behavior. This may occur because the social reinforcers have been erroneously paired with the wrong behaviors, as exemplified in studies by Allen, Hart, Buell, Harris, and Wolf (1964) and Allen and Harris (1966). However, an alternate hypothesis would be that normal social statements of praise or reproof do not have the expected reinforcing values for disturbed children.

A number of laboratory studies of normal children have demonstrated the expected effects of praise and reproof in reinforcing child behavior (Kelley & Stephens, 1964; Zigler & Kanzer, 1962; Stevenson *et al.,* 1963). Finley and Staats (1967) have further shown that words positively evaluated on the Semantic Differential will function as positive reinforcers, while negative evaluative words function as punishments, and neutral evaluative words have little effect upon behavior. In contrast, at least one study of disturbed boys (Levin & Simmons, 1962) indicates that response contingent positive words can lead to a deceleration of performance.

Clinical observation also supports the hypothesis of idiosyncratic social reinforcement values. Many disturbed children appear to seek unusual forms of attention. For example, the aggressive child produces an excess of behaviors that result in disapproval and a deficiency of behaviors that result in approval. Case histories commonly suggest that some disturbed children have received unique early experiences in which primary reinforcers have been unsystematically paired with social stimuli. Under such conditions the social stimuli would be expected to develop little reinforcing value.

Given that social reinforcement may not produce the expected effects with disturbed children, specialized treatment techniques become necessary. Thus behavior therapists frequently resort to tokens, candy, or other material reinforcement to achieve reliable control. Obviously, the token or candy cannot be used indefinitely to maintain a child's behavior. At some point the values of social reinforcers must be altered so that the normal contingencies of school or home will control his performance. Achievement of this ultimate treatment goal requires the development of procedures for strengthening otherwise ineffective social reinforcers.

A study was designed, the first objective of which was systematically to examine the values of social reinforcers for a group of disturbed boys.[1] In a second experiment with the same children, procedures were instituted to modify the value of the social reinforcers.

Experiment I

METHOD

The children were five boys, ages 10 to 12, in the residential program of the Wisconsin Children's Treatment Center. Four had been admitted recently because their severe behavior problems had made them unmanageable in the community. The fifth had undergone successful treatment for similar problems, and was awaiting discharge. None was classified as psychotic or retarded. The children were paid five cents per day for participation in individual half-hour sessions. They participated in an average of six sessions each.

During the first experimental session each child made Semantic Differential ratings of words which would later be used as social reinforcers. The "pleasant-unpleasant" scale, which loads heavily on the evaluative factor (Osgood *et al.,* 1957), was used. The word list, containing 48 positive, 48 neutral, and 32 negative evaluative words was the same as that used by Finley and Staats (1967) in their study of sixth-grade normal children.

On each successive session, the investigator and child were seated at opposite sides of a small table. Before the child was a row of four push-button switches. The investigator controlled a small signal light above the buttons. The child was instructed to press any one of the buttons to turn off the light each time it came on. A button press also activated a small electrical counter mounted directly in the child's vision. Thus, extinction of the light and activation of the counter were intended to serve as reinforcing events for any button-pressing.

Additionally, the investigator read words from the list described above in order to provide social reinforcement for response to specific buttons. A different type of word (positive, negative, or neutral) was made contingent upon a response to each button. For example, when the child pressed the first button, the investigator would matter-of-factly say a positive evaluative word. A response to the second or third buttons resulted in the investigator's saying a negative or neutral word, respectively. When the child

1. The authors wish to credit Donna M. Morrissey, M.S., co-investigator of the following experiments.

pressed the fourth button, the investigator would say nothing. The word lists were randomized so that a different positive, negative, or neutral word was said after each response to the respective buttons.

A block of trials was continued until a consistent pattern of response emerged (generally 40–60 trials). At that point, the social reinforcers would be paired in a different manner with the buttons. For example, Button 1 might now result in no word, Button 2 in neutral words, etc. These contingencies were consistently switched throughout the experiment to assure that any button preferences were the result of the social reinforcement and not of some extraneous factor.

All five children were exposed to the social reinforcement procedure until the investigators felt that a pattern of response had been demonstrated. The mean number of trials was 293 per child, with one child being kept at the task for only 180 trials and another for as long as 507 trials.

RESULTS

The Semantic Differential ratings made by the five children were compared with the normative data of Finley and Staats (1967). The percent

Table 6.4. Per Cent of Positive, Neutral, and Negative Evaluative Words Assigned to the Correct Category by Each Subject

	Word Category			
Child	*Positive*	*Neutral*	*Negative*	*All Words Combined*
#1	100%	100%	94%	98%
#2	71	96	59	75
#3	94	94	94	94
#4	98	17	28	48
#5	96	71	97	88

of positive, neutral, and negative words correctly assigned to the expected category appears in Table 6.4. Each of the four children made correct assignments of 75% or more of all the words. The remaining child (#3) assigned only 48% of all the words to the expected category. He appeared to be deliberately making foolish ratings in searching for a negative reaction from the investigator. Examination of the Semantic Differential data indicated no systematic relationship between the children's ratings and their subsequent performance on the social reinforcement task.

The various conditions of social reinforcement resulted in four identifiably different patterns of individual performance, as shown by the summarized data of Figure 6.3.

Child #1 avoided the button which was paired with a negative word, but his choice of one of the other three buttons appeared uninfluenced by the reinforcement conditions.

Child #2 (the subject who was ready for discharge) demonstrated what is assumed to be a normal pattern of response. Nearly 75% of his responses were made to a button associated with positive words. He responded least in the negative condition; responses to the neutral and no-word conditions were of intermediate frequency. These findings are consonant with those of Finley and Staats (1967) for normal subjects.

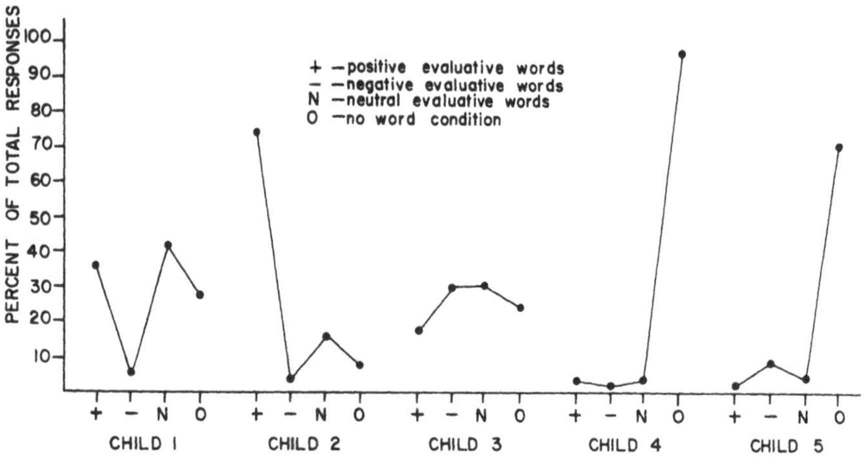

Figure 6.3. Per Cent of All Responses Made by Each Child Under Each of the Four Social Reinforcement Conditions during Experiment I

The responses of child #3 could not be reliably controlled by social reinforcement. He produced approximately the same number of responses to each of the four buttons regardless of the words spoken by the investigator. A variety of individual factors influenced his performance independent of the social reinforcement. After 507 trials his button preference was still unpredictable.

Children #4 and #5 are interesting in that their performance, although different from normal expectations, was highly predictable. They consistently avoided social reinforcement by making the majority of their responses in the no-word condition.

Experiment II

Since all except one of the boys performed differently than normally expected, a second experiment was conducted to modify the strength of the social reinforcers. The words were paired with primary positive and aversive stimuli with the intention of developing normal social reinforcement values.

METHOD

Children #3, #4, and #5 from the previous experiment were selected for participation. Child #1 was no longer available and social reinforcers had already been shown to have normal values for child #2.

In the first phase of the experiment, the child's pressing of one button was paired with the presentation of a piece of candy, while pressing another button resulted in a five-second blast of noise. The children performed for several blocks of trials to demonstrate that the candy would function as a positive reinforcer, and the noise as a punishment. This was quickly established with children #3 and #5, but the candy had little effect upon the performance of child #4. His behavior was promptly controlled, however, when he was switched to tokens that could be exchanged for prizes.

In the second phase of the experiment, button-pressing was followed by a social reinforcer which was in turn paired with the appropriate primary reinforcer. Thus, after a button press followed by a positive word, the child was given candy or a token; following a negative word, each child received the noise. Nothing happened after the neutral or no-word condition. Social reinforcers were given on a 1:1 schedule as in our first experiment. Initially, the primary reinforcers were also presented on a 1:1 schedule. Gradually, however, the primary reinforcers were shifted to a partial schedule. Thus, each child would receive candy or noise only every second or third time he pressed the respective buttons. The decision to continue increasing the reinforcement ratio was based upon having achieved a consistent preference for the positive button and an aversion for the negative button. Schedules were increased to a maximum of VR 1:50 for the primary reinforcers, while the social reinforcers were maintained at 1:1.

The final test phase of the experiment was the same as Experiment 1 and consisted of 240 trials of social reinforcement only.

Results

The test phase data are presented in Figure 6.4. The pattern of responses is consistent for each of the three *S*s. Over 85% of their responses were made to the buttons that were followed by positive evaluative words. Re-

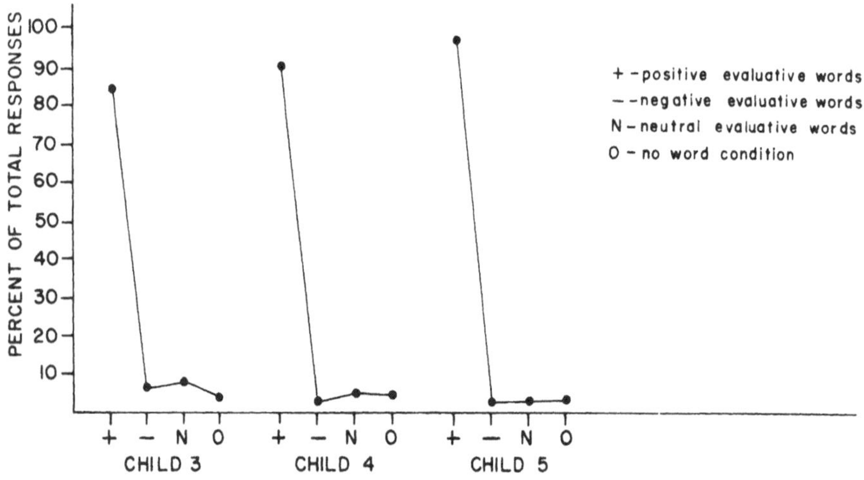

Figure 6.4. Per Cent of All Responses Made by Each Child under Each of the Four Conditions after the Social Reinforcers Had Been Paired with Primary Positive and Aversive Stimuli in Experiment II

sponses to the other buttons were of such low frequency that no determination can be made of their relative preference values.

Discussion of Experiments I and II

Previous findings with normal subjects (Finley & Staats, 1967) indicate (1) that positive and negative evaluative words function as positive and negative reinforcers, respectively; and (2) that a subject's evaluative rating of a word will predict its reinforcement value. In the present study, social reinforcers failed to influence performance in the expected manner. Instead, the reinforcement values of positive, negative, and neutral evaluative words were markedly idiosyncratic. Although the disturbed children generally produced the expected Semantic Differential ratings of the words, their performances were uniquely affected when the words were presented as reinforcers.

Theoretically, a positive evaluative word should function as a reinforcer because it is a sign of "pleasant" experiences and arouses at least some portion of the internal affective feelings of actual pleasant experiences. The present children, however, appeared to have a language deficit in which these internal affective values of the words (as inferred from the word's reinforcement value) were unrelated to the cognitive understanding of the word meaning. The children could correctly rate the words on a "pleasant-unpleasant" scale; but the words apparently did not arouse sufficient feeling of "pleasantness" or "unpleasantness" to function as behavior-controlling reinforcers.

This reasoning is supported by the results of Experiment II. The words were paired with primary "pleasant" and "unpleasant" experiences (i.e., candy and noise). This pairing altered reinforcement values, apparently because the words acquired meaning as signs of "pleasant" and "unpleasant" experience.

According to these studies, failure to control the behavior of a disturbed child can result because social reinforcers do not have the expected values for him. Behavior-modification programs should include functional analyses of reinforcement contingencies. Procedures for altering reinforcement values could be introduced where appropriate. For example, the procedure of Experiment II might be expanded as a treatment technique. Parents and teachers could be instructed to follow statements of approval with material reinforcers according to gradually increasing ratios. Prompt alteration of abnormal reinforcement values, if attainable, would subsequently result in efficient behavioral treatment, for normally available social reinforcers would then be effective in controlling the child's behavior.

The preceding examples of the uniqueness of the social reinforcers for the children involved in the studies are not evidence that all emotionally disturbed children's reinforcers are at variance from the population from which they were referred. These examples are informative only for the cases from which they were derived. The data are not intended to be generalized beyond the behavioral repertoires of the children they describe. This is consistent with the experimental-clinical approach, i.e., that each child's habit repertoire is presumed to be representative only of his own unique learning history.

There is considerable experimental literature in which a particular social reinforcer is used on an entire group of individuals. The implication in such studies is that there is commonality of social reinforcers, an erroneous implication when one is searching for precise information about one individual. We do not mean that studies in which single reinforcers are employed are disreputable; we mean that such group studies do not provide information about any single individual. When one is confronted with the clinical responsibility for an individual, such group data are of little value, unless they approach standardization type of information as available in intelligence testing that informs one if that subject's behavior is at variance from what is expected in his home environment.

There seems to be a myth in the field that a bag of candy and a prerecorded message of "good" are the necessary and sufficient conditions of behavior modification. There is a myth that unqualified attention from a teacher is sufficient to accelerate and permanently maintain appropriate behavior in children in a classroom setting. The necessity of evaluating the idiosyncratic social reinforcers of the disturbed child's habits demonstrates how learning theory is compatible with the experimental-clinical approach. The uniqueness of one's learning history is the error term of the large group studies on learning, and it is that error term for which one usually has to assume clinical responsibility in a treatment program, and which must therefore be approached idiographically.

The single-subject, single-response study in which a particular response is varied in its rate is not even very informative for that one individual. Such single-response studies omit all the multiplicity of interactive variables in the response repertoire of the subject. One cannot assume generalized reinforcers for each subject unless they are identified as such, although we implied as much in the previous studies. Because a reinforcement contingency has a certain predictable effect on one behavior, we may not assume that it will, predictably, be effective for all other behaviors in the same manner. For example, although social praise may accelerate compliant behavior in a youngster, it cannot be presumed that such praise will accelerate all responses in that child. There are many situational variables which interact with the effectiveness of our social reinforcers. The discriminative stimulus of a secondary reinforcer is embedded in a myriad of other stimulus conditions which may alter the value of the social reinforcement for a multitude of social situations. This statement is no more complex than stating that praise from one person will accelerate behavior in one individual, and that, for another individual, it will have no effect, because of the second individual's previous learning history. Thus, the social praise did not have a generalized effect for all individuals, but is a function of all other stimulus conditions relevant to the responses being elicited at any given moment. For the same reasons that one cannot presume that social reinforcers will have the same effect for different people, it is erroneous to presume that the social reinforcers will have the same effect for all responses within an individual.

In fact, it may be that in some instances, the same response may be maintained by different reinforcers, and those reinforcers may be diametrically opposed in their presumed value for other persons. For example, a teacher's approval, as well as her disapproval, may all serve to accelerate "showing off" behavior in a youngster. That teacher's approval may be effective in improving arithmetic performance, whereas her disapproval may be effective in destroying arithmetic behavior. This is a problem with which we have not been successful in dealing at present. Part of the problem is that in an analysis of behavior of the specificity that we are currently performing, we may identify certain reinforcers as having a predictable effect on a given response, or at most on two or three responses. From that information we usually make the erroneous assumption that those reinforcers are generalizable to all other responses, rather than analyzing the reinforcement effects situationally. Large group, single-response studies do not inform one about rehabilitating a child within that group—which is the problem confronting the clinician. The single-subject, single-response study in the analysis of effectiveness of social reinforcers is more likely to tell you more about that one individual, although, actually, one cannot generalize beyond that one given piece of information about the child.

In treating a child, one must be cautious and insure that the reinforcement contingencies used to accelerate and maintain normal response patterns are of the kind and the frequency comparable to those available to that child when he returns to his normal environment. Token economies are very distant approximations of the social reinforcement contingencies available to a child in his normal environment. Token contingencies maintaining socially appropriate behavioral patterns would be unjustified treatment programs, from which the patient would be discharged, because his behavior would have been maintained on reinforcers and schedules not available in his normal environment, so that his behavior would deteriorate simply because they would no longer be there. Token economies are effective in maintaining very stable institutional behavior, and in instances of mental retardation or life-long custodial care, a rich token economy would give considerable meaning to the life of the patient. However, one would not expect such patients to function effectively in a normal environment where poker chips were not the dominant reinforcers. Neither is money the single sufficient reinforcer for human behavior. Money, as a token form, does maintain much work behavior, but it does not maintain the complexities of social behavior which may be occurring during, or in conjunction with, the work behavior for which one is being paid. Monetary systems may be established for an adult in residential care that should be increased in value to be comparable at his date of discharge to those monetary systems available to him when he returns to the normal environment. One should always remember that the kinds of responses being maintained by any token economy must be comparable to those which will be maintained in the normal environment. Adults are not paid for making up their beds—in fact, very few children receive such monetary rewards.

There are no technical manuals available that provide a large source of treatment techniques which could be used in certain instances. In the absence of such a source, and considering the obvious uniqueness of each person's learning history and his social reinforcers, one must approach each child's treatment program idiographically. The experimental-clinical model provides some degree of methodological control of the development of such a treatment program. Furthermore, establishment of these treatment programs are not something which may be relegated entirely to one's clinical skills, as has been traditional.

This discussion does not imply that experimental studies on single-subjects, single-responses, or groups of single responses, are not applicable to the treatment of disturbed children. Ferster and DeMyer's (1962) presentation of a study which demonstrated that autistic children can learn in accordance with the operant model does provide a framework for teaching these children new behaviors in the clinical setting. Lovaas' studies on conditioning social reinforcers (Lovaas, Freitag, *et al.*, 1966) provided a treatment model which was used clinically in the case studies contained in Chapter 7. Experimental literature is of considerable importance in establishing which principles of learning should be studied or employed in the treatment program of a child. Such experimental demonstrations are not intended to be clinical treatment procedures applicable to all patients. They do not assume the burden of clinical responsibility. The clinician must be resourceful in his application of these principles as derived from the experimental literature.

CHAPTER SEVEN

Case Studies

The following five case studies are presented as examples of the applied experimental-clinical method. The first four cases are young psychotic children, the last case is an older, multiply handicapped, neurotic child. The cases illustrate the use of experimental designs, numerous dependent variables, and simultaneous administration of multiple-behavior therapy programs, to the same child. At the present time, some of the children are gradually being returned to their homes; some will not return for at least an additional year. These are the most recent cases in residence and reflect the latest developments of the experimental-clinical method.

The treatment programs described were administered almost exclusively by the nursing and child-care staffs. In certain instances, such as in beginning new programs or when the Center was insufficiently staffed, the authors and research analysts would assist in administering the programs. The staff were trained in learning theory and research methodology, and were monitored by the investigators for competence in conducting the programs.

There are many conditions in the treatment programs which were not described or measured in detail. For example, the younger children were always closely staffed, and in all cases there were some management orders constantly in effect. One such management order was positive social reinforcement for as many compliant and cooperative responses as the staff could remember to reinforce. These programs are discussed briefly in each case study.

Case Study 1: Heidi

DEVELOPMENTAL HISTORY

It was mid-morning, July 17, 1967 when Heidi was admitted to the Wisconsin Children's Treatment Center with the accepted referral diagnosis of childhood autism. Heidi was accompanied by her father, mother, and two elder brothers, all of whom reluctantly and painfully complied with our request to make the separation quick. Father and sons displayed their tears; mother ulcerated hers.

We obtained the following information from her parents as a result of several interviews directed at learning Heidi's speech and developmental history. As would be expected with most families, the parents had difficulty recalling the exact chronological order of events as well as their accurate description. The parents remembered that there was an apparent attempt on Heidi's part to imitate a sound when she was two, when she repeatedly tried to produce the word "squirrel"; the best approximation she could perform was "squ." This degree of delayed speech did not unduly concern the parents at the time, since their next eldest reportedly did not acquire speech until the approximate age of three. Between the ages of two and three, Heidi also acquired the verbal responses of "you" and "Jay." One brother's name was Jay.

When she was two and one-half, Heidi swallowed a bottle cap and, following her father's emergency extraction of the object that produced minor bleeding, the parents remembered that Heidi said, "Daddy, Daddy," as she fled to her bedroom. This was the last incident in which the parents can recall speech acquisition for approximately one year. When three and one-half, Heidi began to use the words "Daddy," "you," and "Jay" more frequently, and also acquired the words "hello" and "good-bye." She was remembered as having babbled and cooed considerably as an infant and was described by the parents as a happy, beautiful, and delightful infant.

When six, Heidi had a "high fever" (exact temperature not recorded in the baby book) associated with febrile convulsions. She had contracted chicken pox when eight months old with associated low-grade fever, and although the fever was not considered unusually high (probably less than 102°) it was sustained for one week. When Heidi was two, her parents noted that her left eye began to cross, particularly when she appeared to be anxious, and what developed into a variable left-eye strabismus they initially considered to be a volitional response. Historically, this left-eye strabismus was important, since it was experimentally demonstrated to be an operant response to a certain extent. We will present more detailed discussion of this response later in this study.

Heidi was between the ages of two and three when relatives of the family began to express their concern that she was demonstrating increasingly less complex behavior than would be expected for her age. She was between three and four, as the parents recalled, when there was an increasing absence of tears. Laughter and smiling had progressively disappeared from Heidi's response repertoire since age two. The parents had begun to notice during her chronological age one through two that there was increasing pain insensitivity, but this observation seemed to vary in respect to their recollection of particular events that elicited pain. By the time Heidi was seven, at her admission, she would have certainly been described as a remarkably pain-insensitive child.

The parents' report contained not only varied incidents of pain insensitivity, but also the fact it was always difficult for Heidi to be sedated when necessary with the usual childhood sedatives, like phenobarbital. When Heidi was experiencing pain she would often scream, but her screaming was always less than would be normally expected. This observation of her subnormal pain sensitivity was based on her parents' expectations as derived from their comparison of Heidi with her two older sibs, both of whom are normal. The events that would be expected to produce pain responses included several falls resulting in scrapes and bruises, plus Heidi's breaking windows with the back of her head by slamming it against the window pane. It was apparently very difficult to retain certain windows in the house.

During the year between the ages of three and four, Heidi did not walk unless she was attempting to avoid someone. She almost resided in a wagon; she would not walk independently and had to be taken from one place to another in a wagon by the family members. She would ride on her mother's bicycle if placed there, but during that year transportation or locomotion was primarily by a wagon. The parents recalled that at this point spankings never seemed to evoke fear responses, perhaps because of her pain insensitivity, but they were never sure of this interpretation, since there were still various incidents of Heidi's responding to pain. They do recall that when Heidi was less than two years old, scoldings would stimulate her to tears, but her sensitivity to scoldings varied, since she was reported to have cried on several occasions when she was six for short intervals of time; but, as they reported again and again, this kind of reaction seemed to "cycle." Furthermore, this was a "dry" crying. The parents reported that when Heidi was first admitted, the intensity of deviant behavior seemed to cycle from intervals ranging from months to a year in which the undesired responses (e.g., aggressive and self-destructive responses) would increase both in intensity and frequency and then decrease to a more tolerable level. The parental conditions associated with such cycling of deviant behavior were never ascertained, and it is beyond us, from the information available, to speculate upon those training conditions.

When Heidi was three, the parents recall an interval of 72 hours during which Heidi was extremely hyperactive, awake, and screaming. She was examined at a hospital at that time, but no apparent physical condition was isolated to account for the extreme behavioral activation. Between ages three and six, Heidi screamed considerably, and this is the parents' most dominant recollection of any verbal behavior on Heidi's part, i.e., screaming rather than producing imitative speech. It should be noted that Heidi comes from a verbal family in which one would expect that she would have had many, many opportunities to imitate speech.

ADMISSION BEHAVIORS

The staff noted the following incidents during Heidi's first day of residence. Twenty-eight rages and temper tantrums were observed during that first day; these rages were often accompanied by "screaming and screeching" responses, as defined by her simply making a high-pitched scream highly suggestive of abject terror. A total of 529 "screaming and screeching" incidents occurred that first day. While her parents were still in the office, the staff noted that Heidi's rages included the behaviors of screaming, head-banging, biting, kicking, scraping staff's legs with her shoes (Heidi wore sneakers for the next six months), hitting, banging, and wildly flailing her limbs. It was also noted that Heidi seemed to be aware when the door of her room was closed and the staff not immediately present. She became slightly more settled when the parents finally said their good-byes.

It was recorded during the next few hours that she preferred playing with balloons, particularly holding, fondling, and twirling them, tenderly pedaling a tricycle, swinging (not independently, but only when pushed), and playing in water. There were occurrences of very simple and short-lived compliant responses, such as banging a toy drum or dropping clothespins into a bottle upon request. Her first lunch was very difficult, as were many meals thereafter, since rages did occur that were accentuated by staff's difficulty in extricating her from beneath the table, where she would lie while rocking about, screaming, grinding her teeth, and banging her head, arms, and legs against the table and floor. The investigator remembered very clearly the trials of removing her from beneath the table during the first meal, putting her over his shoulder, and carrying her to the quiet room for the prescribed one-minute time-out. At the conclusion of the fourth trip, the investigator was rather sweaty, bruised, exhausted, and winded and could begin to empathize with the parents of autistic children.

It was noted that Heidi had a habit of holding out items to the staff on her tongue, and when the staff would attempt to remove the object from her mouth, she would promptly swallow the marble, stone, or toy before they could grasp it. A hypothesized history for the social reinforcement conditions that are suspected to have initiated and maintained this "testing" response (i.e., testing the social environment for the availability of a particular reinforcement contingency by placing inedible objects in her mouth) dates from the time when her father had removed the bottle cap from her throat, resulting in minor lacerations, after which she had screamed out, "Daddy, Daddy" and run to her room. Henceforth, from that dated trauma, the parents were alerted to her swallowing objects and attempted to prevent such incidents by verbal admonishment and physical intervention if necessary. A good example of the social punishment cues for which she would test by placing objects in her mouth was clearly observed in the occupational therapy shop during the first days of her residence. During one session, Heidi took one button from a box on the table, put it on her tongue, and held it out in front of everyone. The occupational therapist, who happened to be a naturalistically programmed social reinforcer, totally ignored the response, even though Heidi was holding her head beneath the therapist's and looking up with the button held on her tongue, obviously testing for the social punishment stimuli she apparently expected to receive. When the occupational therapist persisted in ignoring the response, Heidi placed two buttons on her tongue and repeated the routine of showing it to everyone about the table and testing for the presence of aversive social reinforcers. Again, the therapist ignored the behavior. This stimulated Heidi to produce three buttons, with this sequence persisting until Heidi had a mouthful of buttons and was making very real choking sounds, which everyone continued to ignore. It required approximately 45 minutes before she finally spat out the buttons.

The staff charted in their experiences from the first day that Heidi would often simultaneously demonstrate affectionate and aggressive responses. For example, when she would hug a staff member during water-play activities, the hug would culminate in a sharp jerk on the staff member's neck, accompanied by hair-pulling and occasionally a bite. Staff also noted that there was very poor eye contact, with a noticeable left-eye strabismus occurring at a rate which is best described as variable. It was interesting to note that the staff described her rest periods as "fair," and that she would remain in the room so long as the staff remained outside the door in the hall and provided continual reminders by returning her to her room when she would begin to leave. At that time we were ignorant of the fact that she was operating for social punishment cues at a rather stable rate. One staff member noted that there was also an incident of her smiling and clapping in response to praise; it was later found that this was an unusual and unpredictable response for Heidi to make.

A management order was promulgated at the time of Heidi's arrival that was intended to decelerate her temper tantrums and rages. A one-minute time-out procedure was begun immediately, since her temper tantrums were so severe and frightening to the entire staff and to the children in the cottage. We decided to begin the treatment program for tantrum and rage behavior and to delete the preferred baseline data which we had originally planned to record. The management order was for staff to provide a one-minute time-out contingent upon each occurrence of a temper tantrum, and the time-out would be conducted by the staff member's first saying loudly, "No" at each occurrence of the behavior, and then walking or carrying Heidi to the quiet room and shutting the door for the prescribed minute, taking care not to look in the window and allow Heidi to see the staff. The program for temper tantrums will be discussed in greater detail later, but we mention it here since it was begun on the day of admission. A second management order was also initiated in which all compliant behavior, however slight, was placed on a 100% schedule of positive social reinforcement. That is, all staff were to take particular care to praise or provide some strong, effusive positive evaluative statement contingent upon Heidi's responding in a way that they considered to be compliant to their requests. A compliant response was defined as the child's performing a task as *verbally* requested of her—our characteristic procedure of identifying "compliant" responses. These initial compliant responses were qualitatively quite different from those observed later in the program. We were initially recording as compliant responses such behaviors as turning to staff when her name was called, or sitting down upon request, or approaching one or two paces when called by name.

Self-Mutilation of Laceration. Two days prior to Heidi's admission, she had kicked and broken the glass in a china closet at home, resulting in a three-inch laceration on her right upper inside thigh that had required sutures. The emergency care at the doctor's office where the laceration was repaired required two hours of restraining Heidi by parent, nurse, and doctor; sedation, as could have been predicted, was ineffective. At the conclusion of the treatment, Heidi immediately tore out the stitches, which again resulted in considerable bleeding. When Heidi was admitted to the Center, she would repeatedly reach beneath her clothes and tear at the wound, which would result in more bleeding and increased the threat of infection. However, it was noticed that she would look at the staff whenever she was mutilating the wound, presumably operating for ostensible social punishment responses from staff. A management order was immediately enacted in which staff were not to look at her whenever she attempted to open the wound, but turn away and continue with some other activity. It required approximately four weeks for the wound to heal normally under this program, during which only topical antiseptics were applied. Apparently, our suspicion was correct that social reinforcement, in the form of admonishment for mutilating the wound, was maintaining that behavior, and the removal of all such verbal social reinforcers resulted in the extinction of the response. The treatment effect was quick, possibly because this particular self-mutilation response was operative for only three days prior to being placed on an extinction schedule.

Food Preferences. When Heidi was admitted to the Children's Treatment Center she demonstrated marked food preferences which interfered with normal mealtime routines and imposed dietary problems: she ate hot dogs. Heidi ate hot dogs at such an operant level that it was a time-out from punishment (a classical negative reinforcement paradigm) for the parents to relinquish and provide her with hot dogs on the schedule which she demanded. If one refused to comply with her attempt to obtain a hot dog, this intervention was likely to stimulate rage and aggressive behaviors.

Eating at mealtime was an aversive experience for the entire family while Heidi was residing at home, as exemplified by those occasions in which she would walk on the table during the meal, continually spill, eat with her hands, and throw food. We decided not to take a baseline of such behaviors. A management order was instigated which required that hot dogs be deleted entirely from Heidi's diet. Hot dogs were contained in the diet at the Center and were served about every other week, but they were unavailable to Heidi until she could reliably eat a variety of foods with appropriate table manners. At that time we were beginning to suspect that Heidi's social reinforcers were contaminated, in the sense that polarity may have been shifted to some unknown extent. Thus, we would allow food, as a primary reinforcer, to be the available contingency for eating appropriately, with no social reinforcers being present. The management order also provided that she would be seated at a table by herself, i.e., she would not eat with the other children in our group. One of the staff members would sit across the table from her, but would remain silent throughout the meal. No vocalizations were to be paired with eating various kinds of food, since the possibility of their contaminating the "approach to eat" response was a real possibility and we could thus inadvertently condition an anorexic response. The program was simply to allow food to reinforce itself, which would be expected to occur if it were not allowed to be contaminated by unknown effects of social reinforcers. The child was allowed 30 minutes to complete each meal; she was prevented from throwing the food on the floor and required to stay in the chair throughout the meal. If a rage or temper tantrum occurred during the mealtime, she would be whisked off to the quiet room for the time-out procedure in effect at that time for such behavior. After four days, Heidi consistently ate meals of a variety of foods. Unfortunately, the program was not entirely successful, because she was still eating with her hands. However, we finally had a sufficient primary reinforcer to condition other responses and reinforcement contingencies.

Eating with Utensils. Heidi would not eat meals with the appropriate utensils in a predictable manner. She would occasionally use a spoon or a fork, but most often she would use her fingers, and she would not respond to a verbal reprimand or instruction to use the correct utensil. It is obvious that a seven-year-old child should learn to use utensils appropriately, so we devised the following management order, which may be described as a *B* design study, since a baseline was not secured. On the previous four days it had been observed that during all meals she ate various foods with her fingers. The management order was to teach Heidi to eat with utensils by placing a plate containing a spoon with a small amount of food before her, with a glass containing a small amount of milk to one side. She was allowed to eat only with a spoon. Staff were to withdraw the plate if she attempted to pick up the food with her fingers, and after a one- to two-second interval, return the plate for another trial. During this program she was given vitamins daily, and a food supplement was provided at snack time before her retiring in the evening, since we feared that otherwise she might lose weight because of eating insufficient amounts. Finger foods were not given to Heidi during mealtime, since this would only have warranted her to use her fingers as an appropriate response and thus would have provided training of that undesired response. She was given soft drinks and other preferred fluids throughout the day to offset any possible dehydration's resulting from her refusal to drink milk appropriately during the meal. These desired liquids were administered as reinforcement contingencies in other programs, particularly in shaping compliant behavior during the remainder of the day. These kinds of precautions should always be observed in programs which use food as a reinforcer, especially if the primary reinforcer is on a thin schedule—which is typical in the initial phases of a program. The following are Heidi's responses, observed during successive meals, to the staff's teaching her to eat with utensils:

Day 1

Lunch: Heidi slouched at the table with her head on her arm during the entire meal; she made no approach response to the spoon with the food on it that was placed before her, nor to the milk.

Supper: Heidi again slouched at the table with her head on her arm, but she reached for the spoon three times, only to retract her hand quickly from the spoon just prior to touching it.

Day 2

Breakfast: Heidi continued to slouch over the table with her head on her arm, but she did sip some milk; no responses were made to the spoon containing food.

Lunch: Heidi slouched over the table with her head on her arm; no approach response was made to the food on the spoon; she did make numerous attempts to grab the food with her hands but was prevented from doing so by staff's retracting the plate.

Supper: Heidi continued to slouch over the table with her head on her arm; she reached for, but did not touch, the spoon once.

Day 3

Breakfast: Again, Heidi slouched over the table with her head on her arm. She touched the spoon 13 times during the course of the 30-minute meal. However, there was no food or liquid intake.

Lunch: As usual, Heidi slouched over the table with her head on her arm, but touched the spoon 11 times, and touched her milk glass three times. She did not drink any milk, but did eat one small bite of banana, using the spoon.

Supper: Heidi again slouched over the table with her head on her arm; she touched the spoon 18 times and held the spoon close to her mouth but did not eat. There was no food or liquid intake during the meal.

Day 4

Breakfast: Heidi sat up straight without slouching over the table. She held the spoon with food on it three times, for 30 seconds to one minute each time; she did not consume any foods or liquids.

Lunch: Heidi sat up straight without slouching; she touched the spoon 12 times but did not eat or drink.

Supper: Heidi held the spoon in her hand throughout the meal. The attending staff member assisted the eating response by slightly lifting Heidi's elbow so that she moved it toward her mouth, and she then ate her entire meal with the spoon; the meal comprised pancakes, two strips of bacon, ice cream, and milk.

She had refused to eat for seventy-two hours after the program was begun.

Since that last meal, Heidi has continued to eat with utensils appropriately; she has not returned to eating with her hands. We did have to assist the eating response by touching her elbow on increasingly fewer trials for successive meals for approximately ten days, after which we no longer had to direct her eating responses. There has been no extinction of that particular behavior back to the original eating with hands during mealtime. Heidi still required training in eating politely; these habits would be trained at a later date, since there were more important habits to be acquired or extinguished.

Temper Tantrums and Rages. When Heidi was admitted, one of her characteristic responses was her extreme temper tantrums, which we have termed "tantrums" and "rages," the latter term qualifying more descriptively her tantrum behavior. The combination of responses which the staff agreed upon calling a temper tantrum included, either entirely or in some combination, Heidi's falling on the floor, flailing her arms and legs, banging her head and screaming, grinding her teeth, distorting her facial features, and kicking anyone who attempted to interrupt this wild behavior which heretofore had been operantly very successful. The temper tantrums and rages were disruptive to the total cottage program, because they were so severe and frightening to the other children as well as to the staff. We decided to delete a baseline count of tantrums and to commence with a *B* design study for which the treatment program would be a one-minute time-out. The time-out condition required staff to walk or carry Heidi to the quiet room where she would be deposited for exactly one minute, after which she would be removed; if the temper tantrum commenced or continued within six feet of the quiet room door as she was being removed, she would be given another trial for one minute in the quiet room. The rationale for the short time-out condition was so that the low-rate occurrence of the response would eventually be made high rate, since it was predictable that the tantrum would continue when she left the quiet room, and she would then have another trial for that response. When Heidi was removed from a situation where she was having a temper tantrum, the staff would immediately say, "No," very loudly and proceed with what we described as a "benign time-out" which is simply not speaking to her but walking, and if necessary, carrying, her to the quiet room. When she was finally placed in the quiet room, the staff would again say, "No," loudly and firmly to her and then shut the door. Figure 7.1 shows the effectiveness of the program. The one-minute time-out was apparently effective, and a two-minute time-out was commenced, on day 14, that effectively extinguished the response. Because only a *BC* design was used, one can only hypothesize that the temper tantrums decelerated as a function of the time-out condition. Although pleased with our success in controlling her temper tantrums, we were far from devising effective treatment procedures for Heidi's other inappropriate behaviors, as shall be seen in our attempts to extinguish aggressive behaviors.

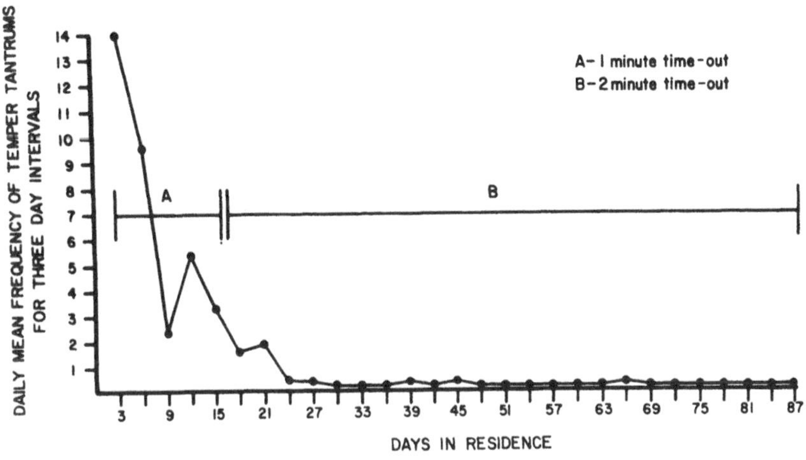

Figure 7.1. Effects of One- and Two-Minute Time-Outs on Rages and Temper Tantrums

Gross Testing and Aggressive Responses. Beginning from the moment of Heidi's admission, the staff were immediately aware of what we described as "gross testing." Gross testing responses included all aggressive responses, directed toward the staff members or other children, including hitting, biting, slapping, kicking, spitting, and throwing objects at the staff member. We used the term "gross testing" since it appeared obvious that these assaultive behaviors were "gross," and they were operant responses testing for the availability of social reinforcers. It was rather easy to record the occurrence of these responses, since one simply learned to press the hand tally counter each time he was hurt. The gross testing responses were not placed on a baseline for the same reason given for temper tantrums; the treatment design was simply a *BCD* design in which *B* was a one-minute time-out condition, *C* was a two-minute time-out condition, and *D* was the administration of faradic stimulation. During the *B* and *C* treatment intervals, each time an aggressive behavior occurred defined as gross testing, the child was taken to the quiet room for the respective time-out condition in effect at that time. As can be seen from Figure 7.2, the frequency of the aggressive behaviors accelerated with the one-minute time-out condition. The two-minute time-out condition assisted that acceleration and it became apparent that an error was occurring in the program, since we were confronted with increasingly stronger aggressive responses. We recognized that the "honeymoon" effect was certainly operative, and we anticipated

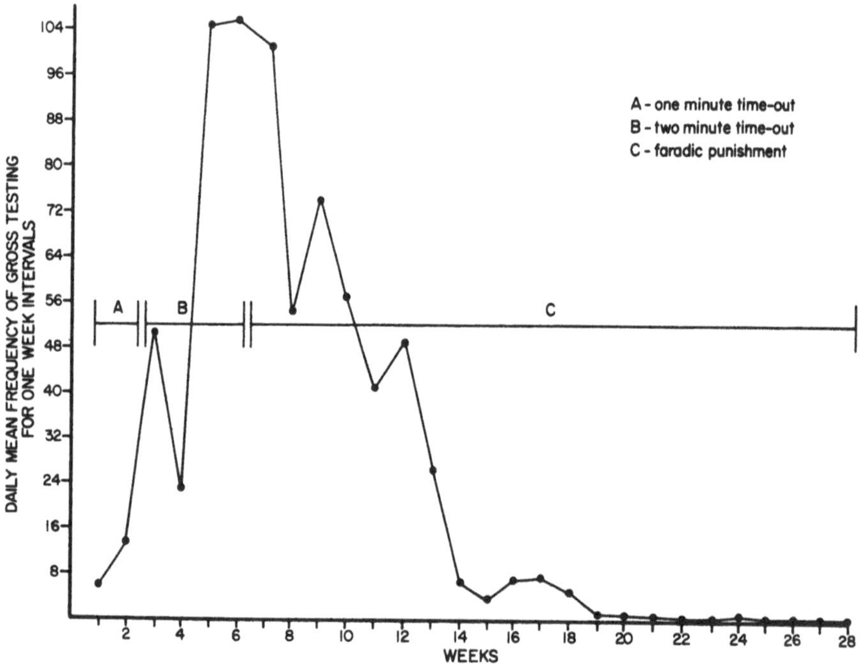

Figure 7.2. Effects of One- and Two-Minute Time-Outs and Faradic Punishment on Daily Mean Frequency of Gross Testing Aggression

that Heidi would demonstrate more of the characteristic behaviors which initiated her referral for residential care after the first two weeks of residence. We expected that we would notice some increment in these aggressive behaviors, but the frequencies as represented in Figure 7.2 certainly forego any conclusion that the acceleration was simply a function of her operating on the new environment at a rate comparable to that which had occurred for aggressive behaviors while at home.

It is at a time like this that the challenge of research and the fear of ulceration begin simultaneously for the investigator. As the data were being monitored, we could see that the treatment condition, which had been successful with a comparable behavior in a child similar to Heidi, was not decreasing the undesirable behavior as expected. The literature provided no answers as to why we were finding this strange effect in our data, i.e., the same time-out contingency decelerated temper tantrums but accelerated aggressive behaviors. However, it has been noted in the literature that autistic children often have a behavior pattern of aggressive or self-destructive behaviors (Lovaas, 1966). We had observed in our research with Heidi that the expected positive and negative social reinforcement contingencies had been noticeably ineffective in altering her behavior. Lovaas (1966) reported similar findings with autistic children, and noted that autistic and schizophrenic children are typically not responsive to usual forms of social punishment; however, what exactly was occurring remained an enigma to us. We were not content to rely on explanations such as diffuse, disorganized, etc., behaviors to explain the autistic child's behavior; such descriptions fail to explain how one treats the child.

We did notice that, when Heidi was receiving a time-out for a temper tantrum, the procedure of being carried or walked to the quiet room would almost invariably stimulate further aggressive responses toward the staff that staff would of course report as gross testing responses. It seemed possible, therefore, that in using the punishment condition of a time-out for both temper tantrums and gross testing we were committing the error of stimulating the behavior the punishment was intended to decelerate. It was therefore hypothesized that we were making one of the primary errors of a punishment paradigm, namely, that the punishment condition was producing the behavior which it was designed to decelerate (Kushner & Sandler, 1966). At this point, we realized that we did not know what we were doing, nor did we have the vaguest idea what to do next with Heidi. The staff were becoming discouraged; the investigator was exhausted from spending evenings in the cottage assisting but only maintaining the aggressive behaviors in the child. Heidi was becoming progressively worse; the investigator was becoming increasingly reluctant to face her parents. It became quite apparent that we did not know very much about treating psychotic children, and there were no references in the literature to explain the paradoxical treatment effects.

It seemed evident that it was time to reorganize our findings and our hypotheses about Heidi in an attempt to isolate the contingencies that were maintaining her behavior. The following is a report of the progression of ideas and studies that culminated in a diagnostic behavioral analysis of Heidi and directed the course of her entire treatment program.

DIAGNOSTIC BEHAVIORAL ANALYSIS OF SOCIAL REINFORCERS

Introduction. There are several procedural requirements of behavior-therapy techniques that contribute to their advantages over traditional psychotherapeutic endeavors. The techniques are derived from laboratory-documented learning theory; the dependent variables are typically objective measurable units of discrete behaviors. The emergence of the experimental-idiographic study in which the subject serves as his own control in conjunction with observable dependent variables is a vast improvement over the non-predicted outcome measures of traditional psychotherapy studies. Unfortunately, there have been an increasing number of studies which fail to satisfy the basic procedural requirements of behavior-therapy methodology. For example, the acknowledgment that "abnormal" behavior is maintained by social reinforcers has been over-generalized to the increasingly popular conclusion that unqualified "attention" is presumed to be the sufficient reinforcing condition for almost all deviant behavior. Few studies experimentally demonstrate, much less replicate, the kind of attention (e.g., expected positive reinforcement vs. expected social punishment stimuli) that reinforces (i.e., accelerates) the behavior under treatment. The error incurred by the over-generalized employment of "attention" as a positive social reinforcer is the assumption of commonality of reinforcers, which is an unwarranted conclusion for secondary reinforcers acquired under unknown circumstances. A rudimentary knowledge of learning theory makes it clear that social reinforcers are *hypothesized* to be conditioned, and therefore their quality and effectiveness are unique to each person's learning history.

A recent development in behavior therapy has been the reliance upon dramatic rate changes to justify the assumption that the independent variable (treatment technique) was the necessary and sufficient condition for the change (i.e., *B* design). In the applied clinical field, time and expense often negate employment of controlled idiographic studies. However, only questionable credence can be given to uncontrolled rate-change studies which contain no documentation of differential effectiveness of a reinforcement condition used in treatment as contrasted to those reinforcers which were identified as having sustained the deviant behavior.

The importance of experimentally documenting the reinforcement conditions sustaining the deviant behavior, as well as the contingencies used in the treatment conditions, is obvious. Effective behavior-therapy techniques are not based on subjective impressions of reinforcement contingencies; they are based on an experimental analysis of the components of the habits under modification. The following study demonstrates how an experimental analysis of differential effectiveness of social reinforcers assisted us in designing a treatment program for Heidi, as well as clarifying the conditions which maintained her referral behaviors.

Method

Subject. To review: the behaviors Heidi exhibited that eventuated her referral and the diagnosis of childhood autism included head-banging, repetitive screeching, having her speech confined to five words which occurred repetitively and non-operantly, biting, hitting, pinching self and others, nocturnal and diurnal enuresis, encopresis, fecal smearing, pica, noncompliance to verbal requests, posturing, tic-like facial grimaces, anal play, spinning self and objects, and numerous other autisms such as repetitive twiddling of fingers and jerking of hands and arms.

Observations on video tapes of Heidi's interacting with her parents and sibs suggested that the expected social reinforcers were contaminated. Her parents would attempt to ignore Heidi's bizarre behavior, but often (i.e., variable schedule) resorted to verbal and physical admonishment when her behavior became intolerable. Infrequently (i.e., variable schedule) her parents and sibs would hug Heidi and demonstrate affection following their typically ineffectual attempts to control her by force and admonishment. They explained that they felt guilty for having to scold her so severely and often. This interaction suggested that the parents had, inadvertently, established a paradigm to counter-condition the expected social punishment stimuli by infrequently backing these with expected positive social reinforcers. If this hypothesis, derived from the video tape observations, was correct, we could expect that, with such a reinforcement history on an increasingly thin schedule, Heidi would operate to obtain the social punishment contingencies, since they had been "backed-up" with both primary and secondary reinforcers (e.g., temper tantrums operated to obtain hot dogs). A typical example of the contamination of social reinforcers for Heidi could be seen when her parents were hugging her and she would infrequently bite or hit them while they demonstrated their affection.

When Heidi was admitted to the Center, her rage behavior (falling on floor, screaming, throwing her arms around, closing eyes, postural rigidity) and her gross testing and aggressive responses (biting, pinching, and hitting staff) were so intense and disruptive to the cottage routine that a baseline was not taken. The behaviors were immediately put on a program of one-minute time-out from reinforcement. This time-out had previously been effective with other children, and its short duration would make it likely that Heidi would receive many time-outs for the same temper tantrum. The time-out involved staff's firmly saying, "No," and, if necessary, carrying her in her rage or walking her when aggressing or testing, to a small bedroom devoid of furniture and decor. Figure 7.3 illustrates the unique effect with the time-out program; rages decelerated, gross testing and aggressive responses accelerated. It became obvious that a more exploratory behavior analysis should have been conducted prior to our having devised the treatment program.

Procedure: Experiment 1

When we were conducting the behavior analysis, the hypothesis relevant to testing the differential effectiveness of the reinforcers was as follows. We observed that, when Heidi was taken to the quiet room for the time-out for

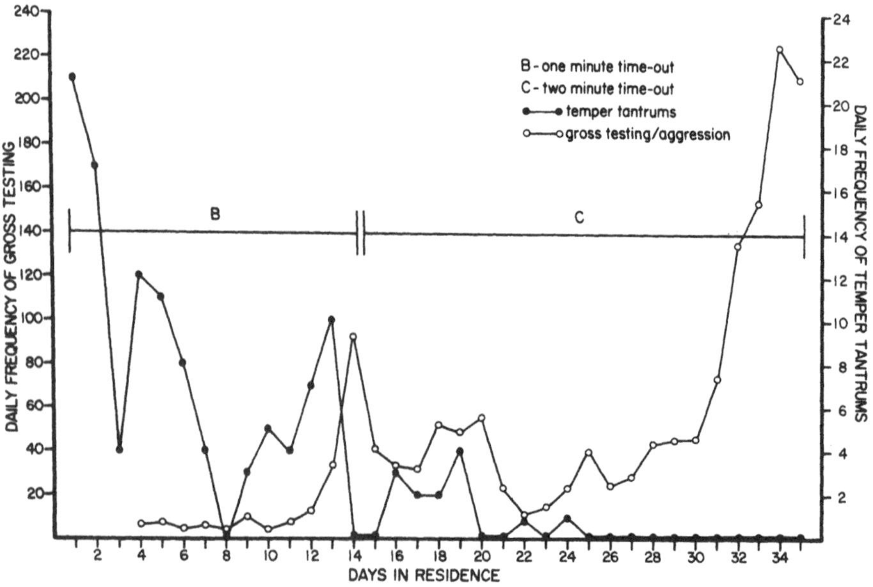

Figure 7.3. Comparative Effects of One- and Two-Minute Time-Outs on Daily Frequency of Temper Tantrums and Gross Testing/ Aggression

assaultive and testing behavior, she would aggress constantly on the way to the quiet room. We suspected that we had committed the major error of a punishment paradigm: the punishment condition apparently stimulated more of the behavior which was being punished. Staff would administer verbal social punishment cues each time Heidi aggressed during the walk to the quiet room, and if these expected social punishment cues produced an acceleration of the behavior, then it would seem understandable how the time-out condition had accelerated the aggressive behaviors. It appeared warranted to test the differential effectiveness of social reinforcers with Heidi. Observations of interactions between Heidi and the family, plus the acceleration of aggressive and testing responses which elicited negative reactions by staff, suggested that her social reinforcers were of reversed polarity. We designed the following behavioral analysis to test this hypothesis.

Heidi sat by the investigator in a large room with the same five toys present in all sessions. A video camera operated by remote control was in the room. Heidi showed no interest in the camera and was unaware of how it functioned. Heidi was seen each morning and evening at the same time intervals on successive days. Two experiments were conducted with Heidi.

In experiment 1, a variable left-eye strabismus (left eye would turn in, independently of right) was paired with both expected positive social reinforcers and expected social punishment stimuli. The investigator never spoke to Heidi during these sessions, except to present the social reinforcement contingencies. Each session was 30 minutes long. The investigator operated a remote cumulative recorder and a bank of numerical counters for data collection. The order of reinforcement contingencies tested for successive sessions is described below:

Session 1

Baseline: Investigator counted frequency of left-eye strabismus, while trying to engage Heidi in playing with the toys.

Sessions 2 and 3

Strong negative verbal comments (ostensible social punishment stimuli) were delivered by the investigator at the occurrence of each incident of left-eye strabismus (e.g., "No," "Stop that," "Don't do that," while pointing to her eye). Observers concurred, from observing video tapes, that the investigator was providing what they would consider severe social punishment. As in all sessions, the investigator tried to initiate parallel play with the toys placed in the room.

Session 4

Return to baseline: the investigator recorded the frequency of the occurrence of the left-eye strabismus.

Session 5

The investigator replicated presentation of the social punishment contingency on the left-eye strabismus as performed in Sessions 2 and 3.

Session 6

Return to baseline: investigator counted the frequency of left-eye strabismus.

Sessions 7 and 8

Expected positive social reinforcement was contingent upon the occurrence of each left-eye strabismus. The positive social reinforcement included positive evaluative statements (e.g., "That's a good girl," "Isn't that nice,") and a light hug.

Session 9

Return to baseline: investigator counted the frequency of left-eye strabismus.

Results. Figure 7.4 contains the results for the successive sessions of the experiment. It was our conclusion that the social punishment contingency accelerated the left-eye strabismus; the positive social reinforcement condition seemed to decelerate the response slightly, and a certain organic level of the response occurred in all treatment conditions. The behavioral analysis supported the hypothesis reached fom observations and video taped sessions of parents and sibs with Heidi. This hypothesis was that the expected social reinforcers for Heidi were of a reversed polarity. The social punishment contingency certainly accelerated the abnormal left-eye strabismus; the positive reinforcement contingency reduced the response slightly below what was observed in the baseline condition; it was impossible to extinguish the response with the positive condition, since there was a certain organic level of the response occurring at all times. We were so startled by the data that we decided to retest the effectiveness of social punishment stimuli in a second experiment with a different response.

Procedure: Experiment II

The purpose of the study was to test for differential effectiveness of verbal social punishment stimuli on self-biting responses. Five 20-minute sessions were conducted with Heidi. These sessions were conducted in the morning and afternoon at the same time intervals on successive days. The same experimental conditions prevailed as those for experiment 1. The self-biting response occurred primarily on Heidi's hands and arms; her arms were constantly bruised from this habit. In session 1, a baseline was recorded on the frequency of self-biting. During session 2, the social punishment condition, identical to that employed in experiment 1, was contingent upon self-biting; in session 3, the investigator returned to baseline; in session 4, the social punishment contingency was replicated; in session 5, the investigator returned the response to baseline.

Results. Figure 7.5 shows the cumulative recordings for the five successive sessions in which the expected social punishment contingency was contrasted with the baseline of self-biting. Again, as it had affected the strabismus response, the social punishment condition accelerated the abnormal response of self-biting. The results were interpreted as corroborating the results of experiment 1, supporting the hypothesis that Heidi demonstrated a reversed polarity of expected social reinforcers. This condition of reversed polarity of social reinforcers has been noted with other disturbed children referred to the Center, and it occurred in various diagnostic categories. Because this finding is considered so crucial, a more detailed discussion of polarity of social reinforcers is provided below.

Discussion: Experiments I and II. Our behavioral analysis provided some explanation of why the time-out condition failed to alter Heidi's as-

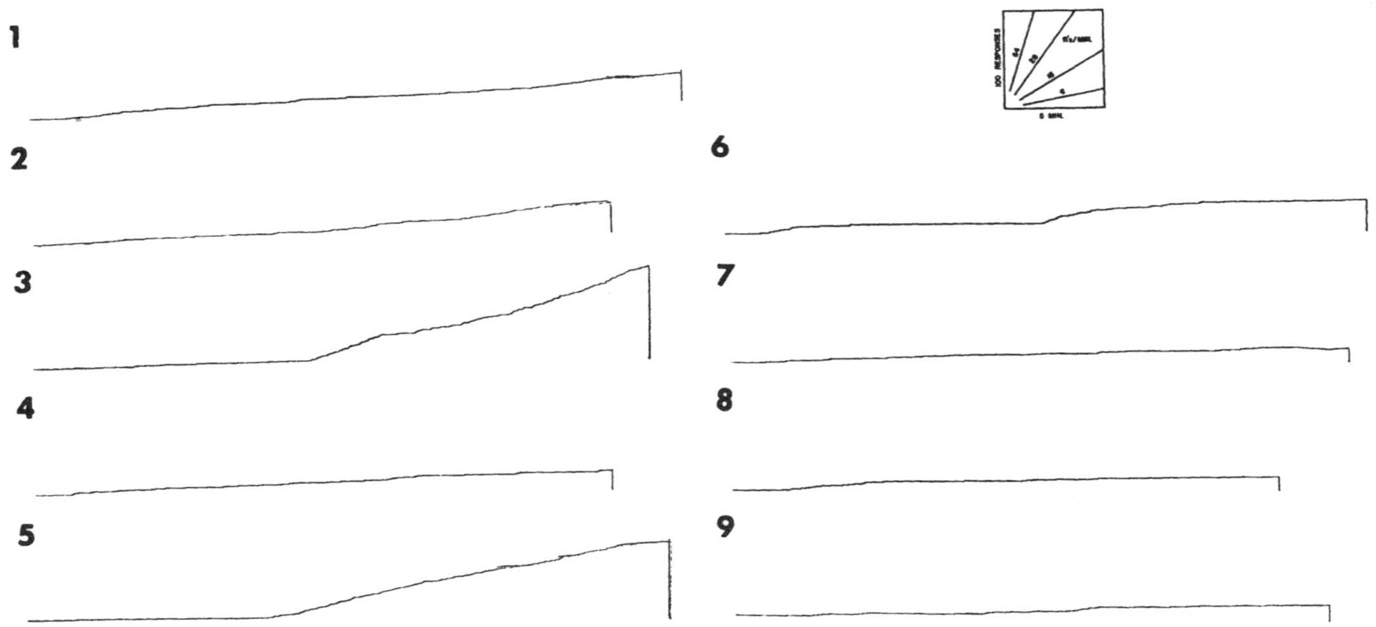

Figure 7.4. Effect of Praise and Social Punishment on the Frequency of Left-Eye Strabismus

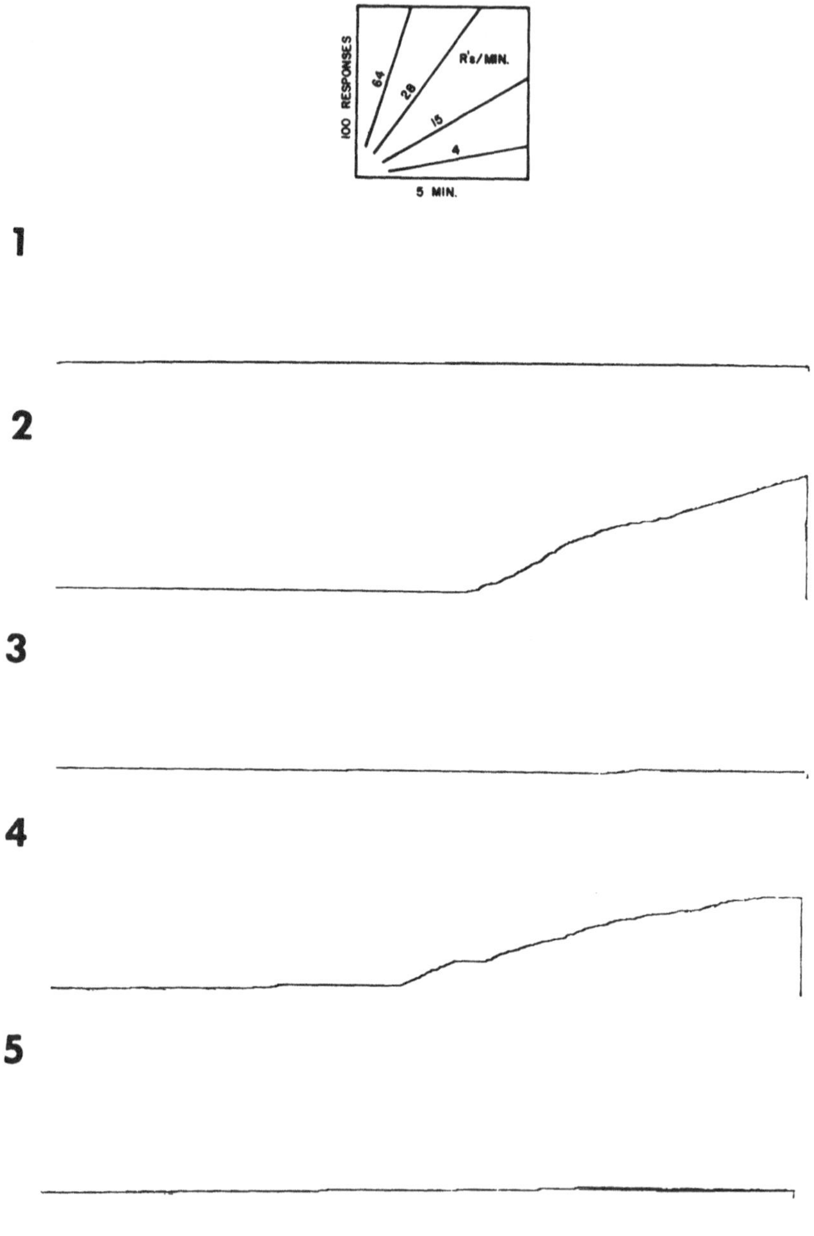

Figure 7.5. Effect of Social Punishment on the Frequency of Self-Biting

saultive behaviors, i.e., the frequent social punishment stimuli elicited by Heidi's gross aggressive behavior while she was being walked or carried to the quiet room served to accelerate that behavior, since, for this child, the expected social punishment contingency functioned as a positive reinforcement. Second, the behavioral analysis confirmed the clinical impression that the parents were currently, and inadvertently, maintaining her bizarre behavior by their social reinforcers and were understandably at a loss about how to control her behavior. Third, the analysis indicated that the immediate treatment program should first involve counter-conditioning Heidi's social reinforcers. This latter treatment program will be discussed later in more detail, but, in summary, it involves pairing expected social punishment stimuli with faradic stimulation while simultaneously counter-conditioning expected positive verbal social reinforcers by pairing these statements with food during all meals.

A finding of primary interest in this case, one which has been found in numerous cases at the Treatment Center, is that "unqualified attention" from others was not the reinforcement contingency for the deviant behaviors, but a very specific kind of social reinforcement was operated for with these behaviors. The finding of contaminated social reinforcers is almost obvious, for it then becomes apparent how a normal environment will maintain the deviant behavior. For example, the undesired behavior would typically elicit ostensible social punishment stimuli from others that have the unfortunate consequence of accelerating the behavior and causing such events as school dismissal and, finally, clinic referral. It becomes apparent how the social environment will maintain, indeed accelerate, deviant behavior which has a history of reversed expected social reinforcers. In Heidi's case, considerable treatment time would have been saved if the behavior analysis had been conducted immediately at her admission. Such a procedure should optimally be routine for severely disturbed children, since it identifies the reinforcement contingencies operated for with the referral behavior and indicates what initial steps must be taken to construct a behavior-modification program. In this case, and perhaps in many similar cases in residential settings, the first treatment program indicated would be to counter-condition the social reinforcers to the correct valence.

It should be clarified that with some children reversed polarity has been found, whereas with some youngsters both expected positive reinforcers and social punishment conditions function to accelerate behaviors, and the converse occurs with others, and that these effects may vary with different reinforcing persons and conditions. There are no general conclusions which may be drawn from the data, other than that it is warranted in all instances to investigate the kind of reinforcement contingencies maintaining disturbed children's behavior.

A year before making the case study of Heidi, the investigator had stumbled upon an incidence of reversed polarity of social reinforcers in an idiographic study with an adolescent schizophrenic. Perhaps the entire study is best described as an example of serendipity. That study is described in Chapter 6 as "The effectiveness of negative practice and social reinforcers for symptom control of Gilles de La Tourette's disease in a schizophrenic adolescent."

The findings of reversed polarity of social reinforcers are based on few subjects thus far, but the ramifications of the data certainly justify further study. It becomes apparent that, if a child's reinforcers are such that expected positive social reinforcers have a reversed effect, social punishment in the form of negative evaluative statements, spankings, etc., will have an accelerating effect on the behaviors with which they are paired. The unfortunate consequence is that the best-intended of homes will maintain the most socially abnormal behavior with such reinforcement conditions. In those homes, desired behaviors are praised with the usual social reinforcers, but, because of the child's reversed polarity of social reinforcers, such desired responses decelerate whereas the social punishment contingent upon socially deviant responses only serves to accelerate those behaviors, much to the disconcertment and confusion of the parent. Under such conditions, one expects that parents', or perhaps foster parents', reinforcement contingencies will eventually be placed on some degree of an extinction program, since they had failed to succeed for them. Under such an extinction program of preferred child-training practices, one expects random behavior in the parents' child-rearing practices that they use in their attempts to control the child's behavior. This result's in the parents' attempting numerous techniques, none of them tried very persistently, and the long-term effect is tantamount to placing the child's abnormal behaviors on a thinner reinforcement schedule and thereby producing greater resistance to extinction of the undesirable habits. Various combinations of social reinforcers have been observed to be employed by the parents; few have been studied extensively. Such combinations as positive social reinforcers' functioning as expected, and social punishment's having no or weak effects have been observed; combinations also occur in which social punishment stimuli are effective, whereas positive social reinforcers have a negligible effect; combinations are observed where both positive and punishment conditions have weak effects, particularly in the depressed child.

SELF-DESTRUCTIVE AND AGGRESSIVE RESPONSES

It has been noted in the literature that autistic children often demonstrate a behavior pattern of aggressive and self-destructive behaviors (Rimland, 1964). In our behavior analysis with Heidi we have noted that the expected positive social reinforcers and punishment contingencies have been noticeably ineffective in altering her behavior. Lovaas reports similar findings (Lovaas, 1966), noting that these children are typically not responsive to expected social punishment contingencies; we concluded from our behavior analysis with Heidi that her social reinforcers were contaminated and expected social punishment would actually accelerate the abnormal behaviors with which they were paired. For example, we noticed with Heidi's parents—and it was confirmed by them—that when Heidi was demonstrating aggressive or self-destructive behaviors, they attempted to control those behaviors with social punishment contingencies, but the resultant guilt evoked by their punishing her would often result in their immediately providing affection, which we suspect inadvertently resulted in counter-conditioning expected social punishment stimuli. It was our hypothesis that social punishment stimuli became discriminative stimuli for eventual positive social reinforcement, the latter contingency being on an increasingly thinner schedule. Also, the contingencies operated for with her aggressive behaviors included preferred foods, certain toys, and activities.

Clearly, a more effective social punishment condition had to be used to decelerate Heidi's self-destructive and aggressive behaviors. It was decided that an electro-shock apparatus, such as that employed by Lovaas *et al.* (1966), Tate and Baroff (1966), and Kushner and Sandler (1966), be employed as the aversive stimulus. The apparatus contained six C-type batteries with an inductorium to generate high-voltage and low-amperage electro-shock. In replication of the methodology employed by Dr. Lovaas, it was recommended that the shock be applied either to the arm, or to the leg, for at least one-half-second durations, contingent upon the behavior to be decelerated and also simultaneously paired with a verbal social punishment stimulus, preferably the word "No." The shock was not employed unless it could be administered within several seconds following the undesired reponse. Typically the word, "No" preceded shock so that it would acquire the expected behavioral suppressant value.

The proposed methodology was twofold. A program of conditioning positive social (secondary reinforcers) with food (primary reinforcement) in accordance with the methodology presented by Lovaas (1966b) was conducted during the same days that the aversive conditioning sessions were conducted. The aversive conditioning program involved experimental sessions in which the investigator, who was initially to be the only person to administer the shock, would work with Heidi in situations most likely to elicit the behaviors desired to be decelerated. The responses which were to be decelerated included anal play, self-mutilation responses, and aggressive responses directed toward staff and children. It was important that the program of conditioning social reinforcers be in effect on the same days as the aversive conditioning program was, in order that Heidi be differentially reinforced for appropriate responses rather than being trained totally on an avoidance program.

Administration of Faradic Punishment. Using electro-shock to countercondition self-injurious and aggressive behaviors in a seven-year-old child was not a pleasant task. However, the effects of a properly conducted conditioning program can be justifiable if the child's welfare is demonstrably improved. Let us discuss the procedure used in applying the faradic stimulation with this autistic child.

The electro-shock apparatus was simply an inductorium. The model used initially contained two 3/4″ brass rods which protruded from the end of a metal cylinder which housed the six batteries and inductorium. The apparatus, one inch in diameter, was activated by the investigator's holding it with both hands and pressing the two spring-loaded halves together. Both hands had to be used to work the apparatus. Later in the study, a more recent model of the "Hot Shot"[1] apparatus that could be operated with one hand was employed. Optimal conditioning effects occur when the reinforcement contingency follows a response as soon as possible, and also immediately follows the social (secondary) reinforcer which is to be conditioned. Perhaps these two requirements are the same, in that time is no more than a passage of events and if the reinforcement contingency is delayed in following a particular response, it is most likely being paired up with some other response. We noted that when the apparatus was employed that required the use of two hands, as soon as the child discriminated that the investigator was going to apply the instrument, avoidance reactions immediately occurred which would have been punished if at that time the investigator continued with the application of the instrument. With the one-handed apparatus, one could quickly punish the assaultive or self-destructive response before it interacted with avoidance responses.

The actual use of the apparatus was quite simple. When the subject bit herself while in the presence of the investigator, he shouted, "No," and the shock stick was flicked on and applied to her leg. This punishment was delivered quickly, since the apparatus was close at hand. This conditioning procedure was used for self-biting and self-hitting, hitting and biting others.

An interesting finding of this conditioning study, comparable to that found in teaching Heidi speech and most other behaviors, was that she did not extinguish self-biting in ten or twelve trials. It was noted that, in the first day in which the electro-shock apparatus was employed by the investigator in an experimental setting, the self-injurious and aggressive behaviors

1. Hot Shot Products, Minneapolis 16, Minnesota.

dropped out and cooperative behaviors could be maintained when food was used as reinforcer. However, as soon as Heidi left the room with another staff member, she would commence hitting and biting that staff member. The training effects did not generalize outside the experimental room, not even to the investigator himself. At this point it became necessary for the investigator to employ the shock apparatus in many situations throughout the cottage, which required long intervals of training sessions with Heidi. However, when the investigator left the cottage, Heidi would commence the punished behaviors at a high rate with the other staff who had not employed the apparatus. At this time we realized that the training effects were limited only to the investigator and it would be necessary to train the other remaining staff as punishers if they were to have any control over Heidi's behavior. The program was then changed, so that, under the investigator's supervision, the staff employed the shock apparatus as necessary for self-injurious and aggressive behaviors during the daily cottage routine. It is interesting, since we had been counting so many different behaviors, that the one event which was not counted accurately was the number of times shock was used with Heidi. This is an unfortunate but rather easily explained omission—applying the punishment contingency was a most unpleasant task. However, between 200 and 250 trials were required for the self-injurious and gross testing behaviors before they were brought under sufficient control. It is estimated that at least twice that many trials of threats to use the apparatus were required with Heidi during that six-month interval. The apparatus was faded from the program in a very natural manner. The staff were told that so long as they were able to conduct an activity without the apparatus present, they should do so, but they were to keep it in the periphery of the activity initially; eventually it was kept only in the child's room, to which staff would return with the child to scold her in the presence of the apparatus for aggressive behaviors, or an approximation of those behaviors, whenever they occurred. As the graph in Figure 2 indicates, 122 days were required for the gross testing behavior to extinguish.

An interesting occurrence during punishment of the gross testing and self-injurious behaviors was that staff would observe approximations to the punished responses that we described as low-level testing, or low-level darting, or whatever response it approximated. A gross testing response would be defined as Heidi's actually reaching out and pinching or hitting one of the staff. A low-level pinching response would be reaching out and perhaps touching as if to pinch, but not completing the pinch response, and eventually, moving the hand half-way toward the staff member, and finally merely approximating a movement previously characteristic of the "reaching-out-to-pinch-the-staff" response.

Figure 7.6 shows that, when the gross testing responses were decelerating, the rate of low-level testing responses began to be recorded, and that these became high-rate as they replaced the gross testing response. This kind of response relationship was interpreted to illustrate a hierarchy of responses and to indicate that, as a dominant and more recently acquired response was extinguished, a more distantly acquired response or, more precisely, a close approximation or vestige of the previously dominant response, now became the dominant response. This kind of relationship was

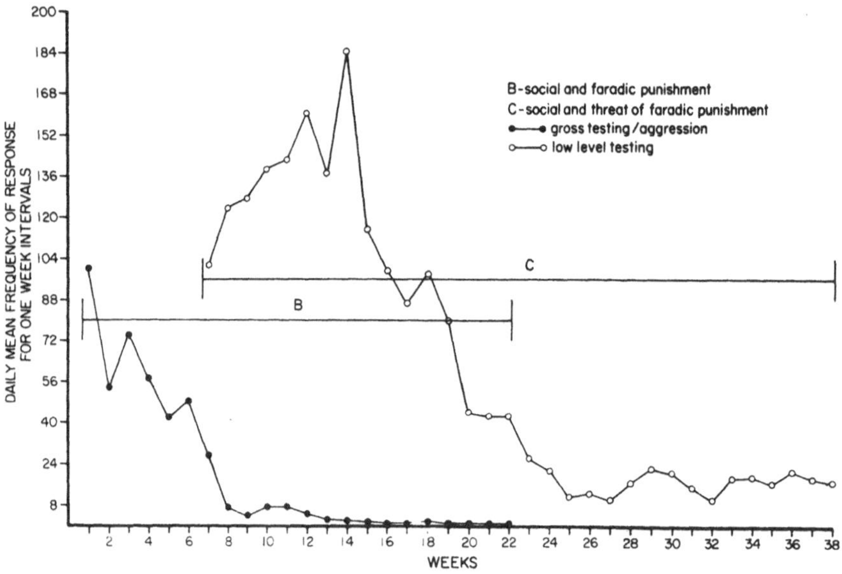

Figure 7.6. Comparison of Effects of Social and Faradic Punishment on Gross Testing/Aggression and Social and Threat of Faradic Punishment on Low-Level Testing

noted for Heidi's self-biting. After self-biting had been extinguished, it was necessary to extinguish a hierarchy of responses of increasingly distant approximations to self-biting. For example, after self-biting was extinguished, Heidi would gum herself, and eventually this response had to be extinguished. The same hierarchy of responses was noted with pinching and hitting staff and attempts to run away (darting) from staff. We contended that we had to extinguish all components of a response hierarchy. This presented a measurement problem, since the punished response was qualitatively changing. We simply made one division of the aggressive responses, gross testing/aggression was defined by physical contact, low-level testing/aggression was defined by the absence of physical contact.

HYPOTHESIS OF LEARNING DEFICIT

From the above data, one could predict the results when the staff began teaching Heidi speech. Figures 7.10 through 7.19 show that, as we were shaping speech responses by progressing from a blowing response, to humming, to the word, "Mama," a previously acquired response would contaminate acquisition of the most recent response. In clinical terms, this phenomenon would be called concreteness. Concreteness is defined here as the inability to discriminate the finer nuances of a stimulus complex, such as responding to many different stimuli as if they were the same, as contrasted to generalization, where the subject discriminates the finer aspects of a stimulus complex and is able to discriminate similar stimulus characteristics and respond appropriately. Looking at the learning history of Heidi's responses which were trained in this program, we find similarities in the deficits that hampered habit acquisition. First of all, a response which was acquired by Heidi ostensibly appeared over-generalized, in the sense that it could be evoked by a variety of situations, some of them operant and some not. We did not think that the term "over-generalization" was really appropriate. This was particularly true of her aggressive behaviors, which occurred in a variety of situations, even when she was being punished with shock. Similarly, her echolalia, which was confined primarily to the response "Daddy," would be emitted at a high rate in a variety of situations. Occasionally, the verbal response, "Hi," or "Good-bye," would occur like the response of "Daddy." Sometimes these words were appropriate verbal responses which would initiate social rewards for their occurrence, but most of the time they were not operative in terms of evoking some reward system. In fact, those occasions in which we considered "Daddy," "Hi," and "Good-bye" to be appropriate may have been correct only by chance, as a function of their occurring so randomly. Heidi's verbal responses, like her aggressive responses, were in part a function of poor discrimination ability.

A similar problem seemed to occur for toilet-training, a response which she had acquired correctly at one time, in which defecation and urination could occur appropriately when she was in the bathroom on the toilet at the right times of the day; but they were now occurring in a variety of places. However, as will be discussed later, just as aggressive responses were maintained, Heidi would defecate, urinate, and demonstrate pica quite operantly to receive verbal social punishment stimuli, particularly when aggressive responses were not effective in evoking those preferred contingencies

In trying to teach Heidi to speak, we noted that many trials were required for her to acquire each successive speech response, and that, once a response had been conditioned, it would contaminate acquisition of later responses. One hypothesis about her learning deficit was that, since it required so many trials to acquire a given response, when it had finally been acquired, it had been associated with innumerable stimulus situations. The hypothesis of a discrimination deficit would make it predictable that it would be difficult to extinguish the new response, since it was elicited by a variety of stimuli, particularly if she had been unable to discriminate the differences among these stimuli. Perhaps this hypothesis described an initial deficit of Heidi's which one may vaguely label as a "discrimination deficit," in that Heidi would not respond to the finer characteristics of the auditory stimulus but to a variety of concurrent stimuli that could be continually shifting. The resultant effect may be that, once the response had finally been acquired, it had been paired with a variety of stimuli, most of which were not preferred stimuli for evoking the response. This hypothesis is entirely speculative; it is not definitely known why so many trials were required for Heidi or whether the response once acquired was elicited by a variety of stimuli which happened to be present while the response was initially being conditioned.

Self-Biting. As already mentioned, Heidi bit herself quite frequently when she was admitted; this behavior was also prevalent prior to her admission to the Center. It was obvious that this self-destructive behavior had to be deleted from her response repertoire. Self-destructive responses are behaviors which guarantee aversive social stimuli or punishment, and, as we found with Heidi, if a child's social reinforcers are of a reversed polarity, one would predict that such responses would be maintained in almost any normal home situation because of the social punishment stimuli they would evoke. We decided to decelerate the rate of self-biting responses by using shock as the punishment contingency while simultaneously counter-conditioning social reinforcers. Each time shock was administered, it was preceded by the social punishment stimulus, or discriminative stimulus, "No," or "No, don't do that." In many situations, if the shock could not be administered quickly, briefly, and precisely, only the threat of shock was to be employed, but this too was always preceded by verbal punishment. The staff were not to delay longer than one second to administer the shock, and if they were not able to follow up on the response that quickly, they were to ignore the response. There is considerable laboratory documentation indicating that delay of reinforcement is a crucial variable in the acquisition of almost any response, since the longer the delay, the greater the probability of reinforcing an intervening and inappropriate response. Figure 7.7 shows the effectiveness of the program of employing shock in decelerating the self-biting.

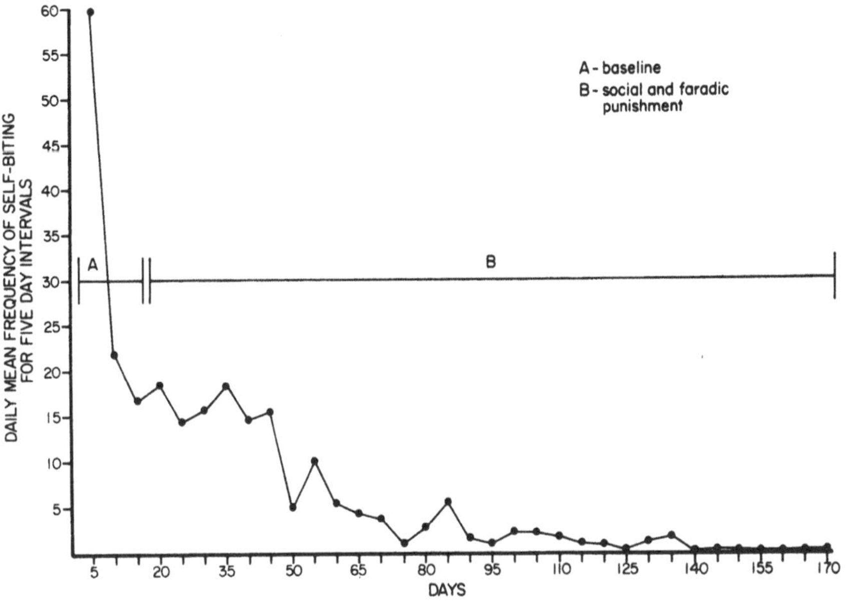

Figure 7.7. Effect of Social and Faradic Punishment on Daily Mean Frequency of Self-Biting

For most of the trials the shock apparatus was used as a threat, and its actual employment was faded as soon as possible until only the noise of the buzzer was used. We gradually shortened the length of the apparatus and eventually carried it around in a bag while decreasing the frequency of its visible presence during the day. The crucial point was that 200–250 trials of employing the shock were actually required to decelerate the aggressive and self-destructive behaviors of this autistic child. We did not find the spectacular generalization effects that would be expected of a much brighter child. Heidi was extremely concrete. The behavior which was punished had to be punished in almost all situations which could possibly elicit its occurrence. We did not have the startling treatment effect from shock that has been reported by other investigators using shock with autistic children (Lovaas, 1967; Risley, 1968; Tate & Baroff, 1966). We do maintain that all children are behaviorally heterogeneous, and that we cannot generalize from one child's treatment program to that of another—certainly a basic premise of this entire book. Shock did not prove to be a treatment panacea, since it was not rapid in its generalization for Heidi. However, we suspect that with a bright youngster, with a shorter history of less severe autism, the generalization effects would have been better. In Heidi's case, no punishment or reward system provided what we would describe as optimal generalization effects for any response she acquired.

Biting Others. Heidi would bite other persons in an unpredictable fashion; she gave no cues to signal that she was about to do so. This behavior was placed on a punishment program by being paired with shock whenever it occurred. Each time Heidi bit one of the staff, the shock apparatus would be used. The treatment program was initially conducted by the investigator in experimental sessions, and it was effective in decelerating the response almost completely in that room with the investigator, but it did not generalize outside of the room to the investigator or to the other staff. It became necessary for all staff to punish the response in a variety of situations. The biting response was recorded as a gross testing/aggressive response and is contained in that chart. The behaviors of gross testing did decelerate, as Figures 7.2 and 7.6 show. There is no separate graph to show the deceleration of biting others, but the effect of the punishment contingency was interesting and is comparable to what occurred with all of the responses which were punished with shock. Heidi quickly learned, in certain situations where the punishment contingency was in effect, not to bite the staff. She would instead perform a low-level approximation of the biting response. Rather than completing the biting response for which she had been punished, she would gum one's arm. It was decided to punish the gumming response; and after gumming was extinguished, she would place her mouth within an inch or two of one's arm. That response also had to be punished, and at this point a threat of shock and a strong verbal admonishment seemed to be sufficient. After extinction of the last approximation to a biting response, Heidi then jerked her head toward one's arm, which eventually extinguished to her turning her head toward one's arm in a manneristic style. The same kind of reversed ontogeny of a habit was observed in counter-conditioning her biting herself, hitting other people, and darting away. As we would counter-condition the current and dominant response in a hierarchy, the next response down the hierarchy, most similar to the response, would accelerate. After that response had been effectively decelerated, a more distant approximation of the original response would occur, and we would have to progress through an entire chain of related responses to eliminate a habit pattern completely. Perhaps this phenomenon is what has been described in the past as symptom substitution. This effect is reflected in Figure 7.8, which shows how this approximation of actual biting was decelerated.

Anal Play. When Heidi was first admitted, it was repeatedly observed that she would place her hand in her rectal area, manipulate her anus, and afterwards she would approach staff with her hand—which would guarantee an avoidance response by staff, invariably followed by some variation of verbal social punishment, which varied from a simple loud statement of "No," to unmitigated profane statements. This anal play behavior was apparently maintained by the social punishment stimuli it engendered, and since we knew at the time that the polarity of her reinforcers had been reversed, we decided to pair up the response with shock. The faradic stimulus for anal play was presented during experimental sessions on days in

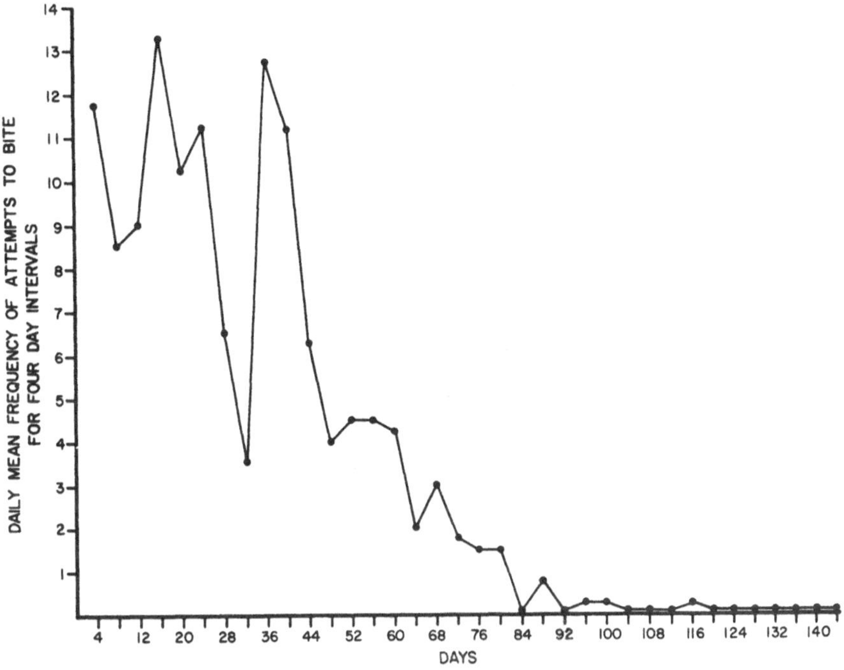

Figure 7.8. Effects of Social and Threat of Faradic Punishment on Attempts to Bite Others

which the senior investigator worked with the child. The behavior occurred many, many times when she was not under the staff's close supervision, so much of the time the punished condition was the threat of shock by staff paired up with a social punishment of "No." Figure 7.9 shows the effectiveness of the program in extinguishing the response. The response did extinguish completely, so we were unable to replicate the study, since its original rate could not be retrieved, and we were unwilling to reinstate the reversed polarity of her social reinforcers to reengage that behavior.

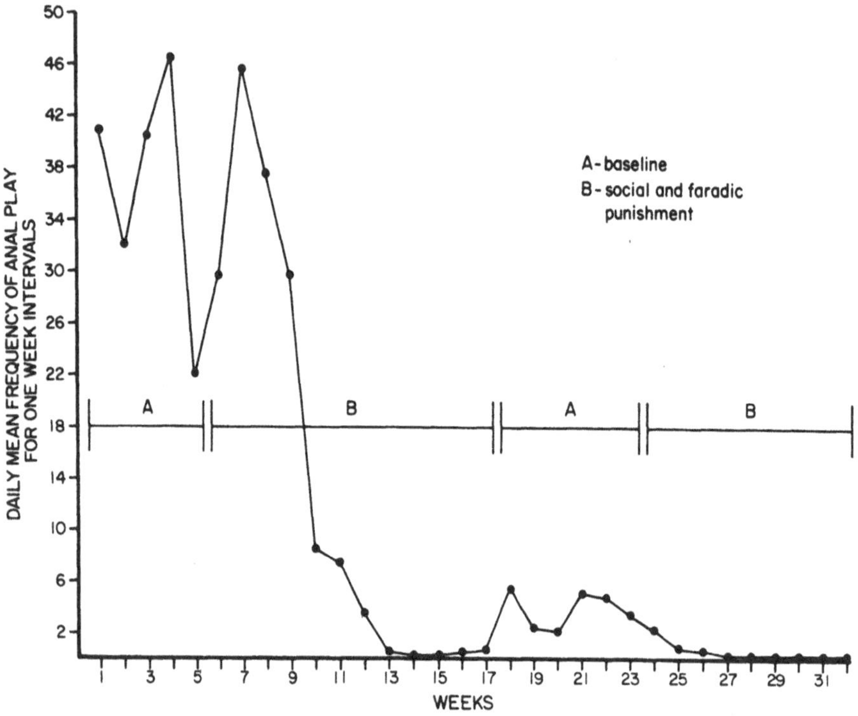

Figure 7.9. Effects of Social and Faradic Punishment on Daily Mean Frequency of Anal Play

COUNTER-CONDITIONING SOCIAL REINFORCERS

The findings from our experimental behavioral analysis indicated that we needed to devise a program to condition Heidi's social reinforcers so that the ostensible positive social reinforcers would accelerate behavior and the expected social punishment stimuli would decelerate behaviors. A twofold program was initiated. The program for simultaneously counter-conditioning self-injurious and aggressive behaviors as well as conditioning social punishment stimuli has already been discussed. A program was also devised to replicate the technique of Lovaas (1966) of using food to condition positive social reinforcers.

On day 23, a program was initiated to counter-condition Heidi's positive social reinforcers. Let us reiterate that the program was coordinated with the management order to use faradic stimulation to counter-condition aggressive responses and also to condition the social punishment stimuli to be as effective as would be expected in a normal environment. During the conditioning of the positive social reinforcers, the food available at mealtime was used as the primary reinforcement contingency. All meals were used in this conditioning program so long as staff were available to conduct the program. The program was maintained at least five days a week for all three meals, and on weekends when staff were available. The conditioning program required Heidi to be seated at a table facing the investigator. The investigator would present a positive social reinforcer such as "Good girl," "That's nice," "That's a good girl, Heidi," "Very good," etc. If Heidi responded with eye contact to the investigator's social reinforcement statement, she would immediately be presented with one bite of food by the staff member. The reinforcement training condition was on a 1:1 schedule at all times, i.e., a 100% reinforcement schedule, in that in every trial to which Heidi responded with eye contact, food would be administered. The conditioning program was continued for 274 meals for a total of 13,525 trials. The effectiveness of the program of conditioning Heidi's social reinforcers was ascertained by another experimental analysis of her social reinforcers, as we shall now describe.

Testing Polarity of Social Reinforcers. After conditioning of positive social reinforcers and the gross testing/aggressive responses had decelerated close to zero, and low-level testing had declined significantly, we hypothesized that Heidi's social reinforcers were of the correct polarity. We decided to test the hypothesis experimentally to determine whether the treatment effect would be demonstrable on an abnormal habit pattern, as in the initial behavioral analysis study.

On day 1, in the morning, Heidi had three 20-minute sessions during which she practiced throwing a ball back and forth with the same staff member in the same room, with five-minute rest period between sessions. Similarly, three 20-minute sessions, with five-minute breaks, were conducted in the afternoon of the same day, and again on the morning of the next day. The objective of the study was to test the relative effectiveness of three reinforcement contingencies. The procedure was differentially to reinforce Heidi's hand-touching mannerism (touching face with hand, touching floor or wall or objects about the room with hand) with three reinforcement conditions, with each condition available for three of the 20-minute intervals in a counterbalanced order of *A,B,C, C,A,B,* and *B,C,A.* Condition *A* was an expected extinction condition of ignoring the manneristic response; the second contingency, *B,* was the ostensible social punishment of saying, "No," "Stop that," and gesturing toward the faradic stimulator; the third reinforcement condition, *C,* was verbal praise such as "That's a good girl," "That's nice," "Very good." The first 20-minute session as the extinction condition, the second 20-minute session was the threat of punishment with verbal admonishment, the third condition was praise.

On the next series of sessions, the order was threat of punishment (*B*), praise (*C*), and ignoring (*A*). The third series of sessions occurred on the morning of the second day. The first condition was praise (*C*), the second condition was ignoring (*A*), and the third condition was threat of punishment (*B*).

Table 7.1. Effect of Three Social Reinforcement Contingencies on Frequency of Manneristic Response

	Social Punishment and Threat (B)	*Extinction No Reinforcement (A)*	*Positive Social Reinforcement (C)*
Session 1:	36	8	51
Session 2:	17	23	39
Session 3:	7	3	22
	60	34	112

Table 7.1 shows that the extinction condition of ignoring the manneristic response effected the greatest deceleration of the behavior, the threatening response produced the next greatest decelerating effect, and, to the happiness of all staff involved, the positive social reinforcement condition accelerated the response spectacularly above the other conditions. It would have helped us if a baseline had been obtained for comparison of these three conditions.

Perhaps the extinction/no reinforcement condition could be interpreted as a controlled baseline condition. Figure 7.10 shows the cumulative recordings taken for each experimental session. The cumulative recordings were obtained by a research analyst who was observing the child-care worker conducting the study.[2] The research analyst operated the remote recording apparatus; Heidi was unable to determine what the analyst was doing, since the recording buttons could be pushed silently and invisibly (to her). During the second replication of the extinction condition, there was an apparent acceleration effect. We suspected that this acceleration was a function of order effects, since it followed the positive reinforcement condition and Heidi may have still been operating for that kind of reinforcement. This interpretation, of course, is only a suspicion, and was not confirmed by successive replications; the possibility of such a design error's occurring in a short-term experimental analysis of reinforcement contingencies should be recognized.

The above experimental analysis of Heidi's social reinforcers indicated that they were now of a correct polarity, that we could cease the program

2. The authors wish to acknowledge Mr. Duane Alwin, child-care worker at the time of this study, who designed and conducted this experimental analysis of behavior.

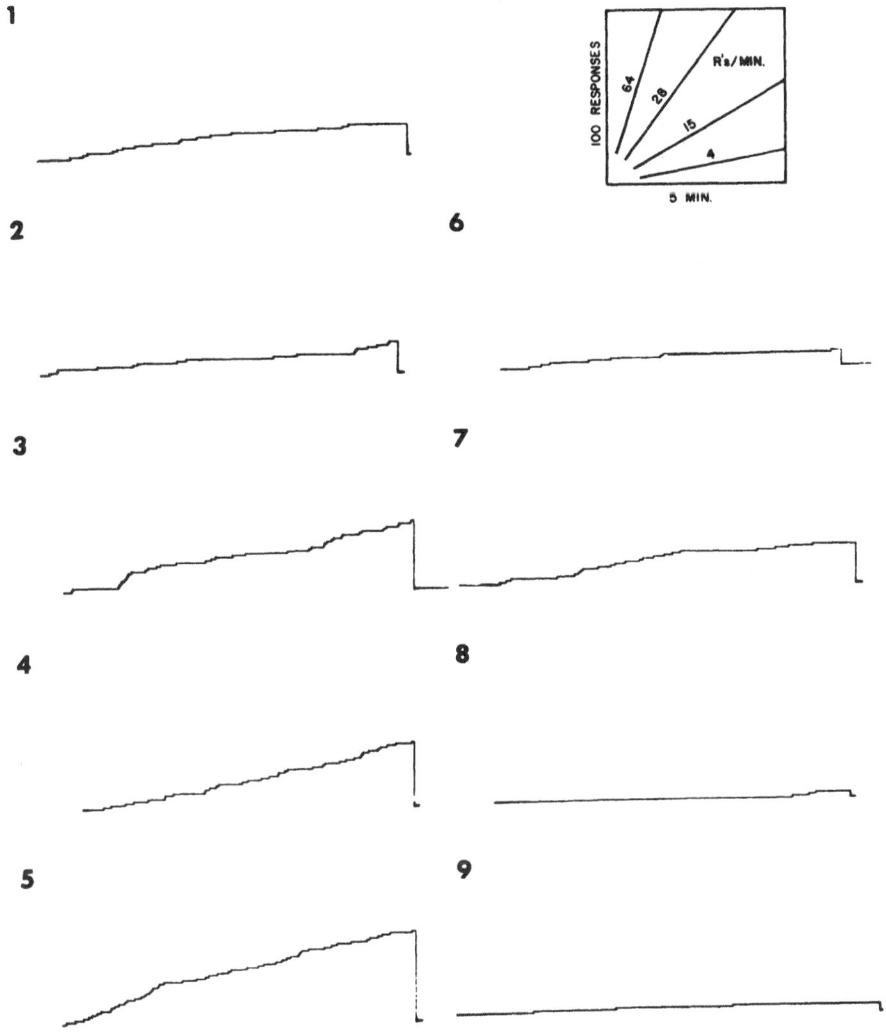

Figure 7.10. Effect of Praising, Ignoring, and Socially Punishing Manneristic Responses

of reinforcing social reinforcers and progress to a speech program using food as a reinforcer. We had previously attempted to use food to reinforce speech with Heidi, and after two successive days for a total of 6000 trials of attempting to shape an approximation of the word "Cat" (which was a wrong word to begin with for a non-speaking child), we had ceased that program, since Heidi was not beginning to demonstrate even the roughest verbal approximation to the cue. Furthermore, there was a marked acceleration of gross testing and low-level testing responses occurring during those sessions. We decided at that time to postpone the speech-shaping program until her social reinforcers had been conditioned to the correct valence, which had now been done. The next step of the program was to train speech.

SPEECH TRAINING PROGRAM

Method. Our method of training speech was comparable to that presented by Lovaas (1967). Positive social reinforcement and food were contingent upon imitative speech responses considered to be an acceptable approximation of staff's cue. The speech program was conducted at all meals, to a maximum of six and a minimum of one and one-half hours' training per day. The duration of each training period depended upon the available staff ratio and other training programs in progress.

During the speech-training sessions, the staff member would be seated at a table facing Heidi, fork in one hand and hand tally counters in the other to record trials, reinforcers, and frequency of certain error responses. The staff would request an attentive response, if necessary, then present the verbal cue which Heidi was required to imitate. If she responded correctly within five seconds, profuse social praise and then a bite of food were given. The rewards for speech served to continue the conditioning of positive social reinforcers, since they were discriminative stimuli for forthcoming primary reinforcement.

At the beginning of the speech program the shock apparatus was present. It was observed[3] that the apparatus would invariably suppress speech in general, specifically the trial-and-error responses so necessary for shaping speech. The instrument was thereafter removed from sight during the speech training sessions.

The method of ignoring all erroneous imitative responses was altered, since its consequence was to put all trial-and-error responses on an extinction schedule. During the first days of teaching a new response, when speech production would decelerate because of Heidi's failure to produce acceptable responses, we would (*a*) back-up to an easier response or approximation to the response being shaped, and/or (*b*) socially reinforce trial-and-error speech production occasionally during the speech-training sessions, and particularly during other activities. Trial-and-error speech production could be accelerated by imitating the verbal sounds she was beginning to acquire, much as a parent would with an infant.

Heidi was given diet supplements and vitamins at bedtime on days when

3. The authors are grateful to Isabel Schleicher, R.N., whose observations led to this alteration in the speech program.

she had not received adequate food during mealtimes because of her inability to produce the correct response. Thus there was no danger of a severe weight loss for Heidi resulting from a program where all food was used as reinforcers. Figures 7.11 and 7.12 contain Heidi's weight and height changes for successive months and are contrasted with the median expected weights and heights for her age. Heidi is a tall, slender child, as are her sibs, and her food-contingent programs of shaping social reinforcers and speech did not impair her growth.

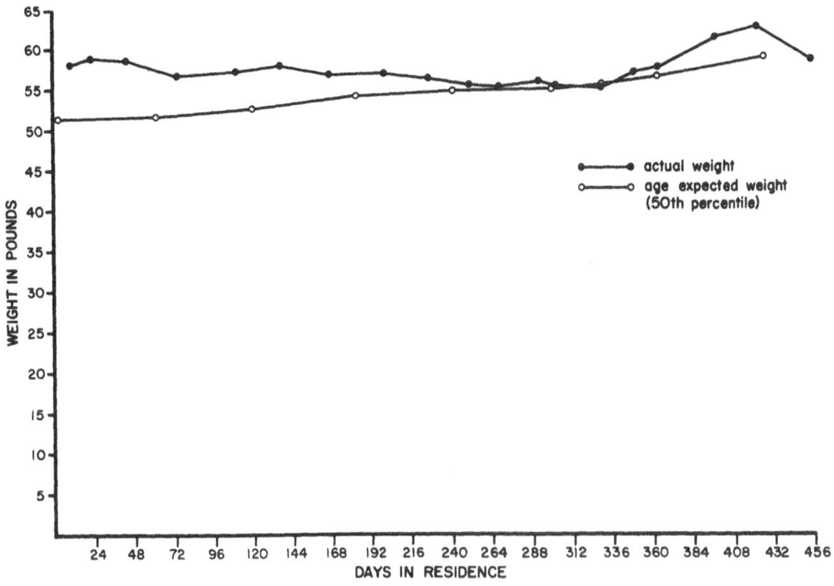

Figure 7.11. Comparison of Actual and Expected Weights during Food-Contingent Conditioning Programs

Results. The speech program is divided into 23 treatment steps illustrated in Figures 7.13 through 7.19. Each treatment step represents training of either a particular speech response or alternation training, i.e., successively rehearsing previously acquired verbal responses. The training of a verbal response was terminated when Heidi was able to imitate successfully the staff's speech model successively 90 to 100% of trials. The total daily percent of correct imitative responses for the last days of each treatment period was not always 100%, since she would often have error responses in the mornings or not respond to every trial, thus lowering the daily average of correct imitations. Heidi did attain response criterion at the conclusion of all treatment steps except for steps 16, 18, 20, and 23, and we

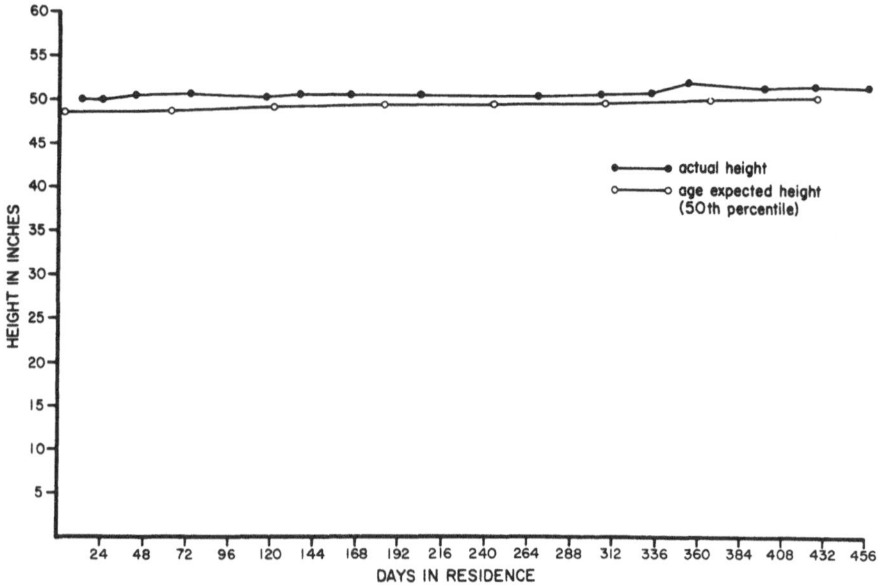

Figure 7.12. Comparison of Actual and Expected Heights during Food-Contingent Conditioning Programs

shall explain the reason for this. The successive treatment steps and their results are as follows:

Treatment Step 1

The first stimulus Heidi was to imitate was the staff member's "blowing" by pursing the lips and exhaling. This was the first approximation to shaping the word "Mama." The program began with Heidi's blowing out a candle (which was an available response) in imitation of the staff member. On successive trials the candle was faded out by our not having it lighted at all times and progressively moving it away and eventually out of sight. By the third day, the candle was removed entirely, and the next three days resulted in her imitating the blowing response increasingly better. When she was finally imitating to criterion, she was producing the response spontaneously during the day, for which she received considerable praise from staff. This phenomenon of her rehearsing the most recently acquired verbal response outside of the training situation was observed for single words, but was confined primarily to that response, i.e., there was less rehearsal of words acquired earlier. Figure 7.13 shows the rate of acquisition of the blowing response.

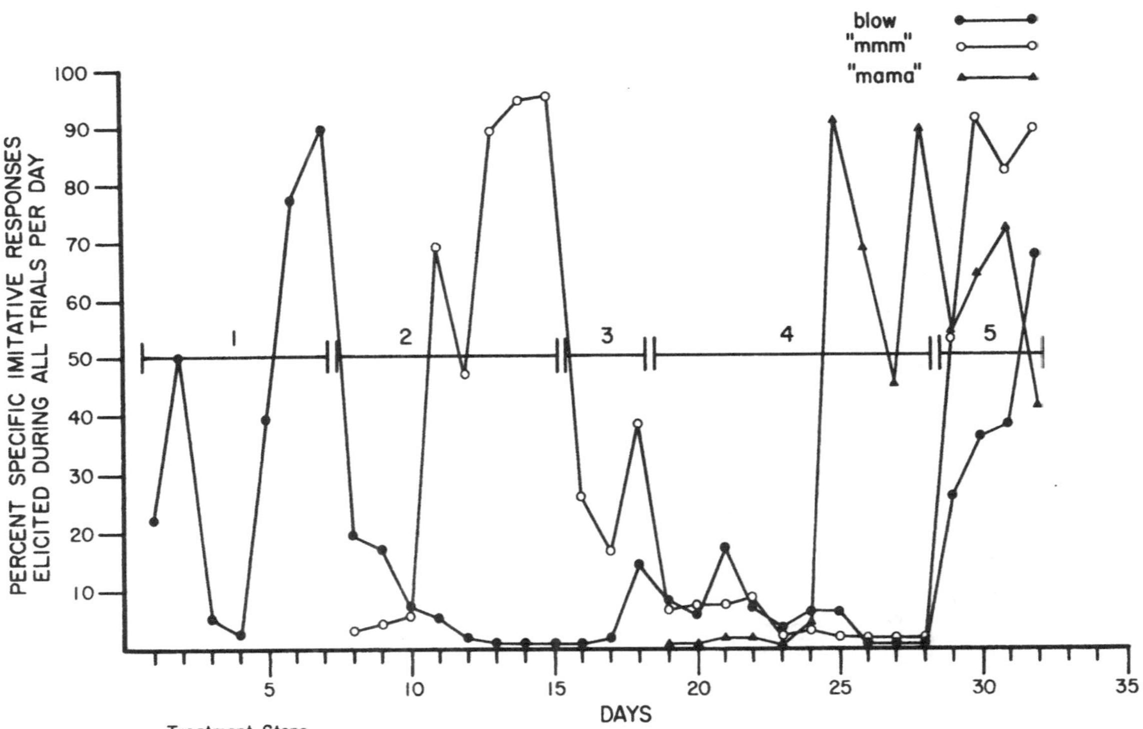

Treatment Steps

1. reinforce blowing response
2. reinforce "mmm," extinguish blow
3. alternately reinforce blow, "mmm"
4. reinforce "mama," extinguish blow, "mmm"
5. alternately reinforce blow, "mmm," "mama"

Figure 7.13. Speech-Training, Treatment Steps 1–5

Treatment Step 2

The second response shaped was humming. On the first day and most of the second, Heidi would produce the previously acquired blowing response rather than attempt the humming response. We had to shape the humming response by closing her lips while she was blowing. By the fourth day, she was receiving few reinforcements, her food intake was confined primarily to the evening diet supplements as well as liquids provided throughout the day to prevent dehydration. It was not until the blowing response extinguished, simply because it did not receive primary reinforcement, that the other random trial-and-error verbal responses from which the humming response could be shaped began to emerge. In shaping the humming response, as for all of her verbal responses, staff had to reinforce responses, at the beginning of these treatment intervals, that were very crude representations of the criterion response for which we were working. The initial humming responses which we expected and reinforced were not completed with her mouth entirely shut and were very short in duration. As the blowing response progressively diminished as the dominant error response, the humming response accelerated. This extinction of blowing, and acquisition of humming, is shown in step two in Figure 7.13. The discrimination deficit of Heidi's previously acquired verbal response interrupted with the acquisition of a new response was characteristic of her speech program. Recency of training was also a factor, since her producing the blowing response as an error response diminished with successive treatment steps; in fact, it eventually disappeared as an error response.

Treatment Step 3

During this treatment period, alternation training commenced. Staff would present the model of blowing until a correct response was elicited and then would present the humming response until that was imitated appropriately, with this alternation continuing until Heidi was capable of making the correct imitation for either word on the first trial for successive trials. Although it does not appear in Figure 7.13 that on the final day of the treatment period she was producing these alternations correctly 100% of the time, that level of success was attained in the latter part of the day. An obvious criticism of the speech-training program was that we did not demand a sufficiently long interval during which the criterion response was rehearsed.

Treatment Step 4

The fourth treatment step was to teach Heidi to say the word "Mama," which was shaped from the previously acquired blowing and humming responses as well as initially physically opening and closing her mouth. As may be seen in Figure 7.13, during treatment step 4 we were not very successful in eliciting acceptable approximations of the word "Mama" until the blowing and humming responses extinguished as error responses. When the staff would present the model of "Mama," the response elicited would be either the humming response, which was initially the most dominant error, or the earlier acquired response of blowing. Staff would record whether Heidi responded with the correct response of "Mama" or an acceptable approximation, or with the error response of humming or blowing. It was not until the seventh day of training that the correct imitative response emerged as the dominant response, at which time the blowing and humming responses had extinguished. Other error responses, which were not recorded, occurred when she did not provide any of the three plotted verbal responses contained in Figure 7.13, treatment step 4. Sometimes she would make no responses, sometimes she would make any of a variety of guttural sounds, and often a combination of humming and blowing. The latter kind of error was typical of many of the error responses elicited throughout the speech-training, i.e., she would respond with various combinations of previously acquired responses.

Heidi required 5,911 trials to teach her to produce the blowing response, 6,707 trials for reaching criterion for the humming response, and 15,653 trials to learn the response of imitating "Mama."

Treatment Step 5

The treatment goal was to train Heidi to discriminate between the "Mama," "blowing," and "humming" imitative responses. The criterion was for her to be able to repeat upon the first trial, on alternate trials, the three speech models. Five to six hours for each of four days were required for Heidi to reach this criterion among the three speech responses. Figure 7.13 shows the rates at which these were acquired.

Treatment Step 6

The next reinforced speech response was "who". As this speech model was provided, the dominant error responses were the previously acquired blowing, humming, and "Mama" responses. Figure 7.14 shows treatment step 6 and illustrates how the new verbal response of "who" was not satisfactorily acquired until the "blowing," "humming," and "Mama" responses extinguished as error responses.

Treatment Step 7

In treatment step 7, the responses acquired thus far of "blowing," "humming," "Mama," and "who" were presented alternately, i.e., the cue of

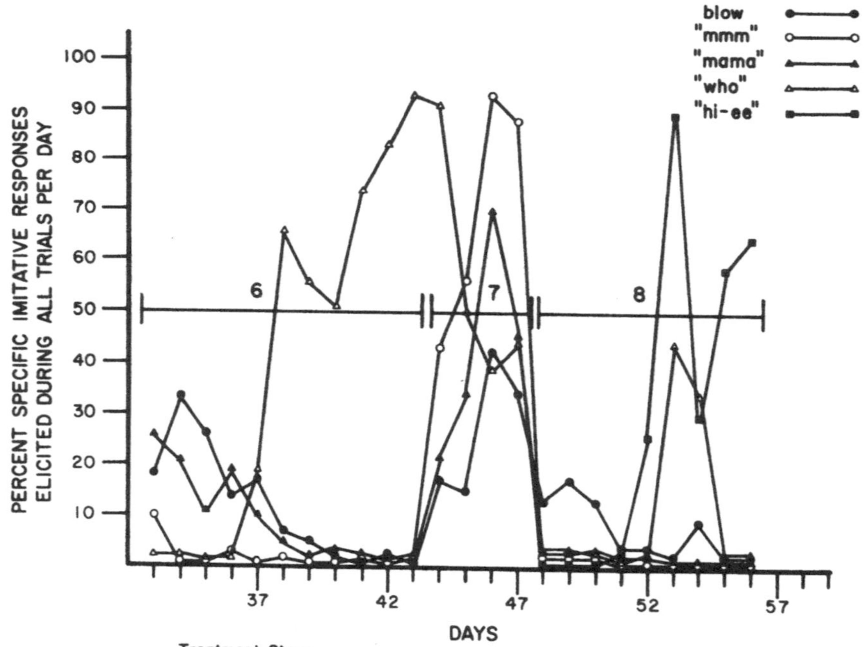

Treatment Steps

6. reinforce "who," extinguish blow, "mmm," "mama"
7. alternately reinforce "who," blow, "mmm," "mama"
8. reinforce "hi-ee," extinguish "who," blow, "mmm," "mama"

Figure 7.14. Speech-Training, Treatment Steps 6–8

"who" was given until she correctly imitated that response, and then the next cue, such as "Mama," would be given until that was imitated correctly. This procedure was continued until criterion was reached, which required four days of training whose results are shown in Figure 7.14.

Treatment Step 8

In treatment step 8, the goal was to teach Heidi the first approximation of saying her name. The criterion response was to be "Hi-eee," which was shaped from the available response of "Hi." During the early training sessions, the previously acquired responses of "who," "blowing," "humming," and "Mama" were recorded as error responses to illustrate again how these responses interfered with acquisition of the new response. As may be seen in Figure 7.14, treatment step 8, the response was not acquired until the previously acquired responses of blowing, humming, "Mama," and "who" had extinguished as error responses.

Treatment Step 9

The next speech component of the word "Heidi" trained was "Dee." During this treatment step we discontinued recording the kinds of errors, since it was becoming impossible for staff to count so many categories while smoothly conducting the speech-shaping program. However, the previous treatment periods had sufficiently documented the kind of error which impaired Heidi's speech acquisition, namely, her inability to discriminate her own speech response to a model. Previously acquired responses had to extinguish before she could acquire a new response. A total of 14,839 trials were required for Heidi to acquire the response of "Dee," as shown in Figure 7.15.

Treatment Step 10

The treatment goal was to combine the previously acquired responses of "Hi-eee" and "Dee" to produce the word "Heidi." This was completed by first alternately reinforcing "Hi" and "Dee" and then gradually presenting them more quickly, and eventually reinforcements were made contingent upon her imitating both responses successively. A total of 29,898 trials were required to bring the two responses together to shape the response of "Heidi" to criterion; the rate of acquisition is shown in Figure 7.15.

Treatment Step 11

Figure 7.16 contains results of treatment step 11, which was to teach Heidi to say the word "I." We also recorded the frequency of her stating the previously acquired responses of "Heidi" instead of the currently reinforced response. Figure 7.16 shows that once again it was not until the

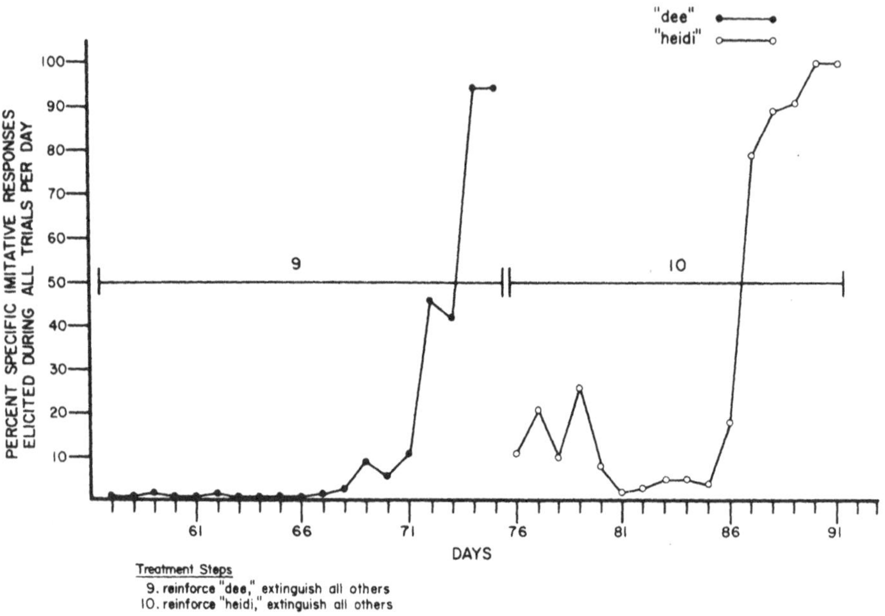

Figure 7.15. Speech-Training, Treatment Steps 9–10

previously reinforced response had decelerated through simple extinction that the new response was acquired.

Treatment Step 12

Heidi was next taught to imitate the word "me," and during this step we recorded the frequency of her saying the word "I" as an error response to the staff's model of the word "me." And again, Figure 7.16 shows that the error response of the previously acquired response had to decelerate before the new response "me" was acquired to criterion. It was becoming increasingly obvious with the successive replications that there was no facilitation effect apparent from the entire training period. We had hoped that Heidi would learn successive verbal responses more quickly; we have observed such a facilitory effect in other children. Unfortunately, thousands and thousands of trials were required for each speech response and the same kind of error continued to interfere with speech acquisition.

Treatment Step 13

Treatment step 13 was the next approximation to teaching Heidi the word "Mitch." We planned to first teach "me," then "shh," and finally to

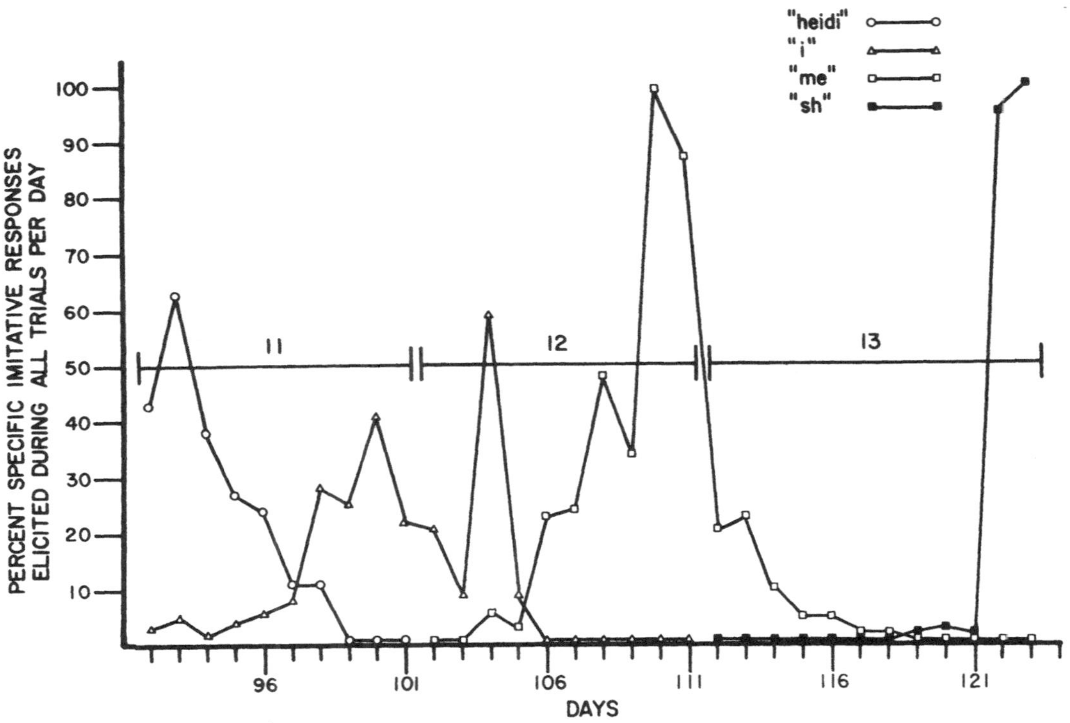

Treatment Steps

11. reinforce "i," extinguish all others, specifically "heidi"
12. reinforce "me," extinguish all others, specifically "i"
13. reinforce "sh," extinguish all others, specifically "me"

Figure 7.16. Speech-Training, Treatment Steps 11–13

bring these responses together to shape the speech response "Mitch." During treatment step 13, Heidi was being trained to say "shh" and the previously acquired response of "me" was recorded as the error response. Treatment step 13 in Figure 7.16 shows that she had considerable difficulty in acquiring the response "shh;" in fact, 11,032 trials were required.

Treatment Step 14

The treatment goal was alternation training on the previously acquired responses of "me" and "shh," the results of which are contained in Figure 7.17.

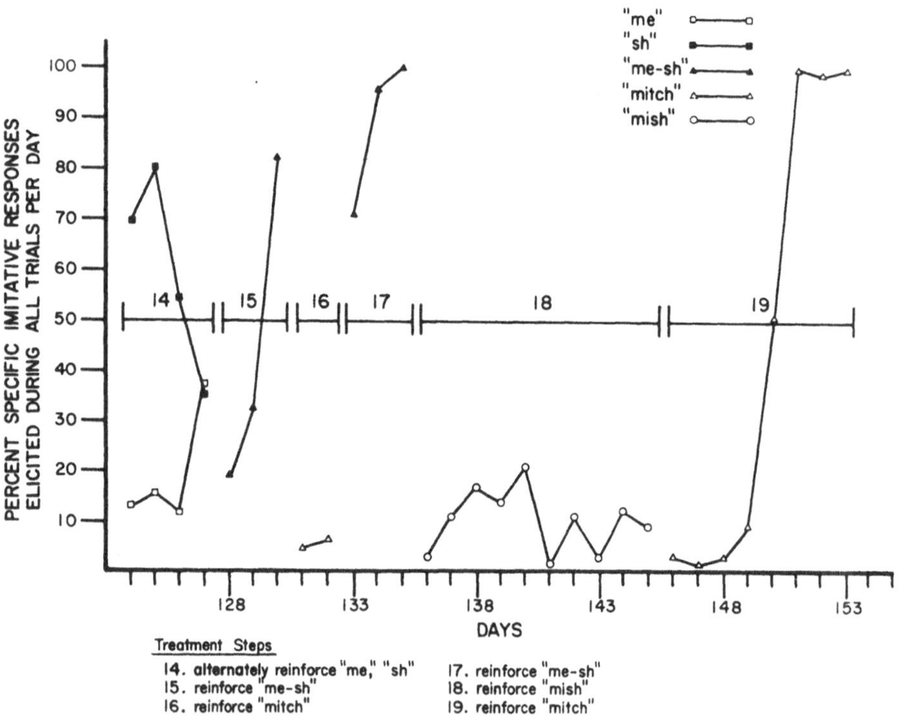

Figure 7.17. Speech-Training, Treatment Steps 14–19

Treatment Step 15

The responses of "me" and "shh" were combined for the response of "Meeshh." This was accomplished by reinforcing her successful imitation of both responses and progressively decreasing the time interval between cues until only the single cue of "Meeshh" was given. The rate of acquisition is shown in Figure 7.17.

Treatment Step 16

In this treatment interval, we attempted to shape "Meeshh" to "Mitch," but her performance indicated that the step would be too difficult, so we then proceeded to treatment step 17, shown in Figure 7.17.

Treatment Step 17

At this time we "backed-up" and reinstated training on "Meeshh" and retrained the response until it was again reliably available to Heidi. This step is shown in Figure 7.17.

Treatment Step 18

In treatment step 18, the response to be shaped was "Mish," as the next approximation to "Mitch." As may be seen in Figure 7.17, the word "Mish" was not trained to criterion for fear it would interfere with transition to the response of "Mitch."

Treatment Step 19

The criterion response was now "Mitch," which Heidi had to imitate progressively better in successive trials to receive the primary reinforcement of food. Treatment step 19, as illustrated in Figure 7.17, shows that she did acquire that response to criterion within five days.

Treatment Step 20

We began alternation training for the family names of "Daddy," "Mama," "Mitch," "Jay," and "Heidi." This was a rather discouraging training period. Heidi quickly retrieved the response of "Jay," but was progressively unable to retrieve the responses of "Daddy," "Mama" and quickly lost the previously acquired response of "Mitch," and the response of "Heidi" was now totally unavailable. Figure 7.18 contains the data accumulated at this time.

Treatment Step 21

We now "backed-up" the program to retrain the response of "Heidi," which seemed the most difficult response for Heidi to recall. We had to begin anew by teaching the response "Dee." The other component of the word Heidi, "Hi," remained available to her at this time. As may be seen in treatment step 21, in Figure 7.18, 17 days of training were required to reinstate the response of "Dee."

Treatment Step 22

The two responses of "Hi" and "Dee" were combined for the word "Heidi," the acquisition of which is seen in Figure 7.18.

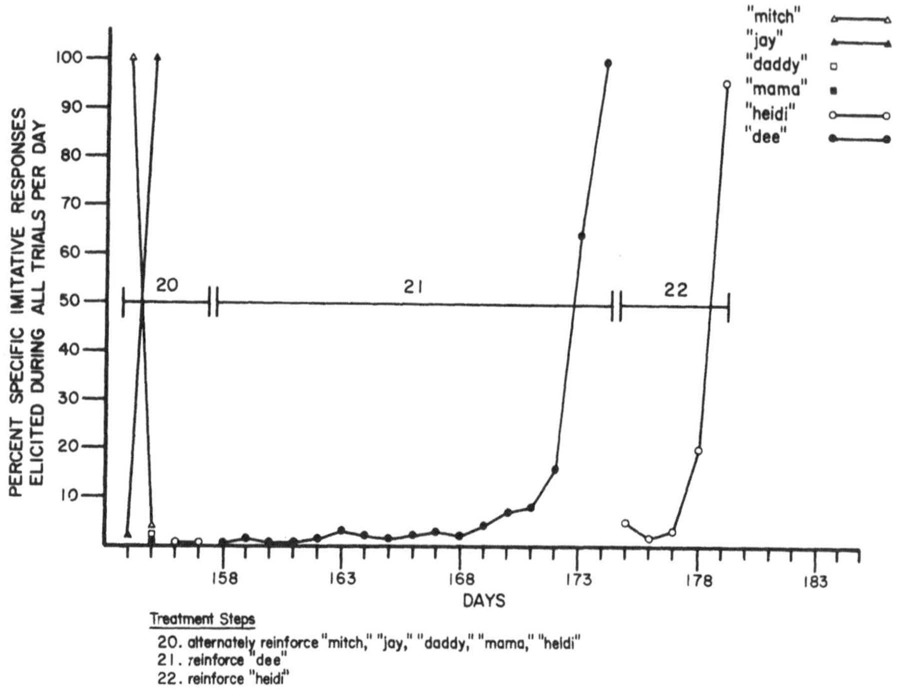

Figure 7.18. Speech-Training, Treatment Steps 20–22

Treatment Step 23

Treatment step 23 was alternation training again for the words "Heidi," "Daddy," "Mama," "Mitch," and "Jay." As is seen in Figure 7.19, which contains the combined percent success of imitating all five words alternately, it was unsuccessful. The responses of "Heidi" and "Daddy" were most reliably imitated, but she was unable to imitate the other words.

Discussion. After a total of 152,914 trials and uncounted hours of training, we had not taught Heidi to imitate the names of her family reliably. Heidi demonstrated a severe deficit in retaining acquired speech responses: she was never able to generalize so as to use those responses operantly, except that she was gradually using "good-bye" appropriately. Optimal generalization requires fine discrimination to discern similarities and differences among stimuli. It was our hypothesis that Heidi was able to comprehend language at a rate of acquisition increasingly disparate from her ability to express speech, as was developmentally observed by her parents and also demonstrable during the speech program. For example, we noticed that as she became increasingly compliant to verbal requests, she

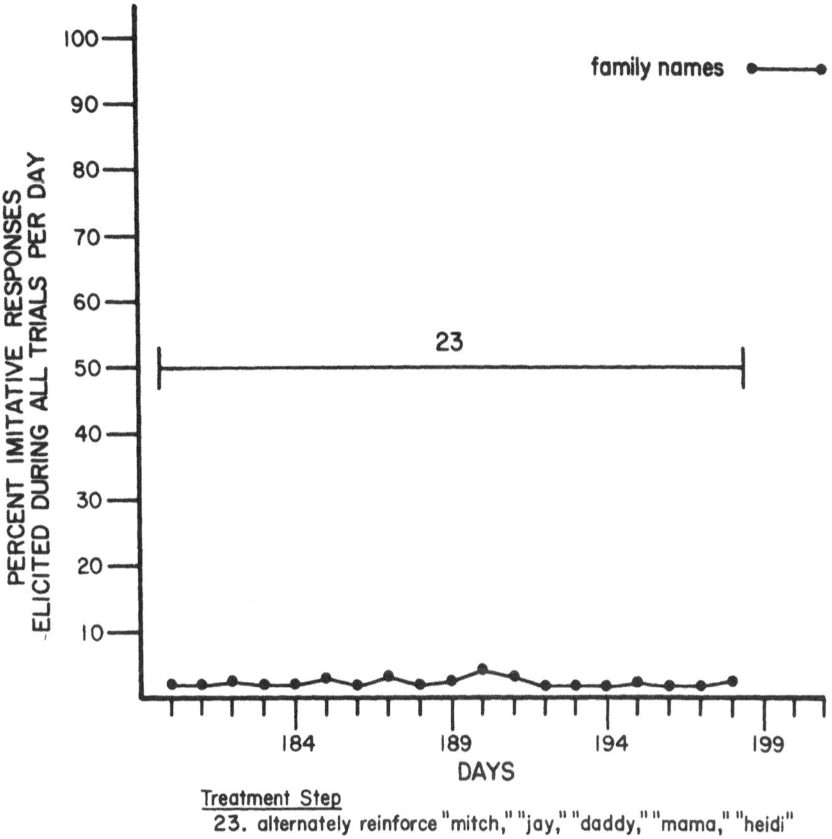

Figure 7.19. Speech-Training, Treatment Step 23

could comprehend and follow verbal instructions which were complex considering her absence of communicative language.

This discrepancy between reception and expression of speech would be likely to guarantee conflict experiences for a child. Our hypothesis was that the random, often aggressive, responses evoked by such frustrating circumstances contributed to Heidi's acquisition of her autistic behaviors. We suspected that she learned to operate for preferred reinforcers motorically, e.g., a temper tantrum or an aggressive response is a crude form of sign language but is often highly effective. Since we had been convinced after 152,914 trials that Heidi was not reliably retaining language, and that she had no facilitation for acquiring successive speech responses, we abandoned the approach of teaching verbal language. On the hypothesis that many of her abnormal behavior patterns were operant responses, and as such were a form of communication, we decided to begin a program of teaching a rudimentary sign language. That program was successful to the extent of teaching her to point to something she wished, and to take one by the hand, if necessary, to a place where she wanted to go.

We have not presented Heidi's speech program to illustrate treatment technique or the value of learning theory. We have presented it to document methodology and, specifically, the value of monitoring treatment variables so one can assess a program's effectiveness, and from constant refinement of hypotheses generated from the data, alter the treatment program accordingly.

LOW-LEVEL TESTING

Concomitant with the speech-shaping program, Heidi's gross testing/aggressive responses had decelerated, but as previously noted, we observed that this behavior was being replaced by a close approximation of it, which we have described as low-level testing or, perhaps more precisely, low-level aggressive responses. Low-level testing responses were defined as her making a gesture as if she were about to commit a gross testing/aggressive response, which would appear as an incompleted striking, biting, or kicking response. These low-level testing responses would also include attempting to use an object in an aggressive manner, e.g., as deliberately spilling food or kicking over a chair. At the time the low-level testing responses were recorded, the gross testing responses were extinguishing as a function of the administration of shock. Low-level testing responses were paired with the threat of shock preceded by verbal social punishment. Specifically, the staff member would loudly scold Heidi for the low-level testing response, on a variable and decreasing schedule, and gesture as if to use the apparatus. The threat to use shock as a contingency was gradually faded. Figure 7.6 shows the effect of this treatment program using an *AB* design. The *A* interval represents the baseline, and *B* the punishment contingency.

Whenever we acquired a new staff member or trainee, Heidi would test him with these low-level responses. It was our hypothesis that at such times she was again testing for the available social punishment conditions. We also observed that if one of the staff were shifted to another phase of the program and then re-visited our group, Heidi would usually test the availability of social punishment with her threats to hit, bite, etc. This effect still occurred one year after her date of admission, but it was progressively diminishing, i.e., the responses reinstated were more comparable to those observed five to seven months earlier, so that across time they were progressively less similar to the original gross testing/aggressive responses.

Darting Responses. When staff accompanied Heidi on a walk, inside or particularly outside, or during any structured activities, Heidi would demonstrate an escape behavior which we described as darting. Darting was defined as Heidi's moving in an almost startled fashion, i .e., leaping away from the staff and running for a short distance and immediately engaging in some activity of her own, or perhaps wandering around in an apparently aimless manner. We considered that Heidi had made a darting response when she moved more than 12 feet away from the staff and did not return immediately when requested to do so. A darting response was typified by the seemingly startled reaction of jumping away from staff and running off. Each occurrence was recorded as a count of one. We hypothesized that the darting response had historically operated for social punishment in the form of persons chasing after and scolding her to return. Following acquisition of the baseline, we initiated the treatment condition of pairing verbal social punishment with shock (which was faded to threat of shock within one week) for darting responses. This contingency was defined as scolding quite loudly and severely, "No," "Don't do that," "Don't you ever run away from me again," and threatening to use the electro-shock apparatus, which would engender profuse tears and an approach response to obtain affection. Figure 7.20 shows the effect of punishing with shock and fading to threat of shock, and in all instances using verbal admonishment.

One interesting observation, also noted by Lovaas (1967) when he administered shock, was that Heidi soon learned to approach the staff tearfully after shock had been administered or threatened. This behavior appeared to be a response operating to avoid further shock, since such an approach response containing tears and "melting" into one's arms or "molding" was positively reinforced by staff. Perhaps this effect, coupled with the conditioning of positive social reinforcers, was responsible for teaching Heidi to be an affectionate child. Six months after the onset of the shock punishment program, whenever in discomfort, or whenever the situation was available, Heidi would quickly snuggle up in one's lap and "mold."

TOILET-TRAINING

Evacuation was a major problem with Heidi. Heidi was enuretic, diuretic, encopretic, and coprophagic, and the singular or combined occurrences of any of these behaviors were instrumental in guaranteeing social punishment stimuli from staff. Heidi would be enuretic while sitting on one's lap, or while sitting on a chair facing staff while they attempted to condition positive social reinforcers. We hypothesized that these behaviors operated to receive her preferred social punishment contingency. It had been observed that, while holding a staff member's hand and walking down the hall receiving a count of one for a compliant response, Heidi would simul-

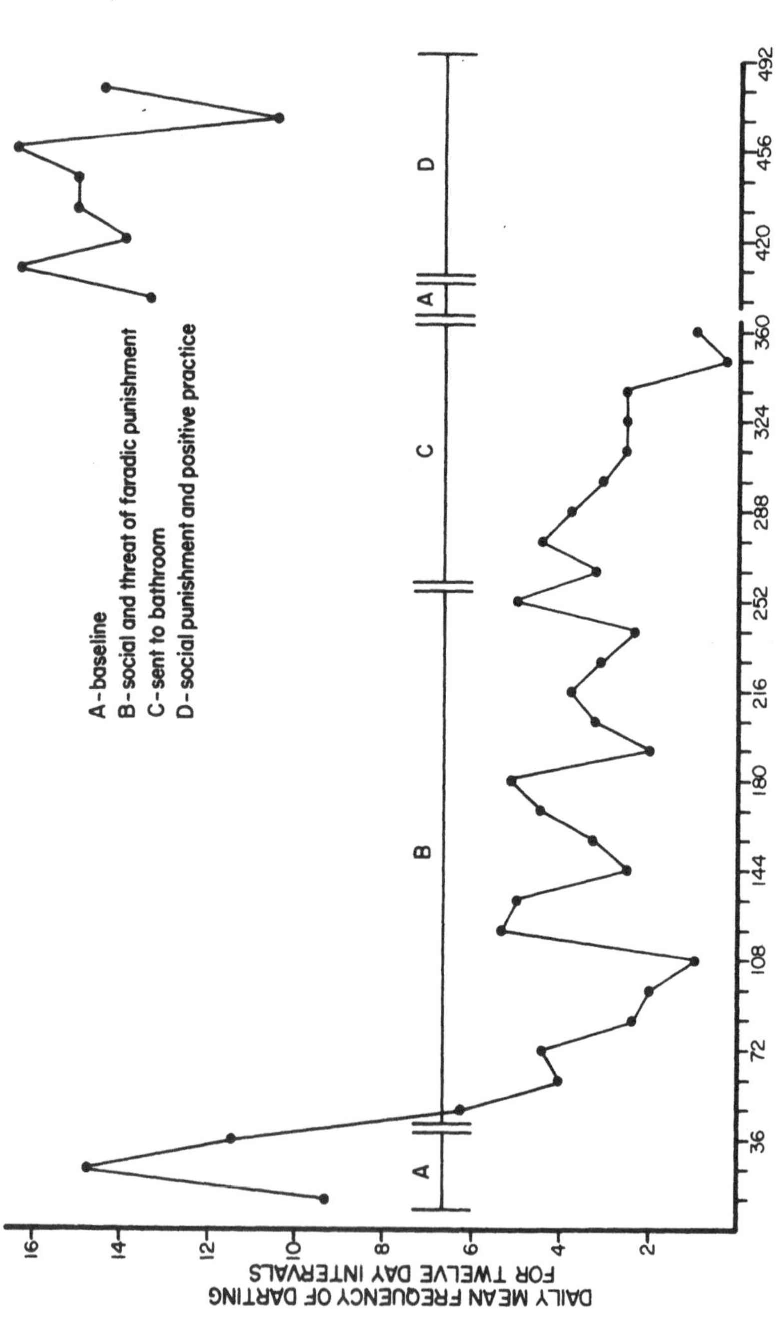

Figure 7.20. Effects of Three Treatment Procedures on Daily Mean Frequency of Darting Response

taneously defecate. Encopresis was such a severe problem that if she were allowed to remain in an unstructured activity, or if the 1:1 staff ratio were reduced, for even an interval as short as one minute, it was sufficient time for her to defecate and, if undeterred, smear the feces on herself and the floor. Occasionally the staff would have the undesirable experience of returning to the room to find Heidi in the act of fecal smearing as well as pica. Such occurrences would invariably stimulate verbal social punishment contingencies from the staff—responses which our research at this time was indicating was just the kind of contingency required to maintain the behavior.

The first management order was extremely erroneous; we required Heidi to clean up the feces on the floor using a rag, bucket, and mop. She was unable to perform this chore; we had to hold her hands and take her through the motions as we positively reinforced the slightest degree of compliant behavior—which actually would only decelerate the behavior of cooperating with the cleaning task. We were just becoming aware of her reversed polarity of reinforcers. At that time, staff were becoming increasingly angry at Heidi, and it was thought that punishing the response immediately after its occurrence, or as close thereafter as possible, would assist in decelerating it frequency. Thus, when she was caught in a state of fecal smearing and coprophagia, we would scold her, and on three occasions paired faradic punishment with that behavior—which, to our dismay, had no appreciable effect. Possibly the punishment contingency was too delayed after the response had occurred to produce a deceleration. Furthermore, Heidi did not have an alternative response to replace the inappropriate behavior. She was unable to request verbally that she go to the bathroom, and she was not motorically trained to indicate her need. During this treatment program, indicated as treatment *B* in Figure 7.21, we also reinforced her appropriate use of the toilet with gum and social reinforcement. A treatment program was designed in which staff would take her to the bathroom each half-hour, and Heidi would be on the toilet for decreasing intervals of time with staff outside of the bathroom on an increasing time. The program, listed as treatment *C* in Figure 7.21, required that once or twice each hour Heidi would be taken to the bathroom for approximately five minutes, and staff were to fade the duration of supervising her for each minute she was on the toilet according to the following schedule:

Day 1: 60 seconds in bathroom; staff 5 seconds outside of door.
Day 2: 55 seconds in bathroom; staff 10 seconds outside of door.
Day 3: 50 seconds in bathroom; staff 15 seconds outside of door.
Day 4: 45 seconds in bathroom; staff 20 seconds outside of door.
Day 5: 40 seconds in bathroom; staff 25 seconds outside of door.
Day 6: 35 seconds in bathroom; staff 30 seconds outside of door.

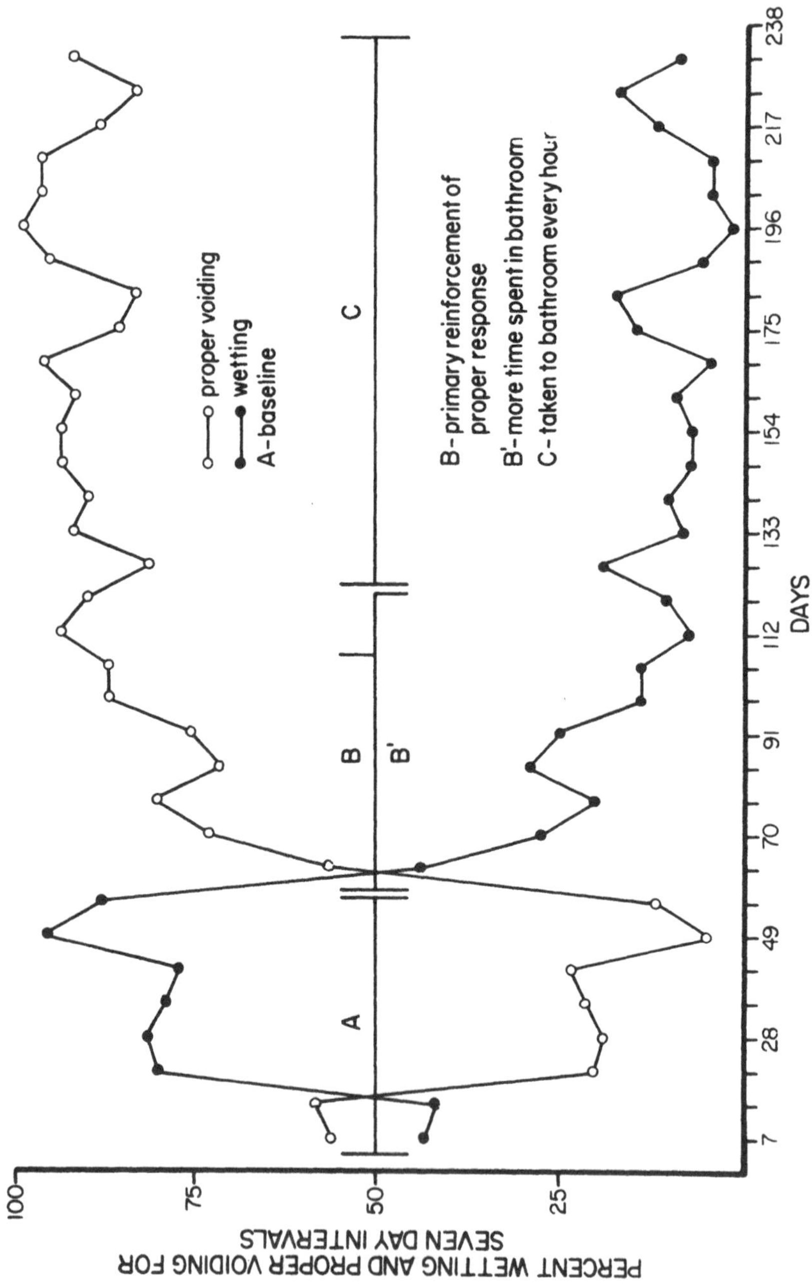

Figure 7.21. Effect of Toilet-Training Program on Per Cent Wetting and Per Cent Proper Voiding

Day 7: 30 seconds in bathroom; staff 35 seconds outside of door.
Day 8: 25 seconds in bathroom; staff 40 seconds outside of door.
Day 9: 20 seconds in bathroom; staff 45 seconds outside of door.
Day 10: 15 seconds in bathroom; staff 50 seconds outside of door.
Day 11: 10 seconds in bathroom; staff 55 seconds outside of door.
Day 12: 5 seconds in bathroom; staff 60 seconds outside of door.

This toilet-training program was then thinned out as staff found it possible to do so. There was an attempt to keep Heidi in the bathroom for roughly five-minute intervals so as to provide at least five of the above trials, until the criterion was reached in which staff could just check in and out while she was on the toilet. Whenever urination or defecation occurred, Heidi would receive candy and profuse praise. Figure 7.21 shows the effect of these programs on voiding, Figure 7.22 shows acquisition of proper defecation responses, and Figure 7.23 illustrates a corresponding control over soiling and fecal smearing.

Until this time, Heidi had had considerable control over the staff by using feces as the punishment condition for staff's leaving her. This was comparable to her having a tantrum when her parents would not provide her with preferred foods. The treatment program interrupted the behavior by making it reinforcing to use the toilet correctly. Also, for successive weeks, we would alter our requests from having her walk with us, to walk ahead of us, to walk the entire length of the hall by herself, to the bathroom, with these steps conducted conjointly with increasing time intervals in which Heidi was left in the bathroom by herself. The time was finally reached when Heidi could reliably go to the bathroom without any staff supervision. Figures 7.21 through 7.23 show the effect of the treatment program on the frequency of wetting, soiling, and smearing, but the treatment goal was not achieved until the sixth month of the study. As with many programs, it certainly took a long time to teach Heidi how to use the toilet correctly. Single-subject, single-habit studies from the literature suggest that this same goal can be reached much more rapidly (e.g., Marshall, 1966). However, each case is unique, and when a facility is conducting a total program for several children with a minimum of staff, the maximum number of programs which can be simultaneously efficient is reached rather suddenly.

The problem of nocturnal enuresis still remained with Heidi. We did not elect to use a "bell-and-pad" conditioning apparatus to control this behavior, since we could predict that she would play with the equipment and render it inoperative. A management order was promulgated that Heidi would be awakened and taken to the bathroom two hours after she fell asleep. Her compliance to this verbal request was socially reinforced,

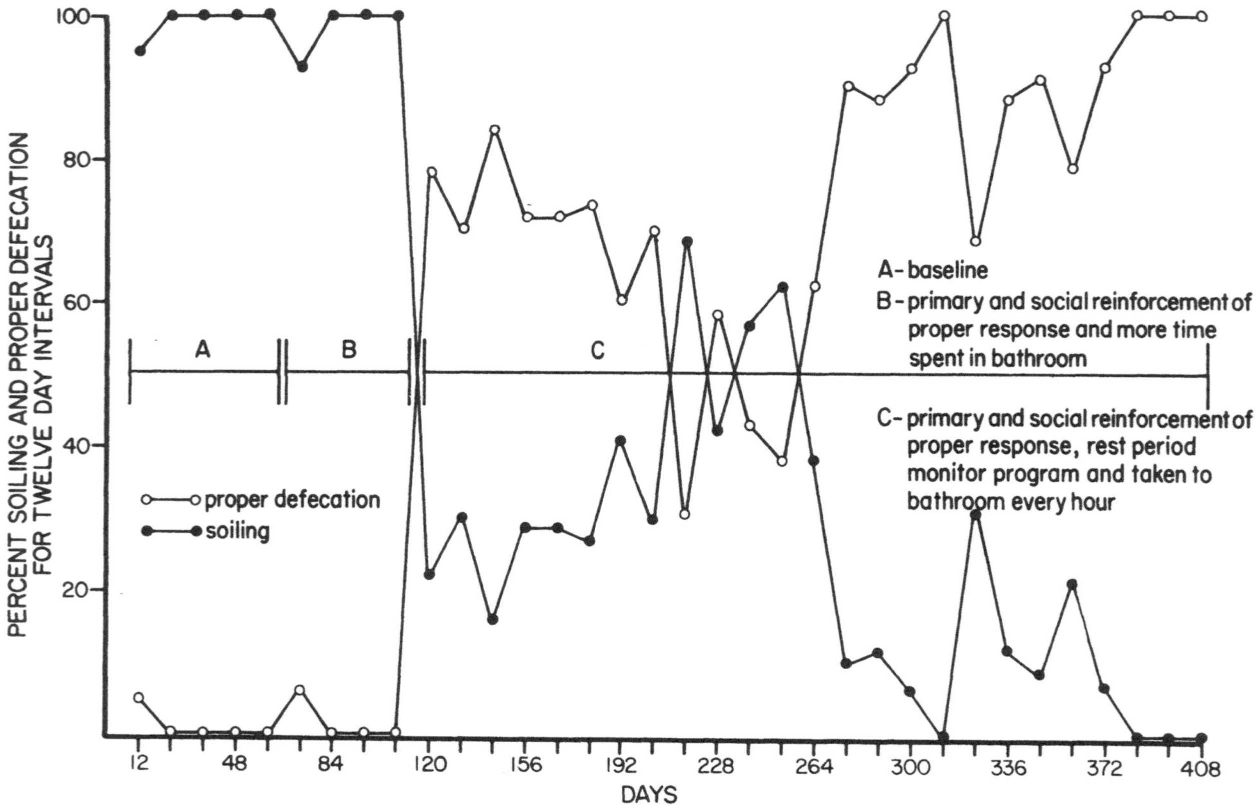

Figure 7.22. Effect of Toilet-Training Program on Per Cent Soiling and Per Cent Proper Defecation

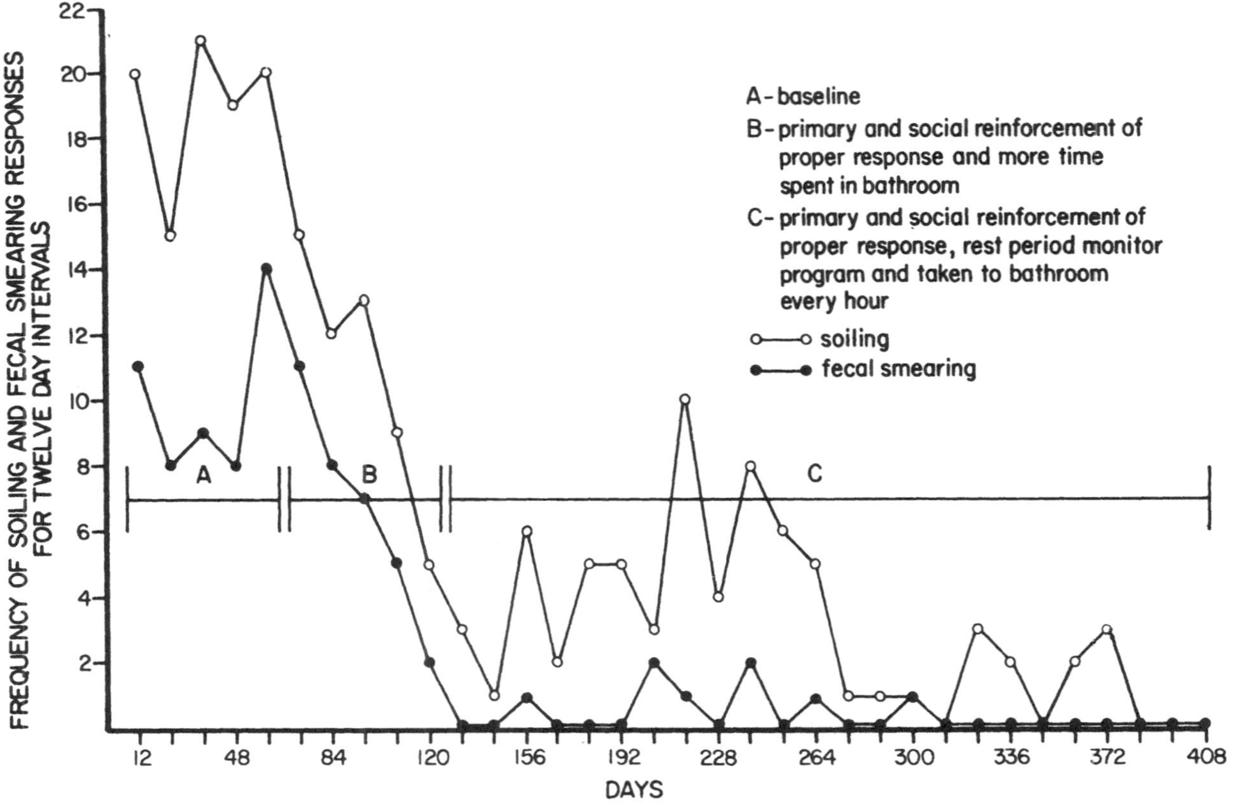

Figure 7.23. Effect of Direct Toilet-Training on Frequency of Soiling and Fecal Smearing

particularly whenever she voided in the toilet. Figure 7.24 shows that the program was successful, but required four months of treatment.

MANNERISTIC RESPONSES

Heidi demonstrated two manneristic responses that made her appear bizarre and were a possible source of embarrassment in public places. One response was her kneeling, or dropping to one knee, when she was verbally requested to comply and she did not wish to do so, or when she was admon-

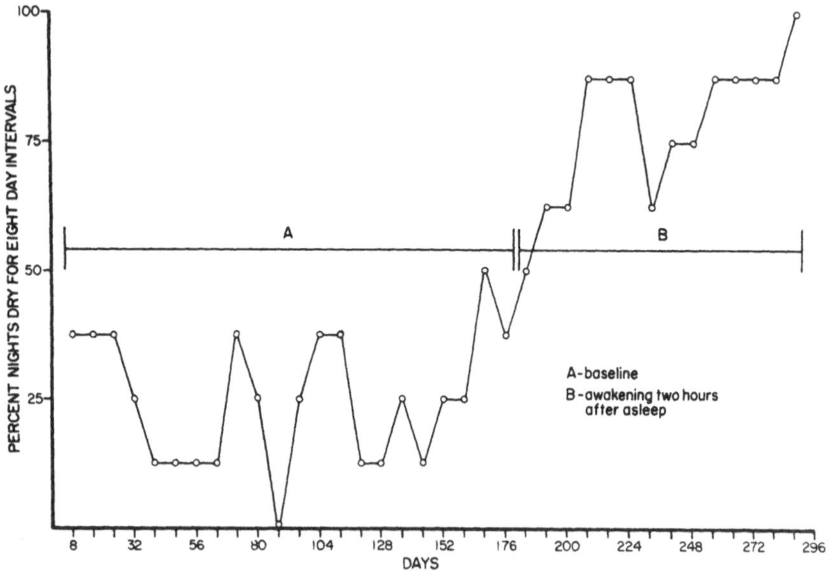

Figure 7.24. Effect on Enuresis of Awakening Child Two Hours after Asleep

ished. Figure 7.25 shows the baseline and treatment program, which involved social admonishment and occasional gestures as if to indicate that staff would use the faradic stimulator. The response decelerated quickly and stabilized at a twice-daily rate. The program was retained in effect longer than the data show in Figure 7.25. Six months after the study the response seldom occurred unless she was having a particularly bad day, when it would occur if she were strongly admonished and given a time-out.

A second mannerism which was treated was clasping and placing her hand(s) on top of her head. Again, following a baseline, social admonish-

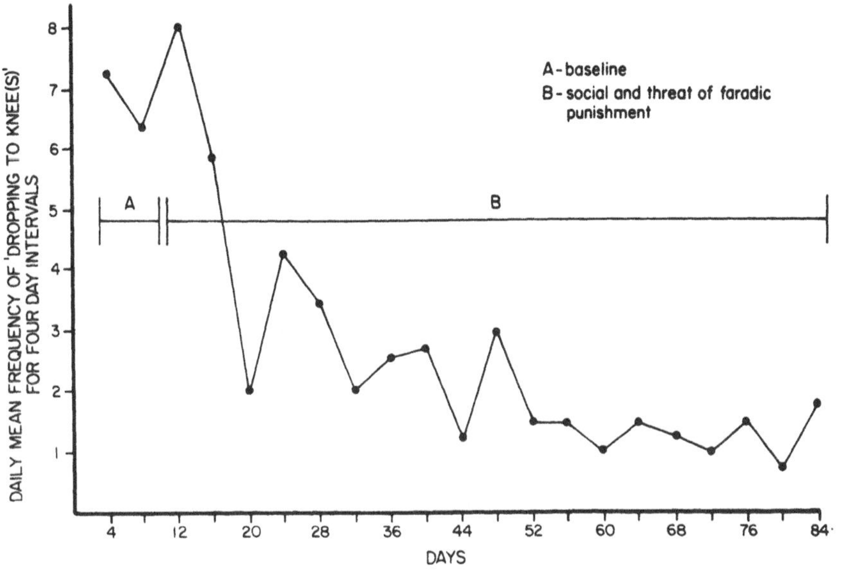

Figure 7.25. Effect of Social and Threat of Faradic Punishment on Daily Mean Frequency of "Dropping to Knee(s)" Response

ment and the threat (but not use) of the faradic stimulator were directed at Heidi whenever the response occurred. Figure 7.26 shows that the treatment program effectively controlled the behavior. These last two studies demonstrated that we had conditioned social punishment cues, but they still had to be supported by occasional threats to use the shock apparatus.

TESTING RESULTS

Vineland Social Maturity Scale. At the date of admission, Heidi's score on the Vineland Social Maturity Scale was 30.5, which yielded a social age equivalency of 1.79. Eleven months after her admission, her score was 49.5, which yielded a social age equivalency of 3.9. The 2.11-year social scale advancement during that 11-month interval should be interpreted with caution. First of all, these are not considered to be spectacular gains for 11 months, considering the staff hours involved. Second, the responses shown on the social maturity scale reflect that Heidi, at the time of examination, was able to perform many of the normally expected and socially appropriate responses of a late three-year-old child. The skill with which she performed these tasks is not qualitatively represented by the raw score.

For example, she was able to imitate certain sounds when she took her second examination that she was totally incapable of doing in the first examination, but the precision with which she imitated varied considerably from what one would expect of a late 1-year-old child. That is, she could best imitate only the sounds which had been most recently rehearsed for thousands of trials. There were also certain activities in which she would play cooperatively with other children, but her degree of cooperation was minimal and confined to few activities. Most of the responses in which

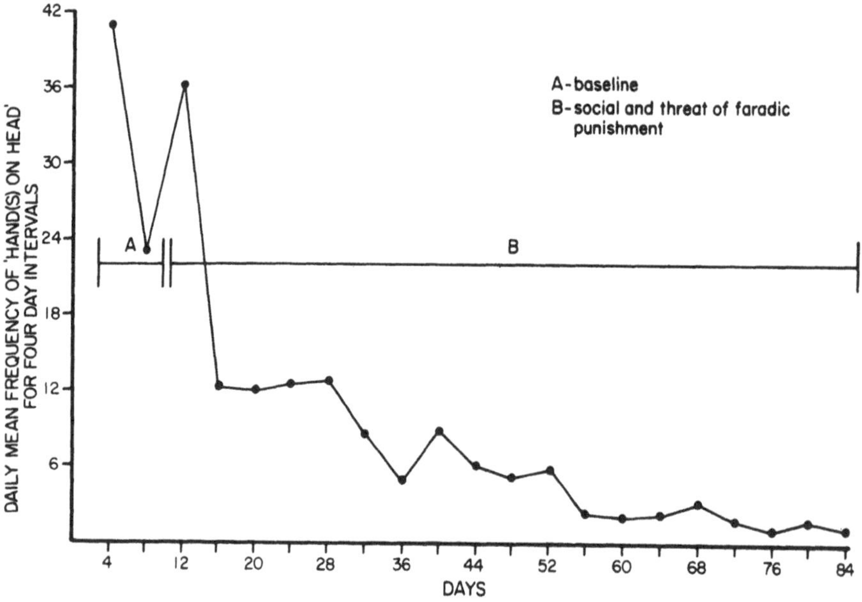

Figure 7.26. Effect of Social and Threat of Faradic Punishment on Daily Mean Frequency of "Hand(s) on Head" Response

there was developmental advancement, such as self-help skills like dressing or washing, had been specifically trained during the treatment program with an intensity one was not likely to find in the average home. For example, cutting with a scissors involved hundreds of trials with her mother, who would use candy, preferred beverages, and profuse social praise as reinforcers for approximations to the response.

Her rate of advancement, as reflected on the Vineland Social Maturity Scale, continued to progress. At the date of this writing, Heidi remains a severely retarded child although behaviorally more amenable to training.

CONCLUSION

The data contained in this case study reflect the extent of the success of many of Heidi's treatment programs. The case study is not provided as an example of a treatment panacea, but rather as an application of the experimental-clinical method. Total treatment programming was illustrated; multiple and simultaneous treatment programs were in effect; treatment goals were being attained at a known rate. The methodology made it possible to monitor the effectiveness of all programs and to alter those programs as was found necessary.

There were certain components of Heidi's program which were not elaborated in the case study, since data were not recorded. For example, the didactic family therapy program in which the parents were coming to the Center for increasingly longer intervals of time to learn the techniques which we found to be successful in teaching Heidi the desired behaviors. The program also included gradually reintroducing Heidi into her home environment by having her make increasingly longer home visits with decreasing staff supervision, approximating complete residence in her home. She progressed from walks on grounds to walks off grounds, to longer time periods in stores, at home, etc., and all the time simultaneously we were reinforcing her compliant behaviors with contingencies progressing from a 100% schedule of primary reinforcement to a thin and variable schedule of social reinforcement. Heidi was always in some structured activity or placed in an activity where she would be performing some task requiring compliance. She was seldom without supervision except at nap time, since that would only have increased the probability of her rehearsing the autistic behaviors which had necessitated her referral. Constant training, gradual reintroduction into the community at a rate guaranteeing retention of preferred acquired behaviors, and teaching her parents to perform all the successful techniques are the crucial and most difficult aspects of total programming.

At the conclusion of the study, Heidi would be described as a severely retarded child who was affectionate and easily pleased. She demonstrated numerous subtle attention-getting behaviors, but these could be controlled verbally. We did learn that under strong emotional stimuli, such as other children's playing and squealing, and particularly when she was in unstructured activities for long periods of time, she would become increasingly excited and more difficult to settle. We learned that she could retrieve diffuse rage and self-destructive behaviors in a matter of hours when in a fear-inducing situation. This was observed when she was taken to a hospital for oral surgery and the staff there responded to her fear by placing her in restraints and a cage bed, and administering a mild sedative. She became terrified, was unable to communicate, and within hours was writhing, screaming, and biting. It took approximately five days to eliminate all components of those behaviors that she had retrieved.

The final treatment goal will never be achieved for a child like Heidi. She will always require a well-supervised environment, such as day-care or residential placement. However, with the continuation of some of the treatment programs, she may have an enjoyable life. But without a structured and highly reinforcing program, we predict that many of her referral behaviors will be reinstated.

Case Study 2: Jim

INTRODUCTION

The following is an outline of the successive treatment programs designed specifically for a five-year-old autistic child. Jim was referred to the Center by an agency outside the preferred 50-mile geographical perimeter that we considered the maximum distance which parents could conveniently travel for the required increasing schedule of family-child visits. The insistence of both parents and referring agency made it clear that the former were willing to make the required journeys to the Center because no other program for young psychotic children was available. Jim's referral was an example of the unfair circumstances confronting parents who are desperate for a residential program, regardless of their agreement with the techniques used, simply because no other program is available. Perhaps parental cooperation under such circumstances is virtually coerced.

Jim's parents were informed of all requirements and obligations demanded by the research program, with emphasis upon their participation in the parent-training which would be conducted on an increasing schedule. Both parents were also involved in a traditional family therapy program concurrent with their visits to the Center.

Jim had previously been examined and treated at several outpatient facilities for varying periods of time, each program having resulted in his eventual rejection by the facility, by the parents, or by both. When Jim was brought to the Treatment Center for his first outpatient evaluation, he occupied himself primarily by walking aimlessly around the room holding a paper cup and repeatedly asking his mother to write the word "cookie" on the cup. His requst was limited to the simple repetition of "cookie," "cookie." It was observed that, after several such requests had been made, his mother would write the word on the cup. It was specifically observed during the interview that she reduced the schedule of reinforcing Jim's request to an average of once for every three requests. Presumably, the mother inadvertently reinforced the repetitious cycle of his request behavior for this bizarre response, because if she failed to comply with Jim's request he would have a temper tantrum. It was observed that the mother's writing the word "cookie" was simply a response to avoid the aversive stimulus of his temper tantrums. Thus, Jim had his parents on a negative reinforcement contingency (cessation of the aversive stimulus of Jim's temper tantrum accelerated parent's writing "cookie" on the cup), and his parents maintained his request behavior with the positive reinforcement of complying with his request. The manner in which Jim would request someone to write the word "cookie" on the paper cup was an example of operant behavior on his behalf, particularly since he had his parents on a "time-out from punishment schedule" for their compliance with his request. This was a case where the parent-child interaction which maintained the abnormal behavior was the immediate and temporary reduction of the child's undesirable behavior aversive to his parents. The clinician should always keep in mind that the child is also training and maintaining certain behaviors in the parents, as well as the converse.

Jim's father was able to instruct Jim to place objects in the wastebasket, and Jim would comply with his father's demands if they remained on such a simplified level. The father demonstrated that upon his requests Jim would read the names of various objects that he had written on a piece of paper, reflecting a sight-reading skill at the level of a beginning first-grade child. This suggested that Jim certainly was acquiring some school-related skills, although in a rather limited manner. However, Jim's verbal behavior was restricted to these rather useless recitations, indicating that his speech was atypical and approximately three years below age-expectancy. Jim's compliant responses to both parents were limited to tasks which would be expected of an early two-year-old child.

It was observed during the initial interview and corroborated at both the home visit and the second diagnostic interview that Jim's food intake was limited almost exclusively to bread, toast, and cookies, and some fluids. Again, the parents were on a "time-out from punishment program" in which Jim would cease screaming and having a temper tantrum when they would comply with his requests for any of these preferred foods. The presentation of nonpreferred foods would stimulate a temper tantrum.

Jim's behavior did operate to obtain preferred reinforcers; unfortunately, these reinforcers were typically asocial and unusual contingencies for a child to obtain. Jim would not use tantrums to have his parents carry him about or demonstrate affection toward him, although his tantrums operated as negative reinforcers to enable him to avoid people. Many of Jim's reinforcers seemed to be simple contingencies, such as having the same television channel on the entire day—even if he just left it on while he wandered around the house. If someone altered the tuning of a particular TV program, even while Jim was in another room, Jim would immediately react with a tantrum and would not stop this aversive behavior until the television had been turned back to its previous station and volume.

Jim had been described as an autistic child by other agencies, and we accepted the diagnosis in a limited form. He was described as a youngster demonstrating a desire for sameness, i.e., if he were engaged in some activity and one altered that activity from its usual routine, he would react by screaming, flailing his hands, and running around. He was totally incapable of playing either cooperatively or in parrallel with either peers or adults. Jim was inordinately skilled in constructing objects and using mechanical toys and craft materials. He was almost at his age level in fine motor coordination skills such as required with pencils, scissors, and puzzles. Jim acted as though he were visually and auditorily oblivious to the presence of other persons. This was most dramatically illustrated when Jim was being observed in free play and he literally walked across a staff member who was seated on the floor attempting to involve Jim in play. The majority of Jim's speech was restricted to a few echolalic responses; his observed imitative behavior was limited to his occasionally repeating a vocalization by another person, which was the same as one of his few verbal responses. Jim would seldom, spontaneously or upon request, imitate physical gross motor activities. It was reported by his parents, as well as observed by us, that if one attempted to interfere with Jim's preferred play, it would invariably guarantee continuous whining, which would often spiral to a temper tantrum that would be maintained until he was allowed to return to the activity which had originally been interrupted. There was no evidence of, nor was there a prior history of, self-destructive behavior. Jim's assaultive behaviors were defined as his slapping at other persons, and the strength of these striking responses would be considered very weak in contrast to our experiences with other autistic children. Jim's language comprehension was much below age-expectancy. For example, he was unable to comprehend or excute commands such as "put the block on top, or under, or beside, the chair."

In summary, Jim's appearance was that of a frail youngster who existed on a very poor but strongly preferred diet of excessive carbohydrate foods. He demonstrated neither cooperative nor parallel play and he was essentially mute. Although Jim was toilet-trained, he was untrained in using the toilet in a manner other than what would be expected of a young girl. Jim demonstrated a variety of autistic mannerisms which ranged from hand-flapping and slight spinning to obsessiveness over certain repeated motions, words, and activities. The few words he could say were spoken in a high-pitched, poorly enunciated, and barely audible manner. Jim demonstrated gross motor coordination below age-level expectancy. He was almost totally noncompliant to verbal requests other than those asking him to hand a few objects to another person. His responses to stimuli in the environment could all be described as weak; Jim touched things delicately, he walked delicately, he was afraid to take a large bite of any kind of food when he was learning to eat a variety of foods, he chewed food weakly, and in general he just seemed to be what we would describe as a "weak responder." His physique was slight, and he was anemic. Also, Jim's clothes were immaculate and he had never played hard enough to become dirty.

We suspected that Jim would be reluctant to test for the kind of social reinforcers which were available for his autistic behaviors at home when he was admitted to the research group. Our prediction was erroneous: It took Jim exactly 20 minutes after admission to test the staff with a spectacular temper tantrum which lasted for 45 minutes. We shall now describe chronologically the treatment programs which were designed to teach Jim more age-appropriate behaviors.

TEMPER TANTRUMS

Temper tantrums were a primary behavior problem with Jim when he was admitted. Tantrums are one of the referral behaviors that seem to be characteristic of all the children admitted to the research group. Jim's temper tantrums were defined by the staff as including the following behaviors: holding his head back and rolling it from side to side with his eyes shut while crying and screaming loudly, typically without tears; wailing in a weak but high-pitched manner; bouncing around in a circle; flapping his arms and hands; falling to the ground and continuing with his tantrum until the staff member who had stimulated it withdrew. After the staff member withdrew, Jim would cease his tantrum and commence with the activity which had been interrupted. Temper tantrums were predictably evoked by staff members' interrupting Jim's self-stimulatory behavior and isolative play behavior, and his wandering about the cottage; by their verbally or physically requesting that he engage in some group activity; by their presenting nonpreferred foods at mealtime when he was first admitted; and by their requiring him to hold one's hand or brush his teeth or take a bath—or almost any of the verbal demands one would make of a child during a structured day. As we have mentioned, it was presumed that Jim's temper tantrum operated to make the parent or staff member leave him alone so that he could continue in the preferred activity in which he was currently engaged. When the staff member did withdraw, this was the reinforcement contingency or, more specifically, the discriminative stimulus for continuing in his isolative play. Cessation of a temper tantrum was the negative reinforcement contingency maintaining his parents' withdrawing from Jim whenever he had a temper tantrum. Because his parents had variably tried to "hold out" against three temper tantrums by not withdrawing from Jim at at such times, he had been trained to have tantrums until, after about one hour, he would almost collapse from fatigue. Jim would fatigue rather rapidly for a child of his age who was having a tantrum, but, considering his physical condition as a result of the restricted diet upon which he was sustaining himself, this was not surprising. Furthermore, his restricted physical activities did not allow him to develop the physique normal for his age.

A behavioral baseline was initiated on the first day of Jim's residency to record the daily frequency of his temper tantrums. An uncontrolled baseline was obtained for one week, i.e., staff were to record with a hand tally counter each time a temper tantrum occurred. There was no particular procedure to be followed in recording these observations. There were two time intervals during the day when temper tantrums were not counted. One interval was during the experimental compliance sessions, when staff would conduct a tightly controlled session to reinforce compliant and extinguish noncompliant behaviors. The other was during the didactic family therapy sessions. Temper tantrums occurring during those intervals were recorded separately as evidence of treatment effects for either the experimental compliance sessions or the therapy sessions. Data for those two treatment programs were logged separately.

In measuring the temper tantrums, staff did not record the duration of each incident. Time as well as frequency would have been a preferred measure, since duration is the more sensitive measure of a tantrum, but acquiring such a measure requires more staff time to record it accurately.

The treatment condition was tested with a simple *AB* design. A replication was impossible, since the temper tantrum behavior decelerated completely. Furthermore, it would have been impossible to retrieve the baseline rate of the behavior without sacrificing many other concurrent programs whose desirable treatment effects we suspected were interacting with the *B* treatment condition used for decelerating temper tantrums. For example, Jim was being reinforced positively for compliant responses, the occurrences of which were incompatible with temper tantrums. Responses presumed to be associated with the occurrence of temper tantrums, such as his darting away from staff or noncompliance were being punished. Thus, Jim was not only being taught that temper tantrums would not provide the previously predictable and preferred contingencies, but also trained to make responses incompatible with temper tantrums, namely, of compliance, for numerous social and educational skills.

The *B* condition, or treatment procedure, was a two-minute time-out in the quiet room for each occurrence of a temper tantrum. Figure 7.27 shows the deceleration of the rate of temper tantrums as contrasted to the one-week baseline during the treatment program. The program was maintained for almost six months, after which it was ceased with the understanding that it would be reinstated if these responses occurred again.

The simple *AB* non-replicated same-subject design employed to assess the effectiveness of a time-out contingency on Jim's temper tantrum is certainly open to criticism. The presumption that the treatment effect shown in Figure 7.27 was a function of the time-out contingency gains credibility only by reference to the three-year history of temper tantrums that in this study were effectively decelcrated in a matter of weeks. Obviously, the effects of the time-out condition are confused with those of concurrent treatment programs. Also, our impression was that the instability of the

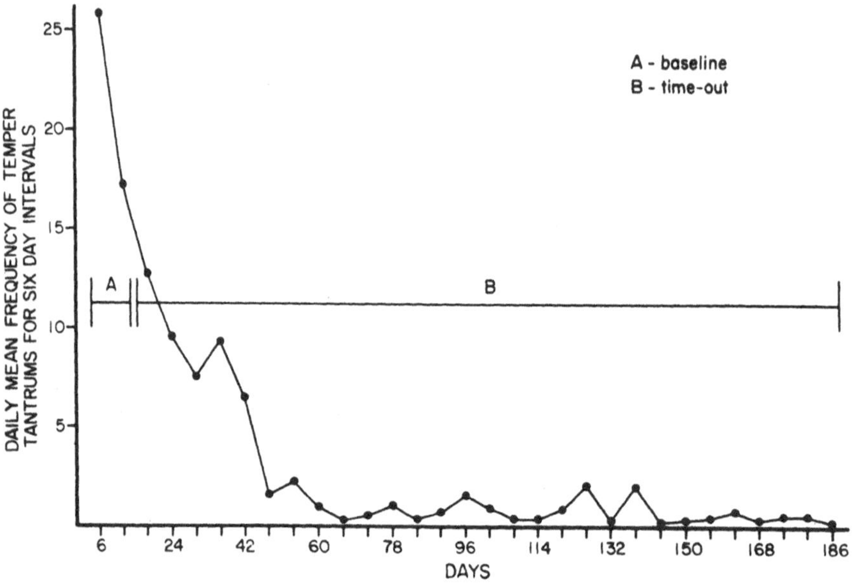

Figure 7.27. Effect of Two-Minute Time-Out on Daily Mean Frequency of Temper Tantrums

very short baseline indicated that the tantrums were effectively decelerating prior to the treatment condition.

With the *AB* design employed for assessing the effectiveness of the time-out condition on temper tantrums, one cannot conclude that it was the necessary and sufficient condition for the deceleration of the response. Also, one cannot state with assurance that, if the time-out were actually ineffectual, there may have been a deceleration of temper tantrums quite independent of the presence of the time-out condition contingent upon tantrums. This problem is characteristic of studies conducted in a total program; and in any non-replicated design, the question always remains whether the treatment condition could have been ascribed to conditions uncontrolled by the experimental design. In the residential setting where the children are monitored constantly and the staff are optimally trained, one gains more assurance if the treatment condition is contingent upon the response 100% of the time. Since that is the only treatment condition most immediately contingent upon the response, one can be more confident that it was the *primary* responsible variable. Since the response of temper tantrums did decline in Jim's case, we can conclude that the time-out procedure was not an effective condition for *accelerating* temper tantrums or for maintaining them at the rate found in the baseline. We do suspect that the total program in conjunction with the time-out contingency was interactively effective in decelerating the behavior. Speculation generated by a non-replicated design could continue ad infinitum. Perhaps the cogent point which should be emphasized is that, in any experimental design, nonmothetic or idiographic, confounding is more the rule than the exception.

Low-Level Temper Tantrums. As Jim's temper tantrums decelerated in conjunction with the two-minute time-out program, there was a continual qualitative change in the appearance of these responses. For example, Jim's temper tantrums had initially been characterized by screaming, dry crying, rolling his head from side to side, dancing around the room while flapping his hands, and finally flopping to the floor. As these temper tantrums were brought under staff control and their occurrence became more infrequent during the day, their appearance progressively changed to quick short bursts of whining. We were again observing what occurs during deceleration of many behaviors, namely, that, as the initial response is extinguished, a vestige or approximation of the original response begins to appear. This phenomenon is probably what clinicians have been describing as symptom substitution. If we did not selectively extinguish this "low-level" temper tantrum, we would be allowing an approximation of the original response to remain in the response repertoire, which would increase the probability of Jim's retrieving the strong temper tantrums which were initially present. Therefore, we decided to extinguish the low-level temper tantrums. A program was begun on day 94 of Jim's residency.

The low-level temper tantrums were qualitatively different from the temper tantrums recorded above and shown in Figure 7.27. The staff defined the low-level temper tantrum as a short interval of whining, at most a loud and short, dry wail. Several quick jumping hops often accompanied this crying as Jim bounced several steps away from the staff member. Staff were required to count the behavior whenever it occurred, and no particular method was employed to disguise their counting of the response. Figure 7.28 shows the six-day baseline of the frequency of the low-level temper tantrums occurring during the entire day.

Again, as much of our data show, there was no spectacular deceleration of the response. There were several factors which we suspect contributed to the ineffectual treatment program for low-level temper tantrums. First, we did not have an optimal staff ratio during this time, so that staff were too busy to time-out each occurrence of the response correctly. Second, the staff were tolerating, or more aptly, adapting to, the low-level tantrums so that many responses were not timed-out. This is a problem common to many of the programs, i.e., as the extreme deviant behaviors are extin-

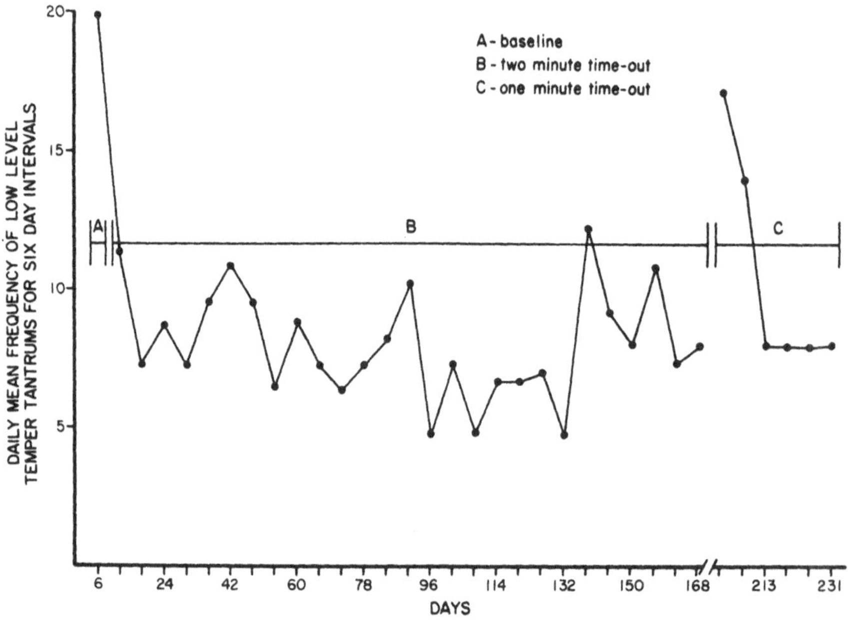

Figure 7.28. Effects of One- and Two-Minute Time-Outs on Daily Mean Frequency of Low-Level Temper Tantrums

guished the approximations to those responses are tolerated by staff because they are not such a nuisance. This problem is compounded by the fact that there are no normal children with whom the patient can be compared; i.e., staff become used to deviant behavior.

It is predicted that low-level temper tantrums will decelerate, not so much as a function of the time-out contingency, but because alternate responses incompatible with tantrums will be acquired. Again, these all-day counts did not include the morning-long didactic family therapy sessions which were occurring twice a week at this time. Figure 28 shows the effect of the two-minute time-out punishment contingency tested on a non-replicated *ABC* design. The same punishment contingency of the two-minute time-out was used with the low-level temper tantrums as with the original temper tantrums, since the former were considered to be a vestige of the original tantrums and, in effect, we were replicating the same treatment program on the tantrum behavior. As Figure 7.28 shows, the time-out condition was associated with very little deceleration of the low-level temper tantrums, which was not comparable to the effects shown in Figure 7.27. Since the original temper tantrums and low-level temper tantrums were correlated behaviors, we were confused by the long time required to decelerate the latter responses.

COMPLIANCE-NONCOMPLIANCE RESPONSE RATIO

If one were required to summarize the most global description of Jim's responses which prompted his referral, it would be "an absence of behavior." Although never experimentally documented, it was our hypothesis that, if one were to count the number of discrete responses Jim emitted each day in comparison to those recorded for children of comparable age in the normal school setting, he would show significantly fewer responses both per time interval and for particular activities. Much of Jim's behavior was confined to self-stimulatory responses and much random movement, and his social interactions were characterized by avoidance responses. These avoidance responses, as previously described, were invariably evoked when an adult or child attempted to control or to redirect his behavior in a structured activity different from that in which he was currently engaged. Jim was incapable of maintaining even momentary eye contact with another person. If a strong verbal request for a compliant response were made of Jim, one could predict that he would weakly flail at one with his arms, dart away, and quickly progress to crying and tantrum behavior.

Jim's adamant refusal to comply with staff's verbal requests was described and recorded as a noncompliant response, and we began the treatment program for it on the first day of his residency. When Jim complied or attempted to comply with a verbal request by a staff member, this was recorded as a compliant response. The staff members communicated frequently with each other to assure that the requests being made of Jim were those that he was physically capable of performing or that he could comprehend the verbal request sufficiently to make some response approximation. The staff were requested to obtain a one-week baseline count of the compliant and noncompliant responses, both of which are shown in ratio form in Figure 7.29. After the baseline had been accumulated, treatment programs were begun whose goal was accelerating compliant and decelerating noncompliant responses. The treatment contingency for compliant responses was strong and profuse social praise. The positive evaluative statements involved were to be varied, spontaneous, and not confined to simple remarks such as "Good boy." These social reinforcements were an accumulation of responses varying from a pat on the head and a quick hug to numerous positive verbal statements. The compliant treatment contingency was performed in an *AB* design.

The program to decelerate noncompliant behavior was a five-minute time-out condition in Jim's room, performed during the first two weeks of treatment. During these two weeks Jim was in his room most of the time in

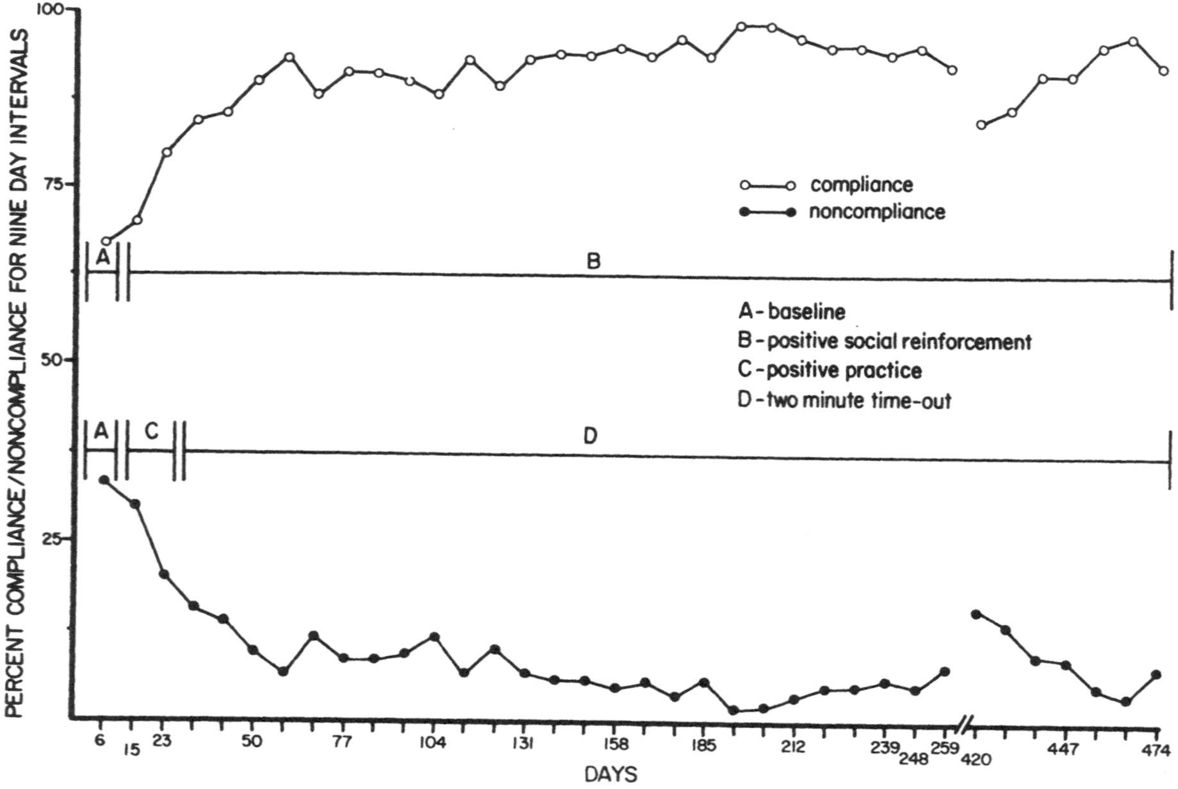

Figure 7.29. Effects of Concurrent Treatment Procedures on Per Cent Compliance/Noncompliance

a one-to-one training program; we did not have sufficient behavioral control to allow him to function in a complex environment at the beginning stages of his program. In the administration of the five-minute time-out for noncompliant responses, the staff would simply walk out of the room, shut the door, and return after five minutes. The five-minute time-out contingency is indicated as *B* in Figure 7.29. Following that treatment technique, we initiated a two-minute time-out punishment contingency for all noncompliant responses. At this stage of treatment, Jim was no longer in his room on a 1:1 ratio with staff, but, although still under close staff supervision, he was being trained to be compliant in an ever-expanding environment. It was most convenient at this time to remove him to the quiet room for the two-minute interval, which is noted as *C* in Figure 7.29. The reliance upon the quiet room for the administration of the time-out was progressively altered during the program. Jim would often receive the time-out in his room; eventually his punishment was changed and he was spun around in a chair and made to face the wall if he were at a table working with staff member, or he was placed in a corner facing the wall, or, if he was outside, he was seated facing a tree and away from the group. In the classroom, a small quiet room was built of plywood and he was placed in it for the required two minutes. As Figure 7.29 shows, there was a definite acceleration of compliance and a deceleration of noncompliance. However, the data failed to demonstrate the qualitative change in the kind of compliant responses which were progressively changing. With a desirable treatment effect, one would expect that compliance would increase and that complexity of response would correspondingly increase.

As the program progressed at a rate with which Jim was able to comply satisfactorily, increasingly complex requests were made of him by staff. Thus, the compliant responses counted in the data six months following his admission were qualitatively different from those which had been tallied during the early weeks of training compliant behavior. Similarly, Jim's noncompliant responses were qualitatively changing as a function of the two-minute time-out condition contingent upon their occurrence. His initial noncompliant responses were invariably accompanied by escape responses such as running away, often in conjunction with tantrums and a considerable amount of wailing. As his program progressed, these responses diminished progressively.

The treatment condition for compliance and deceleration of noncompliance was not a singular program. The treatment program comprised a time-out contingent upon noncompliant responses and profuse positive social reinforcement for all compliant responses. As Figure 7.29 indicates, considerable trials were required before an optimal ratio of compliant behavior was achieved. As the program continued, we were actually recording fewer occurrences of both compliant and noncompliant responses. The reason for this is as Jim became increasingly compliant, the staff were required to make fewer requests of him.

Although a favorable treatment effect is reflected in Figure 7.29, the data are qualitatively deceptive. The complexity of the requests for compliant responses at the termination of the data shown in Figure 7.29 were, by our standards, still at a very low level. Even after six months of such treatment, Jim's compliant responses were quite slow, they were delicate, they lacked spontaneity, and they were generally consistent with what one might expect of a three-year-old youngster. The complexity of the responses was improving progressively, but the actual kind of those responses is not reflected accurately in the data. Perhaps this kind of deceptive data could have been minimized if a standardized set of requests had been administered to Jim at successive intervals. The reader should be aware that, although one may show data demonstrating increasingly compliant behavior in a psychotic child, the child may still be acting very bizarrely while complying with verbal request. Also, it may be that the child is trained to become increasingly compliant for the same minimally demanding requests.

CONDITIONING FOOD AS AN EFFECTIVE REINFORCER

When Jim was admitted, he was a thin, frail, anemic youngster with very decided food preferences. He survived primarily on toast and cookies. Jim's muscle tone was flaccid and his gross motor coordination was decidedly below age-expectancy, although his fine motor coordination was not noticeably deficient. Jim's response repertoire was so restricted that there were few gross motor activities in which he could either perform by himself or perform under close supervision, since he had neither the necessary training and compliance to engage in an activity, nor the required physical skills. Jim's activity was so diminished that an average amount of food was not required to sustain him. We observed that he would fatigue quickly, that he required long naps, and that his sleep pattern was to take a long afternoon nap and to retire early in the evening only to awaken at four or five o'clock in the morning. When at home, he would wander about the house in the early hours of the morning, so that his mother had to keep a constant vigil over his behavior. Jim's unusual sleep patterns interfered with normal sleeping for the rest of his family. His parents had been unable to extinguish Jim's erratic sleep patterns. If they tried to ignore him when he entered their room at night, he would have a temper tantrum which would awaken everyone in the home. Thus, the cessation of Jim's temper tantrum was negatively reinforcing to the family members, and the quickest way to achieve this was by allowing him to climb into bed with his parents, or offering him preferred kinds of food, etc. Thus, Jim had his parents on an avoidance paradigm. Over time the parents learned to anticipate the cues indicating an impending rage and performed the behavior that historically terminated the rage.

As a prerequisite to Jim's total program, we had to condition a variety of foods to serve as effective primary reinforcers. These foods, available during the daily meals, would eventually be used as primary reinforcers to condition attention and eventually speech. We also planned to condition social reinforcers while simultaneously training attention and speech. This would be accomplished by positive social reinforcement preceding primary reinforcement when conditioning attention and speech. Furthermore, since Jim was in such poor physical health as a result of his high carbohydrate diet, he was unable to perform effectively in the gross motor activities which we were training in his program. We could also expect that, with Jim's general poor health, he would be susceptible to the many contagious illnesses which plague any children's residential center, and this would mean more time during which he would be unavailable for learning appropriate behaviors. It was mandatory that we divise a program to condition food as an effective primary reinforcer, not only for Jim's physical health but also for his behavioral development.

Two different programs were devised to condition food as a more effective reinforcer for Jim. The first program will be described, although it was abandoned because its treatment effects were not sufficiently rapid. The second program was found to be more effective, and we have subsequently used it successfully with other children who demonstrated marked food preferences. His family had observed repeatedly that, if Jim were seated at the dinner table and a meal were placed before him with the preferred food or bread absent, he would have a temper tantrum until he was permitted to have bread. Again, it was the termination of the temper tantrum that was the negative reinforcer for others' providing Jim with bread, toast, and certain kinds of cookies. It was our hypothesis that coercive social statements, such as scolding him for not eating the foods he did not desire, or imploring him to eat those foods, or even using a variety of disapproving facial expressions, were discriminative stimuli which would maintain his tantrum behavior. We assumed that the verbal and facial cues in the past had only signaled Jim that it would not be long before the preferred food would be given him and that he should just continue having his tantrum for a little while longer. We decided that, during his meals in the first treatment program, the staff would not be seated at the table with Jim. He was seated at the table with the usual food placed before him, except that bread and cookies were not allowed on the table. The goal of the program was to allow food to reinforce itself. Jim's preferred foods, such as toast, bread, and cookies, were deleted entirely from his diet. We assumed that hunger drive itself would eventually force approach behavior toward eating the food that would then reinforce that response and that eventually he would begin to eat a variety of foods. Jim was allowed 30 minutes to complete each meal and to eat any of the foods which were on the plate. Predictably, during the first meal, he screamed and cried and frantically operated for his preferred foods of toast and cookies. At successive meals, Jim began to nibble increasingly at the variety of foods on his plate. However, we observed that Jim was not rapidly acquiring the habit of eating a variety and a substantial quantity of foods during this particular program. We wanted to devise a program which would accelerate his eating behavior more quickly for the sake of his health as well as for his social development.

On day 18, one of the research staff[4] devised a program in which a nonpreferred reinforcement contingency was conditioned to be preferred by being conditioned with an already preferred contingency, The program was to use the preferred reinforcement contingency of toast and cookies on progressively decreasing schedules of reinforcement for eating increasingly greater amounts and varieties of food. The program was established as follows: For all meals during the week when sufficient personnel were available to conduct the program, a staff member would be seated at the table facing Jim with a plate of food before him. The staff member was holding a spoon or fork with food on it. Jim's preferred reinforcement contingency of toast and cookies were on a separate plate in front of the staff member and were given in progressively smaller bites for successive meals for each bite of food which Jim ate from his plate. The program began by giving one-inch squares of toast and quarters of cookies for minute bites of food. The staff were careful in shaping the required response of eating the varieties of foods by requiring extremely small bites of food that increased in size and also progressively differed from similarity to toast. That is, in the first meal, the staff reinforced Jim's eating foods similar to toast, such as potatoes, and in successive meals introduced increasingly greater varieties of food. It was observed that potatoes and then meat and eventually cereal became increasingly reinforcing, much more so than vegetables and most fruits. As new foods acquired reinforcing effects, these were used in addition to toast and cookies as reinforcers for eating the remaining nonpreferred foods. When a trial was administered in which Jim was to eat a certain bite of food, the meal would not progress until he did eat the food, swallowed it appropriately, and received the reinforcer. The program began by using food on a 100% reinforcement schedule that was eventually thinned until Jim was eating bread and butter along with his meal like any

4. The authors wish to acknowledge Isabel Schleicher, R.N., who innovated the above program for conditioning Jim's food preferences.

normal child. If a particular spoonful of food were held before Jim and he refused to eat it, the staff member would not substitute a more preferred kind of food but would continue to hold that particular bite of food before Jim for the remainder of the meal. If Jim did not eat it, he would go hungry until the next meal. Vitamin supplements, iron supplements, and a daily food supplement containing minimum daily adult requirements were provided for Jim each day. The food supplement was given in the evening at snack time.

This treatment program required 836 trials and 836 reinforcements, conducted over 21 days, after which Jim was eating a sufficient quantity and variety of foods so that we decided it was feasible to conduct the next approximation to teaching speech, i.e., to condition attentive responses. However, on day 194, we decided to "back-up," since his food preferences were deteriorating. For the next 31 days, 559 trials resulting in 414 reinforcements were performed during the noon meals, to reinstate proper eating.

DARTING

It was almost impossible to retain Jim in a structured, staff-directed activity when he was first admitted. When an attempt to do so was made, it would invariably stimulate tantrum behavior, hitting responses, crying, and what we have defined with many of the children as "darting." In Jim's case, darting was defined as Jim's dashing away from a staff member when he asked anything of Jim. He would run from 5 to 15 yards and then stop and usually engage in some self-stimulatory behavior or, more often, merely stand there. The baseline and treatment conditions employed to decelerate darting behavior commenced on day one, and are contained in Figure 7.30. As Figure 7.30 shows, the darting behavior was at a relatively high rate when Jim was first admitted. Although a formal experiment was not conducted, it was our hypothesis that one could easily have varied the rate of his darting by the number of requests made of him to direct his behavior in some structured activity with a staff member. Jim would invariably run away from the staff member when he was requested to comply. The baseline shown in Figure 7.30 is not stable; perhaps this is a function of a contaminated baseline caused by concurrent treatment programs. It is very likely that the program of reinforcing compliant responses that was concurrent with acquiring the darting response baseline was decelerating the latter response to some extent. More precisely, Jim was now being reinforced for low-level compliant responses, so that rather than darting away when a request was made, he was being trained to attend to a staff member's request for a compliant response, which was incompatible with darting.

The procedural design used to demonstrate the effectiveness of the treatment programs was an *ABC* study. The one-week baseline, or *A*, indicated

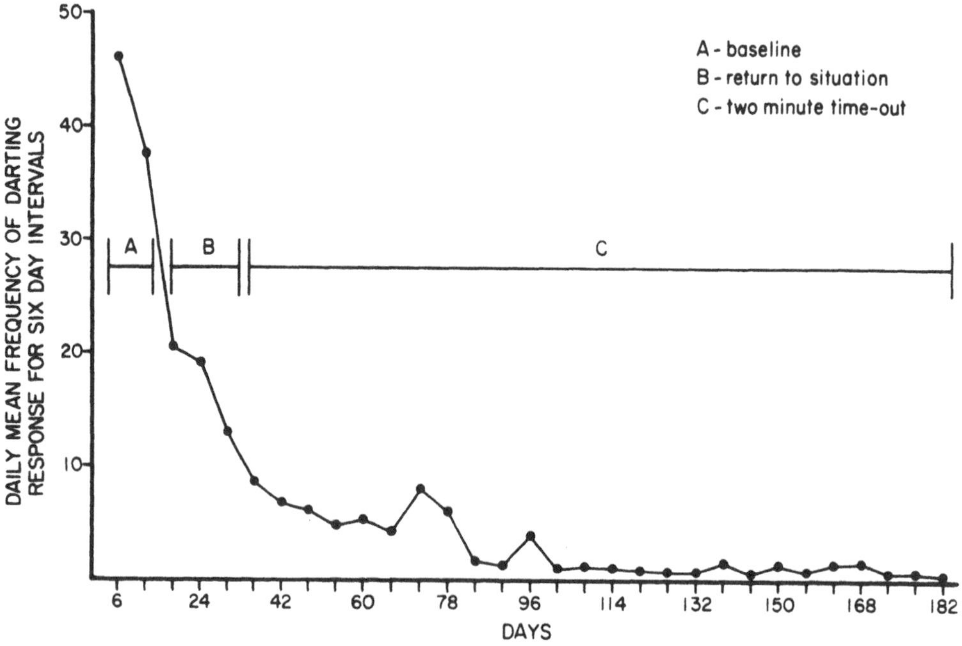

Figure 7.30. Effects of Two Methods of Treatment on Daily Mean Frequency of Darting Responses

that the behavior was variable, after which the *B* treatment condition was initiated for two successive weeks. The *B* condition required that each time Jim darted away the staff member was immediately to take him by the hand, if necessary, and lead him back into the activity or group activity from which he was running. The staff were then to make a very concerted effort to reinforce as promptly as possible any compliant behavior he demonstrated. The rationale was for the staff to make initiating and engaging in an activity highly reinforcing by using the darting response as a cue to themselves that they were probably asking too much of Jim at the time and were stimulating avoidance responses. The negligible treatment effect shown in Figure 7.30 prompted us to conclude that we might be incurring the error of reinforcing an undesirable behavioral chain. The chain of behavior which we may have been establishing was Jim's darting away as an avoidance response which let him avoid the nonpreferred activity and was a discriminative stimulus that staff would "back-up" to an easier activity for which he would receive considerable positive reinforcement. The positive reinforcement program in effect at that time included using small pieces of cookies and bread as reinforcers for compliant behavior in conjunction with social reinforcement. Thus, one way Jim could earn cookies when he was in a session where he was being compliant and not succeeding very well would be for him to dart away. Therefore, treatment condition *C* was begun. *C* involved giving Jim a two-minute time-out for each occurrence of the darting response. These time-out punishment contingencies occurred wherever it was most convenient, e.g., staff's leaving him in his room and walking out, or putting him in the quiet room, or making him face a corner and sit for two minutes if the response occurred outdoors. Although the treatment effect was not spectacular in its rate of deceleration, it was definite and the behavior did extinguish, as Figure 7.30 indicates. We should add that after the two-minute time-out had been completed following a darting response, Jim would be reintegrated in the activity from which he had darted and behavioral expectations would be the same as when he had darted away from that activity.

LEAVING ROOM DURING NAP AND NIGHT TIME

We have mentioned that a dominant behavioral characteristic of Jim's prior to his admission was his unusual sleep patterns. During nap times and when put to bed in the evening, Jim, instead of lying quietly in his bed and resting or playing quietly in his room, would leave the room. Jim expended little energy during the day, he ate minute quantities of food, he was put to bed early, and it was not surprising that he would usually awaken in the early hours of morning. He was put to bed at 6:30 in the evening when at home because his parents legitimately required a respite from his behavior. Jim would invariably awaken by two or three o'clock in the morning and arise, enter his parent's room, and insist upon threat of a tantrum on climbing into bed with them. This would awaken his father, whose job required long hours of work. Jim's mother, to make it possible for her husband to sleep, would take Jim out of the room, procure any desired foods he wanted, or engage in any activity he wished. This pattern gradually changed until Jim's mother slept in another bed so that Jim would be least disruptive of his father's rest. This separation which Jim's behavior effected between his parents had mutually reinforcing effects for the parents. Thus, Jim's negative reinforcement paradigm had made his parents sleep separately and trained his mother to awaken at any time of the night to provide him with any number of preferred reinforcers to keep him quiet, or just to interrupt his wandering about the house in the dark. Jim soon dominated the family routine to such an extent that his mother had to retire early so that she would have sufficient sleep to arise in the middle of the night to care for Jim, unaware that the family routines had been reorganized inadvertently and innocently to reinforce his bizarre nocturnal behaviors. These same contingencies were also available to Jim during his nap time in the afternoon while he was at home.

We predicted that Jim would operate for the same reinforcement contingencies during his resting and sleep pattern behaviors when he was brought to the Center. We predicted that he would retire early in the evening, only to awaken in the middle of the night and begin to operate for the kinds of staff attention and food reinforcers comparable to those available for such behaviors in his home. This behavior was also expected to occur for nap time. We described his behavior at these times as "leaving the room." Staff would count the frequency with which Jim left his room dur-

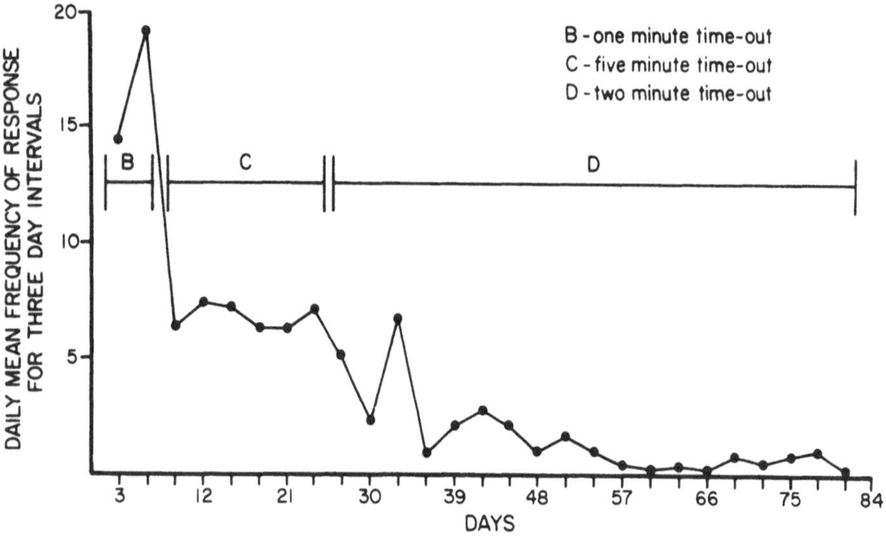

Figure 7.31. Effects of Three Time-out Procedures on Daily Mean Frequency of "Leaving Room during Rest Period" Response

ing nap periods or after he had been tucked into bed in the evening. When he left his room at these times, the staff would count the behavior, take him back into his room, and ask him to stay there. This was a controlled baseline, the results of which are shown in Figure 7.31. The 23-day controlled baseline shows that his "leaving the room" response was initially high and variable but that the variability was diminishing, which was suggestive of an incipient treatment effect during the baseline. A regression line drawn through the baseline data would lead one to suspect that the response would have extinguished eventually without our having resorted to a treatment program. This may have been the case, but we do not know. It is our hypothesis that the behavior would have declined in frequency but leveled off at some rate, indicating that a treatment program should be devised to extinguish the behavior. A series of three different treatment conditions were employed successively to extinguish Jim's "leaving the room" behavior. The first treatment, labeled *B*, required staff to walk Jim back to his room and shut and lock his door for exactly one minute, after which the door would be reopened. The staff's discussion about the data and the effectiveness of that program led us to conclude that after one week we would attempt a five-minute time-out in his room, and this is labeled treatment condition *C*. For the five-minute time-out, Jim would be taken back to his room and the door would be locked for five minutes, after which it would be unlocked and opened again. We assumed that having the door open during nap time or in the evening was a preferred contingency, and that having the door shut was noxious. We were afraid that Jim's room would acquire some form of a generalized punishment stimulus from our using this treatment procedure. Furthermore, there was still the possibility that Jim would simply play with preferred toys during the time-out in his room, thus rendering the time-out ineffectual. We have used a time-out condition of leaving a child for a one-or two-minute time interval whenever an inappropriate response occurred and it has proven ineffectual in some instances, presumably because the child could engage in some preferred activity. We are typically reluctant to use such a program unless we are sure that the child will not engage in positively reinforcing behavior while left in the room. After two weeks of conducting the *C* treatment condition, the management order was changed to treatment *D*. Treatment *D* required staff to take Jim to the quiet room for a two-minute time-out each time he left his room during rest time or at night when he was supposed to be asleep. When staff accompanied Jim to the quiet room for his two-minute time-out, they would explain the contingency by stating "when you leave your room during nap time or when you are supposed to be asleep, you have to go to the quiet room." Jim obviously did not prefer the quiet room, so his leaving his room would only eventuate an undesirable contingency. The data in Figure 7.31 show that with the two-minute time-out condition there was a diminuation of Jim's leaving his room until it was eventually extinguished. The occasional instances in which Jim left his room at the conclusion of the program were not considered at the time to be a behavioral problem. One would expect a normal five-year-old child to leave his room occasionally during rest periods to get a drink of water, to use the bathroom, or to make some appropriate requests of his parents.

Jim's nocturnal wandering extinguished completely from his response repertoire during the treatment condition of the two-minute time-out. We contend that the two-minute time-out contingency did not teach Jim how to sleep; it only taught him to remain in his room where he was awake and supposed to be resting. Jim's total treatment program contributed to the success of teaching him to remain in his room at night. The number of hours during the day in which he was engaged in gross motor activities under staff supervision resulted in a very exhausted youngster at the end of the day. An interactive effect was suspected, i.e., Jim remained in his room at night because he was asleep as a result of being very tired. Furthermore, his food intake had increased and eventually stabilized, so he was retiring in the evening after having had a liberal amount of appropriate snacks. Perhaps several of these emerging factors contributed to the unstable baseline during which Jim's leaving the room response was decelerating. One cannot attribute the treatment effect shown in Figure 7.31 exclusively to the time-out condition. This of course is characteristic of all successive treatment designs, as discussed in the methodology section of this book. In addition, when numerous concurrent programs are being conducted, one may expect more than singular effects of each treatment program. The interactive effects of the simultaneous programs presented herein suggest a complexity of dependent variables that no same-subject design currently available can handle.

Other treatment programs also confounded the effects of the time-out condition. For example, we think that there was an interaction between the fine motor activities training program and the time-out for Jim's leaving his room during nap times. Jim was being trained and reinforced for constructive self-involved play, a first step toward parallel play. He was being taught to play constructively with Lincoln logs, tinkertoys, puzzles, drawings, etc. These kinds of self-involved play toys acquired reinforcement valence as the program progressed and were being used by Jim during rest periods, thus contributing to his remaining in his room rather than leaving it during the prescribed nap time. At best, one could say that the two-minute time-out contingency was one variable, perhaps a crucial one, that contributed to Jim's total program for decelerating leaving his room during nap time.

Jim's behavior of leaving his room during nap and sleep times is characteristic of many psychotic children whom we have observed. In fact, all of the children we have seen thus far referred with the diagnosis of childhood schizophrenia or autism have demonstrated abnormal sleep patterns. Quite often these youngsters, for varying intervals of time, wander about their homes at night. We feel it is worthwhile to investigate, for each individual case, whether this is operant behavior. We have also observed that these psychotic children do not play actively with their peers. They are typically not allowed to play outdoors unless under the close scrutiny of the parents, lest they injure themselves, wander away, or disrupt other children. As a result, psychotic children spend considerable time in the house and do not expend so much energy per day as of a normal child. This is only a hypothesis; we have yet to demonstrate differential gross motor activity rates between psychotic and normal children. However, psychotic children typically demonstrate more stereotyped behavior and less variability in the kinds of responses they are capable of making and are often restricted to close quarters to prevent their injuring themselves or causing undue concern about their behavior to parents and teachers. Such a diminished activity level would contribute to maintaining light sleep patterns, and possibly make it more probable that the child would have sufficient energy to wander about the house in the evening operating for whatever kinds of reinforcers are available for such bizarre behavior. It has been our experience that these abnormal sleep patterns, so typical of many psychotic children, tend to stabilize with an increased activity schedule after the child has been admitted to the treatment program. Furthermore, we suspect that it would require longer to stabilize sleep patterns by using a specific contingency, such as a time-out, as contrasted to a total program which trains many responses all of which contribute to the child's remaining in his room and sleeping as he is requested to do.

APPROPRIATE VOIDING

We are presenting the following conditioning program for three reasons: to illustrate the variety of responses which must be separately trained with the psychotic child; to emphasize that one may not leave training effects to chance; and to demonstrate a typical "shaping" procedure. Jim was toilet-trained. Unfortunately, he would void only while sitting on the toilet. If he were requested to stand before the toilet to urinate in a boy's characteristic way, the request would produce prolonged shrieking and crying. Our eventual goal was to reintegrate Jim to a normal home and school setting, and we knew that in school he would be the target of considerable rebuke from his peers if he did not know how to use the toilet like a boy. We had no evidence that he would begin to use the toilet appropriately by modeling other children, since, like many autistic children, Jim manifested a deficit in imitative learning. We decided that we would teach him to urinate appropriately, just as we had to teach him many other desired responses. Let us discuss the shaping program designed to teach Jim to use the toilet appropriately.

First, Jim was allowed initially to use the toilet whenever and however he pleased. However, for those trials shown in Table 7.2, he would be accompanied by staff to the bathroom for increasingly closer distances with the appropriate response of standing before the toilet. The succession of training trials progressed from approaching the toilet at one-foot intervals beginning two feet from the bathroom door until the toilet was reached.

When he had been trained to stand before the toilet without having a temper tantrum, the program was altered so that on successive trials he was allowed to void only while standing. During these training trials, one quarter of a vanilla cookie was used as a reward for such successive trial, or step, in the shaping program. During the final steps of the program, Jim was rewarded whether or not he urinated. Twelve days were required for

Table 7.2. Response Increments for Training Appropriate Voiding

Day	*Trials*	*Response Increments*
1	3	Standing two feet outside of bathroom door
1	1	Standing one foot outside of bathroom door
1	1	Standing at bathroom door
1	1	Standing one foot inside of bathroom door
1	1	Standing two feet inside bathroom door
1	1	Standing three feet inside bathroom door
1	1	Standing four feet inside bathroom door
1	1	Standing five feet inside bathroom door
1	1	Standing six feet inside bathroom door
1	1	Standing seven feet inside bathroom door
2	9	Standing in front of toilet
3	10	Standing in front of toilet with trouser button unfastened
4	8	Standing in front of toilet with trouser button unfastened and zipper open
5	6	Standing in front of toilet with trouser button unfastened and zipper open
6	7	Standing in front of toilet with trousers down
7	7	Standing in front of toilet with trousers down
8	5	Standing in front of toilet with trousers down
9	11	Standing in front of toilet with trousers down (voiding twice correctly on this day; thereafter permitted only to void in this manner)
10	6	Standing in front of toilet, trousers down (voided once)
11	9	Standing in front of toilet, trousers down (voided three times correctly)
12	9	Standing in front of toilet, trousers down (voided correctly five times)

Jim to learn how to void appropriately, and thereafter the response was no longer rewarded with food, and the social reinforcement contingent upon correct voiding was thinned and eventually dropped. Jim's behavior of voiding correctly has persisted and he has not retrieved the prior habits; it required 12 days, during which 24 and 3/4 cookies plus profuse social reinforcement administered during 99 trials progressively shaped the appropriate voiding response. Table 7.2 contains a description of the response expectancy increments used to shape the behavior.[5]

PHYSICAL AGGRESSION

While at home Jim would hit anyone who attempted to intervene with any preferred ongoing behavior. This response generalized to the Treatment Center and he would often strike staff who tried to interrupt an activity in which he was currently engaged or to direct him into a new activity. The staff defined the response of physical aggression as Jim's hitting a staff member with his hand and making contact. The hitting response always remained very weak and did not injure staff. At his date of admission, Jim was quite frail and did not have the strength to hurt anyone seriously. However, striking another person is not a preferred response and a program was designed to extinguish that behavior. The program commenced on day nine of his residency. Jim's hitting a staff member was one of a chain of responses predictably evoked when the member tried to direct Jim into a new structured activity. The following treatment program was designed to control the behavior.

Figure 7.32 contains the data for the baseline and treatment condition designed to extinguish the behavior of physical aggression. The study was a simplified *AB* design, which is subject to those criticisms directed against such a method as outlined above in Chapter 4. We obtained the 15-day baseline in an uncontrolled manner, i.e., the staff simply tallied the response when it occurred, and there was no directive about how or when they should press their hand tally counters to record the behavior. The 15-day baseline shown in Figure 7.32 indicates that the response was initially high and variable, but that variability diminished as the baseline progressed, suggesting an unstable and decelerating baseline. The unstable baseline leads us to suspect that whether or not the treatment program had been conducted, the response would have extinguished. This suspicion cannot be discounted because there was no experimental replication of the treatment procedure. The treatment procedure was a two-minute time-out which had been initiated by day 16. The two-minute time-out was conducted by staff's either walking Jim or picking him up and swinging him over staff's hip and marching to the quiet room and depositing him there and shutting and locking the door for two minutes, after which Jim was brought out and reintegrated into the activity from which he had just been removed. The two-minute time-out contingency was related to a rapid de-

5. Two years after the completion of this particular program, it was observed that Jim would frequently void inappropriately, which indicated that the nonpreferred response was being reinstated.

celeration of the response, as may be seen in the treatment phase of Figure 7.32.

We did not replicate this study, since the response of hitting staff was irrevocably extinguished and has not recently been occurring at a sufficient rate for us to perdict that it could be reinstated by a return to baseline. It is our impression that the effects of the two-minute time-out contingency were confounded with other aspects of Jim's total treatment program. For example, Jim was concurrently being reinforced with food (on a decreas-

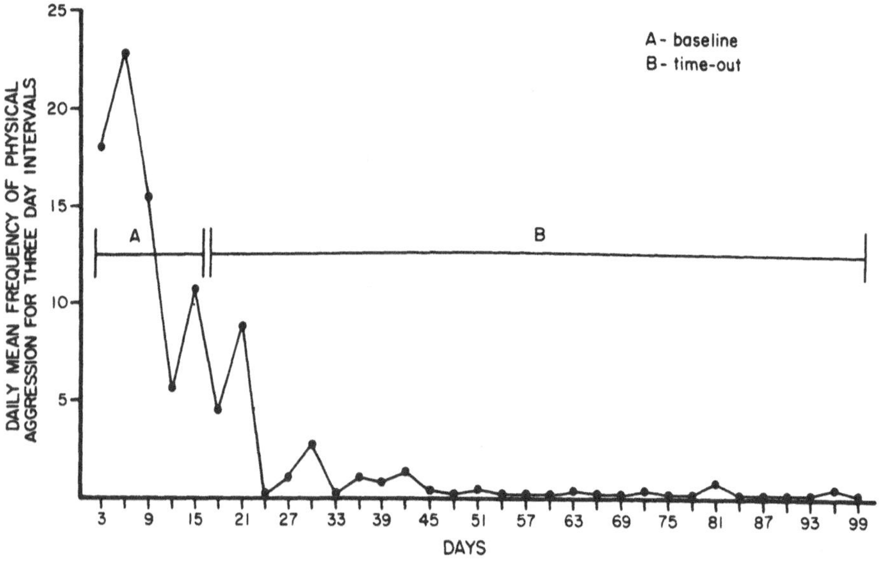

Figure 7.32. Effect of Two-Minute Time-Out on Daily Mean Frequency of Physical Aggression

ing schedule) and social praise for performing compliantly in various activities, particularly when he could change from one activity to another successfully. Thus, the alternate response of compliance, which was incompatible with hitting, was positively reinforced and was replacing the hitting response. The ease with which Jim was shifted from one activity to another depended upon the available staff ratio at any given time and on the number of children in the group. These training intervals would vary in length from 15 minutes to an hour on the same activity, either on a one-to-one or, at most, a one-to-four ratio of staff to children. Furthermore, other concurrent programs, such as conditioning attention, extinguishing running away from staff, teaching speech, and decelerating both temper tantrums and leaving his room, were also being conducted.

It was not discouraging that we were unable to demonstrate complete experimental control of the time-out condition on the hitting response. If we had been able to demonstrate a return-to-baseline effect with the hitting response we would have been demonstrating, in addition to experimental control, that we had a very weak total treatment program, if not indeed a very weak independent variable in the two-minute time-out contingency. We contend that all of the treatment programs designed for each child as represented in this book are complexly interrelated. Improved experimental designs are needed to control for the confounded effects evident in these studies. For example, while we were attempting to extinguish hitting, temper tantrums, darting responses, and leaving the room, we were alternately "building in" preferred responses to replace those which were being extinguished. It would be naïve to extinguish noncompliance to verbal requests from adults in a child without at the same time reinforcing compliant behavior. One could devise a program wherein children were simply punished for abnormal behavior and not trained to do anything to replace that behavior. The hypothesized effect of such a program would be a responseless child, a child who, in the presence of staff members, would simply sit still and not demonstrate disruptive abnormal behavior. Such programs are in effect in many children's units in staff-deficient state hospital systems. The challenge is to teach behavior to the disturbed child, not simply to demonstrate that one is able to extinguish behavior. These children already demonstrate behavioral constriction; it is not the goal of the clinician to accentuate that referral problem.

The rate at which Jim's hitting other persons decelerated with the combined treatment condition as described above was quite remarkable. The reader is cautioned that such quick treatment effects with a simple two-minute time-out contingency are infrequent. In fact, the treatment effect was so quick that it was exceptionally suggestive of confounding. We felt that the manner in which the time-out was administered was crucial and contributary to the quick treatment effects. Staff would verbally admonish Jim for the hitting response and immediately guide him to the quiet room which was available to assure a precise time-out. Furthermore, we suspected that Jim was comprehending the verbal admonishment, although the extent of his intellectual functioning as relevant to such comprehension could not be assessed at the time. We had observed that Jim demonstrated "islands" of precocious behaviors, such as being able to acquire reading skills under minimal supervision, and the manner in which he was able to control parent and staff behavior was suggestive of a child more intelligent than simple test scores may have led one to conclude. Perhaps these variables also contributed to the quick treatment effect.

CONDITIONING OF APPROPRIATE USE OF THE BATHTUB

When admitted, Jim was extremely frightened of taking a bath in the amount of water necessary for scrubbing a five-year-old child clean. This became a problem, since, with increased activity, Jim was getting progressively dirtier each day. We found that it was not effective to disguise the depth of water in the tub with soap bubbles, since he would remain frightened, scream, and constantly attempt to leave the bathtub and bathroom whenever there was more than two or three inches of water in the tub. His fear response made it difficult to clean him each day, and physically keeping him in the tub would only stimulate further fear responses and make it probable that later conditioning of the appropriate use of the tub would become increasingly more difficult. The following program was devised to counter-condition Jim's fear response in the bathtub and to make bathing an enjoyable daily activity. The program was begun on day 44 of his residency.

For successive days the depth of water in the bathtub was increased by exactly one-half inch, from a one-inch level of water on the starting day. The one-inch level of water used at the beginning of the program was not sufficiently deep to evoke Jim's fear response. During all bathings, there were profuse soap bubbles and many toys were available, to make the entire setting enjoyable. The staff were requested to insure that Jim was playing and enjoying himself while taking a bath at a water depth which would not engender a fear response on successive days. If a fear response was evoked for any given level of water, then at the next bath the water was reduced to the previous level at which no fear response had been stimulated. This "backing-up" would continue until the fear response disappeared, after which, for successive days, the water depth would again be increased by one-half-inch increments. Fourteen days were required for Jim to learn how to use the bathtub with any amount of water and to have a laughing-splashing good time of it. Ten months after that program, the fear response had never been reinstated.

ATTENTION

It had already become apparent to us that training attention is a prerequisite step to conditioning of speech. Attention is defined as the child's maintaining a criterion level (e.g., two or three seconds) of eye contact upon some verbal cue from the staff member. With some psychotic children, it may be necessary to strengthen the primary reinforcers as the prerequisite to conditioning attention. In Heidi's (Case #1) treatment program, we had to strengthen the primary reinforcers, then condition the correct polarity of social reinforcers, before shaping attention. The conditioning of positive social reinforcers may be carried out simultaneously with training attentive responses by using the social reinforcers as a discriminative stimulus for the presentation of the primary reinforcers.

After Jim had been taught to eat a sufficient amount and variety of foods considered to be age-appropriate, we began a speech program in which he was required to imitate staff's verbal models of basic phonemes as well as words which he was capable of saying but would not say audibly. We intended to combine shaping attention as well as to condition speech simultaneously by making each trial contingent upon his turning and maintaining eye contact for one and eventually two seconds prior to presenting the speech model. If Jim responded imitatively with an acceptable attentive and vocal response, he received profuse social praise and then a bite of food. We found within ten days that the response requirements were too demanding for the speech program, since we were having little success in conditioning the prerequisite response of attention, and Jim was making very poor approximations to speech and was not earning sufficient amounts of food. This last problem increased the likelihood of his retrieving his preadmission status of diminished food intake. We therefore decided that we should "back-up" and train Jim to pay attention for at least a two-second interval to a staff member when an appropriate cue for an attentive response was presented, before we began teaching him speech. The program consisted of staff's first teaching Jim to pay attention for one second, after which he would progress to the two-second criterion interval. The staff member, holding food, would be seated facing Jim and would say his name or some other verbal cue to elicit Jim's attention, such as "look at me." Jim had to maintain eye contact for at least one second for the first phase of the attention-shaping program. The second phase of the program was to teach Jim to maintain eye contact for two seconds, using the same program of reinforcing that behavior by social praise immediately followed by food reinforcement. All responses were reinforced on a 1:1 ratio of reinforcement. From previous experience we recommend that the attention-shaping program be conducted so that, after the criterion level of attentive response is attained, the reinforcement ratio be thinned so as to establish a more durable response. We have had difficulty in maintaining Jim's attentive responses because attention had been on a 100% reinforcement schedule, which was thinned drastically in the speech program because he would attend but not respond vocally. This failure to respond would not produce reward, so attention was being placed on an extinction program.

However, the above was the least of our errors. We failed to graph and monitor the recorded data in shaping attention and began the speech-shaping program with insufficient attention-training. Figure 7.33 shows training one- and two-second attentive responses and clearly illustrates our failure to train to a desired 85% to 90% criterion level of success. We could have avoided this failure by studying the graphed data rather than relying upon our clinical judgment, which led us to conclude that a cri-

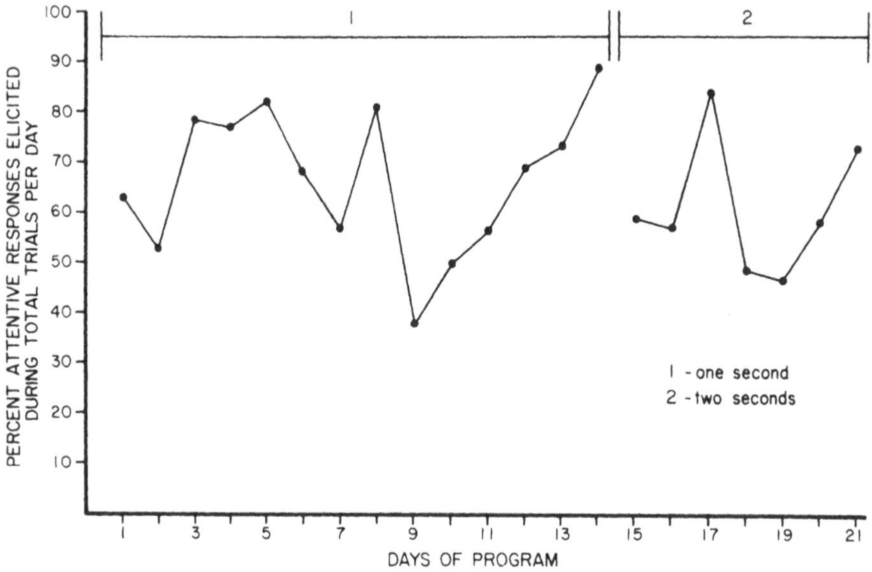

Figure 7.33. Attention-Training, One- and Two-Second Criteria

terion level response had been attained. As a result of the poor attention-training, Jim did not progress rapidly in the speech program and we had to "back-up" and retrain attention ten months after admission. At that time a criterion response of three seconds was maintained, and the results of that program are contained in Figure 7.34. And again, we should have maintained that program longer. We had still failed to consult our data, and Jim was attending only 55% of the time. We thereafter decided to integrate three-second attentive responses as prerequisites to providing the speech model. Thus, Jim's attention-shaping continued during the speech-training program.

Jim's attention data provide an example of the necessity of logging data and monitoring them constantly. It has been our experience that, with a multiplicity of concurrent programs, decisions are made after a cursory

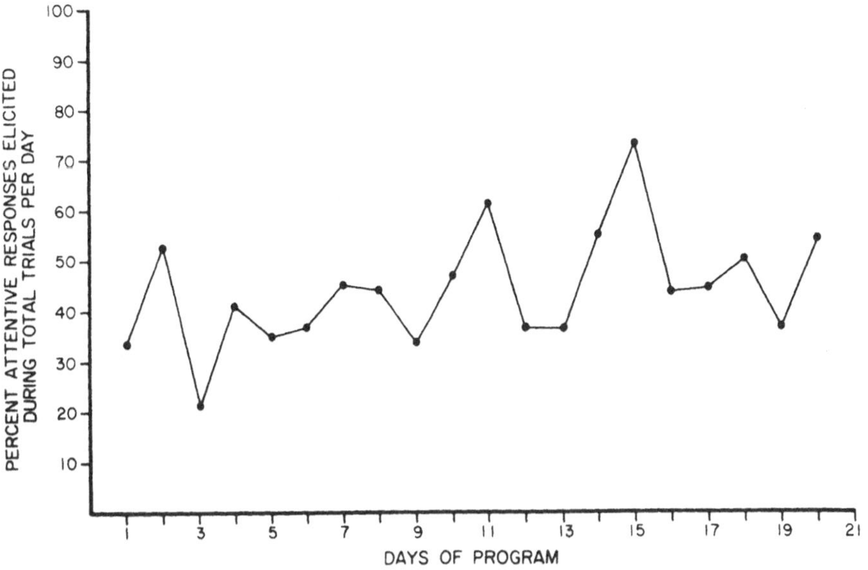

Figure 7.34. Attention-Training, Three-Second Criterion

glance at the data. Clinical judgment in conjunction with a brief review of the data has led to many erroneous judgments—as the above treatment procedure illustrates.

ROCKING

Rocking was defined as Jim's moving his head or entire body back and forth. Jim's rocking in the rocking chair was also counted. This response was present when Jim was admitted but treatment was deferred until the more disruptive behaviors had been brought under control. We do not know if the rocking responses were changing during the early months of his program. Staff's clinical judgment agreed that Jim's rocking was increasing in frequency and duration, but they may have been agreed erroneously.

A seven-day baseline was acquired beginning on day 234 of Jim's residence. Staff counted the frequency of Jim's rocking; unfortunately, the duration of each separate response was not recorded. As we have stated, the duration of a response, such as rocking or temper tantrum, is a more sensitive dependent variable than frequency alone. The treatment contingency *B*, as shown in Figure 7.35, was simply social admonishment contingent upon each rocking response. For example, we would loudly and

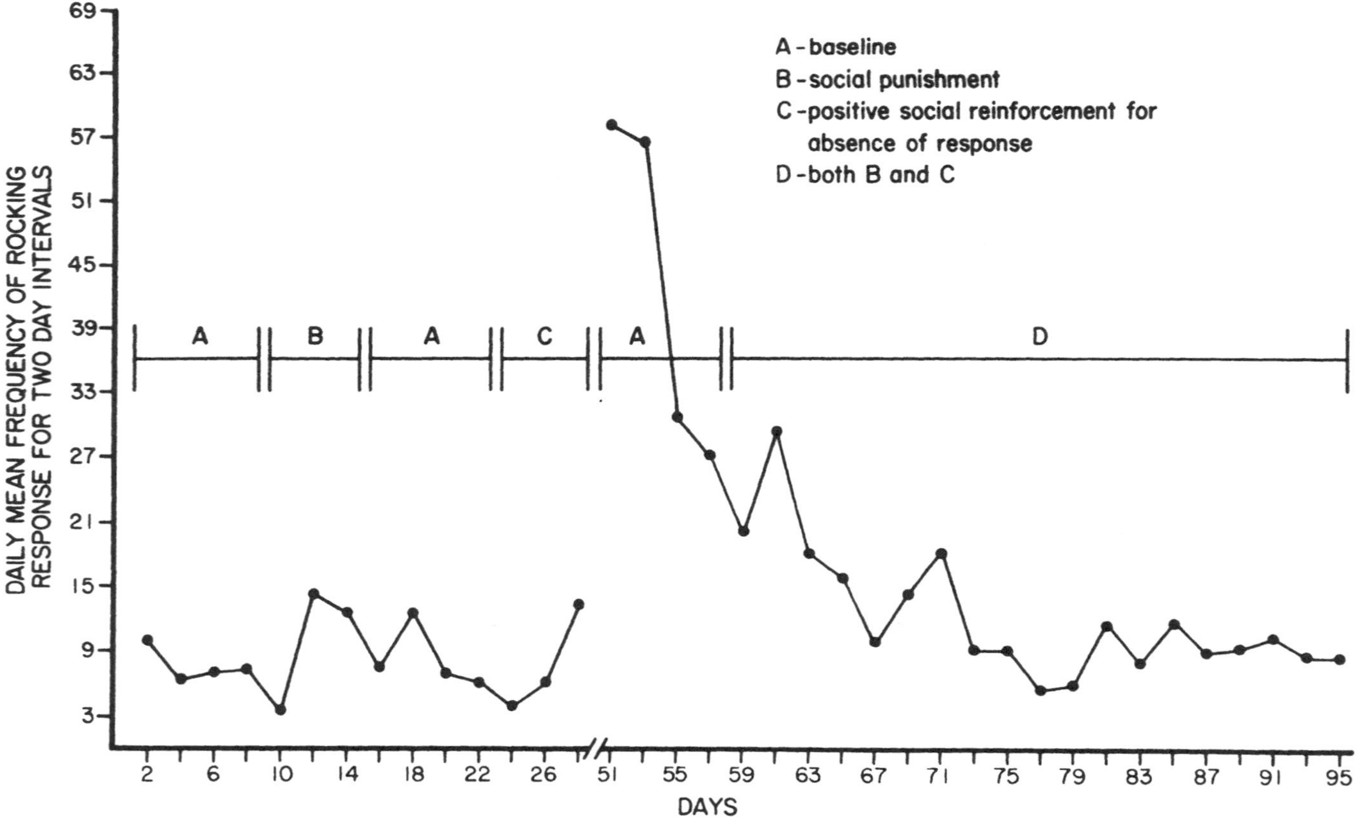

Figure 7.35. Effects of Three Treatment Methods on Daily Mean Frequency of Rocking Response

strongly state, "Jim, stop that—you are not to rock," or make a similar verbal statement. So, Jim was scolded for every rocking response he demonstrated. Figure 7.35 shows that we were not exceptionally successful in quickly decelerating the response.

Rocking is a difficult response to decelerate, probably because it has its own positively reinforcing effect. Stereotyped behaviors are characteristic of many diagnostic categories, particularly in mental retardation. In decelerating such responses, as with a profoundly retarded child, it seems reasonable that alternate or incompatible responses should be trained so that the youngster is not rendered responseless by the program. In Jim's program, speech, parallel and cooperative play, school readiness skills, etc., were being trained, all of which were incompatible with rocking. We noted that Jim persisted to rock when not in a structured activity, and also that the duration of the separate occurrences of rocking were shorter (i.e., staff would observe Jim rocking and, before they could admonish him for the response, it would cease).

INAPPROPRIATE GAIT

Jim's gait was exceptionally unusual. He was unable to run to an extent comparable to age-expectancy. His walking was slow, delicate, as if he

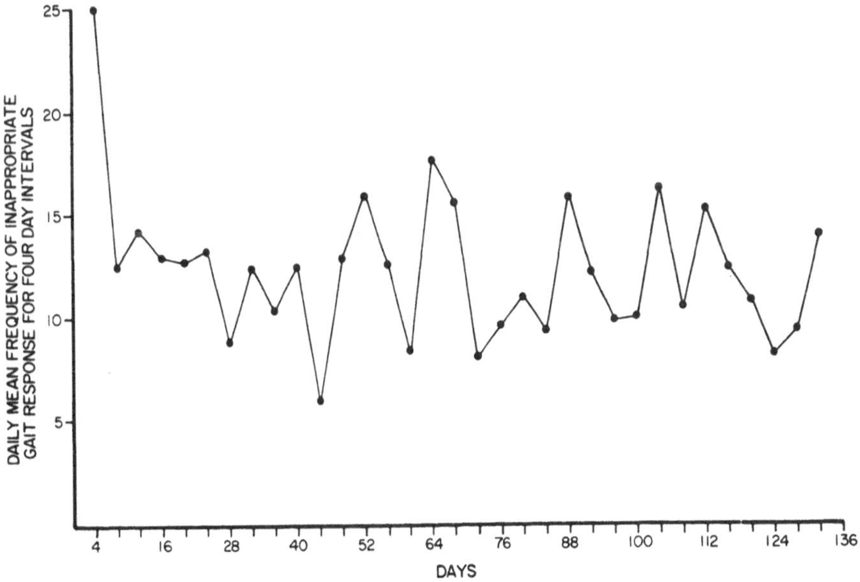

Figure 7.36. Effect of Positive Practice on Daily Mean Frequency of Inappropriate Gait Response

were "walking on eggs." Often he would bounce along in a springing and uncoordinated manner which we simply defined as inappropriate gait. Figure 7.36 shows the baseline and treatment effect for Jim's gait disturbance. The treatment procedure required staff verbally to stop Jim by scolding the response, and immediately require him to return to the point at which the response commenced and walk the same course and distance again. As soon as he rehearsed the correct walking response, he would receive every strong positive social reinforcement. This procedure, which has been cited in the treatment techniques described in Chapter 5, is entitled positive practice. Whenever Jim walked inappropriately he was immediately stopped, but the admonishment was not considered the crucial component of the program. The important point was that Jim was reinforced considerably for complying with rehearsing the correct response. Furthermore, the staff would socially reinforce Jim throughout the day for walking appropriately whenever they observed him doing so and remembered to reward it. Thus, correct gait was on a variable schedule of positive reinforcement, and as the frequency and duration of correct gait increased,

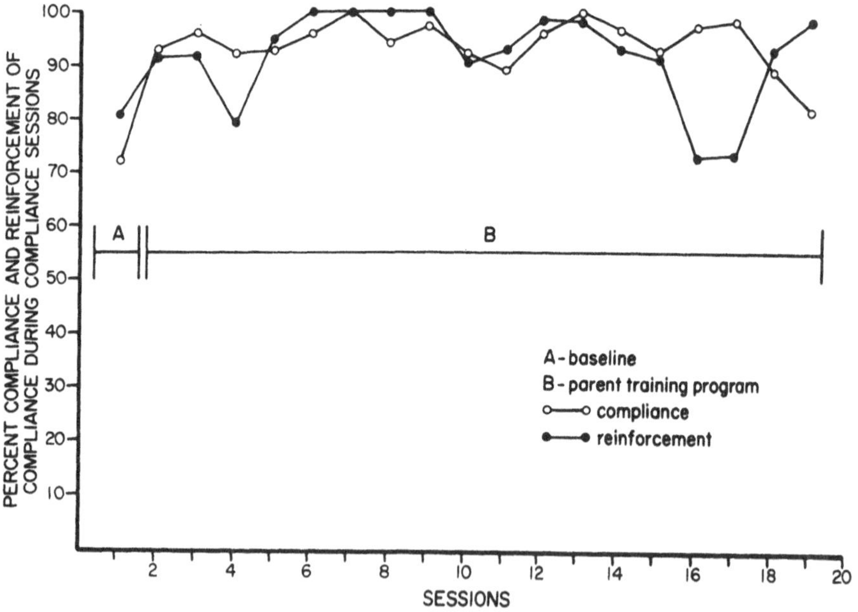

Figure 7.37. Effect of Parent-Training Program on Relationship between Father's Per Cent Reinforcement and Child's Per Cent Compliance during Compliance Sessions

it was on a progreessively thinner reinforcement schedule. Jim was interrupted when observed walking inappropriately, and then reinforced for rehearsing the response to a criterion level acceptable to staff.

PARENT TRAINING

The didactic parent program included periodic review of accumulated data, decreasing staff supervision, and closely monitored and videoed sessions where they were taught to use the treatment techniques currently incorporated in Jim's program. Both parents were in family therapy with the research group social worker. During the first months the parents visited briefly with Jim and spent the remainder of the time being informed of our progress in developing programs for Jim. We wished to attain maximum behavior control at thils time and felt that unstructured visits with the parents would insure that Jim would only rehearse the referral behavior with them, which could have had a deleterious effect on the program.

During the second month, we conducted sessions with his parents and Jim in which his parents were taught how to use both primary and sec-

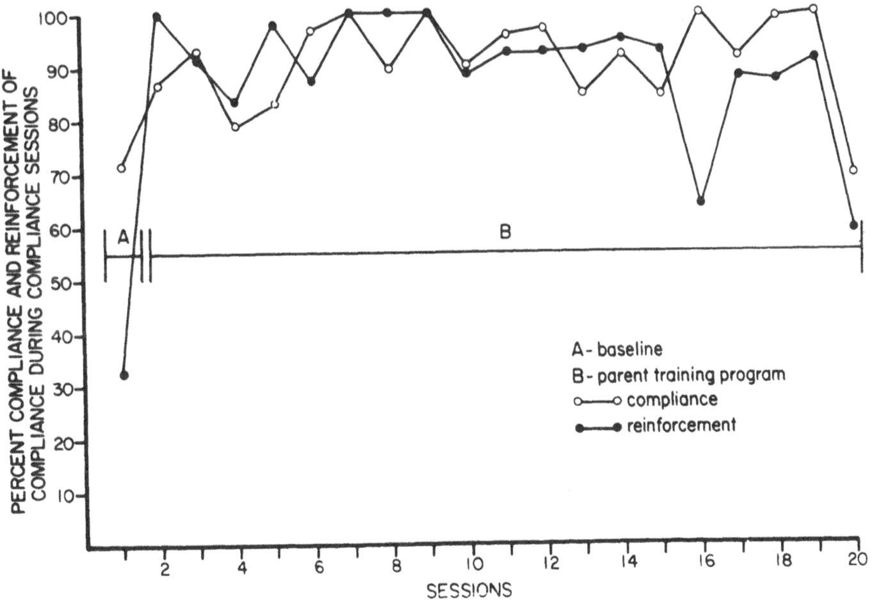

Figure 7.38. Effect of Parent-Training Program on Relationship between Mother's Per Cent Reinforcement and Child's Per Cent Compliance during Compliance Sessions

ondary reinforcers to train Jim to be compliant. The tasks used at first were simply to have him hand blocks to his parents, and as sufficient compliance was acquired with the parents, the tasks progressively increased in complexity, such as playing basketball, eating at a restaurant, etc. The parents were monitored on a decreasing schedule as they gained greater skill in teaching Jim appropriate behaviors. During the monitored sessions, staff would count number of verbal requests, compliance, non-compliance, social reinforcement of parents, gross testing and aggression

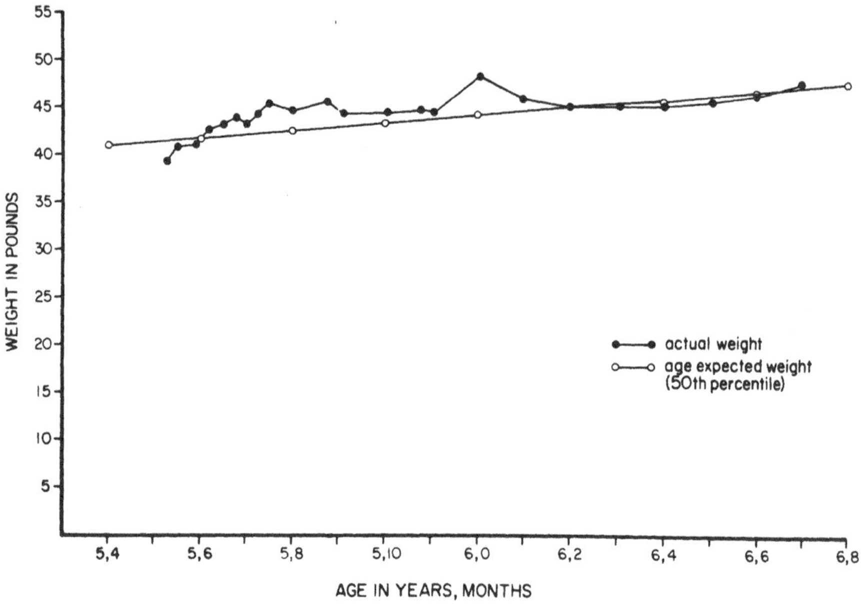

Figure 7.39. Comparison of Actual and Expected Weights during Food Contingent Conditioning Programs

responses. The testing responses diminished so rapidly that they were not worth graphing. However, the reinforcement rate and compliance/non-compliance ratio were crucial and are shown for each parent in Figures 7.37 and 7.38. The data for each session were shown and explained immediately to each parent, and this feedback, particularly in conjunction with review of video tapes, taught them to reinforce at a very high rate. Neither parent was naturally reinforcing Jim's compliant behavior when he was admitted. This procedure was explained and demonstrated to them, which accounts for their initially high reinforcement rate. As noted with

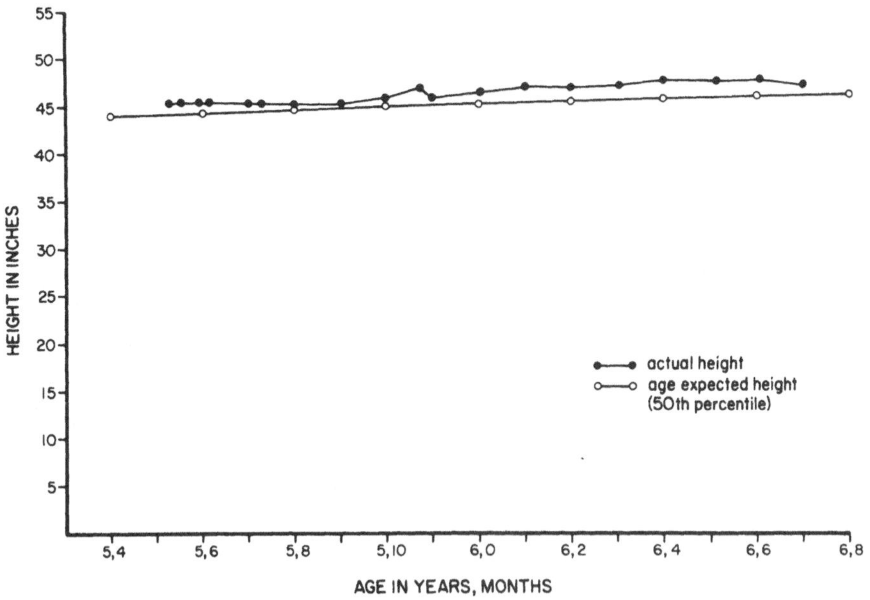

Figure 7.40. Comparison of Actual and Expected Heights during Food Contingent Conditioning Programs

the other parents, as well as with group staff, it required several months before they felt comfortable in praising such simple and normally expected behaviors. And like other parents, when they were not monitored closely by staff, e.g., when working with Jim outdoors, their reinforcement ratio would drop considerably. Figures 7.37 and 7.38 show that both parents did learn how to stimulate and reinforce compliant behavior in Jim during supervised training sessions.

Food was used contingently throughout Jim's treatment program for training appropriate eating, attention, and speech. Weight and height measures were obtained bi-weekly to ascertain if such a program would have a deleterious effect on his health, e.g., anorexia. Figures 7.39 and 7.40 demonstrate that his weight and height remained steady and close to the 50th percentile for age expectancy throughout the course of treatment. Furthermore, when permitted to eat by himself he consumed age appropriate quantities and varieties of foods.

Case Study 3: Sharon

INTRODUCTION

Sharon was admitted to the research group when she was three years and four months old. Her mother reported that she first noticed that "something was wrong" when Sharon was less than one year old. The usual signs of infantile autism (Rimland, 1964) were reported by the mother: Sharon's failure to relate affectionately, inability to distinguish parents, desire to be alone, and rigidity when picked up and held. Although Sharon had not acquired speech, she maintained complete control over the family with her raging temper tantrums, which suggested that she was capable of operating upon her environment in a communicative manner.

When she was admitted, her parents claimed that Sharon had acquired some operant speech in the form of single verbalizations. These verbal responses were delimited to ones which the parents were able to discriminate but they were not comprehensible responses to other persons. There was no generalized operant speech which was employed in a predictable fashion by Sharon. She demonstrated a communication disorder which appears to be prevalent among autistic children. It was our hypothesis that Sharon interacted with her environment with gross motor responses, and that her vocal responses were restricted to a primitive type of speech in the form of screaming or as represented by a temper tantrum. As will be clarified further in this case study, our impression was that Sharon's aggressive behavior was interactive with her communicative disorder. Thus, to delete aggression was tantamount to eliminating her form of speech. A treatment program with such a goal, of course, would be comparable to attempting to teach a youngster mutism after he had been using language for several years. Perhaps this difficulty in language acquisition was responsible for the slow treatment effects which we shall discuss in this study.

Sharon demonstrated many of the behaviors characteristic of autistic children as discussed by Ornitz and Ritvo (1968). At her date of admission, Sharon had deviant eye contact, i.e., it was unpredictable whether she would maintain eye contact when attention was verbally requested. As we have mentioned, she was muscularly rigid when held in one's arms. In fact, she became quite frightened if held directly out in front of someone, which suggested an imbalance difficulty. When she was admitted, and through her first two years of residency, Sharon manifested a fear of walking over undulating ground. We did not know what conditions were responsible for this behavioral characteristic, but we had to teach her to walk up and down stairs in a step-wise fashion, to run, and to climb over objects. She was also fearful of roughhouse play, which would invariably trigger aggressive behavior, which would produce an avoidance response from other people. Sharon had never been able to play with other children, even games so simple as peek-a-boo. There was no measurable I.Q. obtainable from Sharon when she was admitted. We established quite soon after her admission that she was exceptionally skilled at working with puzzles. This characteristic is not surprising, and seems comparable to the Wechsler Intelligence Scale for Children patterns obtained by Rutter (1966).

Sharon demonstrated bizarre food preferences, and there was a definite refusal on her behalf to eat "rough" foods. She had an unusual failure to respond to pain stimuli in an expected way. There was some posturing behavior, in which she would turn her head in a quick upward fashion. She was devoid of social smiles or approach behavior toward other persons. Her stereotyped behavior seemed to be restricted to repeatedly building puzzles so long as they were handed to her. If Sharon were not interrupted, she would obtain paper and shred it into tiny pieces. This latter behavior was acquired approximately one year after admission. Sharon did not demonstrate imitative behaviors, which is another characteristic of autistic children.

Sharon's height and weight were less than medium expectancy for a child of her age. She was a pale youngster and of slight stature. And as is so frequently observed of autistic children, eating was a problem for Sharon. She ate preferred foods, usually soft vegetables, in an unusual fashion. She would eat in very tiny bites and chew the food delicately. She consumed only small quantities of food at each meal. Her food preferences were limited to certain vegetables and various soft-starch types of foods. There were some indications for operant behavior for food, notably in a habit pattern acquired during a previous hospitalization where she learned to scream for candy. Sharon's toilet-training was not complete at date of admission. Although she had been trained to sit on a potty chair, she would not use it predictably for elimination. Her toilet problems were interactive with her delimited and restricted food intake. She was consuming only sparse quantities of roughage, and she was an unusually inactive child—a combination which resulted in chronic constipation. This had developed into varying degrees of severity. It was our hypothesis that constipation was the unconditioned stimulus, as represented by the discomfort of passing large and hard stools, the anticipation of which would invariably stimulate her to screaming and aggressive behavior in her frantic attempts to avoid the bowel movement. There was no validation for this hypothesis. In fact, her characteristic negligible response to cutaneous pain would lead one to suspect she would not be responsive to the pain stimulated by constipation. However, it would be over-generalized to presume that she was insensitive to pain on all sense modalities, because this hypothesis would not be warranted by the data accumulated thus far.

Sharon's play behavior was nonconstructive. She played neither in parallel nor cooperatively with other youngsters, whatever their ages. She was able to engage in repetitive activities by herself, such as piecing together simple puzzles, that she would perform repeatedly. This was the extent of her constructive play, and it was perseverative.

Sharon had few if any skills when admitted, and she was almost devoid of compliant behavior. She was a child who would not smile at one, and her constant bland expression and her high rate of aggressive behavior made it exceedingly difficult for other persons honestly to reinforce her. Sharon's gross motor coordination was significantly below age-expectancy. Unfortunately, she was so uncooperative when admitted that it was impossible to assess her skills in any structured setting. As mentioned above, she walked in a hesitant manner and had to be taught to run and trained to use stairs in a successive step-by-step fashion. Our impression was that her fine motor coordination surpassed her gross motor abilities, as evidenced by her skill with small puzzle pieces.

One dominant component of Sharon's behavior was her aggression, which apparently is not characterstic of all autistic children reported in the literature. Our impression is that children demonstrating the level of aggression seen in Sharon are usually under heavy medication in residential centers for retarded children, and do not find their way to research facilities and therefore are not reported in the literature so frequently. However, Sharon was an aggressive child, which was presumed to be interactive with her communication disorder. Aggression was her most dominant social behavior. She hit, bit, kicked, and spat with no provocation other than the presence of another person. The investigator recalls vividly her admission day—when he was attempting to console her while she was screaming, she bit through a new sports jacket. Our interpretation of Sharon's aggression was that it was a primitive form of body English, and that it did serve the operant purpose of enabling her to avoid demands for compliance by other persons, and to manipulate others to do certain things for her. We did not think that Sharon had preconceived ideas of what she wished other people to do for her. Rather, our impression was that aggression was a dominant response mode which Sharon had acquired, and that her numerous forms of aggression often resulted in her receiving various kinds of rewards, from her parents and other significant persons, that were intended to decelerate her aggression but had the converse effect. An example of such an event would be her parents' losing their tempers after hours of Sharon's screaming and assaultive behavior. After losing their tempers, they would provide her with candy, etc., in their frantic attempts to control her and reduce the guilt engendered by their counter-aggression.

Self-destructive responses were also characteristic of Sharon. She could be observed sitting by herself, screaming, and with both hands flailing and slapping at her eyes and face to the extent of causing bruising. This behavior would persist for hours at a time if she were left unattended. Attempts to console her by cuddling at such times would most likely elicit aggressive responses which served to drive people away from her and result in further social isolation. She would bite her hands so repetitively that an open sore and calluses were present at all times. There were bruise marks about her arms and legs as a result of her self-destructive responses.

Screaming was also a highly prevalent response which seemed to permeate Sharon's behavior when she was admitted. Her screaming was devoid of tears and could not be defined as crying. It was a dry, hoarse scream for which staff could seldom identify the triggering stimulus. This screaming would persist for hours at a time and could be initiated at any time of day or night. This behavior occurred most often when she was in her room by herself, and frequently late in the night.

EXTINGUISHING FOOD PREFERENCES

When she was admitted, Sharon's appearance was that of a frail and anemic youngster. This condition may have been attributed in part to her food preferences, which were restricted to soft vegetables. She ate little, and she ate very slowly by nibbling at her food. She seemed to support herself on a sparse amount of food contrasted to what would be normally expected of a growing three-year-old. As Figures 7.41 and 7.42 show, when Sharon was admitted her weight was around the 25th percentile and her height close to the 10th percentile of normal expectancies. Food was used contingently during the course of Sharon's treatment program. Preferred foods were used to condition eating other nonpreferred foods and all foods were used during those meals when staff were available to conduct the programs for training speech. The details of the speech-shaping program are given in another section of this case study. It is interesting to note that, although Sharon was trained to eat greater quantities and varieties of foods during the course of the treatment program, her height and weight remained less than average. Her height and weight were at the 10th percentile when she was five years old. Sharon was then eating considerably more than she had when admitted, but apparently her actual stature was that of a small child. She was a little chubbier when admitted than she was after a year and eight months of treatment, which may be attributed to the fact that she was then a much more active child than she had been at admission. She never learned to eat large bites of food, nor did she ever eat quickly throughout the program. Her manner of preferring small bites of untextured foods may be attributable to her inability to flex her tongue easily, that did not facilitate her masticating of food. It seemed

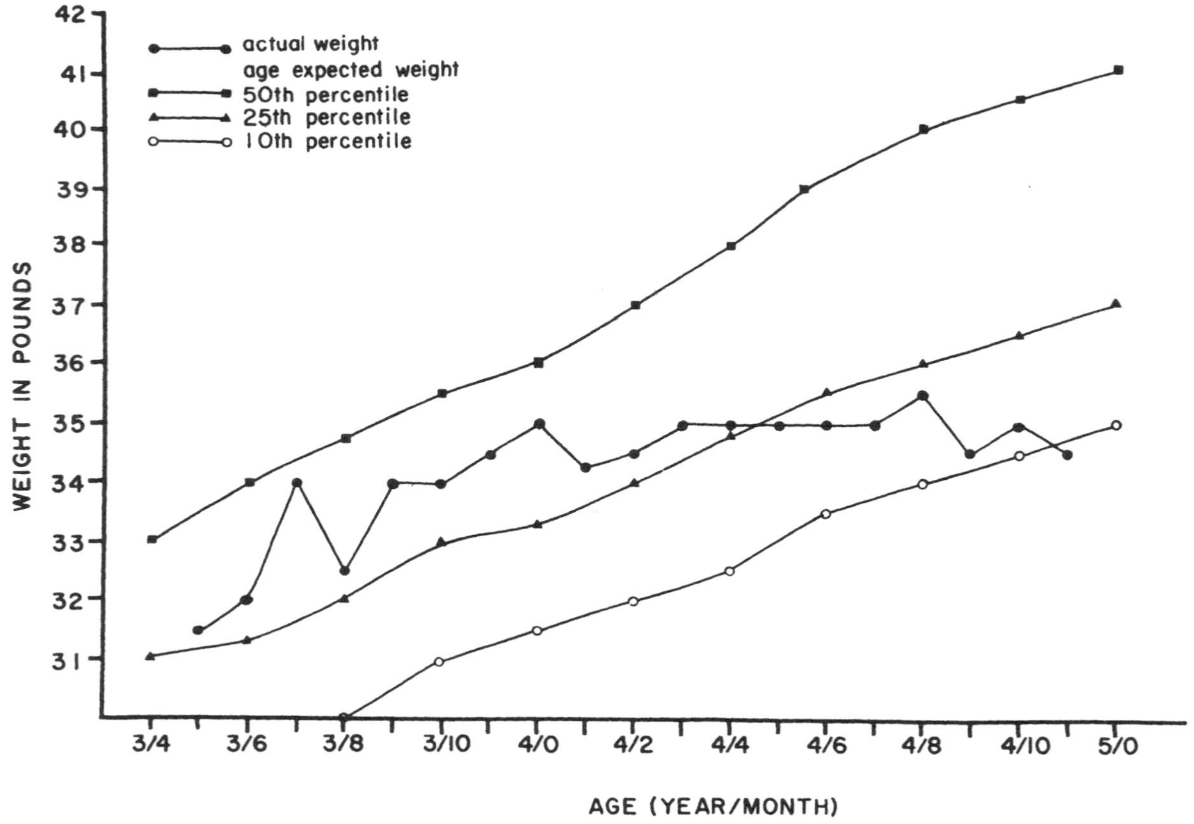

Figure 7.41. Comparison of Actual and Expected Weights during Food Contingent Conditioning Programs

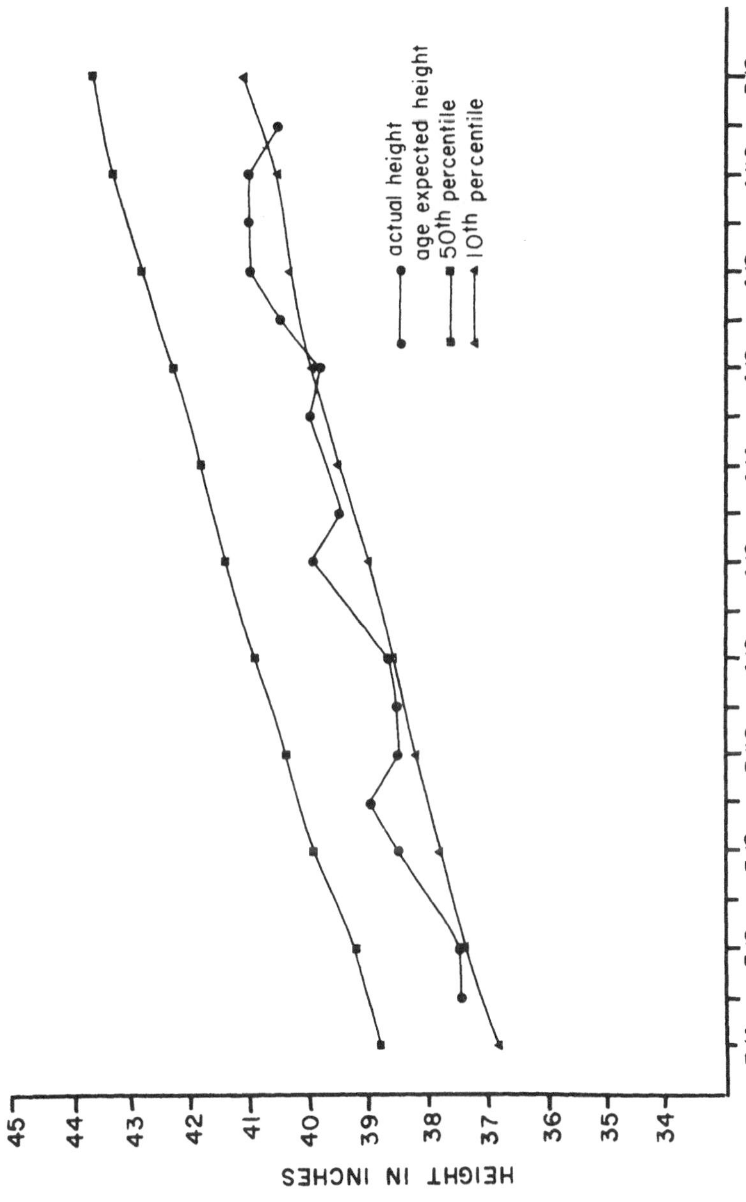

Figure 7.42. Comparison of Actual and Expected Heights during Food Contingent Conditioning Programs

as though Sharon were what we could describe as a "delicate responder" in all phases of her behavior. For example, she ran in short, tiny, mincing steps and had to be trained to run at an age-appropriate pace. Even with that training, by the time she was five she still did not stride in her run but rather learned to run more quickly with her tiny steps. Sharon held objects delicately, in both fine and gross motor tasks. She would not respond strongly in the whole-hearted manner expected of a child involved in play. There was always that hesitancy on her behalf to respond, not, we presumed, that she was consciously afraid of a consequence, but merely that her only available responses were weak. The only exception to this observation was that she could strike and bite herself and other persons very harshly.

At the beginning of Sharon's treatment program, staff had to train her to eat a variety of foods. This was accomplished by placing all foods on her plate. Staff would be seated facing Sharon and would allow her to eat at her own pace. However, she was required to alternate preferred with nonpreferred foods throughout her meal. At some meals, such as at breakfast, if she did not drink her juice she was not permitted to continue eating the remainder of her breakfast unless she finished the juice. If she did not complete eating by termination of the usual mealtime, which averaged 30 minutes, the food was removed from the table and she would not eat until the next meal, when new food would be introduced. We did not retain food from one meal and use it for the next.

TOILET-TRAINING

Sharon was not predictably toilet-trained when admitted; we assumed that this deficit was related to her chronic constipation. As we have described, Sharon consumed small quantities of food with moderate food preferences, avoided textured foods, and was remarkably less physically active in comparison to other three-year-old children. These conditions had interacted to produce a long-standing history of constipation. Our hypothesis was that constipation was the unconditioned stimulus by producing painful bowel movements, the anticipation of which elicited prolonged intervals of screaming, avoidance of the toilet, and both self-destructive and aggressive behaviors. This problem had progressed to the extent that Sharon would avoid use of the toilet.

Figure 7.43 shows the succession of treatment techniques designed to train Sharon to use the toilet appropriately. During the early weeks of the study, Sharon was concurrently being trained to eat a variety of foods at mealtime, which improved her food intake. For the first 230 days, Sharon's total treatment program involved plentiful use of dried fruits as reinforcers, in addition to liquid medication as required for constipation

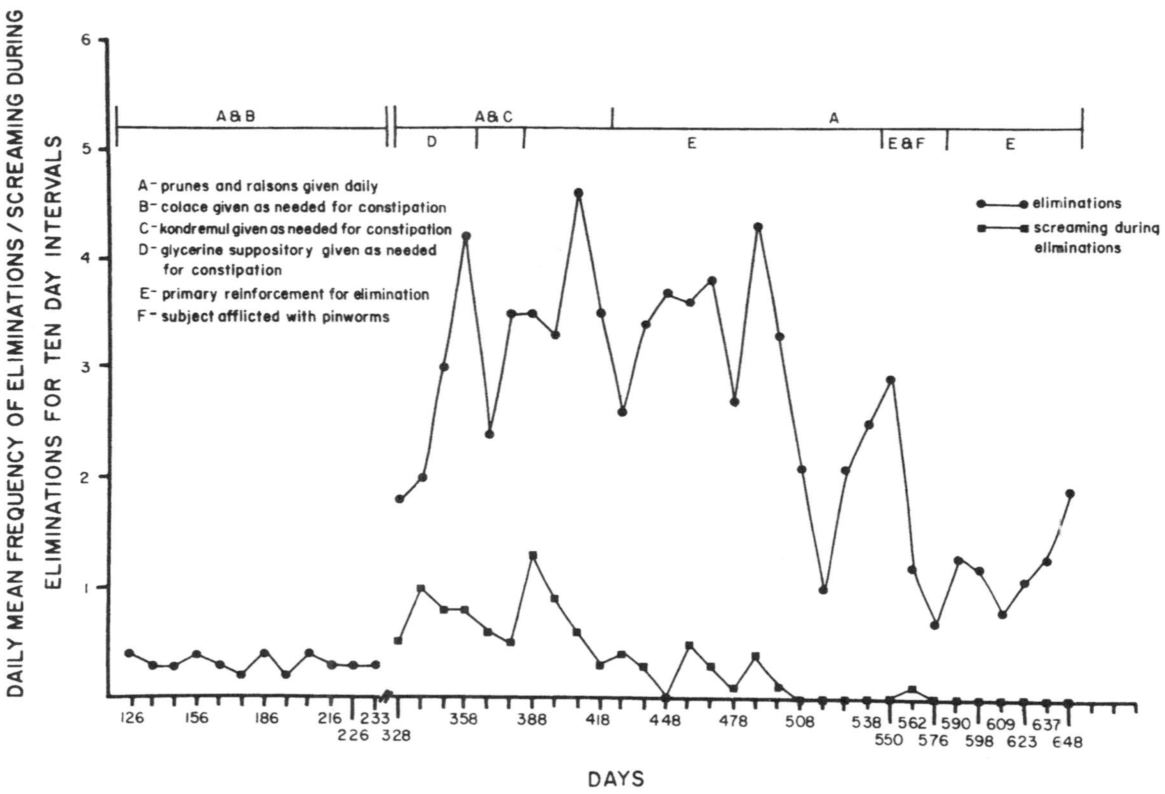

Figure 7.43. Daily Mean Frequency of Eliminations/Screaming during Eliminations for Ten-Day Intervals

occurring during the interim. Throughout the 230 days, Sharon was having less than one bowel movement per day, and continued to be constipated. She was being trained at this time to use a potty chair which was placed in her room, for the use of which she would be reinforced during training sessions directly with staff, and also reinforced for spontaneous use of the chair both socially and with pieces of dried fruit and candy. By day 300, she was capable of using the training chair without assistance.

On day 300, a program was begun in which a glycerin suppository was administered on a PRN basis for constipation. This program was formally in effect for a 17-day interval, but it was occasionally reinstated to assist Sharon for a two-month interval. The program required that on successive days, a glycerin suppository be administered but decreased in size by quarter-inch increments so long as the medication was successful in initiating bowel movements without concurrent screaming responses. Apparently her history of constipation had been of such severity that she was conditioned to attempt to avoid the pain of the bowel movement by retention. Unfortunately, this behavior only engendered more painful bowel movements and trained her to avoid elimination further. The suppository had such a quick effect that she did not have the usual anticipatory responses, nor did she attempt to retain the bowel movement. On successive days, the glycerin suppository was diminished in size. On days when she had some difficulty in elimination, the suppository would be increased to the size which had been successful on the previous day. Thereafter, on successive days, the suppository would again be diminished in size to a final length of about one-half inch, after which it was used only infrequently. The surprising effect of this technique was that the anticipatory responses did diminish, and she began to use the toilet in an appropriate way but at an exceptionally high rate, as may be seen in Figure 7.43. The treatment technique was successful, but we had trained another abnormal response, namely, that of using the toilet for defecating between three and four times a day. When the glycerin suppository was no longer required, Sharon's training program was to provide her with a preferred candy reinforcer each time she eliminated in the toilet correctly without screaming. This technique was in effect to the conclusion of the entire 604 days shown in Figure 7.43. By the conclusion of that time, Sharon was using the toilet appropriately, and at a rate which would be expected of an average child. The rate of her encopresis, so prevalent prior to toilet-training, extinguished.

We wished to assess whether the screaming responses associated with constipation would decelerate concurrently with toilet-training. Staff counted the frequency of Sharon's screaming when using the toilet. As Figure 7.43 shows, the screaming episodes associated with using the toilet extinguished as she became toilet-trained.

SCREAMING

Sharon's screaming was a perplexing referral behavior. This response was defined as a dry, wailing scream unaccompanied by tears but often associated with self-destructive behavior. The duration of these screaming episodes varied from a few minutes to an occasional occurrence of two hours at night. The perplexing aspect of this behavior was that we were unable to identify the conditions which would stimulate it. We observed that this response was most frequent when Sharon was in her room during rest period and also late at night. During her first year of residence, screaming occurred often at the termination of a meal. (Many screaming incidences were related to her anticipation of having a bowel movement, as we have discussed in the study of toilet-training.)

During the succession of treatment techniques devised to control Sharon's screaming, staff would count the daily frequency of these episodes and, when possible, also record the duration of the response. These data are shown in Figure 7.44, and illustrate the difficulty of controlling the behavior. Social punishment would spike the rate and duration of screaming, whereas ignoring the behavior and leaving her door open when she was screaming during rest periods and at night had a preferred effect. The treatments were discouraging, and once a screaming episode began, we were unable to interrupt the behavior.

On day 218, a new treatment program was begun. Staff had previously observed that Sharon demonstrated a fear response, i.e., muscular rigidity, whenever lifted off the floor or required to balance on playground equipment or to climb over objects. On the premise that this was an unconditional fear response, staff tried picking her up, holding her out in front of oneself or in some position of imbalance, and admonishing her for screaming. The screaming would cease immediately with this procedure, and it was expected that the frequency of the response would gradually follow deceleration of duration. The treatment program was then placed into effect.

During all of Sharon's programs, if she cried with tears, staff would cuddle and console her. Although affection was not studied specifically, she did not cuddle warmly when admitted, but this behavior began to emerge approximately two months after shock was used to punish aggression and self-destruction. The crying response did not replace screaming behavior, the responses were autonomous.

COMPLIANCE TRAINING

The continuing ratio of Sharon's compliant to her noncompliant behavior is not precisely depicted in Figure 7.45. As we have discussed in other case studies, simply comparing the ratio of compliant to noncompliant

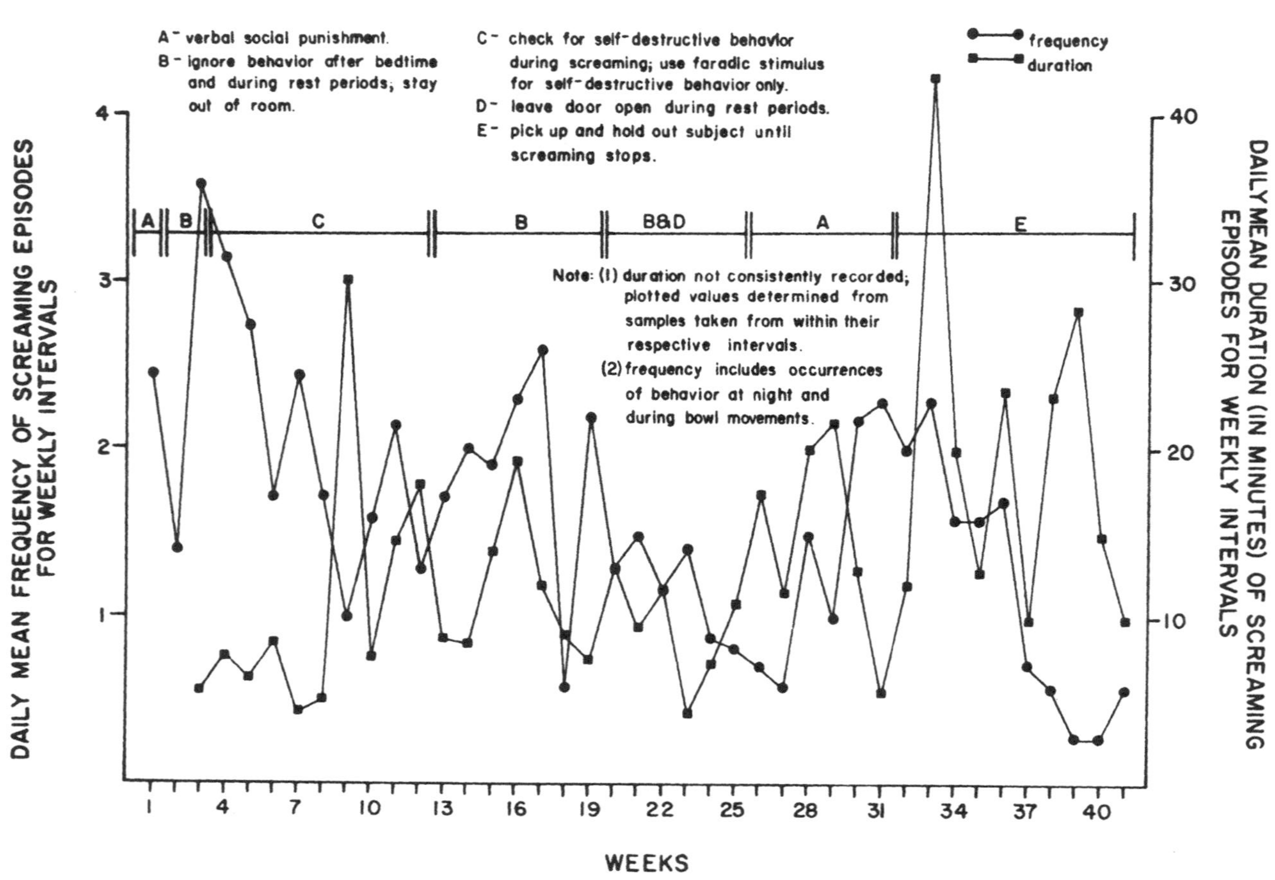

Figure 7.44. Effect of Several Treatment Methods on Daily Mean Frequency/Duration of Screaming Episodes

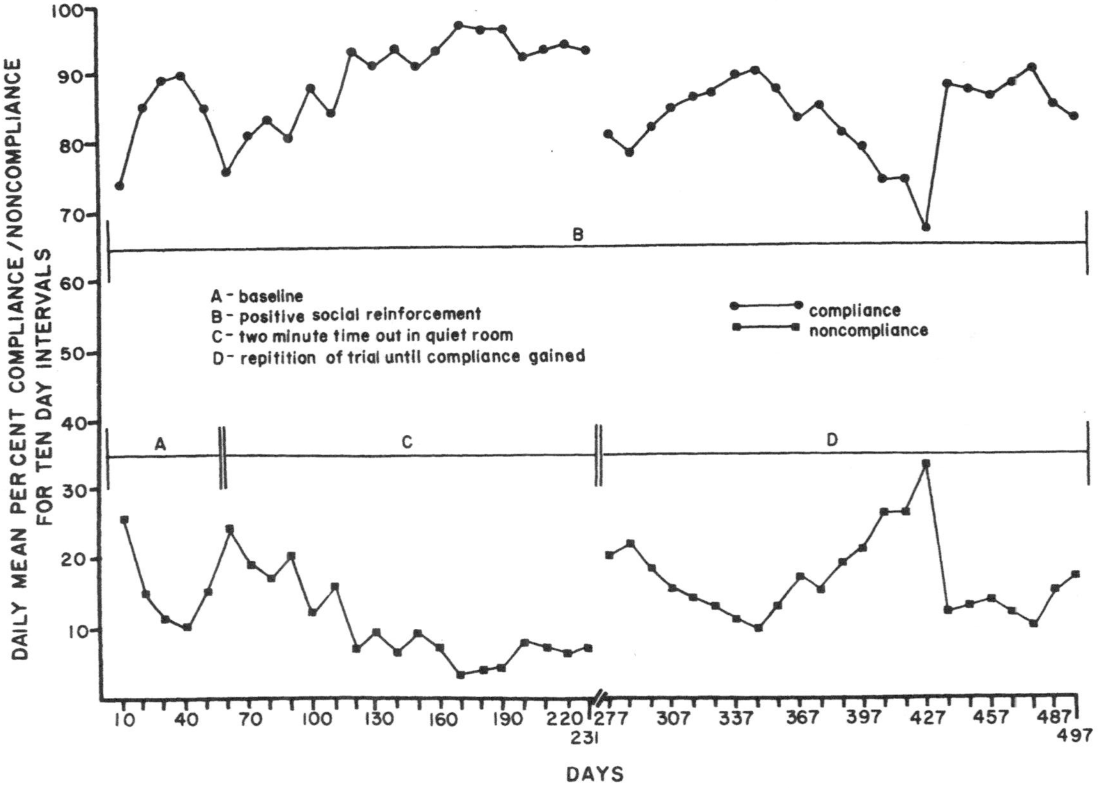

Figure 7.45. Effect of Three Treatment Methods on Compliant/Non-compliant Responses

behavior across time fails to demonstrate any qualitative changes in the behavior. The beginning weeks of the study shown in Figure 7.45 were restricted to very simple requests for compliant behavior, but there was a gradual progression to more complex requests as the study continued. Initial requests were delimited to such simple ones as asking Sharon to hand a block to a staff member. At the conclusion of the study represented by Figure 7.45, requests for compliance were as complex as asking her to go to the classroom which was two buildings distant. However, the data have not surpassed the problem of reflecting the qualitative change of behavior, since compliant and noncompliant behavior are here grouped as if they were always the same level of response complexity.

Positive social reinforcement was used profusely by staff for compliant behavior. This reinforcement included positive verbal statements and physical affection when it was appropriate. Unfortunately, Sharon was at first markedly unreceptive to affection, which when demonstrated would often trigger aggressive and avoidance behaviors. Compliant behaviors were defined as Sharon's fulfilling, or attempting to fulfil, verbal requests made of her by a staff member. A noncompliant response was tallied as one in which she did not respond appropriately to a verbal request or even attempt to do so. Thus, when a staff member made a verbal request of Sharon, it was a forced-choice situation in that Sharon would respond either compliantly or noncompliantly and would receive a count for either response by the staff. These counts were then entered into the data book at the conclusion of each staff member's shift working with Sharon. Noncompliance was treated in two ways in the study: after a baseline interval for noncompliance, a two-minute time-out was attempted after which a positive practice program was initiated. We shall discuss this in more detail shortly. Conduct of a program for teaching a child compliance is dependent upon staff's making requests of the child which the latter is known to be capable of fulfilling. There is a major problem in conducting a continuing shaping program when the behavioral definition is a function of the staff's clinical judgment and is progressively changing, i.e., the requested behavior is constantly moving to more complex levels. This training goal is difficult to achieve, since the child is simultaneously training the staff throughout the program to remain at the same request complexity level. Specifically, staff are being rewarded by the child who is able to perform successfully at a given complexity level of compliant behavior. For example, perhaps the request level is restricted to asking the child to hand blocks to the staff member. When the staff member moves the youngster to a more complex level of response expectancy in his verbal command, such as requesting the child to build objects with the blocks upon verbal command, it is more likely that the child will not be able to perform adequately at first, which will result in noncompliant behavior. It is punishing for staff to work with a youngster who is not compliant, i.e., the frustration is not restricted exclusively to the child. Thus the staff may inadvertently be trapped into "infantilizing" the child, just as the parents of autistic children are so often trapped. It is very tempting to work with a child on a level of response expectancy where he will invariably succeed, which is rewarding at all times both to staff and child. Also, progressing in a hierarchy from simple to complex verbal commands requires optimal communication among staff so that everyone is consistent in his response expectancy of the child. Such programs require considerable vigilance among staff to enable them to modify their behavioral expectancy of the child. A program which allows staff to monitor each other and work with different children in structured training situations makes it more likely that the level of communication necessary for the advancement of the child to more complex behaviors will become a reality.

During the first stage of the program shown in Figure 7.45, noncompliant responses were placed on a baseline. During that baseline condition, noncompliance was not punished in any form, but the reciprocal behavior of compliance was positively reinforced by staff in the manner described above. On day 57, noncompliant behaviors resulted in Sharon's being placed in the quiet room for a two-minute time-out. Positive reinforcement for compliant behaviors remained in effect during this treatment interval. This program change was initiated because Sharon was becoming increasingly noncompliant. Apparently, social reinforcement was not independently successful in training compliant behaviors. The response complexity level demanded up to that time was rather constant; it was restricted to simple requests such as asking her to hand and place objects, etc. With the change to a time-out program for noncompliance, a preferred treatment effect occurred very gradually. The program shows a deceleration of noncompliant responses, and the converse behavior of compliance increased in its daily frequency. On day 232, counting the compliant and noncompliant responses was discontinued, although the respective treatment programs were retained in effect. At day 267, the treatment program for noncompliant behaviors was changed, and staff began again to count the behaviors. It was our impression that Sharon's noncompliant responses had accelerated—as indeed they had, as may be seen at the start of the program on day 267. Our hypothesis about what had occurred was that Sharon was being increasingly noncompliant, which eventuated her having a time-out, which was a preferred contingency since she succeeded in avoiding having to work directly with staff on the training programs which had progressed to more complex response levels. Sharon, like many autistic children, preferred to be alone, undemanded of, and behaviorally static.

A positive practice program was initiated. This program required that staff repeat the trial of the verbal request to Sharon until a compliant response was obtained. Each time a new request was made of Sharon, she would receive a count of either compliance or noncompliance. If she were noncompliant, positive practice would begin in which the staff would continue requesting the desired response until it occurred, after which it would be socially reinforced by them. During the positive practice session for the response, the staff would not count whether she was compliant or noncompliant. The management order was to count the first new request as compliant or noncompliant and not to count the response ratio during positive practice episodes.

Behavioral variance seemed to increase at this time when the staff were "pushing" Sharon more intensely for preferred behaviors. Sharon was now unable to avoid staff by being noncompliant, since they would constantly make the request over and again until she did succeed. She was not to be socially punished during the interim of positive practice for a response, instead, the request was made repeatedly.

The data in Figure 7.45 are deceptive. At the conclusion of the study, it would appear from them that Sharon was less compliant than she was after the first 100 days of treatment. Actually, she was failing more often, but staff were making more complex response expectancies of her. Also, the change to more complex response levels was progressing more quickly than it had during the first year of treatment. At the latter stages of the study, other concurrent programs were becoming more successful. For example, aggression was decelerating at this time, speech was beginning to occur spontaneously after 16 months of intensive work, gross motor training had progressed to a level where she was capable of engaging in more strenuous activity, and she could be programmed in conjunction with more than one child, which made her amenable to learning cooperative responses with her peers.

TEMPER TANTRUMS

Sharon's temper tantrums were defined as a series of related behaviors which could include any combination of noncompliance, screaming, refusal to move, and running away from the staff member. Temper tantrums were characteristic of Sharon when she was in a forced-choice situation requiring her to learn a new response. As may be seen in Figure 7.46, the first program was to place Sharon in her room until she was settled and quiet, after which we would take her out of her room and reinitiate the activity in which she had had the temper tantrum. We gradually learned that there were several potentially reinforcing objects and activities available in her room. Thus, temper tantrums were successfully allowing her to avoid a

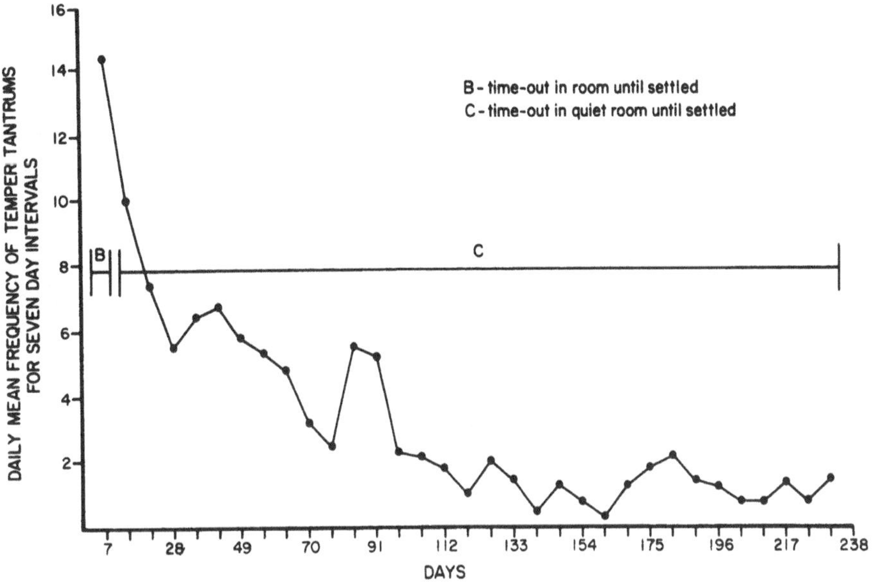

Figure 7.46. Effects of Time-Out Procedures on Daily Mean Frequency of Temper Tantrums

situation in which she did not wish to engage and a time-out in her room actually served to reinforce the temper tantrum behavior. In view of these data, treatment *C* was begun, in which she was placed in a quiet room until the tantrum ceased, after which she would be returned to the activity from which she had just been removed. Duration of time in the quiet room varied from a few minutes to seldom more than ten minutes. She would often say, "Ready," as soon as she walked into the quiet room, but she had to remain there for at least a two-minute interval. The data do not depict the duration of the total time of her tantrums. However, the behavior did subside to the point where the management order was kept in effect and the response no longer counted. The quality of the tantrums shifted from wild uncontrolled screaming and avoidance responses to short bursts of animated noncompliance.

SELF-BITING

Figure 7.47 contains the daily mean frequencies averaged over nine-day intervals for self-biting, and later for a combined count of self-biting and self-destructive responses. Sharon's self-biting response was defined as her placing her hand in her mouth and biting it. She had open sores and cal-

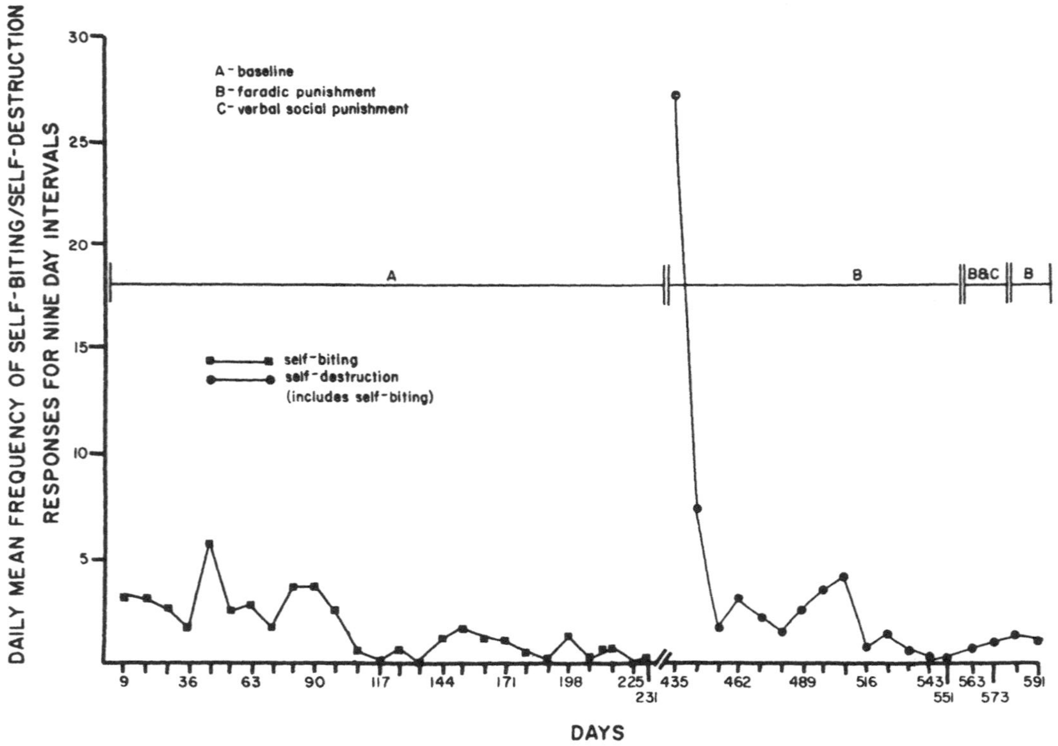

Figure 7.47. Effect of Faradic and Social Punishment on Daily Mean Frequency of Self-Biting and Self-Destructive Responses

luses on both hands from this behavior when she was admitted, and the response persisted throughout her first year of residence. Figure 7.47 would lead one to conclude that self-biting occurred on the average of four times a day and that, within 200 days of simply having been placed on a baseline with no treatment whatsoever, the response spontaneously extinguished. The data were in error. Self-biting responses were chained to her screaming incidences, which typically occurred when she was in her room by herself. In the first year of treatment, Sharon was successfully training staff to avoid her as much as possible. The program was not so demanding of her nor so time-consuming as it was during the second year after shock was used and her assaultive behavior became more controllable. There were longer intervals of time during the first year when Sharon was alone and was not being observed by staff. Furthermore, the treatment program for screaming responses during that first year was to ignore the behavior and not to enter her room on the premise that the screaming may have been an operant response for some kind of attention. The fact that Sharon still had an open sore on her hand and calluses was evidence that self-biting was still occurring when she was by herself and that the behavioral counts were in error.

On day 435, a program was initiated in which faradic punishment was used for self-biting and self-destructive responses. Self-biting and self-destructive responses were included in a combined count which is responsible for some of the apparent acceleration seen in Figure 7.47. Self-destructive behaviors were defined as Sharon's hitting as well as biting herself. These behaviors were both present during the screaming episodes when, under the management orders, she was being ignored by staff. And again, since these screaming episodes occurred most often when she was alone, such as during nap or evening sleep, staff were unable to tally the total occurrence of the self-destructive behaviors. However, we did decide that the behavior had to be punished directly, since it had not extinguished after a year's treatment. At day 435, faradic stimulation was concurrently used for punishing aggressive responses, as will be discussed later.

It is necessary to discuss the decision for applying faradic punishment for Sharon's self-destructive and aggressive behaviors. We had completed a year's research with Sharon and were discouraged by the data. The decision to resort to the use of shock, which was not necessary in all cases studied, resulted from her first home visit. Sharon was taken to her home, a trip which required a two-hour drive on which she was accompanied by three staff members to obtain data, to assess generalization of treatment effects, and to assist her parents in carrying out the current management orders for Sharon. The investigator became painfully aware of the fact that all staff and parents were reluctant to make complex requests of Sharon and allowed her to "float" to avoid eliciting assaultive and self-destructive behaviors. Her speech had not improved appreciably, she was not responsive to affection, and she had to be handled cautiously during the home visit.

The data from the first year had simply failed to reflect the minimal qualitative changes in Sharon's behavior. However impressive some of the data may have appeared in numerical form, the fact was that Sharon remained a grossly disturbed child whose first year of treatment could be described as a failure. While returning to the Treatment Center after the home visit, we had to interrupt Sharon's isolative play of shredding paper, and this stimulated rage and aggressive behavior. She screamed, bit, and hit herself and staff members in the car until she collapsed from fatigue and slept. That rage lasted for an hour and one-half of driving time. Upon arriving at the Treatment Center, we began to consider the use of faradic punishment for Sharon's aggressive and self-destructive behavior. The investigator was dismayed by the fact that the use of shock with Heidi had such a slow treatment effect. Further inspection of Lovaas' (during a personal visit with O. I. Lovaas in 1967) data was made to ascertain whether they could be of any assistance in making the decision to resort to shock, or whether less drastic treatment alternatives were available for controlling Sharon's aggression and self-destruction. We learned that, in the laboratory setting, the principles of punishment and reward were demonstrable to autistic children, but the generalization effects were minimal and the pre-treatment behaviors were quickly reinstated. This confirmed our belief that a punishment program for the assaultive behaviors would have to be a continual treatment program allowing little opportunity for the child to rehearse the pre-treatment behaviors.

We decided to use faradic stimulation for self-destructive and aggressive behaviors, since all other programs had been ineffectual. The parents were informed of all the data, the findings of experimental studies on the use of shock, and the fact that hundreds of trials had been necessary with the previous child who had been treated with shock and that we expected the same slow effects with their youngster. As Figure 7.47 shows, at the beginning of the faradic punishment program, Sharon was engaged in self-destructive behavior more than 25 times per day on a nine-day average. The response did decelerate rapidly with this new program and approximated a zero level at day 543. At this time we attempted to combine shock with social punishment statements, e.g., we would admonish Sharon verbally after which she would be punished with the faradic stimulator for the behavior. This management order was designed to condition social punishment statements with the hopes that they would eventually be able to replace shock. This management order had the nonpreferred effect of accelerating the response, so we decided to reinstate the management order of using only faradic punishment for self-destructive responses rather than simultaneously attempting to counter-condition social punishment statements. The program had the preferred effect again, as may be seen at day 591 on the graph. The behavior was thereafter retained on that management order. Sharon was also monitored more closely during her episodes of screaming, so that these self-destructive behaviors were being counted and treated accordingly. Sharon was more manageable at this time because of the concurrent reduction of aggressive behaviors and her acquisition of speech, all of which combined to make her more tractable to engage in other rehabilitation programs.

Again, as reflected in all data presented so far, there was no spectacular treatment effect. There was a treatment effect, but it required months during which there was a gradual acquisition of preferred behaviors and reduction of such responses as self-destruction. During the course of all of these programs, Sharon was on as close to a 1:1 staff-to-child ratio as we could program. The data contained in the phase of Figure 7.47 in which all responses were grouped under self-destruction and treated with shock are more accurate representations of the actual rate of these behaviors than we have for the first year of treatment. These behaviors were not returned to a baseline condition because other data suggested that only a few weeks would be required to reinstate the referral behaviors, which included self-destruction. Perhaps this problem is more profound with autistic children, but it is not unique to them, since the same difficulty in generalization of treatment effects applies for all child-patient populations. Considering the hypothesis that autistic children have difficulty in discrimination learning on various sense modalities (cf. Wing, 1969), we may assume that it is probable that they are going to be less able to discriminate similarities in environmental conditions and thereby fail to generalize their acquired responses. Apparently, the behavior learned in one situation remains as a response to that setting, independent and unaffected by what is learned in other ostensibly comparable settings. This problem was observed time and again when children were taken on home visits, during which the referral behaviors would gradually replace those which had required months to teach the child.

AGGRESSION

When Sharon was admitted, we began immediately to study management orders to control her aggressive behavior. For the first 200 days of residence, we addressed ourselves solely to treating gross aggressive responses. Gross aggression was defined as Sharon's striking another person by making physical contact. Her hitting responses varied in intensity, but staff generally agreed that her aggressions were often painful. She would strike one with an open-palmed hand, and she did not demonstrate preference for left- or right-handedness when she aggressed. Figure 7.48 shows that Sharon was responding with gross aggression during a baseline interval 41 times per day as averaged for nine-day intervals. A quick appraisal of Figure 7.48 would lead one to conclude that the combined management orders of a two-minute time-out preceded by verbal social punishment immediately after she aggressed were effective in decelerating Sharon's aggressive responses. This conclusion would not have been correct. There was a spurious component in the apparent deceleration of Sharon's gross aggressive responses. Specifically, she was so aggressive that staff would not make strong demands in working with her during the daily program. For one to intrude upon Sharon's isolation and to demand increasing complex behaviors, however profuse the social and primary reinforcements were, would have the discouraging but almost invariable effect of eliciting aggressive behavior. Thus, staff were not "pushing" Sharon for increasingly complex behavior in her treatment program. This is just one more instance in which it becomes obvious that the child is training the staff for certain kinds of behaviors while concurrently being trained by the staff.

We did notice that a new response form of aggression was emerging. This form of aggression, identified as low-level aggression, was defined as Sharon's striking at another person but not making physical contact. The response was described as a flexion of the arm but without physical contact. On day 204, staff began to count low-level responses which they admonished with social punishment. Figure 7.48 presents those data and also a plotted line for the combined total aggression, which was the accumulation of gross and low-level responses occurring each day. Again, it would appear that the low-level responses were decelerating, and quite rapidly. However, the correlated behavior of gross aggression was constant, which was unusual since it had been our experience that related behaviors, such as gross and low-level aggression, would co-vary. Observation and discussion with staff members revealed that Sharon was becoming a most unpleasant child with whom to work, and her low-level aggressive responses were cues for staff to "back off" and not to demand complex responses, thereby avoiding triggering gross aggressive responses from her. A break of one month occurred in the data at this point while we reassessed the treatment program. From what staff had stated, it appeared that social punishment would stimulate more aggression, rather than decelerate it as the data had first led us to conclude. The data at first simply reflected that Sharon had trained staff to avoid her, and that they therefore tallied fewer aggressive responses. A program was then begun in which only the two-minute time-out was contingent upon gross aggression; low-level aggression

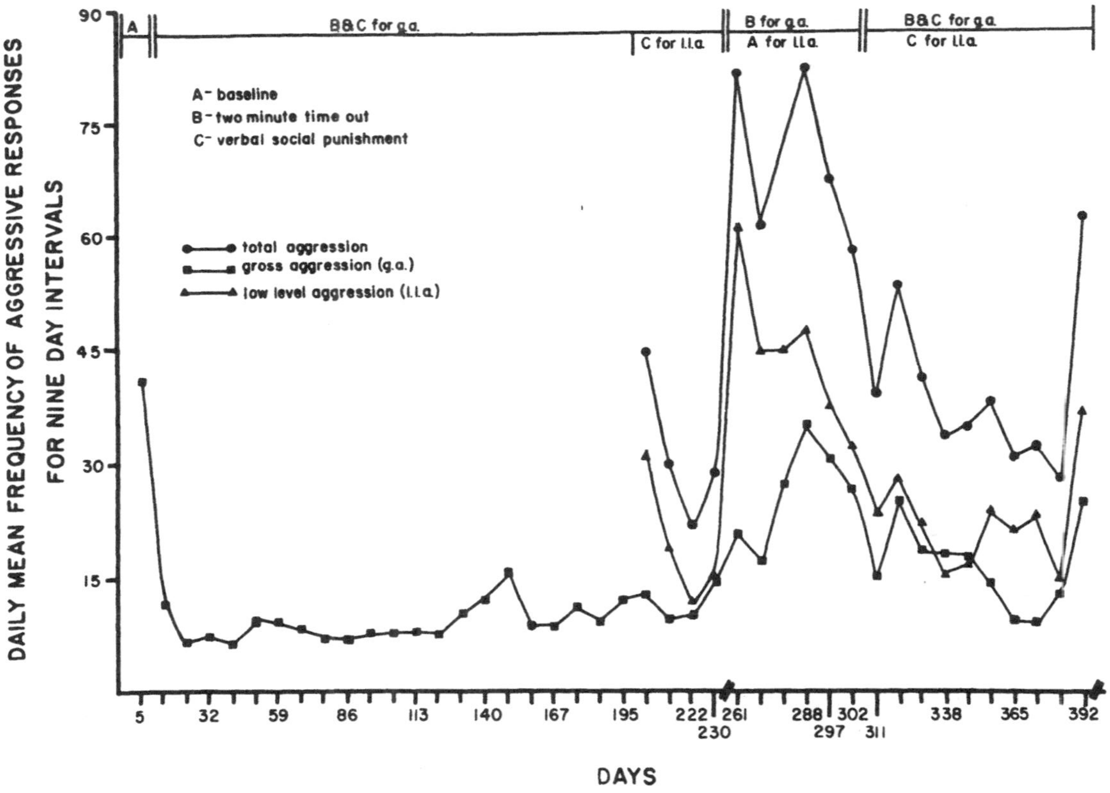

Figure 7.48. *Effect of a Time-Out and Social Punishment on Aggressive Responses during the First Year of Residence*

was placed on a baseline and simply counted and neither punished nor timed-out. Figure 7.48 shows that, with staff's concerted effort to make an accurate count of Sharon's aggressive behavior, it was quite high. Also, we saw at this time that the gross and low-level behaviors were indeed paralleling each other. In fact, usually low-level aggressive responses would precede Sharon's gross aggression. The gross aggressive responses were declining gradually with the time-out treatment procedure, and the low-level responses were also decelerating in step with the gross aggressive responses. Figure 7.48 shows that we then initiated a program in which a two-minute time-out plus social punishment was contingent upon gross aggression, and verbal social punishment was contingent for low-level aggressive behaviors. The data show that the response deceleration was gradually, but then progressively, reversed so that we were reinstating her aggressive habits at the pre-treatment rates. It was becoming apparent that Sharon's aggressive responses would decelerate with time-out conditions, and accelerate when social punishment was contingent upon their occurrence. The deceleration of the response rate, however, was spuriously accentuated by the fact that aggressive responses were not being counted while she was having a time-out. Also, since aggression was stimulated by staff's intruding upon her isolation and forcing her to perform on speech-training and other programs, it was likely that Sharon would learn to operate for the time-outs so as to regain social isolation. Unfortunately, it had taken us a year to realize that social punishment was not a decelerating condition for aggression, but had the punishment error of actually accelerating the response. This indicated that we would have to countercondition the social punishment stimuli if Sharon were to return to any situation in which ordinary verbal commands could be directed at her. At this time we had begun to reevaluate Sharon's entire program, particularly after her first home visit when we had been confronted with the evidence that there was little generalization of treatment effects.

We decided to retest the hypothesis that social punishment statements would accelerate aggressive responses for Sharon. Figure 7.49 shows the study and the ensuing treatment programs for Sharon's aggressive behavior. The first three treatment phases, labelled as *A, C,* and *A,* are the study of this hypothesis. The gross and low-level aggressive behaviors were tallied in a combined count by staff for a baseline period, followed by two weeks of treatment of verbal social punishment contingent upon the aggressive responses, after which the responses were returned to baseline. The vertical axis shows the daily mean frequency of these aggressive responses for four-day intervals, and it should be noted that this ordinate includes 352 responses per day, as contrasted to Figure 7.48, in which the ordinate axis contains only 90 responses. The data show rather clearly that social pun-

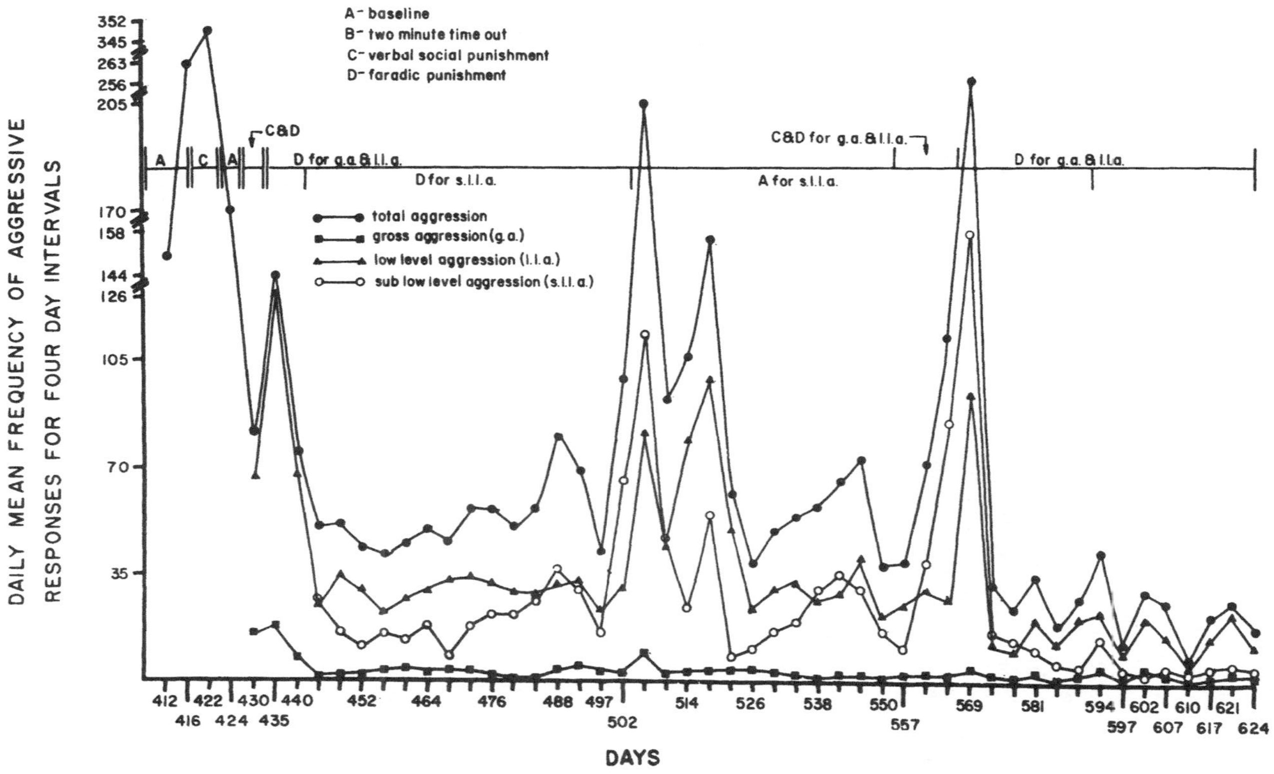

Figure 7.49. Effect of a Time-Out, Social Punishment, and Faradic Punishment on Aggressive Responses during the Second Year of Residence

ishment definitely increased the frequency of the aggressive responses, and that the response returned to a baseline level comparable to the first baseline. On the basis of these data, we decided to pair both gross and low-level aggressive responses with verbal social punishment statements and faradic punishment. This program was disbanded in one week, since the social punishment statements were simply not being counter-conditioned by the electric shock, as indicated by an acceleration of both low-level and gross aggressive responses. It was decided to pair only the shock with gross and low-level responses.

Sharon's behavioral reaction to shock was very strange. There were initially no tears, in fact, it was several months before she began to demonstrate crying and avoidance responses to the faradic stimulator. During the first weeks of the shock punishment program she would be punished with the instrument every time she struck out, which she did repeatedly. She would not respond to this repeated punishment in a fearful or emotional manner. It was as if she simply did not experience the shock at the pain-intensity level one would expect of a child. After thousands of trials, we saw gradual evidence of emotional reactivity to the shock in the form of tears. Slowly she demonstrated avoidance responses, such as jerking her hand away from the instrument, concurrently with deceleration of aggression.

While using shock for punishing aggressive behavior, we observed a slow but definite deceleration of both gross and low-level aggressive behaviors. However, we noticed a concurrent emergence of a response level of aggression which we defined as sub-low-level aggression. Sub-low-level aggression was defined as Sharon's flicking her wrist as a response approximation of the low-level aggressive response. These responses could be as minute as flexing her wrist and/or opening and closing her hands in a quick, almost indistinguishable motion. This response was a component of the aggressive response; it was our interpretation that if we left the response untreated it would reinstate the gross aggressive behavior. Thus, we began to punish the sub-low-level aggressive behaviors on a baseline, for which there would be no social punishment nor shock. The reason for this was that staff simply could not tolerate using the electro-shock instrument so frequently with Sharon. As Figure 7.49 shows, this decision to place sub-low-level aggression on a baseline did have an effect on the gross and low-level responses which were retained on a faradic punishment program. Disconcertingly, all aggressive responses increased, supporting the hypothesis that every response in the chain of related aggressive responses must be extinguished directly. However, gradually the faradic punishment brought the gross and low-level aggressive responses under control, and there was, surprisingly, a concurrent reduction of the sub-low-level aggressive responses. We were encouraged by the data, and on day 550 we decided to reinstate the program of pairing faradic punishment with verbal social punishment statements when punishing gross and low-level aggressive behaviors. However, again the social punishment statements only served to accelerate all of the aggressive behaviors, although gross aggression did not rise in such a spectacular manner as the low-level and sub-low-level aggressive responses. With this unfortunate effect, we decided to reinstate the program of faradic punishment for gross and low-level responses, and not to resort to verbal social punishment statements. During the remainder of the treatment program for aggression shown in Figure 7.49, the staff would occasionally scold Sharon for aggressive and other asocial behaviors.

The remainder of the data show that the gross aggressive responses did come under control, and that the low-level and sub-low-level aggressive responses were decreasing in variance and frequency. Simultaneous with this deceleration was the acquisition of language as a function of the speech program described later. Rather than Sharon's having to hit someone to make known her needs, she now had alternate responses such as simple verbal statements to make requests of staff. At the time of this writing, the treatment programs remain in effect for gross and low-level aggressive responses.

There are several features of the data that may be relevant to the treatment of aggressive behavior in other autistic children. We learned in Sharon's case, as we had found with several other children, that social punishment would invariably elicit the response which it was intended to decelerate. It was this punishment error which necessitated our attempting to counter-condition the social punishment stimuli by pairing them with shock while concurrently using the latter to decelerate aggressive responses. Unfortunately, this treatment paradigm was not effective with Sharon; shock alone had to be used to eliminate the aggressive behaviors. It was our impression that Sharon was simply not responding to the electric shock at the reactivity level necessary to counter-condition the verbal stimuli. Our hypothesis was that there was an organic deficit responsible for her lack of response to external stimuli, particularly to cutaneous faradic stimulation. It is interesting that the time and number of trials necessary for the extinction of Sharon's aggressive behaviors were much greater than early laboratory studies had hypothesized would be necessary for extinguishing aggressive habits in autistic children (Lovaas, 1967). In Sharon's case, we began using faradic stimulation on April 7, and the data contained in Figure 7.49 are inclusive up to October 26 of the same year. During the interim, the total aggression count, inclusive of gross, low-level, and sub-low-level aggressive responses, totaled 12,206, for which 5,985 pairings of faradic punishment were administered. The problems inherent in such a treatment program should be obvious to the reader. First, the program of using shock that extensively is devastating to the staff who have to administer the program. If the program is *not* emotionally difficult for a given staff member to administer, then that staff member should be removed from the job. And although the aggressive responses were extinguishing, we learned that the habit patterns could be reinstated very rapidly. Evidence for this is contained in Figures 7.48 and 7.49, when Sharon's aggressive responses were capable of returning to baseline so quickly. Such quick retrieval of a baseline suggests that the generalization of treatment effects was very delimited. Clinical evidence of the weak generalization of training for controlling aggressive behavior was obtained during Sharon's home visits. During her home visits, Sharon's control of aggression was variable, since her parents were unable to carry out management orders at the same level of vigilance than one is capable of doing with someone else's child in a residential setting.

SPEECH-TRAINING

When Sharon was admitted, there was neither evidence of a progressive speech development prior to her hospitalization nor evidence that her speech deficit was a regressive phenomenon. Her speech had simply never developed, the reasons for which we could only speculate upon throughout the course of the speech-training program. The only exception to this observation was that her parents reported that Sharon had had some words prior to her admittance to the research program, but that those few responses had dropped out. Apparently, she had acquired some speech responses that the parents had learned to discriminate and that Sharon could vocalize so that they sounded the same at successive times. However, there was no evidence that she would vocalize these responses in an imitative manner. Sharon made sounds at the beginning of the treatment program, but she articulated them so poorly that they were not comprehensible to other persons. These sounds were made repetitively, they had an explosive quality, and she would not repeat them in an imitative fashion when enjoined to do so. Sharon seemed to communicate more by body English than by speech responses. There was no historical evidence to support an interpretation that her failure to acquire language was of a psychogenic nature. Her two siblings had acquired speech, although one demonstrated mild articulation problems which were amenable to speech correction in the public school setting.

There were several problems which made it difficult to teach Sharon speech, whatever organic conditions may have compounded her failure to acquire language. It was as difficult to teach Sharon speech as it was to teach her any other response, since there were no obvious positive reinforcers for this child. In fact, the first two months of the program were devoted to teaching her to eat a variety of foods so that mealtimes could be used for conditioning speech while concurrently pairing it with positive social reinforcement statements in an attempt to increase simultaneously their valence. Also, there was the unfortunate reality that Sharon was not a reinforcing youngster for staff to work with because of her failure to respond to affection, her lethargy, and her unpredictable barrages of aggression. This reduced the chances of her receiving the staff's best speech-training skills. Sharon was not tractable to acquiring language under the rigorous kind of program which we have been using with autistic children because of her glaring noncompliance and her frantic attempts to remain isolative throuh the use of aggression, temper tantrums, and screaming.

Sharon could not make the muscle movements necessary for formation of the many phonemes composing the English language. She was capable of making some sounds, but these were simple exhaling responses requiring a minimum of oral muscle movements. Sharon's inability to manipulate her tongue interfered with her speech acquisition. Her tongue was short and thick, and she was incapable of protruding it past her lips in an imitation of staff during the speech program. Although Sharon learned to imitate staff's facial expressions as they overemphasized speech sounds for her, she persisted in having difficulty using her tongue fluently.

The speech sounds which Sharon emitted were barely audible to others, which did not assist her in speech acquisition. As mentioned elsewhere, Sharon was a "delicate responder," and this description was also applicable to her speech responses. We decided not to begin the speech program until Sharon was eating a greater variety of foods, had shown some diminution of aggression, was in better physical health, and was more compliant. After two months of her residential treatment, we decided to initiate the speech-training programs, which are described below.

Sharon's speech program was comparable to those employed in our other case studies of autistic children. The first step was to train and rehearse her in imitating an available response which she had had before beginning the speech program. After Sharon had demonstrated acquisition of an imitative response which would occur errorlessly, the program advanced to teaching her speech components or phonemes. After she had acquired a large number of phonemes which she could imitate in any order they were presented, these were combined to make simple and, later, more complex words. The phonemes, when combined into words, were used to train her to use them in frontal, terminal, and then medial positions. After this phase, we began teaching Sharon to imitate sequences of two-, three-, and up to five-word sentences. The next step was teaching her to make her own request statements. Then we trained her to imitate questions, progressing to requesting her to make a spontaneous question to which staff would answer. The progression of the speech program was designed to teach her spontaneous conversation eventually.

The mechanics of proceeding through such a speech program were arduous and exceptionally expensive. The program required that the food at all meals, so long as staff were available to conduct the program, be used as reinforcers for training speech. Thus, all meals were training sessions for speech. During the remainder of the day, whatever program which she may have been involved in, if speech were requested of her, she was required to rehearse the response until successful. This technique is identified as positive practice. Some persons expressed the fear that positive practice would engender stuttering. We have been using positive practice in training speech with autistic children for three years without any evidence of the children's acquiring stuttering responses. We suspect that the reason for this is that the error responses were not being paired with punishment or admonishment of any kind. Rather, the staff would benignly and calmly present the verbal stimulus over and over again and request the child to imitate it, with trials being rehearsed successively unil the child was successful, after which she would be rewarded in an appropriate manner. Punishment was not being paired with error responses; therefore, it was less likely that anxiety would be associated with speech production and thereby produce a circular interaction among speech errors, punishment, and anxiety.

Speech-Training Chronology. The speech-training began two months after Sharon's admission. The first month of training involved all meals, and intervals of time throughout the day when Sharon would be working on a 1:1 ratio with staff on imitating the response, "hi," which was available to her. The function of this phase of the program was to train Sharon to imitate staff when they presented a speech model. This imitative training persisted for three days, after which we began training the word, "me." Sharon's response to the model was to attempt to produce the word "me," but with error responses consisting of variations on the "eee" sound.

At the beginning of the second month of speech-training, we became impatient and attempted to teach speech responses by presenting stimulus cards with pictures, to which we would point and say the name of the object for her to imitate. This was a positive practice paradigm, and the stimulus cards were of a set number which were used repeatedly but not in an ordered manner. Words such as "apple," "sheet," "boy," "pail," etc., are examples of those presented. The emphasis of the words was not localized on any particular vowel sounds. Five futile weeks were spent on this program before we abandoned it to return to the more sequential program which we had begun earlier. Lists were compiled containing examples of words which included the phoneme currently under training in the initial, terminal, and medial positions. Staff would communicate with each other throughout the program and at the weekly rounds to ascertain what level of success they were having in training the different sounds. "P" and "b" sounds were begun first, followed by "e" and "a" responses. The progression then moved to the sounds, "h." "m," "b," "s," after which these were combined for forming different words such as "me," "see," "top," "pop," etc. The program was not rigidly formalized; rather, staff had lists of words available to provide examples of the sounds and words Sharon was currently learning. While teaching Sharon these responses, the staff would use a clipboard attached to which were mechanical counters to record trials and number of reinforcers received for training particular responses. On the data sheet staff would enter the words or sounds they had trained and the numbers of trials necessary and reinforcers received, and comments to indicate the relative success they judged the training to be for that particular response. Thus, the next staff member to work with Sharon in the speech program had the benefit of previous staff comments on the latest sounds or words currently rehearsed in her training.

Four and one-half months of intensive training were required to cover the phonemes we considered necessary for the acquisition of words. A speech program then consisted of Sharon's imitating single whole words, which were varied constantly. At this point we began to use picture cards and books, and identified objects around the room whose names Sharon was to imitate after hearing them from staff. The previously trained phonemes were never acquired to perfect articulation, and certainly not at age-expectancy of volume. Therefore, staff continued to enter on the data sheet the kinds of words with which Sharon was having difficulty during the speech-training sessions so that other staff would be alerted to these difficulties and continue training on those responses. Nine months of training on single words was necessary before we could progress to Sharon's imitating simple sentences up to five words long. After two months of training, she progressed to the point where she could use simple but lamentably stereotyped sentences to identify objects in her environment. She also began to demonstrate acquisition of spontaneous speech and used it in the cottage setting and during home visits. She would with much pride identify objects about the room and ask for certain kinds of foods and activities, demonstrating that she had begun to use speech spontaneously. At the time of this writing, Sharon was on the level of the speech program in which she was being reinforced for using sentences both in imitation and spontaneously during mealtimes.

The training interval described above was conducted in a sixteen-month period. During that time, Sharon received a total of 58,837 speech-training trials during mealtimes and other training sessions throughout the day. During the course of the program, she received 11,994 reinforcers in the form of bites of food at mealtime and social reinforcement at training sessions occurring at other times. The mean ratio of trials to reinforcers was 4.91, indicating that, at almost every fifth training trial, Sharon was being reinforced. This, of course, does not reflect the variance, which would be greater at the beginning of training a new response and at the end when she would be reinforced on the first trial.

Three different samples were made during the course of the speech program. The samples consisted of staff's counting the total number of comprehensible words spoken by Sharon, exclusive of those occuring during speech-training sessions. A 13-day sample was taken after admission; the daily mean number of words spoken was 102, and the range varied from 41 to 222. These words were repetitions of "potty", and "go side." Five months after her admission, a 15-day sample of total words emitted per day was taken, which yielded a mean of 170 words, and the daily counts ranged from 114 to 267. These counts were composed of more single words used repetitively. One year and nine months after her admission, a count was made of the words spontaneously spoken for two days; the daily mean count was 1,580 words. These words were contained in many three- to five-word sentences, such as "I want to eat potatoes," "That is a book," etc. On the basis of these data, the speech program was maintained in effect.

Sharon's language acquisition had generalized to her home and the parents had been trained to reinforce her verbally and also to conduct speech-training trials at mealtimes both at the Treatment Center and at home. Sharon's volume of speech remained very poor and still required improvement. She had acquired a much more varied use of her tongue, these responses having been emphasized and trained by staff during the speech trials. Sharon was acquiring speech and using it, although it was certainly not a quick rehabilitation. The success of the program, even if the gains thus far are minimal and do not approximate the language expected of a normal five-year-old, seems to be a function of several major components of the training program. First, rewards, both social and primary, were used constantly throughout the program. The reliance upon reinforcement seemed primary to the success of the program, in conjunction with using these reinforcers judiciously in a program of successively approximating speech. That is, staff monitored Sharon's speech closely and administered the rewards only when she was demonstrating some improvement in her speech. Also, the success obtained may be attributed in part to the massive number of trials, and to the duration of the program, for there was no respite from training for months and months. Furthermore, one cannot rule out the possibility that Sharon may have acquired the current level of speech simply through developmental changes, whatever the training programs.

Sharon's acquisition of speech was related to the reduction of her aggressive behavior and the deceleration of her screaming and self-destructive responses. In order for Sharon to be available for speech acquisition, there had to be a deceleration of these incompatible responses. However, considering that these responses were forms of communication for Sharon, e.g., aggressing to remain in isolation, acquisition of speech gave her alternate responses to make known her needs. This was particularly apparent when she was acquiring the ability to use verbal statements and would tell the staff with which food she wished to be reinforced, rather than slapping the food away from the staff or spitting it out to indicate a food preference.

Case Study 4: Will

INTRODUCTION

It was the absence of behavior that prompted Will's referral to the Treatment Center. Will had been enrolled in a Head Start program but had been quickly rejected because he did not demonstrate the prerequisite skills, e.g., he did not speak, he had to be carried to the school, he played neither cooperatively nor in parallel, and he was devoid of those self-help skills expected of a four-year-old. Will would entertain himself by playing with a few toys, and he preferred spinning pots and pans. If his parents demanded Will comply with a verbal request, this would invariably provoke a temper tantrum characterized by dry wailing, his alternately becoming rigid and flaccid when picked up, throwing his arms about, facial grimacing, and wriggling out of one's hands only to run a short distance and to fall phlegmatically to the ground. Will would not predictably obey even so simple a request as "Come with me." One had physically to take his hand to make him comply. When staff would release his hand, Will would wander away from the other persons present and amuse himself in some unstructured manner. Will would not look at one in the eye; his fine and gross motor coordinations varied with tasks but were estimated to be less than what would be expected of a two-year-old. He walked on his toes so consistently that there was a question of muscular atrophy in his arches. Will was unable to run at an age-expectancy rate; actually, it was impossible to make him run, since he simply would not comply with such a request. Will was physically weak and lethargic for his age—not surprising, considering that he was of frail stature and under-exercised. He would eat a variety of foods, but not in great quantities.

Will was socially mute. He made some sounds which his parents presumably could interpret. Tape recordings made in his room during nap times recorded what sounded like animal noises with intermittent rough approximations of verses from "Old MacDonald." His behavior when alone in his room was most unusual. He would wander about, aimlessly climb upon the chairs, door, and windows, repeatedly slam the cabinet doors, throw objects, and emit his strange gutteral sounds.

Will seemed oblivious both to verbal requests and to physical directions; he was totally noncompliant. He did not possess the prerequisite responses necessary for us to be able to administer a test for intelligence evaluation. Although the referring agencies alternately assigned the diagnoses of childhood autism and schizophrenia before Will's admission, he was being considered for referral to an institution for retarded children because of his behavioral deficits. The accepted referral diagnosis was childhood autism.

Reasons for this diagnosis included the developmental discrepancies between motor coordination and language acquisition, aloofness from others, and unusual body movements. Historically, we suspected that there was some deficit affecting language skills that interacted with his parents' difficulty in training Will in expected social behaviors.

In summary, Will was a mute four-year-old with an exceptionally delimited response repertoire. He had not learned how to play with other children, and he was ostensibly oblivious to the presence of other persons until they infringed upon his characteristic stereotyped play. He neither smiled nor cried with tears. Will never cuddled, hugged, approached, or even looked at, other persons. Will would not imitate even the simplest responses. Like that of many autistic children, his behavior was most aptly described as the absence of behavior.

Some of the following series of treatment procedures were performed concurrently, some successively. Initially, the total series of programs were designed to decelerate those behaviors which interfered with teaching the social and academic behaviors which dominate the latter half of Will's treatment program.

TEMPER TANTRUMS

Will's temper tantrums were incompatible with our being able to teach him compliant and imitative responses. If one interfered with an ongoing activity—typically a stereotyped activity or, later, some self-involved play—one would invariably provoke a temper tantrum. These responses could be evoked by making a strong verbal request of Will or by physically moving him to a new activity. While he was at home, and also when he was observed during the baseline, the temper tantrum would terminate as soon as the staff member or parent left Will and did not insist upon his compliance with their request. Will apparently had other persons on a negative reinforcement paradigm, i.e., he would terminate the noxious temper tantrum if they left him alone. Parents' and staff's leaving Will alone allowed him to return to the preferred activity, which was presumed to be reinforcing and thereby maintaining temper tantrums. The termination of request behavior by parents or staff was presumed to be negatively reinforcing to Will. These requests served as discriminative stimuli for their eventually leaving Will alone, so that the more requests were made of him the louder and more persistent his temper tantrums would become as he operated for other people's retreat. Commencing on day three, we recorded a one-week baseline of Will's temper tantrums, after which a one-minute time-out was contingent upon each temper tantrum. As Figure 7.50 shows, the time-out was decelerating the response, but not so completely as would be desired. On day 29, we revised the management order to a two-minute

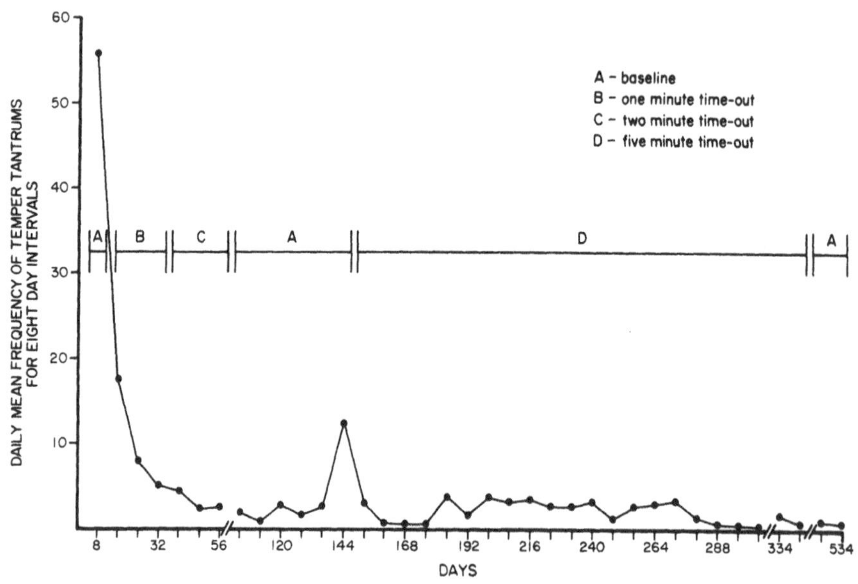

Figure 7.50. Effects of Three Time-Out Procedures on Daily Mean Frequency of Temper Tantrums

time-out, and on day 51, staff discontinued counting the response but continued the two-minute time-out as necessary. On day 101, a baseline was reinstated, and on day 146, a five-minute time-out was begun that was comparable to the time-out currently used for aggressive responses. On day 304, counting was discontinued but treatment maintained. Frequency of temper tantrums was resampled on days 331–346 and again on days 523–537. The series of time-outs, in conjunction with all the unknown interactive effects of other concurrent treatment programs, succeeded in reasonably extinguishing the behavior, although an occasional temper tantrum still occurred even after 500 days.

Temper tantrums, aggressive testing, and noncompliant responses, were all hypothesized as operating for some common reinforcers, e.g., to be left alone. We assume that the treatment programs for these behaviors were interactively facilitating, since non allowed Will to operate for the suspected preferred reinforcer of isolation. This hypothesis raises an additional point regarding behaviors supposedly operating for common reinforcers which one wishes to decelerate. If the investigator puts several such responses on extinction or punishment programs, and returns one of the responses to baseline and produces an acceleration of that response, a generalization effect may occur that will have a deleterious effect on other behaviors under simultaneous treatment that operate for common reinforcers. We have an analogous situation almost every weekend at the Center, when there is not so high a staff ratio, so that some of the programs are not conducted so stringently as prefered. The result of this is that staff observe an acceleration of related deviant responses on weekends.

It is also interesting to note that Will's temper tantrums did not decelerate spectacularly. It took a long time to control this behavior. It is important to stress that Will was not spending extended periods of time in a quiet room, but was in and out quickly so that he was available for learning appropriate behaviors.

TESTING

Will demonstrated a number of kinds of responses that we could not precisely include under aggression or noncompliance. Yet these responses apparently operated for available social punishment cues that we suspected were reinforcing since historically they had signaled that he would be left alone, which would be reinforcing for Will. This was our hypothesis and it was not tested directly. When Will would intentionally spill milk while looking at the staff, or dart away from staff, or threaten to strike, or perform a requested response very slowly when he typically could do it much more rapidly, these diversified responses were collectively recorded as "testing." That is, he was "testing" for the availability of a preferred reinforcement. These responses are all related to the avoidance responses typified by his aggression and noncompliance.

A baseline was not accumulated on these testing behaviors. At day 18, these responses were placed on a one-minute time-out in the quiet room; 10 days later the management order was revised to a two-minute time-out contingent upon each testing response. On day 101, the management order was altered to a five-minute time-out. These successive treatment procedures are identified respectively as *B, C,* and *D* in Figure 7.51. The program was continued beyond day 304, but the behavior had by that time been effectively replaced with more appropriate responses. Hundreds of trials were required to decelerate the behavior. We contend that these testing responses were replaced by other more socially appropriate responses which staff were also training with positive reinforcement.

APPROACH RESPONSES TO STAFF

As we have described, Will would not approach other persons for affection. He demonstrated many deviant behaviors to avoid other persons' directing his behavior as well as showing affection toward him. Will terminated these abnormal behaviors when social intrusion ceased, which

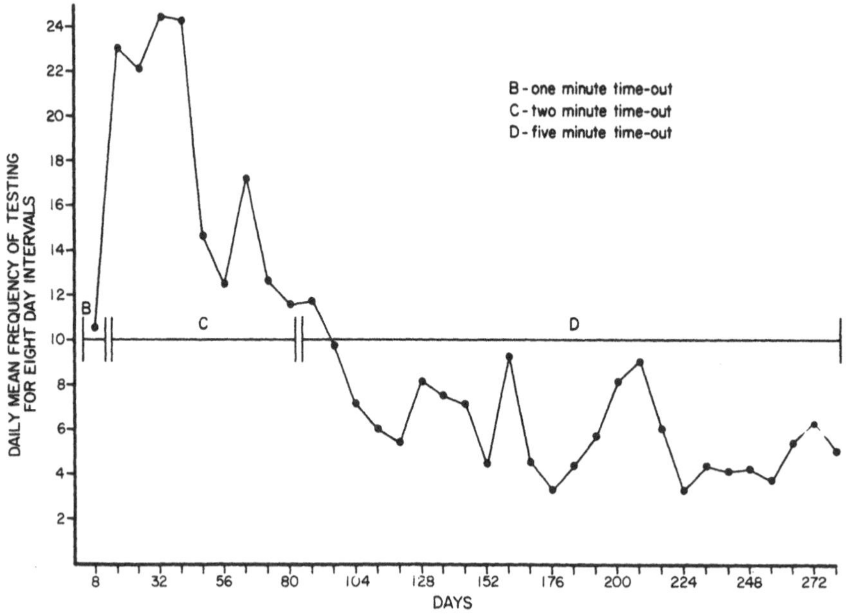

Figure 7.51. Effects of Three Time-Out Procedures on Daily Mean Frequency of Testing

was negatively reinforcing for the "intruder." Will did not cuddle; he could be held on one's lap for only a brief moment, after which he would wiggle out of one's hands and wander off.

We wanted to determine whether one could accelerate Will's approaching staff for even minimal physical contact or affection. Twenty-three days after his admission, staff began a 35-day program of demonstrating profuse social reinforcement for every approach response by Will and intermittently providing candy in conjunction with the social reinforcement. On day 58 of Will's residency, the management order was altered so that following the social reinforcement Will would always be given a small chocolate candy. This program, labelled *C* in Figure 7.52, continued until day 188 of Will's residency. Figure 7.52 contains the data for the study, which show that there was a slight acceleration of the approach behavior. At the termination of the study, Will would not have been considered an affectionate child. The data did reveal that the behavior was gradually accelerating, which suggested that he was beginning to operate for positive social reinforcement or, more likely, the candy. The management order of being affectively demonstrable to Will whenever he approached staff was maintained. The candy reinforcement was deleted from the program, since our continuation of that reinforcement would risk his operating excessively for candy, thereby ruining his appetite and impairing his speech-training program during mealtimes.

At the time of his discharge, Will still could not be described as an affectionate child. In fact, it seemed to us that we would have had a more effective program if we had used food first to condition positive social rein-

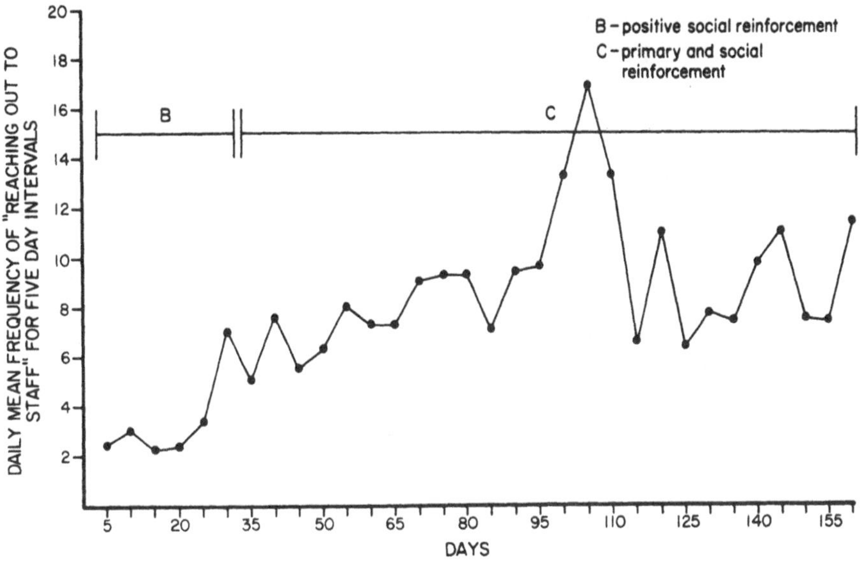

Figure 7.52. Effects of Two Treatment Procedures on Daily Mean Frequency of "Reaching Out to Staff" Response

forcers prior to conditioning attention, as we did in Heidi's case. Perhaps Will's total program would have progressed more rapidly if the prerequisite social reinforcers had been strengthened and been of a known polarity.

SPEECH-TRAINING

Will's speech program began with the accumulation of a baseline on the second day after his admission. A variety of treatment programs were used for the duration of his residency to train speech. Will's speech was dominated by deep, guttural sounds which had little variety, i.e., they were primarily explosive, grunting responses. A one-week baseline was recorded of those sounds. The staff's definition of the response was that the sound could not be misconstrued as a word, the approximations of which were being counted separately. Figure 7.53 shows that the frequency of these vocal responses was high and accelerating. Only a one-week baseline was recorded because the counting required a full-time staff member to monitor the frequency of Will's vocal sounds. The baseline was obtained in an uncontrolled manner. One may speculate that the click of the hand tally counter was inadvertently reinforcing the responses, or that the constant barrage of speech in the cottage setting was evoking first approximations to speech imitation. Whatever hypothesis be chosen to account for the response acceleration, Will's vocal sounds were increasing rapidly, which made for a most promising prognosis for his speech acquisition. These gutteral sounds would be the trial-and-error responses from which speech would be shaped.

On the second day of his residency, staff began to count every discernible word Will spoke during the entire day. A ten-day baseline was accumulated, after which a series of treatment programs began. After this interval, speech was not monitored again until day 52 of his residency. The daily frequency of words was then monitored until day 186 of residency. Figure 7.53 contains the data for the baseline of words as well as for some of the treatment programs which will be described below. In references to Figure 7.53, the left-hand axis refers to the frequency of vocal sounds, and the right-hand axis is the reference for frequency of words.

When staff were counting spontaneous words, these responses did not include any words which staff were directly trying to stimulate Will to imitate. The words logged in Figure 7.53 were confined to a few very poorly enunciated responses, such as guttural approximations of "Mama," "Daddy," and "Old MacDonald." These same few responses were being repeated many, many times during the day.

Encouraged by the increase of speech sounds and the evidence of an acceleration of spontaneous words, we began a speech program in which social and primary reinforcements (food) were contingent upon imitative responses. During all meals, and at 20-minute intervals during 20-minute training sessions on fine and gross motor coordination skills and compliance training, staff would present speech models for Will to imitate. Initially, Will would not imitate staff's speech models, although he would imitate a talking toy which would pronounce the recorded name of an object after one pulled a string on the toy. This toy was used and then faded from practice, and staff introduced pictures whose names staff would pronounce for Will to imitate.

During this four-month treatment interval, Will's parents were coming to the Center twice a week for didactic training sessions. In these visits

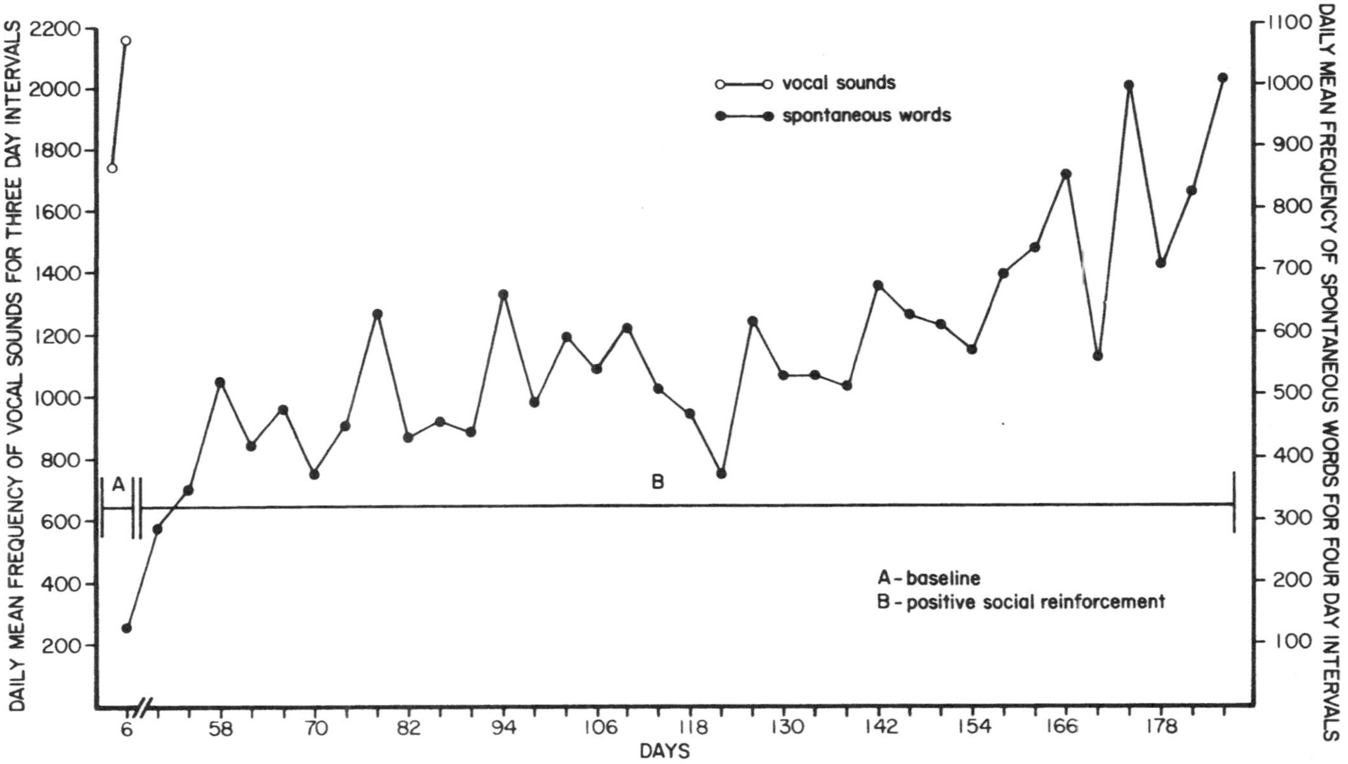

Figure 7.53. Initial Baseline of Vocal Sounds and Effect of Positive Social Reinforcement on Daily Mean Frequency of Spontaneous Words

they were instructed in how to teach Will to comply with verbal requests and also the current speech programs. They would be seated at a table with Will between them. One parent would present the verbal model, first with the toy and later with pictures. If Will imitated acceptably, one parent would operate a marble-dispensing apparatus, the marble from which Will would then give to the other parent in exchange for one potato chip or one quarter-ounce soda (these food reinforcers were given on alternate trials, the potato chip's sustaining thirst and the soda's partially relieving that thirst). The order of reinforcement for each acceptable imitative response was: (1) social reinforcement from parents and staff present (pandemonium ensued, since at least five persons would be praising him simultaneously); (2) marble dispensed; and (3) food administered.

These speech-training sessions were incorporated under treatment *B* shown in Figure 7.53. The program was a failure. Will's spontaneous speech accelerated and reached a plateau at roughly 800 words per day. Eight hundred words is not far from mutism for a four-year-old, and the responses persisted in being composed of the same words, which were poorly enunciated. Staff had spent 11,807 trials over 210 training sessions on this program. The speech program was stopped. It took us one month to reformulate Will's speech program.

In reviewing the data and video tapes of the speech-training with Will, several procedural errors became evident. First, Will would not look at the staff presenting the imitative models. Secondly, we were constantly rehearsing the same verbal responses over and over simply because we were reluctant to have Will become hungry in order to increase drive. We were afraid of what deleterious side effects would occur if we demanded too much of his speech. A third error was that Will was not required to speak except during the speech-training sessions, in which only minimal response criteria were being maintained. Fourth, Will's spontaneous sounds revealed that he did not possess the various phonemes prerequisite for complex speech acquisition.

We decided to devise a new speech program in which we would teach the prerequisite response of attention, then condition the speech components, progressing through chronological age-expectancies to his current age, then reinforce imitative speech, then reinforce responses to simple questions, after which we would progressively shape conversant speech.

It was of procedural interest to us to learn whether food had to be contingent during mealtime while we were shaping attention. A contingent-and-noncontingent attention shaping program was coducted as follows.[6]

6. The authors wish to acknowledge Richard Hanish, Research Analyst, who designed and directed the attention-training in the speech program for Will.

During the noncontingent reinforcement period at each meal, staff would be seated facing Will. When Will turned toward staff and/or opened his mouth, which he would do to signify that he wished a bite of food, it would be fed to him by the staff. Every 30 seconds after Will had swallowed his previous bite of food, the staff would say, "Will" to elicit an attentive response, and if one occurred, he would be socially rewarded and then immediately reinforced with food. Thus, food could be contingent either upon his attending to his name (this was a new response) or on his simply turning toward the staff with no eye contact required whenever he preferred another bite of food (this was an old response). In other words, the operant response of eating did not have to depend upon the discriminative stimulus of his name. This program was conducted for 18 meals, with results which are shown in treatment interval 1 of Figure 7.54. This procedure failed to effect an acceleration of attentive responses during the course of treatment; in fact, it appears that the dominant habit of inattention was increasing in strength. This evidence supported our contention that food would indeed have to be used contingently in order to train Will to attend optimally to a speech model. The contingent reinforcement procedure would be used during the speech program.

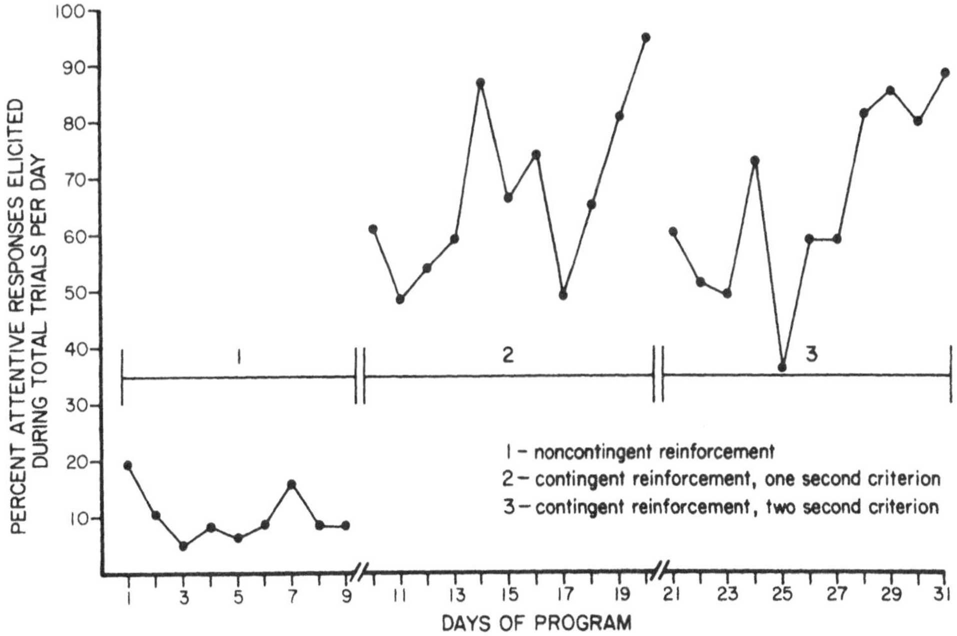

Figure 7.54. Attention-Training. Comparison of Effects of Noncontingent Reinforcement Programs

It may seem obvious that, of course, the food (reward) must be contingent if one is going to train a response. But it is not so apparent that, when conducting a shaping program during which a child is deprived of food, the clinician's guilt could be relieved occasionally by his giving the child the food noncontingently but that such a procedure would impair the child's progress. In Will's case, such a procedure, although it would have made the staff member momentarily feel less of an ogre, in the long run would have been deleterious to Will's total treatment program.

Sufficient experience had been accumulated at this time for us to know that an optimal shaping program should progress at small enough increments to guarantee success, which would assure that the child would eat well. Figures 7.55 and 7.56 show Will's weight and height, respectively, for successive months during the course of the treatment program. The data show that Will thrived. On weekends, when there would be fewer staff, Will would eat unassisted at the table. Let us digress—one hypothesis which shall be investigated in the future is that one detrimental effect of food contingent programs will be overeating problems in the youngsters when they are older.

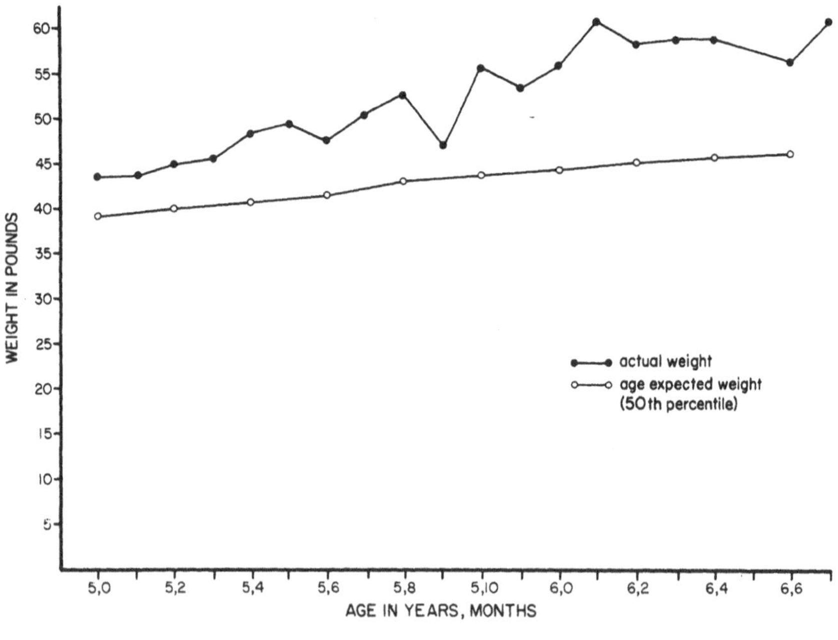

Figure 7.55. Comparison of Actual and Expected Weights during Food Contingent Conditioning Programs

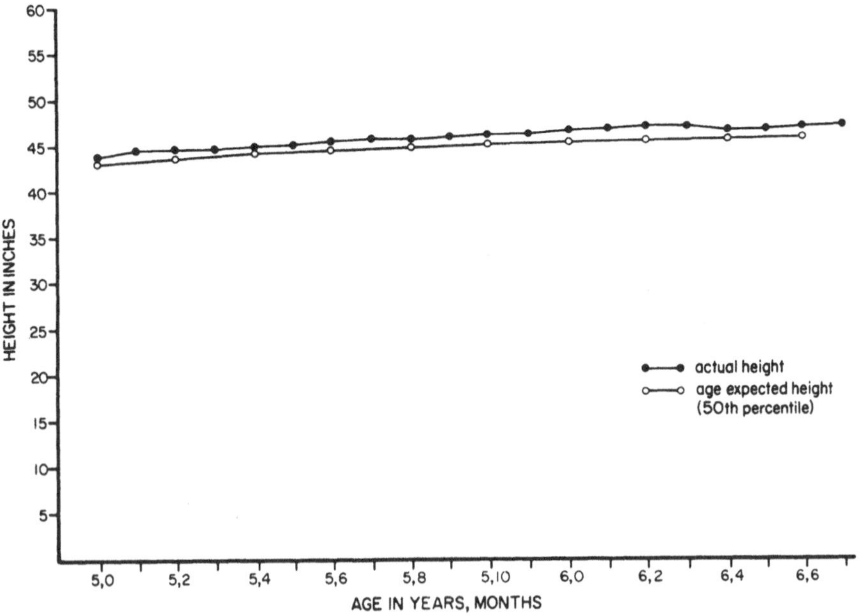

Figure 7.56. Comparison of Actual and Expected Heights during Food Contingent Conditioning Programs

The next phase of Will's program was to train him to pay attention when the cue of his name, or some other socially expected attention-evoking cue such as "hey" or "look at me," was presented. The first step was to condition one-second eye contact attentive responses, after which a two-second criterion response would be necessary for presentation of social reinforcement and a bite of food, in that order, during mealtimes. Figure 7.54 contains the percent attentive response to the attention-demanding cues for successive days for shaping one-second and then two-second eye contact attentive responses. The criteria for beginning training on two-second attentive responses was greater than 85% success for three consecutive days, and the same criterion was roughly maintained for termination of the two-second attentive response training. A total of 2,241 trials, for which Will received 1,222 reinforcements over a course of 69 meals, were required to train his attention. Will was now prepared to begin a speech-shaping program.

An informal speech test was administered to determine the available and absent phonemes and the ones which required improvement. The first sounds trained and improved upon were those available in the initial position of a word, but substituted or absent in the terminal and medial positions of the word.

Will's speech program had actually been "backed-up." The error incurred in the initial speech program was that of not shaping speech, but of attempting to reinforce the unavailable response of spontaneous imitation. The speech program was redesigned so that Will would learn to attend sufficiently, a prerequisite response to his acquiring any degree of imitative speech. After his attention had been trained, the next step was to assure that the components of speech were at age-level and readily available so that Will could use them in imitating staff's speech models. The imitative models progressed from naming objects to repeating series of questions and answers, from which staff gradually shaped spontaneous speech as the required response for obtaining food.

Will's new speech program commenced on day 218 of his residence. The first sounds reinforced in the program were the available but distorted responses in the initial position of words. Will would often substitute these available sounds in the terminal and medial positions of words. The training program progressed from easy to hard sounds, and from frontal, to terminal, to medial positions of words. Table 7.3 contains the sounds which were specifically and separately trained in this manner. Other sounds, such as "r" and "l," were incorporated in the latter part of the speech program concurrently with imitation of sentences. The sounds shown in Table 7.3 rendered Will capable of progressing to the next step of imitating a variety of words.

Table 7.3. Trials, Reinforcers, and Meals Required to Train Specific Vocal Responses

Sound	*Trials*	*Reinforcements*	*Meals*
"b"	2,129	532	25
"p"	2,284	543	24
"d"	984	266	12
"k"	3,746	919	41
"g"	2,029	433	18
"j"	4,051	1182	60

Thus, in training the few specific sounds contained in Table 7.3, we accrued, 15,223 trials and 3,755 reinforcers (i.e., bites of food) over 180 meals. These now available sounds were then employed in a program of positive practice of imitating increasingly complex sentences that eventually progressed to training Will in spontaneous speech. 9,614 trials and 3,095 reinforcers over 176 meals were utilized for this purpose. During this latter stage of shaping speech, staff were requested to stimulate speech constantly, and to demand that Will rehearse all error responses until he was successful. All successful positively rehearsed responses were profusely socially reinforced. Staff were alerted to praise correct spontaneous speech as often as possible.

The final stage of shaping speech was to maintain a conversation with Will during mealtimes; at this stage Will was permitted to eat unassisted. This was the last approximation to normal speech.

COMPLIANCE/NONCOMPLIANCE RATIO

It took us almost one year to realize that we had failed to monitor the compliant and noncompliant behaviors which are so crucial to every treatment program. Noncompliance is a response common to all the psychotic children admitted to the research group. We have had difficulty measuring change in compliant behavior for the same reasons that it is difficult to monitor any shaping program. If the training of the compliant behaviors is a successful program, then the responses should be constantly qualitatively changing, i.e., the compliant behavior should become increasingly complex. We made the mistake of counting all compliant and noncompliant responses to verbal requests made by staff. The result was a ratio, i.e., to what percent of all staff requests did Will respond either compliantly or noncompliantly? Figure 7.57 could lead one to conclude that Will was, first of all, a very compliant child, because his noncompliance ratio was always low. However, the data are very misleading. The shaping program for compliant behavior commenced on day 304, when all compliant responses were rewarded socially. All noncompliant responses to a verbal request were allotted a five-minute time-out in the quiet room. The response ratio remained constant during this interval.

On day 468 of Will's residency, a standardized set of requests was devised that progressed from easy to difficult. We wished to ascertain if we could show the treatment effect on each request item, and the five-minute time-out was maintained during this interval. On day 492, tokens were given for each successful compliant response. During this treatment period, Will would lose a token for each noncompliant response, with the same punishment contingency being used for all aggressive responses. This treatment period is *C* in Figure 7.57. Our practice of using a standardized set of instructions so as to monitor more precisely the acquisition of increasingly complex compliant responses was cancelled on day 507, and the earlier *B* program was reinstated. We decided to reinstate the first program because the data were too expensive to collect, i.e., one had constantly to alter the list of verbal requests. Also, one had to carry a cumbersome clipboard around throughout the day. The program had not

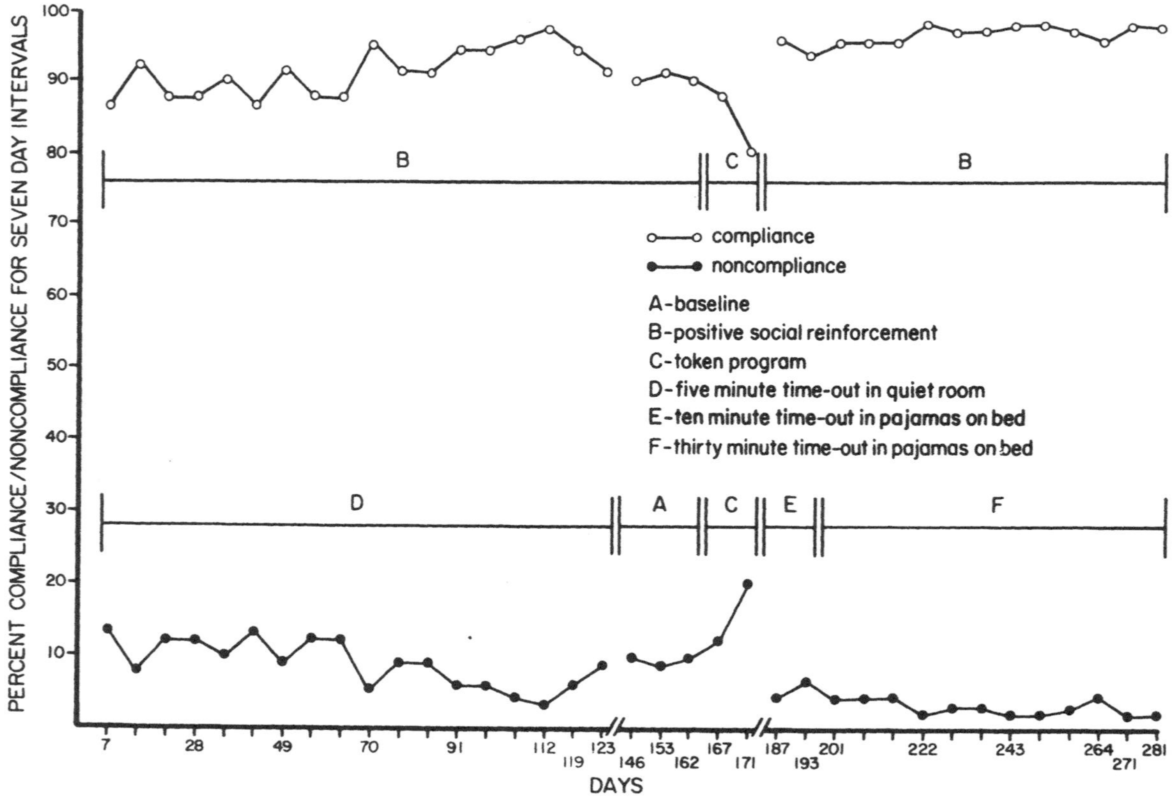

Figure 7.57. Effects of Concurrent Treatment Procedures on Per Cent Compliance/Noncompliance

been performed long enough to assess its effectiveness. Perhaps these problems could have been alleviated by a sampling procedure, which we would recommend instead of the procedures we used.

So there were no precise data on the compliance training of Will. However, there were clear examples of the qualitative change in his compliant behavior. When admitted, Will had to be carried to a Head Start classroom where he would remain almost immobile and mute throughout the day. In his 12th month of residency, he successfully attended a two-week day camp for normal children. In his 4th month of residency, he was attending a regular kindergarten class.

AGGRESSION

Will often hit other children and staff when a verbal request was made of him. When his mother arrived for a visit, he would walk up, strike her, and run away. He would smack and scratch other children, often looking at staff with a strange grin as if to discern their impending response. These aggressive responses had to be decelerated; they were an annoyance to everyone and would certainly guarantee his dismissal from any public school program when that time arrived for Will. The treatment program varied for Will's aggressive behavior. The data are shown in Figure 7.58. The behavior was initially placed on a five-minute time-out, i.e., every time he struck another child or staff, he would be verbally admonished and taken to the quiet room for a five-minute time-out. This program was in effect constantly from day 21 to day 492. At the latter time, he was attending the special Children's Treatment Center school in the morning and public school kindergarten in the afternoon. There was a sudden acceleration of the aggressive behavior that we attributed to his imitating behavior of the older boys, with whom he was now playing after school. To digress briefly: Will had learned to imitate but he was not optimally discriminative of the behaviors he modeled. At this time, we established a program from days 493 to 500 in which tokens were earned for compliant behavior and a time-out and a token were removed for every aggressive response. This program was dropped after one week because we were trying to move Will back to a normal environment, and to expect the continuation of behaviors sustained on tokens would not be realistic in terms of the reinforcement contingencies actually available in the public school. On days 501 to 507, the program was altered to staff's ignoring Will and his aggressive behavior but manifesting overt attention and support for the child whom he had struck. This program might eventually have been successful, since it was conducted concurrently with a stepped-up program of compliance training so that Will had considerable positive reinforcement available during the day. However, its initial effect was that Will began hitting other children harder and more frequently. We were afraid that his aggression would generalize to the public school where the teacher would not have time to perform the treatment program, so that eventually Will would have to be expelled from school.

On day 507, the program was altered to a complete "back-up" whenever Will aggressed. We knew he enjoyed school, but we had to teach him to be a more sociable child. When Will aggressed, staff would take him to his

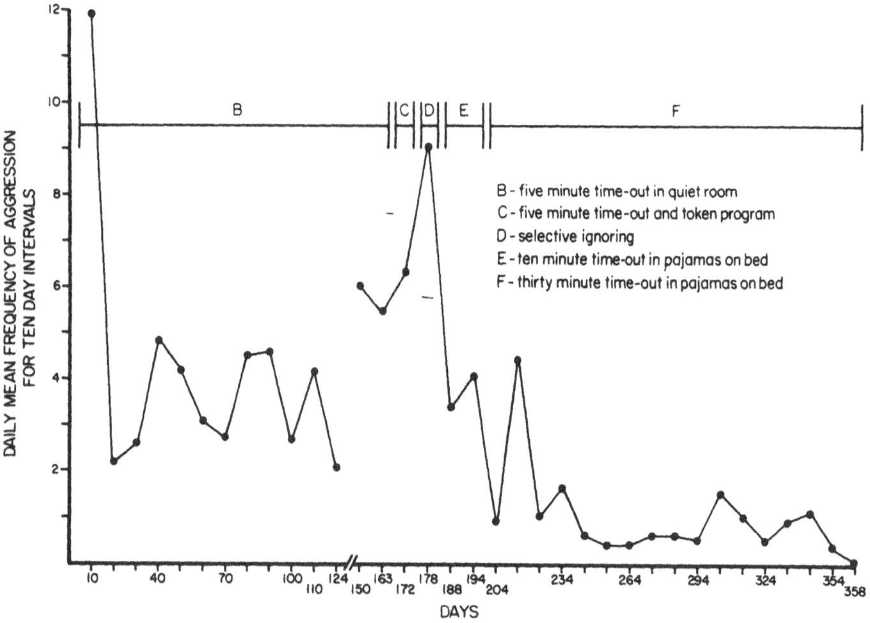

Figure 7.58. Effects of Five Treatment Procedures on Daily Mean Frequency of Aggression

room, put him in pajamas, and leave him in bed, wailing, for ten minutes. Then he would start the day all over again, from practicing dressing, making the bed, etc. During these activities of starting the day anew, he was being socially reinforced for compliance to verbal requests. If Will aggressed in school, he would be sent to the principal's office. The principal then called us and Will would be returned to the Treatment Center for this positive practice program, treatment *E* in Figure 7.58. This program was changed to 30 minutes in pajamas and bed on day 523, and the effects of the program are shown in treatment interval *F*. The program effectively extinguished the aggressive responses, but again, it required over 500 days to train Will not to hit. It is likely that shock, such as used with Heidi, might have controlled this behavior in fewer days. We did not use electroshock with Will because we felt reasonably sure that we could control the behavior with the time-out condition. Furthermore, our policy is to use electric shock only if it is the only way to prevent the child's doing irreversible physical damage to himself by his self-destructive and/or aggressive behaviors. Furthermore, as our programs are designed so that child-care and nursing staff perform the treatments, we do not wish to promote a procedure which could easily be misconstrued by many state hospital personnel. We have already observed instances in other facilities of child patients' being placed in seclusion for hours and days under the misconception that the program was designed to "control" the behavior. Such punishment techniques are outrageous, vindictive, and clearly indicate that such programs are not designed to train and positively reinforce appropriate behavior.

CORRECT GAIT

Will walked and ran on his tiptoes. His gait was also characterized by his holding his upper arms to his sides, forearms extended and wrist relaxed so that his hands flexed down. His back was swayed considerably so that his stomach protruded. When excited, he would throw his head back, emit a monosyllabic howl, jump up and down on his toes, and flap his hands rapidly up and down. If Will wore shoes with non-flexing soles, he roughly approximated a normal heel-to-toe gait. As soon as such shoes were removed, he would retrieve the tiptoe gait, which was also present when he wore tennis shoes.

On day 44 of Will's residency, we began a program in conjunction with fine and gross motor training sessions in which Will was taught to walk from heel to toe. Will would wear soft shoes and a shaping program was conducted as follows. During the initial trials, staff would kneel on the ground, hold Will's leg, request he make one step, and guide his foot in making the appropriate heel-to-toe step. Social reinforcement and decreasing amounts of raisins (Will was always constipated at the beginning of his treatment and dried fruits were used extensively as reinforcers, but this problem had declined by the end of the sixth month) were contingent upon these assisted, but correct, responses. For successive trials, conducted optimally twice a day for 20 minutes, the amount of assistance provided by staff was faded. This procedure of physically assisting a response on a decreasing schedule has been described as "priming" in the literature (Buell *et al.,* 1968). This technique probably dates historically to occupational and physical therapists and, although they may not have been so systematic in their application of reinforcement, they certainly are skilled in establishing a response hierarchy for successively approximating goal responses.

Will's program of twice-daily sessions of training, walking, and then running gait was formally in effect until day 197 of his residency. Throughout the training program, staff would correct Will whenever he walked on his toes, and then reinforce profusely when he corrected his gait in a positive practice paradigm.

Staff were always requested to praise Will whenever they observed him walking correctly. This was difficult for staff to remember; the abnormal gait itself would cue staff to correct it, but they often failed to reinforce the correct gait because it was not sufficiently deviant to elicit their attention. This kind of problem occurs in many treatment programs designed to help the patient's normal behavior acquisition, i.e., the staff become hypersensitive to abnormal responses and fail to reinforce the newly acquired desired behaviors. We know of no simple technique to compensate for this problem other than to reinforce the staff constantly to reinforce the positive behavior, for that is their goal, i.e., to promote the child's growth.

It took one year before Will walked with a normal gait. However, when his parents visited, we could still predict that he would immediately rise to his toes. Also, when he returned to the Treatment Center from his public school attendance at the conclusion of each day we often noticed that he would be walking on his toes again.

FAMILY-TRAINING

Family-training was perhaps the most crucial and least known aspect of the total treatment programs for all the children. We aimed to train the parents to be able to conduct all treatment programs and to be as skillful as the staff in shaping appropriate responses and decelerating abnormal behaviors in the child. We conducted the didactic program by having his parents work independently with Will in making requests for compliant behaviors. Initially, this simply required Will to hand blocks to either parent. His parents had been instructed on the use of social reinforcers and time-outs with Will, and were always acquainted with the accumulated data. A video tape was made of their performance several times during the course of the parent-training program, and we reviewed it with them to provide feedback of how accurately they had adopted our programs. They were also given copies of Patterson's parent-training manual (Patterson & Gullion, 1968).

While his parents were reviewing the video tapes of Will's various responses that they had been trained to reinforce differentially, staff informed them on correct and incorrect responses. Cumulative recordings were obtained by remote control by staff while his parents were working with Will. Immediately after each session, the parents told the percent compliant responses they had reinforced, and how successfully they had punished the deviant responses which occurred. Figures 7.59 and 7.60 show that the

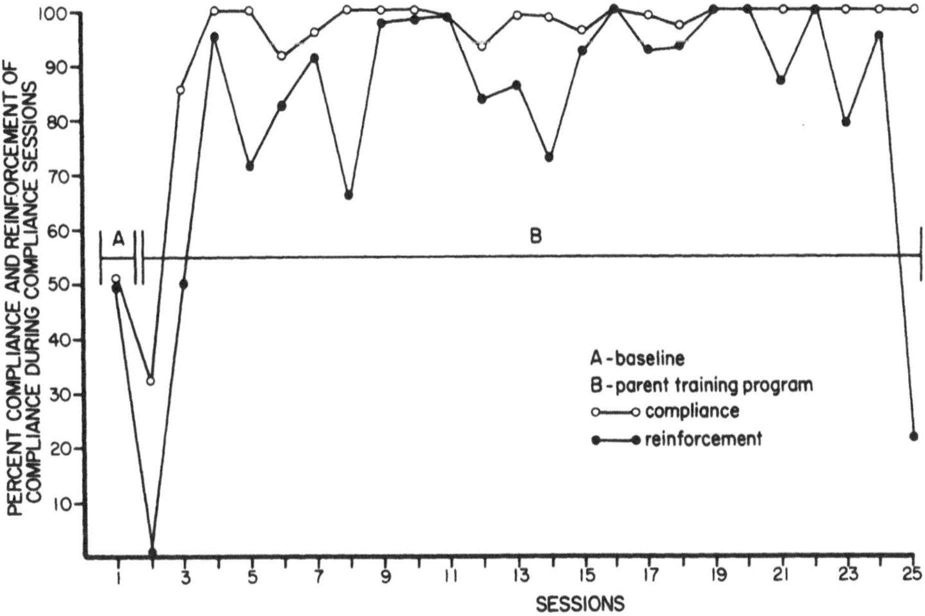

Figure 7.59. Effect of Parent-Training Program on Relationship between Mother's Per Cent Reinforcement and Child's Per Cent Compliance during Compliance Sessions

parents were effectively reinforcing a high rate of compliant behaviors. Again, however, the data do not show the qualitative change in Will's compliant responses to his parents' requests. Their initial requests were confined to asking Will to hand them blocks; at the termination of the recorded data, the parents were playing table games (e.g., checkers) and basketball with Will.

We repeatedly observed that the parents reinforced optimally when staff were present and while they were in the cottage. However, with decreasing staff supervision, there was a corresponding decline in their requests, the complexity of their requests, and the ratio of their reinforcement. Since the parents would have to assume primary responsibility for transfer of training effects, this didactic program still needs much research. This problem was common to all families.

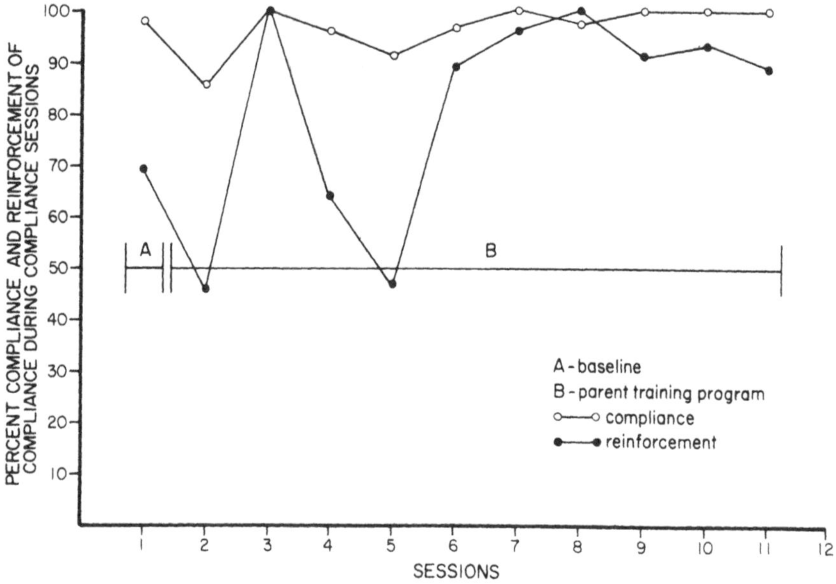

Figure 7.60. Effect of Parent-Training Program on Relationship between Father's Per Cent Reinforcement and Child's Per Cent Compliance during Compliance Sessions

CONCLUSION

The above programs comprise those treatment techniques which were measured specifically. Will's treatment program had numerous other components which were crucial to his social growth. During the first six months of his program, throughout the day he received successive 20-minute training programs in fine and gross motor coordination and speech.[7] He was trained for increasingly complex motor responses, and his success responses were reinforced socially at a ratio of approximately 1:4 with poker chips which were redeemable for five minutes of play with toys of his choice from a toy cafeteria (cf. Staatz & Staatz, 1963). It is doubtful that he comprehended the meaning of the poker chips during that program, but the social reinforcement was increasingly effective in training these responses.

To illustrate these training programs: when Will attended kindergarten he was deficient in the fine motor skills required for using a pencil. The

7. The authors wish to acknowledge Mrs. Naomi Nelson, Occupational Therapist, for her assistance in the design of the fine and gross motor training programs.

occupational therapy staff used food during mealtimes to shape his correct grasping of the pencil. He learned to use the pencil by copying, with tracing paper, figures and letters which were faded in their intensity. He was trained in fine motor skills during some mealtimes by learning to grasp the pencil correctly, by working with snaps, zippers, and buttons, and by tying shoelaces. In fact, Will received 1,011 trials, and 653 reinforcements, over approximately 60 meals to train him in these fine motor skills.

Will had to learn to throw and catch a ball, to walk up and down the stairs appropriately, to hold a utensil, to sit and stand straight, to ride a tricycle and a bicycle, to pour milk, to use buttons and zippers, to butter his bread, to balance-walk a beam, to use slides and swings, etc. As he was learning these skills he was also acquiring speech, so that at the time of this writing, Will speaks in full, spontaneous sentences but still in his barely audible voice. As he was acquiring speech, he was taken on an increasing schedule of home visits. As he began to demonstrate increasingly compliant and socially appropriate behaviors, there was a planned decrease in staff supervision during these visits. This presented a problem, as indicated by the data on aggressive behaviors, in that Will began to imitate a multitude of peer models, so that our control over his acquisition of new social behaviors was decreasing. This operated in our favor when Will was at public school, but during the rest of the day, in a cottage setting, he began to imitate some of the behaviors of the older neurotic youngsters.

When Will was admitted he was untestable; at his discharge he had attained an I.Q. of 78 on the Stanford-Binet, Form L-M. He was returned home and admitted to a language disabilities classroom. A year after his discharge he was still in that classroom, and aspects of his old autistic behaviors remain. Occasional aggressive responses still occurred, and academic progress was slow. Will was functioning as a mildly retarded child at the conclusion of the program. Agency assistance will probably always have to be available to Will.

Case Study 5: Dan

He made the noise about every ten seconds, a loud shrill sound not unlike the yipping bark of a small dog. To anyone near by, the piercing noise was startling, almost painful. It was typically accompanied by various facial tics and sometimes by the flexion of his entire body. This tic-like noise was so prominent that his other behavioral problems and the issues of conflict in the family seemed insignificant. In fact, Dan had been referred to us because the noise-making behavior had thwarted a variety of other facilities in their attempts to help him and his family.

Dan was congenitally deaf, as his parents first noted when he was about a year and one-half old. His father and a younger sibling were also born deaf, although an elder sib demonstrated no auditory deficits. Auditory examinations of Dan often varied in their findings, but most examiners concluded that he had a severe hearing loss. He was assisted with hearing aids and special amplifiers available in his special classes. Now eleven years old, he had been attending special classes for the deaf since nursery-school age. His lip-reading skills were developing but the speech he had acquired was difficult for persons unfamiliar with the deaf to understand. Not only was there a deficit in his communication skills, but he was also academically retarded, functioning on a first- to second-grade level in arithmetic and reading.

Dan's parents recalled numerous travels from one doctor to another, from one school to another, in what now appeared to them to have been a vain search for help. Dan had always been difficult to manage, being hyperactive and generally undisciplined. In the past year, the noises and other tics had become prominent and were a source of constant distress to his parents. Several years earlier Dan's primary problem had been diagnosed as aphasia, and he had been referred and admitted to a special program for brain-damaged children. Although he had performed relatively well in that program, the professionals there felt that, because of his deafness, they were unable to provide an optimal program. Consequently, he was shuffled from that residential program to a boarding school for the deaf that was a considerable distance from his home. When Dan was told that he was moving to another school, his vocal tics increased to intolerable levels. That summer he lived at home and attended a special class in his community. The noise behavior became extremely disruptive in the special class. When he returned to school in the fall, the noises continued and became unbearably disruptive to the boarding school program because Dan's vocal tics echoed through the hearing aids of the other children. In many other respects his behavior was unmanageable and the professionals there had reluctantly to recommend his discharge. His parents brought him back home and once again enrolled him in a public school program. His teacher in the special class worked hard and conscientiously before she too concluded that Dan could not be maintained in the school and must be referred to another program.

Dan had been evaluated by no less than a dozen different professionals during the previous years. The early evaluations were inconclusive concerning his hearing problems. When he was three and one-half, it was suspected that he might have normal hearing even though no speech had developed. At that time, his only vocalization was crying, which occurred relatively persistently in the examining room. Parental conflict and inconsistency concerning Dan were noted, and both audiologists and psychiatrists wondered if absence of speech did not serve as a protective mechanism for Dan in the presence of parental disagreements about his management. Two years later, specialists concluded that aphasia was his most prominent problem and consequently he was enrolled in a school for the brain-damaged. When Dan was six the psychiatrist who had seen him periodically over the past several years noted considerable personality improvement. Autistic-like features which had previously concerned the psychiatrist seemed no longer to be present. His most outstanding personality traits, however, were negativism and defiance. These traits remained prominent up until his referral to the Children's Treatment Center. The noise-making behavior was noted by various teachers as early as nursery school, but did not become alarming until Dan was enrolled in his most recent boarding school for the deaf. The noises then occasioned his referral to a psychiatrist who felt that both the noises and his hyperactivity were indeed indications of a cerebral dysfunction. Dan was administered a neuropsychological examination which failed to support the diagnosis of brain dysfunction, but it was concluded he demonstrated behavioral features characteristic of Gilles de La Tourette's disease.

Over the years, psychotherapeutic approaches had been attempted with Dan and his parents. Dan responded minimally to individual relationship experiences. The parents made every attempt to utilize child-management recommendations and improved considerably in the consistency with which they managed Dan. However, problems of parental conflict did not seem to be significantly ameliorated.

The vocal tic had begun to receive special attention during the year prior to Dan's admission to our program. Various behavioral and medical approaches had been attempted. Teachers had at various times attempted reasoning with Dan about the noise, excluding him from the classroom when the noise became unbearable, providing added structure and other anxiety-reducing measures, and using direct punishment. The direct punishment had been to squirt Dan with a water-gun whenever he made the noise. Our assessment was that these techniques had not been performed with sufficient consistency and duration, and there was no measurement indicating whether they were effective. One physician had systematically performed a series of drug treatments designed to control the noise. Unfortunately, accurate behavioral data were not available to him because Dan was living some distance from the doctor. Consequently, the subjective reports of the mother were the only data the physician had on whether the noises were increasing or decreasing with the various medications. We suspect that some of the drugs may have had a significant effect upon the noise behavior but, unfortunately, we could not corroborate this because of the lack of data. Further, as our studies subsequently demonstrated, the noise-making behavior could be, to a large extent, controlled by environmental circumstances—which would have produced considerable variability in the amount of noise independent of the drug effects. Throughout the various professional opinions concerning this noise behavior ran the recommendation that a behaviorally oriented psychologist be consulted to design a treatment program.

Our evaluation of Dan and his family was that we confronted a multiple-problem situation and that treatment directed at any one of the problems would be insufficient.

Dan's major problems were: the vocal tic, head tics, noncompliance, defiance, impulsive behaviors, academic retardation, limited language development, emotional constriction, and extreme concerns about his status in the family.

In some respects the family presented problems typical of the sort encountered at the Treatment Center. Certainly Dan's impulsive and defiant behavior and the issues of family conflict were familiar problems. The staff, however, recognized that they were not equipped to deal with the problems of a hearing- and speech-handicapped youngster. We were not confident that we could provide any solutions for the most prominent referral problem—Dan's noises. We felt, however, that despite the many kinds of expertise that had previously been brought to bear on Dan's problems, approaches had been tried in a piecemeal manner. Some professionals had focussed on problems of family dynamics, others on educational problems, others on Dan's behavioral problems, others strictly on the tics and noises. We felt that with proper coordination the Center might be able to provide a total program that would attack all of these problems 24 hours a day. We recruited a special education teacher who had had extensive experience with both deaf and severely emotionally disturbed children and, most important for our purposes, prior experience in working in a total treatment program. This teacher's skills gave us the opportunity to deal with Dan's communication problems and to train our staff in many of the specialized techniques that have been developed for use with the deaf. The other major area where we felt limited was, of course, the noise-making behavior. We concluded that an experimental-clinical approach would allow us to develop a solution.

We were fortunate in that Dan's parents were willing to make any sacrifice necessary to help their son, and throughout our work with Dan, his mother, father, and siblings made every effort to work through the larger problems of family conflict. Further, they offered themselves extensively to learn the management procedures that were developed for Dan and participated in the design and data collection of those studies. Frequently, their ideas proved to be major contributions to the treatment program.

During the admission interviews, we found Dan responsive and capable of considerable warmth and relationship. He was very cooperative so long as the examiner engaged in relatively superficial activities, such as playing games. He seemed to enjoy himself and provided entertainment for the examiner. However, as soon as the examiner attempted to question Dan about the problems that brought him to the Center, about his family, about difficulties in school, he became aloof, cold, and evasive. Most prominently, he turned his eyes away from the examiner and thus effectively silenced him, since Dan had to read lips. His speech was poor and the examiner could understand only a few simple words that were spoken. Dan could, however, communicate by drawing, writing, and reading. He did this willingly as long as central problems were not discussed. Dan gave the impression of a very primitively organized personality structure. He was a youngster who relied on basic adjustment mechanisms such as avoidance and denial. We noted, for example, that he could not seem to understand our explanation of why he would reside at the Treatment Center, yet he readily comprehended some complicated rules in a new game that we taught him.

INITIAL TREATMENT PROGRAM

Studying the noises. Certainly the most prominent and discrete referral problem was Dan's tic-like noises. We began observing these during our initial diagnostic evaluations. Throughout our outpatient evaluation, a tape recorder was operating and the noises recorded were later transformed to the cumulative recordings which are presented in Figure 7.61. The overall rate of noises was approximately 6 responses per minute. The rate of the noises seems to vary considerably, sometimes rising as high as 20 responses per minute, while at other times no noises occur for as long as 3 minutes. Virtually all of the noises we observed were inspiratory high-pitched barks

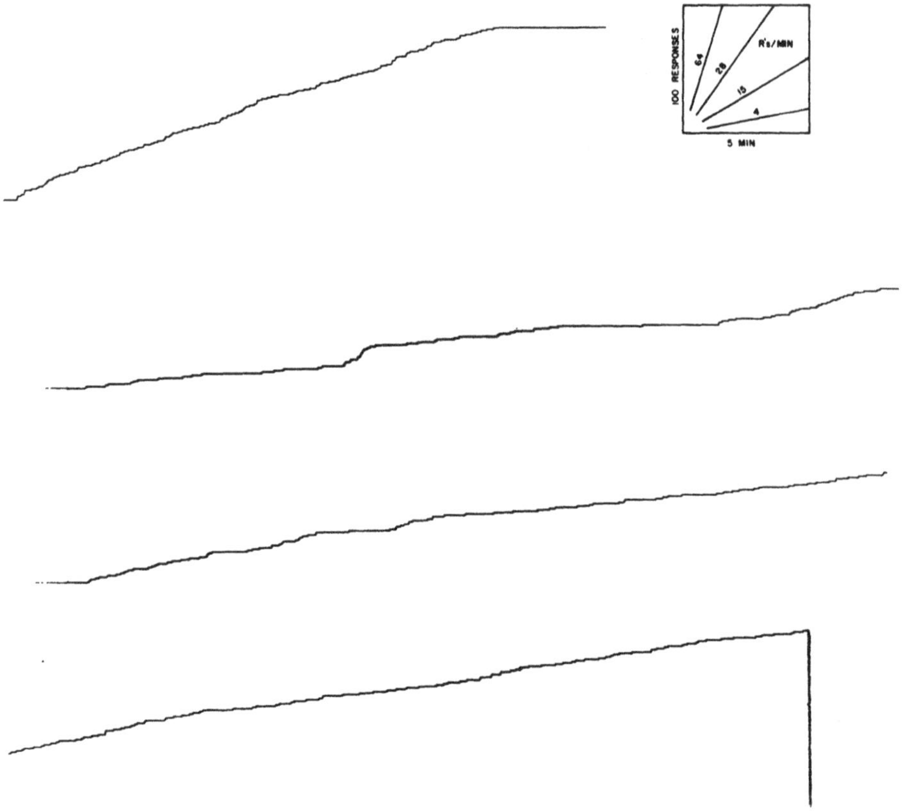

Figure 7.61. Samples of Continuous Cumulative Recordings of the Noise Behavior Obtained during Preadmission Visits to the Center

accompanied by neck and facial tics. It was difficult for us to form any hypothesis about the gross situational variables that might be effecting the response. We could readily observe, however, that all kinds of nonspecific attention were contingent upon the response on a variable schedule. It seemed to be a common response for almost everyone to stare momentarily at Dan when he made the noise.

We were interested in discovering whether environmental circumstances influenced the rate of the noise, and specifically we hoped to determine whether there were any particular reinforcement contingencies that maintained this response. Consequently, an initial miniature experiment was conducted during our outpatient evaluation to test the effect of several kinds of social reinforcers upon the noise behavior. During the study Dan and the experimenter sat in an office playing a simple card game. The experimental design may be described as *ABACDA*. The baseline condition, *A*, consisted of the experimenter's simply relating to Dan in an essentially normal manner over the card game. During the *B* condition, the experimenter used social punishment following each of the barking responses. Thus, when Dan made a noise, *E* would say "No, I don't like that," "Stop that noise," or some equivalent negative statement. In the *C* condition, the experimenter attempted to praise Dan for making the noise. When the noise occurred, *E* would say, "Good, fine, boy that's a loud one," etc. While doing this, *E* would lean close to Dan or sometimes pat him on the arm or shoulder. During the final phase of the study, D, *E* gave Dan a brief time-out for each noise. The time-out consisted of *E*'s becoming silent and staring into his lap until five seconds of noise had elapsed. During the experiment the noises were recorded on a tape recorder which was left running. Subsequently, the response rate was transformed to a cumulative recording. Figure 7.62 contains the cumulative recordings of the noises during each phase of the experiment. The social punishment condition appeared to have produced a marked increase in the rate of the noise, and the praise condition produced a slight increase. We were uncertain about the effects of the praise condition, since after making the experiment we learned from Dan's mother that he finds any body contact from an adult aversive. Consequently, the fact that the examiner was both praising him and occasionally patting him on the arm may have confounded these results. The first portion of the time-out procedure appeared to have a marked effect in decelerating the noise. The last several minutes of this condition, however, again showed an increase in the rate of noises. Consequently, we were unable to conclude that the time-out suppressed the noises. The experiment suggested the hypothesis that any attention made contingent upon the noises will increase the rate. Withdrawal of attention was suspected to have a decelerating effect. This initial experiment, coupled

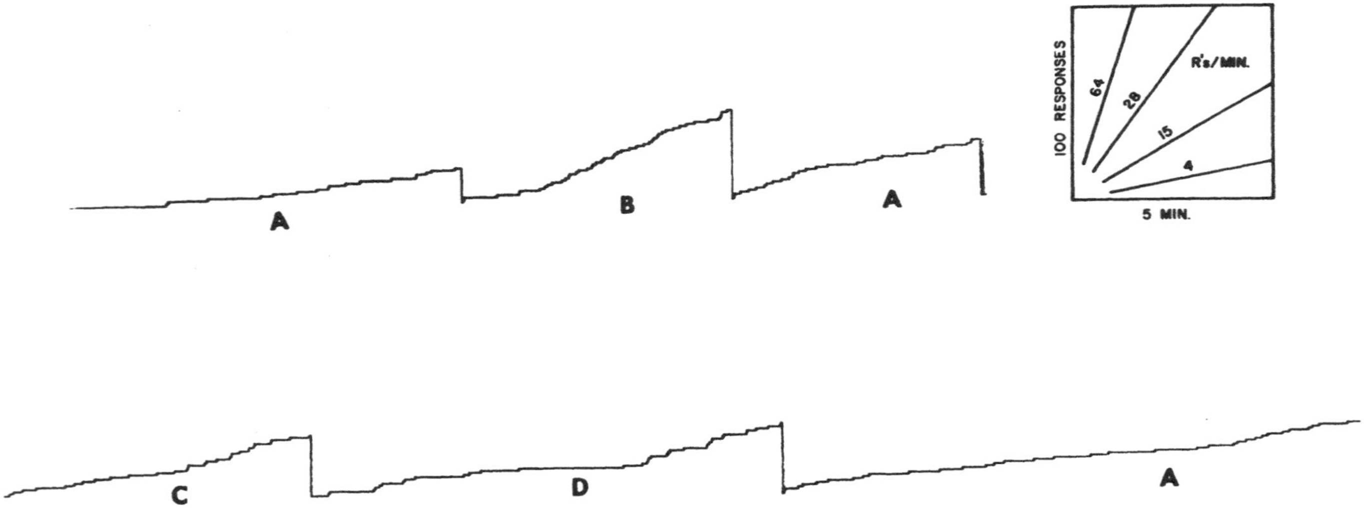

Figure 7.62. *Cumulative recordings of noise behavior during experiment testing effects of social reinforcement condition. The experimental conditions were:* (A) *baseline,* (B) *disapproval,* (C) *approval,* (D) *time-outs (see text for full explanation).*

with a review of Dan's case history, strongly indicated that the noises were being specifically reinforced by a variety of social responses in the child's normal environment. Anyone who had heard this child at the time of admission would know that most people could not avoid attending to the noises in some manner. His history indicated that many adults had attempted to ignore Dan's noises. Unfortunately, every report further indicated that the adult had been able to ignore the noises only temporarily and had finally responded with anger and desperation. The most likely alternative at that time was to reason with him or in desperation shout at him to be quiet. Most persons seemed to have been confused about whether the noises were made deliberately or unconsciously. We felt this distinction was probably theoretically irrelevant and that it would be more important to concentrate on obtaining empirical evidence about whether social responses to the noise produced an acceleration or deceleration of the behavior.

The initial data suggested that gross attention could indeed be a significant reinforcement for the noise, and Dan's case history indicated that a consistent extinction program had never been conducted. The treatment plan for the noises was to structure Dan's environment so that social attention would never be made contingent upon the noise. A total extinction condition was begun from the moment he entered residence at the Center. We knew that complete ignoring of the noise would be difficult to obtain. For the first few days that Dan was at the Center, the noise was painful but not impossible for the adults to ignore. In no other case has the Center's entire staff so proven their ability to provide a totally consistent treatment environment. Absolutely everyone at the Center, including clerical staff, housekeeping personnel, child-care workers, and therapists, learned within a few days time to act as if the noise had never occurred. We still had the problem of visitors to the Center and thus we had to be sure to inform them of the management procedures on Dan. We had anticipated that our worst difficulty would come with the other children, and wondered how we could guarantee that they would not respond to the noise. With their first complaints, we explained to them that this was one of Dan's problems, and that he was going to be doing it for some time, and displeasing as it was, we were all going to have to get used to it and live with it. Within a few days they, too, had modeled after the staff and only rarely did they imitate or attend to the noise.

Subjective observations of the first few days of the extinction procedure were interesting and encouraging. The rate of the response seemed to increase over what we had observed during Dan's outpatient visits and, more interestingly, the quality of the response began to change. No longer did we hear a simple inspiratory shriek. Now, instead, this was mixed with an explosive sound and the tone of the response varied considerably. Sometimes the noises came in rapid-fire bursts, sometimes paced regularly and slowly, sometimes at an irregular rate. Sometimes the sounds were very loud, sometimes very soft. The rate, amplitude, tone, and timbre of the response were all becoming extremely varied. At times Dan ran through all these variations within a five-minute period. This, of course, is precisely what one would expect to happen when a specific well-learned response begins to undergo extinction. That is, other related responses in the same response hierarchy were beginning to occur with greater strength as the child operated for the preferred reinforcers. The next three months contained many versions of the response. Some of these we immediately recognized as related responses on the same hierarchy. On two occasions, however, staff mistakenly identified a variation as a totally new response and failed to follow the usual management procedure of ignoring the noise. For example, at one point he started to say quite clearly, "Fuck, fuck." The staff member who was with him when this first occurred classed the response as a swearing response and did not immediately relate it to his noise behavior, even though it was but a small modification of the way the noise often sounded. Consequently, he was promptly given two or three time-outs for this response. The staff promptly realized, however, that it would probably be more efficient to class this response along with the noises rather than with four-letter words Dan might be learning from other children at the Center. Consequently, we ignored it. However, the few time-outs he had received for the response were sufficient to improve the clarity with which he said the word and to increase the frequency of its occurrence. Three weeks transpired before the four-letter word dropped from his repertoire. On another occasion, he began making a clicking sound at the back of his throat. Again, one of us inadvertently attended to the sound before we all were able to communicate with each other and decide upon ignoring it. This response continued to occur for several days before it, too, dropped out.

Two subsequent studies were conducted that relate to the hypothesis that attention reinforced the noise behavior. We referred to the first of these in the chapter on measurement. Our major observations of Dan's noise behavior when he first came to the Center were made by using the remote counter to obtain cumulative recordings. Both the observer and other staff members noted that the rate of noises seemed to increase while observations were being taken. The observer further noted that sometimes Dan seemed to attend especially closely to her finger on the button of the remote counter and that sometimes he seemed to watch her while making the noise. Thus, it seemed that the process of taking the observations itself had a reinforcing effect upon the behavior. Consequently, we set up this study.

The three experimental conditions of the study were as follows: Condition 1 consisted of observing the noise behavior and recording it on the remote counter in Dan's presence. Under condition 2, the observer was again present but, instead of the remote counter, she carried a small portable tape recorder which was running with its microphone in full view. In condition 3, the observer was present as a participant in the milieu, but carried no counter, tape recorder, clipboard, or other data-collection equipment. In this condition, the observer maintained a frequency count mentally and used a concealed stopwatch to time the length of her observations. Over a four-day period, 30 samples of ten minutes' observation each were collected. The observations were made at randomly determined times and the condition of observation was systematically altered. The experiment thus resulted in ten ten-minute observations under each of the conditions of observation. The mean number of noises per ten-minute sample was then computed for each condition of observation. Chapter 3, Figure 3.1 page 64, illustrates the observations taken with the remote counter and the lowest rate when observations were taken secretly. The mean number of noises per ten-minute interval was 18.2 for the remote counter, 6.9 for the tape recording, and 4.1 for secret observation. Since a randomized method of sampling this behavior had been used, a statistical test of the differences under the three conditions could be made. A simple analysis of variance of the data resulted in an F equal to 7.62, significant at the .01 level. Tests of the individual differences between means revealed that condition 1 resulted in a significantly greater number of noises than conditions 2 or 3. However, the difference between conditions 2 and 3 was not significant ($P > .05$). We concluded that the observer's action of pressing the button on the remote counter each time a noise was made did indeed have a reinforcing effect upon the noise-making behavior.

We were pleased to have this corroborating evidence that an attentive response made contingent upon the noise would accelerate the behavior. However, it was disconcerting to see that the effect of relatively unobtrusive observation (at least unobtrusive for our setting, where children are observed 24 hours a day) was so great. The periods of observation had been quite short in this study and we consequently wondered whether this effect would diminish during longer observations. Some of the cumulative records obtained on Dan over day-long periods had indicated that high rates of noise-making seemed to occur when the observer began making observations or when Dan became particularly attentive to the observer because other persons had temporarily left the scene. Consequently we conducted a series of short observations with the remote counter and cumulative recorder. In these sessions, we hoped to see if the effect of observation might adapt out after the initial minutes of observation. Figure 7.63 contains representative samples of the curves thus obtained. These data and the fact that ultimately we wanted Dan to be making very few noises regardless of who was observing him or what other persons in the environment were doing contingent upon the noises led us to decide that we would continue to obtain data by means of the remote counter and cumulative recordings.

We decided not to have cottage staff maintain behavioral charts on the noises, since the noises were difficult enough to ignore and asking staff to count them would only increase the likelihood of their reinforcing the

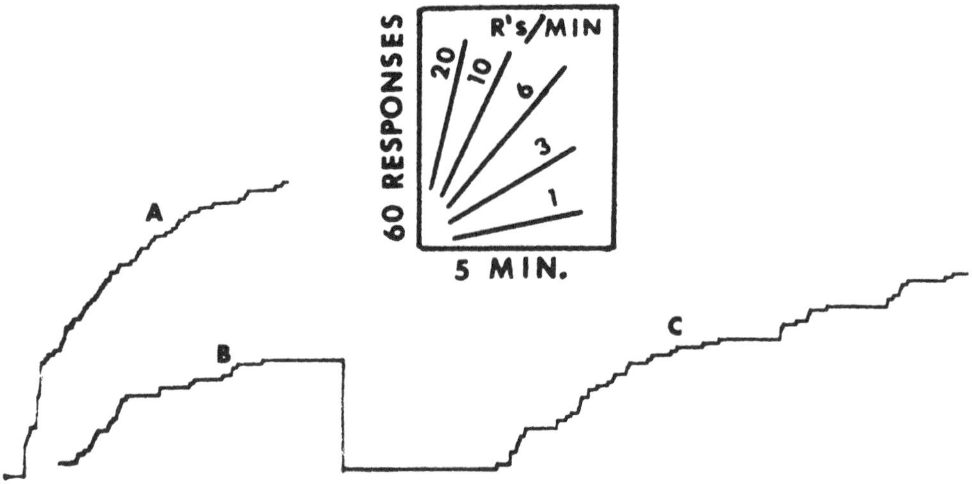

Figure 7.63. Adaptation to observation with the remote counter. The three curves show the first five to ten minutes of three different observation periods. Recordings A *and* B *show a marked adaptation effect after the first three to four minutes of observing. Recording* C *shows somewhat less adaptation.*

noise-making. We felt that a better extinction would be maintained if the staff were excused from responsibilities of observing the noises. This speculation was apparently correct, because on numerous occasions the staff were observed to be totally unaware of the noises. So successfully did they learn to ignore the response selectively that repeatedly the authors had the experience of hearing staff say that Dan had almost completely stopped making noises while at the very same moment he could be heard at the other end of the hall "barking up a storm." The decision to observe him with the remote counter required that the research assistant assigned to the group periodically collect day-long samples of his noise-making behavior. This measurement was used throughout the studies of this behavior.

Another study of the effective reinforcers for the noise-making behavior was similar to the outpatient study in which various forms of praise and disapproval were systematically tested. This study was conducted approximately one month after Dan's admission to the Center and consequently after extinction of his vocal tic had been in effect. In the study two staff members who worked in other groups were used as experimenters.[8] Our own staff were not used because we did not wish to contaminate the current extinction effects. This study was performed in two sessions; the design was *ABA* during the first session and *ACA* during the second. In the first session, a psychology trainee who had no real acquaintance with Dan joined him in a game in the family room in the cottage. An observer was present with the remote counter, an apparatus to which Dan had adapted by this time. The experimenter played with Dan while ignoring his noises for approximately 15 minutes, as represented by the baseline interval in Figure 7.64. Next, the experimenter responded to each noise Dan made in a negative manner. When Dan would make a noise, she would say, "No, I don't like that," or "Cut it out" in a very convincing manner. As may be seen in the next interval of Figure 7.64, the rate of noise-making increased dramatically. The baseline had been approximately one response per minute, but during the *B* condition of verbal social punishment, the rate increased to 20 responses per minute. The *B* condition was discontinued after only a minute and one-half because the effect was so dramatic, and we did not wish to risk reinstating the noise at the pre-treatment level. Subsequently, the experimenter returned to ignoring the noise and, as may be seen in the last interval of Figure 7.64, the rate of noise-making gradually returned to baseline level. The second experimental session was conducted in a similar manner. During the baseline section, only the observer was present with Dan. At the beginning of the "B" condition, a staff member who had had no prior relationship with Dan entered the room. The experimenter told Dan, "I hear you make this really neat noise. Would you do it for me so I can see what it is like?" He then proceeded to prod Dan saying, "Come on, make the noise." When the noise occurred, he said, "Hey, that's great, good, that's really neat, I like that." As can be seen from the bottom portion of Figure 7.64, a gradual increase in the rate was achieved with this negative practice technique, although it was not so dramatic as under the disapproval condition. After five minutes, the experimenter was called away from the room and the observer remained to obtain a second baseline measurement. As Figure 7.64 indicates, the baseline was retrieved.

Replication of the experiment would have produced better evidence

8. The investigators wish to express their appreciation to Richard Hanish and Janet Loeb for their participation in this study.

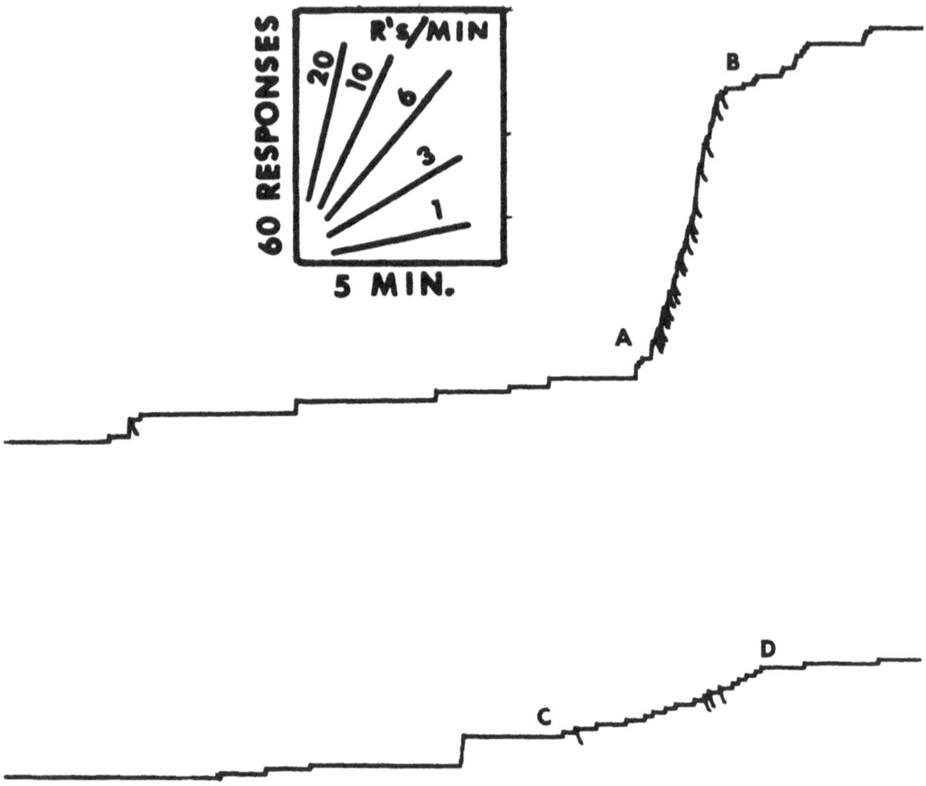

Figure 7.64. Cumulative recording of rate of noise-making during tests of two social reinforcement conditions. The beginning and end portions of both top and bottom tracings were baseline conditions. Between points A *and* B *in the top graph* E *expressed disapproval following each noise. Between points* C *and* D *in the bottom graph* E *was expressing approval for each noise.*

of the reliability of the data. However, we felt that the evidence indicated that attention reinforced the noises, and from a clinical standpoint, we did not wish to continue with procedures that might reinstate high rates of noise-making behavior or confuse the youngster about the behavior of the staff.

Results of First Two Months of Extinction of Noises

The noises were observed for a full day once each month during Dan's first three months in residence. Figure 7.65 through 7.67 present samples of the cumulative curves obtained at each of these observations. The first week in residence, shown in Figure 7.65, shows considerable variability in the rate of the noise-making response, ranging from zero to a high of about 12 responses per minute for different 5-minute sections of the record. The overall rate of response was approximately 5 responses per minute during the entire sample. Figure 7.66 shows the curves obtained for a similar period of observation one month later, by which time there were occurring extended periods of no noises and only one brief incident of

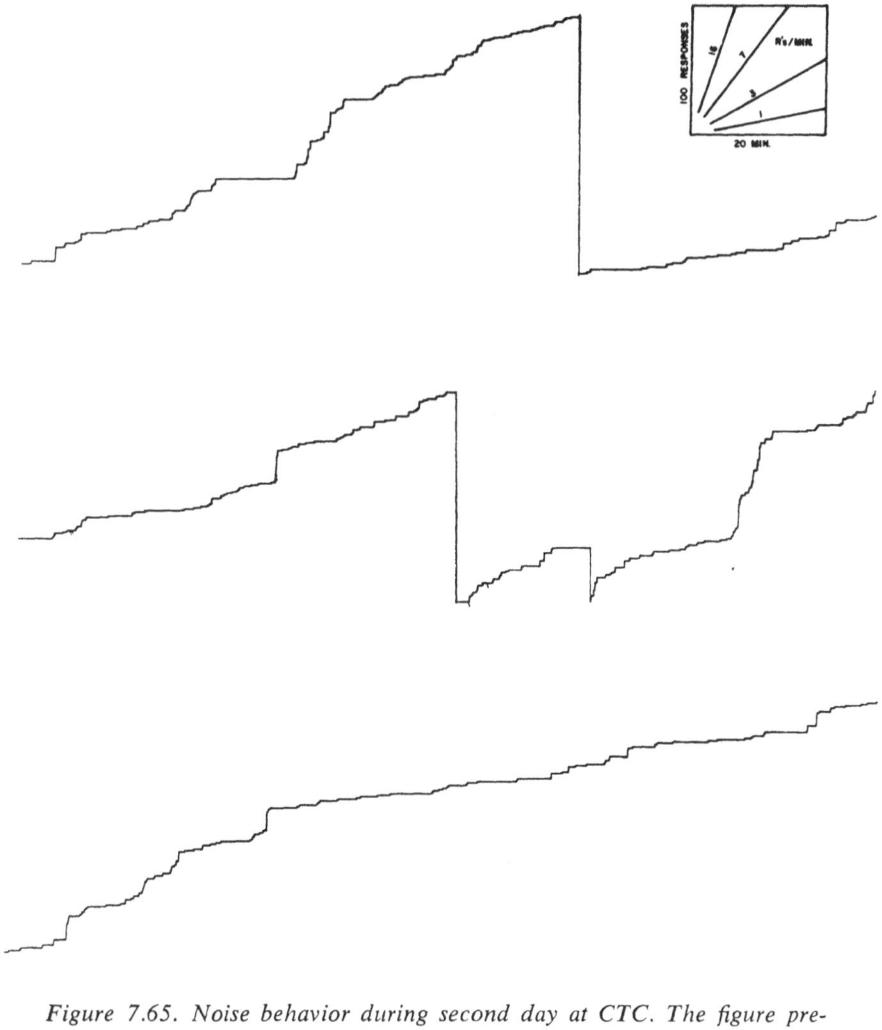

Figure 7.65. Noise behavior during second day at CTC. The figure presents representative samples from a day-long observation.

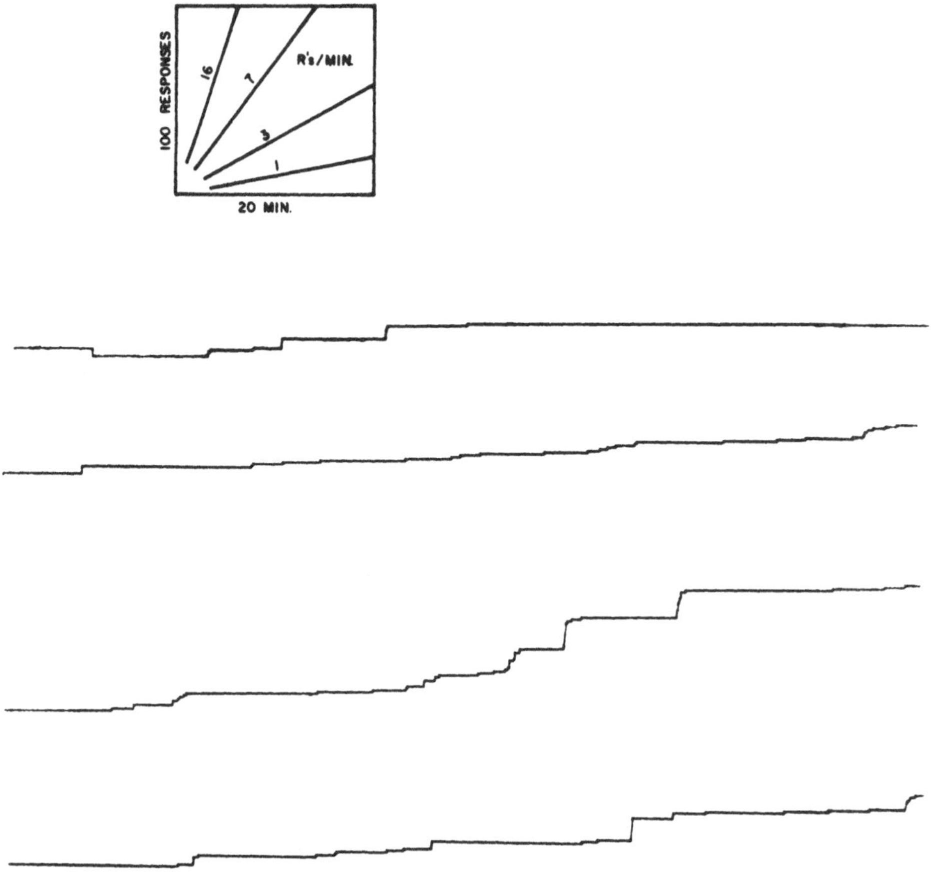

Figure 7.66. Noise behavior during the 23rd day at CTC. The figure presents representative samples from the day-long observation.

high-rate noise-making. It appeared that extinction was occurring and the rate of noise-making had reduced remarkably. In the following month, as depicted in Figure 7.67, the results were similar, but more erratic than in the second month. The observer noted that the peaks of high-rate responding occurred at moments when Dan was apparently angry with her and wanting her to stop following him.

Considering that the vocal tic had been occurring at a relatively high rate for several years, we were gratified to see this much control achieved through the simple technique of consistently ignoring the response. Unfortunately, the low average rate (less than one response per minute overall) was still too frequent for us to risk exposing Dan to any but a very con-

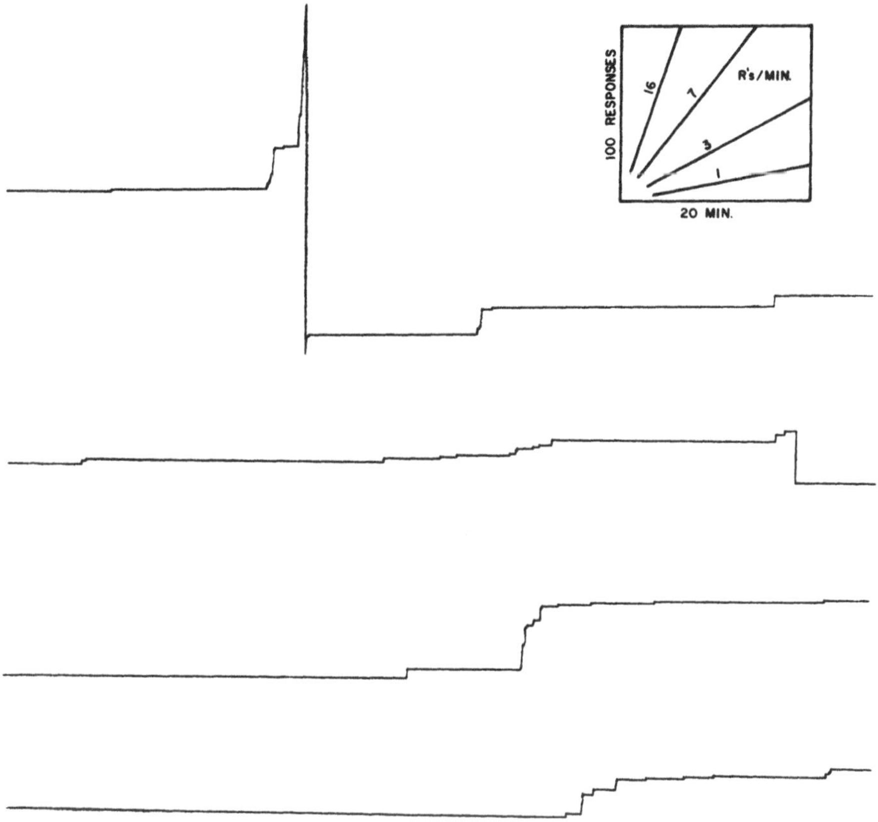

Figure 7.67. Noise behavior during the 60th day at CTC. The figure presents representative samples from the day-long observation.

trolled environment. For example, we observed that when we took him off-grounds to a store, he immediately began making noises at a high rate. Naturally, customers and clerks immediately turned and reinforced the noise with some kind of attention. Even in our setting, we observed that, although visitors had been cautioned against responding to this behavior, the rate of the noise would increase markedly when Dan approached or was approached by strangers. On one occasion, one of the authors led a group of graduate students through the cottage dining room when Dan and his group were eating supper. Dan looked up when the author entered the room and nodded a simple hello. When the first visitor entered the room, he looked up and made two or three barking sounds. As the group passed through the room, he proceeded with a steady barrage of noises which stopped as abruptly as it had begun when the last of the visitors exited through the door on the opposite side of the dining room. This incident was surely the most objective evidence that we had not achieved sufficient control of the noise behavior to warrant Dan's discharge from the Center.

Treatment of Compliance. Initial observations of Dan both in the home and during outpatient visits indicated that high levels of noncompliant behavior were a major problem. During four hours of visiting in his home, he was observed to comply with only 50 percent of the requests made of him by his mother. She went to great extremes to achieve his compliance. Generally, he seemed to pay little attention to any request made of him and would simply go his own way. The only time his mother achieved any degree of compliance was when she successfully threatened him into climbing out of a tree by waving the belt with which he was sometimes spanked. Several times we observed her chasing him through the house in an attempt to get him to do something she had asked. She herself admitted trying many methods to gain better control of Dan and said that, in accordance with professional advice, she had recently launched a systematic program of praising him every time he did what was asked. She did follow compliance with praise, but she was so angered and frustrated that her statements did not sound convincing. It was further evident that Dan could successfully avoid complying with a request by simply outwaiting the adults around him. His teacher in school had also experienced frustration and failure in attempting to evoke even the simplest obedience from Dan. Consequently, we decided that another of Dan's critical behaviors we should begin treating was compliance.

Using a simple *B* design, we began making behavioral counts of his compliance and noncompliance from the moment of his admission to the Center. He was told when he was oriented to the program that his success at learning to do what staff asked of him would be the most important thing in determining how fast he would proceed through the levels program (as described in Chapter 5). He began the program at level 2. This highly structured level was chosen because it maximized the possibilities for adult control and minimized the number of circumstances in which Dan might fail to comply with requests. Staff were instructed that whenever any request was made of him, whether it was simply to reply to a "hello" or more complicated such as "Make your bed," all events in his environment should cease until he complied. If he did not comply with a request, he was steered away from all activities, materials, and persons until he had done what was requested. For example, if we were waiting for him to comply and another youngster invited him to play a game, the staff might say to the other youngster, "Dan will be able to play with you as soon as he does something for me."

Figure 7.68 presents the summarized data on compliance for Dan's first 12 weeks in residence at the Center. The marks at the top of the figure indicate his progression through the levels program during the 12 weeks. Noncompliance here is represented as the percent of all requests made of him with which he failed to comply. Initially, Dan was noncompliant to almost 25 percent of the staff requests. The rate of noncompliance varied throughout the 12 weeks, finally dropping to as low as five percent. At that time, counts of compliance were discontinued although the compliance program remained in effect. The counts were stopped because it was necessary to study other behaviors and a five percent rate of noncompliance seemed to be an acceptable behavioral expectation. Figure 7.68 is particularly interesting in the manner in which it reflects movement through the levels program. Study of the figure demonstrates that frequently, with progression to a higher level and thereby less staff support and structure, Dan's rate of noncompliance would increase. As he remained on a given level for a period of time, noncompliance would again decrease. The sharp increase in noncompliance which occurs at week 9 resulted in our decision to drop him back one level. This occurred around Christmas when he was experiencing considerable concern about issues arising in family therapy and we decided that he would be unable to go on a vacation trip with his parents and siblings.

Unfortunately, the simple ratio count of compliance and noncompliance was not the best measure for Dan. A preferable measure would have been the length of time required for Dan to comply with each staff request. A wait of two, even three, hours was not uncommon to get Dan to comply with even the simplest requests. On one occasion we waited 14 hours for compliance, on another as long as eight hours. An accurate record of these times would have been far more dramatic evidence of the shaping of compliant behavior.

Training Speech Substitutes for the Vocal Tic Behavior. Although 2 months of extinction had produced a marked reduction in Dan's noise-making behavior, it still occurred at an annoying rate. We felt that the major benefits of extinction had been obtained and an additional program must be developed. We considered the development of a punishment program. Although punishment, especially electrical shock, might have been successful with a behavior problem of this kind, we had several reservations about using it with Dan. First, a variety of punishments had already been tried to treat this particular behavior and, probably because of inconsistent management, had failed. We recognized that it would probably be impossible to punish every noise response, since many of them would occur unknown to the staff or in situations where they would be unable to administer punishment. Also, we could predict Dan's acquisition of secondary behaviors because of the implementation of punishment. For

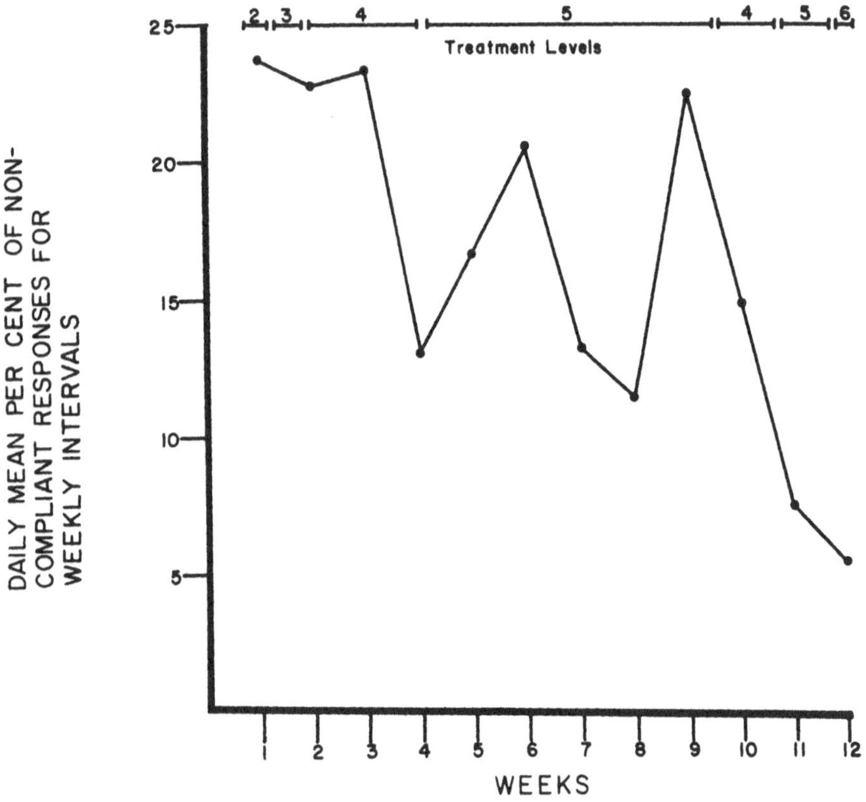

Figure 7.68. Daily mean percent of noncompliant responses during first twelve weeks of treatment. Progress through the levels program is indicated at the top of the figure.

example, we could visualize a scene in which Dan might make a noise and a staff member might spend 15 or 20 minutes attempting to hold him still in order to administer the shock. We were further concerned because, once Dan left the Center, even if shock had been successful, the noise could reoccur in situations, such as in public school, where shock could not be administered. Finally, we felt that we had already made progress in reducing the noises with extinction and we subjectively decided that severe punishment be reserved as a last resort.

The extinction schedule suggested the program that we ultimately selected. In setting up the extinction program, we had assumed that the noise behavior would simply disappear and no other behavior would take its place in the youngster's response hierarchy. A more tenable view is that the extinguished response shifts to a lower expectancy on the response hierarchy while other responses acquire a greater probability of occurrence. The present case demonstrates that, when a response is extinguished, the clinician should attend to responses which may replace it in the subject's total response hierarchy. In Dan's instance, although we collected no data, we observed four responses which had seemed to be replacing the vocal tic. One was vociferously to call the name of his favorite staff member, "Molly, Molly." Another was to poke staff members in the arm. A third response was to flip light switches on and off in a most annoying fashion. This particular response was probably modeled after teachers he had had in the past who had attracted the attention of their classes of deaf children by flipping light switches. Finally, it seemed that the noise behavior might also be replaced by a series of impulsive acts (described in a subsequent section). Of the four major responses which seemed to be taking the place of noises on the response hierarchy, only the one of calling the staff member's name was considered a desired behavior.

We decided that extinction would have little further success unless we could carefully train a series of desired responses to replace the verbal tic. The responses which were prominently absent from Dan's repertoire were speech responses. Consequently, we devised a program to train speech responses that might obtain the same reinforcing attention for which the noise behavior had operated. His teacher had already begun a program to expand his repertoire of speech responses. We were able to require complete sentences from Dan and to train him to use speech in a wide variety of situations. We wondered if we could not devise specific speech responses which could easily substitute for the noise behavior. Consequently, three staff members began maintaining a series of research notes from which we would identify possible substitute speech responses. These three staff members followed Dan for prolonged periods, noted each time that he produced a vocal tic, and decided what, if any, would have been an appropriate speech response in that situation. For example, Dan might be observed struggling to make his bed. At this point a staff member might pass his room, and Dan would respond with several barking noises. The staff member would note that the noise had occurred and then could conclude that an appropriate speech substitute would be "Will you help me make my bed?" As these observations were compiled, it became clear that Dan was also using the bark as a nonspecific form of verbal communication in a variety of situations where other children used words to communicate. For example, on one occasion one of the authors appeared with a clipboard in the cottage living room fairly late in the evening. This was an unusual time for him to be in the cottage, and as several of the children came in to watch television, they were curious about his presence. The first youngster who came into the room asked, "What are you doing here tonight?" The second who entered the room noted the author's clipboard and pencil and asked, "Which of us are you observing tonight?" A third, upon entering the room, said, "Will you play a game with me?" Finally, Dan entered the room, noted the author's presence, and responded with a series of loud, shrill barking noises.

Our notes from a week of observations yielded a wide variety of speech responses that would have served as good substitutes in the many situations in which Dan had made the noise. Reviewing these notes, we found that four types of statements could have served as substitute responses in the majority of situations in which he had made barking noises. He made noises whenever he felt successful about his behavior. For example, if he scored a point in a game, he would immediately give several yelps. Consequently, we selected the statement, "Good for me!" as a possible substitute response. Secondly, we found that whenever Dan made a mistake in school, performed poorly in a game, or was otherwise chagrined by his performance, he again made noises. In such situations, we selected the statement, "Oh, no, that's awful." Third, we identified many situations in which the noise seemed to function simply to gain social attention. For instance, if a staff member were working in his office and Dan came by the door, he would look in and make several noises. For this type of situation, we selected the statement, "Will you please pay attention to me?" Finally, because of his poor hearing and his difficulty in paying close attention to others, Dan often seemed to be puzzled about what others were doing or saying, and he would again make the noise. For these situations, we selected the query, "Will you please tell me what's going on?"

These four statements were then used as the basis of a new baseline observation of his noise behavior. The observer made a series of 100 five-minute observations randomly spaced over two days' observation. The observer noted each time, during a given five-minute observation, that Dan made the noise. At the same time the observer noted which, if any, of the four speech responses might have been an appropriate statement for Dan to make under the given circumstances. If none of the four statements would have been appropriate under the circumstances, an entry was made in a miscellaneous category. The observer further noted in the data whether or not any of the four statements, or some approximation to them, had been used by Dan during the observation interval. The first column (observation #1) of Table 7.4 summarizes the baseline data. During the 100 five-minute samples, Dan was observed to make the noise 94 times. On eight of those occasions, the phrase "Good for me" would have been appropriate. On five of the 94 occasions, "Oh, no, that's awful"

Table 7.4. Summary of 100 5-Minute Samples of the Noise Behavior and Judgments of Appropriate Speech Substitutes for Observations 1, 2, & 3

	Observation #1 Treatment Days 88 and 89		*Observation #2 Treatment Days 120, 121, & 122*		*Observation #3 Treatment Days 127 and 128*	
Total Noises:	*94*		*19*		*24*	
Appropriate Substitute:	#	%	#	%	#	%
Good for Me	8	9	5	26	9	38
Oh No, That's Awful	5	5	0	0	0	0
Pay Attention	48	51	2	11	2	8
Tell Me What's Going On	19	20	9	47	11	46
Other or None	21	22	3	16	2	8

would have been satisfactory. On 48, or 51%, of the occasions when Dan made the noise, the phrase "Will you please pay attention to me?" would have been a suitable substitute. On 19 occasions, "Will you please tell me what's going on?" would have been appropriate. And, in 22% of the occasions, some other or no statement at all would have been appropriate. The data thus indicate that our four statements could be suitable substitutes for 85% of the 94 noises made during the observations. As evident from observation 1 in Table 7.5, Dan never made a response which approximated any of the four statements being proposed as substitutes for the noise. Our hypothesis, then, was that if we could train these four responses and guarantee reinforcement for them while maintaining extinction for the noise behavior, we would produce further reduction in the rate of noises.

To test this, we decided to train the speech response that would serve as an appropriate substitute for the majority of situations where noises had occurred. Thus, we began with the teaching of "Will you please pay attention to me?" We determined that once this response was occurring with regularity we would make another sample of 100 five-minute observations.

Table 7.5. Summary of 100 5-Minute Samples of Actual Speech Responses for Observations 1, 2, & 3

	Observation #1 Treatment Days 88 and 89	*Observation #2 Treatment Days 120, 121, & 122*	*Observation #3 Treatment Days 127 and 128*
Good for Me	0	0	2
Oh No, That's Awful	0	0	0
Pay Attention	0	82	112
Tell Me What's Going On	0	0	0

The training of "Will you please pay attention to me?" began immediately. As a first step, Dan's teacher introduced this statement during his regular school classes. She taught him the correct pronunciation of the words and role-played, with him, a wide variety of situations in which the statement could be used. She then proceeded to prompt him to use the statement whenever it was appropriate in the tutorial situation with her. The statement itself was difficult to teach, both because the words were hard for Dan to articulate, and because he resisted both prompted and spontaneous use of the phrase. The noise was by far his preferred response under situations where "Pay attention to me" would be appropriate. Nevertheless, we began a count of his use of this phrase and the day-long management orders required staff to prompt him in the use of this phrase whenever it was appropriate. The staff attempted to anticipate when Dan should be prompted, and thereby decreased the frequency of the vocal tic. Dan was not told that the statement was to serve as a substitute for the noise. In fact, staff were careful to give him no indication that his learning of this statement was any different than his having learned other speech responses that had already been taught. Figure 7.69 shows the progress of

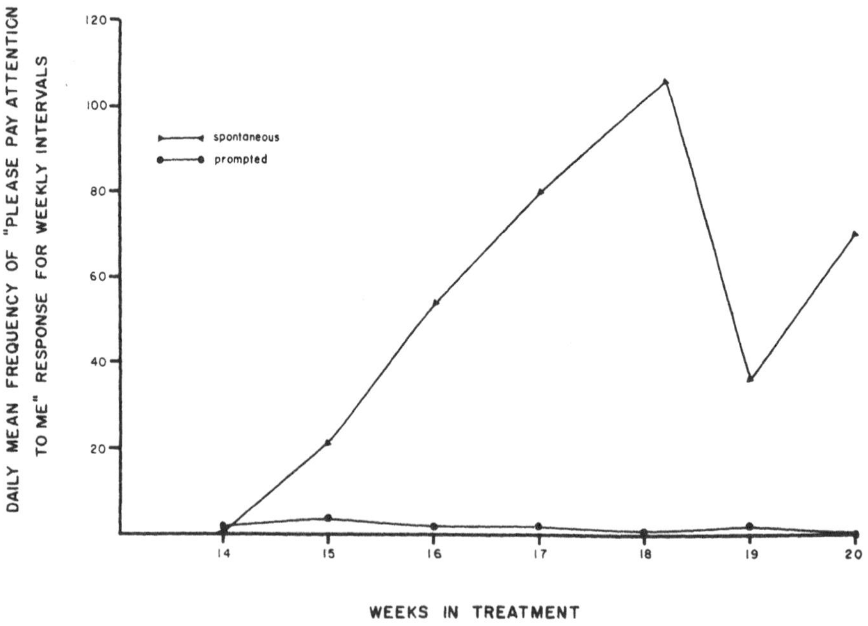

Figure 7.69. Frequency of "Please Pay Attention to Me" Response Occurring with Prompting and Spontaneously

teaching the response. As he acquired spontaneous use of the response, he achieved an all-time level of saying "Will you please pay attention to me?" 141 times in one day.

An example of his early learning of this response merits special mention. On one occasion, when the response was first being taught, the staff were gathered for their weekly meeting. It was customary for other Center staff to manage our youngsters so that their regular staff would not be disturbed during the weekly rounds. Customarily we ignored children who tried to obtain our attention at this time, expecting them to go to the other staff for any help they needed. As we deliberated about our slow progress in teaching Dan to say "Will you please pay attention to me?" we heard him outside the door of the meeting room. He peeked in at the window and obviously wanted the assistance of one of the staff members. Everyone continued with the business at hand and payed no attention to Dan. Next, however, we heard him make the vocal tic quite loudly several times. Then we heard him attempt to say something quite softly. Finally, with perfect clarity and at the top of his lungs, we heard him say, "Will you please pay attention to me?" Almost in unison, the staff shouted "Reinforce that!" Dan's teacher rushed from the room to reinforce the behavior. Dan was so surprised by this quick response that he ran upstairs and hid behind a chair. When the teacher found him, the expression on Dan's face clearly said, "What hath God wrought?" If this first reinforcement was somewhat overwhelming, others were more carefully timed, and slowly the response began to accelerate.

Just one month after the first sampling, a second observation was made, as summarized in observation 2 of Table 7.4. We were overwhelmed to find that only 19 noises had occurred during the 100 five-minute observations. Out of those 19, only two noises had occurred under circumstances where "Will you please pay attention to me" would have been an appropriate statement. The reduction in noises was more than we could account for by the continuation of extinction, and the data seemed to indicate that the statement "Will you please pay attention to me" was serving as a substitute for noises. As observation 2 of Table 7.5 shows, he actually said "Pay attention to me" 82 times during these same 100 five-minute observations. The data, however, seemed suspicious; they were too good. One variable which may have accounted for the unusual success of the program was that during the second observation period Dan had been mildly ill with a cold. This cold had been accompanied by a slight throat and ear infection which may have diminished the rate of noise-making. Consequently, we waited another week until he had recovered from the cold and made the third set of observations. As can be seen from Tables 7.4 and 7.5, this third set of observations was just as encouraging as the second. Thus, we decided that teaching alternate responses was a correct procedure, and we began to train another one of our four speech responses.

The data from the second and third observations indicated that, for nearly 50% of the noises observed, "Tell me what's going on" would have been an appropriate substitute. It became the next speech response we taught Dan. Figure 7.70 shows the progress of our attempt to train this

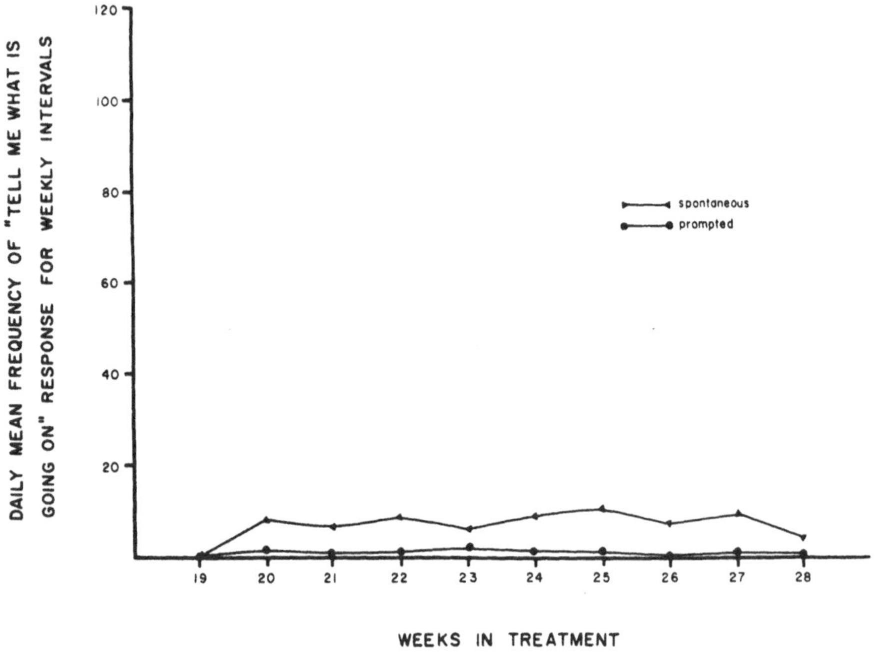

Figure 7.70. Frequency of "Tell Me What is Going On" Response Occurring Spontaneously and with Prompting

speech response. Both these data and those of Table 7.7 (observation 4) indicate that we were not so successful in teaching this response. The data initially suggested that staff were not prompting the response sufficiently. This interpretation may have been correct, but the amount of prompting of the alternate speech response was as frequent as it had been in training "Please pay attention to me." Perhaps more attention to the conditions under which prompting was most effective could have helped. For example, we found it more difficult to reinforce Dan for his asking "Will you please tell me what's going on," than we had for "Will you please pay attention to me." His communication skills were still quite poor and staff

Table 7.6. Summary of 100 5-Minute Samples of the Noise Behavior and Judgments of Appropriate Speech Responses for Observations 4 & 5

	Observation #4 Treatment Days 170 & 171		*Observation #5 Treatment Days 179 & 180*	
Total Noises:	384		31	
Appropriate Substitute:	#	%	#	%
Good for Me	48	13	2	6
Oh No, That's Awful	0	0	0	0
Pay Attention	52	14	1	3
Tell Me What's Going On	106	28	16	52
Other or None	218	57	12	39

frequently found it difficult to give him an explanation that he could understand of what had transpired in a conversation. It seems that this response, so necessary in his speech repertoire, could not be adequately reinforced because of his problems in understanding what people said to him.

A fourth observation of 100 five-minute intervals was made. In this sampling, the rate of noise-making behavior was extremely high. A total of 384 noises occurred, as Table 7.6 shows. The data indicated that a lower percentage of noises may have occurred with "Tell me what's going on" and that there had been some regression with the response of "Please pay attention to me." More disturbing, however, was the increase in the number of noises for which Dan could have substituted other speech responses or simply been silent. The observer's subjective evaluation was that many of the noises indicated anger with her and displeasure at being observed. During the subsequent week, a fifth observation was made. At this sampling, his rate of saying, "Tell me what's going on" was comparable with that of the previous sampling. During the actual sampled observations, we now observed only 31 noises and once again 50% of these were in the

Table 7.7. Summary of 100 5-Minute Samples of Actual Speech Responses for Observations 4 & 5

	Observation #4 Treatment Days 170 & 171	*Observation #5 Treatment Days 179 & 180*
Good for Me	0	7
Oh No, That's Awful	0	0
Pay Attention	11	101
Tell Me What's Going On	1	3

category of "Tell me what's going on." Our previous effects with "Please pay attention to me" were again observed in this fifth observation, and we were encouraged to observe that he again employed that phrase frequently. Unfortunately, the phrase, "Tell me what's going on" was used only three times. We had also begun teaching the phrase, "Good for me," although no specific data had been accumulated on its frequency. Thus, the fourth and fifth observations gave fewer grounds for optimism than the previous two. We were experiencing extreme difficulty in teaching alternative

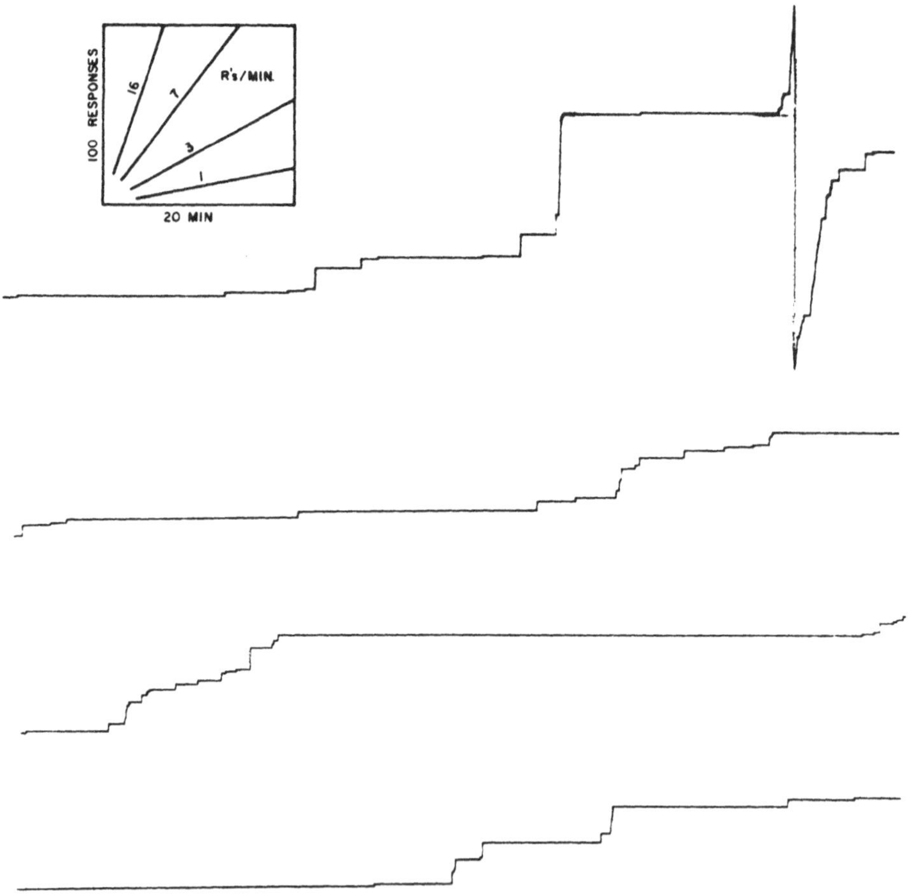

Figure 7.71. Noise behavior during a day-long observation on the 138th day of treatment. The figure presents representative samples from the full day's cumulative record

phrases other than "Please pay attention to me" and other kinds of phrases that would be the appropriate substitutes for the noise behavior.

Before proceeding beyond the middle phase of treating Dan's vocal tic, we obtained a sample of the rate of noise behavior. The cumulative recording represented in Figure 7.71 was made between the third and fourth observations. This cumulative recording is different from previous recordings in that it shows extended periods of no noise-making, as well as brief intervals of high-rate vocal tics. The high-rate noise-making seemed to be specific to Dan's relationship with the observer, whose comments supported an earlier opinion that Dan's noises were direct expressions of anger. In general, we felt this record, the five observations previously discussed, and general living experiences with Dan all indicated a relatively low rate of noises.

Impulsive Behavior.[9] Shortly after Dan's admission to the Center, his impulsive behavior became a source of concern to the staff. This behavior occurred in virtually every situation. For example, at meals Dan would suddenly reach in front of other persons to grab the butter or the catsup, generally spilling something in the process. He ate rapidly and sloppily.

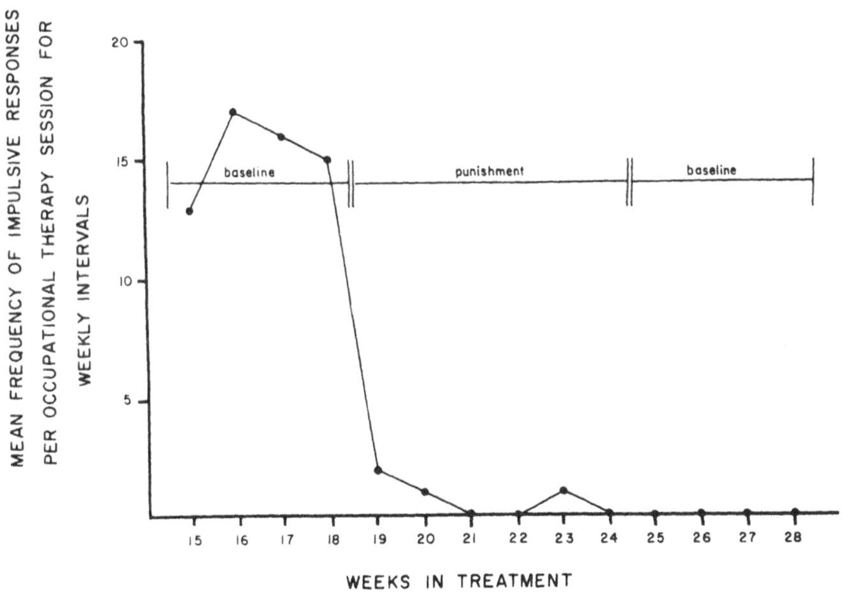

Figure 7.72. Impulsive Responses Occurring during Occupational Therapy Sessions

9. The authors are indebted to Robert Leff, Ph.D., for the design and supervision of this portion of Dan's treatment program.

In the craft shop, he often would grab tools away from others or attempt to perform three tasks at once. In playing a team game such as field hockey, he would snatch the ball away from his own teammates, often knocking them down in the process. He could not seem to slow down or wait more than a few seconds for gratification.

The most severe forms of impulsiveness were observed in the occupational therapy shop, in group activities, and during meals. A punishment program was projected, and since the appropriate punishment for each of the three situations would be different, separate counts were taken in each situation. In addition, a fourth count covered all of the other occurrences

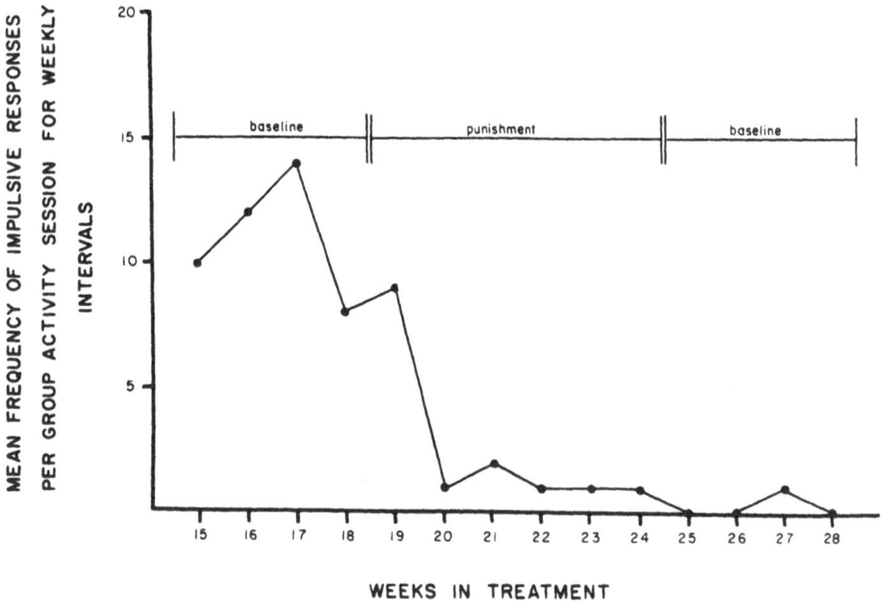

Figure 7.73. Impulsive Responses Occurring during Group Activity Sessions

of impulsive behavior during the remainder of the day. These four counts are presented in Figures 7.72 through 7.75. Our original plan had been to obtain a baseline for one week and then proceed with the punishment program. However, since a speech program of training responses incompatible with the noise behavior took priority and had just begun, the punishment for impulsiveness was delayed and the baseline continued for four weeks.

During the baseline there was a deceleration of the impulsiveness counts. Several factors may have accounted for this deceleration. During that time, the speech responses, especially "Please pay attention to me," increased radically. Talking may well have been incompatible with some of Dan's impulsive behavior. We found some support for this hypothesis in the fact that the least baseline reduction of impulsiveness occurred in the craft shop and group activity, the two places where there was the least amount of emphasis on speech-training. Another factor which may have affected the baseline was Dan's attentiveness to the impulsiveness counts.

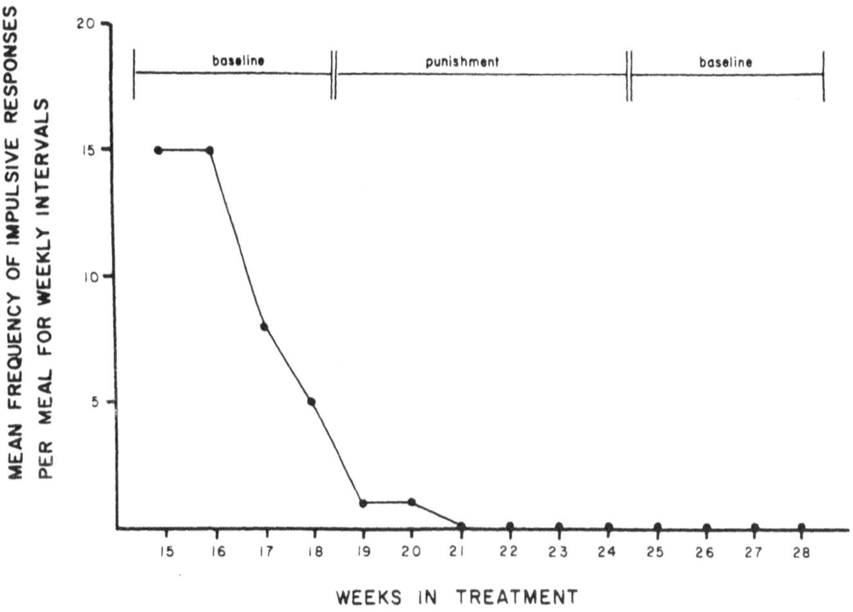

Figure 7.74. Impulsive Responses Occurring during Meals

He carefully observed the staff making these counts and often inquired about the behavior that was being counted. Thus, the mere act of our counting may have resulted in some of the reduction. Finally, several emotionally laden issues were at this time resolved in family therapy. Unfortunately, we do not have controlled data available to support any of these speculations. Nevertheless, the reduction in impulsiveness during the baseline reemphasizes two important conclusions about behavior-modification methods. First, the simple *AB* design, like this, provides little in the way of accurate assessment of treatment programs. Second, as we have often pointed out, one of the most effective but certainly least understood behavior-modification techniques is the baseline count.

Despite the deceleration of impulsiveness during baseline, the behavior remained sufficiently high to make managing Dan difficult. Consequently, a punishment program was instituted at Week 5. The program consisted of (1) punishing all inappropriately impulsive behaviors occurring in his interpersonal behavior or in physical activities, and (2) reinforcement of all evidence of restrained behavior. The program was applied consistently and unremittingly regardless of whether the impulsive behavior appeared to be volitional or accidental. The punishment and reinforcement were delivered swiftly and made as immediately contingent upon the behavior as possible. Instances of punishment for impulsiveness and of reinforce-

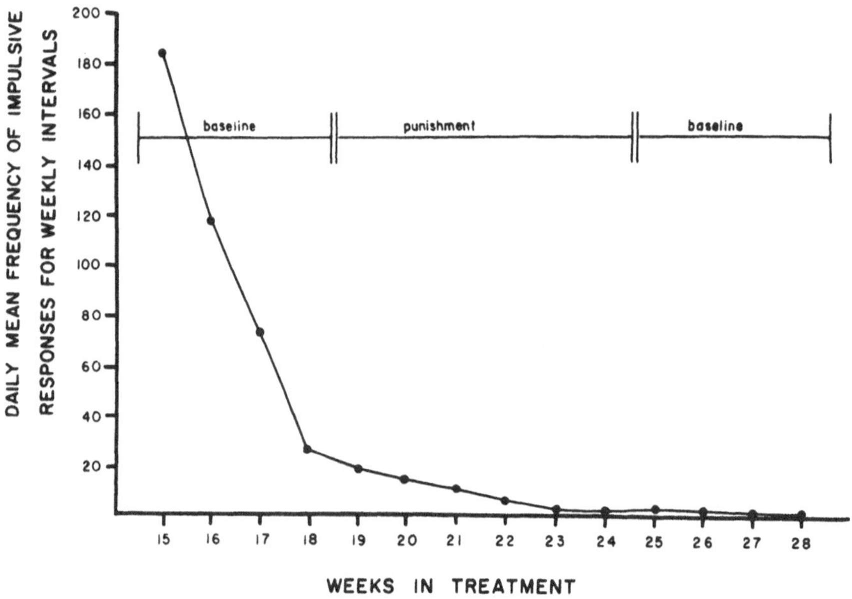

Figure 7.75. Impulsive Responses Occurring throughout the Day with the Exception of Occupational Therapy Sessions, Group Activity Sessions, and Mealtimes

ment for slowness were recorded on behavioral charts. The staff were instructed to attempt to balance the number of reinforcements for slowness with the number of punishments for impulsiveness. The words "Slow down, Dan" were used as a cue. Whenever the staff said, "Slow down, Dan" the appropriate punishment followed immediately.

The punishments varied according to the situation. At meals, his total allotment of food was given to him in a single serving. Immediately after each instance of his gulping food too rapidly, grabbing from others, or reaching across the table, the staff would say, "Slow down, Dan" and remove a small portion of the food from his plate. Restrained, polite, careful mealtime behavior was rewarded by praise and, of course, by allowing him to eat his entire meal.

During group games, the cue, "Slow down, Dan" was again used and his impulsive actions were forceably restrained. When he stopped, he was moved back one step or level in the game. For example, if it were a field hockey game, he would be moved to a different portion of the field away from where the ball was being played. Again, verbal reinforcement ("That's good, Dan, you're slowing down") was given when his behavior was appropriately slow or he demonstrated teamwork.

During work in the craft shop, the cue was again used and Dan was given a short time-out and moved back a step in his project. Moving him back a step was accomplished by dismantling a portion of his most recently finished work. Again, verbal praise was used when he was being appropriately slow and restrained.

During the remainder of the day and when his behavior in meals, group games, or the craft shop could not be punished in the specified way, we used the following technique. Dan was at the beginning of each day given a predetermined number of small coin-like tokens. He carried these in a busman's change dispenser which was locked so that no tokens could be inserted except by the child-care worker. Every time Dan engaged in an undesirable, impulsive act, the staff used the verbal cue, "Slow down, Dan," and then immediately operated the coin dispenser to remove one token. As always, the slow, restrained, and controlled behavior was frequently reinforced with praise. Initially, Dan received 185 tokens at the beginning of an eight-hour shift. If 18 of those tokens remained in the changer at the end of the shift, the staff member gave Dan a trip to the toy cupboard where he could choose a prize. Gradually, as his impulsive behavior reduced, we asked Dan to have more and more tokens remaining in the changer at the end of the shift. Dan was not told how many tokens were in the changer nor how many he had to have left at the end of the shift. Rather, he was told that if he had enough tokens at the end of the shift, the staff would give him a trip to the cabinet.

Dan demonstrated both pleasure and extreme irritation with the new program. He liked the idea of the coin dispenser, at least up until the first tokens were removed. His reaction to having the tokens removed and to the other punishments in the program was extreme. He demonstrated depression, anger, and defiance. However, he quickly, if somewhat begrudgingly, accepted the program and learned to control his impulsive behavior. Within ten weeks, his impulsiveness had diminished to a near zero level in all four counts, and the formal program was dropped. At this time, the coin changer was given back to the staff and Dan invited several staff members to join him in a trip to the lake, into which, with great pleasure and vehemence, he pitched the tokens. Thereafter, he was given praise for restrained behavior and his impulsive behavior was punished intermittently with time-outs. The cue, "Slow down, Dan," and an additional cue, "It's hard to wait," were continued. The cue, "It's hard to wait," was introduced to Dan's speech-training program, and not only did staff say it when he was having difficulty being restrained, but also he was asked to say these words to staff and to think them to himself. Although impulsiveness periodically emerged as a problem throughout the duration of his treatment and is still in evidence at post-discharge evaluations, the previous high levels have not returned. The parents report that a brief discussion or a few punishments are enough to focus his attention once again upon being restrained.

REINTRODUCTION TO PUBLIC SCHOOL

We finally had enough behavioral control to be able to devise a program to reintroduce Dan to his home community. Although still a major problem, his noise-making had decelerated considerably. Noncompliance was no longer a severe problem, impulsive acts had diminished close to a zero level, and he had made substantial gains in our school program. His communication skills had shown marked improvement. His speech, although still difficult for strangers to understand, was more spontaneous and complex than it had been in the previous two months. He was paying better attention to others and consequently, his lip-reading skills had improved. Further, there was a concurrent improvement in his social relationships with other youngsters. He had been able to control himself in a group classroom composed of children without auditory deficits and, in the cottage setting, was regarded as a leader and friend by all of the other boys. Dan was becoming restless at his prolonged stay at the Center and was indicating that he was motivated to make more frequent home visits. Although he was not directly asking for a public school experience, he did demonstrate interest in the other youngsters who were beginning public school.

We then consulted with representatives from the public schools' Deaf Education Department to review Dan's program and begin consideration of a plan to reintroduce him to school. Among those consulted was the Director of the Deaf Education program and Dan's previous classroom teacher. Both had had many trying experiences with Dan on previous occasions. Their interest in and concern for Dan were unquestioned, but they were justifiably reluctant to involve themselves once again with this youngster. The teacher had known Dan over a number of years and had been instrumental in his referral to the Children's Treatment Center. She had previously invested heavily in Dan and had experienced only frustration and punishment in return. In addition, like many teachers who struggle conscientiously with severely disturbed youngsters, she questioned her own adequacy for dealing with Dan and wondered if she might not find herself contributing to a future failure experience for him.

The school personnel reviewed Dan's program with us, with the family therapist, and with Dan's teacher at the Center. They were interested in the programs we had developed for him, but quite skeptical about our enthusiastic assessment of his improvement. When they had observed him in both school and the cottage setting, they agreed that he demonstrated considerable change. The teacher was especially pleased that, for the first time in many years, Dan had extended himself to her with a genuinely warm greeting. It was agreed that we would begin slowly but deliberately to reintroduce Dan to the school setting.

Through several subsequent conferences with the school, we began to develop a program of gradually doing so. Basically we saw Dan as frightened about this return to school and fearful of repeating the total failure of social behavior that he had had in previous school experiences. We felt that good behavioral control could best be achieved at this point by his Treatment Center teacher, who would conduct a desensitization program gradually reacquainting Dan with the school and increasing his time in the classroom. She would actually go to class with him and, during the first weeks, would directly supervise Dan in the classroom while the regular teacher taught the rest of the children. Gradually she would withdraw from direct supervision of Dan and assist the teacher in any way possible so that she could handle the extra burden of this special youngster. In the third phase, she would withdraw herself from the classroom entirely. Both the school principal and the public school teacher expressed considerable doubt about the presence of the Center teacher in the classroom. This was indeed a new procedure for them, and in one sense, they saw it as a bribe to get them to take Dan back. On the positive side, however, they were willing to try the program, and despite their doubts, they invested fully in the plan to readmit Dan to public school. The management programs for Dan were taught to the public school personnel and they were given direct assistance in learning how to use these procedures.

Table 7.8 presents an outline of the steps that were taken to reintroduce Dan to school. This outline oversimplifies the effort extended by the Center teacher and the public school teacher to help Dan achieve a successful experience. Consequently, to supplement that chart, we have included samples of the Center teacher's daily notes. These notes serve as examples not only of her daily contact with Dan, but also as representative of the kind of detailed work which all of the cottage staff carried on with Dan throughout his contact with CTC.

Table 7.8. Program for Reintroduction to School

Treatment Day	*Event*
150	CTC staff visit public school.
156	Public school personnel visit Dan at CTC.
166	CTC staff visit public school—set up initial program.
172	CTC teacher drives Dan past school (spring vacation).
177	CTC teacher walks through school with Dan (spring vacation).
178	Dan meets school secretary—spends time in classroom—no children present (spring vacation).
179	Spends time in classroom—no children (spring vacation).
183	Visits school—stays in hallway—teachers and children present.
184	Spends time in his class.
186	First time on playground for recess.
190	First serious start on academics—one-half hour.
192	40 minutes—CTC teacher right next to him.
198	60 minutes—CTC teacher right next to him.
199	CTC teacher moves to back of room—in class for 2 hours.
212	Full afternoon program.
215	CTC teacher shares entire class with regular teacher instead of working just with Dan.
222	CTC teacher leaves Dan alone in school for short time.
225	Handles school without CTC teacher.

"On treatment day 172, Dan and I took our first unannounced trip to school. I only said we were going for a ride. As we neared school he recognized the route and said, 'This is the way to public school,' and I said yes. Throughout the whole trip he was 'quietly barking,' although this was under the breath as we carried on an ongoing conversation. As we neared the school he recognized the route and asked, 'Are we going to public school?' I said yes, and he was alarmed and asked why. I said to just look. We pulled up to school and passed it a little way. He asked if we were going in, and I replied no, and he was definitely relieved. We talked about school, how he felt; he needed quite a bit of reassurance that we were *not* going in. Dan, while we were in front of school, took off his seat belt and pulled over to my side of the car and sat very close to me, with his arm around the seat, really looking for protection and reassurance. Then the boys came out for gym class. We watched them play and discussed how he had acted before and how the boys were acting, and how did the boys feel about him before in gym class. Then I asked him if he was ready to leave, and he said yes. We were there about 15 minutes. He did not bark at all while we were in front of the school. As we went past the school after we turned around, he let out with a bark that must have shattered the windows. I drove a little further, stopped the car, and we talked about how glad he was to be leaving and we talked about how he felt. He did very well. He did not bark at all on the way back, and we talked all the while.

"Treatment Day 177—I took Dan for a ride again. This time he seemed to know he was going to school. No barking. We pulled into the back entrance and I suggested that we go out (this was the time of Easter vacation). There were men working in the playground, and he said he didn't want to, and he began to bark. We talked about feelings, recognition that he was scared and that he did not like school before. Then he asked why the school was dark, and I explained it was vacation and there was no one there. We sat and talked awhile and then he asked if Mrs. K. (teacher) was there. I reassured him that no one was there. We waited a little more and then I asked if he would like to go on, and he said yes, rather hesitantly. He looked for many excuses to hold back: he straightened the seat belt, he closed the window, he fixed the wiper blades, so I sat down with him on the steps of the building and we talked about the scared feelings. Dan agreed that he was pretty frightened to be going into school. Mrs. K. had a desk in her room with Dan's name on it, which you could plainly see. He made no response. I commented, 'Oh look, wasn't it nice that there was a desk there with your name on it.' But he said it's *NOT* for me! He said the desk did not belong to him, although he did see his name. We did not go in, but walked right through the building. Dan seemed very relieved to leave. We sat in the car and talked.

"Day 178—Dan is making good improvement regarding progress of school desensitization program. Dan did not bark at all during the trip, and seemed very warm, responsive, and comfortable. We entered school with no hesitation or delay. He barked as we entered the building and as we walked down the hall. Mrs. K.'s room was locked and the school secretary opened the door. She recognized Dan and he tried to ignore her. We went into Mrs. K.'s room, Dan did not remove his coat throughout the stay. He randomly ran around the room, looking, making faces, and very ill at ease. He sat down at his desk and I sat across from him whereupon he moved his desk closer to me *and* initiated conversation about how he felt. He said he did not like school before, Mrs. K. or the children. He talked about the things that he did that upset the class, such as shuffling his feet, banging the desk, throwing erasers, eating pencils, and so forth.

"Day 179—the trips were getting better and better and more encouraging. Very little barking at school, none before or after we left school. We role-played again how it would be when he came to school and talked about once again all the feelings centered around his previous school experiences.

"Day 183—Dan was terrific on his first visit to public school with people present. All the role-playing and approximation and so forth the last couple of weeks have certainly paid off.

"Day 184—Once again Dan was terrific. Beyond wildest hopes he handled himself beautifully. We had good conversation on the way to school, pulled up to school, Dan looked at me and said, 'I am scared,' and he *was*. We waited a few minutes and he talked about how scared he was, what would the children do, then said, 'O.K. I'm ready.' As we crossed the threshold he made one very small soft bark. We went into Mrs. K.'s room. There was indoor recess as it was raining outside and the children were playing individually and in small groups. Dan and I joined a group of two boys. He played very well. Dan was very nervous. I introduced Dan and myself to the class, and we went to each child, and said hello. Recess was over and *Dan went and sat down at his desk*. I said, 'Are you ready to leave, don't you want to go,' and he *asked if we could stay for a few more minutes*. Mrs. K. became very businesslike and passed out arithmetic papers. Dan asked me to sit right by him which I promptly did. We were back from the circle. He raised his hand and asked for a pencil. Mrs. K. gave him two papers and he was very relieved to see that he knew them and he could do the work academically.

"Day 190—Started Dan's really first day of academics in public school. He was to be at school from 12:30 until I felt that he could no longer manage it, and Dan was so nervous before this that he could not eat lunch at all. He was to eat lunch at 11:15, his mother came to lunch to encourage him, Mrs. B. (family therapist) and I ate lunch with him, Molly ate lunch with him; he was able to talk about how nervous he was and how afraid he was and he could not eat at all. We went to school and after we finished, Dan did not stay in school an entire hour. We stayed from about 12:30 until 1:00—he did very well academically and he really felt good about the way he did.

"Day 199"—for the first time, Dan came to school from 12:30 to 1:30 and I moved to the back of the room and he turned around often, almost constantly for support and reassurance, but did allow me to move to the back of the room and did work independently very nicely."

Following this successful beginning with public school, we began to plan with school personnel for a summer-school experience. We anticipated that Dan would be making more frequent and extended home visits during the summer, which, if accompanied with a summer-school program, would best prepare him for entering public school full time in the fall. We had anticipated that he would be discharged from the Center by autumn. The summer program was somewhat different from that of the previous spring, since there was a different teacher and some of the children in the class were different. In particular, his own younger sister was placed in the same summer-school class. Although this gave the two youngsters an opportunity to work through a number of competitive situations, it also placed increased stress upon Dan. The noise-making behavior in school was inconsequential during the summer and the teacher carefully followed the ignoring program. However, impulsive behavior was sometimes noted as a problem. Another problem described by the summer-school teacher was Dan's frequent "put-offs" to other children. Although we had long been aware of this behavior, the summer-school teacher highlighted how destructive it was for him. When he was most uncertain of himself, he would act snobbish with other youngsters. He would throw back his head, sneer, or make cruel jibes at the other children. Aside from this, his summer-school experience was unremarkable. He was seen as generally fitting into the class with the other hard-of-hearing youngsters, he enjoyed the school experience, and he seemed to gain academically. At the conclusion of summer school we decided Dan could attend public school program full time with the beginning of the fall semester.

MORE NOISES

Despite his generally good introduction to public school, observations of Dan's behavior at the Center and reports from his parents on home visits were discouraging. He had acquired a new behavior of frequently spitting outdoors, and occasionally indoors. He was paying very poor attention to persons when they spoke to him, and his speech had deteriorated. The data on his vocal tics were most discouraging.

Observations number six, seven and, eight, summarized in Tables 7.9 and 7.10, showed a decrease in the use of any of the previously acquired speech responses and a marked increase in other possible alternatives for the noises. These observations indicated that the rate of noise-making had

Table 7.9. Summary of 100 5-Minute Samples of the Noise Behavior and Judgments of Appropriate Speech Substitutes for Observations 6, 7, & 8

	Observation #6 Treatment Days 220 to 226		*Observation #7 Treatment Days 253 & 252*		*Observation #8 Treatment Days 288, 289, & 290*	
Total Noises:	*86*		*156*		*75*	
Appropriate Substitute:	#	%	#	%	#	%
Good for Me	6	7	3	2	0	0
Oh No, That's Awful	1	1	0	0	0	0
Pay Attention	0	0	1	1	4	5
Tell Me What's Going On	3	3	68	44	11	15
Other or None	76	88	84	54	60	80

Table 7.10. Summary of 100 5-Minute Samples of Actual Speech Responses for Observations 6, 7, & 8

	Observation #6 Treatment Days 220 to 226	*Observation #7 Treatment Days 253 & 252*	*Observation #8 Treatment Days 288, 289, & 290*
Good for Me	0	0	0
Oh No, That's Awful	0	0	0
Pay Attention	4	0	19
Tell Me What's Going On	1	0	0

returned to an earlier level. The noise now seemed to serve for a variety of new kinds of communications. One particularly disturbing observation that staff occasionally made was that the noises now appeared to be thoroughly compatible with some of the speech responses we had taught Dan. For example, one staff member noted that Dan would approach him, say, "Please pay attention to me," and then emit a series of noises.

Our study indicated that the vocal tics operated as various kinds of oral communication; one kind seemed to be an expression of anger. As others have noted in occurrences of Gilles de La Tourette's syndrome, the noise now seemed more clearly to be used as an obscenity.

A plausible explanation for our lack of progress with the vocal tic was that Dan was now being exposed to increased stress with his reintroduction to public school and with the increased time he spent on home visits. In reviewing the records, we saw clearly that staff had been spending most of their time working with Dan around school-related activities. The content of family therapy sessions had also emphasized the daily events occurring during his home visits. Speech-training programs had necessarily lapsed, and—of particular importance—Dan's speech teacher was no longer on the staff and working with him.

A number of staff members were observing that Dan was increasingly isolative. They felt that they were receiving brush-offs from him, although it was often difficult for them to describe exactly how he was brushing them off. Clearly, he often acted aloof and angry; staff attempts to discuss problems with him were met by resistance.

The one approach that had never been made in the treatment of Dan's noises had been to talk with him about the behavior. Originally we had avoided this because we felt that professionals in the past had failed in their attempts to reason with Dan about his behavior. We had at first decided to ignore the response. We wondered at this time whether staff's relationship with Dan might not be extensive enough that the behavior could be discussed objectively with him. At the least, we hoped that by talking with him we could obtain missing insights about his behavior.

We finally decided to interview him about the noise. The data in Figure 7.76 were collected just prior to this interview. Staff members sat down with Dan to discuss the problem. When the discussion opened, Dan feigned complete ignorance of what staff meant by "noise." The staff then played a video tape of Dan and several times replayed the noises he made on the recording. He was then clearly shaken, embarrassed, and terribly ashamed of himself. He made feeble attempts at denial and resisted using the word "noise" or making any other direct reference to the behavior. The interview was torturesome for all three concerned. Finally, with much support from staff, he accepted our concern that the noise-making behavior was inappropriate. It was preventing him from leaving the Center, and was bringing ridicule from others. His motivation to leave the Center was clear—especially at that moment. More positively, he clearly wanted to be home with his family and to succeed in public school. He said he could not control the noise behavior, but passively agreed to try. A firm

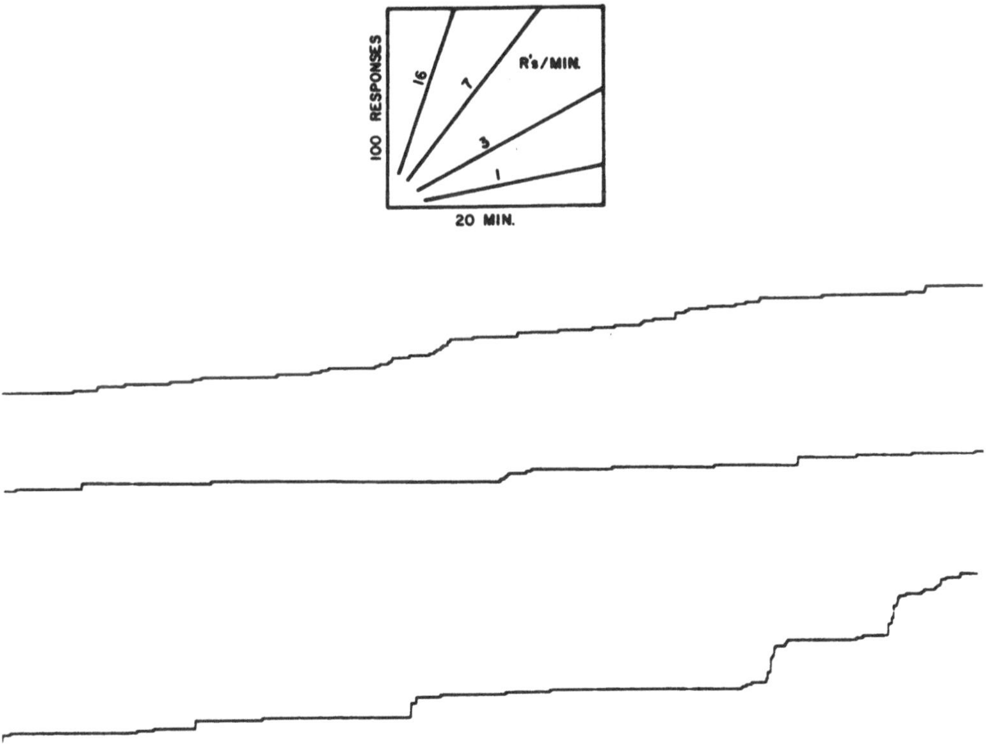

Figure 7.76. Samples from a Day-Long Observation of the Noise Behavior just prior to the Interview about the Noises, Treatment Day 303

program was established for all of the behaviors causing current concern. Dan was told at the end of the interview that he would need to make progress on all of these behaviors before the next level (level 11) could be granted to him. The requirements were that he must (1) stop making the noises, (2) stop spitting, (3) pay attention when staff or others spoke to him, and (4) talk. Each of these requirements was discussed in detail. He was given a counter and encouraged to count the noises himself and keep a record on his progress. For paying attention, we would give him a token reinforcement, and for talking, staff and his parents would provide praise.

This interview clearly had an effect. For the next two weeks, Dan was observed to be extremely anxious, angry, and embarrassed. The rate of

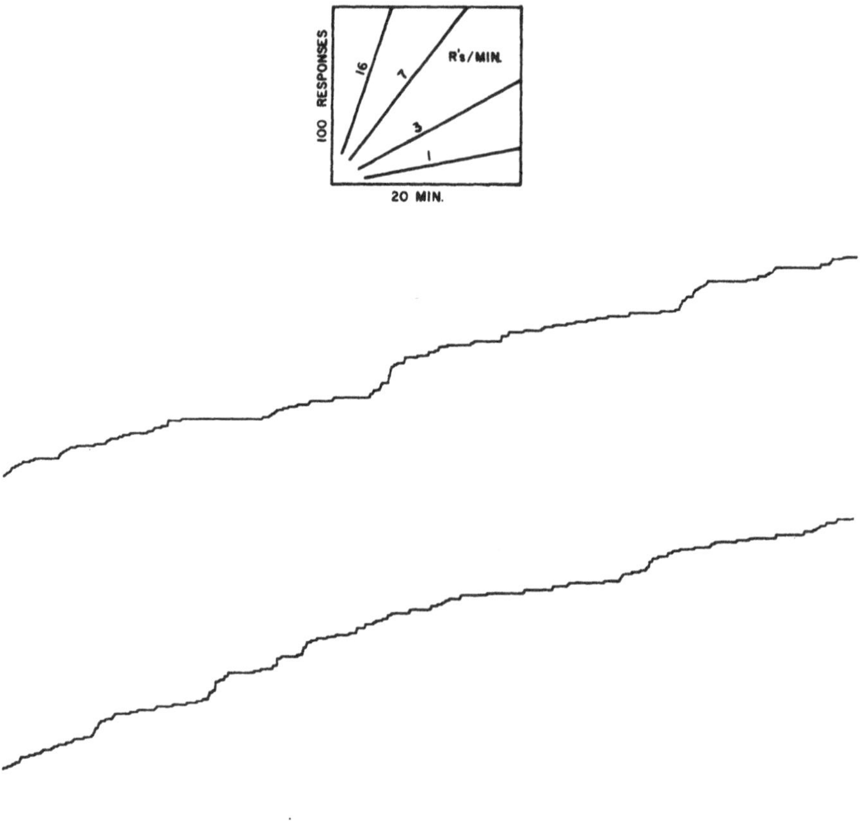

Figure 7.77. Representative Sample of the Observation of the Noises on the Day after the Interview about This Behavior, Treatment Day 305

noises increased, as seen in Figure 7.77, which presents data from the day following the interview. Dan worked for the tokens for attention, he talked more frequently, and he tried to control his spitting. He continued to protest that he could not control the noises. He was seen using the counter but seemed to count for himself only about 10% of the noises. He either was not aware of the other 90% or simply was attempting to deny them by failing to count. We decided to continue ignoring the noises and reinforcing attention and talking. All appropriate speech responses were encouraged and, in particular, he was stimulated to verbalize emotional responses, such as anger, frustration, etc. Within two weeks, the rate of noises dropped once again to their usual level, as indicated in the cumulative recordings of Figure 7.78. However, Dan himself had lost all interest in attempting to control the noises, did not talk with staff about them, and certainly was not making any great progress toward controlling them. Therefore, when he asked for level 11, he was refused.

The fall semester of school was rapidly approaching. We were concerned that the conditions had not improved since our interview with him about the noises and related problems. On the day before school began, we met with his parents to discuss the problem. The investigator was in favor of moving Dan back to level 2 and having him at the Center full time so that we could press heavily with a speech program and possibly introduce a punishment program for the noises. Dan's parents were against this on the grounds that the data still indicated that our best approach was to ignore the noises and that the progress he had made in readjusting to school should not be forgotten. They themselves felt that Dan had improved tremendously in every respect over the behavior he had demonstrated a year earlier prior to his admission to the Center. They felt that his being moved back to level 2 would be a totally ignominious experience to him and would cause him to lose the confidence he had acquired, and that we would be put back to where we had started a year before. His parent's wishes were honored and Dan went back to school on level 10.

The ensuing weeks were interesting. His performance in school was barely adequate. When he was back at the Center or on home visits, he made renewed efforts to put a distance between himself and staff and parents. His daily sessions with homework were especially difficult. His mother worked valiantly at helping him with homework; Dan worked just as intensively at resisting her every effort to help him.

Staff and mother both pressed for expressions of feeling from Dan rather than permitting him to isolate himself emotionally. On several occasions—and this had never before happened while we had known Dan—he broke down and cried on his mother's shoulder. It was only then that the obvious became apparent to us. For all the responses we had counted, ob-

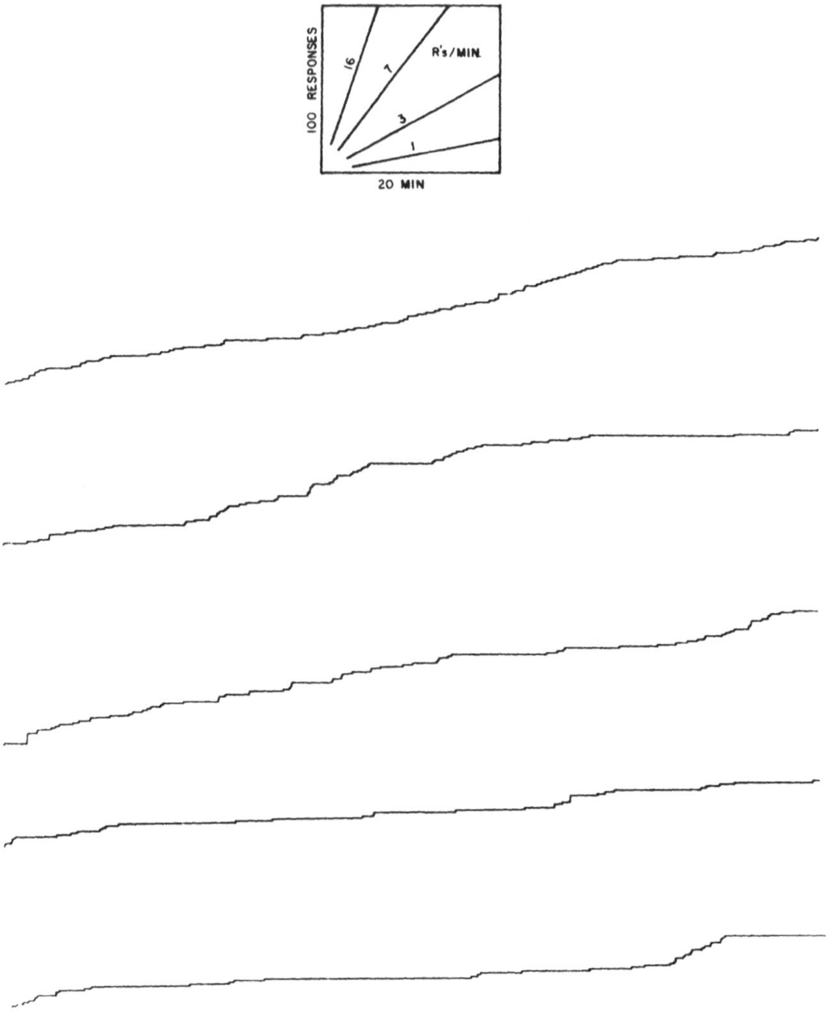

Figure 7.78. Samples of the noise behavior five to nine days after the interview. The rate of noises gradually diminished during this time, as indicated by these recordings which were made on treatment days 309 to 312.

served, and described with this youngster, we had failed to note fully behavior that was largely absent—experiences of emotional closeness to other persons. Although Dan was more spontaneous than when we had first known him, the occasions when he cried in anyone's presence or spontaneously expressed pleasure with someone else were exceptionally rare. Now occurred the first occasions in which he had actually laid his head on his mother's shoulder and sobbed since he was a small child.

By the beginning of October, we felt some progress was being made on the noises, as Figure 7.79 shows. Spitting had been reduced to a near zero level, attention and talking behaviors had all improved remarkably. He proudly received level 11. We felt he was working on the noises and consequently started a program of giving him a token and praising him for

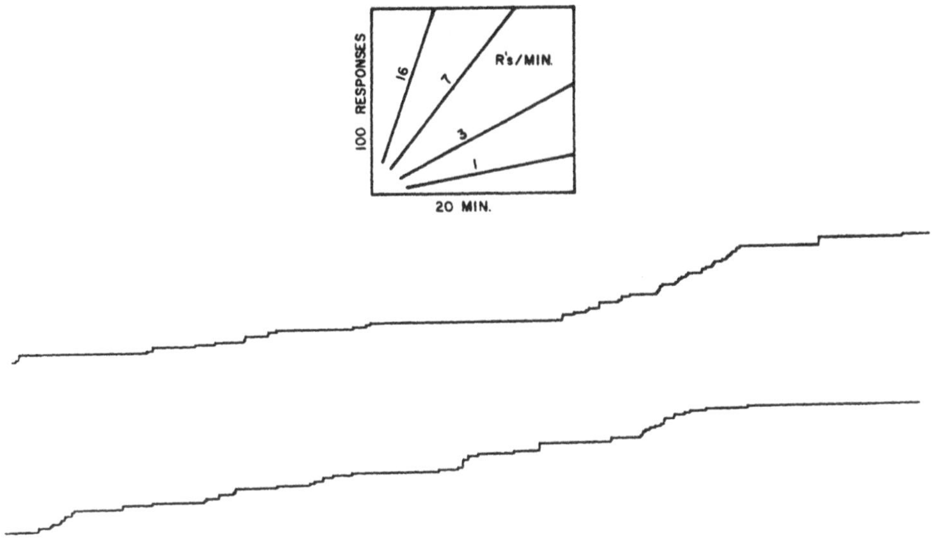

Figure 7.79. Representative Sample from a Day-Long Observation just prior to Moving Dan to Level II, Treatment Day 325

each five minutes in which we observed no noise. He was initially delighted with this program, and accepted the token and praise. Within two days, however, staff noted that he punctuated each receipt of the token and praise with a barking noise. Shortly, he was making the noises just before the staff tried to praise him. On a home visit at this time, he began making so many noises that his father, in frustration, isolated Dan in his room. He was rejecting tokens and praise from his parents. Another new development was that he now started using the noises to provoke his roommate at the Center. His roommate in particular, and other children, began, for the first time, to complain about his noises, and by plan the staff openly permitted this. Dan defended himself with the other children saying that he could not help making the noises, but staff refused to accept this excuse.

His attitude was suddenly very negative and he brushed off friends, staff, and parents alike. The noises were too near unbearable limits in the public school setting. Additionally his repertoire of head tics had increased. Figure 7.80 presents simultaneous observations of both the noises and head tics as they were occurring at this time. Obviously both were at intolerable levels.

We met again with Dan's parents and talked about the plan of moving him back to level 2. With disappointment, which we all shared, the parents agreed, and the father himself took command by telling Dan that he was moving him back to level 2 because he needed to work on the way he avoided people, and he had to learn to control the noises. With support from staff and the parents, Dan, for the first time since we had known him, broke down in his father's presence. He admitted his feeling of failure, hugged his father, and cried. It was an emotionally exhausting hour for staff and parents.

THE FINAL PROGRAM

We were back at level 2. Efforts to focus Dan's attention on the noises had twice caused his return to previous levels of deviant behaviors. His brush-offs of other people were deliberate, clear, and frequent. Expressions of anger were more direct, obvious, and verbal. He had had a few experiences of emotional closeness with staff and especially with his parents. He had experienced some remarkable successes in public school only to end up with the same sort of failure he had experienced before. His articulation was improved and his frequency of speech accelerated. In short, we had been stalemated and he was back at level 2. Had we gone as far as we would be able to go with Dan? Was this simply a temporary regression? Were we really correct in deciding that he could control the noises or were we unfairly asking him to do the impossible Was he simply expressing his anxiety about leaving the Center? Was he unwilling to return to his home and the complicated problems of living in a family? Were we back at the place where we had begun a year ago and where so many other professionals had left off? These many questions troubled each of us, the staff, Dan, and his parents.

In the midst of this speculation one thing was clear to this investigator. The "experimental" part of the experimental-clinical program was a flop. Chapter 1 of this book would surely have to be rewritten, and the case study that had shown so much promise would have to be junked. Dropping the clinical part was not so easy, for Dan's parents continued to express confidence that we could and would return their son to them, and the staff were not about to be brushed off by an eleven-year-old boy who barked like a dog. Thus, with feigned innocence, they turned to the investigator and asked what the new program would be.

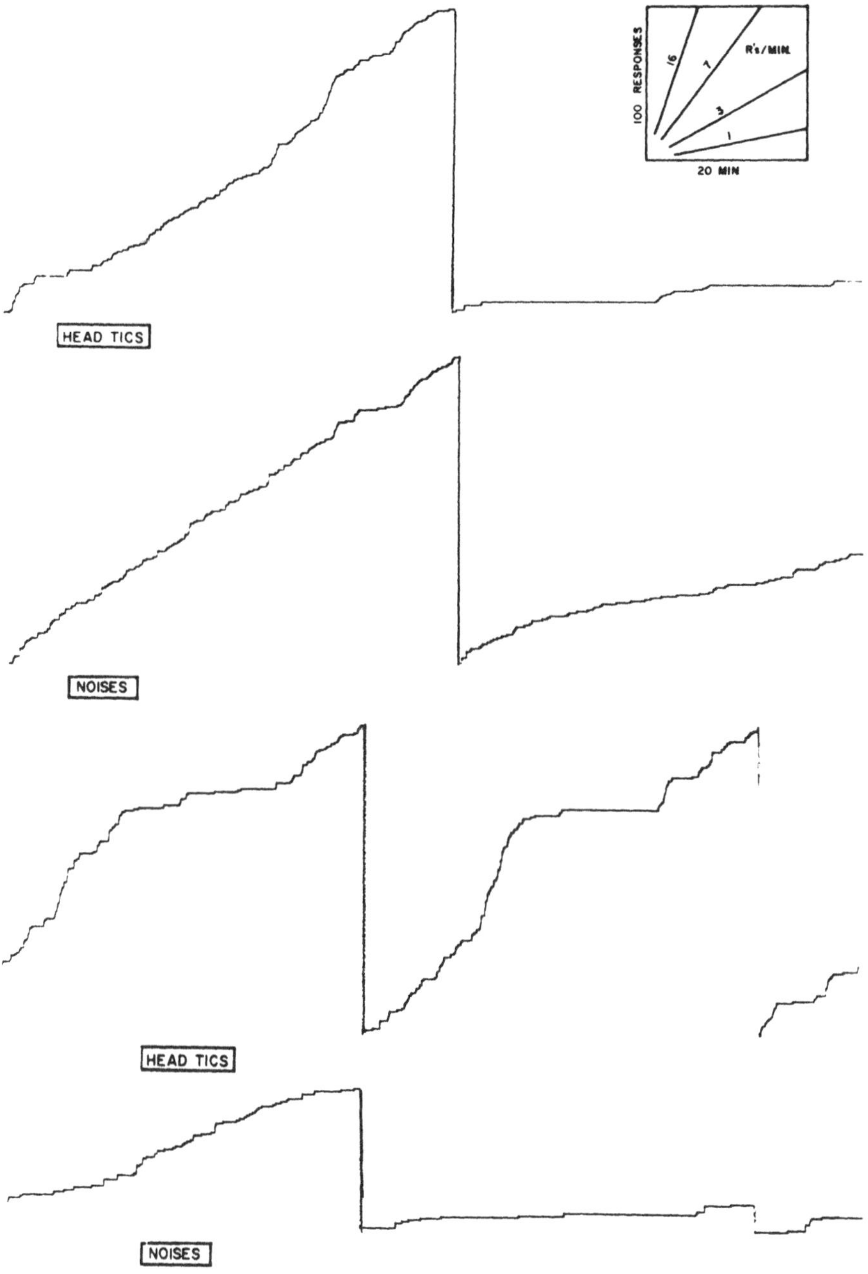

Figure 7.80. Representative samples of simultaneous observations of noises and head tics. These observations were taken several days after Dan was moved to Level II and the praise program was initiated. Treatment day 345.

We were unwilling to discount completely the findings of previous studies of the noise. At least to a degree it could be extinguished, and speech responses could at least partially replace it. Certainly, in broader perspective, the noises could be seen as one of the many ways Dan had of brushing off persons and avoiding the close relationships that seemed so frightening to him.

Our data indicated that Dan could go for fairly long periods without making any noises. This much was evident to everyone. The question was, could he deliberately control those periods in which he would make no noise? Consequently, we began a series of trials. First he was asked to go for a minute without making any noise. A stopwatch was used to time the trial. If he made a noise during the time, the watch was set over again and he was told, "You made a noise, we'll have to start over." If he made the time limit, he was praised, then another trial of a longer time was attempted. These trials were terminated only with success. Within two or three days we found we could get him up to 15- to 30-minute trials without barking. His parents begin immediately to use the stopwatch with him in the same manner as staff when they visited him at the Center. He was not making home visits at this time, since he was on level 2. His parents also were having success with Dan and, perhaps more importantly, were having success in working through with Dan their wish to help him with this major behavioral problem. For example, at first he resisted his father's effort to perform stopwatch trials with him, but when his father insisted that he not be "pushed away," but rather be allowed to help his son, Dan began to work hard at the trials.

This, then, became the basis of his new program. When we had finally succeeded in training Dan to succeed consistently in 15-minute trials on the watch, we proceeded to make the trials an integral part of the requirements for proceeding in the level system. In family therapy, the parents and staff presented to Dan the requirement that he succeed with five 15-minute periods of no noises in one day to make level 3. Before the day was over, he had accomplished this requirement and joyously called his parents on the telephone to tell them of his success. The next day the requirement for level 4 was presented to Dan. He must now make 10 15-minute trials for two days in a row to earn level 4. He failed in his trials for that day and the next morning with great discouragement told us that he could not possibly achieve level 4—"It's too hard." Consequently, we took a step backwards, told him he could have level 3½ if he made five 15-minute periods for two days in a row. The requirement for level 4 would be the same, and would be instituted as soon as he had earned level 3½. Taking it in smaller steps seemed easier to Dan, and he went back to work. In order to avoid his becoming resistant to starting trials when staff asked him to, staff told Dan that he had to come to staff and tell them when he wanted them to conduct the training trials. Within the minimum four days, he had earned level 4. Again, he happily called his parents to tell them of his accomplishment.

Table 7.11. Program for Elimination of Noises and Tics

Level	*Treatment Day Achieved*	*Requirement*
Level 3	367	1 day, five 15-minute trials
Level 3½	370	2 days, five 15-minute trials
Level 4	372	2 days, ten 15-minute trials
Level 4½	381	2 days, five 30-minute trials
Level 5	383	2 days, ten 30-minute trials
Level 6	388	5 days, ten 30-minute trials
Return to Level 5	389	(because he forged a signature)
Level 6	394	5 days, ten 30-minute trials
Level 7	402	8 days, eight 30-minute trials—school day/ten 30-minute trials—no school
Level 8	425	10 days, four 45-minute trials (Trials in school, home, & CTC)
Level 9	438	15 days, five 45-minute trials
Level 10	448	10 days, 10 trials per day (staff determine trial length and situation, e.g., "no noises during this game," etc.), about 4 to 5 hours per day
Level 10½	459	7 days, ten trials per day (no tics or noises)
Level 11	467	7 days, ten trials per day
Level 11½	failed to achieve	10 days, no noises or tics at all
Level 11¼	498	5 days, no noises or tics
Level 11½	508	10 days, no noises or tics
Level 12	521	no noises or tics

Dan's joy was small by comparison with that of his parents and the staff. At last it appeared that we had a program that might work. We only needed gradually to extend the time periods until he was making no noises. Table 7.11 lists the requirements that were designed for each level and the time in which he achieved the level. For much of his progress through this series of hurdles, he complained that the task was too hard. When he complained the task was usually made easier, but then he was allowed to earn only half a step to the next level. By the time he had reached level 4½, we began visits once again to his classroom at school, and he began to request us to allow him to begin school again. By the middle of November, when he was on level 5, he started school for short periods of time each day. His time in school was gradually expanded as it had been during his first try. By the eighth of January, when he was on level 9, he was in school full time. At level 10, the requirements were changed so that he was no longer told in advance a set length of time for each trial. Instead, staff determined when a trial would be held and the duration of the trial was determined by the situation. Thus, staff would tell him "You are to make no noises during this game," or, "No noises during supper tonight." On the average, his ten trials took a total of about four to five hours per day of no noise-making. When we reached the requirements for level 10½, he was allowed to make neither noises nor any body tics or facial grimaces. At this time, too, the staff began to emphasize the running of trials at times which had previously caused Dan to fail. In particular, he had had difficulty controlling the noises during active games, during his shower time, while doing homework, and when anxiously awaiting some event. Staff now required these times as trial times. By the sixth of February, speech and paying attention were at good levels and, by mutual agreement with Dan, we dropped his token program for these behaviors. He was pleased at no longer needing the tokens and saw this as a step in growing up and returning home. By this time, his home visits had increased to periods of four or more days at a time and better than half of his total time was spent at home or in school. Most of his trials were now being conducted by his mother. For level 11½, we set a major behavioral

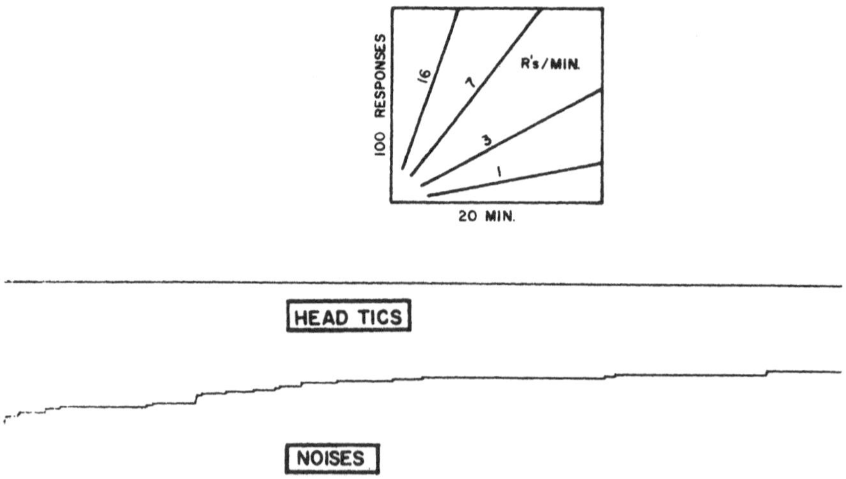

Figure 7.81. Representative Sample of Simultaneous Observations of Noises and Head Tics on Treatment Day 392

expectancy. He was told he would have to go ten days with neither noises nor tics being observed by anyone. He would have a card signed by his teacher to certify that he had made neither response at school, and his mother or any staff member working with him would also have to sign for each day. He said this was impossible and requested to work for level 11¼, which was then established as five days without noises or tics. With some difficulty he finally reached level 11½ on March 13. He now planned a farewell party and his formal discharge from CTC. We told him he was never again to make a noise or a tic. Carefully, over several interviews, Dr. Stover explained that if he makes one noise today, he is liable to make two tomorrow, five the next day, and shortly he would be back with the old severe habit. He accepted the warning without complaint and for the first

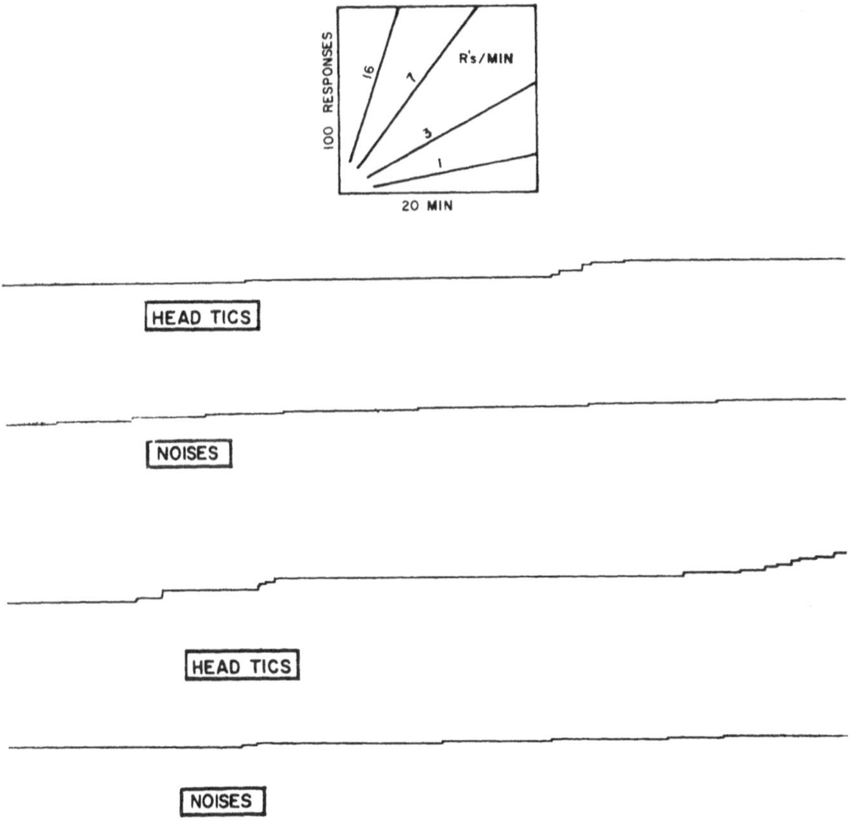

Figure 7.82. Representative Sample of Simultaneous Observations of Noises and Head Tics on Treatment Day 422

time, appeared totally motivated to handle this problem himself. Figures 7.81 through 7.86 present the cumulative recordings taken periodically on Dan throughout the time of his moving back up through the levels. Figure 7.86 represents the last observation we made on Dan. When the observation was complete, he joyously celebrated the fact that the observer would no longer follow him about with the remote counter. The next morning he

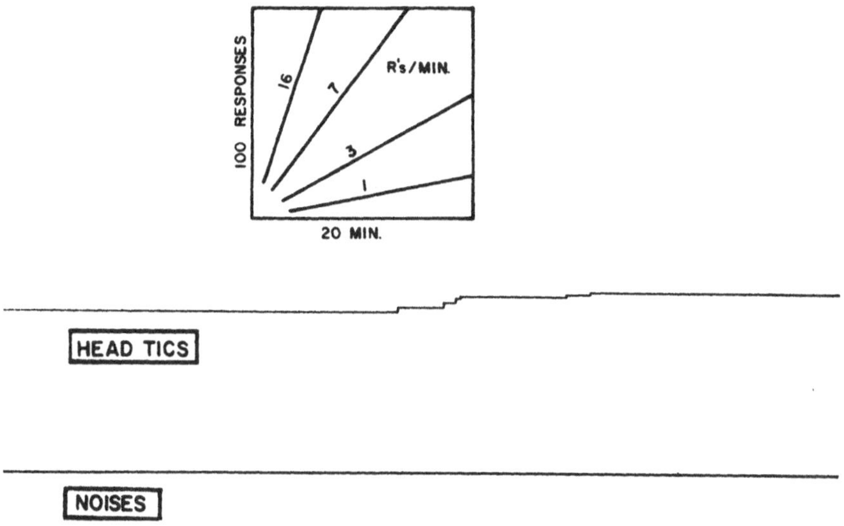

Figure 7.83. Representative Sample of Simultaneous Observations of Noises and Head Tics on Treatment Day 457

proudly came into the research office and called the investigator's attention to the cumulative recordings from the previous day. Dan's pride over those two straight lines compels us to print here the actual photographic reproduction of his tremendous accomplishment.

Dan and his family remained active in outpatient treatment on a weekly and subsequently biweekly basis for approximately five months. His mother continued to require him to have a card signed each day by his teacher to certify that he had made no noises or tics. For each complete day that he went without noises or tics, she rewarded him with 10¢. She established that for making noises he would be given the immediate punishment of spending the rest of the day in his room in pajamas. To our knowledge, he needed this punishment only two or three times during the next six months. Subsequently, he several times went back to making minor modifications of

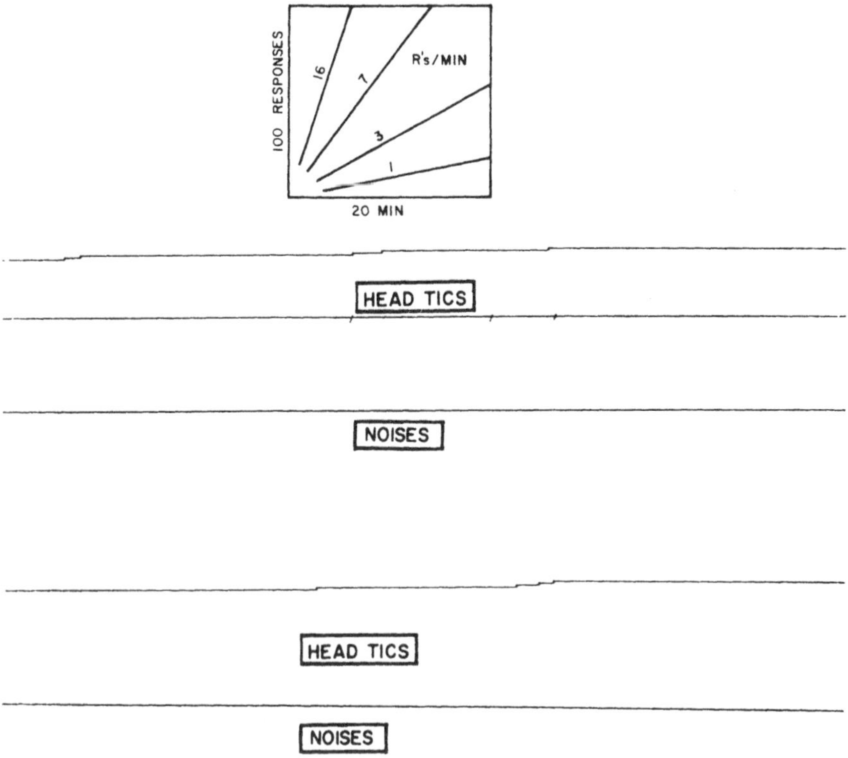

Figure 7.84. Representative Sample of Simultaneous Observations of Noises and Head Tics on Treatment Day 463

the noise, and his mother returned to time trials or to more carefully reinforcing him for each day without noises. At this writing, ten months after discharge, Dan remains in public school and is performing well. He is periodically a source of concern to his teacher and his mother when he slips back into some of the old behavior patterns. To date, the simple device of his mother's and his teacher's getting together occasionally with the collaboration of one of the Center staff has sufficed to remind everyone of the old programs and to improve Dan's behavior. No major exacerbation of the problems has occurred.

CONCLUSION

Several major aspects of Dan's treatment have been left almost totally undiscussed in this case study. One is the progress of treatment with the other member's of Dan's family. His siblings and parents were all in-

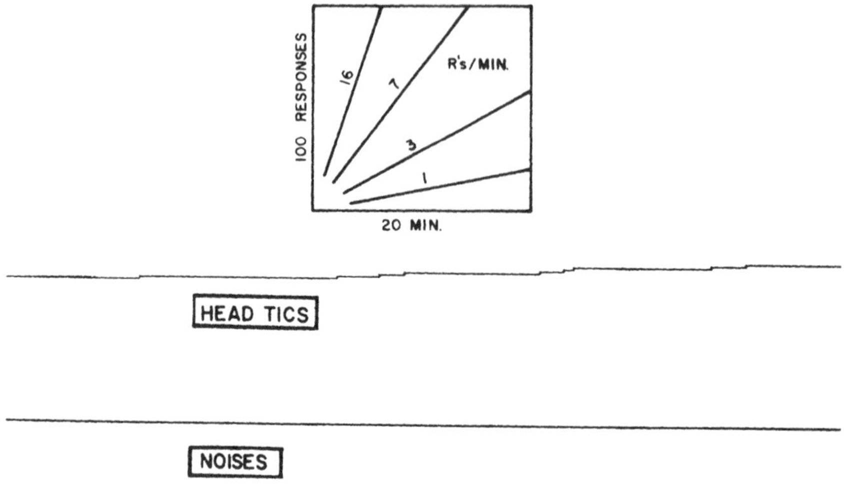

Figure 7.85. Representative Sample of Simultaneous Observations of Noises and Head Tics on Treatment Day 484

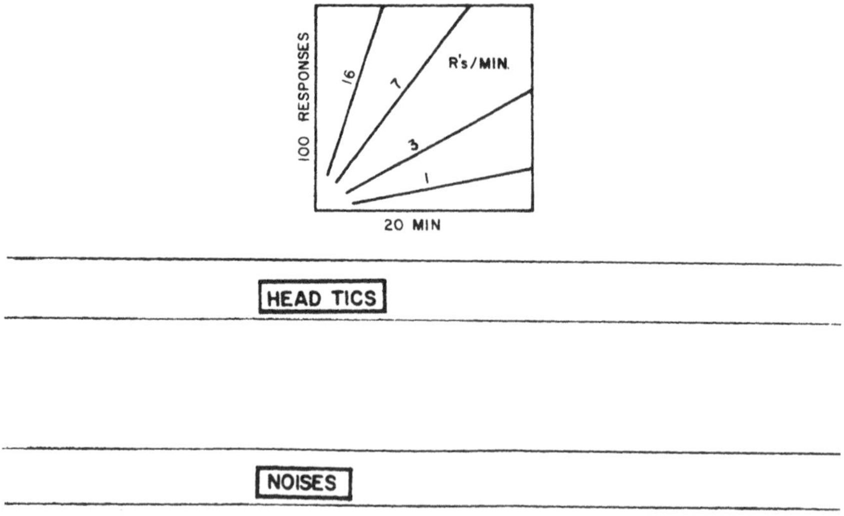

Figure 7.86. Representative Sample of Simultaneous Observations of Noises and Head Tics on Treatment Day 512

volved in a variety of treatment approaches. Family therapy (meeting with the research group social worker) was conducted on a weekly basis throughout treatment. In addition, his parents involved themselves in all aspects of Dan's program. They spent many hours at the Center contributing to the design of programs, learning management techniques from the staff, and carrying much of the daily treatment responsibility for their youngster. In addition, Dan's siblings were involved for many hours in a variety of activities at the Center as well as in direct discussion of family problems. Many of these aspects of the program have not been discussed because they were confidential. And for the sake of brevity, we have not discussed many behavioral problems which were dealt with by direct approaches. Some of these were under data collection most of the time, others were not subjected to data collection either because of neglect or because needs for data collection on other youngsters prohibited adding further counts.

Another aspect which to date defies our attempts at measurement but was a very real part of Dan's treatment was the investment of all of the staff members in this youngster and his family. They suffered many rebuffs and direct insults from Dan and experienced many moments of intense failure, but they continued to "hang in there" with the conviction that Dan could once again return to the mainstream of family and community living. The many ways in which they disciplined, trained, cared for, and moved emotionally close to Dan were as unique and as creative as the staff members themselves.

From the experimental-clinical point of view, this case raises many more questions than it answers. Were we correct in beginning with an extinction program or could the whole solution have been achieved much more quickly and readily with the immediate institution of punishment? Despite the initial data, can we ultimately conclude that the noise behavior was indeed a primitive sort of language substitute? Was the noise entirely governed by this youngster's learning history and environment, as originally hypothesized, or is an organic explanation necessary? Finally, one wonders if the ultimate program that succeeded in teaching Dan to control this behavior himself could not have been found much sooner.

CHAPTER EIGHT

Conclusion

Reflections

Many of the finer details crucial to the implementation of an experimental-clinical program have been omitted in the previous chapters. This chapter is a potpourri of our clinical experience, on topics ranging from ethical responsibility to technical errors commonly encountered in a behavior-therapy program. Our ideas are not supported by data, but some of them are obvious generalizations from laboratory research.

We selected the contents of this chapter on the basis of the questions which other professionals typically ask after we make case presentations. The contents may seem diversified to the extent of being unrelated, but we argue that all of these ideas must be considered, even acted upon, before one may administrate an experimental-clinical program.

NEGATIVE FINDINGS

For this discussion, negative findings are defined as indicating that a treatment hypothesis has failed, either by having no effects or by having treatment effects contrary to those expected. It is the recognition of the prevalence of negative findings in the traditional treatment approaches that has stimulated the development of experimental-clinical method. With traditional approaches, one cannot predict with any degree of assurance which behaviors will be treated. The burden of proof remains upon the clinician to demonstrate whether he has had any success with a patient. By using behavioral measures to monitor treatment effects constantly in conjunction with a same-subject experimental design, one is professing that he refuses to commit an unknown amount of error. In the more traditional treatment models, such as psychotherapy, play therapy, psychodrama, etc., practitioners have not assumed the burden of proof for demonstrating treatment effects and have accepted committing an unknown amount of error.

We do not intend to suggest that we now have the treatment model to treat emotionally disturbed children effectively. The cases presented in Chapter 7 do not represent spectacular treatment effects. As we have repeatedly stated, our purpose here is not to promote certain behavior modification techniques, but to propose a methodology for which we may approximate the goal of predictable and successful treatment. The cases which have been presented, and particularly the many studies which the investigators conducted that were failures, have led us to identify some of the conditions which are responsible for negative findings. Let us discuss some of the variables associated with negative as well as slow treatment effects.

The research which has been reported in this text does not deal with single-response, single-subject performance rate changes. The professional journals are filled with such studies, in which an investigator varied the rate of a previously acquired response with a reinforcement contingency. These are often single-response studies of a single subject. These studies demonstrate that one may, with social reinforcers or, in many instances with primary reinforcers, vary the rate of a behavior. It should be recognized that such studies have been the impetus of the behavior-modification movement. Our studies attack the problems of treating multiple responses, most of which involve the learning of an entirely new response. The complexity of a treatment study seems to increase geometrically as one deals with the acquisition or variance of several responses in conjunction with extinction or replacement of nonpreferred behaviors. When one is conducting a total treatment program in which numerous behaviors are treated at the same time, the suspected interactions among behaviors baffle comprehension. None of the studies reported in Chapter 7 even begins to deal with the problem of interactions among the habits treated. Of the same-subject designs operating concurrently in the case studies, we may frankly admit that we have little or no information on the interactions among programs responsible for facilitating or delimiting the various treatment programs.

Superficially, the same-subject designs used here lend more support to our hypothesis regarding what treatment conditions effected a positive result. The designs are not sensitive to identifying what conditions confounded a treatment effect or what was responsible for the failure of the treatment program. This is simply admitting that one does not systematically vary a confounding variable. Thus, negative results typically remain in the realm of hypothesis formation. Actually, one may state the converse, that even though positive results were obtained, the question still exists whether there was some concomitant confounding variable which occurred at the same time as presentation of a treatment variable and which was primarily responsible for the treatment effect.

Error of Assessing the Wrong Dependent Variable. A major variable responsible for negative findings in many of our studies has been that of monitoring the wrong response. In fact, the staff may be so well trained that they may reliably count the wrong behavior. The behavior to be treated may also be so ill defined that the staff are simply counting the wrong behaviors some of the time rather than all of the time. This sort of problem usually occurs when the consensus among the treatment staff is not good in defining the behavior which is to be treated. For example, we wished to monitor the cooperative behavior of a child. It was observed that this child handed objects to one of the other youngsters in the group. This handing of objects might have been reliably counted as a cooperative response. However, that behavior operated for an aggressive counter-response by the other child, who did not want to be offered anything by that one youngster and would always counter-aggress, suggesting that the first child was handing objects operantly to obtain aggressive behaviors from the other—which was not a desired cooperative social behavior. Thus, we would have been measuring the wrong response by counting "handing objects" as a cooperative behavior.

Video tape recordings help staff agree upon a particular behavior which is to be counted. Having staff sit down and conjointly observe a behavior on a video tape recording does facilitate group discussion on the establishment of a suitable definition of the behavior which is to be monitored. This is a time-consuming and therefore expensive procedure, but ideally should be used routinely.

The case of Gilles de La Tourette's Syndrome discussed in Chapter 6 illustrated an error of monitoring the wrong independent variable. In that particular case, an eye tic was being negatively rehearsed by the child. The investigator was monitoring frequency of tics and had fortunately made a tape recording of the sessions. Listening to the tape recording at a later time, we realized that not only was the investigator monitoring the dependent variable of the eye tic itself, which was presumably also the independent variable since it was the rehearsal of that response which was to lead to its eventual extinction, but also that the investigator was inadvertently carrying out expected positive social reinforcement concurrently with rehearsal of the tic response. We then suspected that a very unusual event was occurring. A behavior was being positively reinforced socially, yet it was extinguishing. The case study then progressed to an investigation of the effects of positive and punishing social reinforcers on the child.

The case did illustrate that the wrong independent variable was being monitored by the investigator.

It is very helpful to break behavior down to its simplest components when developing a treatment procedure. In our experience, when we made the error of counting the wrong dependent variable, we had usually decided upon too complex and loose a definition of the behavior. To illustrate, one youngster was clinically described as a passive-aggressive child. If the staff discussed their response to the child, they agreed that he was ostensibly innocuous, but that he invariably engendered aggressive responses in staff so that they began to administer verbal social punishment in various and subtle forms to the child. The staff found themselves avoiding the youngster and generally agreed that they disliked him. They could not identify exactly what aggressive maneuvers he had made to engender their counter-aggressive responses, and they all agreed that they could be inadvertently reinforcing the child's passive-aggressive behaviors, whatever they were, by their counter-aggressive moves. It certainly would have been erroneous for the staff to count their own reactions of aggressing toward the child as the dependent variable for a treatment condition for that youngster. If it had been established through a behavioral analysis that their counter-aggressive moves were inadvertently reinforcing the youngster's passive-aggressive behaviors, then they would have been counting the wrong dependent variable. Instead of counting the response which is to be treated in the child, they would have been counting the reinforcer maintaining the response in the child. Furthermore, the staff would have been committing the error of introspection if they had been counting their response to the child's behavior.

Video tape recordings were made of this passive-aggressive youngster and the investigators observed them repeatedly in an attempt to identify the behavior which we are calling passive-aggression so that it could be monitored or counted. The passive-aggressive behavior, of course, could be separated neither from the stimulus conditions nor from the reinforcement conditions which maintained that behavior. Under the classification of passive-aggression, we could identify the following measurable behaviors: long reaction time to a verbal question or demand from another person; answering questions directed toward him with a counter-question; saying very few words in a statement during a conversation, so that his statement was essentially unfinished and one had to ask again. These behaviors were such that one was constantly asking this child questions to which he would respond in a very slow and delimited fashion. One could measure these behaviors by seconds of reaction time, frequency of answering questions with questions, and number of words given in answer to questions. Thus, the behavior "passive aggression" had been analyzed in terms of those responses which were measurable and could serve as dependent variables to monitor a treatment condition. A video tape recording was invaluable for identifying those various behaviors. With that particular child, further study was conducted to identify exactly what were the reinforcement conditions for those responses.

Reinforcement or Punishment of the Wrong Response. Another error which we have repeatedly committed is that of reinforcing or punishing the wrong response. One may not only be measuring the wrong response but, in fact, treating the wrong behavior under the illusion that it was something else he was treating. Of course, this error would occur if one were monitoring the wrong behavior.

Typically, this problem is one of a confounded treatment procedure. A common example of this error is seen when staff provide counts of "one," "two," and "three" for a child to comply to a request. If the child does not do what he was requested to do before the count of three is completed, he will receive a time-out. Staff do not like to administer the time-out. The result of this reluctance is that the intervals between the successive counts of "one," "two," and "three" constantly increase. If the intervals increase enough, it is less likely that the child will be receiving the time-out. In fact, what usually occurs is that the youngster is learning to perform the request increasingly more slowly and noncooperatively. At this time, he actually has the staff on a treatment program of time-out from the aversive conditioning of administering a time-out to the child. The staff make the request of the child, and he with increasing lethargy does as he is requested before the count of three is completed, after which the staff give him positive social reinforcement for being compliant. The result is that staff have inadvertently reinforced the wrong kind of response.

In the example provided above, the staff had actually established a chain of behaviors in the child: the staff make a request of the child with which the child becomes increasingly noncompliant by being slow, which eventually operates so that he receives positive social reinforcement when he finally does provide the requested response. The staff were on a negative reinforcement schedule, since it was the termination of the noncompliant behavior that reinforced them for having increasingly long intervals between their counting. This all sums up the seldom-recognized fact that child and adult are both training each other concurrently. The confounding variables in this example are that the child was having the wrong response reinforced and that he was not only having qualitatively worse compliant behaviors reinforced, but other behaviors, such as walking slowly or answering slowly when the staff demanded a response, were being rewarded.

Inadvertent reinforcement of the wrong response is a problem which occurs very frequently in the Treatment Center without staff's knowledge. The immediate use of verbal reinforcers runs a high risk of such inadvertent error reinforcement. For example, in the training of speech we have frequently noted that staff reinforced the youngster who made a correct imitative verbal response. However, by the time the staff reinforced verbally, and perhaps with food, the child had looked the other way and the staff were therefore reinforcing or praising an inattentive response. This kind of error could be corrected by decreasing the latency of the reinforcement, which is of course crucial to the learning of any new responses.

Inadvertent punishment of the wrong response is a problem which plagues many parents as well as our staff. For example, in the parents' zeal to establish honesty in their child, they may accidentally punish that very behavior. To illustrate, suppose parents asked their child whether he had indeed stolen some money from another youngster. The child did confess to such a theft response, and his parents punished him for the theft response which had occurred at an earlier time. The parents may indeed have been successful in punishing the previous response because of optimal verbal mediation, such as Aronfreed has demonstrated is possible (1968). However, if the parents are dealing with a youngster who has a verbal deficit—or perhaps even with a normal child—it would appear that the parents were punishing the child for being verbally honest with them. If there is a deficit in verbal mediation of any sort, this restricts the generality of Aronfreed's findings to exclude children with such problems.

The Error of Extended Latency of Reinforcer. It has been well documented that the presentation of a reinforcement or punishment stimulus should be associated with or immediately follow the termination of a desired response. If the reinforcer does not follow immediately, an intervening response can be reinforced. If one wishes the reinforcer to be mediated back to the response which is to be reinforced, one must risk confounding that mediating variable. For example, if language is used to mediate a reinforcer back to some previously elicited response, problems in memory, previous associations of the mediating stimulus, etc., all may interact.

Thinning the Reinforcement Schedule Too Early. A primary goal of any treatment program is to approximate the environmental response expectations as well as the reinforcement schedules available in that environment for the maintenance of the acquired behavior. One wishes to approximate that normal environmental reinforcement schedule as quickly as possible. In the residential setting, one has the problem of thinning the reinforcement schedule prematurely. Usually this thinning of the schedule is not a function of the over-zealous efforts of the staff to approximate the environmental schedule available to the child at his date of discharge. It is more likely the result of the staff's learning to tolerate the low-level deviant behavior of the child, or being satisfied with a less than criterion response. When one is working with seriously disturbed children throughout the day, one must cease responding negatively to the behaviors barraging them from the children. One result of staff's learning to ignore behavior is that they may become increasingly tolerant of deviant behavior. Thus, if a punishment schedule for a particular response has been enacted, that response may decelerate significantly, but an approximation of the response may remain at a high rate because the staff will tolerate that since it is less obnoxious to them. We have no solutions for this kind of problem. One may periodically monitor the staff in their interactions with the children to ascertain if they are beginning to tolerate increasingly deviant responses. This is logistically difficult and also expensive, but it may be the only solution.

There are a variety of events in a residential treatment program that can contribute to an accumulation of negative results comparable to those listed above. When youngsters are first admitted, their behaviors may be sufficiently obnoxious that it is impossible for staff to maintain a 100% reinforcement schedule for positive responses; moreover, the preferred behaviors may occur so infrequently and so minimally as to be unobserved by the staff. The child may be so deviant in his behaviors that some staff will avoid close participation with him and thereby have fewer opportunities for reinforcing preferred behaviors. This preponderance of unacceptable behaviors and the paucity of preferred responses may contribute to retaining a response on a thin schedule immediately, thereby making it more difficult to acquire the response because of staff's inability to provide a heavy reinforcement schedule. It would be preferable to begin acquisition of a new behavior on a full reinforcement schedule and then gradually thin the schedule. The multiple and concurrent response training program recommended for children almost guarantees initially thin reinforcement schedules. The staff have so many management orders to fulfil simultaneously that they will fail to reinforce or punish many behaviors since they are simply too busy.

Balanced Programs. Another problem contributing to negative findings is that of an improperly balanced treatment program. A balanced program has management orders which are equally accelerating and decelerating behaviors. It would be an injustice for a youngster to be placed on a totally punishing program. One uses punishment to delete a response, and preferably to replace it with some other more appropriate behavior. Therefore, it is mandatory that the program have an alternate and preferred response to replace that which is being extinguished through punishment. A multitude of concurrent punishment or extinction programs may have the unfortunate effect of producing a responseless child. This is comparable to the kinds of programs which exist in many custodial institutions in which reinforcement is available only for the child who demonstrates the least behavior, and is thereby not annoying to the staff. We should always pursue the goal of teaching the child new behavior, for it is that goal for which the child was referred for treatment.

It is often difficult to provide a balanced program. When a child is admitted, the preponderance of deviant responses make it difficult for staff to reinforce the child's few desired responses positively. We have found it helpful to ignore the undesirable behaviors as much as possible, to reinforce the preferred behavior positively, and to demand compliant responses to verbal requests continually throughout the day. Thus, the child is being forced to make a choice of either complying or not complying, and the only available social reinforcement for him is for preferred and compliant responses. This is a difficult kind of program to maintain since, if the nonpreferred behavior is subjected to an extinction program, one can expect the child to operate frantically for the old, preferred reinforcers with his obnoxious behavior. This immediate acceleration of the deviant responses prior to an extinction effect may be sufficiently strong to elicit the child's preferred reinforcer from the staff and thus place that abnormal behavior on a thinner reinforcement schedule, thereby inadvertently making it more durable. There are no simple solutions to this problem other than providing considerable structure to the treatment program so that staff agree on the management orders and have definitive activities to use throughout the day.

Unclear Management Orders. The failure to clarify a management order, or treatment contingency, is often responsible for negative results. A breakdown in communication may be primarily responsible for staff's administering dissimilar treatment programs for the same response. We attempt to counter this problem by having the investigator's office on the ward where he may develop and maintain close communication with the staff and children. There is a weekly staff meeting at which programs for the youngsters are reviewed. As we have emphasized, staff all have equal standing in presenting their ideas in reviewing the treatment programs. Video tape recordings can be of assistance during the staff meetings. Experience in separating behavior to its simplest habits before establishing a management order is necessary. Also, it is desirable to have continual feedback from staff on the data on the effectiveness of the treatment management order. We often find that, while there may be a quantitative change in the response, there is also a qualitative change occurring concurrently. That qualitative change may be in the response itself, or in the emergence of a similar response used by the child to operate for the same available reinforcers in his environment. When such response generalization occurs, one may need to redesign the management order so that it is applied to the correct behavior or the emergence of the new one which may also need to be treated.

PERSONNEL

In Chapter 2 we have discussed the necessity of having personnel in the treatment program who have been trained to qualify for the job. The qualifications include the ability to reinforce spontaneously and effectively the correct behavior in the preferred manner, and to acquire new habit patterns of reinforcement. The staff members who are unable to set limits on the children or to perform a punishment or time-out program concurrently with reinforcement programs are likely to produce negative results. It takes an above-average staff member to conduct all the treatment programs as well as to count the behaviors simultaneously. It has been our experience that the creation of professional child-care workers in the mental health field would be of assistance to the formation of experimental-clinical treatment programs. The staff members in our research groups were college graduates, or college students, or registered nurses. That is, the staff members who collected data and performed the treatment procedures were not high-school graduates who had been unable to pursue their education any further because of either motivational or intellectual reasons. We could not expect that the untrained custodial attendant would be capable of conducting the experimental-clinical model of treatment. It simply takes a motivated and intelligent individual, compensated by an appropriate salary, to perform the duties of a child-care worker.

OVERSIMPLIFICATION OF REINFORCERS

A cursory examination of the literature suggests there is an oversimplified conceptualization of effective reinforcers. A myth seems to be perpetrated in the mental health field that, with a bag of candy and a prerecorded message of the word "good," one can effectively "stamp out emotional disturbance." This oversimplification is misleading and will certainly result in many disappointing treatment programs. This oversimplified concept of reinforcers, such as candies, tokens, and simple verbal statements, seems to be derived from short-term studies on single-response, single-subject performance rate changes. Such an oversimplified use of candy and tokens as reinforcers promotes treatment programs which are not designed to approximate the expected or available reinforcers in the patient's home environment. Such systems as tokens, candy, or food should be used on a limited-term basis. Such reinforcement contingencies are helpful to initiate behavior, but these reinforcers should be faded and replaced by the normal social reinforcement contingencies.

One cannot even presume that food will be an effective primary reinforcer with a youngster. We have had to train many of the young, psychotic children to eat, and even condition food to be an effective reinforcer. One should recall that adults will deprive, immolate, and destroy themselves for social reinforcers depending upon what their prior training had been. To be philosophical about it, men may work for primary reinforcers, but they will die for social reinforcers. We should emphasize that effective reinforcers are defined by being demonstrable as such. One may never presume that a stimulus condition will function as a reinforcer simply because it had such an effect in the past with other groups or an individual. The definition of a social reinforcer is empirical and idiosyncratic.

The Assumption of Commonality of Social Reinforcers. Perhaps the conceptualization of social reinforcers as having common value has been perpetrated by the group studies employing college students as subjects. We refer to those studies in which a specific presumed social reinforcer is presented to study its effectiveness and perhaps the rate of acquisition of a response. Social reinforcers are acquired secondarily to primary reinforcers, according to the learning-theory models assumed in this text. A rudimentary knowledge of social psychology could lead one to expect that some commonality exists among social reinforcers. It is the absence of this commonality that has resulted in that phenomenon described in our case studies that we have termed reversed polarity of expected social reinforcers. We suggest that it is the absence of commonality of social reinforcers that contributes greatly to emotional disturbance.

There is variance within those social stimuli which we assume to have cultural commonality as reinforcers. We recommend that one identify the social reinforcers maintaining inappropriate behaviors in a youngster. If those reinforcers are atypical, a conditioning program may have to be implemented so that the child's effective reinforcers are not too divergent from the more socially appropriate ones. One can probably expect individual differences in respect to expected social reinforcers. We can expect that some staff will be more effective than others for certain children, and that this may co-vary with different responses and contingencies.

In teaching a child new behavior, one should attempt to deal with the total habit. Historically, a therapist has been concerned only with responses. In the traditional psychotherapeutic approaches, the therapist may be interested in hypothesized stimulus conditions which presumably were of importance at one time in the youngster's life. In our studies contained herein, which place emphasis upon the family, we are beginning to deal with the stimulus conditions maintaining habits. We should emphasize that, while one is dealing with the stimulus and response of a habit, the reinforcers should be allocated as much attention. A behavioral analysis is helpful in identifying reinforcers which are differentially effective for a youngster.

THE MYTH OF GENERALIZATION EFFECTS

Studies on the long-term effects of psychotherapy often tested for generalization of treatment effects in terms of habit recidivism, i.e., extinction of treatment effects. This seems to be an erroneous method of assessing the effects of psychotherapy, particularly insofar as the technique did not address itself to the kind of behaviors which were being assessed for generalization effects. The more traditional clinicians have criticized behavior modification for failing to deal with the "total person." The implication of the traditional clinicians' comment is that they are, in fact, themselves treating the "total person." Unfortunately, the literature fails to provide evidence to justify that. The traditionalists have criticized behavior therapists for changing one habit but leaving the remainder of the numerous habits of the person untreated. No one can doubt the validity of that accusation. The current stage of research in behavior modification has not progressed far beyond the single-response study. There is no treatment panacea yet.

However, with the accumulation of firm data, one may be able to assess the relative effectiveness of a treatment procedure, and to proceed from single to multiple behaviors in a scientific manner. In evaluating such research as it accumulates, one must be careful not to commit the error of assessing the programs by making a test for generalization of treatment effects as the only dependent variable.

Generalization of treatment effects means that the trained response will be elicited by similar stimuli in an environmental setting different from that which was involved during the original learning. It is questionable whether it would be valid to test how effective one's treatment program was by assuming that the stimulus characteristics of the treatment environment are comparable to those in the natural setting. If one uses this model of assessing the effectiveness of their treatment program, i.e., testing for generalization effects, one is presuming that there is commonality between the stimuli or home environment to which the child was discharged and those involved in the training setting at the treatment facility. This, of course, involves considerable clinical judgment, and is likely to be an unwarranted assumption.

On the other hand, we have been using clinical judgment in presuming that there is very little commonality between the stimulus characteristics of the treatment environment in the residential setting and those stimulus conditions in the child's home environment to which he will eventually be discharged. There is so much difference between these settings that we feel that one should not test for the effectiveness of treatment by assessing generalization effects, but rather should establish a program which constantly assures that what is learned in one setting will in fact be elicited in another setting. There seems to be an implicit assumption in the traditional model of assessing the value of the treatment for a program by generalization that one will "get something for nothing." That is, there is the assumption that what is learned in a treatment setting will generalize back to an environmental setting, when nothing has been done to assure or ascertain whether the stimuli in the two environments are comparable. If the stimulus characteristics are not comparable, one can expect minimal generalization of effect. There is reason, then, to train the desired responses in the natural home environment at some point in the child's treatment program. It is also mandatory that the parents be trained in performing the programs as effectively as staff can train them. Thus, when the child is discharged, his parents will be able to maintain the programs or to devise new ones when inappropriate behaviors emerge. For example, after an autistic child was admitted, his parents were scheduled biweekly to learn the treatment programs we had devised during the year. One of the autistic behaviors was that of smelling and licking objects. We never treated that response specifically; it decelerated without our establishing a program for it. When the child went on his first home visit one year after his admission, it was observed that the habit of smelling and licking objects appeared and accelerated. His parents were trained in identifying such abnormal behaviors and controlling such responses with their youngster, and were able to extinguish the behavior in the home setting. The response apparently was re-elicited by the home environment, and without successful intervention would have been retrieved at the pre-treatment level.

In considering the generalization of treatment effects, we must remember that the youngster has had more years of rehearsing the abnormal responses amidst all the stimulus conditions in the home environment than he has had for acquiring the pro-social behaviors in the treatment setting. If one has not made sure that the pro-social behaviors are rehearsed among those stimulus characteristics of the environment which previously elicited the deviant behaviors, it is predictable that the abnormal behaviors will be reinstated exactly or to some approximation of their original strength. Perhaps this discussion again supports the hypothesis that in a treatment program, one does not study only the response of the deviant habit pattern, but the stimulus as well as the reinforcement conditions for that behavior.

We suspect, but have not demonstrated with any degree of assurance, that with acquisition of pro-social behavior the child is rendered amenable to receiving more positive reinforcement for more appropriate responses.

With the child's now being capable of responding and likely to receive positive reinforcement from his environment, the probability increases that persons other than those in the treatment team will be teaching him new pro-social responses. In agreement with this hypothesis is our experience that, as a treatment program progresses successfully, the child's behavior becomes increasingly less controlled by the treatment conditions. We have observed that, as the psychotic child acquires speech and begins to communicate while concurrently acquiring pro-social compliant responses, he begins to "blossom." This acquisition of complex behaviors independently of the treatment program is desirable, but also weakens any evidence of experimental control. We have noticed that, as the children acquire speech, they also become immersed in a more complex environment by the nature of that newly acquired response mode. They begin to attend school, to have more home visits, and to initiate more complex social interactions with other children. The speaking child can "operate" more successfully in his environment, and begins to acquire numerous habits independently of those which we are specifically trying to teach. It would be erroneous to identify this phenomenon as "generalization effects," since one would not be able to demonstrate this specifically.

Recidivism in the treatment of emotionally disturbed children may indicate two deficits in the treatment program. First, the treatment program may have failed to teach the child the correct social responses which would assure successful reentry into the home environment. Second, the program may not have been devised to guarantee the transfer of training effects from the residential setting to the home environment. When a previously discharged child is returned to a treatment setting, these two hypotheses may be entertained by the clinician in an effort to teach the correct responses and to establish a program in which the responses will be more effectively reinforced in the home environment.

FAILURE TO MAINTAIN LONG-TERM EFFECTS

Behavior therapists have yet to present substantial evidence on the long-term effects of their programs. However, as mentioned in the discussion on generalization, long-term effects may not be the cogent variable for assessment of a treatment program. Program assessment should be the demonstration of what variables were responsible for the acquisition or deletion of responses. Monitoring of long-term effects should not be discarded, because if the treatment effects deteriorate then this is evidence that the program should be "backed-up" to reinstate the preferred responses. Parents should be trained to identify the emergence of abnormal habit patterns which are the same or comparable to those which initiated their child's original referral, so that they can deal with the problem with a minimum of supervision. It would be presumptive to imply that long-term effects are the criterion for assessment of the treatment program. Such a presumption would imply that one is able to control the child's entire environmental conditions which have their respective effects on the child's social growth. One cannot presume that the child's behavior would remain static after discharge. The child should be accumulating new and more complex responses, and, one hopes, not reacquiring those responses which led to his original referral. A treatment program should be assessed by the extent to which it teaches the behavior which makes the child able to thrive in the stimulus and reinforcement contingencies available in his home environment.

Assessment of long-term effects is a complex task, since it requires studying all of the training conditions available to the child after he has been discharged. A more realistic approach would be evaluating parents' ability to reinstate treatment programs at home whenever deterioration of treatment effects occurs.

DIAGNOSTIC CLASSIFICATIONS IN THE EXPERIMENTAL-CLINICAL APPROACH

Diagnostic classifications have been deemphasized in the case studies we have presented. Only broad diagnostic nomenclature has been used to identify the youngsters. Even with psychotic children, it is questionable whether subcategories are of value. We shall now focus on the rationale for deemphasizing the diagnostic status of the children we have described.

Diagnostic classifications are useful only to the extent to which they benefit the patient. Diagnostic classifications are of little value when they are simply a means for providing employment for the professional. Of course, a diagnostic evaluation may be vital to parents in providing them with realistic expectations of their children, as in the interpretation of mental retardation. Diagnostic nomenclature is heuristic when it designates a treatment program. For example, diagnostic identification of Hurler's Syndrome, which is becoming increasingly rare, will indicate procedures for arresting the progress of the disease. PKU is another example of diagnosis' being coordinated with a treatment program to arrest a progressive deteriorative process. Diagnostic nomenclature is of value when it is used to prevent familial reoccurrence of a disease, such as Huntington's chorea, tuberose schlerosis, and sickle-cell anemia. Diagnostic nomenclature can also be useful when it provides homogeneous grouping of children for certain treatment programs. The most obvious example of this is the establishment of special education classes, on the basis of certain intellectual capabilities of the children, that would provide more expedient classroom training programs.

Classification is a first step in science. However, science is not restricted to simply collecting, classifying, and concluding. Perhaps there are times when a classification science is justifiable, but this is not sufficient for the treatment of emotionally disturbed children.

Epidemological studies are the next step beyond simple diagnostic classification. It may be that the future of mental retardation rests with the development of epidemological studies. Such studies allow one to classify a particular disorder by those conditions which made the classification of the disorder possible. The epidemological study identifies the necessary and sufficient conditions for the presence of the disorder which has been classified. The disorder is not classified simply by symptomatic evidence, but by conditions which made the symptoms present. The epidemological approach fosters the development of methods of controlling those conditions. This approach to diagnostic classification is relevant to the research on treatment procedures for behavioral disorders.

Making a diagnostic classification on the basis of few variables is unwarranted for another reason. Such classifications usually presume commonality of numerous behaviors suspected to be invariably related to those responses which resulted in the child's being placed in a certain classification. This error of being overinclusive ignores the response variability which makes an individual unique. Overinclusive diagnostic nomenclature supports "institutional" care where large numbers of children are grouped and treated the same.

The error of over-generalizing from a diagnostic classification and presuming commonality of all other behaviors in the child is unwarranted for a treatment program, since it restricts the variability of expectations which will be placed on the youngster. Such overinclusive approaches promote program constriction, since the presumption is that all children should be treated exactly the same because their problems are comparable.

We suggest that emphasis upon diagnostic classification may result in clinic irresponsibility. There is a phenomenon which we call the "clinic shuffle," in which the parents "shuffle" their child from one clinic to another because the various diagnoses by each successive clinic are of a kind which they are unprepared to treat. Examples of such youngsters are those identified as autistic with concomitant diagnoses of mental retardation and brain injury. The clinics do not know what to do with the youngster and refer him elsewhere for further diagnoses. In such instances the diagnostic classification has become the end product of the clinic, and this is not beneficial nor conducive to the growth of the child. Broad diagnostic classifications are seldom encouraging to parents.

For these reasons, the cases presented in Chapter 7 were given only cursory diagnoses. As may be gathered from the text, it seems more relevant to classify the child against himself. Rather than commit the error of presuming commonality of children within a diagnostic classification who had been categorized by only a few characteristics, each child is approached uniquely. The diagnostic classification is the description of the child's current behaviors. As the child acquires more complex behaviors, these may be compared to those which initiated his referral. Simply, the diagnostic classification of the child should be the baseline behaviors he has prior to treatment against which he will be compared as treatment progresses. As each successive response is acquired it becomes a baseline against which accumulation of new behaviors may be compared.

Our diagnostic suggestion is for idiosyncratic classifications of the child. Such a descriptive approach does promote formulation of treatment programs. Since the response and reinforcement conditions are unique to each child's learning history, it would not be justifiable to presume commonality of treatment programs for all youngsters. It therefore seems worthwhile and legitimate to describe each child according to his own unique response repertoire.

SYMPTOM SUBSTITUTION

From Freud's hydraulic model of symptoms, one may conclude that if one deviant response is deleted a comparable one will emerge to replace it. According to the analytic interpretation, the emergence of that symptom will not be determined by external events, but by internal events within the patient. Persons who have dealt with the extinction of tics by using behavior therapy approaches have reported that they have not observed symptom substitution of tics. Their reports may be questionable. For example, the question emerges whether the patients were monitored constantly for emergence of new behaviors comparable to the tic which was extinguished. Also, it is suspected that the investigators who have been most successful in extinguishing tics were treating self-referral patients; perhaps the tic for the self-referred patient has an already acquired punishing effect, as manifested by his seeking treatment. Considering the possibility that tics are maintained in part, or entirely, by social reinforcers, we wonder whether these tics would not have extinguished whether or not treatment were used on the behavior. Furthermore, studies of tics are seldom subjected to a stringent behavioral analysis, so the reader is usually unaware of what conditions may have been maintaining and reinforcing the response.

We have observed, particularly in several cases in Chapter 7, that as one deviant response is extinguished, a low-level approximation of that behavior emerges. These cases are not self-referred patients. We suspect that these children are continuing to operate for the same social reinforcers which were maintaining the originally treated behaviors, but with a response which approximates that which is currently under punishment or extinction. In other words, the child is using an approximation of the response which previously received reinforcement. This is really not a very profound observation. It has been repeatedly demonstrated in the case studies that as an aggressive response is extinguished, there is an emergence of an increasing frequency of what we have described "low-level aggressive responses," which in turn must be extinguished. Perhaps this qualitative response alteration is what the analysts have been describing as symptom substitution. Rather than accepting the analytic construct of symptom substitution, we suspect that a response hierarchy, maintained by external environmental conditions, continues to operate for the social reinforcers previously available in the social environment. We contend that these response approximations must all be treated. Although we have not tested this hypothesis as yet, we believe that if one permits a low-level approximation of an earlier punished response to remain in the repertoire, this will increase the likelihood of the child's retrieving the old habit pattern at a later date. For this reason, we suggest that the entire response hierarchy be deleted from the response repertoire. Such a treatment program would be the converse of shaping behavior. That is, if one wishes to approximate a certain desired behavioral goal, one must train a gradual hierarchy of behaviors, and if one wishes to extinguish a response, one should control the entire response hierarchy.

ACCELERATION OF ABNORMAL BEHAVIORS AS A PREREQUISITE TO EXTINCTION

There seems to be a myth that a child has to become "worse" before he improves. The observation that a child will demonstrate an exacerbation of abnormal behavior before he will improve is based upon clinical impressions. However, the concept should not be dismissed as untenable. Some of the case study data which have accumulated in this book suggest that the responses which are being extinguished often temporarily accelerate prior to their deceleration. If one did not persist with the treatment program beyond that initial acceleration interval, there would be no treatment effect. In fact, if one closely monitored the data, and were too reactive to that initial acceleration, one might cease what could have been a very effective program. Such an acceleration would suggest that the child indeed does become worse before he improves.

It is not unreasonable to suspect that the termination of a preferred reinforcer for a given response, whether or not that is an abnormal social behavior, may stimulate the child's frantic rehearsal of the response in an effort to regain the preferred reinforcer. This is demonstrable in the temporary acceleration of a behavior subjected to extinction or punishment. It is not surprising that a child may test his environment very strongly for the availability of a preferred reinforcer when that reinforcer has been suddenly removed.

We have no firm data, only the hypothesis that this phenomenon often occurs. Quite often we have been measuring the wrong kind of behavior to demonstrate this phenomenon. For example, the frequency of temper tantrums is often measured. The duration of the temper tantrum may actually spike very highly during the initial stages of the treatment program, although the frequency of the response may be declining. Actually, the child may be having a tantrum almost the entire day in his attempt to retrieve the preferred reinforcer, even though that reinforcer was no longer available while he was receiving a time-out. In such an instance, as we have repeatedly seen but unfortunately not measured, the child will show a deceleration in frequency of behavior, although the duration of the separate tantrums increased dramatically, although temporarily.

Cost of the Experimental-Clinical Method

The high cost of the experimental-clinical method cannot be denied. A cursory examination of behavior-modification studies leads one to think that a modicum of staff time is required for successful outcomes. However, these studies are usually single-subject, single-response performance studies rather than total programming procedures. The procedures described in this book are expensive because of the high ratio of staff to children. Also, the constant accumulation of data keeps the clinician well informed of the efficacy of the treatment procedure, and this is likely to discourage early discharge. The result is an increased duration of residency so that the children achieve optimal treatment effects, and this, of course, makes for greater expense.

PROMOTION OF MECHANISTIC CHILD-REARING PRACTICES

The question is often raised whether the experimental-clinical method will promote unusually mechanistic child-rearing practices. It has been our experience that, at the beginning of a parent-training program, parents do administer the techniques in a rather perfunctory manner. Their social reinforcements sound like a prerecorded tape echoing a staccato of praise statements. Some parents never seem to acquire the reinforcement skills, however rudimentary they may be, but remain at a concrete level of training the children. We have often observed that some parents may reinforce at a very high rate, and in an acceptable manner, while staff are present, but with very little generalization of the technique beyond the supervision of staff. In the more successful cases, it appears that the parents become more habitual in their reinforcement.

We recognize that total parental cooperation with programs such as those presented here does foster a restriction of child-rearing practices. This restriction is engendered by the research which is delimited to the few responses which are concurrently being studied in each child. The parents employ the same management orders as staff. Such a restriction on the kinds of behaviors being trained at a given time may stifle the resourcefulness of the parents. This problem of restriction of child-rearing practices available to the parents may be improved upon with a greater repertoire of techniques that they may use in the future.

Parental Misuse of Experimental-Clinical Techniques. The experimental-clinical method has not been popularized to the extent of being widely misused. However, behavior-therapy techniques have reportedly been used to the child's social disadvantage by some parents. For example, the parent may positively reinforce the child for socially aggressive behaviors, which may be vicariously reinforcing to the parent but socially disadvantageous to the child. The parents may be very successful in teaching this aggressive behavior as a result of their experience with the behavior-modification program.

We have not monitored for this kind of problem in the training program. The occurrences of such problems have not been reported in the group, although they have been clinically reported to us by other investigators. In fact, one can predict that it will not be long before children will be brought to clinics who have been abused with cattle prods, extended time-outs, etc., all of which contributed to training extremely disturbed behavior.

Perhaps the abuse of treatment procedures by parents should be anticipated by the clinician. When a disturbed child is trained in socially appropriate behaviors, that training should also include the family group which originally trained those behaviors. The clinician must direct himself to the total family; the child may not be treated independently of that group. If a child were treated independently of the other family members, when he is returned home the family could reinstate the previously acquired responses. We suspect that it is more the exception than the rule for parents to receive vicarious reinforcement from their child's abnormal behaviors. Characteristically, the parents seem to be naïve about how they were inadvertently reinforcing their child's inappropriate behaviors.

Ethical Considerations

The following discussion of ethical standards is directed at the experimental-clinical method as well as to operant conditioning procedures as they are used in other studies. We shall discuss ethical standards recommended for the experimental clinician and also the ethical justification for using this treatment approach. Criticisms have been directed at the use of operant conditioning techniques (Lucero *et al.,* 1968) and some of our discussion is in response to those criticisms. Cahoon (1968), Bragg and Wagner (1968), Ball (1968), and Miron (1968) present rejoinders to Lucero, Vail, and Scherber's criticisms of operant conditioning techniques. Some of these rejoinders are incorporated in our discussion of ethical practices.

Combining an experimental model with clinical responsibility not only requires that greater ethical standards be observed toward the patient, but also helps assure the maintenance of those ethical standards. In a clinical treatment program, the patient, or his parents, assume the therapist's ethics provide that the clinical treatments employed have been substantiated by research as the most effective procedures currently available in the field and that the therapist has assumed the responsibility of being trained in their administration. It is the patient's presumption that he is receiving the optimal treatment available, that the therapist is knowledgeable of the latest developments in the field, and that he is aware of any injurious effects which may result from the treatment procedures he is employing with the patient. The experimental-clinical model fosters a research approach by the clinician in which the data resulting from ongoing treatment are more likely to keep the clinician informed of the other investigators in the field.

The experimental-clinical method places an ethical check on the investigator, in that treatment of the patient requires constant monitoring of behavioral change, hypothesis formation, and some degree of experimental design to inform the therapist whether his predictions were correct. The method puts an awesome responsibility upon the clinician in that he holds himself accountable for having public evidence of how successful his treatment techniques have been with the patient. Traditional treatment models seldom are so ethical as to assume the responsibility of informing the patient or his parents exactly how successful the treatment procedure is or is not. Adoption of the experimental-clinical model encourages ethical practice because the investigator assumes the responsibility for treatment effects as well as failures. Assumption of such responsibility is not difficult when one takes pride in knowledge and is not committed to defending a theory or a treatment approach.

Ethical problems arise when one conducts experiments in a clinical setting. However, the experimental-clinical method does not use the patient as a subject in laboratory experiment, but rather uses a research approach to develop ways of benefiting the patient. This goal is in contrast with the use of college students to participate in experiments whose results are not directly beneficial to those students.

The experimental clinician is confronted with an ethical decision when he decides which behaviors should be deleted and which should be acquired in a child's behavior repertoire. These decisions are problematic because there is no standardized text which outlines appropriate age-level behaviors for youngsters across different social-economic groups. A diversity of child development studies provide some evidence of characteristic responses, but these studies are so scattered throughout the literature, and there is such a change of cultural values across time, that they are of little value when one is making these treatment decisions. It would be a major research endeavor, involving a combination of many scientists, to acquire actual ongoing normative behavioral data. Unfortunately, the experimental clinician must rely upon his own subjective judgment in deciding upon behavioral changes in the child. It is our recommendation that the parents assist in defining the behavioral choices for their child.

We do not have the degree of behavioral control described in Orwell's *1984*. Some farsighted individuals, perhaps responding to a simplified equation between Pavlov's dog and man, have voiced fear that man is capable of exerting the massive psychological control described in *1984*. The danger of such a state is conceivable, its most frightening possibility is that such overcontrol reduces behavioral variability. Since it is those investigators who use operant conditioning techniques who will most quickly approximate such behavioral control, it is important that ethical standards regarding the use of such techniques be adopted. We are not currently confronted with a problem of behavioral overcontrol. The fear of such success exists for all of us in the future and should be resolved before that time when the politician and grade-school teacher are as informed as the psychologist in advanced techniques of behavioral control. It is possible that the fruits of operant conditioning may spawn the most hardy seeds of political dictatorship.

If the therapist is not involved in every aspect of the patient's daily program, cannot clearly justify the effectiveness of that program, and has delegated clinical responsibility, however inadvertently, to untrained ward personnel, he cannot presume to have knowledge of that treatment environment which he considers to be therapeutic. Miron (1968) states that he has repeatedly accumulated evidence demonstrating that untrained ward staff inadvertently maintain the bizarre and referral behaviors of the patients in the typical state hospital setting. The inadvertent maintenance of a child's abnormal behavior by his parents is often the reason why the child was referred for treatment. Parents are not considered unethical for making these errors; but the therapist who assumes clinical responsibility for the patient and allows untrained persons to compound the errors of the child's training environment would be unethical.

The use of punishment techniques is serious. Such techniques should be well planned, supervised, and measured, and the suppressed behavior should be monitored to ascertain whether the treatment effects have inadvertently generalized to the disadvantage of the patient. Punishment techniques are effective, as evidenced by Lovaas' (1966) studies of using shock to condition autistic children. In some instances it would be unethical not to use punishment procedures when it has been well documented that they are effective and may even save the life of the patient. There are ethical and legal points which should be considered before employing a punishment condition such as electric shock. We contend that a treatment program involving electric shock should be used only as a last resort when all other available techniques have failed. It should be recognized that a strong aversive behavioral suppressant may easily and inadvertently countercondition other desired social reinforcers or responses and thereby accidentally decelerate some other preferred responses.

Parents encounter an ethical conflict when they must decide to agree to the use of shock for their youngster when all other treatment procedures have failed. It has been our experience that the parents of autistic or schizophrenic children were at their last resort of treatment and had only the choice of institutionalizing their child in a colony for the retarded if our research program failed. In such instances, the parents simply do not have a choice; they are willing to comply with almost any technique, whether or not it is experimental. In the case studies we presented in this book, shock was used with two children, since we considered the procedure absolutely necessary and the last resort. After parental permission had been obtained for the procedure, it became obvious that the parents had simply had no choice—which certainly reflects the status of a field which is delimited in the variety of available treatment techniques. The parents were informed of the literature on the use of the procedure, the faradic apparatus was demonstrated to them, and they were required to use it upon themselves. Video tape recordings were taken during the initial training sessions and then shown to the parents. The parents were continually informed of the data on the responses which were punished, and the data were made public, as evidenced in this text. The crucial point is that when one assumes the responsibility of deciding that a punishment procedure is necessary, he must demonstrate whether it was of value to the patient and assure that the effects of the program remain public.

The use of punishment in a treatment program is dangerous. The effects may be spectacular, in fact, they may easily dominate a program so that a child is seen entirely in a negative view. We have discussed this kind of problem in the chapter on measurement, where we indicated that, in counting behavior, one should not overemphasize counting the abnormal responses of a child. The child should have a balanced daily count between appropriate and undesirable responses. The use of punishment should be deemphasized in any program; the use of positive reinforcement to teach behavior should be the primary focus of a treatment program. It is the responsibility of the clinician not only to decelerate the abnormal behaviors that a youngster demonstrates, but, at the same time, to teach the child appropriate social responses so that he may reenter his community as a participant on an equal level with his peers. Teaching these new behaviors requires positive reinforcement to accelerate existing as well as new behaviors, and the reinforcers should be compatible to those which will be available to the child in his home environment.

Some investigators criticize the use of operant conditioning programs because they seem unnatural. The only reply which seems reasonable to that criticism is that operant conditioning techniques employ the principles of learning which have been identified as responsible for the acquisition of normal as well as abnormal behavior. It seems reasonable, then, to use learning procedures to teach new behavior. It seems unreasonable to presume that the emotionally disturbed individual is one who acquires behavior according to principles other than learning. It is recognized that many operant conditioning programs will be unsuccessful; it is hoped that adoption of an experimental-clinical approach will provide evaluation of such a program.

References

Allen, K. & R. Harris. Elimination of a child's excessive scratching by training the mother in reinforcement procedures. *Behaviour Research and Therapy,* 1966, *4,* 79–84.

Allen, K., B. Hart, J. Buell, R. Harris, & M. Wolf. Effects of social reinforcement on isolate behavior of a nursery school child. *Child Development,* 1964, *35,* 511–518.

Allport, G. W. *Personality and social encounter.* Boston: Beacon Press, 1960.

Allport, G. W. *Pattern and growth in personality.* New York: Holt, Rinehart & Winston, 1961.

Allport, G. W. The general and the unique in psychological science. *Journal of Personality,* 1962, *30,* 3, 405–422.

Aronfreed, J. *Conduct and conscience.* New York: Academic Press, 1968.

Ayllon, T. & J. Michael. The psychiatric nurse as a behavioral engineer. *Journal of the Experimental Analysis of Behavior,* 1959, *2,* 323–334.

Bakan, D. The test of significance in psychological research. *Psychological Bulletin,* 1966, *66,* 423–437.

Ball, T. S. The re-establishment of social behavior. *Hospital and Community Psychiatry,* 1968, July, 54–56.

Bandura, A. Psychotherapy as a learning process. *Psychological Bulletin,* 1961, *58,* 2, 143–159.

Bandura, A. *Principles of behavior modification.* New York: Holt, Rinehart & Winston, 1969.

Bandura, A. & R. H. Walters. *Social learning and personality development.* New York: Holt, Rinehart & Winston, 1963.

Becker, W. C., C. H. Madson, Jr., C. R. Arnold & D. R. Thomas. The contingent use of teacher attention and praise in reducing classroom behavior problems. Unpublished manuscript, University of Illinois, 1967.

Benjamin, L. S. A special Latin square for the use of each subject "as his own control." *Psychometrika,* 1965, *30,* 499–513.

Bettelheim, B. *Love is not enough.* Glencoe, Ill.: The Free Press, 1950.

Borgatta, E. F. & D. Fanshel. *Behavioral characteristics of children known to psychiatric outpatient clinics*. New York: Child Welfare League of America, Inc., 1965.

Boyer, M. H. *The teaching of elementary school physical education*. New York: Jo Lowell Pratt & Co., 1965.

Bragg, R. A. & M. K. Wagner. Can deprivation be justified? *Hospital and Community Psychiatry,* 1968, July, 53–54.

Breger, L. & J. L. McGaugh. Critique and reformulation of "learning theory" approaches to psychotherapy and neurosis. *Psychological Bulletin,* 1965, *63,* 338–358.

Browning, R. A same-subject design for simultaneous comparison of three reinforcement contingencies. *Behaviour Research and Therapy,* 1967a, *5,* 237–243.

Browning, Robert M. Operantly strengthening UCR (Awakening) as a prerequisite to treatment of persistent enuresis. *Behaviour Research & Therapy,* 1967b, *5,* 371–372.

Buell, J., P. Stoddard, F. R. Harris, & D. M. Baer. Collateral social development accompanying reinforcement of outdoor play in a preschool child. *Journal of Applied Behavior Analysis,* 1968, *1,* 2, 167–174.

Cahoon, D. D. Balancing procedures against outcomes. *Hospital and Community Psychiatry,* 1968, July, 52–53.

Conrad, H. S. The validity of personality ratings of preschool children. *Journal of Educational Psychology,* 1932, *23,* 240–256.

Dollard, J. & N. E. Miller. *Personality and psychotherapy*. New York: McGraw-Hill, 1950.

Dukes, W. F. N = 1. *Psychological Bulletin,* 1965, *64,* 1, 74–79.

Dunlap, J. A case of Gilles de La Tourette. *Journal of Nervous and Mental Disorders,* 1960, *130,* 340–344.

Edwards, A. L. *Experimental design in psychological research*. New York: Rinehart & Company, 1960.

Eisenberg, L., E. Ascher, & L. Kanner. A clinical study of Gilles de La Tourette's disease (maladie des tics) in children. *American Journal of Psychiatry,* 1959, *115,* 715–726.

Eysenck, H. J. *Behavior therapy and the neurosis*. New York: Pergamon Press, 1960.

Ferster, C. B. & M. DeMeyer. A method for the experimental analysis of the behavior of autistic children. *American Journal of Orthopsychiatry,* 1962, *32,* 89–98.

Ferster, C. B. & B. F. Skinner. *Schedules of reinforcement*. New York: Appleton-Century-Crofts, 1957.

Finley, J. & A. Staats. Evaluative meaning words as reinforcing stimuli. *Journal of Verbal Learning and Verbal Behavior,* 1967, *6,* 193–197.

Flannagan, J. C. The critical incident technique. *Psychological Bulletin,* 1954, *51,* 327–358.

Gardner, W. I. The behavior modification model. *Mental Retardation,* 1968, *6,* 54–55.

Gelfand, D. & D. Hartmann. Behavior therapy with children: A review and evaluation of research methodology. *Psychological Bulletin,* 1968, *69,* 204–215.

Gesell, A. & F. L. Ilg. *The child from five to ten*. New York: Harper & Bros., 1946.

Giebink, J., D. Stover & M. A. Fahl. Teaching adaptive responses to frustration to emotionally disturbed boys. *Journal of Consulting Psychology,* 1968, *32,* 366–368.

Gilles de La Tourette. *Archives of Neurology,* 1885, *9,* 19, 159.

Ginott, H. G. *Between parent and child.* New York: Avon Books, 1969.

Harris, F., M. Johnston, C. Kelley & M. Wolf. Effects of positive social reinforcement on regressed crawling of a nursery school child. *Journal of Educational Psychology,* 1964, *55,* 35–41.

Hawkins, R. P., R. F. Peterson, E. Schweid & S. W. Bijou. Behavior therapy in the home: Amelioration of problem parent-child relations with the parent in a therapeutic role. *Journal of Experimental Child Psychology,* 1966, *4,* 99–107.

Inglis, J. *The scientific study of abnormal behavior.* Chicago: Aldine, 1966.

Kanfer, F. & G. Saslow. Behavioral analysis. *Archives of General Psychiatry,* 1965, *12,* 529–538.

Kelley, R. & M. W. Stephens. Comparison of different patterns of social reinforcement in children's operant learning. *Journal of Comparative and Physiological Psychology,* 1964, *57,* 294–296.

Kellman, D. H. Gilles de La Tourette's disease in children: A review of the literature. *Journal of Child Psychology and Psychiatry,* 1965, *6,* 219–226.

Kesey, K. *One flew over the cuckoo's nest.* New York: Viking, 1962.

Kushner, M. & J. Sandler. Aversion therapy and the concept of punishment. *Behaviour Research and Therapy,* 1966, *4,* 179–186.

Leff, R. M. Behavior modification and the psychoses of childhood: A review. *Psychological Bulletin,* 1968, *69,* 396–409.

Levin, G. R. & J. J. Simmons. Response to food and praise by emotionally disturbed boys. *Psychological Reports,* 1962, *11,* 539–546.

Lewin, K. *A dynamic theory of personality.* New York: McGraw-Hill, 1935.

Lovaas, O. I. Learning theory approach to the treatment of childhood schizophrenia. Paper delivered at symposium on "Childhood Schizophrenia." American Orthopsychiatric Association, San Francisco, April 13–16, 1966a.

Lovaas, O. I., G. Freitag, M. I. Kinder, B. D. Rubenstein, B. Schaeffer & J. W. Simmons. Establishment of social reinforcers in schizophrenic children using food. *Journal of Experimental Child Psychology,* 1966b, *4,* 109–125.

Lovaas, O. I. A behavior therapy approach to the treatment of childhood schizophrenia. In J. P. Hill (Ed.), *Minnesota symposia on child psychology, Vol. 1.* Minneapolis: University of Minnesota Press, 1967, 108–159.

Lucero, J., D. J. Vail & J. Scherber. Regulating operant-conditioning programs. *Hospital and Community Psychiatry,* 1968, February, 41–42.

MacGregor, R., A. M. Ritchie, A. C. Serrano, F. P. Schuster, E. C. MacDonald & H. A. Goolishian. *Multiple impact therapy with families.* New York: McGraw-Hill, 1964.

Marshall, G. R. Toilet training of an autistic eight-year-old through conditioning therapy: A case report. *Behaviour Research and Therapy,* 1966, *4,* 242–245.

Miron, N. B. Issues and implications of operant conditioning: The primary ethical consideration. *Hospital and Community Psychiatry,* 1968, July, 50–51.

Novick, J., E. Rosenfeld, D. A. Bloch & D. Dawson. Ascertaining deviant behavior in children. *Journal of Consulting Psychology,* 1966, *30,* 3, 230–238.
Ornitz, E. M. & E. R. Ritvo. Perceptual inconstancy in early infantile autism. *Archives of General Psychiatry,* 1968, *18,* 79–98.
Osgood, C. E., G. J. Suci & P. H. Tannenbaum. *The measurement of meaning.* Urbana: University of Illinois Press, 1957.
Pascal, G. R. & W. O. Jenkins. *Systematic observation of gross human behavior.* New York: Grune & Stratton, 1961.
Patterson, G. R. A preliminary report: Fathers as reinforcing agents. Paper presented at Western Psychological Association Convention, San Diego, California, 1959.
Patterson, G., R. Ray, & D. Shaw. Direct intervention in families of deviant children. *ORI Research Bulletin,* 1968, *8,* 9, Oregon Research Institute, Eugene, Oregon.
Patterson, G. R. & M. E. Gullion. *Living with children.* Champaign: Research Press, 1968.
President's Council on Youth Fitness. *Youth physical fitness, suggested elements of a school-centered program, parts I & II.* Superintendent of Documents, U. S. Government Printing Office, 1961.
Quay, H. Dimensions of personality in delinquent boys as inferred from the factor analysis of case history data. *Child Development,* 1964, *35,* 479–484.
Quay, H., W. Morse, & R. Cutler. Personality patterns of pupils in special classes for the emotionally disturbed. *Exceptional Children,* 1966, *32,* 297–301.
Rachman, S. & H. J. Eysenck. Reply to a "critique and reformulation" of behavior therapy. *Psychological Bulletin,* 1966, *65,* 3, 165–169.
Raimy, V. C. (Ed.) *Training in clinical psychology.* Englewood Cliffs, N. J.: Prentice Hall, 1950.
Redl, F. & D. Wineman. *Children who hate.* Glencoe, Ill.: The Free Press, 1951.
Rimland, B. *Infantile autism: The syndrome and its implications for a neural theory of behavior.* New York: Appleton-Century-Crofts, 1964.
Risley, T. R. The effects and side effects of punishing the autistic behaviors of a deviant child. *Journal of Applied Behavior Analysis,* 1968, *1,* 1, 21–34.
Ross, A. O., H. M. Lacey, & D. A. Parton. The development of a behavior checklist for boys. *Child Development,* 1965, *36,* 1013–1027.
Rutter, M. Behavioral and cognitive characteristics of a series of psychotic children. In J. K. Wing (Ed.), *Childhood autism: Clinical, educational and social aspects.* London: Pergamon Press, 1966.
Shapiro, M. B. A method of measuring psychological changes specific to the individual psychiatric patient. *British Journal of Medical Psychology,* 1961a, *34,* 151–155.
Shapiro, M. B. The single case in fundamental clinical psychological research. *British Journal of Medical Psychology,* 1961b, *34,* 255–262.
Sidman, M. *Tactics of scientific research.* New York: Basic Books, 1960.
Siegel, S. *Nonparametric statistics for the behavioral sciences.* New York: McGraw-Hill, 1956.
Skinner, B. F. *The behavior of organisms.* New York: Appleton, 1938.
Skinner, B. F. *Science and human behavior.* New York: Macmillan, 1953.
Spivack, G. & M. Swift. The Devereux elementary school behavior rating

scales: A study of the nature and organization of achievement-related disturbed classroom behavior. *The Journal of Special Education,* 1966, *1,* 1, 71–90.

Staats, A. W. & W. H. Butterfield. Treatment of non-reading in a culturally deprived juvenile delinquent: An application of reinforcement principles. *Child Development,* 1965, *36,* 925–942.

Staats, A. W. & C. K. Staats. *Complex human behavior.* New York: Holt, Rinehart & Winston, 1963.

Stevenson, H. W., R. Keen & R. M. Knights. Parents and strangers as reinforcing agents for children's performance. *Journal of Abnormal and Social Psychology,* 1963, *67,* 183–186.

Stover, D. & J. Giebink. Inter-judge reliability of the Pittsburgh adjustment survey scales. *Psychological Reports,* 1967, *21,* 845–848.

Tate, B. G. & G. S. Baroff. Aversive control of self-injurious behavior in a psychotic boy. *Behaviour Research and Therapy,* 1966, *4,* 281–287.

Thomas, D. R., W. C. Becker & M. Armstrong. Production and elimination of disruptive classroom behavior by systematically varying teacher's behavior. *Journal of Applied Behavior Analysis,* 1968, *1,* 35–45.

Wahler, R. G., G. H. Winkel, R. F. Peterson & D. C. Morrison. Mothers as behavior therapists for their own children. *Behaviour Research and Therapy,* 1965, *3,* 113–124.

Wechsler, I. *Clinical neurology.* Philadelphia: Saunders, 1952.

Wetzel, R. J., J. Baker, M. Roney & M. Martin. Outpatient treatment of autistic behavior: *Behaviour Research and Therapy,* 1966, *4,* 169–177.

Wiest, W. M. Some recent criticisms of behaviorism and learning theory with special reference to Breger and McGaugh and to Chomsky. *Psychological Bulletin,* 1967, *67,* 214–225.

Wike, E. L. *Secondary reinforcement: Selected experiments.* New York: Harper & Row, 1966.

Wing, L. The handicaps of autistic children. *Journal of Child Psychology and Psychiatry,* 1969, *10,* 1–40.

Wolfe, J. B. Effectiveness of token rewards for chimpanzees. *Comparative Psychology Monographs,* 1936, *12,* 60.

Yarrow, L. J. Maternal deprivation: Toward an empirical and conceptual reevaluation. *Psychological Bulletin,* 1961, *58,* 459–490.

Yates, A. J. The application of learning theory to the treatment of tics. *Journal of Abnormal and Social Psychology,* 1958, *56,* 175–182.

Zeilberger, J., S. E. Sampen & H. N. Sloane. Modification of a child's problem behaviors in the home with the mother as therapist. *Journal of Applied Behavior Analysis,* 1968, *1,* 47–54.

Zigler, E. & P. Kanzer. The effectiveness of two classes of verbal reinforcement on the performance of middle-class and lower-class children. *Journal of Personality,* 1962, *30,* 157–163.

Index